Workplace/ Women's Place

An Anthology

Third Edition

Paula J. Dubeck
University of Cincinnati

Dana Dunn
University of Texas, Arlington

Roxbury Publishing Company
Los Angeles, California

Library of Congress Cataloging-in-Publication Data

Workplace/women's place: an anthology/[ed.] Paula J. Dubeck, Dana Dunn.—3rd ed.
p. cm.
Includes bibliographical references.
ISBN 1-931719-69-1 (alk. paper)
1. Women—Employment. 2. Women employees. I. Dubeck, Paula, 1944–
II. Dunn, Dana.

HD6053.W678 2006
331.4—dc22   2006000047

Publisher: Claude Teweles
Managing Editor: Dawn VanDercreek
Production Editor: Monica K. Gomez
Typography: Jerry Lenihan
Cover Design: Marnie Kenney

Printed on acid-free paper in the United States of America. This book meets the standards for recycling of the Environmental Protection Agency.

ISBN 1-931719-69-1

ROXBURY PUBLISHING COMPANY
P.O. Box 491044
Los Angeles, California 90049-9044
Voice: (310) 473-3312 • Fax: (310) 473-4490
E-mail: roxbury@roxbury.net
Website: www.roxbury.net

Table of Contents

* Indicates chapters new to this edition.

Unit Three: Work and Family: Seeking a Balance

---

* Indicates chapters new to this edition.

Unit Four: Women Workers Across the Spectrum

* Indicates chapters new to this edition.

---

* Indicates chapters new to this edition.

Unit Five: Policy and Assessment

* Indicates chapters new to this edition.

About the Contributors

Teresa L. Amott is a feminist, economist, and activist. She co-edited, with Julie Matthaei, *Race, Gender, and Work: A Multicultural Anthology* (1991). She is currently Vice Provost at Gettysburg College.

Patricia Aniakudo is a doctoral candidate in psychology at the University of Wisconsin–Milwaukee. Her interest in African American women firefighters was sparked by her sister, Maurten, who is a professional firefighter in Milwaukee, and by her understanding of the intertwining of race and gender.

Mary Blair-Loy is an associate professor of sociology at the University of California, San Diego. She received her Ph.D. from the University of Chicago, and her research interests include gender, culture, work-family issues, and organizations/careers. She has published in a number of journals, including *Social Forces* and *Gender and Society*. She is the author of the book *Competing Devotions: Career and Family among Executive Women* published by Harvard University Press in 2003.

Marie-Therese Claes is a professor at ICHEC Business School, Brussels and University of Louvain-la-Neuve. She served as president of the International Network of Women in Management from 1997–2000.

Kathleen Cooke is an employee of Danya International, Inc. in Silver Spring, Maryland.

Shelly J. Correll is an associate professor of sociology at Cornell University. Professor Correll's research is in the area of gender inequality and social psychology. In particular, she studies how cultural understandings about gender differentially influence the educational and career paths of men and women. Her "stubborn stereotypes" project seeks to understand the processes by which gender beliefs continue to impact the kinds of everyday interactions and evaluations men and women experience in achievement-oriented settings, such as school and work. She has published in a number of journals, including the *American Sociological Review* and *Gender and Society*.

Gretchen DeHart received her M.A. from Washington State University in 1999. She continued her education, taught classes, and was involved in research projects at WSU until moving to Vermont in 2002. Currently, she works full-time at Planned Parenthood of Northern New England, coordinating their Professional Training Program. She also teaches a course on the sociology of gender through WSU's Distance Degree Program. Through this work, she continues to be engaged in her sociological interests of gender, inequality, communities, and education.

Paula J. Dubeck is an associate professor of sociology at the University of Cincinnati. Her research interests include occupations and professions, gender, and the status of women in organizations. She recently co-edited, with Dana Vannoy, *Challenges for Work and Family in the Twenty-First Century* (1998).

Dana Dunn is the provost and vice president for academic affairs at the University of Texas at Arlington. She has authored articles on gender stratification, sex-based earnings inequality, women in political office, and gender inequality in developing societies.

Paula England is a professor of sociology at Stanford University. She is the author of *Comparable Worth: Theories and Evidence* (Aldine 1992). Her research and teaching focus is on gender in labor markets and the family. She is a former editor of the *American Sociological Review*.

Ruth E. Fassinger is a faculty member in the Department of Counseling and Personnel Services at the University of Maryland.

The Federal Glass Ceiling Commission is a 21-member bipartisan body created by the Civil Rights act of 1991, appointed by President Bush and Congressional leaders in 1992, and chaired by the Secretary of Labor.

Sue Joan Mendelson Freeman is a professor of education and child study at Smith College and a practicing psychologist.

Carmen Garcia-Beaulieu is a research analyst in the Office of Institutional Research at Seminole Community College in Sanford, Florida. She is interested in intersections of gender and race/ethnicity, and in research on higher education.

Kathleen Gerson is a professor of sociology at New York University. She received her Ph.D. in Sociology from the University of California, Berkeley. Her research interests are work-family linkages, human development over the life course, and gender and the family. She has published numerous journal articles and books, including *No Man's Land: Men's Changing Commitments to Family and Work*, Basic Books 1993, and *The Time Divide: Balancing Work and Family in Contemporary Society* with Jerry A. Jacobs, published by Harvard University Press.

Naomi Gerstel is a professor of sociology at the University of Massachusetts–Amherst. Her books include *Commuter Marriage* and *Families and Work* (both co-authored with Harriet Gross). Her most recent articles are on caregiving and homeless families. She is currently at work on a project on family policies at the workplace.

Jennifer Glass is a professor of sociology at the University of Iowa. She has published over 30 articles and books on work and family issues, gender stratification in the labor force, and mother's employment and mental health. Her research has been funded by the National Science Foundation and the Sloan Foundation and has appeared in numerous journals, including the *American Journal of Sociology, American Sociological Review*, and *Social Forces*. She has received the Reuben Hill Award from the National Council on Family Relations, and a fellowship from the Center for Advanced Study in the Behavioral Sciences.

Maria J. Gomez is a counseling psychologist in independent practice in Houston, Texas.

James E. Gruber is a professor of sociology at the University of Michigan–Dear-

born. His research examines the causes and consequences of sexual harassment of working women in the United States and Europe. Studies focus on the effects of women's sociocultural, organizational, and personal resources on the frequency and severity of harassment, as well as the types of responses women give to their harassers.

Kevin D. Henson is an assistant professor of sociology at Loyola University Chicago. His research interests include how contingent work, particularly temporary work, perpetuates and re-creates gender, race, and class inequalities. He is the co-editor of *Unusual Occupations: Current Research on Occupations and Professions* (2000).

Arlie Russell Hochschild is a professor of sociology at the University of California, Berkeley. Her research interests include sociology of family, sociology of gender, and social psychology. She is the author of *The Second Shift* (1989) and *The Time Bind* (1997).

Jerry A. Jacobs is a professor of sociology at the University of Pennsylvania. He received his Ph.D. in Sociology from Harvard University. His research interests include gender and higher education and social stratification. He has published over 50 research articles in academic journals and four books, including *The Time Divide*, co-authored with Kathleen Gerson.

Miliann Kang is an assisant professor of women's studies at the University of Massachusetts, Amherst. She received her Ph.D. in sociology from New York University. Her research interests are the social construction of race, class, and gender; immigrant women; and emotional labor in service industries. In 2000, she received the Cheryl Allyn Miller Award from Sociologists for Women in Society for research on women and work.

Christine Larson is a financial journalist who has written for the *Wall Street Journal, Smart Money* and many other publications. She specializes in making complex information simple, down-to-earth, and fun to read. She holds a B.A. from Princeton University.

Meg Lovejoy is a doctoral candidate in sociology at Brandeis University. Her research interest is on the impact of race, class, and gender on girls' and women's mental health. She has published in the area of ethnic differences in body image and eating disorders, as well as on the impact of the women's studies curriculum in higher education on student development.

Jeanette Luna is affiliated with the National Council of La Raza in Washington, D.C.

Lisa A. Mainiero is a professor of management at the Charles F. Dolan School of Business, Fairfield University. She received her doctorate in organizational behavior from Yale University. Her research interests concern gender influences on career patterns, office romance, and power/dependence issues. She has published in a number of journals, including *Administrative Science Quarterly* and the *Journal of Management*.

Susan Ehrlich Martin received her Ph.D. in sociology from American University. She wrote *Breaking and Entering: Policewomen on Patrol* (1980) and *Doing Justice, Doing Gender* (1996), co-authored with Nancy Jurik. She has been a study director at the National Research Council and at the Police Foundation. She formerly directed a research program on alcohol and violence at the National Institute on Alcohol Abuse and Alcoholism. She is currently an independent consultant.

Julie A. Matthaei is a feminist economist and activist who teaches at Wellesley College. She is currently co-chair of the Committee Against Racism and Discrimination.

Mary Mattis is vice president for research and advisory services at Catalyst, where she designs national research projects that benchmark women's career development and advancement. She also advises corporations on barriers to women's advancement and writes extensively on the glass ceiling.

Brenda Mejia recently joined the Institute for Urban and Minority Education at Teachers College as a research assistant and research coordinator. She obtained her graduate education at Teachers College—Columbia University where she completed her master's degree in psychology and education with honors. Ms. Mejia's research interests are focused on accultura-

tion, the advancement of intercultural understanding of obstacles faced by Latino and African American populations.

Katherine McGonagle is a senior research associate in the Survey Methodology Program at the University of Michigan's Institute for Social Research. She has worked with health-related survey data since receiving her doctorate in social psychology from Miami University in 1988. She has published numerous journal articles describing gender differences in the prevalence and correlates of mental illness and methodological aspects of mental health research.

Peggy Orenstein was formerly managing editor of *Mother Jones* magazine, and was a founding editor of the award-winning *7 Days* magazine. Her work has appeared in such publications as *The New York Times Magazine*, *Esquire* and *The New Yorker*. Her most recent book is *Flux: Women on Sex, Work, Love, Kids, and Life in a Half-Changed World* (2000).

Patricia S. Parker is an assistant professor in the Department of Communication Studies at the University of North Carolina–Chapel Hill. She received her Ph.D. from the University of Texas at Austin. Dr. Parker's research and teaching interests include critical studies of gender, race, and culture in organizations. Her recent work focuses on the communication strategies and leadership behaviors of African American women executives within dominant culture organizations.

Jo Anne Preston is an assistant professor in sociology at Brandeis University. She is currently completing a book on the feminization of school teaching. Her previous publications address the relationship of mill-girl narratives to collective identity and labor activism, the conflict between female apprentices and merchant-tailors in the early industrial period, and the discrepancy between female teachers' self-conceptions and nineteenth century gender ideology.

Joann Prosser is a faculty member in the Department of Counseling and Personnel Services at the University of Maryland.

Belle Rose Ragins is an associate professor of Management at Marquette University. She received her Ph.D. in Individual-Organizational Psychology from the University of Tennessee. She researches, teaches, and consults on diversity, mentoring and gender issues and was awarded the first visiting research fellowship position at Catalyst. She has published in a number of journals including *Journal of Applied Psychology* and the *Academy of Management Journal.*

Barbara F. Reskin is a professor at Harvard University. Her books related to gender and work include *Women and Men at Work* (with Irene Padavic), *Job Queues, Gender Queues: Explaining Women's Inroads Into Male Occupations* (with Patricia Roos), and *Sex Segregation in the Workplace: Trends, Explanations and Remedies* (edited volume).

Jackie Krasas Rogers is an assistant professor of labor studies and industrial relations at the Pennsylvania State University. Her research interests include the reproduction of gender and racial-ethnic inequalities in the labor process, specifically within contingent employment. In addition to her work on temporary clerical employment, she has also interviewed contract attorneys.

Mary Romero is a professor at the School of Justice Studies at Arizona State University, and the author of *Maid in the U.S.A.* (Routledge 1992), co-editor of *Women's Untold Stories: Breaking Silence, Voicing Complexity* (Routledge 1999), *Challenging Fronteras: Structuring Latina and Latino Lives in the U.S.* (Routledge 1997), and *Women and Work: Race, Ethnicity and Class* (Sage Publications 1997).

Mary Ross is a financial analyst at Newark InOne. She has done research on gender and organizations.

Louise Marie Roth is an assistant professor in the department of sociology at the University of Arizona. She received her Ph.D. in Sociology from New York University. Her research interests include gender, the family, and organizations, occupations, and work. She has published in a number of journals, including *Social Forces, Socio-*logical Quarterly, and the *American Sociological Review.*

Pamela Stone is an associate professor of sociology at Hunter College and the Graduate Center of the City University of New York. Her research is on women in the workforce, with a particular focus on sex segregation, earnings discrimination, and pay equity. She is currently writing a book on her study of high-level women who leave professional jobs to become full-time, at-home mothers.

Sherry E. Sullivan is an associate professor at Bowling Green State University. She received her doctorate from Ohio State University. Her main research interest is in the study of careers, and she has published in such journals as the *Journal of Management,* the *Academy of Management Executive,* and *Journal of Applied Psychology.*

Bickley Townsend is senior vice president of Catalyst, a non-profit research and consulting firm that focuses on gender issues in businesses and the professions. She earned her Ph.D. in regional planning and social demography from Cornell University. She was previously senior editor of *American Demography* magazine.

Christine L. Williams is a professor of sociology at the University of Texas at Austin. Her research interests include sexuality and gender, work and occupations and theory. She is the author of *Still a Man's World: Men Who Do "Women's Work"* (University of California Press, 1995).

Janice D. Yoder is a professor of psychology at the University of Akron. Her interests in women in nontraditional occupations spawned research on the pioneering women cadets at West Point, the costs of deviating from occupational gender norms, sexual harassment, tokenism theory, and strategies for empowering solo women. She is the author of *Women and Gender: Transforming Psychology* (1999). She is a fellow of the American Psychological Association. ✦

Introduction to the Study
of Women and Work

The rapid influx of women into the paid labor market in the last thirty years of the twentieth century was one of the most dramatic social changes of that century. This change also continues to have a far-reaching impact on lives today. Women have always worked, yet much of the work they performed has not counted officially as "work." The best example of this uncounted work is domestic work, or household work.[1] Domestic work is nonmarket work. It is performed outside the formal economy in support of households and families, not for exchange on the market. While such work is clearly of great importance, it is not the focus of this book. The selections in this book focus on women's participation in paid work performed outside the home.

In 2004, women made up 47 percent of the workforce (U.S. Census 2004–05). By comparison, women comprised 33.4 percent in 1960 and 42.5 percent in 1980 (Kemp 1994). Women can be found working in virtually all occupations, and their employment contributes significantly to family and personal well-being. In 2003, it was estimated that wives employed full-time contributed 35.2 percent of the family income of dual-earner households (Bureau of Labor Statistics 2005). In addition, women's participation in the labor force increasingly reflects a pattern that approximates that of men's: continuous rather than being interrupted for years of child bearing and rearing.

There are many reasons for examining women's increased involvement in paid work. The first reasons discussed here are economic. Women are a valuable economic resource in that their labor is necessary for the production of the goods and services we

all consume. Traditionally, the study of work addressed primarily male workers (Acker 1988). With women representing almost one half of the workforce today, it is equally important to understand issues such as (1) what motivates women to be productive workers, (2) what causes women to be satisfied with their work, and (3) what factors facilitate or impede women from achieving success in their work situation.

Another reason for studying working women is that the majority of women who work for pay do so out of perceived economic need (Baca Zinn and Eitzen 1993). It has become increasingly difficult to support a family at what is considered to be a desirable standard of living on just one income. Further, many households today do not consist of traditional families with adult males present. Rather, women are the only economic providers in these households. Women earn less for the work they perform than men, and this contributes to disproportionately high rates of poverty in female-headed households, a phenomenon that has come to be known as the *feminization of poverty*. The economic reasons for studying women and work are that women are important producers in today's economy, as well as important economic providers for their families and households.

Studying women's increased involvement in paid work is also important for social reasons. Women's increased labor-force participation has broad social consequences that extend well beyond the economy. Families and schools provide examples of two social institutions profoundly affected by increases in women's labor-force participation. As mentioned earlier, women have always performed domestic work; in fact, they have typically borne the primary responsibility for such work. As women begin to spend significant numbers of hours working outside the home for pay, their ability to perform domestic work and, potentially, the quality of life of their families is affected. Families have needed to adapt to women's changing work roles by making other provisions for the performance of domestic work. As we will see in Unit Three, women in many families still perform a disproportionate share of domestic tasks in addition to their paid work because these needed adaptations have not taken place. Educational institutions are also affected by women working. For example, schools can no longer depend upon the unpaid labor of the employed mothers of school children to serve as teachers' aides to support classroom activities. Issues such as providing for the transportation of children to and from school and the compatibility of school hours with parents' work hours have prompted a rise in after school care programs, which need to be examined in light of women's increased involvement in paid work.

Studying women's paid work is also warranted for what can be referred to as personal or individual reasons. Social scientists agree that work is far more than the means to an economic end. Work has personal meaning because individuals in modern society are defined, in large part, by the work they perform (O'Toole, et al. 1973, Pavalko 1988). "What do you do?" means "What type of work do you perform?" and this is often the first thing we ask a new acquaintance. The answer to this question conveys a myriad of information, including economic status, social class, level of education, interests, abilities, political views, and personality traits (Hedley 1992). "What do you do?" is shorthand for "Who are you?" and others respond to us on the basis of our answer. College professors are assumed to be intelligent and "bookish"; nurses, nurturing; engineers, detail-oriented; and salespersons, gregarious. These assumptions about who we are, derived from others' knowledge of our work, eventually impact our own perception of who we are (Dunn 1995). For this reason, we can say that work contributes to feelings of self-esteem. In order to understand who

women are today and how they feel about themselves, it is necessary to examine their participation in the workforce.

Work affects self-concept and feelings about oneself by contributing to feelings of efficacy and worth. The connection between feelings of efficacy, the power to produce effects, and work is obvious. Producing goods and services is a form of mastery over self and the environment, and is proof of one's ability to "get things done." If the output from one's work is valued by others, then work enhances feelings of worth. On the other hand, if one's work is not socially valued, self esteem is likely to be low. Consider, for example, the often under-valued, unpaid work performed by homemakers. The fact that domestic work has become under-appreciated caused many homemakers to respond to the "What do you do?" question with "I'm just a housewife" (Matthews 1987). That domestic work is insufficient for producing a positive self-concept is further supported by evidence of sub-standard mental health among full-time homemakers (Bernard 1972). Women's increased participation in paid work is therefore personally important because it provides an opportunity for empowerment and increased self-esteem.

Finally, and perhaps most importantly, examining women's paid work is important because the type of work performed by each sex and the social valuation of that work is the best indicator, across societies and throughout time, of the degree of equality between the sexes. When women are judged to be performing valuable work, especially work for pay outside the home, on a comparable basis with men, then gender inequality is minimized.[2] It is not surprising then that many battles for gender equality have been fought in the workplace. Much women's movement activity in the 1960s and 1970s was centered around issues of hiring discrimination and equal pay on the assumption that if women could gain access to the same types of jobs as men for similar rates of pay, they would be treated equally (Daniel 1987). Since that time, we have learned more about how organizations operate with regard to a changing composition of the work force. Issues that seemed to be resolved at "entry" level positions of various occupations have "moved up the organization" to the very top levels; for example, women have had considerable access to entry level managerial jobs, but their move to the very top positions in organizations seems to be blocked. The more we learn about women's work experience and the context in which women work, the more we understand the structures and processes that influence that experience and either facilitate or impede women's opportunities. In doing so, we are gaining some measure of the extent to which there is equality between the sexes.

The chapters that follow explore a wide range of issues related to contemporary women's involvement in paid work. Before introducing these chapters, it is necessary to provide some historical perspective on working women. The following sections of this introduction will explore the changing patterns of women's work participation and examine the causes that underlie that change. A final section will highlight issues that emerged and are emerging in the study of women and work.

The Changing Patterns of Women's Work

Human societies have always divided labor by sex, reserving certain work tasks for men and others for women. While a division of labor by sex has existed in all known societies, the form of the division of labor has varied. The section below describes the typical sex-based division of labor in early human societies and how that division of labor changed as societies evolved with regard to four broad types of societies: hunting and gathering societies, horticultural societies, agricultural societies, and industrial societies. Changes in women's labor-force participation and patterns of work will be examined in more detail for contemporary, post-industrial societies.

The Sex-Based Division of Labor in Pre-Industrial Societies

The earliest human societies, hunter-gatherer societies, had a simple division of labor by sex: men hunted wild game, women gathered naturally occurring vegetation, and

those too old or too young to participate in these activities stayed home and cared for one another. The sex-based division of labor in hunter-gatherer societies was efficient because women's reproductive role was incompatible with physically demanding hunting activities that often required travel far from home (Bradley 1989). Imagine, for example, the difficulty involved in hunting large game while pregnant or nursing an infant. The gathering tasks reserved for women were compatible with pregnancy and child care because they were less physically demanding and could be performed close to home. Hunter-gatherer societies were small, and survival was often difficult in these subsistence-based groups (Lenski and Lenski 1982). For this reason, women's reproductive role was highly valued. The level of equality between the sexes was high in these societies because the work performed by women and men was judged to be of roughly equal importance (Boulding 1976; Chafetz 1984; Nielsen 1978). Men's hunting activities often yielded substantial subsistence resources for support of the group, but hunting activities were sometimes unreliable, and hunters often came back from their long hunts empty-handed (Friedl 1975; Sanday 1981). Women's work contribution became especially important in these periods. The nuts, roots, berries, and tubers gathered by women provided edible foodstuffs which enabled group members to survive during periods when the hunt was unproductive. Thus, the stability of women's economic contribution was highly valued, as was their reproductive role, and these factors contributed to a greater degree of equality between the sexes than in any subsequent period in history (Yorburg 1987; Nielsen 1990).

Over time, horticultural societies developed as a result of technological advancements and new forms of social organization. Rather than depend on hunting wild game and gathering naturally occurring vegetation, people in horticultural societies met their subsistence needs by domesticating plants that resulted in a more reliable and significant yield (Lenski and Lenski 1966). Women, having established a tradition of contributing to subsistence needs by gathering plants, made the rather smooth transition to domesticating plants. Men were typically responsible for claiming the land used for planting. The resulting male ownership of land placed control over the means of production in the hands of men and began to erode women's status (Friedl, 1975; Dunn et al. 1993). Men also continued to hunt, and when successful, provided the scarce and highly valued animal protein. At some point, men also began to domesticate animals in many societies, raising small herds not only for meat, but also for milk and other animal by-products (Lenski and Lenski 1966).

Horticultural societies grew in size with the advent of new technologies (e.g., more sophisticated implements, irrigation). Eventually a transition occurred from a subsistence orientation to a surplus orientation. In surplus-oriented societies, people can produce more than is required for meeting subsistence needs, making it possible for some people to be freed from food production in order to engage in other forms of work. Specialized full-time occupations emerged at this point in history. Some involved turning raw materials into handcrafted goods, others involved providing services (e.g., shopkeeper, educator). These new occupations were performed away from the homesite, so they were considered the domain of men. Domestic work, performed in and around the home, was reserved for women.

The invention of the plow marked the transition to the agricultural stage of development, and the ability to produce a surplus increased dramatically. Animal-drawn plows transferred much of the hardest labor involved in producing food to animals. Having established a tradition of working with animals—first hunting them and then domesticating them—men worked behind the animal-drawn plows and produced increasing amounts of surplus (Yorburg 1987). Other men, freed from the need to produce food, entered newly developing specialized occupations in even larger numbers. A complex market economy resulted where foodstuffs were exchanged for dollars (or other goods), which were then used to purchase goods produced by workers in the new occupations.

What were women doing while men were plowing, shopkeeping, blacksmithing, leather crafting, and so on? First, women often assisted with these activities when needed (during harvest time, for example). Their primary work responsibilities, however, remained in the home. Women were responsible for providing an array of services to their families including cooking and storing food, sewing and manufacturing clothing, medical care, education, and even religious training (Yorburg 1987). These types of work activities are referred to as use-value production because what is produced is consumed by the family unit. In contrast, the work performed by men in agricultural societies is referred to as exchange-value production because the products are intended for exchange through the market. Exchange-value production is more highly valued than use-value production because the former provides greater flexibility in terms of what can be consumed and also affords the party performing the work the opportunity to develop social networks and ties (Nielsen 1990).

An important exception to this pattern of restricting women's work to the domestic sphere occurred in cases of slavery, wherein enslaved groups performed coerced labor. Africans brought to the United States as slaves, for example, did not conform to the sex-based division of labor described above. While it is the case that some black women slaves were forced to work primarily in the slave owner's home, many others were forced to work alongside men in the fields, engaged in extremely physically demanding labor (Deckard 1975; Matthaei 1982).

As women became increasingly associated with domestic labor and use-value production, their status relative to men declined (Nielsen 1990). Gender inequality reached its peak in agricultural societies, not because women were no longer working hard and making an economic contribution, but because of the changed nature of their work. Men were the more visible producers, they owned the means of production (land), the product of their labor was now relatively stable, and what they produced could be exchanged for an almost infinite variety of goods and services through the market. Women, working "behind the scenes" in the less glamorous domestic arena, supported their husbands' work by attending to his needs and those of the rest of the family (Cott 1977).

The Impact of Industrialization on Women's Work

The next major societal transition that had an impact on the nature of work and the division of labor between the sexes was the emergence of industry. Industrialization involved using forms of power other than human and animal (e.g., water, steam, mechanical, electric) to produce manufactured goods. Efficient utilization of these new forms of power meant that workers had to be located in a common work setting and resulted in the rise of the factory mode of production. During the early phases of industrialization in both Europe and the United States, some women—especially unmarried women, women from the lower classes, and minority women—worked in factories (Matthaei 1982). A sex-based division of labor developed for the specialized factory jobs. Women worked with smaller equipment and machinery, on average, and were concentrated in jobs in the textile industry. The jobs women performed paid lower wages than those performed by men (Deckard 1975). Men, with higher wages, were viewed as the primary breadwinners for families, and women's economic contributions, although often necessary, were considered supplemental. Women employed in factories continued to be responsible for domestic work at home, creating for the first time a "double shift" for women consisting of eight or more hours of paid work to be followed by a night shift of use-value work in support of the family (Andersen 1988). Married women, especially white women who could afford to do so, stayed home as full-time homemakers (Matthaei 1982).

By the turn of the twentieth century (1900), just under 19 percent of all working-age women participated in paid work, and the majority of these women were under the age of 24. Less than 6 percent of married women worked for pay outside the home at this time (Kessler-Harris 1982; Costello and Krimgold 1996). Married women's rates of labor-force participation remained low during the first three decades of the twentieth

century due to what has come to be known as the cult of domesticity. The cult of domesticity, also referred to as the doctrine of separate spheres, was borrowed from the English upper-middle classes and held that a woman's proper place was in the home (Reskin and Padavic 1994). Under the cult of domesticity, the homemaker's absence from the paid workforce served as a symbol of the husband's masculinity (Matthaei 1982). Married women only entered the labor force when their husbands were incapable of providing a family wage—a wage sufficient for providing for the family. The cult of domesticity encouraged married women to be economically dependent on their spouses, and thereby led to a decline in women's status.

Poor women and women of color, forced to work out of economic need, retained a higher degree of independence than white women. Ironically, for these women who could not afford the "luxury" of the full-time homemaker role, paid work resulted in somewhat more equal standing with their male peers. Even today, some minority groups have higher rates of female labor-force participation than white women, and the sexes also share resources more equally in these groups (Almquist 1987).

In the early decades of the twentieth century, women who worked outside the home had limited options. Single white women were sometimes employed in new vocations as clerical workers, teachers, and nurses (Andersen 1988). Working class women and women of color worked in factories as laborers, and many immigrant women were employed as domestic servants in other women's homes. There were slow but rather steady increases in the rates of women's labor-force participation until the early 1940s, when World War II created severe labor shortages and an increased demand for female labor. Over five million more women were in the labor force in 1944 than in 1940 due to wartime efforts (Herz and Wootton 1996). During the war years, the sex-based division of labor in manufacturing broke down as many women worked—and performed well—in nontraditional jobs (Kemp 1994). However, despite their successful job performance, women were often displaced from the previously male-dominated jobs when men returned home from the war.

During the middle decades of the twentieth century, the United States economy experienced an important shift from an emphasis on the production of goods to the provision of services. More than half of the labor force was employed in service-producing industries, by the 1950s (Montagna 1977). Many of the new service-oriented jobs in industries like banking, insurance, health, and education, were white-collar jobs that required little physical effort and were far-removed from the dirty, factory setting, and for these reasons seemed more "appropriate" for women. That, combined with the rapid rates of growth in these occupations, opened the doors for many women to enter these new service-producing occupations. Women entered lower tier service-producing occupations, such as retail sales and personal services, in large numbers. From this period forward, women's rates of participation in paid employment increased steadily.

Women's Labor-Force Participation in Recent History

The rise in women's labor-force activity that has occurred over the last few decades has been accompanied by a decrease in men's rates of labor-force participation, causing women to represent an increasing share of all workers. Table I.1 provides an overview of changes in women's and men's rates of labor-force participation from 1900 to 2003 and also indicates the percentage of the total labor force that is female.

The influx of women, especially married women, into paid employment accelerated in the 1960s and 1970s when the women's movement played a role in making paid work appear more desirable to married women (Herz and Wootton 1996). As full-time homemakers compared themselves to employed women, they recognized their comparatively dependent status and felt devalued. Further, increasing divorce rates and rising numbers of impoverished displaced homemakers were making abundantly clear to full-time homemakers the risks of complete economic dependence on a male provider (Matthaei 1982). A number of other factors

Table I.1
Labor-Force Participation Rates by Sex and Women's Share of the Total Labor Force for Selected Years: 1900–2003

People 16 and Older, Civilian Labor Force[1]
Labor Force Participation

Year	Males	Females	Women's Share of Labor Force
1900	80.0	18.8	18.3
1910	81.3	23.4	21.2
1920	78.2	21.0	20.5
1930	76.2	22.0	22.0
1940	79.2	25.4	24.3
1950	86.4	33.9	29.6
1955	85.3	35.7	31.6
1960	83.3	37.7	33.4
1965	80.7	39.3	35.2
1970	79.7	43.3	38.1
1975	77.9	46.3	40.0
1980	77.4	51.5	42.5
1985	76.3	54.5	44.2
1990	76.1	57.5	45.3
1995	75.0	58.9	46.1
2000	74.7	59.9	46.5
2003	73.5	59.6	46.6

[1] Before 1947, people in the labor force included workers age 14 and older.

Source: Adapted from Kemp, Alice Abel, *Women's Work: Degraded and Devalued.* NJ: Prentice Hall, 1994:174. The 1995, 2000, and 2003 data were taken from the Bureau of Labor Statistics chart on "Labor Force Participation Rates, 1975–2008." *Stats.bls.gov/opub/working/data/chart3.txt* and from U.S. Census Bureau, Statistical Abstract of the United States: 2004–2005, Table 570; U.S. Census Bureau, Statistical Abstract of the United States: 2001, Table 570, *www.census.gov/prod/www/statistical-abstract-04*; and U.S. Department of Labor, Women's Bureau. Women in the Labor Force, 2003: Quick Stats, *www.dol.gov/wb*.

also contributed to increases in women's labor-force participation during this period. The civil rights movement resulted in more opportunities and equal treatment for women and minorities in the workplace, which served to make paid work more attractive. In addition, women's educational attainment was becoming more similar to men's, allowing women more access to interesting and lucrative employment. Increased employment opportunities, along with accessiblity to the birth control pill, led to a decline in the birthrate, which meant that women spent less of their adult years with preschool-age children, and thus had more years available to spend in paid employment (Herz and Wootton 1996). While all of the above affected the supply of female labor, the most important cause of women's increased employment was the increased demand for workers resulting from economic expansion (Chafetz 1990; Daniel 1987).

Changes in occupational opportunity in the 1960s and 1970s had differential impact across groups of women (Anderson 1988; Ortiz 1994). Table I.2 provides labor-force participation rates for women by race/ethnicity for 1960 through 2000. In 1960 and 1970, the labor force participation rates for black women exceeded that of non-Hispanic white women. By 1980, the labor force participation rates for black and non-Hispanic white women had nearly converged. By 2000, the rate for non-Hispanic white women, Asian women, and Hispanic women were nearly the same; among black women, the rate of labor force participation exceeded that of the other groups. Importantly, improved educational opportunities for women of color, combined with continued civil rights activity and legal changes, have created new job opportunities, especially for black women and especially in the female-dominated semi-professions (Sokoloff 1992). As such, the labor force participation rates also reflect the expansion of opportunities for women of color. (Chapter 4 provides an analysis of factors that influence labor force participation

of different racial/ethnic groups of women at the beginning of the twenty-first century.)

The rate of increase in women's participation in paid work slowed in the early 1980s due to economic recession. The impact of economic recession was greater, however, for male-dominated industries and occupations (e.g., manufacturing). By 1990, the growth in women's labor-force participation had slowed even further, as continued economic stagnation and job losses in retail trade occupations took a toll on women's employment opportunities. Since that time, labor-force participation rates for women have remained relatively stable (Herz and Wootton 1996; Bureau of Labor Statistics 2005).

Women's participation in paid work today varies by age, race/ethnicity, marital status, the presence of children, and education level. These characteristics affect women's participation in paid work for two primary reasons. First, they are related to opportunities for employment and earnings and the opportunity costs of not working (e.g., age, race/ethnicity, and education level); and second, they are related to domestic/family demands on women's time that detract from the opportunity to work (e.g., marital status and the presence of children). Table I.3 presents selected population and labor-force characteristics of women in 2003. Today, the labor force participation rate for women from their mid-20s to mid-50s is nearly 75 percent (U.S. Census 2004–2005). This represents a change from the early part of the twentieth century when rates were highest for young, unmarried women (England and

Table I.2
*Labor Force Participation Rates for Women by Race/
Ethnicity, Selected Groups, 1960 to 2000*

	1960	1970	1980	1990	2000
White	33.6	40.6	51.2	57.4	59.5
Black	42.2	47.5	53.1	58.3	63.1
Asian			(NA)	(NA)	59.2
Hispanic or Latino			47.4	53.1	57.5

Source: U.S. Census Bureau, *Statistical Abstract of the United States: 2004–2005*, Table 570. Data on Black women from 1960 and 1970 are from Vilma Ortiz. "Women of color: a demographic overview." In M. Baca Zinn and B. Thornton Dill (eds.), *Women of Color in U.S. Society*: 28.

Farkas 1986). Through the middle part of the century, women exited the labor force in significant numbers upon marriage and especially for the birth of children, causing a dip in labor-force participation rates for those under the age of 35. As these women re-entered the labor force when their children became school age, rates climbed once again, though not to a level as high as that for young, unmarried women. Women today are far more likely to work continuously, causing their labor-force participation rates to appear similar to men's: increasing through the middle years, leveling off, and then declining around retirement (Herz and Wootton 1996). Indeed, over half of the women with children under the age of 1 are in the labor force, and more than three-quarters of those with children between the ages of 6 and 17—the school age years—are in the labor force (see Table I.3).

Since the 1960s and 1970s, variation in women's labor-force participation by race/ethnicity has diminished. Increases in white women's levels of participation have served to close the gap between white and black women (Ortiz 1994). Rates of participation for Hispanic women represent marked increases over previous decades, but are still about 6 percentage points lower than those for black women (see Table I.3). Social scientists have long attributed the lower rates for Hispanic women to cultural patterns that emphasize traditional roles in the family. The rapid increases in participation in paid work for Hispanic women suggest that such traditions are eroding, or perhaps that increased employment opportunities and economic need compel women to deviate from tradition (Almquist 1979; Ortiz 1994; Zavella 1987). It is important to note that while labor-force participation rates vary little across most racial/ethnic groups, unemployment rates are about two times higher for racial/ethnic minority women (except Asian/Pacific Islanders) (Bureau of Labor Statistics 2005).

Women's family situations continue to affect their employment, though much less so than in the past. In recent decades, the most dramatic increases in labor-force participation for women occurred for married women with preschool-age children. Between 1950 and 1980, the labor-force participation rate

of married women with children under the age of 6 rose from 12 to 45 percent—a 275 percent increase (England and Farkas 1986)! While women with school-age children are more likely to be employed than those with children under the age of six, the majority of all mothers, regardless of the children's ages, are in the labor force today (U.S. Census 2004–2005) (see Table I.3).

Table I.3
Selected Population and Labor Force Characteristics of Women, 2003

Characteristic	Percentage of the Population in the Labor Force
Total Women, 16 years and over	59.5
Age:	
16 to 19 years	44.8
20 to 24 years	70.8
25 to 24 years	74.1
35 to 44 years	76.0
45 to 54 years	76.8
55 to 64 years	56.6
65 years and over	10.6
Race/Ethnicity:	
White	59.2
African American	61.9
Asian	58.3
Hispanic Origin	55.9
Marital Status:	
Single/never married	65.0
Married, spouse present	61.8
Other (Divorced, Widowed, Separated)	50.1
Presence and Age of Children:	
Without children under 18	54.1
With children under 18	71.7
Children 6 to 17 years only	77.5
Children under 6 years	62.9
Child(ren) under 3 years	58.7
Child(ren) under 1 year	54.7
Education:*	
Less than H.S. diploma	32.5
H.S. diploma	54.1
Some college, no degree	64.3
Associate's degree	71.5
Bachelor's degree or higher	72.8
Total Men, 16 years and over	75.5

*Education data are for women 25 years and older. All other data are for women 16 years and older.

Source: U.S. Census Bureau, Statistical Abstract of the United States: 2004–2005, Tables 570, 573, 579, and 580. *www.census.gov.* Education data are for 2004, from U.S. Department of Labor, Women's Bureau, Quick Stats 2004. *www.dol.gov/wb/stats/ main.htm.*

Education is an important tool that not only increases employment opportunities for women, but also increases the opportunity costs of *not* participating in the labor force. Today women receive about the same overall level of education as men (Sapiro 1994), and their labor-force participation rates reflect these educational gains. The most educated groups of women are those with the highest levels of labor-force activity. For example, nearly 73 percent of all women with four-year degrees or higher were in the labor force in 2003 (U.S. Census 2004–2005).

Despite dramatic increases in women's labor-force activity this century, women continue to be employed in a far more narrow range of occupations than their male counterparts (Dunn 1996; Reskin and Roos 1990). One third of all employed women in 1990 worked in just ten of the 503 detailed occupations listed in the census (Reskin and Padavic 1994). The term *occupational segregation* is used to refer to the concentration of same sex workers in an occupational category. This phenomenon, and its relationship to the pay gap between the sexes, will be discussed in more detail in Chapters 6 and 7. For now, it will suffice to note that women are over-represented in lower-level positions in the workplace, and especially in those occupations that have lower rates of pay. Several factors contribute to the concentration of women in a narrow range of traditional occupations. They include gender role socialization (addressed in Unit One), constraints resulting from work-family conflict (addressed in Unit Three), and discrimination (Dunn 1996).

Themes in the Study of Working Women

Paralleling the large scale movement of women into the labor force and particularly their move into "non-traditional" occupations, were efforts to research their access and experiences and to document what, if any, changes occurred in the workplace and at home. Over the past three decades, certain themes emerged in the effort to explain why women have not attained *equality* and *equal opportunity* in the workplace, goals that were embedded in the 1964 Civil Rights Act that opened many doors for women. Komarovsky (1991) noted that a "first wave" of feminist research addressed issues of gender socialization as explanations for why women were not represented in a number of male-dominated occupations, from high-status professions to blue-collar jobs. But over time, gender socialization could only partly account for women's under-representation in such jobs. Education and legal efforts were opening up avenues of training and opportunity that challenged the stereotypes that designated only some jobs as appropriate for women.

A second wave of research was stimulated by Rosabeth Moss Kanter's (1977) work that identified opportunity structure and numbers as key factors that influenced one's position and behavior in organizations. She found that women and men in positions with blocked opportunity responded similarly regarding the organization, its goals, and their own aspirations. Her emphasis on structural arrangements stimulated research that looked not only at mobility within organizations, but also the structure of occupations and employment. The internal stratification of professions, for example, came into clearer focus, as did the sex segregation of occupations and internal labor markets of organizations. Both gave insight into factors that facilitated or impeded the opportunities for women to be successful. Similarly, Kanter's focus on "numbers," and particularly token status, prompted extensive inquiry into non-traditional, male-dominated occupations.

By the 1990s, at least three foci guided inquiries about women's work and the experiences in the workplace. These remain salient today. The first of these examines the gendered nature of organizations. This focuses on how traditional male values and patterns of behavior influence work arrangements and the culture of the workplace that, in turn, block women's advancement and influence the quality of work life. Work hours and career-related job expectations, for example, generally reflected the model of the man whose home and family responsibilities were cared for by a full-time, stay-at-home spouse. Men did not take off from work for sick-child responsibilities and they were available to work long hours. Explicit (and implicit) timetables that were used to measure advancement, such as years to tenure in a university-reflected a "male model" of work, a model where family and child bearing/caring concerns were not factored in. As Christine Williams noted in her selection (Chapter 5), organizations reward behaviors that are valued, and those behaviors are framed and practiced on a male standard. As inquiry into the opportunities and blocked opportunities for women continued, the gender-based system of organizational practices became more visible. It also provided the opportunity for organizations to consider changes if they were interested in keeping talented female workers. In some cases, those practices left organizations vulnerable to external pressures for change.

A second area to emerge in the research literature by the 1990s is that of work and family. The intersection of these two institutional arenas has created a number of difficulties for employees and employers, and as such, has become a much-researched issue. As noted earlier (Table I.3), among married-couple families today, 62 percent are dual-earner families; the prevalence reflects a dramatic change from 1970, when 40.5 percent of married women were in the labor force (U.S. Census 2001). In addition, in 2003, 58.7 percent of married women with children under the age of 3 were employed, compared with 30.3 percent in 1970 (U.S. Census 2003). Yet women remain the primary person in the household responsible for childcare and household tasks. The result is an expansion of work by women—combining both home and work—unless their spouses are willing to relieve them of some of the burden.

Realistically, however, change with regard to work and family cannot just be based in the "family" side of the "work/family" equation. As such, a third area to emerge in the research literature focuses on laws and social policy. Laws place constraints on the operations of organizations and, as such, will influence their practices (and their culture). Both federal and state legislation will influence the policies that organizations adopt. One step in creating a better balance between these two areas is the Family and Medical Leave Act (FMLA) of 1993, requiring employers (with more than 50 employees) to make selected "family friendly" practices available to employees. Importantly, corporations are increasingly acknowledging that "family friendly" practices bring benefits to the corporation in the form of increased employee commitment, less turnover, and more satisfied workers (Gerson 1998). The effectiveness of the FMLA legislative mandate is now being addressed in the research literature and the findings of this work should provide a better understanding of issues that evolve around the work/family intersection. This research is also informative because of its potential for developing wide scale efforts to bring about change in the practices of organizations.

Approaching the Study of Working Women

The study of women and work is an interdisciplinary endeavor. The selections included in this text incorporate theory and research from sociology, psychology, management, economics, history, women's studies, and communications. The disciplinary perspective most useful in understanding women's work depends upon the questions one asks. For example, if one wants to examine the causes of the wage gap between the sexes, economics and sociology may provide the most guidance. If, however, one wants to know whether communication differences between the sexes block women's movement into high level managerial jobs, communications or management may provide the most insight.

Within disciplines, different theoretical approaches have developed to explain women's work experiences. One important characteristic that differentiates theories in several disciplines (e.g., sociology, economics, management) is whether they view women's work experiences as primarily affected by characteristics of individual women or by structural features of social institutions (e.g., economy, family). It is not always so easy to sort out the two types of influences. For example, at first glance, it might appear that observed differences in men's and women's styles of leadership (discussed in Chapter 8) result from personality differences between the sexes (individual characteristics). Further examination, however, may reveal that because women and men are differentially situated in work organizations, they face differing structures of opportunity and constraint (structural features). The fact that women managers are disproportionately located in low-status positions lacking in authority, may cause them to rely on more cooperative approaches to leadership. Put simply, women with limited power cannot successfully issue directives and orders (what some call a male-oriented management style); instead, they must enlist the cooperation and support of subordinates in order to gain their compliance (Colwil 1993). This is clearly a case where differences between the sexes result, at least in part, from features of social structure, specifically the structure of work organizations. It is common for individual characteristics to interact with structure so as to impact women's work.

An additional, important feature of much recent scholarship on women and work is its feminist orientation.[3] While many academic disciplines have been producing scholarship on women and work for decades, most of this early scholarship did not *focus* on women's work experiences (Stacey and Thorne 1985). The tendency in many disciplines prior to the 1980s, and often beyond, was to examine women's work experiences only in relation to men's, and thus, to depict male experience as the norm (Anderson 1988; Ward and Grant 1985). In other words, women and their work experiences were treated as the exception to the rule or a deviant case. Clearly it is no longer valid to portray working women as an exception to the rule, given that they now comprise nearly 50 percent of all workers. Feminist approaches to women and work position women's experiences at the center of inquiry, and as a result, often generate new knowledge. A feminist orientation also involves exploring the exploitation and oppression of women and a commitment to changing those conditions (Acker et al. 1983). The selections that follow vary with respect to their degree of feminist emphasis, but all are feminist in the sense that they have women's work as their *central* subject matter.

Recent feminist scholarship on women and work is also sensitive to issues of diversity among women (Guy-Sheftal 1995). Women (and women workers) are not a homogeneous group. Race/ethnicity, social class, age, and sexual orientation interact to create differences among women and result in different life and workplace experiences. Subtle and overt forms of workplace discrimination faced by women of color, lesbians, and elderly women provide examples of the impact of difference on women's lives. The selections in this anthology address, to varying degrees, issues of difference among women workers, and some selections focus on the impact of race/ethnicity and social class on women's work experiences (Chapters 15, 18, 20, 22, 24, 25, 26).

The study of women and work can be undertaken using a variety of research methods. The selections that follow employ a range of data collection methods including observation, surveys, in-depth interviews, and existing records. Each approach carries strengths and weaknesses. Field-based methods (also called *qualitative methods*) such as observation and in-depth interviewing, have the advantage of providing rich, descriptive information. They are especially well-suited for providing an "insider's view" of women's work experiences. The downside of these approaches is that the findings they generate cannot be assumed to hold true beyond the sample of women workers studied. Survey research techniques are especially useful for studying social issues that require generalizations based on large groups of people, such as all working mothers, secretaries, or black professional women. The key disadvantage of surveys, however, is that compared to field methods, they have greater difficulty obtaining situational or contextual information. This is particularly troubling for the study of women and work because a focus on women's experience as workers was relatively rare in most disciplines until the last few decades. For this reason, more of the selections in this text, particularly those contained in Unit Four, use observational and interview techniques to capture the voices and experiences of working women. Not all of the selections in this reader are research-based.

Also, some selections in this anthology address women and work issues from an applied perspective. Authors of the selections contained herein represent several employment fields including journalist, career-placement counselor, educator, and government task-force representative. The varied background of the authors provides a well-rounded overview of women and workplace issues. A critical reading of the selections should involve an assessment of how the occupation and/or academic discipline as well as personal history and social location of the author affects the perspective of what is written.

Nearly half of the readings in the current edition are new to this volume. In Unit One, issues in women's socialization for work are examined. Attention is given to research that examined the family and the educational system as socializing agents for girls' orientations and aspirations with regard to work, as well as the impact of gender-based expectations on girls aspirations. In Unit Two, we move from large-scale, societal patterns of sex-segregated occupations and earnings inequality, to the gendered nature of the workplace, examining issues of leadership, sexual harassment, and the glass ceiling.

In Unit Three, the focus is on the work/family interface. Particular attention is given to the "second shift" and the "time bind." The idea that families appear to be facing "less and less time to do more and more," is addressed, as is the "renewed practice" of women "dropping out" of high status, high achieving careers to become full-time mothers. Together they reflect the strains of the work/family interface.

In Unit Four, we turn to examining experiences of women in a number of different occupations, and as experienced by women of different racial/ethnic backgrounds. Our goal, as before, is to give some understanding of the experiences women have as they work in a variety of occupations. The selections include women working in traditional as well as nontraditional jobs, and explore the opportunities and barriers that women encounter in their jobs. In addition, some selections address the ways women adapt to the difficulties of being in "traditionally male" jobs.

In the final section, we examine the emergence and effects of policies that have evolved to address women working and work/family issues. Corporate and government policy reflect an acknowledgement that work and family are no longer separate spheres of life, divided along gender lines. Rather, the blurring of what had once been viewed as a clear division signals not only that changes have taken place, but also that this is a societal issue, not just a family or just a work issue.

Two final comments are in order. First, the goal of this third edition was to extend and elaborate on what we know about women's work experiences and the factors that influence them. Despite over 30 years of research and change, issues concerning women and employment continue to emerge or, like the glass ceiling, reinvent themselves at a different level of an organization. The result is an interesting and challenging array of issues to investigate, and should generate lively discussions about possible solutions. We hope this collection of readings will provide the basis for such discussions.

Second, we would like to acknowledge, as well, the guidance and support of a number of people who made this volume possible, including the reviewers: Meryl Altman (De Pauw University), Barbara A. Arrighi (Northern Kentucky University), Ann Beutel (University of Oklahoma), Karen Flynn (University of Illinois at Urbana-Champaign), Carla Harrell (Old Dominion University), Janet R. Heller (Western Michigan University), Toni C. King (Denison University), Marie A. Laberge (University of Delaware), Benita Roth (Binghamton University), Joyce Tang (Queens College/CUNY), Mary Nell Trautner (University of Arizona), and Margaret Walsh (Keene State College). In addition, the assistance of Sarah Byrne, Juhua Yang, and Robin Carstens at the University of Cincinnati was particularly valued.

Endnotes

1. Volunteer work and coerced work (e.g., slavery) are other forms of unpaid work. Women have also had high rates of participation in these forms of nonmarket work.

2. This link between women's work and their status relative to men is complicated by the

fact that work is often under-valued simply because women perform it.

3. Various feminist perspectives on women and work exist, including liberal feminism, Marxist feminism, socialist feminism, and radical feminism. For a discussion of these different perspectives see Kemp, Alice A., *Women's Work: Degraded and Devalued* (Englewood Cliffs, NJ: Prentice Hall, 1994); Donovan, Josephine, *Feminist Theory: The Intellectual Traditions of American Feminism* (New York: Ungar, 1987); and Tong, Rosemarie, *Feminist Thought: A Comprehensive Introduction*, (Boulder, CO: Westview Press, 1989).

References

Acker, J. 1988. "Women and work in the social sciences." In A. Stromberg and S. Harkess (eds.), *Women Working*, 2nd Edition. Mountain View, CA: Mayfield Publishing: 10–24.

Acker, J., K. Barry, and J. Esseveld. 1983. "Objectivity and truth: Problems in doing feminist research." *Women's Studies International Forum*, 6: 423–435.

Almquist, E. 1987. "Labor market gender inequality in minority groups." *Gender and Society*, Vol. 1, No. 4, 400–414.

——. 1979. *Minorities, Gender and Work.* Lexington, KY: D.C. Heath.

Andersen, M. L. 1988. *Thinking About Women: Sociological Perspectives on Sex and Gender.* New York: Macmillan Publishing Company.

Anderson, K. 1988. "A history of women's work in the U.S." In A. Stromberg and S. Harkess, *Women Working*, 2nd Edition. Mountain View, CA: Mayfield Publishing: 25–41.

Baca Zinn, M., and D. S. Eitzen. 1993. *Diversity in Families.* New York: Harper Collins.

Bernard, J. 1972. *The Future of Marriage.* New York: Bantam.

Boulding, E. 1976. "The historical roots of occupational segregation." *Signs*, 1: 94–117.

Bradley, H. 1989. *Men's Work: Women's Work.* Minneapolis: University of Minnesota Press.

Bureau of Labor Statistics. 2005. Women in the Labor Force: A Databook. Washington, D.C.: *www.bls.gov/cps/wlf-databook2005.htm.*

Chafetz, J. S. 1990. *Gender Equity: An Integrated Theory of Stability and Change.* Newbury Park, CA: Sage Publications, Inc.

——. 1984. *Sex and Advantage: A Comparative, Macro-Structural Theory of Sex Stratification.* Totowa, NJ: Rowman and Allenheld.

Colwill, N. L. 1993. "Women in management: Power and powerlessness." In B. C. Long and S. E. Kahn (eds.), *Women, Work, and Coping.*

Montreal: McGill-Queens University Press:73–89.

Costello, C., and B. Kivimac Krimgold (eds.). 1996. *The American Woman, 1996–1997: Where We Stand.* New York: Norton.

Cott, N. 1977. *The Bonds of Womanhood: 'Women's Sphere' in New England, 1780–1835.* New Haven: Yale University Press.

Daniel, R. L. 1987. *American Women in the 20th Century: The Festival of Life.* San Diego: Harcourt Brace Jovanovich.

Deckard, B. 1975. *The Women's Movement: Political, Socioeconomic and Psychological Issues.* New York: Harper and Row.

Donovan, J. 1987. *Feminist Theory: The Intellectual Traditions of American Feminism.* New York: Ungar.

Dunn, D. 1996. "Gender segregated occupations." In P.J. Dubeck and K. Borman (eds.), *Women and Work: A Handbook.* New York: Garland Publishing: 91–93.

——. 1995. "Sociological dimensions of economic conversion." In L. J. Dumas (ed.), *The Socio-Economics of Conversion from War to Peace.* Armonk, NY: M.E. Sharp: 23–44.

Dunn, D., E. Almquist and J. Chafetz. 1993. "Macrostructural perspectives on gender stratification." In P. England (ed.), *Theory on Gender/Feminism on Theory.* New York: Aldine De Gruyter: 69–90.

England, Paula, and G. Farkas. 1986. *Households, Employment and Gender: A Social Economic and Demographic View.* Hawthorne, NY: Aldine Publishing Co.

Friedl, E. 1975. *Women and Men: An Anthropologist's View.* New York: Holt, Rinehart and Winston.

Gerson, Kathleen. 1998. "Gender and the future of the family: Implications for the postindustrial workplace." In D. Vannoy and P. Dubeck (eds.), *Challenges for Work and Family in the Twenty-first Century.* Aldine de Gruyter: New York: 11–22.

Guy-Sheftal, B. 1995. *Women's Studies: A Retrospective.* New York: Ford Foundation.

Hedley, R. A. 1992. *Making a Living: Technology and Change.* New York: Harper Collins.

Herz, D. E., and B. H. Wootton. 1996. "Women in the workforce: An overview." In C. Costello and B. Kivimac Krimgold (eds.), *The American Woman, 1996–1997: Where We Stand.* New York: Norton:44–78.

Kanter, Rosabeth Moss. 1977. *Men and Women of the Corporation.* New York: Basic Books.

Kemp, A. A. 1994. *Women's Work: Degraded and Devalued.* Englewood Cliffs, NJ: Prentice Hall.

Kessler-Harris, A. 1982. *Out to Work: A History of Wage Earning Women in the United States.* New York: Oxford University Press.

Komarovsky, Mirra. 1991. "Some reflections on the feminst scholarship in sociology." *Annual Review of Sociology* (17) Palo Alto, CA: Annual Reviews Inc: 1–25.

Lenski, G., and J. Lenski. 1966. *Power and Privilege: A Theory of Social Stratification.* New York: McGraw-Hill.

——. 1982. *Human Societies: An Introduction to Macrosociology,* 4th Ed. New York: McGraw-Hill.

Matthaei, J. A. 1982. *An Economic History of Women in America: Women's Work, the Sexual Division of Labor and the Development of Capitalism.* New York: Schocken Brooks.

Matthews, G. 1987. *Just a Housewife: The Rise and Fall of Domesticity in America.* New York: Oxford University Press.

Montagna, P. D. 1977. *Occupations and Society: Toward a Sociology of the Labor Market.* New York: John Wiley and Sons.

Nielsen, J. 1978. *Sex in Society: Perspectives on Stratification.* Belmont, CA: Wadsworth.

——. 1990. *Sex and Gender in Society: Perspectives on Stratification,* 2nd Edition. Prospect Heights, IL: Waveland Press.

Ortiz, V. 1994. "Women of color: A demographic overview." In M. Baca Zinn and B. T. Dill (eds.), *Women of Color in U. S. Society.* Philadelphia: Temple University Press: 13–40.

O'Toole, J., E. Hansot, W. Herman, N. Herrick, E. Libow, B. Lusignan, H. Richman, H. Sheppard, B. Stephansky, and J. Wright. 1973. *Work in America.* Cambridge, MA: MIT Press.

Pavalko, R. M. 1988. *Sociology of Occupations and Professions.* Itasca, IL: Peacock.

Reskin, B., and I. Padavic. 1990. *Women and Men at Work.* Thousand Oaks, CA: Pine Forge Press.

Reskin, B., and P. A. Roos. 1994. *Job Queues, Gender Queues: Explaining Women's Inroads into Male Occupations.* Philadelphia, PA: Temple University Press.

Sanday, P. R. 1981. *Female Power and Male Dominance.* Cambridge: Cambridge University Press.

Sapiro, V. 1994. *Women in American Society.* Palo Alto, CA: Mayfield Publishing.

Sokoloff, N. 1992. *Black Women and White Women in the Professions.* New York: Routledge.

Stacey, J., and B. Thorne. 1985. The missing feminist revolution in sociology. *Social Problems,* 32: 4 (April): 301–316.

Tong, R. 1989. *Feminist Thought: A comprehensive Introduction.* Boulder, CO: Westview Press.

U.S. Census. 2001. *Statistical Abstract of the United States 2000.* U. S. Department of Commerce. *www.census.gov/prod/www/statistical-abstract-1995-2000.html.*

——. 2002. *Statistical Abstract of the United States 2001.* U.S. Department of Commerce. *www.census.gov/prod/www/statistical-abstract.html.*

——. 2005. *Statistical Abstract of the United States. 2004–2005. www.census.gov/prod/www/statistical-abstract.html.*

U. S. Department of Labor. *Women in the Labor Force, 2003: Quick Facts.* Women's Bureau. *www.dol.gov/wb.*

Ward, K. B., and L. Grant. 1985. "The feminist critique and a decade of published research in sociology journals." *The Sociological Quarterly,* 26 (2): 139–157.

Yorburg, B. 1987. "Sexual identity in human history." In J. Stimson and A. Stimson (eds.), *Sociology: Contemporary Readings.* Itasca, IL: F. E. Peacock Publishers.

Zavella, P. 1987. *Women's Work and Chicano Families: Cannery Workers of the Santa Clara Valley.* Ithaca, NY: Cornell University Press. ✦

Unit One

Becoming Workers: Girls' Socialization for Employment

What did you want to be when you grew up? We both wanted to be teachers, not college professors, our current occupation, but rather, public school teachers. Playing "school," for example, was Dana's favorite pastime, and she was constantly on the lookout for playmates who were willing to be her students. What was the source of our early occupational aspirations? Our mothers were full-time homemakers, so our career plans did not result from modeling our mothers. The fact that public school teaching is and has long been a heavily female-dominated occupation meant that our early aspirations were gender-traditional. Socialization messages from a variety of sources likely influenced our early desire to be teachers. Television shows, the books we read, even the staffing patterns in our schools delivered the same message: teaching is for women. We were not oblivious to these messages; we translated them into career goals. The reading selections in this unit address how the process of sex role socialization shapes girls' work aspirations and eventual experiences.

Sex role socialization is a process that begins at the moment of birth when male and female infants are handled differently by caretakers and continues throughout the childhood years (Karraker, Vogel, and Lake 1995; Rubin et al. 1974). Parents typically teach their children to behave in accordance with traditional sex roles. This learning is reinforced by sex role socialization in the school and peer group, by the media, and from other sources. The result is that we internalize our gender, the learned behaviors and expectations associated with our biological sex. This learning sets us on a course for adulthood and the many roles we will play, as spouses/partners, parents, and workers.

Early views on behavioral differences between the sexes did not emphasize the importance of socialization in acquiring gendered behavior. Instead, traditional understandings of differences between the sexes centered on the role of biology in creating sex differences. Even today it is not uncommon to hear that "boys will be boys" and "girls are the way they are" due to the influence of biology. For example, you may have heard explanations offered for the dearth of women in high level management jobs that center on women's natural absence of aggressiveness (often attributed to hormonal patterns) or explanations as to why women are not likely to pursue careers in math and science that focus on a presumed lack of ability (often attributed to brain structure and methods of processing visual/spatial information). Increasingly, as scientific research places these biologically deterministic explanations of behavioral differences between the sexes under scrutiny, they are revealed to be incorrect, or at best incomplete.[1] Yet, to the extent that people believe in biologically based differences between the sexes, these supposed differences continue to influence job choices and opportunities. If an employer is confident that men make better managers because they are naturally more aggressive, or that women won't devote adequate amounts of attention to a demanding job because of their innate desire to nurture children, then it is not difficult to predict who will be promoted to fill the next vice president vacancy.

In the 1970s, with the knowledge that sex role socialization encourages girls to prepare for and pursue traditional women's occupations, research began to focus on exploring the subtle, and sometimes not so subtle, processes through which this occurs. Studies have revealed how teachers' expectations of sex-linked differences in math ability lead them to encourage boys and neglect girls in math instruction (Fox, Fennema, and Sherman 1977). They have also shown how even the most well-intentioned parents, as a result of their own gender-traditional upbringing, might encourage daughters to limit their aspirations and become adult women who derive rewards not from their own, but from their husband's accomplishments (Lindsey 1994).

Our socialization patterns and practices are a product of our culture. Some would argue that they cannot be changed without a fundamental restructuring of society. Yet it is often true that our actions lag behind our attitudes, that we behave according to yesterday's beliefs (or even the last decade's). To the extent that this is true with respect to attitudes concerning gender and employment, it points to the importance of educating adult socialization agents (e.g., parents, teachers) about the consequences of encouraging gender stereotypes. Gender stereotypes, preset assumptions about individuals based on knowledge of their sex, commonly portray men as strong, competent, and rational and women as nurturing, weak, and emotional. Endorsing these gender stereotypes means assuming that women and men are predisposed to different types of work roles. For parents, it means shaping their children, through socialization, to fit the ste-

reotypes. For employers, it means assuming that job candidates adhere to the stereotypes even when they do not. The end result involves artificially restricting the employment opportunities of both sexes, and, in particular, discouraging the achievement of women.

The selections that follow address how women become workers as a result of their sex role socialization. In the first reading, Freeman probes, in depth, the role the family plays in socializing gender. She shows, based on her in-depth interviews with women in managerial career tracks, how parents (particularly mothers) influenced career choice and success. Interview excerpts from her research provide examples of the salience of parental expectations and perspectives on education, independence, and gender for daughters' work experiences. Freeman's research is important not only because she provides evidence of the importance of parents as role models for occupational choice, but also because she reveals that women who followed gender-traditional paths often expected more of their daughters, encouraging them to "Do as I say, not as I have done."

In the next selection, Orenstein turns our attention to the schools and the ways in which primary- and secondary-level education affect girls' self esteem and levels of confidence. She begins by noting the rather depressing findings of the American Association of University Women (AAUW) survey "that the sharp decline in adolescent girls' self esteem can be attributed, in large part, to gender-biased patterns in our schools." Motivated by the AAUW survey, Orenstein spends a year interviewing and observing students, teachers, and administrators in two middle schools. She describes her observations of rampant gender bias in the classroom, providing concrete examples of teachers favoring boys and ignoring girls, and uses the students' own words to convey girls' feelings of discouragement. Orenstein also discusses her observations of how school experiences differentially impact girls in different racial/ethnic groups. Her selection provides insight into the social origins of the lack of confidence and achievement orientation exhibited by many talented and able women workers.

In the third selection, Correll addresses the question of why girls don't go into math and science careers to the same extent as boys. She does this by using a supply-side model, analyzing high school boys' and girls' choices with regard to a math curriculum and college majors, based on their assessments of their own mathematical ability and in relation to their actual performance in high school math. The belief that math is a "male" domain, argues Correll, may negatively influence girls' self-assessment of their own mathematical ability. These assessments, coupled with gender beliefs (which include math as a male domain) will influence career choices, steering girls away from careers that are math-based. In taking a supply-side approach, Correll addresses the socialization influences and cultural values that lead girls to envision the careers they want to pursue, and how gender beliefs favoring males in math and science, diminish the supply of girls seeking to pursue such occupations.

Endnote

1. For further discussion of the debunking of myths about biologically based gender differences and gender bias in science, see A. Fausto-Sterling, *Myths of Gender*, New York: Basic Books, 1985; and N. Tuana (ed.), *Feminism and Science*, Bloomington, IN: Indiana University Press, 1989.

References

Fox, L. H., E. Fennema, and T. Sherman (eds.). 1977. *Women and Mathematics: Research Perspectives for Change*. Washington, D.C.: National Institute of Education.

Fox, L. H., D. Tobin, and L. Buedy. 1979. "Sex role socialization in mathematics." In M. A. Wittig and A. C. Peterson (eds.), *Sex-Related Differences in Cognitive Functioning*. New York: Academic Press.

Karraker, K. H., D. A. Vogel, and M. A. Lake. 1995. "Parents' Gender-stereotyped perceptions of newborns: The eye of the beholder, revisited." *Sex Roles*, 33 (9–10): 687–701.

Lindsey, L. L. 1994. *Gender Roles: A Sociological Perspective*. Englewood Cliffs, NJ: Prentice Hall.

Rubin, J. Z., F. J. Provenzano, and Z. Luria. 1974. "The eye of the beholder: Parents' views on sex of newborns." *American Journal of Orthopsychiatry*, 44 (4): 512–519.

Weitzman, L. J. 1979. "Sex role socialization: A focus on women." In J. Freeman (ed.), *Women: A Feminist Perspective*, 3rd Ed. Palo Alto, CA: Mayfield. ✦

1
Parental Influence and Women's Careers

Sue Joan Mendelson Freeman

It is common knowledge that a family's environment contributes significantly to the shape of an individual's future. That environment has both external and internal components. Outside of it, a family has several sources of identity within the larger society; its race, class, religion, and ethnicity inform a family's practices, beliefs, and opportunities. Cultural heritage and social access are largely determined by the sociological circumstances of one's birth.

Beyond a sociological rubric, factors operating on the individual level shape a person's future. Internal to the family is its psychological environment. Freud awakened our consciousness to the importance of early child-rearing practices for subsequent personal development. Whether or not they accept a psychodynamic framework, social scientists since have reiterated the significance of family in molding its members' psyches.

Notions of self, relation to other, and place in a social network originate in the family. Parent-child relationships are especially critical to one's growing understanding of identity and future. Self-image is subject to many other sources of influence throughout the course of development, but the first impressions emblazoned through the intimacy of family carry considerable weight. Our relationships within the family not only become the prototype for subsequent ones outside but also teach us who we are and what we might expect to do with our lives.

A family's instruction about children's personal attributes and future paths had varied by gender for more than half of this century. Males and females learned characteristics and directions that were separate and specific to their gender. Institutions representing various aspects of society fostered and reinforced gender-specific behavior, and children had firsthand models in their own homes. Mothers who served as family caretakers and fathers who went out to work were powerful role models for children's emulation (Bayes and Newton 1978). Thus, males' and females' identities and destinies were overdetermined by internal and external contributors.

It is not just behavior of role models that influences a child's development. Parents' messages about their own and their children's identities can take many forms. Influence extends beyond behavior to attitudes. For example, the operative factor in the case of mother-daughter messages may be the mother's degree of satisfaction with her role. Thus, mothers who are at home but dissatisfied with that position are more likely to encourage their daughters to do something different (Brown 1979).

Lessons conveyed verbally and behaviorally are particularly influential because of their source and recipient. Children are in a formative process and are therefore malleable, especially by the most powerful people in their lives, their parents. Parents derive their power from their position: Children are totally dependent upon them for an extended period of time. Thus, parental teachings about the child's value and potential are of extraordinary endurance.

A division of labor according to traditional gender lines would find fathers in the work force and mothers in the kitchen. If role model imitation followed expectation, girls would identify with their mothers and thereby formulate notions of themselves and their futures around domesticity. Indeed, some women, like thirty-seven-year-old Dorothy, began with such notions, which were subsequently revised as a function of career opportunity and professional experience.

> My early socialization through my family was very patriarchal, and my mother never worked. It was understood that if I went to school it wasn't for any particular reason other than it was just something

to do. But not any emphasis was ever placed on career for a woman; nothing was placed on learning for a woman. It was understood in my mind to become a mother and a wife, and that was it. So when I went to school, I never really took it very seriously; I didn't study very hard; I really didn't care. And my whole reason for being there—and what I think a lot of women in my position at that time were going through—was to find a husband.

Predictions of sex role imitation ordinarily follow same-sex lines: Girls are expected to identify with their mothers and boys with their fathers. Within a context of a gender-based division of labor, however, girls would have to identify with their fathers in order to develop the characteristics requisite to career aspiration. Females who did just that—identified with their fathers and subsequently became executives—were the subject of an early study, *The Managerial Woman* (Hennig and Jardim 1977). That study also supported the association of high achievement orientation with birth order, firstborn or only children getting an inordinate share (Hennig and Jardim 1977). Among the women interviewed for this study we find more variability in birth order, in which parent is cited as being influential, and in the ways influence is manifested (Brown 1979; Epstein 1970).

Social beliefs about gender roles vary with time and context. Children born after 1960 were likely to receive very different messages about gender-appropriate identities and directions than those born two decades earlier (Brown 1979). Social change spawned by recent human rights movements has affected our attitudes and practices regarding male and female traits and behavior. Revised beliefs and economic conditions have combined to allow women's development and occupation to extend outside the home. . . . The families of the women in this study spanned an age range from early twenties through mid-fifties, the time frames of their early formative years vary. Most childhoods predated the current women's movement; yet these women developed high achievement motivation for work and career. By looking at

their families, we gain insight into the shaping of these women's aspirations. . . .

This Study

The testimony presented here [about parental influence on careers] comes from interviews with forty women who were or were about to become middle managers. Interviews were conducted during a four-year period in the early 1980s. The women were diverse in class and ethnic backgrounds, although most were white Americans; included were three black and three foreign-born women.

Their organizations ranged from large to Fortune 500 companies. The women worked in financial services; retail industries; large, diversified conglomerates; media and publishing; high-technology industries; transportation; manufacturing; natural resources; and consumer products. They could be found in production on the shop floor, in regional offices in the field, and in corporate headquarters. Their positions ranged from sales representative to vice-president, with project leaders, instructors, accountants and auditors, writers and overseers of company publications represented. About half of the women already held the title of manager, and their areas included marketing, personnel and human resources, equal employment opportunity, product manufacturing and distribution, in-house education and training, sales, and legislative affairs.

These women were a special group because they had been chosen by their companies for further training at a college-affiliated management program. That these women were singled out for such support by their companies is subject to various interpretations, including the implication of professional promise, perhaps in the form of advancement within the organization. Thus, we are listening not just to female middle managers but to a select subset of that population, those to whom some kind of company commitment has been implied. . . .

Mothers as the Prime Movers

For several women, mothers were predominant influences. Sharon's mother stressed the importance of education, and at the time of the interview Sharon had already earned one graduate degree and was pursuing another.

> Absolutely from my mother. Nobody in our immediate family ever went to college, so being the oldest child . . . my mother always encouraged me to think about going to college. It was always to have a better job. There was a real big focus on having skills and being unique in that respect. And she was absolutely the prime reason. In that respect, my father was always encouraging but certainly not so much on a vocal level. It was definitely my mother.

Parents do not merely convey a "Do as I did" message to their children. In fact, mothers often use their own lives as negative examples for their female offspring. They want their children to have opportunities that they lacked. Alison's achievement orientation began early with educational strivings, and by the age of twenty-five this young woman had found herself already on the edge of managerial positions.

> My mother, from as early as I can remember, was pushing me . . . I think she always felt cheated by the fact that she didn't go to college, and she didn't have a career and didn't have a way to be independent. . . . As long as I can remember, my mother was always saying, "Get a college education so you can be independent and never depend on a husband or anybody else." I bet I heard that once a week for my entire life.

Mothers, who had been socialized according to traditional gender dicta of female domesticity and dependence, found their experience wanting and preached the opposite to their daughters. Recognizing the limitations imposed upon them by economic dependence, they encouraged their daughters to increase the possibilities for their own lives. Leigh's mother did not mince words in her explicit message, but Leigh did not begin to build a career until she joined a growing manufacturing corporation in her mid-thirties.

> She had been a support when I was young, very definitely. When I was in college, she would say things like "Prepare yourself for a job." "But I want to take all these art courses." And if I had listened to some of the things she said, I might have

done things a little differently. I don't know if I would have, but she had been through [it] herself and knew where things were. Very bright woman.

When mothers recognize the many options that could be available to their daughters, they often coach them about paths to pursue. Marsha's mother described the different destinations in which various paths would culminate. This tutelage in decision making and nurtured independence prepared Marsha for a direct path to a high executive position in finance for which she had solid undergraduate training.

> I have to give her some of the credit because she did a lot of talking. We were very close. We talked quite a bit. And she would bring up comparisons: "You either do this, and this is where you may end up. But if you do this, there's no limit to where you can go." So I have to say that she was the major factor.

The support of a close relationship is crucial to risk taking. Encouraged to make decisions and tutored in their consequences, a woman develops a strong self-image and many skills necessary for career success. Ursula, in industrial sales and a single parent by age thirty-two, also learned strengths and skills from her mother's example.

> My mother was a very strong influence in our family. She was a very strong woman . . . And I think I've incorporated—I've learned from her. One of the things that's helped me so much has been being persistent, not giving up. If somebody tells me, "No," how can I make them say yes? How can I change their minds? Or what do I need to change to make it work? And I really picked that up from my mother. My mother was not in business . . . But she was strong and took responsibility for a lot of things. And I think she had a lot of influence on the choices that I've made.

The majority of women interviewed had mothers who were not employed in business. Several had never worked outside of the home, and the few who had were primarily part-time employees. A mother's participation in the labor force did not define what and how she communicated to her daughter, however. For example, some employed mothers would have preferred full-time homemaking, and others who were at home would have preferred paid work. Daughters became aware of what mothers did, said, and might have desired. Their personal characteristics evolved under a mother's watchful tutelage, others from a more subtle model. Values and a general sense of personal worth, not tied to any specific undertaking, were derived from supportive maternal environments. Daughters also learned skills and attributes essential to career from mothers who managed not businesses but homes (Baruch, Barnett, and Rivers 1983).

Where Fathers Take the Lead

Ordinarily, neither parent dictated a particular path for a child to pursue. Instead, daughters were encouraged to develop so that they were prepared to take advantage of all sorts of opportunities. Like mothers, fathers had various ways of fostering development that ranged from specific expectation to general support.

Through intellectual challenge, Connie's father sharpened her thinking ability and stimulated her assertiveness. His style of coaching reflected his own strength, which served as both a formidable model and a dependable support. By her early thirties, Connie, who had always been a high achiever, was headed for one of the top executive positions held by women of this group.

> I was the oldest child, and I was given a lot of opportunity to experience things first time around. I think my father encouraged me to debate and talk: "Why do you feel this way, and how did you get to that point, and why?" [He was] interested in what I was doing. So I think my father was important, and my mother was very supportive. And I don't know that I'm through this stage yet, but I would be very secure and calm if I could go home and ask him the answer to a question, and he told me his version of it. Whatever that version was, I always felt that was the right story and that probably nobody else knew, because nobody else was as smart.

A father's authoritative expertise can work to a daughter's advantage when he not only lends her the benefit of his experience but also facilitates similar expertise in her. Connie learned that she could rely on her father as a knowledgeable consultant, but more importantly, she developed her own problem-solving abilities through his prompting.

Other fathers also emphasized cognitive skill in their daughters. To expand oneself through knowledge is useful for its own sake as well as for practical purposes. Scholastic study and achievement can promote a sense of accomplishment and self-esteem. Meanwhile, broad exposure acquaints one with prospects for the future. Through education, daughters learn more about available opportunity and about themselves and their aptitudes. Teresa's interest in school carried her through a graduate degree, which prepared her for escalating positions within her company. Her recollection of an emphasis on education is common to many.

> We had to go to school; we had to do our homework. That was just what you were supposed to do. And I always did well in school, and they kept encouraging it.

For Ina, who also held a graduate degree, the importance of education was an unquestioned given:

> [My mother's] idea of an education [as] security was the key thing that ran through my whole life—and my sisters' also. We all have professions . . . And they always encouraged it. You got one B and all the rest A's. Well, next time try for all A's. Go for the top. And even still, my mother's very proud of my career.

It is not necessarily one or the other parent who promulgates education and high achievement, but fathers, more often than mothers, are perceived as demanding. The demand may be connected to scholastic performance or to achievement more generally. Without articulating particular expectations, Leigh's father still served as a motivating force for her, although it was her mother who had instructed her to prepare for a job when she wanted to take art courses.

> I'd say my father was very demanding—a very demanding person. And it wasn't as though he was gearing me to go to work. But the person I had to succeed for was my father . . . he's been very successful, and a very bright person. And I had to

prove myself to him. So I've always had to fight hard to do that, but it's certainly been a motivation. And I wouldn't have known that many years ago. I certainly know that now.

A father's admirable characteristics can inspire his daughter's emulation. Further, his qualities make his approval all the more desirable to a daughter who strives to prove herself worthy through similar accomplishment.

Nina, who had been more interested in work than school, can now relate her father's values to her own.

> My dad's very goal-oriented. He's always instilled that in us—to get our act together and to have some goals and aspirations and to set them high, and . . . both my parents would always support us in that.

These women describe encouragement and support for achievement in a general sense. They do not speak of being groomed for a lifetime of work or career, never mind a specific occupation. Sex differences may remain, with families expecting boys to prepare for lifelong employment and coaching them toward particular careers (Hardesty and Jacobs 1986). Perhaps females born within the past two decades have received similar messages. However, the women of this study, who have spanned the old and new messages about women's lives, speak in the sketchier and broader terms of achievement.

Family Support for Achievement

Influenced by the spoken and unspoken, children are commonly unaware of the sources of motivation during their formative years. In retrospect, they can recognize family components that contributed to what they have become. The full meaning of parental example and instruction becomes clear when women connect their current selves to the past. Stella attests to the value of the interview question in stirring an integration for her.

> I like the idea of you getting me to actually talk about [my family] and to relate it somehow. I never really saw a correlation between my feelings for my family and my work and the obligations and the things like that. I always thought that this is one thing and this is another and some-

how the two paths never meet, but it's almost inseparable.

Several women interviewed acknowledged the influence and support of both parents in their development. Karen, who coordinates financial planning for a retail corporation, derived different qualities from her mother and father, and their individual strengths combined to enforce a belief in her potential.

> My father was very much one of these workaholic-type people. He was also somebody that you could never satisfy . . . and so I think I probably did a lot of stuff trying to please him but never quite getting that satisfaction. My mother was a very organized person . . . I learned a lot of organizational-type things from her. I would say both parents were pretty strong. And I was never raised with any sort of feeling other than you could do whatever you wanted to do.

We see here the origins of a strong achievement orientation. Striving to do and be as much as possible begins in childhood in relation to a parent and continues in adulthood in relation to oneself. Personal attributes and concrete skills that contribute to professional success are initially acquired through family tutelage. Connie draws parallels between her behavior as a child in the family and as a professional in the corporation.

> I can remember always, as a child, having to do, to be, in order to please my parents, I would want to get all A's. Then I took up horseback riding, and I had to enter a contest, and I wanted to win, get the first prize. And immediately, when I got this prize, I turned and looked to them to see the smiles and the positive reinforcement. So it must have started there. I think that I play to the house when I work. I don't build a lot of relationships with subordinates, and I don't build a lot of relationships with peers. What I do is build relationships with superiors, and that's got to go back to wanting your parents' approval. . . . It's got to be a transferring of that. And then just being hard on yourself . . . if I have a chance of doing it perfectly, then I will do it. But if I only have a chance of being average, it's not fun anymore. . . . So it has to be that. It goes all over.

Even when women cannot trace career origins to family influence, they are aware of an unqualified support for their endeavors and for themselves. Renee's family is virtually ignorant of the technicalities of her work as a systems consultant, but she feels their pride in her accomplishments.

> My family per se has never had any kind of a part in my career . . . she [her mother] never had any idea what I did for a living. And I can't blame her. If I were not in the industry . . . I cannot explain it to anyone else. So they really didn't have anything to do with it other than just being very proud. I would always get a strong sense of that.

Thus, families vary in the ways they exert influence and in the values they choose to emphasize. Some families' influence is perceived as negligible with regard to career. Most women interviewed nonetheless acknowledged their families in the development of a strong sense of self. A general emphasis on education and preparation for employment was an integral part of many women's upbringing, but critical to development was a global feeling of parental faith in daughters' worth. Not only did parents reinforce certain values, they believed in their daughters' abilities to meet expectations. Personal strength ultimately contributes to professional growth. Specific career assistance is less vital than the gift of self that Connie's parents have given her.

> My parents are not involved right now in coaching me or giving me tips on how to be more effective. They provide a lot of love and support and encouragement and interest—in that sense, helping me form a strong self-concept. I think they did that.

Sex Roles

An environment that both supports and holds out high standards can instill in a woman the belief that she is capable of doing anything she chooses. However, open-ended options are contrary to a gender-based division of labor that prescribes what roles males and females should occupy. Many women interviewed came from homes where traditional gender lines held sway. In some instances, the explicit message about a daughter's future did not contradict the modeled one. Monica,

thirty-two, believes that her choices would have been different had her family not perpetuated customary sex roles (Bayes and Newton 1978). Now a manager in human resources, she has earned a graduate degree since her secretarial beginnings in the corporation.

> In fact, I get aggravated with my parents, because my mother and father were very traditional. My father made the decisions. My mother was a full-time housewife. They talked a lot about girls do this and boys do that, though they always encouraged me. I did very well in school, and my father was very helpful to me [in] school work. There was a feeling that I should go to college, but it was for the wrong reason. It was because you'll meet a nice boy and get married. And unfortunately, no one ever gave me any other options. Had I to do it over again I certainly would have had a different view of things.

The larger cultural environment can reinforce family stereotypes of the preferred gender. The strength of inner conviction overcomes socialization that limits female potential. It is Hope's internal sense of self-worth that fully frees her.

> We had a very male-dominated environment. Boys—like they are everywhere, but specifically in the South—boys are the chosen kids. And everything centers around them. Girls are just second-class citizens. And so you never really get over that. The conflict comes when you realize that "Hey, I really am not a second-class citizen. In fact, sometimes I'm actually a better citizen than they are. I'm more capable, I'm more competent." And that brings another kind of conflict, because you don't have to prove that you're that. You have to come to terms with the fact that you're simply being as good as you can be—good, by your own definition, not good by someone else's.

Even when women grew up in homes that depicted traditional sex roles, they learned of other possibilities for their own lives. Parents, in the majority of cases, communicated prospects for their daughters that they themselves were not living. Jill reiterates an emphasis on education and values demonstrated by parents. The principle underlying specific lesson was that she could do and be whatever she pleased.

> Obviously, they have played a tremendous role in my life, as every family does. In my career development in particular, both parents contributed something differently. My mother did not work and has always been oriented toward the home and family life. My father has always directed all of his children, that we could do anything we wanted to, that as long as you worked hard, and were productive, and did your best . . . it was out there, and you just have to try. And he himself was a very hard-working individual and very dedicated to whatever he went into, so his own behavior was an excellent example of what he had to teach us. I would say that certainly helped in terms of my career development.

Parents instilled in daughters the value of conscientious effort. Moreover, parents conveyed their confidence in women's ability to attain their goals. Daughters internalize both the beliefs and the confidence originally derived from their families; hence, they formulate and fulfill similarly high expectations of themselves. Susan, a twenty-eight-year-old production manager, can feel the full weight of her personal worth and professional success as a result of this kind of family interaction.

> The environment I grew up in was pretty much middle-class. My parents were very concerned with grades for all of us, and there was really no distinction in terms of who could do what, or who was supposed to excel at what. My father's whole thing was that everybody should be a math major, everybody should be a chem or physics major. They were real pushy around achievement. I think that contributed a lot to what ultimately happened once I got into the work environment. The standards of performance that they expected became my own expectations somewhere in the later years of college. I didn't need them behind me anymore, expecting that. I expected it of myself. So they really played a critical role [in] developing those expectations and achievement levels.

These women set high standards for their professional performance. Individual variation notwithstanding, they were impressively uniform in their desire to achieve all that they might, not necessarily in terms of material reward but in relation to their sense of self. One woman spoke for several in saying that she was more apt to improve herself due to constantly questioning "whether I'm as good as I should be." There is plenty of evidence that these women have high standards for their performance, and those standards seem to originate in families where expectations for children's development are gender-free. With a background in human services and currently working as a manager in a traditionally male transportation business, Beverly learned that she could do whatever she wished as long as it was at a high level:

> But he [father] was really influential in that he truly believed that I could do anything I wanted to do. He had none of the traditional ideas about what I ought to do and what I shouldn't do. He was also a real perfectionist and expected me to be a cut above average in everything always. So there was a lot of achievement pressure and a lot of performance pressure.

Janna's family also valued cognitive strength and encouraged her career:

> My father's major value system has to do with competence and intelligence . . . reinforced for being bright. So I was never told that I really ought to consider being a nurse or a teacher. It was always expected that I would go to college; it was always expected that I would have a career. And I don't think that as a child or a young woman growing up in that family I was ever treated as a female.

The absence of a gender-linked socialization characterized Esther's childhood in the depression years.

> I can't honestly say that I was . . . brought up in an atmosphere that said women can't do this or can't do that. I just believed I could do anything I wanted to, and I never thought of it as being a woman. I did a lot of reading when I was a child, and I had a lot of role models in my own mind—people like Marie Curie, George Sand, Amelia Earhart was a great heroine of mine, Clara Barton, Elizabeth Browning. They sound like such stereo-

types, but they were the women that I really did relate to.

Whether women had female role models available to them in their immediate families or from other sources, they still developed the idea that everything would be available to them regardless of gender. An "anything is possible" notion came from parents like Nina's who believed that to be so for their daughters.

And my parents have instilled [in] us that we had the ability to do anything we wanted to and given us the opportunity to do that.

Independence

These women recall receiving both general and specific notions about themselves and their futures from their first families. For many, particular parental emphases on education and achievement were apparent progenitors of internalized high standards for their own performance. A family environment that communicated support and confidence in daughters' inherent worth was critical to their developing belief in themselves. Frequently coupled with such faith was encouragement for gender-free pursuits and a future of economic independence.

Socialization according to a gender-based division of labor would shape female identities for domesticity and economic dependence on a male. The majority of women interviewed had mothers without careers—indeed, without paid work of any kind—who spent their lives occupied with family caretaking. When their mothers did enter the labor force, it was often out of necessity as divorced or widowed women who had children to support. Daughters learned an indelible lesson from the experience of mothers who were suddenly abandoned and unprepared to fend for themselves and their families. Women whose primary occupation had been wife and mother were not equipped to take over as breadwinner. Witnessing what had happened to their mothers, women resolved not to repeat the pattern. Mary, who claimed work to be central to her identity, sees the link between her current independence and her mother's experience.

I think [what] influenced me most is I wanted to be independent. I would never do what she did. I would never ever want to put myself in a position where I would fall apart. I don't want to give up "I'm me" and "I'm going to support me, and I'm going to be independent." I'll give up some of my independence in other ways but not in terms of money and support and my identity.

Family tragedy exerts a powerful influence on psychological development. From the misfortune of parents' lives children infer what they must avoid in their own futures. Colleen learned early from family events and her mother's reaction to them.

I always felt a need to be self-supporting. I never wanted to depend on a man to have to take care of me. I'm talking about financially. I think I got that because my dad died when I was young. My mother had to go out to work . . . and she was totally unprepared for that shock. The kinds of things that I saw her going through and the pain that she went through because of being totally unprepared for it was something that I never wanted to experience.

Rebecca, equipped with an advanced technical degree and a corresponding supervisory position by age thirty, drew very specific conclusions from a similar life history:

The other significant thing was [that] my father died so young and my mother had to go back to work to raise me. I always felt that it was kind of a driving factor for me in being independent, and being able to draw on an educational background that was marketable. [I felt] that I could always draw on that strength, [having] that education behind me, that if anything similar happened in my life, whether I got married or not, . . . I would feel that I was not totally dependent on my husband and that income. And I think I've done that. As a result, I can never see myself not working. I don't abandon all other roles—I enjoy being a wife and hopefully a mother someday, but there's always that thing in the back of my mind that says, "Well, you know you have this identity. You know you're not going to give it up."

Environmental events and circumstances are formative influences in children's psychological development. In these cases, the lessons of adversity seem to extend to earliest recollection. Women talk of "always" having wanted their independence. The long-standing convictions formed as a consequence of family circumstance become part of their identity.

It is not only death or divorce that molds daughters' resolve. Absence of economic advantage confirmed Hope's need for financial independence.

> I think [there was] always the sense that I could take care of myself. I never wanted to be in a position where I had to rely on someone else and be at their mercy. I grew up without a lot of advantages. There was a lot of negative stigma to the area that I grew up in, so I was constantly overcoming obstacles, and that has something to do with what goes on in the job. By the time I was fourteen, I was already into expressing myself and becoming my own person. Certainly I have my mother's strength. And when I left home, I left because I felt like I needed my own identity . . . it got me started on the right track, because I became who I'd always been inside anyway.

Sometimes a family's main influence is not from direct teaching or parental example. Women define themselves and their aspirations in reaction against the negative model of a family's status. Stella received personal support, but inspiration for a different direction from her upbringing.

> They've encouraged me in anything . . . that I want to pursue or anything that I feel that I want to do. But as far as making a decision about myself, an actual decision, I think it comes directly from me. The only thing that I can say is that I grew up in a very poor family, and I grew up knowing that I didn't want things to remain the way they were. And that was always in the back of my mind, that I knew in order to do better I had to rely on just me. Because I can't really say that anybody in my family influenced me. They were certainly supportive of everything I did.

The development of self-reliance may be a common outgrowth of certain kinds of environments. Where a family's situation, for whatever reason, precludes deliberate individualized attention to its members, children learn

independence early. Thus, socioeconomic advantage is not a necessary condition to develop personal characteristics that forecast women's career and economic independence. Roberta's ability to fend for herself grew even in the absence of family guidance. Currently a consultant in a staff operation of a *Fortune* 500 firm, she finds herself working on degree completion and developing a career path in her early thirties.

> Well, with all of us kids, . . . there was never much support in terms of what we were doing with our lives or with our schooling or anything like that. So I learned very early on to be independent and just to fight for myself as best I could.

A need to be independent is communicated to daughters in several ways. Many learn from the negative example of mothers unprepared for employment. Adverse family conditions teach children to develop attributes and abilities that will insure a different adult life. Mothers might communicate the virtues of independence even when family situations do not ostensibly precipitate it. Elena, a single parent who resists dependence, remembers receiving contradictory messages that she subsequently sorted out for herself.

> What I consciously know is that my mother was always very ambivalent about her dependence on my father. She said, "It's really important for you to take care of yourself." So that's something that I always had in my head. But yet, it was also very important to her that we should be feminine and that we should be attractive and that we should be looking for a husband. So, her whole message was always very, very mixed. . . . And basically what I learned [later] was that I could support myself, which was a very important thing to me, because I felt at that time that I didn't want to focus my whole life on finding somebody to marry me and support me. I couldn't possibly do it—what I was supposed to do. And that encouraged me to explore even more.

Regardless of whether they learn it as a function of early necessity or later experience, women are convinced of the importance of self-sufficiency in an economic sense. Fending for themselves, living up to high standards, and achieving gratifying work all become integral to who they are and the way they live their lives. They may become wives and mothers, but not at the expense of their identities as fully functioning independent human beings.

References

Baruch, G., R. Barnett, and C. Rivers. 1983. *Lifeprints: New Patterns of Love and Work for Today's Women.* New York: New American Library.

Bayes, M. and P. M. Newton. 1978. "Women in authority: A sociopsychological analysis." *Journal of Applied Behavioral Science*, 14:9.

Brown, L. K. 1979. "Women in business management." *Signs*, 5(Winter):287.

Epstein, C. F. 1970. *Women's Place.* Berkeley: University of California Press.

Hardesty, S. and N. Jacobs. 1986. *Success and Betrayal: The Crisis of Women in Corporate America.* New York: Franklin Watts.

Hennig, M. and A. Jardim. 1977. *The Managerial Woman.* Garden City, NY: Anchor Press/Doubleday.

Food for Thought and Application Questions

1. Select the autobiography of a well-known woman who is/was accomplished in a socially valued role. Political leaders, entrepreneurs, scientists, athletes, musicians, artists, and writers provide examples of possible choices. Read the sections in the autobiography that describe childhood experiences and family upbringing. Is there evidence of parental socialization for achievement? Give examples and discuss. Are any of the specific patterns revealed in Freeman's interview study of women managers evident (e.g., "Do as I say, not as I do," role modeling)?

2. What did you want to be when you grew up? Were your early occupational aspirations "gender appropriate"? If so, who or what influenced the choice? To what extent did your parents play a role in shaping your career goals? How did they do so? If your early occupational aspirations were not gender-traditional, were you ever encouraged to change them? Did you? Why? ✦

2

Shortchanging Girls

Gender Socialization in Schools

Peggy Orenstein (in association with the American Association of University Women)

... Like many people, I first saw the results of the American Association of University Women's report *Shortchanging Girls, Shortchanging America* (1991) in my daily newspaper. The headline unfurled across the front page of the *San Francisco Examiner*: "Girls' Low Self-Esteem Slows Their Progress" (Eaky 1991), and the *New York Times* proclaimed: "Girls' Self-Esteem Is Lost on the Way to Adolescence" (Daley 1991).[1] And, like many people, as I read further, I felt my stomach sink.

This was the most extensive national survey on gender and self-esteem ever conducted, the articles said: three thousand boys and girls between the ages of nine and fifteen were polled on their attitudes toward self, school, family, and friends. As part of the project the students were asked to respond to multiple-choice questions, provide comments, and in some cases, were interviewed in focus groups. The results confirmed something that many women already knew too well. For a girl, the passage into adolescence is not just marked by menarche or a few new curves. It is marked by a loss of confidence in herself and her abilities, especially in math and science. It is marked by a scathingly critical attitude toward her body and a blossoming sense of personal inadequacy.

In spite of the changes in women's roles in society, in spite of the changes in their own mothers' lives, many of today's girls fall into traditional patterns of low self-image, self-doubt, and self-censorship of their creative and intellectual potential. Although all children experience confusion and a faltering sense of self at adolescence, girls' self-regard drops further than boys' and never catches up (AAUW 1990 and 1991). They emerge from their teenage years with reduced expectations and have less confidence in themselves and their abilities than do boys. Teenage girls are more vulnerable to feelings of depression and hopelessness and are four times more likely to attempt suicide (AAUW Educational Foundation 1992).

The AAUW discovered that the most dramatic gender gap in self-esteem is centered in the area of competence. Boys are more likely than girls to say they are "pretty good at a lot of things" and are twice as likely to name their talents as the thing they like most about themselves. Girls, meanwhile, cite an aspect of their physical appearance (AAUW 1991). Unsurprisingly, then, teenage girls are much more likely than boys to say they are "not smart enough" or "not good enough" to achieve their dreams.

The education system is supposed to provide our young people with opportunity, to encourage their intellectual growth and prepare them as citizens. Yet students in the AAUW survey reported gender bias in the classroom—and illustrated its effects—with the canniness of investigative reporters. Both boys and girls believed that teachers encouraged more assertive behavior in boys, and that, overall, boys receive the majority of their teachers' attention. The result is that boys will speak out in class more readily, and are more willing to "argue with my teachers when I think I'm right" (AAUW 1991).

Meanwhile, girls show a more precipitous drop in their interest in math and science as they advance through school. Even girls who like the subjects are, by age fifteen, only half as likely as boys to feel competent in them. These findings are key: researchers have long understood that a loss of confidence in math usually *precedes* a drop in achievement, rather than vice versa (AAUW 1992; Kloosterman 1990; Fennema and Sherman 1977). A confidence gap, rather than an ability gap, may help explain why the numbers of female physical and computer scientists actually went down during the 1980s (White 1992; National Science Board 1991; Linn 1990). The AAUW also discovered a circular relationship between math confidence and overall self-confidence, as well as a link between liking math and aspiring to professional careers—a correlation that is stronger for girls than boys. Apparently girls who can resist gender-role stereotypes in the classroom resist them elsewhere more effectively as well.

Among its most intriguing findings, the AAUW survey revealed that, although all girls report consistently lower self-esteem than boys, the severity and the nature of that reduced self-worth vary among ethnic groups. Far more African American girls retain their overall self-esteem during adolescence than white or Latina girls, maintaining a stronger sense of both personal and familial importance. They are about twice as likely to be "happy with the way I am" than girls of other groups and report feeling "pretty good at a lot of things" at nearly the rate of white boys (AAUW 1990). The one exception for African American girls is their feelings about school: black girls are more pessimistic about both their teachers and their schoolwork than other girls. Meanwhile, Latina girls' self-esteem crisis is in many ways the most profound. Between the ages of nine and fifteen, the number of Latina girls who are "happy with the way I am" plunges by 38 percentage points, compared with a 33 percent drop for white girls and a 7 percent drop for black girls. Family disappears as a source of positive self-worth for Latina teens, and academic confidence, belief in one's talents, and a sense of personal importance all plummet (AAUW 1990). During the year in which *Shortchanging Girls, Shortchanging America* was conducted, urban Latinas left school at a greater rate than any other group, male or female (U.S. Bureau of the Census 1992). . . .

Seeking the Source: Entering Girls' Worlds

When I first read about the AAUW survey, I felt deeply troubled. This was a report in which children were talking directly to us about their experience, and I didn't like what I heard. These girls had internalized the limitations of gender. As a feminist, I took this as a warning. As a journalist, I wanted to find out more. According to the survey, middle school is the beginning of the transition from girlhood to womanhood and, not coincidentally, the time of greatest self-esteem loss (AAUW 1990 and 1991). So, with that in mind, I went back to eighth grade.

I chose to work on this project in California, which has the largest school system in the country. California, along with Minnesota and several other states, has been on the cutting edge of both gender-fair and multicultural education and perhaps there is less bias here than there might be elsewhere. But I wanted to see what was working in classrooms as well as what was not.

School administrators are leery of journalists, and teachers even more so. It was not easy to find educators (or parents) who were willing to put up with a year's scrutiny, even though, since I was writing about children, I promised to change the names of everyone involved. I interviewed over one hundred and fifty girls and spoke with nearly a dozen administrators before settling on two schools, fifty miles apart, in which I would spend the 1992–93 school year. . . .

Learning Silence: Scenes From the Class Struggle

The school described in the sections that follow, Weston, is a suburban middle school with an overwhelmingly white student body and a reputation for excellence. Weston, California, sits at the far reaches of the San Francisco Bay Area. The drive from the city takes one through a series of bedroom communities, carefully planned idylls in which, as the miles roll by, the tax brackets leap upward, the politics swing right, and the people fade to white. But Weston is different: once an oddly matched blend of country folk and chemical plant workers, this is an old town, the kind of place where people still gather curbside under the bunting-swathed lampposts of Maple Street to watch the Fourth of July parade. Many of the businesses in Weston's center—doughnut shops, ladies' clothing stores, a few hard drinkers' bars, and picked-over antiquaries—haven't changed hands in over thirty years. There are a few fern bars and one cafe serving espresso here, but if people want high tone, they go to the city.

Not that Weston has remained suspended in time. The ramshackle houses downtown may still be populated by the families of mechanics, plant workers, and, in shoddy apartment complexes, a small community of working poor, but the hills that ring the town's edge have been gobbled up by tract homes where young professionals have hunkered down—a safe distance from urban ills—to raise their children. There's even a clean, modern supermarket by the freeway, built expressly for the new suburbanites, with a multiplex cinema across the street for their occasional evenings out.

The only place where Weston's two populations converge regularly is at Weston Middle School, a crumbling Spanish-style edifice just up the street from the post office, city hall, and, more important to the student body, a McDonald's. This is the town's sole middle school, and as such, it serves nearly nine hundred students a year from this disparate population. The bumper stickers on the cars dropping off the children reflect the mix: Toyota vans advertising the local NPR affiliate pull up behind rusty pickups that proclaim: "My wife said if I buy another gun she'll divorce me; God, I'll miss her!" There is also a staunch Christian population here—Mormons, Seventh-Day Adventists, and other, less austere sects whose cars remind other residents that "Jesus Loves You!"

In recent years, Weston Middle School has fulfilled its mandate well: the school entrance is draped with a "California Distinguished School" banner, earned last year by the students' estimable standardized test scores as well as the staff's exemplary performance. The teachers are an impressive, enthusiastic group who routinely seek methods of instruction that will inspire a little more engagement, a little more effort on the part of their pupils: an eighth-grade history teacher uses a karaoke microphone to juice up his lessons; an English teacher videotapes students performing original poems to bring literature to life; a science teacher offers extra credit to students who join

him in cleaning up the banks of a local river. There is also some concern about gender issues in education: Weston's history teachers have embraced the new, more inclusive textbooks adopted by the state of California; in English, students write essays on their views about abortion and read, among other books, *Streams to the River, River to the Sea*, a historical novel which recasts Sacagawea as an intrepid female hero.

Yet the overt curriculum, as fine as it may be, is never the only force operating in a classroom. There is something else as well. The "hidden curriculum" comprises the unstated lessons that students learn in school: it is the running subtext through which teachers communicate behavioral norms and individual status in the school culture, the process of socialization that cues children into their place in the hierarchy of larger society. Once used to describe the ways in which the education system works to reproduce class systems in our culture, the "hidden curriculum" has recently been applied to the ways in which schools help reinforce gender roles, whether they intend to or not.

The Daily Grind: Lessons in the Hidden Curriculum

Amy Wilkinson has looked forward to being an eighth grader forever—at least for the last two years, which, when you're thirteen, seems like the same thing. By the second week of September she's settled comfortably into her role as one of the school's reigning elite. Each morning before class, she lounges with a group of about twenty other eighth-grade girls and boys in the most visible spot on campus: at the base of the schoolyard, between one of the portable classrooms that was constructed in the late 1970s and the old oak tree in the overflow parking lot. The group trades gossip, flirts, or simply stands around, basking in its own importance and killing time before the morning bell.

At 8:15 on Tuesday the crowd has already convened, and Amy is standing among a knot of girls, laughing. She is fuller-figured than she'd like to be, wide-hipped and heavy-limbed with curly, blond hair, cornflower-blue eyes, and a sharply up-turned nose. With the help of her mother, who is a drama coach, she has become the school's star actress: last year she played Eliza in Weston's production of *My Fair Lady*. Although she earns solid grades in all of her subjects—she'll make the honor roll this fall—drama is her passion, she says, because "I love entertaining people, and I love putting on characters."

Also, no doubt, because she loves the spotlight: this morning, when she mentions a boy I haven't met, Amy turns, puts her hands on her hips, anchors her feet shoulder width apart, and bellows across the schoolyard, "Greg! Get over here! You have to meet Peggy."

She smiles wryly as Greg, looking startled, begins to make his way across the schoolyard for an introduction. "I'm not exactly shy," she says, her hands still on her hips. "I'm *bold*."

Amy is bold. And brassy, and strong-willed. Like any teenager, she tries on and discards different selves as if they were so many pairs of Girbaud jeans, searching ruthlessly for a perfect fit. During a morning chat just before the school year began, she told me that her parents tried to coach her on how to respond to my questions. "They told me to tell you that they want me to be my own person," she complained. "My mother *told* me to tell you that. I do want to be my own person, but it's like, you're interviewing me about who *I* am and she's telling me what to say—that's not my own person, is it?"

When the morning bell rings, Amy and her friends cut off their conversations, scoop up their books, and jostle toward the school's entrance. Inside, Weston's hallways smell chalky, papery, and a little sweaty from gym class. The wood-railed staircases at either end of the two-story main building are worn thin in the middle from the scuffle of hundreds of pairs of sneakers pounding them at forty-eight-minute intervals for nearly seventy-five years. Amy's mother, Sharon, and her grandmother both attended this school. So will her two younger sisters. Her father, a mechanic who works on big rigs, is a more recent Weston recruit: he grew up in Georgia and came here after he and Sharon were married.

Amy grabs my hand, pulling me along like a small child or a slightly addled new student: within three minutes we have threaded our way through the dull-yellow hallways to her locker and then upstairs to room 238, Mrs. Richter's math class.

The twenty-two students that stream through the door with us run the gamut of physical maturity. Some of the boys are as small and compact as fourth graders, their legs sticking out of their shorts like pipe cleaners. A few are trapped in the agony of a growth spurt, and still others cultivate downy beards. The girls' physiques are less extreme: most are nearly their full height, and all but a few have already weathered the brunt of puberty. They wear topknots or ponytails, and their shirts are tucked neatly into their jeans.

Mrs. Richter, a ruddy, athletic woman with a powerful voice, has arranged the chairs in a three-sided square, two rows deep. Amy walks to the far side of the room and, as she takes her seat, falls into a typically feminine pose: she crosses her legs, folds her arms across her chest, and hunches forward toward her desk, seeming to shrink into herself. The sauciness of the playground disappears, and, in fact, she says hardly a word during class. Meanwhile, the boys, especially those who are more physically mature, sprawl in their chairs, stretching their legs long, expanding into the available space.

Nate, a gawky, sanguine boy who has shaved his head except for a small thatch that's hidden under an Oakland A's cap, leans his chair back on two legs and, although the bell has already rung, begins a noisy conversation with his friend Kyle.

Mrs. Richter turns to him. "What's all the discussion about, Nate?" she asks.

"*He's* talking to *me*," Nate answers, pointing to Kyle. Mrs. Richter writes Nate's name on the chalkboard as a warning toward detention and he yells out in protest. They begin to quibble over the justice of her decision, their first—but certainly not their last—power struggle of the day. As they argue, Allison, a tall, angular girl who once told me, "My goal is to be the best wife and mother I can be," raises her hand to ask a question. Mrs. Richter, finishing up with Nate, doesn't notice.

"Get your homework out, everyone!" the teacher booms, and walks among the students, checking to make sure no one has shirked on her or his assignment. Allison, who sits in the front row nearest both the blackboard and the teacher, waits patiently for another moment, then, realizing she's not getting results, puts her hand down. When Mrs. Richter walks toward her, Allison tries another tack, calling out her question. Still, she gets no response, so she gives up.

As a homework assignment, the students have divided their papers into one hundred squares, color-coding each square prime or composite—prime being those numbers which are divisible only by one and themselves, and composite being everything else. Mrs. Richter asks them to call out the prime numbers they've found, starting with the tens.

Nate is the first to shout, "Eleven!" The rest of the class chimes in a second later. As they move through the twenties and thirties, Nate, Kyle, and Kevin, who sit near one another at the back of the class, call out louder and louder, casually competing for both quickest response and the highest decibel level. Mrs. Richter lets the boys' behavior slide, although they are intimidating other students.

"Okay," Mrs. Richter says when they've reached one hundred. "Now, what do you think of one hundred and three? Prime or composite?"

Kyle, who is skinny and a little pop-eyed, yells out, "Prime!" but Mrs. Richter turns away from him to give someone else a turn. Unlike Allison, who gave up when she was ignored, Kyle isn't willing to cede his teacher's attention. He begins to bounce in his chair and chant, *"Prime! Prime! Prime!"* Then, when he turns out to be right, he rebukes the teacher, saying, *"See,* I told you."

When the girls in Mrs. Richter's class do speak, they follow the rules. When Allison has another question, she raises her hand again and waits her turn; this time, the teacher responds. When Amy volunteers her sole answer of the period, she raises her hand, too. She gives the wrong answer to an easy multiplication problem, turns crimson, and flips her head forward so her hair falls over her face.

Occasionally, the girls shout out answers, but generally they are to the easiest, lowest-risk questions, such as the factors of four or six. And their stabs at public recognition

depend on the boys' largesse: when the girls venture responses to more complex questions the boys quickly become territorial, shouting them down with their own answers. Nate and Kyle are particularly adept at overpowering Renee, who, I've been told by the teacher, is the brightest girl in the class. (On a subsequent visit, I will see her lay her head on her desk when Nate overwhelms her and mutter, "I hate this class.")

Mrs. Richter doesn't say anything to condone the boys' aggressiveness, but she doesn't have to: they insist on—and receive—her attention even when she consciously tries to shift it elsewhere in order to make the class more equitable.

After the previous day's homework is corrected, Mrs. Richter begins a new lesson, on the use of exponents.

"What does three to the third power mean?" she asks the class.

"I know!" shouts Kyle.

Instead of calling on Kyle, who has already answered more than his share of questions, the teacher turns to Dawn, a somewhat more voluble girl who has plucked her eyebrows down to a few hairs.

"Do you know, Dawn?"

Dawn hesitates, and begins "Well, you count the number of threes and . . ."

"But I know!" interrupts Kyle. *"I know!"*

Mrs. Richter deliberately ignores him, but Dawn is rattled: she never finishes her sentence, she just stops.

"I know! ME!" Kyle shouts again, and then before Dawn recovers herself he blurts, *"It's three times three times three!"*

At this point, Mrs. Richter gives in. She turns away from Dawn, who is staring blankly, and nods at Kyle. "Yes," she says. "Three times three times three. Does everyone get it?"

"YES!" shouts Kyle; Dawn says nothing.

Mrs. Richter picks up the chalk. "Let's do some others," she says.

"Let me!" says Kyle.

"I'll pick on whoever raises their hand," she tells him.

Nate, Kyle, and two other boys immediately shoot up their hands, fingers squeezed tight and straight in what looks like a salute.

"Don't you want to wait and hear the problem first?" she asks, laughing.

They drop their hands briefly. She writes 8^4 on the board. "Okay, what would that look like written out?"

Although a third of the class raises their hands to answer—including a number of students who haven't yet said a word—she calls on Kyle anyway.

"Eight times eight times eight times eight," he says triumphantly, as the other students drop their hands.

When the bell rings, I ask Amy about the mistake she made in class and the embarrassment it caused her. She blushes again.

"Oh yeah," she says. "That's about the only time I ever talked in there. I'll never do that again."

Voice and Silence

I had chosen Amy, along with two of her friends, Evie DiLeo and Becca Holbrook, as three of the subjects for this book partly because, within minutes of our first meeting—and months before I ever saw them in a classroom—they announced to me that they were not like other girls at Weston: they were, they proudly announced, feminists. Amy explained that to them "feminism" meant that as adults they plan to be economically independent of men. Until that time, though, it means "knowing that boys aren't all they're cracked up to be."

I had hoped that these girls, with their bold credo, would defy the statistics in the AAUW survey *Shortchanging Girls, Shortchanging America*. Yet although they spoke of themselves in terms of grit and independence, those qualities were rarely on display in the classroom. Whereas their male classmates yelled out or snapped the fingers of their raised hands when they wanted to speak, these girls seemed, for the most part, to recede from class proceedings, a charge they didn't deny.

"I don't raise my hand in my classes because I'm afraid I have the wrong answer and I'll be embarrassed," Becca, who is gangly and soft-spoken, explains one day during lunch. "My self-confidence will be taken away, so I

don't want to raise my hand even if I really do know."

"I hate when teachers correct you," says Evie, who, dark-haired and serious, is enrolled in Weston's gifted students' program. "And it's worse when they say it's okay to do things wrong in that voice like 'It's okay, honey.' I can't handle it. I get really red and I start crying and I feel stupid."

"I think," Amy says slowly, "I think girls just worry about what people will say more than boys do, so they don't want to talk so much."

I mention to Amy that the boys freely volunteer in the math and science classes I've observed, even though their answers are often wrong. They seem to think it's okay to say "I think," to be unsure of a response.

Amy nods in agreement. "Boys never care if they're wrong. They can say totally off-the-wall things, things that have nothing to do with class sometimes. They're not afraid to get in trouble or anything. I'm not shy. But it's like, when I get into class, I just . . ." She shrugs her shoulders helplessly. "I just can't talk. I don't know why."

Girls' hesitance to speak out relative to boys is not mere stylistic difference; speaking out in class—and being acknowledged for it—is a constant reinforcement of a student's right to be heard, to take academic risks. Students who talk in class have more opportunity to enhance self-esteem through exposure to praise; they have the luxury of learning from mistakes and they develop the perspective to see failure as an educational tool. Boys such as Kyle and Nate feel internal permission to speak out whether they are bright or not, whether they are right or wrong, whether their comments are insightful, corrosive, combative, or utterly ridiculous. The important thing is to be recognized, to assert the "I am."

"I think my opinions are important, so I yell them out," Nate tells me one day after Mrs. Richter's math class. "The teacher'll tell you not to do it, but they answer your question before the people who raise their hands. Girls will sit there until the bell rings with their hands up and never get their question answered." He waves his hand in the air as if brushing the girls aside and says contemptuously, "Forget that."

According to gender equity specialists Myra and David Sadker, students who participate in class hold more positive attitudes toward school, and those attitudes enhance learning. Yet they also found that, in the typical classroom, boys overwhelmingly dominate the proceedings: they consistently command more of the teacher's time and energy than girls, receiving more positive reinforcement, more remediation, and more criticism. Nor is the difference just one of quantity: in the Sadkers' observations of one hundred classrooms in four states, they found that the boys were routinely asked more complex questions than girls, and were commended for their academic acumen, while girls were commended for social skills and docility (Sadker and Sadker 1985 and 1986).

In every class I visit at Weston there is at least one boy like Nate or Kyle, a boy who demands constant and inappropriate attention and to whom the teacher succumbs: if she doesn't, after all, she won't get much done during that period. In a straight count of who talks in Weston classrooms—who yells out answers, who is called on by the teacher, who commands the most interaction—the ratio hovers roughly around five boys to one girl. Compared to other schools, however, this constitutes progress: the Sadkers placed the rate at eight to one (Sadker and Sadker 1985; Schrof 1993). Even in English class, traditionally girls' turf, Weston boys received roughly three times the recognition of their female classmates.

The argument can be made that boys as well as girls suffer from the hidden curriculum. Boys such as Nate may be learning an unfortunate self-centeredness along with a lack of respect for their female classmates. Yet they still profit from the attention they receive. Ignored by their teachers and belittled by their male peers, girls lose heart: they may become reluctant to participate at all in class, unable to withstand the small failures necessary for long-term academic success. Even girls such as Amy, Evie, and Becca, who frequently proclaim that "guys are *so* obnoxious," have absorbed the hidden lessons of deference to them in the classroom, and, along with it, a powerful lesson in self-abnegation.

Several days after joining Amy in her math class, I visit Ms. Kelly's English class. Ms. Kelly is a second-year teacher: freckle-faced and snub-nosed, dressed in a T-shirt and khaki skirt, she barely looks older than her students. The class has been studying Greek mythology; today Ms. Kelly, who has placed the desks in clusters of six, instructs the students to write out the discussion they imagine took place between Zeus and Hera when she discovered he had fathered an illegitimate child.

"Any questions?" she asks, after explaining the assignment.

Two girls, Kathy and Amanda, raise their hands and she calls on Amanda. Amanda glances at Kathy, who sits in the group of desks next to hers. "Well, can you help me when you've answered her question?" she says politely. The teacher tends to Kathy, and then to a boy in another group who is misbehaving; she never returns to Amanda, who becomes frustrated.

"What are we supposed to do?" she mutters. "I don't get it." She puts her pencil down and looks over the shoulder of the girl sitting next to her. After a few minutes, she sighs wearily and begins to write.

I walk around the room, asking the students if I can read their works-in-progress. Amanda, who will eventually get an A on her paper, covers hers when I ask to see it.

"Oh," she says, "mine's so stupid you wouldn't want to read it."

Kathy reluctantly hands me her work. As I skim through it, one of the boys shoves his paper at me.

"Don't you want to read mine?" he asks.

I smile politely, as unwilling as the teachers to chastise him for interrupting, and take his paper. The dialogue he's written is almost incoherent and laced with misuses of the archaic forms of "you," as in "Hera, I'll whip thou butt for that."

He smirks as I read.

"Good, huh?" he says; then takes the paper back to read to his seatmates.

During an earlier lesson, the students have composed their own original myths, and have voted on the one they think is the best in the class. At the end of today's period, Ms. Kelly reads the winner, written by a wiry, sharp-featured Latina girl named Amber. The tale is surprisingly artful, the story of a young boy's search for the answers to questions that his father says are unsolvable. His quest takes him through enchanted woods, where he encounters talking animals who help him unlock the secret of a magic waterfall. He attains wisdom through risk and adventure, and, in the end, brings insight as well as treasure home to lay before his father.

After class I ask Amber why she chose to make a boy, not a girl, the central character in her story. She shrugs. "I used a boy because little girls don't go into creepy places and explore things," she says. "And it was an adventure; it wouldn't be right if you used a girl."

I ask Ms. Kelly to lend me the students' stories from all of her class periods and flip through the stack. Although many girls chose men and boys as the embodiments of bravery, strength, and wisdom, it did not surprise me to find that not a single boy had imagined a female hero.

Certainly some girls at Weston act out, demand attention, clown in class, but when they try those tactics, using disruption as a tool to gain individual attention and instruction, they are not met with the same reward as boys.

In mid-November, Mrs. Richter is giving out grades to Amy's class. The teacher sits at her desk in the back corner of the room, and the students come up one by one, in reverse alphabetical order; their faces are tense on the way up, then pleased or disappointed on the way back.

When Dawn's turn comes, Mrs. Richter speaks sharply to her.

"You're getting a B," the teacher says, "but for citizenship, you're getting 'disruptive.' You've been talking a lot and there have been some outbursts."

Dawn scrunches her mouth over to one side of her face, lowers her eyes, and returns to her seat.

"Disruptive?" yells Nate from across the room where the teacher's voice has carried. "*She's* not disruptive, *I'm* disruptive."

Mrs. Richter laughs. "You've got that right," she says.

When his turn comes, Nate gets a B plus. "It would've been an A minus if you turned in your last homework assignment," Mrs. Richter says. As predicted, his citizenship comment is also 'disruptive,' but the bad news isn't delivered with the same sting as it was to Dawn—it's conferred with an indulgent smile. There is a tacit acceptance of a disruptive boy, because boys *are* disruptive. Girls are too, sometimes, as Dawn illustrates, but with different consequences.

So along with fractions and exponents, Dawn has learned that she has to tamp down assertive behavior, that she has to diminish herself both to please the teacher and to appease the boys, with whom she cannot compete. Meanwhile, Nate has learned that monopolizing the class period and defying the teacher gets him in trouble, but he also garners individual attention, praise, and answers to his questions.

Over the course of the semester, Dawn slowly stops disrupting; she stops participating too. At the semester break, when I check with Mrs. Richter on the classes' progress, she tells me, "Dawn hardly talks at all now because she's overpowered by the boys. She can't get the attention in class, so she's calmed down."

Nate, however, hasn't changed a bit, but whereas Dawn's behavior is viewed as containable, the teacher sees Nate's as inevitable. "I'll go through two weeks of torture before I'll give him detention," Mrs. Richter says. "But you have to tolerate that behavior to a certain extent or he won't want to be there at all, he'll get himself kicked out."

"I know his behavior works for him, though," she continues. "He talks more, he gets more answers out there, and he does well because of it. I try to tell him that we need to let others talk so they can understand too. But when I do, I begin and end with positive things about his behavior and sandwich the bad stuff in the middle. I'm never sure which part he really hears. . . ."

Note

1. The students who participated in the survey were drawn from twelve locations. The sam-

ple was stratified by region, and the students included were proportionate to the number of school-aged children in each state.

References

American Association of University Women (AAUW). 1990. *Shortchanging Girls, Shortchanging America: Full Data Report*. Washington, D.C.: American Association of University Women.

——. 1991. *Shortchanging Girls, Shortchanging America: Executive Summary*. Washington, D.C.: American Association of University Women.

——. 1992. *The AAUW Report: How the Schools Shortchange Girls*. Washington, D.C.: The AAUW Educational Foundation and the National Educational Association.

Daley, S. 1991. "Girls' self-esteem is lost on way to adolescence, new study finds." *New York Times*, National Edition, January 9, p. B1.

Eaky, K. 1991. "Girls' low self-esteem slows their progress, study finds." *San Francisco Examiner*, January 9, p. A1.

Fennema, E. and J. Sherman. 1977. "Sex-related differences in mathematics achievement, spatial visualization and affective factors." *American Educational Research Journal*, 14:1.

Kloosterman, P. 1990. "Attributions, performance following failure, and motivation in mathematics," in E. Fennema and G. C. Leder (eds.), *Mathematics and Gender*, New York: Teachers College Press.

Linn, M. C. 1990. "Gender, mathematics and science: Trends and recommendations." Paper presented at the Summer Institute for the Council of Chief State School Officers, Mystic, CT. July-August.

National Science Board. 1991. *Science and Engineering Indicators*. Washington, DC: National Science Board.

Sadker, M. and D. Sadker. 1985. "Sexism in the schoolroom of the '80s." *Psychology Today*, March.

——. 1986. "Sexism in the classroom: From grade school to graduate school." *Phi Delta Kappan*, 67, 7.

Schrof, J. M. 1993. "The gender machine." *U.S. News & World Report*, August 2.

U.S. Bureau of the Census. 1992. *Educational Attainment in the United States: March 1991 and 1990*. Washington, D.C.: U.S. Government Printing Office.

White, P. E. 1992. "Women and minorities in science and engineering: An update." Washington, D.C.: National Science Foundation.

Food for Thought and Application Questions

1. Reflect on your own primary- and secondary-level educational experiences. Identify aspects of the "hidden curriculum" that encouraged gender-traditional behavior. To the extent that teachers played a role in transmitting this hidden curriculum, do you think they did so intentionally? If not, what motivated their behavior? What do you believe to be the end result of the existence of this hidden curriculum? Did it affect you personally? If so, how?

2. The educational setting described by Orenstein is coeducational. How would the hidden curriculum and girls' experiences differ in a single-sex educational environment? Give specific examples and discuss the likely consequences of these differences. ✦

3

Gender and the Career Choice Process

The Role of Biased Self-Assessments

Shelley J. Correll

Women and men hold different kinds of jobs, as abundant evidence shows (for reviews, see Reskin 1993; Jacobs 1995a; Jacobsen 1994). While explanations of the persistence of sex segregation in paid work remain incomplete, the consequences for gender inequality are clear. The differential occupational distribution of men and women explains the majority of the gender gap in wages (Peterson and Morgan 1995; Treiman and Hartman 1981). Most attempts by sociologists to explain the persistence of sex segregation in the labor force document the importance of demand-side processes, such as statistical discrimination, internal labor markets, and the gendering of job queues (for reviews of this research, see Reskin and Roos 1990; England 1992). Far less attention has been given to supply-side processes by which males and females differentially move into various activities associated with different kinds of work (Peterson and Morgan 1995). However, supply-side processes are important because the supply networks from which employers recruit are already segregated by gender (Granovetter and Tilly 1988). Further, sex segregation often emerges early in the path toward many careers. For example, Jacobs (1995b) finds that one-third of all women would have to change college majors to be distributed in the same manner as their male counterparts. Since males and females appear to be voluntarily making career-relevant decisions that will carry them, on average, in substantially different occupational directions, it is important to examine these early stages in the supply-side process and ask why men and women make the choices they do.

In this article, I develop and test a simple supply-side mechanism to illustrate how cultural conceptions of gender serve to constrain the early career-relevant choices of men and women. I argue that widely shared cultural beliefs about gender and task competence bias actors' perceptions of their competence at various skills. Focusing on perceptions of competence is crucial for understanding modern stratification systems since the presumption of competence legitimates inequality in achievement-oriented societies such as the United States. When competence at a certain skill is thought to be necessary for a particular career, then gender differences in the perceptions of task competence, over and above actual ability, foster gender differences in commitment to paths leading to that career.

As a specific location of this process, I examine how gender differences in the perception of mathematical competence influence high school and college students' educational decisions that lead to careers in engineering, math, and the physical sciences. As these professions have been especially impervious to the entrance of women (Hanson 1996), they provide a convenient window from which to examine the process by which cultural beliefs about gender differentially influence early career decisions of men and women. Further, since the "quantitative professions" are among the more rewarding financially (Frehill 1997; Babco 1988), gender differences in the movement into them has consequences for the continued gender gap in wages. Certainly, discrimination and other structural constraints continue to limit the occupational opportunities available to women. However, a fuller understanding of the persistence of sex segregation in the labor force can be gleaned by also examining the seemingly voluntary processes by which men and women make career-relevant choices.

Gender and Career Choice Processes

The career choice process occurs throughout the life cycle as individuals make a series of decisions that have occupational consequences. Sociologists who examine the processes by which individuals choose careers have focused primarily on later stages when individuals actually choose to enter *jobs* rather than on the decisions to move into activities at earlier stages on the paths leading to specific careers. However, as noted above, gender differences in the selection of activities that constrain occupational choices often occur earlier in the life cycle. This is especially evident in the case of professions like engineering, where a college degree in the field is necessary to pursue a career. Due to the sequence of required classes, the decision to pursue a degree in engineering or the physical sciences must usually be made during the first or second year of college (Seymour and Hewitt 1997). Further, those who fail to take advanced-level math classes in high school are highly unlikely to select college majors in science, math, or engineering (McIlwee and Robinson 1992). Since gender differences in the selection of activities relevant to careers in these fields emerge as early as high school, it is important to examine decisions made at this stage in the life cycle.

Gender and the Path to Math

The ratio of females to males declines as young people move further down the path toward the quantitative professions (McIlwee and Robinson 1992). By high school, males are more likely than females to be enrolled in advanced-level math and science elective classes (AAUW 1992; National Science Foundation 1994). Of the bachelor's degrees earned in 1990, 31.2% of physical science degrees and 13.8% of engineering degrees were awarded to women (Jacobs 1995b). In the United States workforce in 1993, only 8% of all engineers and 9% of all physicists were female (National Science Foundation 1996). Thus, in contrast with the vast movement of women into other professions, such as law and medicine, engineering and the physical sciences remain extremely male dominated.

In considering the process by which males and females differentially move into activities relevant to careers in engineering and the physical sciences, it is important to establish what is *not* causing this gender difference. We need to keep in mind that, unlike other systems of difference such as race and class, males and females grow up primarily in mixed-sex families and attend similar kinds of high schools. Since most young people attend coeducational high schools and high schools tend to have very balanced sex ratios, gender differences in career choice are not primarily due to differences in the type of high school attended by males and females. Further, gender differences in the entry into the quantitative professions are not due to differences in family structure or socioeconomic status since males and females are distributed roughly equally across these groups. Finally, a gender difference in the choice of a quantitative college major is not the result of a higher rate of transition from high school to college by males, since females are slightly *more* likely than males to attend college (National Center for Education Statistics 1998). In sum, compared to differences between students of different ethnic groups or social classes, there is considerable similarity in the structural location and resources available to male and female youth. What is puzzling is that a gender gap emerges early in the path toward careers in the quantitative professions in spite of this structural similarity.

While many and varied explanations have been offered for the continued dearth of women in engineering and the physical sciences, most explanations implicate a linkage to mathematics (for a thorough review, see Oakes 1990). Mathematics has been described as the "critical filter" on the path to careers in math, science, and engineering (Dossey et al.). But, how does this filter serve to remove women disproportionately from the path to the quantitative professions?

Gender and Mathematical Aptitude

One explanation for the shortage of women in the quantitative professions is that males have a biological aptitude for math that females lack (Rudisill and Morrison 1989;

Kolata 1980). However, cross-national studies have found wide variation in both the direction and magnitude of mathematical gender differences, casting serious doubt on biological superiority theories (Baker and Jones 1993). Further, a meta-analysis of over 100 studies demonstrates that gender differences in mathematical performances are small, have declined over time, and vary in direction depending on the mathematical domain (e.g., computation, understanding of mathematical concepts, etc.; Hyde, Fennema, and Lamon 1990). Since analyses of gender differences in math aptitude are often conducted using large national surveys or populations of college freshmen, even differences that are statistically significant are often very small in magnitude (see, e.g., Hyde et al. 1990). Thus, gender differences in actual mathematical competence do not seem to be responsible for the large differences in the numbers of men and women choosing to enter fields requiring some level of mathematical competence. Instead, I argue that cultural beliefs about gender and mathematics differentially influence the movement of males and females along educational and career paths leading to careers in science, math, and engineering. In the next section, I draw upon current understandings of gender as a multilevel system to develop this argument.

Cultural Beliefs and Biased Self-Assessments

Gender and Cultural Beliefs

Sociologists have increasingly realized that gender is a multilevel system that consists not only of roles and identities at the individual level, but also includes ways of behaving in relation to one another at the interactional level, and cultural beliefs and distributions of resources at the macrolevel (Ridgeway 1997; Risman 1998). The multilevel nature of this system allows processes that contribute to the reproduction of gender inequality at the macro, micro, and interactional levels to occur simultaneously. In this way, the gender system is overdetermined and represents a powerfully conservative system.

Cultural beliefs about gender (hereafter called "gender beliefs") are the component of gender stereotypes that contain specific expectations for competence. It is this component, with its specific expectations of competence, that presents special problems for gender equality (Ridgeway and Correll 2000). Gender beliefs are also cultural schemas for interpreting or making sense of the social world. As such, they represent what we think "most people" believe or accept as true about the categories of "men" and "women." In North America, at least, men are widely thought to be more competent than women, except when performing "feminine" tasks (Conway, Pizzamiglio, and Mount 1996; Wagner and Berger 1997). As we will see below, substantial evidence indicates that mathematical tasks are often stereotyped as "masculine" tasks. Even individuals who do not personally believe that men are more competent than women are likely aware that this belief exists in the culture and expect that others will treat them according to it. This expectation has been shown to modify behavior and bias judgments, as will be described below (Foschi 1996; Steele 1997).

Gender Beliefs about Mathematics

Many studies have shown that students view math as masculine and perceive mathematics to be a male domain ([see for example] Hyde et al. 1990; Armstrong 1981). Likewise, most students believe math and science to be more useful and important for boys and better understood by them (Eccles et al. 1984). A recent ethnographic study of over 300 male and female students who were enrolled in an engineering or science major or had switched out of one paints a detailed picture of the gendered culture of math and science (Seymour and Hewitt 1997). Many of the women in this study said they had difficulty "giving themselves permission" to major in science, math, and engineering, even though they could not explain precisely what had discouraged them (p. 241). They described a dampening effect of a cultural message that suggests that women either could not or should not do math and science.

Collectively, the studies cited above demonstrate that widely shared cultural beliefs do include claims that males are more competent than females at mathematics. While empirical support for actual gender differences in mathematical competence is weak (Baker and Jones 1993; Hyde et al. 1990), the belief of male mathematical superiority itself is widely dispersed in American culture. Exposure to news reports that claim that males have greater natural mathematical ability has been found to increase mothers' stereotypic perceptions of their daughters' mathematical abilities (Jacobs and Eccles 1985). Research also suggests that parents convey different expectations of mathematical success to their male and female children (Frome and Eccles 1998). Likewise, male and female teachers at all grade levels routinely have lower expectations in math for females than for males (AAUW 1992; National Science Foundation 1994). Thus, individuals are exposed to gender beliefs associated with mathematics from various sources (teachers, parents, counselors, published results of standardized test scores by gender), and likely become aware that "most people" believe that males, as a group, are better at math.

Some individuals probably also come to *personally* believe that males are better at math, although girls have been shown to be less likely than boys to hold stereotypic views about mathematics (Hyde et al. 1990). If an individual girl believes that boys are better at math, she might view mathematical competence as inconsistent with a female gender identity, doubt her mathematical ability, and decrease her interest in careers requiring high levels of mathematical proficiency. In this way, personally holding gender stereotypic views in regard to mathematics would be sufficient to produce gender differences in perceptions of mathematical competence and commitment to careers requiring mathematical proficiency.

The Impact of Gender Beliefs on Judgments and Behaviors

Gender beliefs can operate in different ways simultaneously to contribute to the reproduction of gender inequality. It is clear that children learn and internalize gender beliefs and that this internalization affects behavior. However, there is some variation in *what* is internalized. With respect to mathe-

matics, one possibility is that an individual comes to personally believe that boys are better at math than girls. Holding stereotypic beliefs about activities, such as mathematics, has been shown to influence the attitudes and career aspirations of young people (Eccles et al. 1999). The other possibility is that an individual internalizes the belief that "most people" believe boys are more competent than girls at mathematics.

Ridgeway (1997) argues that when gender beliefs are salient they shape behavior most powerfully by affecting people's sense of what others expect of them. When males are widely thought to be more competent at a task than females, both males and females in a situation unconsciously expect more competent task performances from men. This differential performance expectation has been shown to invoke the use of a more lenient standard for evaluating the performances of men in the situation compared to women. The use of a more lenient standard to judge male performances causes males to be perceived as having more task ability than females, even when males and females perform at the same objective level (Foschi et al. 1994). Thus, when a female enters a situation having internalized the belief that "most people" expect more competent performances from men, even if she does not personally endorse this stereotypic belief, she may still leave the situation with a lower assessment of her ability compared to a male performing at the same level, due to the biasing effect of others expectations.

Recent research by Steele (1997) and Lovaglia et al. (1998) further suggest that when individuals know others expect people of their social category (e.g., women, African-Americans) to do relatively poorly on a task, this knowledge creates anxiety and actually leads to poorer performances. Steele and colleagues (Steele 1997; Spencer, Steele, and Quinn 1999) experimentally manipulated the relevance of a gender belief associated with a task. When subjects were told that males performed better at the task, male subjects outperformed female subjects. However, when subjects were told that previous research had found no gender differences in performing the task, females and males did equally well. Even if subjects did not personally believe that males were better at the task, their awareness that others held this belief heightened their anxiety and had an impact on their performance. This leads to the conclusion that regardless of whether gender beliefs are personally endorsed or internalized as other people's expectations, they often lead to biased self-assessments of ability. I now turn to describing how gender beliefs about mathematics bias perceptions of task competence and, thereby, influence career-relevant decisions.

The Constraining Effect of Gender Beliefs

My general argument is that widely shared cultural beliefs about gender and task competence differentially bias how individual males and females evaluate their own competence at career-relevant tasks. This bias may be the result of the internalization of a cultural belief about gender and mathematics into one's gender identity, or it may be the result of the expectation of others causing males and females to invoke the use of different standards for evaluating their own mathematical success, or both. The predicted outcome, however, is the same: males will overestimate and females will underestimate their own mathematical ability. If, for a given level of achievement, females are less likely than males to perceive that they are good at a task, they should be more likely to reduce their ef-

forts and interests in activities requiring competence at the task, and therefore they should also be less likely to persist on a career path requiring task competence.

It is important to note that gender beliefs are not rigid scripts that individuals are compelled to follow. Indeed, when individuals assess their own competence at a given task, their assessments should depend more on performance information (such as grades or test scores) than on cultural beliefs about gender differences in task competence. However, cultural beliefs provide a context of meaning that modifies or biases the more situationally relevant foreground information, such as the evaluations of task competence by others (Ridgeway 1997; West and Zimmerman 1987). At the individual level, this biasing effect allows individuals considerable variability in the perceptions of their task competence. But, at the aggregate level, it should be sufficient to produce systematic gender differences in perceived task competence.

Figure 3.1 provides a general sketch of my argument about the impact of these processes on persistence on educational and career paths. To test this model, I propose three hypotheses, which are described in more detail below.

Gender beliefs and biased self-assessments. In order for a person to continue on a

Figure 3.1
The Impact of Biased Self-Assessments on Career-Relevant Decisions

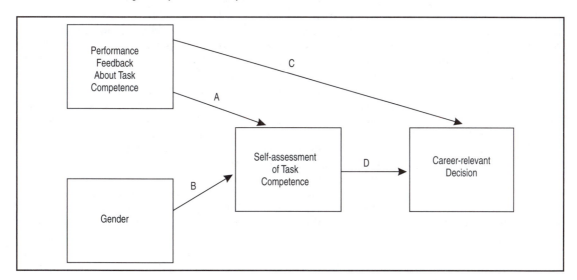

path toward a given career, I assume that she or he must adopt a personal conception of herself or himself as competent at the tasks believed to be necessary for that career path. That is, while many factors certainly influence individual career-relevant decisions and preferences, as a minimum, one must feel competent at the skills or tasks necessary for a given career in order to be commit oneself to pursuing that career. I refer to this personal conception of task competence as a "self-assessment." As depicted in Figure 3.1, positive performance feedback in regard to a given task by legitimate others (such as teachers or supervisors) should increase one's personal self-assessment of task competence. However, cultural beliefs about gender and task competence are argued to provide a framing context (Ridgeway 1997; West and Zimmerman 1987) that biases other information individuals use in assessing their own competence.

In the case of mathematics, when males receive positive feedback about their ability, they should evaluate themselves as skilled at mathematics since a positive evaluation is consistent with both the feedback they received and with societal expectations about their mathematical competency. Conversely, females who receive positive feedback about their mathematical ability should be less likely to perceive that they are skilled at mathematics since this perception is incongruent with widely shared beliefs about gender and mathematics. Research has shown that individuals are more likely to attend to and retain information that confirms stereotypes and to ignore information that contradicts expectations (Hamilton 1981). Further, Foschi (1996; Foschi et al. 1994) has demonstrated that when a cultural belief about a task advantages males (i.e., when males are widely thought to be more competent at the task), both males and females unconsciously use a more lenient standard to evaluate male performances compared to female performances. The use of a more lenient standard ensures that even when they are performing at identical ability levels, males are judged as being more competent or having more task ability than females.

Since widely shared cultural beliefs include claims that males are more competent than females at mathematics, I expect that: *Males are more likely than females performing at the same level to perceive that they are good at mathematics.* [Hypothesis 1]

Performance feedback and self-assessments. For both males and females, I expect more positive performance feedback about task ability to lead to higher self-assessments of task competence. However, I expect gender beliefs to influence the extent to which performance feedback affects self-assessments. Males who assess themselves as competent at mathematics can base their assessment, at least partially, on societal expectations, rendering feedback about their competence less important to them than to females, who must base their assessments on something other than societal expectations. Societal expectations of their competence provide males with a sense of confidence in their mathematical ability that makes performance information, either supportive or contradictory to this expectation, less relevant to their self-assessments. In other words, knowing others expect you to do well at a task provides an insulating layer from the constant input of performance feedback common in school and work environments. Conversely, self-assessments will be more contingent on performance feedback in a situation where societal expectations of task competence are lacking. Therefore, I expect that: *The effect of performance feedback about mathematical competence on mathematical self-assessment is larger for females than for males.* [Hypothesis 2]

Biased self-assessments and career-relevant decisions. As previously stated, both males and females must adopt a personal conception of themselves as competent at the tasks believed necessary for a specific career if they are to continue on a path leading toward that career. Therefore, while performance information about task competence undoubtedly has an impact on decisions to move forward on a path leading to a given career (path "C" of Fig. 3.1), self-assessments of task competence will have an effect on career-relevant decisions above and beyond the effects of external indicators of ability (path "D" of Fig. 3.1). Since mathematical competence is assumed to be necessary for persisting on a quantitative career path, I expect that for both males and females, *Higher self-assessments of mathematical competence increase the odds of persisting on a path toward a career in a quantitative profession.* [Hypothesis 3]

Data

The data for this study are from the National Educational Longitudinal Study of 1988 (NELS-88). In 1988, a multistage probability sample of approximately 25,000 eighth grade students, their parents, teachers, and school administrators, from over 1,000 schools was surveyed. A subsample of the students from the base year was again surveyed in 1990, 1992, and 1994, when most were sophomores, seniors, and two years beyond high school, respectively. The students were also given tests in mathematics, reading, social studies, and science, which were developed by the Educational Testing Service. The data set contains over 6,000 variables on each student (see Ingels et al. [1992] for more information on this data set).

While approximately 25,000 students were surveyed in the base year of the NELS-88 study, the subsequent waves were a subsample of the base year and were restricted to those students who continued to be enrolled in the same high school and who were not enrolled in some alternative certification program. I utilize three different longitudinal subsamples to test the above hypotheses. The self-assessment hypotheses (hypotheses 1 and 2) are tested using the eighth to tenth grade longitudinal subsample (sample size = 17,424). The hypothesis about the effect of biased self-assessments on career-relevant decisions is tested on either the eighth to twelfth grade subsample (sample size = 16,489) or on the eighth grade to two years past high school subsample, depending on whether the decision being made occurs during the senior year of high school or in college.

Models and Measurements

Five models are used to test the three hypotheses. The dependent variable in model 1 is mathematical self-assessment. The dependent variable in model 2 is verbal self-assessment.

While model 1 tests whether males assess their mathematical competence higher than females, the verbal self-assessment model, model 2, evaluates whether males globally assess their competence higher than females do, regardless of a task's gender association. Taken together, models 1 and 2 provide a test for the idea that widely shared cultural beliefs about gender and task competence have an impact on the perceptions males and females make of their competence at various tasks (hypothesis 1). Model 3 tests the second hypothesis that the *effect* of performance feedback about mathematical competence on mathematical self-assessments is greater for females than for males. To evaluate this hypothesis, separate models are estimated for males and females. Models 4 and 5 evaluate the effect of biased self-assessments on career-relevant decisions at two different time points (hypothesis 3).

Dependent Variables

The latent variable "mathematical self-assessment" measures the extent to which students believe they are skilled at math. Likewise, the latent variable "verbal self-assessment" measures the extent to which students think they are verbally skilled. Three items serve as indicators of mathematical self assessment: "Mathematics is one of my best subjects," "I have always done well in math," and "I get good marks in math." Likewise, three items serve as indicators of verbal self-assessment: "I learn things quickly in English," "I get good marks in English," and "English is one of my best subjects." Students were asked to agree or disagree on a six-point scale to these prompts during their sophomore year of high school, the only year in which these items were included in the survey.

Path persistence, the dependent variable in hypothesis 3, refers to whether or not students move into activities that require a certain level of mathematical competence and are relevant to careers in the quantitative professions. Path persistence is measured at two time points on the educational path leading to careers in science, math, and engineering. First, a calculus enrollment variable measures whether or not a student enrolled in calculus by her or his senior year of high school. This information was taken from students' transcripts. Second, a quantitative major variable indexes whether or not those students who enrolled in a postsecondary educational institution selected a quantitative major in college. Students were asked in an open-ended question to list their college major. The National Center for Educational Statistics (NCES) coded responses into 112 detailed categories. I created a dichotomous measure from this variable where all engineering majors, chemistry, physics, other physical sciences, computer programming, statistics, and mathematics were coded as quantitative and all other majors were coded as nonquantitative.

As the path persistence variables are dichotomous [models 4 and 5], the models estimate the effect of the independent variables on the likelihood of a student enrolling in high school calculus or choosing a quantitative major.

Independent Variables

The argument that gender affects how students assess their task competence hinges on comparing females and males who are otherwise equal in relevant ways. It is especially important to control for other factors commonly associated with differences in educational attainment. For this reason, all models control for race and parental education. Gender is added as an independent explanatory dummy variable in models 1, 2, 4, and 5.

"Tracking" is the process whereby students are separated by ability into different classes to be taught the same school subject (e.g., honors-level algebra I, academic-level algebra I, regular algebra I). Tracking has been shown to both reflect and reproduce class and racial inequalities in the United States (e.g., see Oakes 1985). Additionally, and relevant to the current study, it is likely that when students make self-assessments of their mathematical or verbal competence, they compare themselves to others in their own mathematics or English classes. In this way, academic tracks represent ability reference groups within which students compare themselves when making self-assessments. According to the data used in the current study, females are slightly more likely to be

in tracks associated with higher academic ability (see Table 3.1). Consequently, females also are more likely to assess their competence in comparison to members of a higher-ability reference group. Gender differences in track placement could, therefore, contribute to gender differences in self-assessments of task competence.

A dummy variable representing the honors track and one representing the academic track were created for math and English classes using teacher descriptions. While both honors and academic classes are considered higher ability levels than the general high school math or English class, honors is generally thought to be the highest math or English track.

In comparing the perceptions students make of their ability to perform a task, it is important to control for actual task ability. Task ability (in this case, math and verbal ability) was measured by averaging the eighth and tenth grade scores on the math or verbal standardized tests administered by the Educational Testing Service as part of the NELS-88 survey.

Of primary importance to this study is the effect of performance feedback on students' self-assessments of task competency. Mathematical and verbal performance feedback is measured by using the average math and English grades students received in high school. I converted these values to the commonly used 4.0 grade point average scale ("4.0" being the highest "A" grade) to aid in interpretability.

English grades and test scores are included in the math self-assessment models, and conversely, math grades and scores are included in the model with the verbal self-assessment dependent variable. This is done to make all models as comparable as possible. Further, it is likely that students make relative comparisons of the performance feedback they receive in various classes when assessing their ability and making career-relevant decisions. If students did not make relative comparisons, then the only performance information that would influence their mathematical self-assessments would be their mathematical grades and scores. However, others have shown that students do make these comparisons, classifying academic

Table 3.1
Means for Variables Used in Subsequent Analyses[a]

Dependent Variables	Models 1, 2, and 3		Model 4		Model 5	
	Females	Males	Females	Males	Females	Males
Math assessment items:						
Math best	3.65 (1.83)	4.11 (1.70)	3.67 (1.82)	4.10 (1.71)	3.78 (1.78)	4.19 (1.67)
Math always	3.85 (1.73)	4.21 (1.60)	3.87 (1.74)	4.19 (1.61)	4.01 (1.69)	4.30 (1.57)
Math marks	4.04 (1.72)	4.29 (1.60)	4.05 (1.73)	4.28 (1.62)	4.19 (1.67)	4.45 (1.53)
English assessment items:						
English best	4.08 (1.63)	3.69 (1.58)	4.08 (1.62)	3.68 (1.58)	4.30 (1.50)	3.86 (1.51)
English quickly	4.70 (1.26)	4.43 (1.30)	4.70 (1.25)	4.44 (1.30)	4.86 (1.14)	4.60 (1.21)
English marks	4.62 (1.40)	4.20 (1.47)	4.63 (1.38)	4.21 (1.47)	4.84 (1.25)	4.43 (1.34)
Enrolled in calculus[b]			.098	.106	.130	.149
Chose quantitative major[b]					.036	.124
Independent variables:						
Math grades	2.13 (.91)	1.99 (.93)	1.97 (.86)	1.82 (.86)	2.10 (.83)	2.01 (.85)
English grades	2.39 (.87)	2.03 (.90)	2.24 (.83)	1.88 (.85)	2.46 (.76)	2.14 (.78)
Math test scores	51.3 (9.37)	51.7 (9.80)	51.4 (9.41)	51.9 (9.91)	53.7 (9.06)	54.5 (9.48)
Verbal test scores	52.3 (9.11)	50.5 (9.46)	52.4 (9.15)	50.6 (9.45)	54.5 (8.71)	52.6 (9.25)
Class level:[b]						
Math honors	.190	.179	.181	.167	.188	.169
Math academic	.477	.475	.479	.466	.541	.533
General math track[c]	.333	.346	.340	.367	.271	.298
English honors	.233	.178	.225	.172	.254	.198
English academic	.380	.407	.386	.394	.421	.437
General English track[c]	.387	.415	.389	.434	.325	.365
Ethnicity:[b]						
Asian	.036	.036	.041	.037	.045	.044
African-American	.112	.111	.109	.102	.103	.084
Hispanic	.096	.085	.089	.080	.077	.076
White[c]	.756	.768	.761	.781	.775	.796
Parent's education in years	13.3 (2.28)	13.6 (2.32)	13.3 (2.28)	13.6 (2.32)	13.7 (2.24)	14.1 (2.32)

Source: NELS-88.
Note: For models 1, 2, and 3, $N = 6,877$ for females and 6,624 for males; for model 4, $N = 5,876$ for females and 5,681 for males; for model 5, $N = 3,539$ for females and 3,085 for males. SDs are given in parentheses.
[a]Values given are for cases with no missing values on any of the listed variables. All cases are weighted using the NELS sampling weights. See text for a description of the variables and for the wording of the assessment items.
[b]A (0–1) variable. The mean represents the proportion of students in the category indicated by the variable label. Standard deviations are not reported for (0–1) variables.
[c]Omitted reference category.

subjects, college majors, and even students within college majors as math/nonmath, hard/soft, "techy"/"fuzzy" (Seymour and Hewitt 1997). If students do compare their math and verbal feedback, and especially if they perceive competency in these two areas to be in tension with each other, then as students receive increasingly higher verbal feedback they might see themselves as less skilled at mathematics, as less of a "techy." Therefore, it is important to control for Eng-

lish performance in the mathematical self-assessment models.

Finally, the self-assessment items are added as independent variables in models 4 and 5 to test the path persistence hypothesis (hypothesis 3). That is, I argue that if self-assessment of mathematical competence differs by gender, this differential perception should be at least partially responsible for the gender differences in the movement of males and females into activities relevant to the quantitative professions. To test this idea, mathematical self-assessment is allowed to predict persistence on the mathematical career path. The verbal self-assessment variable is also added to these models since students likely use relative assessments of their competence when making career-relevant decisions.

Results and Discussion

Table 3.1 provides descriptive statistics for the males and females in the sample for whom there is complete data for each stage of the analysis. Not surprisingly, there is a large gap between the number of males and females who elected a quantitative college major. Compared with only 4% of females, 12% of males have majors in engineering, mathematics, or the physical sciences. A smaller gender gap was found in calculus enrollment, where 10% of females and 11% of males had enrolled in calculus by their senior year of high school (see the model 4 column of table 1). The means of the mathematical assessment items do suggest that males are more likely than females to believe they are competent in math. This pattern emerges even though math grades and math test scores are very similar for males and females. Males do not appear to globally assess their competence higher, as the means for the English assessment items are higher for females than for males. Finally, gender differences in the parental education, ethnicity, and math and English class-level variables appear minor, as would be expected.

Gender Beliefs and Biased Self-Assessments

The first hypothesis is that males assess their mathematical competence higher than females who perform at the same ability level and who receive the same feedback about their mathematical competence. [The data analysis for Model 1 showed] first, and not surprisingly, higher math grades and test scores increase the level of mathematical self-assessment. Thus, those with more mathematical ability, as measured by test scores, are more likely to believe that they are skilled at mathematics. Further, the more positive the feedback from legitimate others, in the

form of math grades, the higher the level of mathematical self-assessment. This is not surprising since evidence of task competence should be highly salient as students make personal assessments of their skill at a given task. Consistent with hypothesis 1, males are more likely to perceive that they are good at math than are those females with equal math grades and test scores.

Since the argument presented suggests that widely shared cultural beliefs about gender and task competence bias males' and females' self-assessments of task competence, it is useful to evaluate the same model for a set of tasks that have different gendered beliefs associated with them. Model 2 is identical to model 1, except the dependent variable is verbal self-assessment. As with the mathematical self-assessment model, differences in ability and performance feedback are controlled. [The analysis for Model 2 showed] that *females* were found to make higher self-assessments of their verbal ability. This indicates that males do not globally assess their task competence higher than females, regardless of the gender association of the task. Instead, cultural beliefs associated with a particular task or field of study bias students' perceptions of their abilities in that field.

While it is beyond the scope of this article to attempt to extend the argument presented to understanding racial or ethnic differences in career choice, it is worth discussing what may appear to be surprising results. Controlling for track of math and English class, grades, test scores, and parents' education, Asians, African-Americans, and Hispanics were found to assess both their math and verbal ability higher than whites. Others have shown that African-American students often have more positive attitudes toward education than whites (Portes and Wilson 1976) and have higher self-concepts and higher self-esteem (Coleman 1966). Portes and Wilson (1976) have argued that positive attitudes towards self and school represent a real advantage to blacks in facilitating educational success. Espousing positive attitudes may be a strategy that African-American children learn from their families as a partial way of countering the impact of discrimination. The higher self-assessment values for African-

Americans found in this study, then, appear consistent with earlier research.

Performance Feedback and Self-Assessments

The results presented thus far show that males assess their mathematical competence higher than females of equal mathematical ability. But, as stated in hypothesis 2, since cultural beliefs about mathematics advantage males, performance feedback about their task competence should be less important to them in making self-assessments of their mathematical competence. Conversely, performance feedback, in the form of math grades, should have a larger impact on females' self-assessments of their mathematical ability, since they must contend with lower societal expectations of their mathematical competency. To test this hypothesis, I estimate the effects of the independent variables on mathematical self-assessment separately for males and females.

Comparing the male and female regression coefficients for the math grade variable [table not shown], the larger coefficient for females, 0.97 versus 0.74 for males, suggests that females do rely more on performance feedback about their task competency in making self-assessments. Also, the gender difference in the *strength of the effect* of math grades on self-assessment was found to be significant. As hypothesized, feedback about their mathematical competence has a significantly larger effect on the mathematical self-assessments of females compared to males.

Recall that the mathematical self-assessment models control for the feedback students receive about their verbal competence. The logic behind this control is that it is likely that when students assess their mathematical competence, they make *relative* comparisons of the feedback they receive in various school subjects. As mentioned earlier, some have suggested that students perceive competency in math and verbal areas to be in tension with one another (Seymour and Hewitt 1997).

As with math grades, the *effect* of English grades on mathematical self-assessments is significantly larger for females. That is, while higher English grades lead to lower self-assessments of their mathematical ability for all

students, controlling for math grades and test scores, the negative effect is larger for females. While the gender difference in the effect of math grades on mathematical self-assessment was hypothesized, the significant gender difference in the effect of English grades was not. One explanation for this unexpected finding is that when individuals are in a situation where societal expectations of their task competence are lacking, they pay heightened attention to all performance feedback in the general environment, in this case the environment of school. Therefore, the process of making relative comparisons of various types of feedback when assessing one's own competence at a specific task, a process which occurs for all students, is amplified under conditions where societal performance expectations are lacking. Widely shared cultural beliefs about gender and mathematics create this type of environment for female students.

Biased Self-Assessments and Career-Relevant Decisions

Gender differences in self-assessments of competence at mathematics become important if they can be linked to gender differences in early career-relevant decisions, in this case, the decision to persist on the path leading to careers in the quantitative professions. . . . [The data show] that males are 1.23 times more likely to enroll in calculus than are their otherwise equal female counterparts. Importantly, since mathematical ability is controlled, the gender difference in calculus enrollment cannot be attributed to superior mathematical ability that some claim males possess (Rudisill and Morrison 1989; Kolata 1980).

[Also] as hypothesized, higher levels of mathematical self-assessment increase the odds of enrolling in calculus. [Further, the data suggest that] students' decisions to enroll in calculus are based on a relative comparison of their assessments of their math and verbal skills. That is, at any level of mathematical self-assessment, the higher the perception of verbal ability, the lower the odds that a student will enroll in calculus, and vice-versa. Put another way, when males and females perceive themselves to be equally mathematically competent, they are equally likely to enroll in calculus. This suggests that gender differences in the self-assessment of task competence are at least partially responsible for the differential movement of males and females along the path to the quantitative professions.

To further test the path persistence hypothesis, I examine the impact of gender and mathematical self-assessments on selecting a quantitative college major.

[The data analysis shows that] as predicted in hypothesis 3, higher levels of mathematical self-assessment increase the odds of choosing a quantitative major. This suggests that all students need to develop a personal conception of themselves as skilled at mathematics if they are to move toward a career in a quantitative profession. As with the calculus model, higher verbal self-assessments decrease the odds of choosing a quantitative major, indicating that students use relative understandings of their competencies when making career-relevant decisions. Further, the magnitude of the gender coefficient does decrease with the inclusion of the mathematical assessment variable, although the difference is small. This small effect, combined with the larger effect of mathematical self-assessment on calculus enrollment, suggests that gender differences in mathematical self-assessment contribute to the gender disparity in the decision to pursue a quantitative career.

In fact, others have argued that calculus enrollment might be especially important for females in choosing a quantitative major (Seymour and Hewitt 1997; McIlwee and Robinson 1992). If this is true, then gender differences in mathematical self-assessment, which at least partially explained the gender gap in calculus enrollment, become even more consequential.

In sum, the results presented provide support for the supply-side model presented. Gender beliefs about task competence bias the assessments individuals make of their own competence at mathematics, and these biased assessments differentially influence the decisions males and females make to persist on the path toward careers in science, math, and engineering. Since males tend to overestimate their mathematical competence relative to females performing at the same ability level, they are more likely to choose careers in the quantitative professions. Importantly, gender

differences in the selection of activities leading to these careers are not the result of actual differences in ability or merit, but they are instead the result of biased perceptions of competence.

Summary and Conclusion

The purpose of this study was to develop and test a simple supply-side model about gender differences in early career-relevant decisions. To test the hypotheses generated, I focused on high school students' perceptions of their mathematical competence and how these perceptions, controlling for actual ability, influenced decisions to persist on the path leading to careers in the quantitative professions. Since these professions have remained stubbornly male dominated (Hanson 1996), they represent an important site from which to examine the constraining effects of gender beliefs on career decisions.

The results of this study show that males assess their own mathematical competence higher than their otherwise equal female counterparts. Males are more likely than females with the same math grades and test scores to perceive that they are mathematically competent. Males were *not* found to assess their competence at verbal tasks higher than females, demonstrating that males do not globally assess their competence higher for all tasks, regardless of the task's gender association. Instead, widely shared cultural beliefs about gender and task competence bias the perceptions individuals have of their own task ability.

Further, the *effect* of performance feedback on self-assessments was found to differ by gender. Math grades had a significantly larger positive effect on the mathematical self-assessments for females than for males. Proof of their competence could be more important to females because they must contend with lower societal expectations of their mathematical ability. More generally, this suggests that the appraisals individuals make of their own competence at various tasks are more contingent on local evidence when societal expectations for success are lacking.

Importantly, self-assessments of task competence were found to influence career-relevant decisions, even when controlling for commonly accepted measures of ability. For males and females, the higher they rate their mathematical competence, the greater the odds that they will continue on the path leading to careers in the quantitative professions. However, since males tend to overestimate their mathematical competence relative to females, males are also more likely to pursue activities leading down a path toward a career in science, math, and engineering. While standardized test scores and high school grades are certainly imperfect measures of ability, I contend that they are likely more accurate measures of ability than are the self-perceptions of high school students. Therefore, these results suggest that those who persist on a mathematical career path may not even be the best qualified for careers requiring mathematical proficiency. In other words, boys do not pursue mathematical activities at a higher rate than girls do because they are better at mathematics. They do so, at least partially, because they *think* they are better.

This study's major contribution is to highlight one mechanism by which cultural beliefs about gender constrain the early career-relevant choices of men and women. The model presented focuses on how gender beliefs bias self-perceptions of competence. This focus is important since presumptions of competence often legitimate inequality in achievement-oriented societies. The model proposed was evaluated with respect to the quantitative professions. However, my eventual goal is to highlight more generally how gender beliefs associated with various career-relevant tasks bias individuals' perceptions of their competence at those tasks and, consequently, influence their commitment to different career trajectories. Anytime widely shared cultural beliefs about a task advantage males, the self-assessments males make of their competence in regard to the task should be higher, on average, than that of females performing at the same objective level. If the task is also one that is thought to be necessary for movement along a particular career path, then males, acting on upwardly biased appraisals of their task competence, should be more likely than females to continue on the path leading to that career. Conversely, if a task belief advantages

females, such as beliefs associated with nurturing skills or abilities, females should assess their task competence higher than males. A gender difference in the self-assessment of nurturing ability, for example, might partially explain the gender gap in professions such as nursing. The model could also be used to explain gender differences in the choice of specialties within a field, assuming that tasks believed to be necessary to pursue various specialties are associated with clear and stable cultural beliefs about gender. For example, if it is widely believed that, to be successful, surgeons have to be able to maintain emotional distance, and men are thought to be better than women at maintaining emotional distance, then the model could be employed to understand the continued male dominance of the specialty of surgery within the field of medicine. As these examples suggest, while the quantitative professions have been extreme in their resistance to the entry of women, there is no reason to think that they are the only professions that have skills that are both thought to be necessary and have gender beliefs associated with them. These required skills might either be less "critical" for entrance into a given profession or less stereotyped than mathematical skills are for the quantitative professions. This, however, would only serve to dampen, not eliminate, the effect shown. Career-relevant decisions are made at many points throughout the life cycle. Therefore, even small gender differences occurring at decision-making junctures can serve to carry males and females in substantially different occupational directions.

The results of this study demonstrate that widely shared cultural beliefs attached to various tasks affect not only how individuals are channeled into particular activities and subsequent career trajectories by others, but also how individuals "self-select" into occupationally relevant activities. This implies that the gender-segregated labor force will be reproduced partially through the different and seemingly voluntary choices men and women make. Any attempts to counter the effects of gender beliefs on gender segregation and inequality in the labor force, therefore, will require looking beyond how stereotypes are used by gatekeepers, such as teachers and employers, and focusing also on how gender beliefs affect males' and females' perceptions of their own abilities at crucial decision-making junctures.

References

American Association of University Women. 1992. *How Schools Shortchange Girls*. Washington, D.C.: American Association of University Women Educational Foundation.

Armstrong, J. M. 1981. "Achievement and Participation of Women in Mathematics." *Journal for Research in Mathematics Education* 12: 356–72.

Babco, Eleanor. 1988. *Salaries of Scientists, Engineers and Technicians: A Summary of Salary Surveys*. Washington, D.C.: Commission on Professionals in Science and Technology.

Baker, David P., and Deborah P. Jones. 1993. "Creating Gender Equality: Cross-National Gender Stratification and Mathematical Performance." *Sociology of Education* 66: 91–103.

Coleman, James S. 1966. *Equality of Opportunity*. Washington D.C.: Government Printing Office.

Conway, Michael, M. Teresa Pizzamiglio, and Lauren Mount. 1996. "Status, Communality and Agency: Implications for Stereotypes of Gender and Other Groups." *Journal of Personality and Social Psychology* 71: 25–38.

Dossey, J. A., I. V. S. Mullis, M. M. Lindquist, and D. L. Chambers. 1988. *The Mathematics Report Card: Are We Measuring Up?* Princeton, N.J.: Educational Testing Service.

Eccles, Jacquelynne S., Bonnie Barber, and Debra Jozefowica. 1999. "Linking Gender to Educational, Occupational, and Recreational Choice: Applying the Eccles et al. Model of Achievement-Related Choices." Pp. 153–91 in *Sexism and Stereotypes in Modern Society: The Gender Science of Janet Taylor Spence*. Washington, D.C.: American Psychological Association.

Eccles (Parsons), Jacquelynne, T. Alder, and Judith L. Meece. 1984. "Sex Differences in Achievement: A Test of Alternate Theories." *Journal of Personality and Social Psychology* 46:26–43.

England, Paula. 1992. *Comparable Worth: Theories and Evidence*. New York: Aldine.

Foschi, Martha. 1989. "Status Characteristics, Standards and Attributions." Pp. 58–72 in *Sociological Theories in Progress: New Formulations*, edited by Joseph Berger, Morris Zelditch Jr., and Bo Anderson. Boston: Houghton Mifflin.

———. 1996. "Double Standards in the Evaluation of Men and Women." *Social Psychology Quarterly* 59: 237–54.

Foschi, Martha, Larrisa Lai, and Kirsten Sigerson. 1994. "Gender and Double Standards in the Assessment of Job Applicants." *Social Psychology Quarterly* 57: 326–39.

Frehill, Lisa M. 1997. "Education and Occupational Sex Segregation: The Decision to Major in Engineering." *Sociological Quarterly* 38 (2): 225–49.

Frome, Pamela M., and Jacquelynne S. Eccles. 1998. "Parents' Influence on Children's Achievement-Related Perceptions." *Journal of Personality and Social Psychology* 74 (2): 435–52.

Grannovetter, Mark, and Charles Tilly. 1988. "Inequality and Labor Processes." Pp. 175–220 in *The Handbook of Sociology*, edited by Neil J. Smelser. Newbury Park, Calif.: Sage Publications.

Hamilton, David L. 1981. *Cognitive Processes in Stereotyping and Intergroup Behavior*. Hillsdale, N.J.: Erlbaum.

Hanson, Sandra L. 1996. *Lost Talent: Women in the Sciences*. Philadelphia: Temple University Press.

Hyde, Jane Shibley, Elizabeth Fennema, and Susan J. Lamon. 1990. "Gender Differences in Mathematics Performance: A Meta-Analysis." *Psychological Bulletin* 107 (2): 139–55.

Hyde, Jane Shibley, Elizabeth Fennema, Mariyln Ryan, Laurie A. Frost, and Carolyn Hoop. 1990. "Gender Comparisons of Mathematics Attitudes and Affect: A Meta Analysis." *Psychology of Women Quarterly* 14 (3): 299–324.

Ingels, Steven, Leslie Scott, Judith Lindmark, Martin Frankel, and Sharon Meyer. 1992. *National Educational Longitudinal Study of 1988: First Follow-Up Data File User's Manual*. Washington, D.C.: U.S. Department of Education.

Jacobs, Javis E., and Jacquelynne S. Eccles. 1985. "Gender Differences in Math Ability: The Impact of Media Reports on Parents." *Educational Researcher* 14: 20–25.

Jacobs, Jerry A. 1995a. "Trends in Occupational and Industrial Sex Segregation in 56 Countries, 1960–1980." Pp. 259–93 in *Gender Inequality at Work*, edited by Jerry A. Jacobs. Thousand Oaks, Calif.: Sage Publications.

———. 1995b. "Gender and Academic Specialties: Trends among Recipients of College Degrees in the 1980s." *Sociology of Education* 68: 81–98.

Jacobsen, Joyce P. 1994. "Trends in Work Force Segregation, 1960–1990." *Social Science Quarterly* 75 (1): 204–11.

Kolata, G. B. 1980. "Math and Sex: Are Girls Born with Less Ability?" *Science* 210: 1234–35.

Lovaglia, Michael J., Jeff W. Lucas, Jeffrey A. Houser, Shane R. Thye, and Barry Markovsky. 1998. "Status Processes and Mental Ability Test

Scores." *American Journal of Sociology* 104 (1): 195–228.

McIlwee, Judith S., and J. Gregg Robinson. 1992. *Women in Engineering: Gender, Power and Workplace Culture*. Albany: State University of New York Press.

National Center for Education Statistics. 1998. "Digest of Education Statistics, 1998." U.S. Department of Education, Office of Educational Research and Improvement.

National Science Foundation. 1994. *Women, Minorities and Persons with Disabilities in Science and Engineering: 1994*, NSF 94-333HL. Arlington, Va.: National Science Foundation.

——. 1996. *Women, Minorities and Persons with Disabilities in Science and Engineering: 1996*, NSF 96-311. Arlington, Va.: National Science Foundation.

Oakes, Jeannie. 1985. *Keeping Track: How Schools Structure Inequality*. New Haven, Conn.: Yale University Press.

——. 1990. "Opportunities, Achievement and Choice: Women and Minority Students in Science and Mathematics." *Review of Research in Education* 16: 153–222.

Peterson, Trond, and Laurie A. Morgan. 1995. "Separate and Unequal: Occupation-Establishment Sex Segregation and the Gender Wage Gap." *American Journal of Sociology* 101: 329–65.

Portes, Alejandro, and Kenneth L. Wilson. 1976. "Black-White Differences in Educational Attainment." *American Sociological Review* 41: 414–31.

Reskin, Barbara. 1993. "Sex Segregation in the Workplace." *Annual Review of Sociology* 19: 241–70.

Reskin, Barbara, and Patricia A. Roos. 1990. *Job Queues, Gender Queues: Explaining Women's Inroads into Male Occupations*. Philadelphia: Temple University Press.

Ridgeway, Cecilia L. 1997. "Interaction and the Conservation of Gender Inequality: Considering Employment." *American Sociological Review* 62: 218–35.

Ridgeway, Cecilia L., and Shelley J. Correll. 2000. "Limiting Gender Inequality through Interaction: The End(s) of Gender." *Contemporary Sociology* 29 (1): 110–20.

Risman, Barbara J. 1998. *Gender Vertigo*. New Haven, Conn.: Yale University Press.

Rudisill, E. Murray, and Linda Morrison. 1989. "Sex Differences in Mathematics Achievement: An Emerging Case for Physiological Factors." *School Science and Mathematics* 89: 571–77.

Seymour, Elaine, and Nancy M. Hewitt. 1997. *Talking about Leaving: Why Undergraduates Leave the Sciences*. Bolder, Colo.: Westview Press.

Spencer, Steven J., Claude M. Steele, and Diane M. Quinn 1999. "Stereotype Threat and Women's Math Performance." *Journal of Experimental Social Psychology* 35 (1): 4–28.

Steele, Claude M. 1997. "A Threat Is in the Air: How Stereotypes Shape Intellectual Identity and Performance." *American Psychologist* 52: 613–29.

Treiman, Donald J., and Heidi I. Hartman, eds. 1981. *Women, Work, and Wages: Equal Pay for Jobs of Equal Value*. Washington, D.C.: National Academy Press.

Wagner, David G., and Joseph Berger. 1997. "Gender and Interpersonal Task Behaviors: Status Expectation Accounts." *Sociological Perspectives* 40: 1–32.

West, Candace, and Don Zimmerman. 1987. "Doing Gender." *Gender and Society* 1: 125–51.

Food for Thought and Application Questions

1. Discuss how beliefs about mathematical ability have consequences for males and females in high school and in the choices that are made in college. Then explain why this is important to women's opportunities in the workforce.

2. Assume you had the assignment of encouraging middle school girls to consider careers in science, math, and engineering—all of which depend on solid math training. What information from research about math preparation and performance would you include as you develop your presentation? Justify your choice of information. ✦

Unit Two

Workplace Inequality: Gendered Structures and Their Consequences

Perhaps you have seen the bumper stickers, T-shirts, and buttons, "Equal pay for equal work," "The best man for the job may be a woman," "Oh, so that explains the difference in our salaries" (accompanied by a graphic of two toddlers, a male and a female, looking inside their diapers), "We try harder and get paid less," and "Women make policy, not coffee." These slogans are responses, or mass level forms of resistance, to the gender inequality in the workplace that takes a number of forms, as the slogans suggest. They range from gender-based earnings inequality to unequal access to jobs.

It is often assumed that women's increased involvement in paid work has been associated with a sharp reduction in workplace inequality, but in reality, this is not the case. No longer isolated in the domestic sphere, women work along side men in offices, factories, and other work settings. This makes workplace comparisons between the sexes more likely and serves to highlight inequalities. Federal legislation was enacted more than 40 years ago to address various forms of workplace inequality. The Equal Pay Act of 1962 and Title VII of the Civil Rights Act of 1964, which forbade workplace discrimination against women and other protected groups, have met with limited success in part because women and men are located, often by choice, in different occupations.

In recent years, there has been a barrage of articles in popular magazines about the progress women have made entering management and the professions. These articles often exaggerate the amount of change that actually has occurred in women's employment patterns. While women have made inroads into high-level occupations—they hold 50.5 percent of the positions designated as managerial, professional, and related occupations (U.S. Census Bureau 2004–05)—their share of *top level jobs* is still extremely small. Catalyst, a research organization that investigates the progress of women in top managerial positions, found that in 2002, women comprised only 15.7 percent of the corporate officer ranks of Fortune 500 companies, and only *eight* women held the position of CEO. Further, women held less than 7.9 percent of the highest ranking titles of chairman, vice-chairman, CEO, COO, president, senior executive vice president, and executive vice president (Catalyst 2004). The data for women of color are even less encouraging; African-American women comprise 5 percent of all people employed in management, professional, and related occupations, Asian-American women comprise 2.5 percent, and Latina women comprise 3.3 percent of people employed in such occupations (Catalyst 2005 a, b, c). Furthermore women of color made up only 1.6 per-

53

cent of corporate officers in 2002 (Catalyst 2002).

Importantly, looking to managerial and professional occupations for an indication of levels of workplace inequality is misleading, because only a minority of men and women are employed in these jobs. Women are even more under-represented in some other types of occupations, including the construction trades (where they represent less than 3 percent of those workers), police officers (12.4 percent), and blue-collar jobs like truck drivers (4.6 percent) (U.S. Census Bureau 2004–05).

Sex segregation is the term used to refer to the concentration of same-sex workers in job categories. Sex segregated employment is a prevalent type of inequality in the workplace, and it often serves as the basis for a second type of workplace inequality, sex-based earnings differences. Occupations dominated by women are paid at lower rates than occupations dominated by men. This is reflected in the earnings of full-time wage and salary workers. In 2003, women earned only about 77 cents for every dollar that men earned. There is much evidence that the low pay in many female jobs (e.g., nurse, teacher, secretary) cannot be explained by their demand for skill or training (Treiman and Hartman 1981). It can be convincingly argued that rates of pay in these jobs are low simply because women hold the jobs.

The workplace is segregated not only by sex but also by race. It is important to note that white women are a privileged group in the workplace when compared to women of color. Compared to white women, women of color are concentrated in lower tier occupations with less pay. Working to preserve their relative advantage, white women have, on occasion, worked to deny opportunities to women of color (Reskin and Padavic 1994). Workplace inequality, then, is patterned by both sex and race—and also by social class and other group characteristics. One's placement in a job hierarchy, as well as the rewards one receives, depends, in part, on how these characteristics "combine."

How do we explain sex-based inequality in the workplace today? There are a number of factors that have been suggested by re-search. Workplace inequality may come from different skills and experiences—productivity-related factors—that men and women bring to their work situation. These differences might result from one sex obtaining more education than the other, or from one having more on-the-job training than the other. To the extent that these types of differences exist between the sexes, unequal access to jobs and unequal rates of pay are viewed as nondiscriminatory. Studies show, however, that these productivity-related differences are responsible for only a small portion of the inequality that exists in the workplace today (Marini 1989). Further, education and work experience differences between the sexes have been eroding for some time, yet even these changes have done little to create more similar occupational distributions for men and women or to narrow the earnings gap between them.

Gender socialization forces discussed in Unit One are partially responsible for creating patterns of workplace inequality. To the extent that belief systems and cultural values support sex stereotypes, then the sexes will appear suited for different types of work. Women are encouraged by parents, teachers, and other socializing agents to prepare for and pursue jobs that will use their presumed traits. One such trait is women's nurturing ability, a quality well suited to caring for young children. As such, it is no coincidence that jobs involving the care of young children (e.g., daycare workers, elementary school teachers) are female-dominated. For men, a different set of gender stereotypical traits are presumed, traits that equip them for positions of leadership.

Gender socialization forces also contribute to workplace inequality by encouraging women to bear the primary responsibility for childcare. When or if women assume these responsibilities, they may opt for certain types of employment that facilitate the coordination of work and family. Some positions, like teaching, are particularly compatible with childcare responsibilities (summers off and after school hours free). Other positions, such as those that require long hours or extensive travel, prove very difficult for women with primary care responsibilities. Unfortunately for women, the latter category of jobs is by far the more financially rewarding one. (Women's coordination of work and family roles will be discussed in Unit Three.)

The "other side" of the workplace-employment equation is the employer. Employers work with structural arrangements that have been influenced by the social and cultural expectations associated with gender. For example, those who do the hiring may define the characteristics of "appropriate" job incumbents by gender-based stereotypes. Indeed, for years—including a number of years after the Civil Rights Act of 1964—the influence was made explicit in employment advertisements that categorized jobs as "job openings-male" and "job openings-female." That practice clearly perpetuated the sex segregation of occupations. Yet, even with legal changes that eliminated explicit gender labeling of jobs, the sex segregation of jobs remains one of the major forms of workplace inequality. Employers who endorse gender stereotypes will make hiring decisions accordingly and deny jobs to the "wrong" sex. From their biased perspective, doing otherwise would jeopardize productivity and profit.

Beyond defining expectations about characteristics of the "appropriate" job incumbent, scholars studying workplace inequality are increasing their attention to the way in which work is arranged and how work arrangements have been influenced by gender-associated expectations. This is reflected in the "gendered organizations" perspective. Some researchers, for example, have argued that the corporate "regular work day" appears to be modeled for the full-time employed male with a spouse at home to care for day-to-day home and child responsibilities. Norms about how much time should be devoted to work, out-of-town travel for work, and that work will be done "on-site," convey a pattern of work activity that generally presumes someone else is taking care of the home. These patterns and expectations, which are often embedded in regular practices of organizations and reflected in their culture, affect the employment and career opportunities for women. To the extent that

women do not have flexibility as part of their job and workplace expectations, they are at a disadvantage for employment, career, and economic success. Organizations with policies that consciously counteract the bias of a male model of work behavior are more likely to also reduce the unequal consequences of such work arrangements.

Another explanation of sex inequality in the workplace is that men, as beneficiaries of these practices, work to preserve their advantaged position. For reasons of self interest, men who feel that their advantage is threatened by women's progress in the workplace might fight to exclude them from particular occupations. As employers, men might simply refuse to hire women; as employees, men might refuse to work with women or may treat them poorly so as to encourage their rapid departure. Recently published cases of sexual harassment in previously all male military academies and in an automobile factory are examples of environments that make women unwelcome and unsupported, often hastening their departure. An inhospitable environment for women, as such, will restrict opportunities and can exacerbate workplace inequality.

The readings in this unit address women's employment and the nature, scope, and consequences of workplace inequality. To begin, we set the stage with an article by England, Garcia-Beaulieu, and Ross, examining women's labor force participation across racial/ethnic groups of women. With the change in the profile of labor force through the last quarter of the twentieth century, there have been changes in the patterns of labor force participation by subgroups of women defined by race/ethnicity. The authors examine the effects of marriage, children, education, husband's income, and recency of immigration as factors that encourage or discourage employment. The importance of education and responsibility for children are key factors in this regard, and the latter is defined by the authors as the lynchpin for gender inequality.

In Chapter 5, we shift attention to employers with an elaboration of perspectives on how workplace organizations operate. Williams presents the conceptual framework of "gendered organizations" to understand why, as she asks, "gender [is] a liability for women but an asset for men?" The gendered-organizations perspective argues that practices of organizations are not gender-neutral, as implied by the rational bureaucratic model of organizations. Rather, they reflect a preference for male workers and traditionally male characteristics; these characteristics are also more rewarded by organizations. Williams notes that women are not passive participants in such situations. They, like their male co-workers, bring expectations about gender and job incumbents with them to the work place. At the same time, women also have been more active than their male co-workers to *challenge* existing gendered practices and the gendered division of labor in organizations. Aware of the privileges and rewards associated with such practices, women see the benefits of seeking to change those practices. As such, Williams presents the potential for changes in work practices that come from women seeking to enhance their economic opportunities.

The third chapter in this unit is by Reskin and describes the stability and change in sex segregated employment patterns. After introducing a measure designed to capture the amount of occupational segregation present in the workplace, Reskin shows that rates of decline in occupational segregation have been rather slow since the 1970s. In contrast, Reskin also demonstrates a sharp downward trend for occupational segregation by race, especially among women. The causes of workplace segregation, both cultural and structural, are then discussed and examined in light of post-1960s occupational desegregation. Given that segregated employment patterns are a major contributor to the earnings gap between the sexes, this selection provides a useful starting point for examining pay inequalities.

In the next selection, Larson examines women's earnings compared to men's and recent fluctuations in the wage gap. Larson reports that "more education doesn't necessarily mean a smaller wage gap" although education has been one of the means by which the wage gap had been expected to close. Yet "education *can* make a difference in the wage gap" if it is gained in the right areas—particularly in areas feeding into high-paying jobs, such as science and engineering. Within the broader context of employment, even in high paying professions, Larson discusses the informal pressures on women to specialize in lower-paying, female-identified specialties; the cost of family and child responsibilities borne mostly by women; and the limited support by corporate and government policies for family-friendly practices so working mothers are not penalized. These factors combine to produce a wage gap that appears to be "stuck." Larson concludes with a look at local actions representing small but significant steps that are aimed at reducing the wage gap. Her article reminds us that multiple factors combine to bring about the wage gap between men and women, and it reflects themes that are repeated in other articles throughout this book.

As noted earlier, the Williams article (Ch. 5) introduces the concept of "gendered organizations." One of the consequences of gendering practices is that the contributions women make are overlooked or underplayed because the framework from which they are viewed does not recognize them as contributions. This sets the context for examining management styles and changes in those styles over the last quarter of the twentieth century. In the movie/play *My Fair Lady*, there is a song titled, "Why Can't a Woman Be More Like a Man?" which has Professor Henry Higgins bemoaning the various qualities of women, while lauding those of men. These laments were probably not far from what corporate leaders thought in the 1970s as women moved into the traditionally male stronghold of corporate management, a move facilitated by the legal enforcement machinery of the 1964 Civil Rights Act and EEOC guidelines. It was not that women had been absent from the corporate arena until the 1970s. Rather, they had generally been absent from positions of managerial authority. From the early 1970s and into the mid-1980s, the percentage of females earning BA degrees in business grew dramatically. In 1971, 9.1 percent of the business and management BA degrees were earned by women; by 1985, business and management had become the largest area of degree concentration for women and over 45 percent of the Business BA degrees were awarded to women (National Center for Educational Statistics 1995). Their education prepared them for leadership roles in the corporate world, and women expected to command the respect and exercise the authority that should go with the position. *How* this was to be accomplished, however, proved to be a major challenge.

Despite the training and preparation for managerial positions, women faced a number of barriers that were rooted in gender-based expectations. One such issue was the way in which managers, and particularly successful managers, were socially defined. That is, when one thought of the "typical" successful manager, one envisioned "male." Thus, the characteristics that were used to typify the "successful manager," were essentially the same factors that characterized "males." More important for women was the fact that the characteristics of the "successful manager" were not similar to those used to describe the typical adult woman (Schein 1973, 1975) Because of these stereotypes, women did not fit the image of the successful manager.

It was thought that if women *were* going to get ahead, they would have to become more like "successful managers" (males). Yet women who sought to achieve success by behaving in assertive and/or self-confident ways, often encountered a different obstacle: a number of behaviors that were rewarded when practiced by men, were *negatively sanctioned* when practiced by women. Thus, a woman who was assertive or showed self-confidence might be defined as arrogant or abrasive (Tarvis 1992). In essence, acting like a man often did not benefit women who moved into nontraditional positions. Later research showed that women who "struck a balance" between the "traditional male"- defined and "traditional female"-defined behaviors were more able to work successfully in traditionally male domains (Jurik 1988).

The selection by Marie-Therese Claes, examines the changes in management styles that emerged by the end of the twentieth century. The context in which these changes emerged was one in which there was a need for change in the structure of organizations (due to pressures of the global economy) and in the kind of management leadership that works best with such changes. Claes reviews the literature on men and women in leadership positions, the need for collaborative work, the leadership style that facilitates it, and the evolving balance between "feminine" and "masculine" traits that can be most effective in developing leadership for the future. In showing how "feminine" traits have become defined as valuable for effective management, Claes highlights an important contribution brought by women in to the workplace, particularly in leadership positions.

The next two articles in this unit deal with the opportunity for women to move up the organizational ladder to top positions. The first of these is the report of the Federal Glass Ceiling Commission. The Commission, appointed by the President in 1991, was charged with identifying barriers for women's and minority's progress up the management hierarchy. After documenting the virtual absence of women from these elite positions, the Commission details the obstacles confronting managerial women. An important contribution of this highly visible report is the suggestion that the integration of high level management position is good for business. Such arguments are important for motivating profit minded corporations to "shatter the glass ceiling."

A number of the issues presented in the Commission's report are made concrete in the article by Ragins, Townsend, and Mattis. Drawing on survey and interview data from high ranking corporate women and from interviews with CEOs of major corporations, they compare what each group defines as the barriers to women's advancement. In addition, the female executives are asked about the major factors that helped them succeed. A critical finding is the difference in how CEOs and high ranking women view certain obstacles to advancement. For example, while CEOs indicate line or management experience as the greatest barrier to women, women rank male stereotyping and preconceptions as the main barrier. The research presents much food for thought about women's advancement, particularly when there is a gap in understanding between CEOs and high achieving women with regard to barriers to advancement, and CEOs hold the position of "final decision maker" on such practices.

The last article in this section focuses on organizational culture and the extent to which a work environment is hospitable or hostile to women. The selection by Gruber targets one of the most difficult challenges of workplace inequality—that of sexual harassment. Gruber argues that organizational policies put into place affect the climate of the workplace and the extent of receptivity or hostility that working women face. Drawing on theories of organizational culture and the causes of sexual harassment, Gruber discusses various work contexts and the level of harassment likely to be associated with each. He notes in particular the "double male" defined environment, a traditionally male environment and a strong dominance of male employees, the environment which is likely to be most hostile to women. Gruber's research examines complaints of sexual harassment within varying contexts, including the sex segregation of occupations, male vs. female gender predominance, gender contact, and policies and procedures that are in place to address sexually harassing behavior. Work context—that is, *where one works*—does make a difference. Particularly important are proactive policies and procedures to deal with harassing behavior. They are effective in giving women voice, as well as in reducing verbal harassment and the likelihood of women being physically threatened in the workplace.

References

Catalyst. 2002. *Catalyst Census of Women Corporate Officers and Top Earners of the Fortune 500*. New York: Catalyst.

——. 2004. *Women in the Fortune 500 (Fact Sheet)*. New York: Catalyst.

——. 2005a. *Information Center Quick Takes—African-American Women*. New York: Catalyst.

——. 2005b. *Information Center Quick Takes—Asian-American Women*. New York: Catalyst.

——. 2005c. *Information Center Quick Takes—Latinas*. New York: Catalyst.

Jurik, Nancy C. 1988. "Striking a balance: Female correctional officers, gender role stereotypes, and male prisons." *Sociological Inquiry* 58 (3): 291–305.

Marini, M. M. 1989. "Sex differences in earnings in the United States." *Annual Review of Sociology*, vol. 15. Palo Alto, CA: Annual Reviews.

National Center for Educational Statistics. 1995. *Digest of Educational Statistics*. Table 272. http://www.nces.ed.gov/programs/digest.

Reskin, B., and I. Padavic. 1994. *Women and Men at Work*. Thousand Oaks, CA: Pine Forge Press.

Schein, Virginia. 1973. "The relationship between sex role stereotooypes and requisite management characteristics." *Journal of Applied Psychology* 57 (2): 95–100.

——. 1975. "Relationships between sex role stereotypes and requisite management characteristics among female managers." *Journal of Applied Psychology* 60 (3): 340–344.

Tarvis, Carol. 1992. *Mismeasure of Woman*. New York: Simon and Schuster.

Treiman, D. J., and H. I. Hartmann (eds.). 1981. *Women, Work and Wages: Equal Pay for Jobs of Equal Value*. Washington, DC: National Academy Press.

U.S. Bureau of the Census. 2004–05. Statistical Abstract of the United States. Washington, DC. *www.census.gov/prod/www/statistical-abstract.html*. ✦

4

Women's Employment Among Blacks, Whites, and Three Groups of Latinas

Do More Privileged Women Have Higher Employment?

Paula England
Carmen Garcia-Beaulieu
Mary Ross

In 1890, 40 percent of Black but only 16 percent of white women were in the labor force. By 1950, Black women's participation (38 percent) was still way ahead of white women's (29 percent; England 1992). By 1980, Black and white women's employment rates had converged at 47 percent, and both groups had higher employment than Mexican (44 percent) and Puerto Rican (35 percent) women, and 51 percent of Cuban women were employed (calculated from Smith and Tienda 1988, 63). More recent data show that white women are now more likely to be employed than Black women and Latinas (Browne 1999; Corcoran 1999; Corcoran, Heflin, and Reyes 1999). Employment declined substantially for Puerto Rican women (Tienda, Donato, and Cordero-Guzman 1992) and Black mothers with less than high school education (Corcoran 1999) between the 1960s and 1990.

The scholarly consensus has been that women's employment is deterred by marriage and children in the context of a division of labor that features husbands' specializing in market work and providing income and wives' being responsible for child rearing and household work. We find that the part of this standard gender analysis that remains true is that young children reduce women's employment, although less than in earlier decades (Cohen and Bianchi 1999). But the husband support portion of this view never fit for women of color, immigrants, or many working-class white women who historically have not had the option of being supported by a husband with a family wage. This critique of the standard consensus was made by advocates of intersectionality, a perspective that looks at gender together with race, class, and other vectors of privilege (Higginbotham and Romero 1997). They correctly observed that the lack of husbands with solid incomes, along with lower marriage rates, probably explained Black women's higher employment rates than white women through the 1950s, 1960s, and 1970s. But today, white women, despite being more likely to be married to high-earning men, have higher employment rates than Blacks or Latinas, as we will show. Education has had a positive effect on women's employment at least as far back as 1960 (Spain and Bianchi 1996, 67). But Cohen and Bianchi's (1999) analysis from 1978 to 1998 shows that education became increasingly predictive of women's employment over time, and family factors less so. To the extent that education is indicative of the social class of one's family of origin or one's adult household, this means that women who are privileged on class are now more, not less, likely to be employed. We will document this here with recent data. Thus, today, objective economic need is not the only, and not even the major, factor driving women's employment. Of course, upper-middle-class women may subjectively perceive as much economic need for employment as women with low-earning or no husbands; the former often see their family's consumption is inadequate if it is less than those in their relatively affluent neighborhoods and networks. The earnings of men with no more than a high school education have fallen dramatically in recent decades with economic restructuring, leading to the hypothesis that this may explain some of the increase in women's employment. But this hypothesis does not square with the fact that women with college education, most of whom are married to men with relatively high education and earnings, have increased their employment most dramatically (Chinhui and Murphy 1997).

Past Research on Women's Employment and Ethnic Differences

Children reduce women's paid work in all ethnic groups, although less so than in previous decades (Cohen and Bianchi 1999; Kahn and Whittington 1996; Tienda, Donato, and Cordero-Guzman 1992; Tienda and Glass 1985). Mothers, whether single or married, are generally more responsible for child care than are fathers, and thus must replace their own services with paid help to be employed. Children therefore increase the amount they need to earn to make work pay. The role of marriage in reducing paid work is less clear, especially since it is not as tightly linked to childbearing as it was previously (Ellwood and Jencks forthcoming). Husbands could encourage a traditional division of labor, but absent such a differentiation by gender, having a husband might provide someone to share childrearing with and thus make it more possible for women to be employed. Kahn and Whittington (1996) found marriage to deter employment for Latinas but not white or Black women in 1990. Some recent studies have even found a positive (net) association between marriage and employment for Black women (Corcoran 1999). Of course, these relationships may not really be causal but rather indicative that the same women whose social networks include "marriageable" men are those whose race- and class-related advantages provide access to jobs that pay enough to make employment worthwhile. Past studies generally find husband's income to discourage employment (Tienda and Glass 1985), although less so over time (Cohen and Bianchi 1999). Analysis of 1980 and 1990 data finds no significant relationship between husbands' wage on Latinas' employment, but a negative association for white women (Kahn and Whittington 1996; Stier and Tienda 1992).

Education and employment experience increase women's potential earnings, making the opportunity cost of staying home greater. They may also be indicators of more interest in and commitment to paid work, as well as access to more interesting jobs. Probably for all these reasons, studies have long found a positive association of education with employment, especially when husbands' earnings (often correlated with women's education because of marital homogamy) are controlled (Cohen and Bianchi 1999; Kahn and Whittington 1996; Tienda and Glass 1985). Christopher (1996) found that education differences between Black and white women explain 20 to 30 percent of Black women's fewer weeks of employment in 1990; Reid (2002) found education differences to explain some of the more frequent exits of Black than white women from employment.

We will examine whether a woman is an immigrant and, if so, when she entered the United States. Our hypothesis is that more recent immigrants will have fewer resources of language facility, social capital, and local job experience, that they will thus find getting a job more difficult and the potential wage lower, and that this will lower the employment rates of immigrants, especially recent arrivals. Despite a rich literature on gender and immigration (e.g., Pedraza 1991) and the difficult work experiences of immigrant women (Hondagneu-Sotelo 1997; Romero 2002), few studies compare the employment of immigrant and nonimmigrant women. Prieto (1978) showed that women in Cuba had lower employment rates than Cuban women immigrants to the United States after their arrival. Nonetheless, Cooney and Ortiz (1983) found that U.S.-mainland-born Latinas were more likely to be employed than immigrants from Mexico, Puerto Rico, or Cuba. They also showed that English language proficiency facilitates employment of Puerto Rican and Mexican immigrants. (See Stier and Tienda 1992 for conflicting findings for various groups of Latina immigrants on effects of recency of migration.)

Our analysis starts by documenting racial/ethnic differences in weeks of employment in 2001. We then use regression analysis to examine the net association of employment with age and number of children, marriage and husband's income, education, region, whether a woman is an immigrant, and if so, how recently she migrated. We seek to explain the gap between white women and each group of women of color, assessing how much is explained by group differences in each of the independent variables and, where relevant, how much ethnic differential in employment remains even after adjustment for ethnic differences in the other variables.

Data and Method

We use the 2001 Current Population Survey (CPS) Annual Demographic Files (U.S. Bureau of Census 2001). The CPS is a national probability sample of households. We used individuals as the units of analysis, selecting women between the ages of 18 and 65. We compare the three largest subgroups of Latinas with the two largest racial groups, whites and Blacks. We separate out non-Hispanic whites and non-Hispanic Blacks, and among those reported as Hispanic, distinguish those of Mexican, Puerto Rican, or Cuban descent (regardless of race, so that our Latino sample includes some who also identify as Black). Other races (e.g., Asian, Native American) and Hispanics with ancestry from other countries were omitted from our analysis. Although our categories crosscut race and ethnicity, we use the terms interchangeably below. All analyses are unweighted. Table 4.1 presents the sample sizes and means on all variables for each racial/ethnic group.

Our dependent variable is the number of weeks a woman was employed in the previous year. We chose to use this rather than a simple dichotomy measuring whether the individual was employed at the time of the survey so as to use more detailed information.

We include independent variables hypothesized to explain variation in women's employment. We entered three dummy variables to capture whether a woman is an immigrant and, if so, how recent. The three categories are immigrated to the United States before 1990, immigrated between 1990 and 1997, and immigrated after 1997. The reference category is nonimmigrant. Although people who are born in Puerto Rico and come to the mainland are not, technically speaking, immigrants since they are U.S. citizens, for continuity of terminology across groups, we will refer to them as immigrants to distinguish them from mainland-born women of Puerto Rican descent.

Education is measured with four dummy variables indicating that the woman has completed an advanced degree, completed an undergraduate degree, attended some college, or finished high school, with a reference category of those who did not complete high school. The sample contains women as young as 18; some women in their late teens and 20s are attending college, which is likely to deter employment, so we include a dummy for whether the woman was enrolled in school full-time.

Marital status is captured with two dummy variables: Married and no longer married (divorced or widowed), with a reference category of those never married. We also include a variable for the amount of income a woman's husband earned during the year; for unmarried women, this is 0. We include the number of children younger than 6 that the woman has and the number of children she has between ages 6 and 18 (these are the age categories provided in the publicly available CPS). We distinguish children by age since mothers are more apt to stay home with younger children.

Since CPS data do not include a measure of years of employment experience, which increases across the life cycle with age but also is more continuous in more recent cohorts, we include age to roughly pick up these effects. Because employment opportunities for women may differ by region, and ethnic groups vary in regional concentration, we include dummy variables for the West, Northeast, and South.

Given the continuous dependent variable, we use ordinary least squares regression to predict weeks worked.

. . . We regress weeks worked on dummy variables for ethnic groups (non-Hispanic Blacks, Cubans, Mexicans, and Puerto Ricans, with whites the reference category) and other explanatory variables [in the second part of the analysis] (table not shown).

Table 4.1
Means on All Variables

	White	Mexican	Puerto Rican	Cuban	Black
Weeks employed	36.01	29.03	30.78	34.34	34.61
Native born (reference)	0.95	0.47	0.50	0.28	0.91
Immigrated before 1990	0.03	0.29	0.38	0.54	0.06
Immigrated from 1990 to 1997	0.01	0.17	0.08	0.13	0.02
Immigrated after 1997	0.01	0.07	0.04	0.06	0.01
Less than high school (reference)	0.08	0.45	0.29	0.16	0.18
High school graduate	0.33	0.28	0.31	0.36	0.35
Some college	0.32	0.20	0.26	0.23	0.32
College graduate	0.19	0.06	0.09	0.16	0.11
Advanced degree	0.08	0.01	0.04	0.08	0.04
Never married (reference)	0.20	0.26	0.30	0.27	0.41
Married, spouse present	0.62	0.57	0.41	0.54	0.32
No longer married	0.18	0.16	0.28	0.20	0.27
Husband's income[a] ($)	38,533	20,958	18,894	30,454	13,991
Number of children younger than 6	0.22	0.45	0.29	0.12	0.25
Number of children 6 to 18	0.52	0.87	0.70	0.40	0.57
Age	41.29	35.65	38.01	41.86	39.40
Age squared	1,868.25	1,413.89	1,598.14	1,928.50	1,718.63
Midwest (reference)	0.27	0.10	0.10	0.02	0.20
Northeast	0.23	0.02	0.61	0.14	0.19
South	0.29	0.30	0.23	0.77	0.54
West	0.22	0.57	0.07	0.07	0.08
Full-time student	0.05	0.05	0.06	0.06	0.05
Sample size	27,570	4,098	726	265	4,160

a. Unmarried women or women with husbands without income enter this average with 0.

We use the ethnic-specific means in Table 4.1, together with the results [of the second analysis] to decompose ethnic differences in weeks worked between each group of women of color and white women in Table 4.2. We chose white women to serve as the contrast to all groups because they are the largest group, have the most racial/ethnic privilege, and have the highest employment.

The decomposition implies this thought experiment, taking the white/Mexican gap as explained by education as an example: Suppose that Mexican women changed their education levels to those white women have, but suppose that the effect of education on their employment (their slopes) remained as observed.

How many more weeks of employment per year would they have? What percentage of the gap between their employment and white women's (in weeks per year) would be closed by this change? Similarly, when discussing the decomposition results, we will talk about what percentage of ethnic gaps in employment a factor (such as education) "explains." By this we mean that our decomposition shows that if this ethnic gap in an independent variable (e.g., education, number and ages of children, or immigration status) were closed, then given the effects we observe for women of color for this variable, it would close a certain percentage of the employment gap. This conclusion holds only if the coefficients in the regression are estimates of causal effects.

Results: Explaining Ethnic Differences in Employment

Table 4.1 shows the magnitude of white women's advantage in employment. In 2001, white women had the highest employment, narrowly above Black and Cuban women (less than 2 weeks), but about 6 weeks above Mexican and Puerto Rican women. (In results not shown, we did a parallel analysis for 1994 CPS data to capture the period before welfare reform. In that year, all groups' employment was lower than in 2001, but race gaps were larger, with white women em-

ployed 9 weeks more than Mexican, 10 weeks more than Puerto Rican, 4 weeks more than Cuban, and 3 weeks more than Black women. Analyses are available on request.) Below, we present results one explanatory factor at a time, paying attention to what we learn from combining the information from [all tables in this chapter]: How groups are different in their means on each independent variable (see Table 4.1), what net statistical association each variable has with employment and how much of the gap in employment between each group of women of color and white women can be statistically explained by group differences in means on the explanatory factors in each year (see Table 4.2).

Table 4.2

Decomposition of Differences in Average Weeks of Employment Between White Women and Women of Color: Weeks Explained by Group Mean Differences in Independent Variables

	Mexican	Puerto Rican	Cuban	Black
Immigrated before 1990	0.1	0.2	0.3	0.0
Immigrated from 1990 to 1997	1.1	0.5	0.8	0.0[a]
Immigrated after 1997	0.4[a]	0.5	0.9	0.0[a]
Total, immigration	1.7, 25%	1.2, 22%	2.0, 120%	0.0, 2%
High school graduate	0.5	0.1	−0.3	−0.2
Some college	1.5	0.7	1.0	0.0
College graduate	1.8	1.9[a]	0.4	1.4[a]
Advanced degree	1.1	0.7	0.1	0.6
Total, education	4.8, 69%	3.4, 66%	1.1, 68%	1.8, 131%
Married, spouse present	0.0	−0.1	−0.1	−0.2
No longer married	0.0	0.1	0.0	−0.1
Husband's income (1,000s)	−0.6	−0.7	−0.3	0.5[a]
Total, marital status, and other income	−0.6, −9%	−0.9, −18%	−0.4, −21%	0.2, 15%
Number of children younger than 6	1.5	0.5	−0.7	0.1[a]
Number of children 6 to 18	0.7	0.3	−0.2	0.0[a]
Total, children	2.1, 30%	0.8, 15%	−0.9, −53%	0.1, 9%
Total explained, all variables[b]	7.4, 106%	4.4, 84%	3.3, 200%	1.2, 84%
Actual difference in weeks (from Table 1)	7.0	5.2	1.7	1.4

Notes: (1) Weeks explained are the product of the slope for the group of women of color multiplied by the difference between the mean for white women and this group. The pooled slope is used for this calculation except when the group's own slope is significantly different. (2) The regressions from [the deleted table], including age, age squared, region, and full-time student, are used for purposes of this decomposition.

a. The group slope is different from the pooled slope.

b. Includes portions explained by group mean differences in age, student enrollment, and region. Total for education includes negligible portion for current student enrollment.

Immigration Status

Immigrant women have lower employment levels than native-born women for all ethnic groups except Blacks. In 2001, the most recent immigrants (arriving after 1997) averaged 17 weeks less employment, those who arrived between 1990 and 1997 worked 7 weeks less than nonimmigrants, and those who came before 1990 were indistinguishable from nonimmigrants in weeks of employment. Our interpretation of this pattern is that new immigrants lack network connections, English-speaking skills, and/or country-specific experience helpful in getting jobs.

How much of the gap in weeks of employment between white women and women of color can be explained by immigration? The groups with high proportions of immigrants are the three Latina groups; only 5 percent of whites and 9 percent of Blacks, but 53 percent of Mexicans, 50 percent of Puerto Ricans, and 72 percent of Cubans were immigrants in 2001 (see Table 4.1). Among immigrants, Mexicans are the most and Cubans the least recent, because the largest wave of Cubans came shortly after Castro came to power, whereas Mexican immigration has been continuous and growing. Immigration is an entirely trivial factor in the white/Black employment gap since few of either group are immigrants (see Table 4.2). But presence and recency of immigrants explains two weeks or 25 percent of the Mexican/white gap (see Table 4.2), one week or 22 percent of the Puerto Rican/white gap, and all of the very small Cuban/white gap. In sum, the greater representation of immigrants among Latinas than whites is an important part of the reason that Latinas, particularly Mexicans and Cubans, have lower employment rates.

Education

Education is related to employment for all groups. In the pooled model, high school graduates have 9 more weeks employment per year than dropouts, those with some college 12 weeks more, college graduates 13 weeks more, and those with advanced degrees 17 weeks more. Slopes do not vary by ethnicity, except that Black and Puerto Rican women have higher employment returns to college graduation.

How does education affect ethnic differences in employment? Whites have the highest levels of education and Mexicans the lowest (see Table 4.1). Education is important in explaining the employment gap between all groups of women of color and white women. The lower education of Mexicans explains five weeks or 69 percent of their employment gap with whites; for Puerto Ricans, the figure is three weeks or 66 percent; for Cubans, one week or 68 percent; and for Blacks, two weeks, more than the full gap (see Table 4.2). While the general picture is of Black and Puerto Rican women's having less employment because they have less education, given their higher employment returns to college than other groups, an interesting note is that Black and Puerto Rican women who are college graduates actually work a few more weeks per year than white women (not shown).

Marital Status and Husbands' Income

White women are the most likely to be married (62 percent), with Mexican (57 percent) and Cuban (54 percent) women next, and Puerto Rican (41 percent) and Black (32 percent) women having much lower rates (see Table 4.1); husbands' earnings (averaged in at 0 for unmarried women) are much lower for women of color. The older scholarly consensus was that these differences—and the economic need they imply for women to contribute to family support—explained Black women's higher employment in previous decades. But as the regressions show, marriage no longer deters employment for women. There is no significant difference between currently married women and never married women, although divorced and widowed women work 1 more week than those who have never married. Husband's income deters employment for all groups but Blacks, but the magnitude of the difference is trivial (0.3 of a week for each additional $1,000 per year). Black women are employed trivially more when their husbands earn more. All of these coefficients are too small to be substantively interesting. Given this, it is not surprising that the decompositions in Table 4.2 show little power of marital status and husband's income to explain ethnic differences in employment. Even though ethnic groups differ greatly in the proportion married and in husband's income, the small effects of these factors on employment makes them unimportant in explaining ethnic differentials in employment.

Children

Although marriage and husbands' incomes no longer do much to deter employment, children do deter employment for all ethnic groups. The pooled models show that each child younger than 6 is associated with seven fewer weeks of employment per year, and each child from 6 to 18, with two fewer weeks. Blacks show a somewhat smaller (but still significant) deterrent effect than other groups. Cuban women have lower fertility than white women, so fertility differences explain none of the employment gap; in fact, the small employment gap would be 53 percent larger if Cuban women had the (higher) fertility of white women (see Table 4.2). In contrast, fertility is crucial to the white/Mexican employment gap, explaining 30 percent of the seven-week gap (see Table 4.2). Black and Puerto Rican women have fertility higher than that of Cubans or whites but lower than that of Mexicans (see Table 4.1). Puerto Ricanwomen's fertility levels relative to white women explain 15 percent of the five-week gap (see Table 4.2). Black women's higher fertility explains less than one week, or 9 percent of the small Black/white gap (see Table 4.2). In results not shown, we interacted children with marriage to see if married women were more likely to forgo employment because of children but found no such consistent pattern. This may be because for single women with low potential earnings, welfare, as meager as it is, may be a better option than their earnings minus child care costs, thus creating a negative effect of children for single women as well.

Age

Age distributions have little to do with ethnic gaps in employment, with one exception. Cubans are older, on average, than other groups because of the large migration after the revolution and their low fertility. Differences in age between Cubans and whites explain about two weeks of the Cuban/white gap (not shown). (The impact of age is in-cluded in the total explained in Table 4.2, but is not reported as it had no other effects.)

Region

Results provide no clear message about how groups' different regional distributions affect employment prospects, so we do not show the decomposition for region in Table 4.2 (except that these components are added into totals explained by all independent variables together). In results not shown, we assess whether the concentration of Puerto Ricans in New York and New Jersey or of Cubans in Florida accounts for their lower employment rates. We do not find this to be true; models with dummy variables for each state have similar coefficients to our models with only regional control.

Summary and Conclusion

Our analysis explains all of the large white/Mexican and the small white/Cuban employment gap. In 2001, Mexican women were employed seven weeks less than white women; this gap is explained by the fact that the Mexican population contains more immigrants, especially recent immigrants (two weeks of the gap), has lower education (five weeks), and has higher fertility (two weeks; see Table 4.2). When all factors are added together, the entire gap has been more than explained by these factors, with education being the largest factor by far. Cuban women have a smaller employment gap with white women (three weeks), and all of it is explained by a combination of the older age structure of Cubans (explaining two weeks, not shown), the high proportion of immigrants (two weeks), and slightly lower education (one week). Cuban fertility, being lower than whites', makes their employment higher than it would be if they had the same fertility rates as whites, so this factor is offsetting (negative one week) rather than contributing to the gap (see Table 4.2). When we say that we have "explained" the ethnic gaps for these groups, we mean that the group differences in mean levels of education, fertility, and immigration status are such that, given the effects of these factors on employment, if the groups of women of color had white women's means, they would have the employment of white women—or even somewhat higher employment in cases where we have explained more than all the gap.

While our decomposition has explained all of whites' employment advantage relative to Mexican and Cuban women, we explain less, although still a large share, of the gap with the most disadvantaged groups, Black and Puerto Rican women. Puerto Rican women worked five weeks less than white women, while the gap for Black women was a trivial one week. Our decomposition explains 84 percent of the gap for each of the two groups relative to white women. For both groups, education is the biggest factor, explaining 66 percent of the white/Puerto Rican gap and all of the (tiny) white/Black gap. Puerto Ricans' higher rate of immigration explains 22 percent of their employment gap with white women. The fact that we cannot explain all of the white/Puerto Rican and white/Black gaps suggests that factors unmeasured in our regressions are affecting Puerto Rican and Black women more than other groups. Some combination of employment discrimination and living in segregated neighborhoods with inferior schools and few jobs, sometimes making welfare the best option for single mothers, undoubtedly contributes to unexplained portions of these gaps.

What do these findings imply for our contemporary understanding of race, gender, and other axes of privilege such as education and being born in the mainland United States? Sociologists often tell a gender story in which women are disadvantaged in the labor market relative to men in part because of a division of labor in marriage in which women do childrearing. Our findings suggest that today, responsibility for children, not marriage, is a lynchpin of gender inequality, at least insofar as it affects employment. And childbearing is less closely coupled with marriage than previously. The higher fertility of Black, Puerto Rican, and especially Mexican women reduces their employment, even while the low marriage rates of Black and Puerto Rican women do little or nothing to encourage their employment. Advocates of an intersectionality perspective have criticized the generic gender account emphasizing marriage and children, pointing out that many Blacks and Latinas need to work for pay because of the unemployment or low wages of men of their race. We agree that scholarship should seek to understand how race, class, and gender intersect, but our findings make clear that the central race/gender interaction is no longer that less privileged women on race and class are more likely to work outside the home. The unquestionably greater need for employment among women of color no longer leads to higher employment rates (albeit at low wages), as it once did.

In recent decades, the rise in women's employment has been greatest among the well educated (Chinhui and Murphy 1997; Cohen and Bianchi 1999). This is one reason that white women, who still have some edge in educational attainment, now have higher employment levels, as our analysis has shown. In the 1970s and 1980s, the most disadvantaged racial and ethnic groups were adversely affected by recent trends toward greater earnings inequality and the drop in demand for labor with workers low in the labor queue for reasons of education or discrimination. It is well known that this negatively affected the earnings of men with low education, especially Black men. But this restructuring made employment more difficult for some groups of women as well, especially women of color with no more than a high school education (Browne 1999; Corcoran 1999; Tienda, Donato, and Cordero-Guzman 1992). While it remains true that many women need employment because they are single or married to men with modest earnings, it is simply not true today that the women who need jobs the most are most apt to be employed. Women privileged by race, national origin, and education are the most likely to be employed, as our analysis has shown. Some of the employment edge of privileged women is ascriptive (being born in the United States, or the edge of white women over Black and Puerto Rican women that remained unexplained by our models), and some is on achieved criteria such as education or lower fertility.

The past decade has also made it clear that economic and political trends can move the employment of women of color in either direction relative to white women. While some combination of the pressures of welfare reform, the incentives to employment of the Earned Income Tax Credit, and the strong economy of the 1990s increased the employment of women of color more than that of white women in the middle and late 1990s, we would not be surprised if the post-2001 recession is currently reversing those gains. The more general picture of recent trend research is of disproportionate employment losses for men and women toward the bottom of labor queues defined by education or ethnicity. At the same time, all groups share in a retreat from marriage, but less advantaged groups have not delayed their age of childbearing as much as more educated women, so the result is an increased proportion of births outside of marriage, especially among those who do not go to college and particularly among Blacks (Ellwood and Jencks forthcoming; Raley 1996). When we put these realities together with the retrenchment of welfare, we see that women in less privileged racial and ethnic groups are experiencing simultaneous decreases in their chances of employment, marriage, or welfare to provide a decent level of support for themselves and their children. This is the reality that intersectionality studies must grapple with in future research.

References

Browne, Irene, ed. 1999. *Race, gender and economic inequality: African American and Latina women in the labor market.* New York: Russell Sage.

Chinhui, Juhn, and Kevin M. Murphy. 1997. Wage inequality and family labor supply. *Journal of Labor Economics* 15: 72–97.

Christopher, Karen. 1996. Explaining the recent employment gap between Black and white women. *Sociological Focus* 29 (3): 263–80.

Cohen, Philip N., and Suzanne M. Bianchi. 1999. Marriage, children, and women's employment: What do we know? *Monthly Labor Review* 122 (December): 22–31.

Cooney, Rosemary S., and Vilma Ortiz. 1983. Nativity, national origin, and Hispanic female participation in the labor force. *Social Sciences Quarterly* 64: 510–23.

Corcoran, Mary. 1999. Black women's economic progress. In *Race, gender and economic inequality: African-American and Latina women in the labor market,* edited by Irene Browne. New York: Russell Sage.

Corcoran, Mary, Colleen M. Heflin, and Belinda I. Reyes. 1999. Latina women in the U.S.: The economic progress of Mexican and Puerto Rican women. In *Race, gender and economic in-*

equality: African-American and Latina women in the labor market, edited by Irene Browne. New York: Russell Sage.

Ellwood, David T., and Christopher Jencks. Forthcoming. The spread of single parent families in the United States since 1960. In *The future of the family,* edited by Timothy Smeeding, Daniel Patrick Moynihan, and Lee Rainwater. New York: Russell Sage.

England, Paula. 1992. *Comparable worth: Theories and evidence.* Hawthorne, NY: Aldine DeGruyter.

Higginbotham, Elizabeth, and Mary Romero, eds. 1997. *Women and working: Exploring race, ethnicity, and class.* Thousand Oaks, CA: Sage.

Hondagneu-Sotelo, Pierette. 1997. Working "without papers" in the United States: Toward the integration of legal status in frameworks of race, class, and gender. In *Women and working: Exploring race, ethnicity, and class,* edited by Elizabeth Higginbotham and Mary Romero. Thousand Oaks, CA: Sage.

Kahn, Joan R., and Leslie A. Whittington. 1996. The labor supply of Latinas in the USA: Comparing labor force participation, wages, and hours worked with Anglo and Black women. *Population Research and Policy Review* 15: 45–73.

Pedraza, Silvia. 1991. Women and migration: The social consequences of gender. *Annual Review of Sociology* 17: 303–25.

Prieto, Yolanda. 1978. *Women, work, and change: The case of Cuban women in the U.S.* Latin American Monograph Series, monograph 9. Erie, PA: Northwestern Penn Institute for Latin American Studies, Mercyhurst College.

Raley, R. Kelly. 1996. A shortage of marriageable men? A note on the role of cohabitation in Black-white differences in marriage rates. *American Sociological Review* 61: 973–83.

Reid, Lori. 2002. Occupational segregation, human capital, and motherhood: Black women's higher exit rates from full-time employment. *Gender & Society* 16: 728–47.

Romero, Mary. 2002. *Maid in the U.S.A.* 2d ed. London: Routledge.

Smith, Shelley A., and Marta Tienda. 1988. The doubly disadvantaged: Women of color in the U.S. labor force. In *Women working,* 2d ed., edited by Ann Helton Stromberg and Sirley Harkess. Mountain View, CA: Mayfield.

Spain, Daphne, and Suzanne M. Bianchi. 1996. *Balancing act: Motherhood, marriage, and employment among American women.* New York: Russell Sage.

Stier, Haya, and Marta Tienda. 1992. Family, work and women: The labor supply of Hispanic immigrant wives. *International Migration Review* 26 (4): 1291–1313.

Tienda, Marta, Katharine M. Donato, and Hector
Cordero-Guzman. 1992. Schooling, color and
the labor force activity of women. *Social
Forces* 71 (2): 365–95.

Tienda, Marta, and Jennifer Glass. 1985. Household structure and labor force participation
of Black, Hispanic, and white mothers. *Demography* 22 (3): 381–94.

U.S. Bureau of Census. 2001. Current Population Survey: Annual demographic file. MRDF.
Washington, DC: U.S. Department of Commerce, Bureau of the Census.

Reprinted from: Paula England, Carmen Garcia-Beaulieu,
and Mary Ross, "Women's Employment Among Blacks,
Whites, and Three Groups of Latinas: Do More Privileged Women Have Higher Employment?" In *Gender &
Society*, Vol. 18, No. 4, August 2004, pp. 494–509. Copyright © 2004 by Sage Publications.

Food for Thought and Application Questions

1. What factors have *traditionally* influenced the employment of women? Discuss each factor in terms of how it works
to increase the likelihood of women's employment and any interrelationship
among the factors.

2. In the current research, what are the key
factors that influence women's employment? How does their importance *vary*
among subgroups of women (i.e., among
Black women, white women, Cuban, Mexican, and Puerto Rican women)? What
factors influence the groups similarly? ✦

5

Gendered Jobs and Gendered Workers

Christine L. Williams

. . . Women currently constitute 45 percent of the paid labor force, but they continue to lag behind men in earnings and organizational power (U.S. Department of Labor 1993). Several books and articles now document this economic disparity and explain it in terms of the different meanings, purposes, and aspirations that women *qua women* experience in the labor force. In other words, in the sociology of work, gender seems to be something that affects only women, and affects them only negatively.

To explain how and why a woman's gender impedes her economic success, two general theoretical approaches have been developed. On the one hand, conventional theories—such as human capital or status attainment theory—attribute women's lesser achievement in the workplace to the gender characteristics that women bring with them to work. According to this perspective, women cannot compete as successfully as men for the best jobs either because they were not properly socialized to acquire highly valued worker characteristics (such as aggressiveness and ambition), or because they have competing household responsibilities. If men are more successful, this argument goes, that is because they have superior skills or they have made better organizational choices (Sokoloff 1980; Marini 1989).

Feminist researchers have generally rejected this perspective, claiming instead that women's lesser achievement is due to gender discrimination and sexual harassment, not to women's supposed deficiencies compared to men (Acker 1990; Hearn and Parkin 1987; Pringle 1988). In fact, several studies have demonstrated that women and men are not treated equally at work, even if they possess the same qualifications and are hired to perform the same job. In nearly every occupation, women encounter barriers when they try to enter the most lucrative and prestigious specialties. A "glass ceiling" prevents them from reaching the top positions (Reskin and Phipps 1988). From this perspective, the organizational dynamics—and not the "feminine" attributes of women—result in women's lesser pay and status in the work world.

One of the most important studies documenting this organizational inequality is Rosabeth Moss Kanter's *Men and Women of the Corporation*. In this book, Kanter (1977) argues that the barriers women face in predominantly male occupations can be attributed to their *numerical* minority in organizations. Although men and women may have similar qualifications, the organizational structure nevertheless promotes gender differentiation through the mechanism of tokenism. She maintains that because all tokens "stand out" from the dominant group and receive more than their fair share of attention, they are therefore subjected to stereotyping, role entrapment, and various other forms of marginalization.

. . . To fully understand the source of women's disadvantages in the workplace, it is essential to examine the source of men's advantages. Shifting the focus to men therefore is not intended to abandon the concerns of women, but rather to implicate men in the overall pattern of discrimination against women. However, including men's experiences in the analysis of gender and work does substantially alter the research questions: Instead of asking, "What are the deficiencies of women?" or "What are the barriers to women?" the questions now become, "Why is gender a liability for women but an asset for men?" and "What are the mechanisms that propel men to more successful careers?"

To address these questions, I rely on a theory of "gendered organizations" (Acker 1990; Scott 1986; Hall 1993). According to this perspective, cultural beliefs about masculinity and femininity are built into the very structure of the work world. Organizational

69

hierarchies, job descriptions, and informal workplace practices all contain deeply embedded assumptions about the gender and gendered characteristics of workers. These beliefs about gender—which are often unstated and unacknowledged—limit women's opportunities while enhancing men's occupational success. In other words, work organizations contain built-in advantages for men that are often unnoticed; indeed, they seem like natural or inevitable characteristics of all organizations.

On the most basic level, work organizations are gendered in that employers prefer to hire workers with few if any nonwork distractions. This is not a gender-neutral preference: Men fit this description far more easily than women, because of the unequal division of household labor in most families. Joan Acker writes (1990, p. 149),

> The closest the disembodied worker doing the abstract job comes to a real worker is the male worker whose life centers on his full-time, life-long job, while his wife or another woman takes care of his personal needs and his children.

Women's careers often suffer because work organizations typically do not accommodate their additional household responsibilities (Hochschild 1989).

This organizational preference for men exists even in the "women's professions." An Arizona nursing director who is in charge of hiring the staff of the emergency room explained why men in his hospital are overrepresented in the best positions:

> I've sometimes stopped to wonder whether there is a little bias there. I'm not sure. . . . The men sometimes tend to be a little more stable than the women. A lot of the men who work in the ER [emergency room] have really been here for quite a while. They're married; most have kids. When it's time to have a baby, they're not the ones who take off. It's the same problem, . . . it's really not a lot different than a lot of other professions.

Although organizations that employ nurses and members of the other "women's professions" often permit leaves-of-absence to tend to family responsibilities, no one is actually rewarded for taking this time off. Instead, those who demonstrate unconditional devotion to their work receive the best jobs, giving men an unfair advantage over women even in these "female" occupations.

There is a second, even more profound way that organizations are deeply gendered, and that is through the hierarchical division of labor. Gender segregation exists in nearly every organization and every occupation, with men occupying the best paying and most prestigious jobs, and the highest positions of organizational power (Blau and Winkler 1989; Marini 1989). In the United States, more than half of all men or women would have to change major job categories to equalize the proportions of men and women in all occupations. This overall degree of segregation has changed remarkably little over the past hundred years, despite radical transformations in the U.S. job market (Reskin and Roos 1990). Technological developments and management directives have created millions of new jobs and eliminated others, but the basic structure of the gendered division of labor has remained intact. Largely because of this division of labor, women earn far less than men: On average, women still receive less than seventy-five cents for every dollar earned by a man (U.S. Department of Labor 1993, p. 231).

According to the theory of gendered organizations, the division of labor by gender favors men because organizations value men and qualities associated with masculinity more highly than they value women. Organizational hierarchies reify the male standard, rewarding only those who possess putatively masculine characteristics with promotion to the best positions. This preference for masculinity seems to happen regardless of the proportional representation of men in an occupation.

In fact, the higher value placed on men and masculinity is especially evident in traditionally female professions, where men are the tokens. . . . Men have been overrepresented in the top positions in these occupations ever since the nineteenth century, . . . The middle-class white men who did enter these jobs were rewarded for their "masculine" qualities with higher salaries than women received. Also, men were paid more because employers assumed that unlike women, these men needed extra money to support a dependent spouse and children.

Men still are overrepresented in the most prestigious and best-paying specialties in these occupations. Today, male nurses tend to specialize in certain "high tech" areas (such as intensive care and emergency room nursing) or in areas that demand a high degree of physical strength (such as psychiatric and orthopedic nursing) and they are overrepresented in administration. . . .

[Often] the pressures that move men into the more "masculine" specialties are more subtle, . . . embedded in informal interactions that take place between men and their supervisors, co-workers, and clients. . . . Because most of the organizations that train and employ nurses, librarians, teachers, and social workers are "male-dominated," men are often in positions to make decisions that favor other men.

In addition to supervisors, women colleagues and clients often have highly gendered expectations of the men working in these professions that can contribute to men's advancement. . . . For example, some men told me they were pushed into leadership positions by female colleagues, who believed men to be better able to represent their interests to male management. . . .

Organizations thus [treat] men and women very differently regardless of their proportional representation in an occupation. The workplace is not gender-neutral; it is a central site for the creation and reproduction of gender difference and gender inequality. Both men and women are constrained to act in certain ways by organizational hierarchies, job descriptions, and informal workplace practices that are based on deeply embedded assumptions about masculinity and femininity, but this social construction of gender favors men by rewarding them for the "masculine" qualities they are presumed to bring with them to the workplace.

Workers are not passive players in this social reproduction of gender in organizations. The theory of gendered organizations recognizes that workers themselves are gendered: Men and women bring different and often competing interests and desires to work, and they actively struggle to remake organizational structure to reflect these interests. But unlike human capital theory, this perspective maintains that gender attributes are not given and uniform, nor are they necessarily rational. The gendered interests brought to work by individuals are constantly being negotiated in a dialectical process with the gendered structure of organizations. As Cynthia Cockburn writes: "People have a gender, and their gender rubs off on the jobs they do. The jobs in turn have a gender character which rubs off on the people who do them" (1988, p. 38). When workers act on the basis of their perceived collective interests as men or women, they contribute to the "gendering" of organizations.

American labor history is full of examples of men organizing collectively in the workplace to promote and protect their perceived gender interests. For many men, their sense of themselves as masculine is closely associated with the technical skills, male bonding, and the breadwinner ethic of the workplace; success at work often constitutes *proof* of their masculinity. Working alongside women can be deeply threatening to men's sense of pride and self-esteem, so many have vigorously defended gender segregation by establishing barriers to women and treating the few who cross over with scorn and derision (Kessler-Harris 1990).

In addition to asserting their masculinity, men have also used the workplace to consolidate their power over women and their privileges in society. Men have occasionally organized to resist the entry of women into "their" occupations as a means to protect their higher wages and exclusive access to the best jobs, couching their demands in terms of their duties and rights as men in society (Baron 1991; Hartmann 1979; Rotundo 1993).

Women have also at times used gendered discourses to defend *their* rights to work (Baron 1991). But overall, women have been much more active than men in challenging the gendered division of labor by crossing over into nontraditional occupations, and accepting the few token men who enter "their" occupations (Bradley 1993; Jacobs 1993). Part of the reason for this difference is that unlike men, women stand to benefit economically from crossing over. But also, occupational integration does not seem to threaten women's gender identity in the same fundamental psychological way as it threatens men's sense of themselves as masculine. While many women may enjoy the "feminine" aspects of their work, their femininity is not contingent on proving themselves competent in "gender-appropriate" work, which is often how masculinity is experienced by men (Williams 1989). . . .

References

Acker, J. 1990. "Hierarchies, Jobs, Bodies: A Theory of Gendered Organizations," *Gender & Society*, 4 June:139–158.

Baron, A. 1991. "Gender and Labor History: Learning from the Past, Looking to the Future," in *Work Engendered: Toward a New History of American Labor*, ed. Ava Baron. Ithaca, NY: Cornell University Press:1–46.

Blau, F. D. and A. E. Winkler. 1989. "Women in the Labor Force: An Overview," in *Women: A Feminist Perspective*, ed. Jo Freeman, 4th ed. Mountain View, CA: Mayfield Publishing Co.

Bradley, H. 1993. "Across the Great Divide: The Entry of Men into Women's Jobs," in *Doing "Women's Work,"* ed. Christine L. Williams. Newbury Park, CA: Sage:10–27.

Cockburn, C. 1988. "The Gendering of Jobs: Workplace Relations and the Reproduction of Sex Segregation," in *Gender Segregation at Work*, ed. Sylvia Walby, Philadelphia: Open University Press.

Hall, E. 1993. "Smiling, Deferring, and Flirting: Doing Gender by Giving 'Good Service,'" *Work and Occupations*, 20:452–471.

Hartmann, H. 1979. "Capitalism, Patriarchy, and Job Segregation by Sex," in *Capitalist Patriarchy and the Case for Socialist Feminism*, ed. Zillah Eisenstein. New York: Monthly Review Press:206–247.

Hearn, J. and W. Parkin. 1987. *Sex at Work: The Power and Paradox of Organization Sexuality*. New York: St. Martin's Press.

Hochschild, A. with A. Machung. 1989. *The Second Shift*. New York: Avon Books.

Jacobs, J. A. 1993. "Men in Female-Dominated Fields: Trends and Turnover," in *Doing "Women's Work,"* ed. Christine L. Williams. Newbury Park, CA: Sage:49–63.

Kanter, R. M. 1977. *Men and Women of the Corporation*. New York: Basic Books.

Kessler-Harris, A. 1990. *A Woman's Wage: Historical Meanings and Social Consequences*. Lexington: University of Kentucky Press.

Marini, M. M. 1989. "Sex Differences in Earning in the United States," *Annual Review of Sociology*, 15:343–380.

Pringle, R. 1988. *Secretaries Talk*. London: Verso.

Reskin, B. F. and P. Phipps. 1988. "Women in Male-Dominated Professional and Managerial Occupations," in *Women Working*, ed. Ann Helton Stromberg and Shirley Harkess, Mountain View, CA: Mayfield Publishing Co.:190–205.

Reskin, B. F. and P. A. Roos. 1990. *Job Queues, Gender Queues*. Philadelphia: Temple University Press.

Rotundo, E. A. 1993. *American Manhood: Transformations in Masculinity from the Revolution to the Modern Era*. New York: Basic Books.

Scott, J. 1986. "Gender: A Useful Category for Historical Analysis," *American Historical Review*, 91:1053–1075.

Sokoloff, N. 1980. *Between Money and Love*. New York: Praeger.

U.S. Department of Labor, Bureau of Labor Statistics. 1993. *Employment and Earnings*, 40 (1) January:195.

Williams, C. 1989. *Gender Differences at Work*. Berkeley: University of California Press.

Food for Thought and Application Questions

1. What is "gendered organization" theory? How does this theory explain women's work status in ways that human capital theory and the theory of tokenism do not? Select an article about women's work status and reinterpret it in terms of a "gendered organization" framework. What insights about women and work do you gain from using such a framework?

2. Discuss a number of ways in which organizations reflect male advantages in their procedures and policies. Develop a list of such practices and suggest how each procedure or policy would have to be changed to make it "gender neutral." ✦

6

Sex Segregation in the Workplace

Barbara F. Reskin

Sex segregation in the workplace refers to women's and men's concentration in different occupations, industries, jobs, and levels in workplace hierarchies. More broadly, sex segregation constitutes a sexual division of paid labor in which men and women do different tasks, or the same tasks under different names or at different times and places. People's race and sometimes their ethnicity and age are also bases for differentiation at work, so workplaces are segregated by sex, race, and ethnicity, as well as other characteristics. The assignment of jobs based on workers' sex, race, and ethnicity is one of the most enduring features of work in industrialized societies and a mainstay in preserving larger systems of inequality.

Because the work that people do greatly influences their pay, sex segregation contributes substantially to the gap in earnings between women and men (England and McCreary 1987). Segregation also reduces women's fringe benefits and their access to medical insurance, pensions, and Social Security income. By disproportionately relegating women to jobs with short or absent career ladders, segregation lowers women's chances of promotion. Both task and rank segregation restrict women's likelihood of exercising authority at work (Reskin and Hartmann 1986). The effects of segregation extend beyond the workplace. Men's higher incomes, occupational status, and authority preserve their power over women in private and public realms.

Ever since the Industrial Revolution removed most productive work from the home, employers have segregated the sexes, reserving better jobs for men (Goldin 1990). We can gauge the extent of sex segregation across occupations, industries, or jobs by examining the index of segregation. (An occupation refers to a cluster of related work activities that constitute a single economic role—for example, baker. In contrast, a job refers to the specific tasks performed by one or more people in a specific work setting—for example, a production baker at Oroweat's Oakland plant, or a "bake-off" baker at the Ballard Safeway store.) The index of occupational segregation shows the minimum proportion of either sex that would have to change from a sex-typical to a sex-atypical occupation for the sexes to be distributed similarly across all occupations. If sex had no effect on people's occupation, the index of segregation would equal 0. If women and men never held the same occupation, the index would equal 100.

In the United States, the amount of occupational sex segregation fluctuated slightly between 1910 (69.0) and 1970 (67.6). The century's largest drop in segregation occurred during the 1970s—by 1980, the index was 59.8 (Jacobs 1989). Segregation continued to decline in the 1980s, but at a much slower rate. The 1990 index—calculated for employed workers in 477 occupations—was 4.5 points lower than the 1980 index, indicating that out of every 100 women about 55 would have had to switch from predominantly female to predominantly male occupations for the labor force to be fully integrated across occupations. Of course, even such an improbably wholesale redistribution would not truly integrate America's places of work because women and men in the same occupation typically work for different employers in different industries and hence hold different jobs (Bielby and Baron 1986).

Occupational segregation by race has dropped sharply in the U.S. since 1940, when most blacks were still confined to a small number of occupations. As Table 6.1 shows, race segregation has declined more rapidly among women than men (King 1992). However, American women of African, Asian, and Hispanic descent as well as Native-American women continue to be overrepresented in the least desirable, traditionally female jobs (Smith and Tienda 1988). In sum, women are less segregated by race than are men, and

Table 6.1
Trends in Sex and Race Segregation

	1940	1950	1960	1970	1980	1988 [a]
Segregation between						
Black and white women	0.618	0.649	0.640	0.474	0.326	0.293
Black and white men	0.383	0.415	0.439	0.362	0.313	0.293
Black women and men	0.772	0.738	0.697	0.694	0.532	0.609
White women and men	0.802	0.729	0.729	0.723	0.574	0.604

[a]Indexes based on 159 occupations common to census classification systems between 1940 and 1980.
Source: King 1992.

as far as occupations are concerned, being female is a bigger obstacle among the employed than not being white.

In all industrialized countries, barriers restrict women's access to many jobs. The pattern of segregation for the United States resembles that in other industrialized countries, although the Scandinavian countries exhibit particularly high levels of segregation, partly because their family policies encourage women to work part time (Rosenfeld and Kalleberg 1991).

Contributing to sex segregation are the actions of employers and workers, as well as cultural and institutional forces. Occupational sex labels and sex-role stereotypes influence employers' decisions as well as workers' occupational expectations. The occupational and industrial structures (in other words, where the jobs are) set limits on the pace of integration. For example, the growth of managerial occupations during the 1980s facilitated women's entry into managerial jobs, but the explosion of service jobs involving traditionally female tasks has slowed integration.

Workers' characteristics and employers' policies also affect the extent of segregation. The human-capital explanation for segregation holds that women's family obligations (1) keep them from investing in education and experience—thus reducing their qualifications for male jobs—and (2) incline them toward traditionally female occupations that supposedly are easy to reenter and do

not penalize workers for work interruptions. This theory has little support (England and McCreary 1987). Considerable evidence shows the importance of employers' and male workers' actions—including discrimination and stereotyping—in segregating workers (Reskin 1993).

The small decline in segregation during the 1960s stemmed more from men's entry into customarily female "semiprofessions" than from the integration of traditionally male occupations (Reskin and Hartmann 1986). The 1970s brought the first large-scale movement by women into the predominantly male occupations (of which there are more than 300). The 1980s brought increased understanding of what factors maintain and reduce it (Reskin and Hartmann 1986). Three factors contributed to the post-1970 decline in sex segregation. The first was "structural" changes in American occupations. The growth of several integrated occupations and the shrinkage of some highly segregated occupations redistributed jobs from segregated to integrated occupations.

The second component of desegregation resulted from women's gradual entry into many sex-atypical occupations (for example, statistician, groundskeeper). Several factors fostered women's increasing share of many male occupations. The more egalitarian values popularized by the women's liberation movement, later marriage and more divorce, and a recessionary economy meant that more women supported themselves and their families. These changes paved the way for laws and regulations barring sex discrimination in educational institutions and the workplace. Changing attitudes, bolstered by new regulations, encouraged many large employers to adopt equal-employment policies. As women's opportunities expanded, they increasingly resembled men in college major, job aspirations, attachment to the labor force, and paid work experience. A growing number of women entered occupations that had been reserved primarily for men, and occupations' traditional sex labels weakened and became less binding on labor-market participants. These factors reinforced small to moderate increases in the representation of women—mostly white women—in many customarily male occupations. Rarely did men replace white women in traditionally female jobs; instead, shortages created opportunities for women of color, contributing to the decline in race segregation among women.

The third component of occupational desegregation stemmed from women's substantial headway into a few male occupations such as insurance adjuster and bank manager. However, their substantial shifts in sex composition did not necessarily produce integration. Instead, some traditionally male occupational specialties such as residential real-estate salesperson and public-relations specialist, became resegregated as women's work. Employers hired thousands of women for these occupations when doing so would save money. Regulations that barred discrimination or required affirmative action contributed to women's large inroads into broadcast reporting, bank management, and bartending (Reskin and Roos 1990). So too did enormous job growth in a few customarily male occupations that outpaced the supply of qualified male applicants. Finally, employers resorted to women for occupations that could not attract enough men because their earnings had declined or they had deteriorated in other ways. In other words, employers turned to women when they needed to cut costs and when a deteriorating occupation did not generate an adequate supply of men (Reskin and Roos 1990). Women flocked to these formerly male occupations because they offered better pay and opportunities than the traditionally female occupations open to equally qualified women.

At the beginning of the 1990s, the majority of both women and men still worked in jobs in which the other sex was underrepresented, if not completely absent. Nonetheless, the work force was less sex segregated than at any earlier time in the twentieth century. How much has occupational desegregation enhanced workplace equity? Although the wage gap has declined, employers still pay a premium to workers in male-dominated jobs, so men and women in customarily male occupations usually outearn women in predominantly female jobs. And job segregation in mixed-sex occupations ensures that women rarely earn as much as their male counterparts (Reskin and Roos 1990). Moreover, while the tens of thousands of women who entered occupations and specialties that men were abandoning averaged higher pay than they would get in "women's" jobs, few earn as much as their male counterparts, and their wage advantage is unlikely to last in occupations that resegregate as "women's work."

The stalled pace of sex integration has three crucial policy implications. First, enforcing existing current programs to bar discrimination and implement affirmative action in training and employment is essential for continued declines in segregation. Second, the prevalence of job-level segregation within nominally integrated occupations means that we must find other solutions to the economic disadvantage under which women labor. One possible solution is pay equity (comparable worth)—the policy of compensating workers for the skill, effort, and responsibility their jobs require rather than for the sex composition of their workforce. However, pay equity cannot eliminate the wage disparity between the sexes so long as women are disproportionately consigned to jobs that society defines as low skilled and denied the opportunity to exercise workplace responsibility. Finally, women's continued responsibility for most family work hampers their access to some jobs. A more egalitarian division of domestic work and family-work policies that takes into account employees' family roles is needed to redress this disadvantage.

To achieve these goals, women must return to the tactics that fostered the pro-equality political climate of the 1960s and 1970s: They must act politically, applying pressure on employers, politicians, and regulatory agencies. Without such action, we will begin the twenty-first century with a workforce in which sex and race rather than talents continue to determine the jobs people do.

References

Bielby, W. T. and J. N. Baron. 1986. "Men and women at work: Sex segregation and statistical discrimination." *American Journal of Sociology*, 91:759–799.

England, P. and L. McCreary. 1987. "Gender inequality in paid employment." In H. Hess and M. Ferree (eds.), *Analyzing Gender*. Newbury Park, CA: Sage, 286–320.

Goldin, C. 1990. *Understanding the Gender Gap: An Economic History of American Women*. New York: Oxford University Press.

Jacobs, J. A. 1989. *Revolving Doors: Sex Segregation and Women's Careers*. Stanford: Stanford University Press.

King, M. C. 1992. "Occupational segregation by race and gender." *Monthly Labor Review*, 115:30–37.

Reskin, B. F. 1993. "Sex segregation in the workplace." *Annual Review of Sociology*, 19:241–270.

Reskin, B. F. and H. I. Hartmann. 1986. *Women's Work, Men's Work: Sex Segregation on the Job*. Washington, D.C.: National Academy.

Reskin, B. F. and P. A. Roos. 1990. *Job Queues, Gender Queues*. Philadelphia: Temple University Press.

Rosenfeld, R. and A. L. Kalleberg. 1991. "Gender inequality in the labor market: A cross-national perspective." In *Acta Sociologica*, 34:207–225.

Smith, S. A. and M. Tienda. 1988. "The doubly disadvantaged: Women of color in the U.S. labor force." In A. H. Stromberg and S. Harkess (eds.), *Women Working*. Mountain View, CA: Mayfield, 61–80.

Food for Thought and Application Questions

1. Gender-segregated employment is reinforced by the selective evaluation of what stereotypical women and men can contribute to the workplace. For example, it might be argued that men are better physicians and engineers because they are more logical and interested in science. Similarly, women might be judged as better suited for positions as librarians or clerical workers because they are detail-oriented. Although such traits may indeed be beneficial for the performance of these work roles, they represent a selective interpretation of women's and men's qualifications for the jobs. Isn't it likely that the detail-oriented stereotype commonly applied to women would be an equally important asset to the physician?

   Gender stereotypes are problematic, not only because they represent gross overgeneralizations, but also because they are applied selectively to limit the occupational choices of women and men. Select any highly gender-segregated occupation (e.g., auto mechanic, 98.7 percent male; architect, 95 percent male; registered nurse, 96 percent female) and explain how gender stereotypes contribute to segregation in the occupation by creating the expectation that one sex or the other is better suited for the work. To illustrate the selective application of gender stereotypes to employment categories, discuss how the stereotypical gender traits might be reinterpreted as beneficial to nontraditional employment. For example, what female traits might prove useful in auto repair? Or what masculine traits would be valuable to a registered nurse?

2. Identify three occupations that have become increasingly gender-integrated over the last few decades. Why have these changes occurred? Is the increased representation of women (or men) the result of a greater supply of non-traditional-sex workers ready to perform the job? Or do the changes result from an increase in employer demand for non-traditional-sex workers? ◆

7

The Penny Pinch

Christine Larson

"Men are here to make a career and women aren't. Retail is for house wives who just need to earn extra money." That's how a Wal-Mart manager allegedly explained the pay difference between men and women, according to recently released documents in the gender pay discrimination suit against Wal-Mart.

With attitudes like that, it's no wonder that the gender wage gap actually increased last year for the first time since 1998. Women who worked full-time year-round in 2003 earned just 76 cents for every dollar earned by their male peers, according to the U.S. Census Bureau—down from 77 cents in 2002. While men's median earnings were $40,668, women's were just $30,724—a 0.6 percent drop from women's earnings in 2002.

The new numbers prove what many women have long feared: that all the improvements in women's working conditions in the past 10 years, including more education and experience, simply aren't enough to close the gap.

"I doubt that it will continue to close without some more drastic interventions," says Hilary Lips, Ph.D., director of the Center for Gender Studies at Radford University in Radford, Virginia. She says the things that have helped the gap close over the past few decades—including laws preventing overt gender discrimination, the movement of women into higher paying professions, and the fact that women take less time out of the workforce to raise children—have already been taken care of. To make more progress, she says, companies, the government, and women themselves will need to take more aggressive action. For example, she recommends more support for women entering math- and science-related fields, more family-friendly policies like paid family leave, and more proactive efforts to seek out pay inequities via corporate pay surveys and equal pay for equal work policies.

In her recent forecast of the future of the wage gap, Lips predicts the gap will be about the same in 2010 as it is today. And a study by economists Michael Shannon, Ph.D., of Lakehead University, Canada, and Michael P. Kidd, Ph.D., of the University of Aberdeen, UK, predicted the gap would shrink by just 25 percent between 1995 and 2040—an improvement of only about 7 cents, based on the Census-reported wage gap in 1995—even when they accounted for the improving education rates of women.

This year's NAFE Salary Survey, which reports on salaries in 20 different industries, also concurs that more education doesn't necessarily mean a smaller wage gap. Some of the most highly paid, most educated women in our survey face a larger-than-average wage gap. Female neurosurgeons earned only 69.2 percent of what men earned. Women scientists doing medical research earned just 71.3 percent of their male colleagues' income. Meanwhile, some of the lowest paid women—receptionists, office clerks, and teacher's aides—made 82–100 percent of their male peers' salaries. These results support recent findings by the U.S. Census Bureau, which concluded that "education alone contributes little toward equality between men's and women's median earnings."

If more degrees can't fill the gap, what can? To achieve fair pay, women need to campaign for changes. Here are some action items:

Burn the 'Pink' Diploma

"We know that educational attainment for women improved fairly dramatically over time," says Shannon. Indeed, more young women than men now finish both high school and college, and this year, for the first time, Harvard offered admission to more women than men. But Shannon's findings agree with those of the Government Accountability Office (GAO): that more education didn't do much to narrow the future wage gap when he projected it ahead to 2040. "We were kind of surprised by the results," Shannon says. "We expected to see the gender gap fall more than it did in the projections."

But don't hang up your mortarboards yet. More education *can* make a difference in the wage gap—if women start studying math and science in the same proportions as men. The real problem is that although women are getting more education, they're not getting enough in majors that lead to higher incomes. In a March 2004 study, professors Dan Black of Syracuse University, Seth Sanders of University of Maryland, and Amelia Haviland and Lowell Taylor of Carnegie Mellon University found that undergraduate women aren't majoring in fields that lead to high-paying jobs. About 50 percent of white, black, and Hispanic women major in the five lowest paying majors (education, humanities, professional degrees, fine arts, and agriculture). Just 26 percent of white men—the highest paid group in the U.S.—major in these areas. Instead, white men choose to study engineering, mathematical sciences, business and economics, physical sciences, and social sciences—the five majors leading to the highest income.

It's worth remembering, however, that although women in science and engineering jobs face less of a wage gap than the average woman, they still earn less than men. Women civil engineers, for example, earn, on average, $61,000—far more than the median income for women in general, but 17.5 percent less than male engineers earn, at $74,000, according to the American Society of Civil Engineers.

When women do major in these male-dominated areas, the wage gap narrows. Asian women—far more likely to major in sciences and engineering than white, black, and Hispanic women, according to the study by Black and his associates—face a smaller gender gap (they earn 75 percent of what white men earn), than other women (on average women earned 67.5 percent of what white men earned in 1999, according to the Institute for Women's Policy Research). Women who don't go to college find themselves shunted into the pink classroom in high school as well. A 2002 study by the National Women's Law Center (NWLC) found that high school vocational programs push women toward cosmetology (which typi-

cally pays $8.49 an hour) and child care ($7.43 per hour), rather than plumbing and electrician training (fields that pay a median hourly wage of $18.19 and $19.29 respectively). Girls represent just 6–8 percent of students in electrician, plumbing, and carpentry vocational classes, but 86–96 percent of students in cosmetology, childcare, and health assistant classes.

Although the NWLC petitioned the Department of Education in 2002 to investigate the imbalance, the government declined, reports Jocelyn Samuels, the NWLC's vice president for education and employment. "This is deeply troubling to us," she says. "In our view, it's a real abdication of their statutory obligation to enforce Title IX [the 1972 statute that prohibits sex discrimination in federally funded schools]." The NWLC also found that 23 states plus the District of Columbia lacked Title IX coordinators to oversee anti-discrimination. As a result of NWLC pressure, the DOE issued a memo in April reminding states of their legal obligation to appoint a coordinator. In August, the DOE issued a similar reminder to colleges and universities. Currently, the NWLC is working with Congress to include anti-discrimination requirements and gender-equity provisions in the Carl D. Perkins Act, the federal law that funds vocational training, up for reauthorization this year.

Beware the Pink Collar Ghetto

Given their career preparation in high school and college, it's no surprise that most women still tend to work in lower paying occupations. "Women are less likely to be in the highest paying jobs, in sales or science or technology—or senior management, where you need sharp elbows," says Martha Farnsworth Riche, Ph.D., former director of the U.S. Census Bureau.

From physicians to hairdressers, women still experience societal pressure to choose traditional female (read, "traditionally low paid") jobs. "Nobody's saying you can't be a surgeon, but it's more comfortable if in medical school, you slide into pediatrics or general practice, where lots of other women practice," says Lips. "There's a lot of informal discrimination most of us don't even recognize when we're experiencing it." Some

[The Gaps Within the Gap]
Women of Color

Why do Asian women do better than their peers? They're more likely than other women to major in science or engineering, according to a March 2004 study by professors Dan Black of Syracuse University, Seth Sanders of University of Maryland, and Amelia Haviland and Lowell Taylor of Carnegie Mellon University. And they're more likely to work in professional and managerial positions than other women, according to the Institute for Women's Policy Research. In general, they have much more education than other groups of women: Some 43.8 percent of Asian-American women age 25 and older held college degrees, compared with 27.3 percent of white women and 11.2 percent of Hispanic women, in 2002. However, it's worth noting that not all Asian women do equally well—Japanese women earn 89 percent of what white men earn, while Vietnemese women earn just 60 percent.

What might help close the gaps between women? "Stronger enforcement of equal opportunity laws and better access to higher education for women of color," says Hartmann. Raising the minimum wage would also help women of color because they're more likely to hold low-wage jobs than white men. ✦

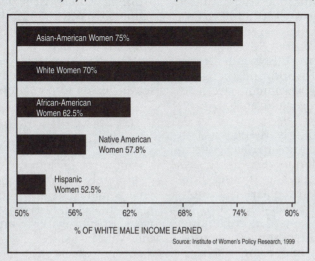

Asian-American Women 75%
White Women 70%
African-American Women 62.5%
Native American Women 57.8%
Hispanic Women 52.5%

% OF WHITE MALE INCOME EARNED

Source: Institute of Women's Policy Research, 1999

economists suggest that subtle societal pressures and discrimination lead women to choose more flexible fields like teaching or human resources, assuming they will need to take on more family responsibilities.

To continue closing the wage gap, young women need more encouragement and financial aid in majors like science, math, and engineering, and more help at succeeding in these professions. They need better, less biased counseling at the high school level and more career counseling that helps them understand the wage implications of their career choices. They need more rigorous policing of Title IX, as well as the support of organizations like Wider Opportunities for Women (*www.wowonline.org*) and the Society of Women Engineers (*www.swe.org*) which provide support networks for young women pursuing historically male fields. Many occupations now have industrywide women's groups to foster women's success, such as the American Medical Women's Association (*www.amwa-doc.org*), the National Association of Women Lawyers (*www.abanet.org/nawl*), and the Association for Women in Computing (*www.awc-hq.org*). Joining and supporting such groups may help close the gender gap in your field.

Campaign for Valuing the Family

Until family becomes an equal opportunity employer—demanding as much time from men as women—the wage gap may never disappear without aggressive legislative attention. Most wage gap studies consider only men and women who work full-time, year-round, without looking at the many women who work part-time. When you add in part-time workers, the wage gap looms even larger. Over a 15-year period between 1983–1998, the average woman worked only 67.5 percent as many hours as the average man—and earned nearly half a million dollars ($449,101) less, according to a study by Heidi Hartmann, Ph.D., president of the institute for Women's Policy Research.

"To see a decrease in the time that women take off from work, we need more paid family leave and subsidized child care," says Dr. Hartmann.

Sadly, the U.S. is one of very few industrialized countries without paid family leave, according to a 2004 report by Harvard researchers. Of 168 countries studied, 163 provided paid family leave. Australia and the U.S. were the only two without paid leave. And although Australia doesn't guarantee paid leave, it does give workers a full year of unpaid family leave—compared to just 12 weeks for U.S. workers.

"It's really time for the U.S. to join the rest of the industrialized world and recognize that employers and government have a responsibility for raising children too," says Martha Farnsworth Riche.

The lack of paid family leave suggests that U.S. corporations and the American government don't value the family very highly, says Lips—despite stump speeches touting "family values." "In most workplaces right now, employers are bending over backwards for employees in reserve units. They're holding their jobs because military service is considered something really important," she says. "But what about bringing up children or looking after a mom who has Alzheimer's?"

Fortunately some states are stepping in. On January 1, California became the first state with paid family leave. Funded by a new payroll tax that amounts to an average of $4 per month per employee, the program enables employees to take up to six weeks off to care for a new child or seriously ill family member and receive up to 55 percent of their pay. Meanwhile, Florida's state legislature adopted universal pre-kindergarten, which would ease the financial burden of child care on working families. Lobbying state legislature for changes like this can help bring about remedies that will lead to a smaller gender wage gap.

Companies too, are getting the message. Twenty nine percent of companies on *Working Mother* Magazine's 100 Best Companies for Working Mothers list offer paid maternity leave beyond short-term disability compared to 13 percent nationwide; 37 percent offer paid paternity leave, versus 14 nationwide; and 47 percent offer adoption leave, versus 13 percent nationwide.

Call for Tougher Anti-Discrimination Laws

Unfortunately none of these measures can completely eliminate the gap in a world where managers still feel free to drop remarks like "You're a girl. Why do you want to work in hardware?"—another quote from the Wal-Mart suit.

Even women with the same experience and education as men face a 20 percent gap, according to the GAO report. A rash of discrimination cases underscores the fact that unfair pay practices persist, despite the Equal Pay Act of 1963 that outlaws gender pay discrimination. In addition to the Wal-Mart suit, high-profile cases were filed against Merrill Lynch & Co. and Morgan Stanley in recent years.

"We haven't had very good enforcement of equal opportunity laws," says Heidi Hartmann Since 1992, the EEOC has filed just 21 lawsuits against companies for violat-

---

[The Gaps Within the Gap]
Company Size

A 2003 study by economist Aparna Mitra, Ph.D, of the University of Oklahoma found a disproportionate number of women work for large or very large firms—which pay more on average than small- and medium-size firms.

However, just because women at larger firms earn more than women at medium-size firms doesn't mean the wage gap is smaller at large firms. Actually, it's even larger. Because while salaries at larger firms are higher overall, these firms pay men significantly more than women.

In fact, after controlling for other factors, the wage gap is 15 percent at medium firms, but 17 percent at large firms and 24 percent at the largest firms. "Women professionals have fewer opportunities for holding meaningful supervisory jobs or earning comparable wages with their male counterparts in large establishments," the report concludes.

Focusing on the types of jobs women and men hold within large coporations, as well as corporate promotion and pay practices, could help close the divide. So can pay equity studies, where corporations audit the requirements and working conditions for all jobs, then compare jobs across the company to make sure women are paid equally for equal work. ✦

ing the Equal Pay Act, with monetary awards of $2.4 million, compared to 662 suits for the Age Discrimination in Employment Act, with awards of $264.3 million.

Two measures pending in Congress would give teeth to the existing law. The Paycheck Fairness Act would toughen penalties for employers who practice wage discrimination and create awards and incentives for employers who evaluate and improve their pay systems. Another pending bill, the Fair Pay Act, would require employers to pay equally for jobs that require equivalent skills, effort, responsibility, and working conditions—even if those jobs seem very different. For instance, one study cited by the National Committee on Pay Equity found that probation officers (usually men) and children's social services workers (usually women) in the county of Los Angeles needed similar skills and worked under similar conditions—but probation officers made $20,000 more a year. The Fair Pay Act would address inequities like this.

However, progress has stalled since the bills were introduced in the '90s and, more recently, information related to the wage gap disappeared from federal web sites. For instance, the Department of Labor abolished its Equal Pay Matters initiative and removed information about the wage gap from its site, according to the National Committee for Pay Equity.

Local Studies and Take Action

No matter what happens at the national level, women across the country are coordinating grassroots efforts to bridge the gap. In New York State, Women on the Job, a Long Island-based education and advocacy group, founded the New York State Pay Equity Coalition, a statewide organization pushing for the passage of pay equity legislation. "It's an interesting coalition because it includes feminist groups, girls and women's organizations like Girl Scouts, civic organizations like Junior League, and labor unions," says Dana Friedman, president of the board of Women on the Job. That kind of broad-based support is crucial, she says, in persuading legislators that pay equity is an important issue for voters. One woman legislator told Friedman, "I don't hear from women about pay equity. The coalition is giving a little more voice to the issue."

Women on the Job is also encouraging girls and women to enter nontraditional occupations, through seminars that introduce women to the trades. By making women aware that they could earn two to three times what they might earn in a traditionally female occupation, the group hopes to inspire more women to pursue higher paying positions.

Equal Pay Day efforts around the country have also helped raise awareness of the wage gap. This year, women around the country arranged mayor's proclamations, held luncheons with business leaders, and offered negotiation workshops for college students and women in business.

In one example of Equal Pay Day activity, last April the Women's Fund of Greater Omaha published a report on the status of Omaha women. They sent the report to CEOs of the city's 100 largest employers. The Fund's executive director, Ellie Archer, isn't yet sure how they'll follow up the report—perhaps with an incentive program for businesses that reduce their wage gap—but she's not about to stop now.

"Equal Pay Day luncheons are nice," Archer says. "But I don't want to be wheeled into one

---

[The Gaps Within the Gap]
Family

Women with children typically earn 10 to 15 percent less than women without children, according to a 1998 study by Jane Waldfogel, Ph.D., at Columbia University School of Social Work. (Men, on the other hand, usually earn more when they have a family.) Even after controlling for differences between mothers and childless women in education and work experience, mothers earn 10 to 15 percent less.

Waldfogel's analysis suggested that family status actually accounted for more than half of the gender wage gap in 1991. That might be because without a guaranteed job to return to, some mothers may be staying out of the workforce longer and switching employers when they do return—costing them experience and seniority.

Maternity leave policies that protect mothers' jobs might help close the family gap, according to Waldfogel's study. ✦

in 20 years saying, 'Good news, girls! We're up to 79 cents on the dollar!'"

Editor's note: No references were included in the original article.

Selected References

Caiazza, Amy, April Shaw, and Misha Werschkul. 2004. *Women's Economic Status in the United States: Wide Disparities by Race, Ethnicity, and Region*. Institute for Women's Policy Research: Washington, DC.

Lee, Sunhwa Lee. 2004. *Women's Work Supports, Job Retention, and Job Mobility*. Institute for Women's Policy Research: Washinton, DC.

National Women's Law Center. 2004. "Women and Girls Have Plenty to Celebrate, But More Progress Must Be Made." June 21 press release. *www.nwlc.org*

Shannon, Michael, and Michael Kidd. 2001. "Projecting the Trend in the Canadian Gender Wage Gap, 2001–2031: Will An Increase in Female Education Acquisition and Commitment Be Enough." *Canadian Public Policy* 27 (4) December: 447–467.

Reprinted from: Christine Larson, "The Penny Pinch." In *National Association for Female Executives (NAFE) Magazine*, Vol. 27, No. 4, pp. 14–19. Copyright © 2004 by the National Association for Female Executives, Inc.

Food for Thought and Application Questions

1. What is the "wage gap" and what factors are said to explain the gap? Using the list of occupations surveyed by NAFE magazine (see Appendix I): Identify the occupations that have the *smallest* wage gap and the ones that have the *largest* wage gaps. In what way, if any, is this gap different for newly hired men and women compared to those who have worked longer in an occupation? What are the differences among women with different racial/ethnic identities? What are the implications with regard to the future closing of the "wage gap" for men and women?

2. Discuss strategies women can take to put themselves in positions where the wage gap is minimized. Discuss strategies for both women who go on to college and those who do not.

3. Develop two strategies that corporations or organizations could take to reduce the wage gap among employees. Include steps educational institutions can take, as well as private corporations. ✦

8

Women, Men, and Management Styles

Marie-Therese Claes

Although only 3 to 6 percent of top managerial positions are held by women, employers have come to realize that they neglect managerial talent in nearly half their workforce if they do not appoint women to such positions. However, it is true that managerial work is undergoing rapid change and as Kanter has pointed out:

> Change-adept organizations cultivate the imagination to innovate, the professionalism to perform, and the openness to collaborate. (Kanter 1997, 7)

Leadership Styles

For more than a decade now, new values, sometimes called feminine values, have appeared in business. These values contrast with the competitive and authoritarian approach usually associated with traditional masculine management as they are based on consensual relations and inspire a different management approach to communication, leadership, negotiation, organization and control. Increasingly, this rebalancing of values is seen as key to business success.

At the end of the twentieth century, the workplace is radically different. Flexibility and innovation characterize global economic conditions and fast-changing technology. Cameron (1995) calls this the "shift in the culture of Anglo-American capitalism" (p. 199) away from traditional (aggressive, competitive, individualistic) interactional norms and towards a new management style stressing flexibility, teamwork and collaborative problem-solving. According to Connell,

> commercial capitalism calls on a calculative masculinity and the class struggles of industrialization call on a combative one. Their combination, competitiveness, is institutionalized in business and becomes a central theme in the new form of hegemonic masculinity" (1987, 156).

There seems to be a true structural change under way here. The business world is questioning the structure it copied from the military hierarchy at the end of the Second World War. The masculine culture of large corporations cannot easily adapt to a context of uncertainty and constant evolution. The team and supportive behaviours more readily identified with women are perceived as increasingly important for management (Hirsh and Jackson 1989) and women's interactive style is often better suited to dealing with problems.

In the 1970s, women managers were supposed to act and talk like men, if they wanted to reach the top. Harragan (1977), characterizing business as a "no-woman's-land," urged women to recognize that the modern corporation was modelled on military structures and functioned according to the precepts of male team sports. This implied that, in order to master corporate culture, women had both to indoctrinate themselves with the military mindset and to study the underlying dynamic of confrontational games such as football. Hennig and Jardim (1976) also urged women to study football in order to master the male concept of "personal strategy": winning, achieving a goal, or reaching an objective.

Grant (1988) studied what women can offer to organizations and identified the psychological qualities that are relevant to organizations and are commonly found in women. His findings support those of other studies that stress women's more cooperative behaviour (important for relational consultation and democratic decision-making) and their need for a sense of belonging rather than self-enhancement; their ability to express their vulnerability and their emotions; and their perception of power less as domination or ability to control, than as a liberating force in the community.

The feminine style of management has been called "social-expressive," with personal attention given to subordinates and a good working environment; by contrast, the masculine management style has been described as instrumental and instruction-giving. However, these qualities are not necessarily reflected in the way women managers actually manage. An attempt to examine managerial behaviour was made by Helgesen (1990), who repeated Minzberg's diary study, only this time with women. Minzberg (1973) analysed the diaries of managers, all of them male: he described what managers actually did, discerning several patterns. In 1990, Helgesen conducted the same research with women managers. The differences that appeared are shown in Figure 8.1.

Rather than a comparison between male and female managers, this could be seen more as a comparison of management cultures that changed over time. In the 1960s, great value was placed on narrow expertise, on the mastery of prescribed skills and on conformity to the corporate norm. There was no need to integrate workplace and pri-vate-sphere responsibilities. In today's organizations, hierarchies tend to give way to less formal structures. The economy is more diverse, the focus is on innovation and fast information exchange, value is placed on breadth of vision and on the ability to think creatively. Top-down authoritarianism has yielded to a networking style, in which everyone is a resource (Naisbitt and Aburdene 1986).

Helgesen (1995) considered that feminine principles (such as caring, intuitive decision-making, non-hierarchical attitudes, integration of work and life, social responsibility) reflected basic cultural assumptions about differences in the ways that men and women think and act. She added, however, that belief in these notions was intuitive rather than articulated, that it was backed up with anecdotes instead of argument.

Women managers surveyed in the United Kingdom reported that the characteristics their organizations valued most highly in a manager were competitiveness, cooperation and decisiveness, and those they least valued were emotionalism, manipulativeness and forcefulness (Traves, Brockbank and Tomlinson, 1997). These obviously cut across

Figure 8.1
Sex Differences in Managerial Styles

Male Managers	Female Managers
The executives worked at an unrelenting pace, and took no breaks in activity during the day.	They worked at a steady pace, but with small breaks scheduled throughout the day.
They described their days as characterized by interruption, discontinuity, and fragmentation.	They did not view unscheduled tasks and encounters as interruptions.
They spared little time for activities not directly related to their work.	They made time for activities not directly related to work.
They exhibited a preference for live encounters.	They preferred live encounters but scheduled time to attend to mail.
They maintained a complex network of relationships with people outside their organizations.	They maintained a complex network of relationships with people outside their organizations.
Immersed in day-to-day need to keep the company going, they lacked time for reflection.	They focused on the ecology of leadership.
They identified with their boss.	They saw their own duties as complex and multifaceted.
They had difficulty sharing information.	They scheduled time for sharing information.

Source: Helgesen, 1990

styles that are identified as typically masculine or feminine.

One can perhaps detect a shift in values towards the "feminization" of management style, but one can also speak of a shift away from individualism and from explicitness. This resembles a shift from a left-brain conception of organizational structure (with analysis, logic and rationality predominating) towards a right-brain conception (with intuition, emotion, synthesis predominating). But it seems that, in practice, management styles are evolving towards valuing a mixture of the so-called masculine and feminine characteristics.

Flexibility and teamwork are among the feminine characteristics; and team behaviour is seen as increasingly important for management. Drucker (1994) pointed out that, in "knowledge work" (adding value to information), teams rather than the individual become the work unit. The idea of "group intelligence" has been explored (Williams and Sternberg, 1988), and according to Goleman, "the single most important element in group intelligence . . . is not the average IQ in the academic sense, but rather in terms of emotional intelligence" (1996, p. 160). This emotional intelligence, or empathy, seems to result from the socialization of girls and much less from that of boys, with the result that "hundreds of studies have found . . . that on average women are more empathic than men" (ibid., p. 132; see also Goleman [1998]). In their approach to work women have been found to be more relationship-oriented than men, more often defining themselves in terms of their relationships and connections to others (Belenky et al., 1986).

In their meta-analyses, Eagly and Johnson (1990) suggest that men demonstrate a more autocratic leadership style and women a more democratic leadership style, and a more interpersonally-oriented style: helpful, friendly, available, explaining procedures, tending to the morale and welfare of others. According to Kabacoff (1998), these assessment and laboratory studies may not be applicable to organizational settings, and moreover the role of women in management positions may have changed since.

Kabacoff's extensive study of gender differences in leadership styles records gender differences which were both self-described and observed (Kabacoff, 1998). Kabacoff found that women tend to be rated higher on empathy (demonstrating an active concern for people and their needs, forming close supportive relationships with others), and communication (stating clear expectations for others, clearly expressing thoughts and ideas, maintaining a flow of communication) than men. Women are also rated higher on people skills (sensitivity to others, likeableness, ability to listen and to develop effective relationships with peers and with those to whom they report). However, they are not seen as more outgoing (acting in an extroverted, friendly, informal fashion), or more cooperative in their leadership styles. Contrary to expectations, women tend to score higher on a leadership scale measuring an orientation towards production (strong pursuit of achievement, holding high expectations for self and others) and the attainment of results. Men tend to score higher on scales assessing an orientation towards strategic planning and organizational vision. Women tend to be rated higher on people-oriented leadership skills, men on business-oriented leadership skills. Overall, bosses see men and women as equally effective, while peer and direct assessment rate women slightly higher than men.

Women are rated higher on excitement (they are energetic and enthusiastic), communication (they keep people informed), feedback (they let others know how they have performed) and production (they set high standards). Men are rated higher on tradition (they build on knowledge gained through experience), innovation (they are open to new ideas and willing to take risks), strategy (they focus on the big picture), restraint (they control emotional expression, remain calm), delegation (they share objectives and accountability), cooperation (they are good team players) and persuasiveness (they sell ideas and win people over).

One can conclude with Eisler that in the movement toward more "feminine" or nurturing management styles, men's socialization into the "masculine" traits of domination, conquest and control is dysfunctional for the new styles of leadership, but that "other qualities also considered masculine, such as decisiveness, assertiveness, and risk-taking, have been, and will continue to be, highly functional, particularly for the effective exercise of leadership" (Eisler 1997, 107).

Communication Styles

A different management style implies changes in language and behaviour in business communication. Since women are concerned not just with content but also with relationships, their aims when communicating are different, as are the modes and strategies they adopt. There seems now to be a need in organizations to create a favourable context for the coexistence of the male and the female model, in order to make the most of their synergy.

Grice (1975) geared his "Rules of conversation" to the transmission of information:

- do not give more or less information than necessary;
- do not say anything you do not believe;
- link your contribution to the previous contribution;
- formulate your views as clearly as possible.

But communication is more than just a matter of passing on information. Relations should also be—and stay—good; communication involves seeking and working together at a productive relationship. Rules of conversation should include the principle of collaboration.

Concluding Remarks

At a time when the ability to manage change is becoming so important, communication plays a major role. Yet a significant source of dissatisfaction in organizations today is the poor structures and networks for mediating and diffusing knowledge, values and experience within the organizational environment. . . . [W]omen possess qualities which could contribute significantly to improved communication, cooperation, team spirit and commitment within organiza-

tions—qualities which today are essential for achieving excellence and maintaining the necessary networks of contacts and relationships.

Given that the leadership skills of the future appear to be developing into a combination of masculine and feminine traits involving strategic thinking and communication skills, both women and men have something to learn and to gain from working together (Powell 1988). The final result of this evolution in required leadership skills should contribute to making organizations more competitive and more successful. Considering the trend towards flatter organizations with the emphasis on training, teamwork, networking and the sharing of power and information, women's aptitudes in these fields should work to their advantage. This is especially true if the emerging working environments allow for diversity. For "appropriate" managerial skills now tend to take into account cultural awareness, that is, the awareness and tolerance of differences. Openness and acceptance of cultural differences will lead to synergy, enabling change and promoting excellence in business and communication.

References

Belenky, M. F.; Clinchy, B. M.; Goldberger, N. R.; Tarule, J. M. 1986. *Womens Way of Knowing.* New York, Basic Books.

Cameron, Deborah. 1995. *Verbal Hygiene.* London, Routledge and Kegan Paul.

Connell, Robert W. 1987. *Gender and Power.* Cambridge, Polity Press.

Drucker, Peter. 1994. "The age of social transformation," in *The Atlantic Monthly.* Boston, MA, Vol. 274, No.5 (Nov.), pp. 53–80.

Eagly, A.,; Johnson, B. 1990. "Gender and leadership style: A meta-analysis," in *Psychological Bulletin* (Washington, DC), No. 108, pp. 33–56.

Eisler, Riane. 1997. "The hidden subtext for sustainable change," in Willis Harman and Maya Porter (eds): *The New Business of Business: Sharing Responsibility for a Positive Global Future.* San Francisco, CA, Berett-Koeler/World Business Academy.

Goleman, Daniel. 1998. *Working With Emotional Intelligence.* New York, Bantam Books.

——. 1996. *Emotional Intelligence.* London, Bloomsbury.

Grant, J. 1988. "Women as managers: What they can offer to organizations," in *Organizational Dynamics* (New York), Vol. 16, No.3, pp. 56–63.

Grice, H. P. 1975. "Logic and conversation," in P. Cole and J. P. Morgan (eds.): *Syntax and Semantics*. Vol. 3: *Speech Acts*. New York, Academic Press.

Harragan, Betty L. 1977. *Games Mother Never Taught You*. New York, Warner Books.

Helgesen, Sally. 1990. *The Female Advantage: Women's Ways of Leadership*. New York. Doubleday.

——. 1995. *The Web of Inclusion*. New York, Doubleday.

Hennig, Margaret; Jardim, Anne. 1976. *The Managerial Woman*. New York, Anchor/Doubleday.

Hirsh, Wendy, and Charles Jackson. 1989. Women into Management: Issues Influencing the Entry of Women into Managerial Jobs. Institute of Manpower Studies Paper No.158. Brighton, Institute of Manpower Studies, University of Sussex.

Kabacoff, Roben I. 1998. Gender difference in organizational leadership: A large sample study. Paper presented at the Annual American Psychological Association Convention, held in San Francisco.

Kanter, Rosabeth Moss. 1997. *On the Frontiers of Management*. Boston, MA: Harvard Business School Press.

Minzberg. Henry. 1973. *The Nature of Managerial Work*. New York, Harper & Row.

Naisbitt, John, and Patricia Aburdene. 1986. *Reinventing the Corporation*. New York, Warner Books.

Powell, Gary N. 1988. *Women and Men in Management*. Newbury Park, Sage Publications.

Traves, Joanne, Anne Brockbank, and Frances Tomlinson. 1997. "Careers of women managers in the retail industry," In *The Service Industries Journal* (London), Vol. 17. No. 1 (Jan), pp, 133–154.

Williams, Wendy, and Robert Sternberg. 1988. "Why some groups are better than others," in *Intelligence* (Norwood, NJ), Vol. 12, No.4, pp. 351–377.

Adapted from: Marie-Therese Claes, "Women, men, and management styles." In *International Labor Review.* Vol. 138 (4):431, pp. 439–446. Copyright © 1999 by the International Labor Review. Reprinted by permission.

Food for Thought and Application Questions

1. A series of articles and books have been written about the managerial style of contemporary CEOs and up-and-coming managers in corporations (see *Working Woman; Fortune;* and the *Wall Street Journal* for articles, for example). Take a sample of such articles, on both male and female CEOs or managers; develop a tally of "masculine" and "feminine" terms used to describe their styles of managing. What, if any, are the differences? How do you account for these?

2. In what context does the more masculine style of managing seem appropriate? In what context is the more "blended" (masculine/feminine) style of managing appropriate? What kind of organizations fit with each? And why? Consider such contexts as heavy manufacturing, banking and financial services, consumer product manufacturing, education, and marketing. ✦

9

The Glass Ceiling

The Federal Glass Ceiling Commission

The term glass ceiling was popularized in a 1986 *Wall Street Journal* article describing the invisible barriers that women confront as they approach the top of the corporate hierarchy.

The Federal Glass Ceiling Commission, a 21-member bipartisan body appointed by President Bush and Congressional leaders and chaired by the Secretary of Labor, was created by the Civil Rights Act of 1991. Its mandate was to identify the glass ceiling barriers that have blocked the advancement of minorities and women as well as the successful practices and policies that have led to the advancement of minority men and all women into decision-making positions in the private sector. . . .

The Federal Glass Ceiling Commission systematically gathered information on barriers, opportunities, policies, perceptions, and practices as they affect five target groups that historically have been underrepresented in private sector top-level management—women of all races and ethnicities, and African American, American Indian, Asian and Pacific Islander, and Hispanic American men. . . .

The Commission research and information-gathering process included the following:

Five public hearings held in Kansas City, Kansas; Dallas, Texas; Los Angeles, California; Cleveland, Ohio; and New York, New York, at which 126 employers and employees from a broad spectrum of industries and institutions testified about their experiences and perceptions of the glass ceiling.

The commissioning of 18 research papers on the status and problems of minorities and women and on other specific aspects of the glass ceiling such as the impact of downsizing on diversity, comparative compensation, and law enforcement.

A survey of 25 chief executive officers (CEOs) from white- and minority-owned businesses regarding their perceptions and experiences in recruiting, developing, and promoting minorities and women into decision-making positions.

Six racially homogeneous focus groups of Asian and Pacific Islander American, African American and Hispanic/Latino male executives in New York, Chicago, and Los Angeles to determine the perceptions, opinions, beliefs, and attitudes of minority men on the key issues related to the glass ceiling barriers. (With each racial/ethnic group, two sessions were held, one of younger men (30–45) and one older (46–65). All respondents were college graduates with a mix of bachelor's, master's, and Ph.D. degrees. All were full-time employees of U.S. companies in the following industries: communications, legal, electronic, health care, aerospace, utility, airline, financial/banking, travel, transport, publishing, realty, employment services, personal products, and beverage.)

Two focus panel groups with American Indian men and women in Washington, D.C. (All members of the groups were college graduates with a mix of bachelor's, master's, and law degrees, a mix of government and private sector employment, and a mix of ages and tribal affiliations. The majority were based in Washington but others came from as far away as California.)

Analyses of special data runs of U.S. Bureau of the Census data conducted expressly for the Federal Glass Ceiling Commission to establish as clearly as possible the educational achievement, status, and compensation levels of the target groups.

Analyses of special data runs of U.S. Bureau of the Census data to identify the status of minorities and women by industrial sector.

Highlights of the Research

What Is the Glass Ceiling?

Federal Glass Ceiling Commission research papers, as well as testimony presented at the public hearings, clearly document that today's American labor force is gender and race segregated—white men fill most top management positions in corporations.

According to surveys of Fortune 1500 companies conducted by Korn/Ferry International and Catalyst over the last decade, 95 to 97 percent of senior managers—vice presidents and above—were men. A 1989 Korn/Ferry survey found that 97 percent of male top executives are white. A 1992 survey of Fortune 1500 companies found that 95 percent of the three to five percent of the top managers who were women were white non-Hispanic women. In 1994, two women were CEOs of Fortune 1000 companies.

The representation of women and minorities on Fortune 1500 boards of directors is also limited. Cox and Smolinski point out that less than 10 percent of the largest employers have women on their board of directors. According to a 1992 Heidrick and Struggles survey, *Minorities and Women on Corporate Boards*, non-U.S. citizens held 2.85 percent of the board seats of 806 Fortune companies, slightly less than the 3.11 percent combined total held by all racial and ethnic minorities.

Conversely, the American work-force is increasingly diverse. In 1950, white men comprised 65 percent of the labor force; in 1990 white male representation had dropped to 43 percent. During the same period, representation of white women in the labor force increased from 24.2 percent to 35.3 percent. At the same time, minority representation in the labor force doubled, to 15.2 percent. Over the last decade, the size of the Asian and Pacific Islander American population has doubled, becoming the fastest growing of minority groups in the United States.

A larger proportion of women and minorities are locked into low wage, low prestige, and dead-end jobs, which according to Harlan and Bertheide (1994), are not connected to any career ladder.

The Current Status of Minorities and Women Managers

Most female and minority professionals and managers do not work in the private-for-profit sector. They hold jobs in the public sector and "third sector"—nongovernmental agencies in health, social welfare, and education; legal service, professional service, membership organizations and associations; libraries, museums and art organizations. According to Burbridge (1994), 90 percent of black female professionals, 70 percent of black male professionals, and 83 percent of white and Hispanic women professionals work in the government or the third sector, compared to 56 percent of white male non-Hispanic professionals.

The exception to this pattern of employment is Asian and Pacific Islander Americans (API) who rely heavily on the for-profit sector. Contrary to the popular image of API Americans, only a small percentage are entrepreneurs or managers of small businesses (9.8 percent).

Federal Glass Ceiling Commission research also analyzed salaries as an indicator of advancement. In 1992, U.S. Census data reported the ratio of female to male earnings in management jobs ranged from a low of 50 percent in the banking industry to a high of 85 percent for managers in human services. An analysis of 1990 U.S. Census data shows that black men who hold professional degrees and top management positions earned 79 percent of what white men earn. Black women, also with professional degrees and in top management positions, earn 60 percent of what white men in comparable positions earn.

Despite identical education attainment, ambition, and commitment to career, men still progress faster than women. A 1990 *Business Week* study of 3,664 business school graduates found that a woman with an MBA from one of the top 20 business schools, earned an average of $54,749 in her first year after graduation, while a comparable man earned $61,400—12 percent more. Wernick reports that a 1993 follow-up study of the Stanford University Business School class of 1982 found that 16 percent of the men were CEOs, chairmen, or presidents of companies compared to only 2 percent of the women. At the level below those top posts, 23 percent of the men in the 1982 class were now vice presidents and 15 percent were directors, compared to 10 percent and 8 percent, respectively, of the women.

Some data support the optimism that the 25 CEOs expressed about the progress of women. For example, between 1982 and 1992 the percentage of women who held the title of female executive vice president increased from 4 percent to 9 percent; the percentage who held the office of senior vice president increased from 13 percent to 23 percent. In comparison, between 1982 and 1992, the percentage of African Americans who held the title of vice president or above increased from 1 percent to 2.3 percent. During the same period, the percentage of Hispanic top managers increased from 1.3 percent to 2 percent, and the percentage of Asian senior managers increased from .4 percent to 1.8 percent.

The small numbers of minorities and women throughout management makes statistics on the rate of change in representation misleading. For example, if two out of three black male managers take early retirement, a firm experiences a 67 percent decline in representation.

The Business Imperative

Another reason for optimism is the growing body of evidence which indicates shattering the glass ceiling is good for business. Organizations that excel at leveraging diversity (including hiring and promoting minorities and women into senior positions) can experience better financial performance in the long run than those which are not effective in managing diversity.

Cox cites a Covenant Investment Management study to prove this point. The Covenant study rated the performance of the Standard and Poor's 500 companies on factors relating to the hiring and advancement of minorities and women, compliance with EEOC and other regulatory requirements, and employee litigation. Companies which rated in the bottom 100 on glass ceiling related measures earned an average of 7.9 percent return on investment, compared to an average return of 18.3 percent for the top 100.

Cox offers several other explanations about why some businesses are motivated to eliminate the glass ceiling. In the U.S., Asians, blacks, and Hispanics collectively represent more than $500 billion a year in consumer spending. In the automobile industry explicit recognition of cultural differences within the U.S. market is paying off. In 1987, by targeting advertising, hiring bilingual sales people, and holding special events, a Miami Toyota dealer gained more than 50 percent of the local Hispanic market and his sales increased 400 percent over a six-year period. On the West coast, a San Francisco Volkswagen dealership credited improved sales to Asian and Pacific Islander Americans for a five-fold increase in overall sales per month. Sales people learned through cultural sensitivity training that among Chinese Americans, family elders often are the ultimate decision makers for major purchases.

To a lesser degree than competition for market share, turnover costs are also factors motivating companies to address issues related to glass ceilings. Cox (1994) cites a published report of Ortho Pharmaceuticals that stated yearly savings of $500,000 mainly from lower turnover among women.

These savings are not surprising. Recent studies estimate the turnover costs range between 150 and 193 percent of a manager or professional's annual salary, compared to 75 percent for lower level employees. Corning Glass reported that during the period from 1980 to 1987 turnover among women in professional jobs was double that of men. During the same time period, the turnover rates for blacks were almost two and a half times those of whites. Another study of male and female managers of large corporations found that the major reason for women quitting was a lack of career growth opportunity or dissatisfaction with rates of progress.

The Pipeline

The research monographs and testimony that examined the preparedness of minorities and women to advance to top management positions considered preparedness in terms of corporate development of minorities and women and educational credentials.

As Wernick (1994) explains, the development of business executives is a long, complicated process. Chief executive officers (CEOs) are generally in their 50s or 60s when they assume the top position. Furthermore, they have usually spent 20 to 25 years "in the pipeline."

It is also worth noting that career paths to CEO positions vary by industry. Certain functional areas are more likely than others to lead to the top. The "right" areas are most likely to be line functions such as marketing or production or a critical control function such as accounting or finance. Studies across industries find certain factors common to successful executives, regardless of gender, race, or ethnicity. They include: broad and varied experience in the core areas of the business; access to information, particularly through networks and mentoring; company seniority; initial job assignment; high job mobility; education; organizational savvy; long hours and hard work; and career planning.

Minorities and women have limited opportunity to obtain broad and varied experience in most companies. They tend to be in supporting, staff function areas—personnel/human resources, communications, public relations, affirmative action, and customer relations. Movement between these positions and line positions is rare in most major companies. Furthermore, career ladders in staff functions are generally shorter than those in line functions, offering fewer possibilities to gain varied experience.

Education is also an important part of an executive's preparation. According to a 1993 Korn/Ferry International UCLA report, almost 90 percent of executives are college graduates. U.S. Census data show that Asian and Pacific Islander Americans and women have the largest percentage of the work force with college or graduate degrees, with 42 percent and 35 percent respectively. The same source shows that college attendance is increasing for black men and women of all ages. Between 1982 and 1991, there was a 36 percent increase in the number of African Americans, ages 20 to 44, with a college degree or more.

The picture for American Indians and Hispanic Americans is less encouraging. Only 9 percent of American Indians in the workforce hold college degrees. Between 1980 and 1990, the number of Hispanic Americans with bachelor's or graduate degrees increased from 7.7 percent to 10 percent. Furthermore, the opposition to bilingual education discourages the acquisition of one of the assets that business values. According to a 1994 *Hispanic Business*

magazine survey of 169 Hispanic senior managers, the majority of managers work in line positions in international divisions using their bilingual and bicultural skills. However, only 4 percent of Hispanic high school students gain bilingual capability by taking the minimum requirement for Spanish literacy, according to a Department of Education longitudinal study.

Where Are the Opportunities?

Federal Glass Ceiling Commission research on the opportunities for minorities and women to advance to top management positions in corporate America focused on two areas: 1) identification of growth industries and businesses and high-demand occupations and their relation to opportunities for advancement and 2) identification of possibilities resulting from changes in the structure of work, new technologies, and the demands of a global economy.

Gender distribution is more prominent than race distribution across industries. Women are more likely than men to be clustered in services; finance, insurance, and real estate (FIRE), and in the wholesale/retail trade industries. Nearly 75 percent of employed women work in these industries.

Growth industries. The industries expected to grow the most between 1990 and 2005 are service/retail trade; FIRE; wholesale trade; transportation, communications, and public utilities; and construction.

Those areas which are expected to have growing needs for general managers and top executives include wholesale; retail trade, especially eating and drinking establishments; finance and real estate (but not insurance carriers); and services, [particularly] business services, auto services, health services, education, social services, and engineering and management services.

Women appear to have the best opportunity for advancement into management and decisionmaking positions in three types of industries: those which are fast-growing (business services); those like telecommunications where change, i.e., deregulation, restructuring has occurred; and those with a female intensive work force (insurance, banking).

Restructuring. A review of research on recent changes in the organization of work identifies seven ways in which downsizing and restructuring can limit opportunities for all managers, professionals, and administrators. They are: 1) an increase in external recruiting which reduces the number of internal career ladders; 2) elimination of layers of management and staff positions; 3) hiring of independent contractors or small businesses to perform some staff functions; 4) more stringent performance measures on those managers who remain; 5) more geographic mobility required of managers; 6) increased importance of team work; and 7) a shift of employment from manufacturing to services.

As Hamlin's (1994) research on the impact of downsizing and restructuring in nine companies found, in more than half the companies, white women and—to a somewhat lesser extent—minority men have increased their representation in management both in absolute numbers and in proportion to white men between 1900 and 1994. Restructuring can present problems as well as opportunities for minorities and women in management. In some cases the last hired are the first fired. On the other hand, when early retirement is part of the restructuring process, higher level positions may become available, thereby increasing advancement opportunities. Hamlin's study showed that white male managers who had seniority and were eligible for relatively generous buyout packages were most likely to take early retirement or choose other forms of severance during downsizing.

Comparison of industries—women. The industries with the highest percentage of women managers were FIRE (41.4 percent), services (38.9 percent), retail trade (38.5 percent), transportation, communication, and public utilities (25.6 percent), and wholesale trade (20.9 percent). Manufacturing (15.9 percent), agriculture (14.5 percent), construction (10.4 percent), and mining (9.8 percent) had the lowest percentages.

The proportion of women employees who are managers is the closest to that of men who are managers in transportation, communications, and public utilities (10.1 percent; 15.2 percent), with the construction industry second (6.4 percent; 9.9 percent). Manufacturing and FIRE showed the biggest proportional differences.

Predominately female industries have larger percentages of women in at least midlevel managerial positions than do predominately male industries. Furthermore, women appear to be advancing best in industries with relatively high growth, those undergoing change with regard to regulation, and those highly competitive and thus dependent on marketing and flexibility.

Comparision of industries—minorities. Department of Labor analyses of 1990 EEOC data for minorities (men and women) find that the industries with the highest percentage of minority managers are retail trade (13 percent), transportation, communication, and public utilities (12 percent), services and FIRE (11 percent). Agriculture (1.3 percent), wholesale trade (0.9 percent), manufacturing (0.8 percent), mining (0.7 percent), and construction (0.6 percent) had the lowest percentages.

The proportion of minority employees who are managers is the closest to that of non-minorities who are managers in transportation, communication, and public utilities (7.7 percent; 15.0 percent), with the retail trade industry second (9.2 percent; 21.0 percent). Agriculture and construction had the biggest differences between the proportions.

However, a study of Hispanic executives in the Fortune 500 industrial and 500 service industries (HACR 1993) found the highest percentage of Hispanic officers in beverages (3.8 percent), soaps and cosmetics (2.4 percent), building materials (1.9 percent), and motor vehicles and parts (1.1 percent). These sub-industries are all in the manufacturing sector. Officer representation for Hispanics in all other industrial sectors was below 1 percent, and has the lowest percentage of FIRE and transportation, communication, and public utilities.

An analysis of the 30 companies listed as best places for blacks to work in the February 1992 edition of *Black Enterprise* found 8 of the 30 companies were in the consumer products industry. Telecommunications, automobiles, other manufacturing firms, oil, chemical companies, and banking/financial services had 3 mentions each.

Representation of minorities in an industry is not directly related to their advancement to management as is the case with women. However, like women, minorities have the best chance of advancement in industries with relatively high growth, those undergoing change with regard to regulation, and those highly competitive and thus dependent on marketing and flexibility.

Research Papers

Bell, E. L., J. Edmundson and S. M. Nkomo. 1994. *Barriers to Work Place Advancement Experienced by African-Americans*. Ella Louis J. Bell, Sloan School of Management, Massachusetts Institute of Technology and Stella M. Nkomo, Belk College of Business Administration, University of North Carolina at Charlotte. Paper prepared for the Glass Ceiling Commission. On file.

Braddock, D. and L. Bachelder. 1994. *The Glass Ceiling and Persons with Disabilities*. University of Illinois at Chicago. Paper prepared for the Glass Ceiling Commission. On file.

Burbridge, L. 1994. *The Glass Ceiling in Different Sectors of the Economy: Differences Between Government, Non-Profit and For-Profit Organizations*. Wellesley College Center for Research on Women. Paper prepared for the Glass Ceiling Commission. On file.

Catalyst, 1993. *Successful Initiatives for Breaking the Glass Ceiling to Upward Mobility for Minorities and Women*. Paper prepared for the Glass Ceiling Commission. On file.

Cox, T. and C. Smolinski. 1994. *Managing Diversity and Glass Ceiling Initiatives as National Economic Imperatives*. The University of Michigan. Paper prepared for the Glass Ceiling Commission. On file.

Golen, A. 1994. *The Impact of the Glass Ceiling on the Professions*. Draft working paper prepared for the Glass Ceiling Commission. On file.

Hamlin, N., S. Erkut and J. P. Fields 1994. *The Impact of Corporate Restructuring and Downsizing on the Managerial Careers of Minorities and Women: Lessons Learned*. Paper prepared for the Glass Ceiling Commission. On file.

Harlan, S. L. and C. W. Bertheide. 1994. *Barriers to Workplace Advancement Experienced by Women in Low-Paying Occupations*. Colorado State University. Paper prepared for the Glass Ceiling Commission. On file.

Hispanic Association of Corporate Responsibility. 1993. *1993 HARC Corporate Study: Hispanics in Corporate America*. Washington, D.C.

James, K. et al. 1994. *Barriers to Workplace Advancement Experienced by Native Americans*. Paper prepared for the Glass Ceiling Commission. On file.

Leonard, J. 1994. *Use of Enforcement in Eliminating Glass Ceiling Barriers*. School of Business, University of California, Berkeley. Paper prepared for the Glass Ceiling Commission. On file.

Mauricio Gastón Institute for Latino Community Development and Public Policy, University of Massachusetts. 1994. *Barriers to the Employment and Work-Place Advancement of Latinos*. University of Massachusetts at Boston. Paper prepared for the Glass Ceiling Commission. On file.

Schwartz, D. B. 1994. *An Examination of the Impact of Family-Friendly Policies on the Glass Ceiling*. Paper prepared for the Glass Ceiling Commission. On file.

Shaw, L. B. et al. 1993. *The Impact of the Glass Ceiling and Structural Change on Minorities and Women*. Paper Commissioned for the Glass Ceiling Commission. On file.

Thomas, Roosevelt et al. 1994. *Impact of Recruitment, Selection, and Compensation Policies and Practices on the Glass Ceiling*. Morehouse College. Paper prepared for the Glass Ceiling Commission. On file.

Tomaskovic-Devy, T. 1994. *Race, Ethnic and Gender Earnings Inequality: The Source and Consequence of Employment Segregation*. North Carolina State University. Paper prepared for the Glass Ceiling Commission. On file.

Wernick, E. 1994. *Preparedness, Career Advancement, and the Glass Ceiling*. Paper prepared for the Glass Ceiling Commission. On file.

Woo, D. 1994. *The Glass Ceiling and Asian Americans*. University of California, Berkeley. Paper prepared for the Glass Ceiling Commission. On file.

Woody, B. and C. Weiss. 1994. *Barriers to Work Place Advancement Experienced by White Women Workers*. University of Massachusetts at Boston. Paper prepared for the Glass Ceiling Commission. On file.

Analyses and Commentaries

Bell, E. L., J. Edmondson and S. M. Nkomo. 1992. *The Glass Ceiling vs. The Concrete Wall: Career Perceptions of White and African-American Women Managers*. Unpublished working paper.

Hispanic Policy Development Project. 1994. *A La Cumbre. A Latino Perspective on the Corporate Glass Ceiling*. Paper prepared for the Glass Ceiling Commission. On file.

Lee, Y. Y. 1994. *An Asian Pacific American Perspective on the Glass Ceiling.* Lee Consultants. Paper prepared for the Glass Ceiling Commission. On file.

Special Analyses of U.S. Bureau of the Census Data

Asian and Pacific Islander Center for Census Information and Services. 1994. *Reference Documentation: Datasets of U.S. Bureau of the Census Public Use Microdata Sample Files.* Prepared for the Glass Ceiling Commission. On file.

Institute for Policy Research and Education of the Congressional Black Caucus Foundation. 1994. *The Impact of the Glass Ceiling on African American Men and Women.* Reference documentation: Datasets of U.S. Bureau of the Census Public Use Microdata Sample Files. Prepared for the Glass Ceiling Commission. On file.

The Tomás Rivera Center. 1995. *Wage Differentials Between Latinos and Anglos: A Statistical Portrait and Its Implications to Glass Ceiling Issues.* Reference documentation: Datasets of U.S. Bureau of the Census Public Use Microdata Sample Files. Prepared for the Glass Ceiling Commission. On file.

Surveys and Focus Groups

Henderson, L. S. III et al. 1994. *Report on Six Focus Groups with Asian, Black and Hispanic Executives in Three Cities on Issues Related to The Glass Ceiling in Corporate America.* Paper prepared for the Glass Ceiling Commission. On file.

——. 1995. *Final Report on Two Focus Groups with American Indians on Issues Related to the Glass Ceiling in Corporate America.* Paper prepared for the Glass Ceiling Commission. On file.

McGuire, G. and S. Nicolau. 1994. *In Their Own Words: CEO Views of Diversity at the Top.* Paper prepared for the Glass Ceiling Commission. On file.

Reprinted from: The Federal Glass Ceiling Commission. *A Solid Investment: Making Full Use of the Nation's Human Capital.* November 1995.

Food for Thought and Application Questions

1. The Glass Ceiling Commission argues that diversifying management is "good for business." Assume that you are a management consultant arguing the benefits of diversified management to high-level corporate executives. How would you convince them that filling more senior management positions with women and minorities is in the best interest of their organization?

2. How can corporate "downsizing" create opportunities for women in management? Do you think that women's movement into management positions in firms that are downsizing is associated with the perception that women are taking jobs away from men? If so, how are male employees likely to react to this perceived "threat" to their jobs? How will their reaction affect women managers? ✦

10

Gender Gap in the Executive Suite

CEOs and Female Executives Report on Breaking the Glass Ceiling

Belle Rose Ragins
Bickley Townsend
Mary Mattis

Women currently constitute nearly half of the U.S. labor force, and occupy a significant and growing proportion of entry and mid-level managerial positions. In 1972 women held 17 percent of managerial positions, and this proportion swelled to 42.7 percent in 1995. Although women are flooding the managerial pipeline, they have been stymied in their entrance to top-level positions; currently, less than five percent of executive positions are held by women. Of greater concern is the lack of progress on this front. The proportion of top level positions in Fortune 1000 companies held by women increased from .5 percent in 1979 to only 2.9 percent in 1989, and only four of the *Fortune* 1000 CEO positions are held by women. A 1995 census revealed that while women accounted for 10 percent of corporate officers, they represented just 2.4 percent of the highest ranks of corporate leadership, and held 1.9 percent of the most highly compensated officer positions in *Fortune* 500 companies.

This lack of progress has been attributed to the glass ceiling, an invisible barrier to advancement based on attitudinal or organizational bias. The glass ceiling appears to be pervasive in corporate America; over 92 percent of executive women report its existence. The glass ceiling is costly, not only in terms of lost productivity among workers who feel blocked in their careers, but also in terms of turnover costs, which are estimated to average 150 percent of managers' annual salaries. Eighty percent of female middle-level managers in one study reported leaving their last organization because of the glass ceiling, and other studies indicate that many leave to start their own competing business.

Increasingly, individuals in many organizations are recognizing the importance of shattering the glass ceiling and removing barriers that prevent women from utilizing their full potential. However, the fact that the glass ceiling has remained virtually intact over the last ten years indicates that these efforts have been largely ineffectual. Dismantling the glass ceiling requires three key pieces of information. First, it is critical to understand the barriers women face in their advancement. Second, it is instructive to understand the career strategies used by women who successfully overcame the barriers to advancement. Finally, it is vital that corporate leaders have an accurate and complete understanding of the barriers and organizational climate faced by their female employees. Commitment to breaking the glass ceiling, while important, is not sufficient; for change to occur, CEOs must also have a clear understanding of the subtle and overt barriers women face in their advancement.

To obtain information about these issues, Catalyst undertook the first large-scale, national study of women executives and CEOs of Fortune 1000 companies. We surveyed 1,251 executive women who hold titles of vice president or above in Fortune 1000 companies and all of the Fortune 1000 CEOs. Surveys were returned by 461 female executives and 325 CEOs. 1 We also conducted indepth, follow-up telephone interviews with 20 female executives and 20 CEOs.

Our study addressed women's advancement from the perspective of women who have actually advanced to senior levels of leadership in the nation's largest companies. These trailblazers are in the best position to provide inside information on the types of obstacles encountered on the road to senior management. By sharing the personal and career strategies used for effectively navigating through those obstacles, this breakthrough generation of female executives can provide critical information for future generations of female managers coming up through the ranks. Of equal significance, by juxtaposing CEOs' perspectives on barriers to advancement with the perspective of female executives, we can assess for the first time whether CEOs understand the subtle and complex organizational barriers faced by their female employees.

Strategies For Breaking The Glass Ceiling: How Women Do It

The female executives in this large national study were presented with a list of 13 possible career strategies that may contribute to the advancement of women to senior management and were asked to rate the importance of each strategy to their own career advancement. As shown in Table 10.1, nine career strategies emerged as central to the advancement of these successful female executives. In particular, four of these strategies stand out as key to their career success. These are consistently exceeding performance expectations (rated critical by 77 percent); developing a style with which male managers are comfortable (61 percent); seeking out difficult or challenging assignments (50 percent), and having influential mentors (37 percent). We interviewed female executives from this national sample to learn more about career strategies used by these female pioneers.

Performance is the Bottom Line

Superior performance is expected of all executives, but it may be particularly important for women. Consistently exceeding performance expectations was the top-ranking strategy used by these successful female executives, and an overwhelming 99 percent of the respondents reported that this strategy was critical or fairly important. These women reported that they had to prove their ability repeatedly, and needed to over-perform in order to counter negative assumptions in a predominantly male business environment. These successful female executives reported that they were often not viewed as credible,

Table 10.1
Women's Career Advancement Strategies

Strategy	Critical	Fairly Important	Not Important	Did Not Use
Consistently exceed performance expectations	77%	22%	1%	0%
Develop style that men are comfortable with	61%	35%	3%	1%
Seek difficult or high visibility assignments	50%	44%	2%	4%
Have an influential mentor	37%	44%	9%	9%
Network with influential colleagues	28%	56%	9%	6%
Gain line management experience	25%	29%	11%	33%
Move from one functional area to another	23%	34%	20%	22%
Initiate discussion regarding career aspirations	15%	47%	25%	12%
Be able to relocate	14%	22%	17%	45%
Upgrade educational credentials	12%	33%	24%	29%
Change companies	12%	24%	23%	39%
Develop leadership outside office	11%	41%	29%	18%
Gain international experience	5%	19%	24%	51%

and that they had to prove themselves and reestablish their credibility in each new work situation. One survey respondent advised:

> Do the best you possibly can at every assignment no matter how trivial. Always go the extra mile. It is not enough to be willing, you have to do it, even if no one is looking.

How do successful corporate women demonstrate superior performance? Follow-up interviews revealed two particular strategies: work harder than your peers; and develop unique skills and expertise.

In describing their high-performance track records, successful female executives emphasized the importance of sheer hard work and stamina. In interviews, executive women described workdays that begin at 4:00 a.m. with several hours of predawn reading before the children awake, latenight business calls and faxes to homes fully teleconnected to the office, and travel schedules and after-hours business obligations that keep them away from home several evenings a week.

But the interviews indicated that while hard work was important, the performance bar may be placed higher for women than for men. One survey respondent advised: "Be willing to work much harder than male peers."

Besides sheer hard work, developing specialized expertise is another effective means for women to become known as high performers. Some successful women executives made a point of developing unique skills so as to become indispensable; others built their expertise by gaining external recognition:

> I think you have to have a specialty . . . and you have to do it better than anybody else can conceivably know how to do it.
>
> —Corporate Controller, consumer products company.

Beyond Performance: Walking the Fine Line

For women, being a star performer, even outperforming their male peers, is not enough to break through the glass ceiling. Fully 96 percent of the executive women in our study identify a second factor, unrelated to performance, as critical or fairly important to their career success. That key factor involves developing a professional style with which male managers are comfortable. These successful executives had to adapt to a predominantly male culture and environment, and deal with the phenomenon often referred to as the male managerial model, in which models for successful managers incorporate masculine styles and characteristics (Brenner, Tomkiewicz, and Schein 1989). This male managerial model places women in a double bind: if their managerial styles are feminine, they run the risk of not being viewed as effective managers, but if they adopt masculine styles viewed as appropriate for managerial roles, they may be criticized for not being feminine.

One successful woman executive points out the double-behavioral standard:

> . . . the guys can yell at each other all the time, shake hands and walk out the door, and it's perfectly comfortable for them—but on the rare occasion that I raise my voice, it's not accepted in the same way.
>
> —Personnel director, retail organization.

Another interviewee reported that she had to learn:

> how to interact with men who had never dealt with women before, and how to be heard, and how to get past what you looked like, and what sex you were, and into what kind of brain you had. . . . I had to learn how to offer opinions in a way that they could be heard because I wasn't necessarily given the right to have an opinion.
>
> —Vice president, consumer products company

These restrictions on behaviors were listed by two other survey respondents in an ironic litany of don'ts for female executives:

> Don't be attractive. Don't be too smart. Don't be assertive. Pretend you're not a woman. Don't be single. Don't be a mom. Don't be a divorcee.

> Do not make waves. Do not disagree and be correct (kiss of death!). [Working] longer, harder, smarter means nothing if you have a mind of your own and express your own ideas and opinions.

Women in managerial positions are forced to develop managerial styles that are not masculine or feminine, but are acceptable to male colleagues, supervisors and subordinates. This is a daunting challenge that is not faced by their male counterparts.

Not only must women walk a fine line, they must also be concerned with making their male colleagues comfortable with their very presence:

> With 13 men on the management committee, and I'm the only woman . . . it was very awkward at first. But it's been over two years now, and what I have found is that they are never truly comfortable because it's not a hundred percent men. And that's not because they don't like me, or they don't like the fact that a woman's there. It's that there's always that certain guard that what they might say in a roomful of men will be taken wrong when a woman is there.
>
> —Senior Vice President, health care organization.

In short, not only must women exceed performance expectations, they must also find the appropriate way to perform that will not threaten their male peers or make them uncomfortable.

Some CEOs acknowledge the challenges women face in fitting into the corporate culture and creating a comfort level with male managers. As one CEO notes:

> I don't think it has anything to do with competency. I think it's just that our society has certain norms that have been built in—wives being uncomfortable with women working in the same office as their husbands, things of that nature. . . . The men might not articulate it that way. But I believe that sociologically, we are where we are through no deliberate intent.

Although the intention may not be deliberate, the spillover of cultural expectations of women's roles into the corporate boardroom creates a unique set of challenges for women seeking leadership positions.

The Importance of Stretch Assignments

Seeking out difficult or highly visible assignments was the third critical success factor identified by the women executives in our study. Half of those surveyed deemed it critical, and fully 94 percent regarded it as important to their career progression. Key assignments have been found to be related to differential career tracking for men and women and are pivotal for three reasons. First, stretch assignments provide professional growth and learning challenges. Second, they serve as grooming exercises for career tracks leading to executive positions. Finally, highly visible assignments provide critical access to key decision-makers and influential mentors in the company. As one interviewee points out:

> When I first came to the company, I was assigned certain very specific, very important high-profile projects, which gave me the opportunity to work on matters that were very important to the company. . . . They involved contact with the handful of senior people and gave me the opportunity, as a relative newcomer with

good credentials but not a lot of prior exposure, to develop their trust and their confidence and their sense that when given an assignment I could get it done.
> —General counsel, media company.

While undertaking these assignments is an important prerequisite for gaining access to highpower career tracks, women encounter gender-related barriers to gaining this career milestone. Many of the women in our study reported that they often had to explicitly signal their willingness to take on unusual or challenging assignments, since otherwise managers may assume they are not interested. Several CEOs underscored the importance of this point:

> There's been an assumption on the part of men that opportunities everywhere are open to them, whereas there might be a perception that a woman might not want to move, because of personal interests of one kind or another. . . . Managers are reluctant to talk about these things today, for whatever reason . . . I think it's more incumbent on a woman to come forward and say how free she is to do things.

This suggests that the burden of obtaining these key assignments falls largely on the woman. Unlike their male counterparts, who may be approached by senior management and offered key assignments, women must first independently recognize the importance of these assignments and then convince others that they are both motivated and able to fill these assignments. The women who successfully reached the executive suite in our study did not wait for potentially career-enhancing opportunities to come to them; they actively took charge of their own careers by overcoming gender-related expectations and seeking visible assignments that promoted their mobility.

Mentoring is Mandatory

A full 91 percent of the female executives surveyed reported having a mentor sometime in the course of their careers, and 81 percent saw their mentor as being either critical or fairly important in their career advancement. Additionally, nearly all of the 20

female executives who were personally interviewed identified at least one senior man
who was instrumental in their development
and advancement.

> I think it's the single most critical piece to
> women advancing career-wise. In my ex-
> perience you need somebody to help
> guide you and . . . go to bat for you. And
> I'm not saying someone to take care of
> you because you're a woman. I'm saying,
> because you are a woman, you need
> somebody to fight some of your battles in
> the male environment.
>
> —Vice president/corporate secretary,
>   utility company

The importance of mentoring has been documented in other studies. Individuals with
mentors receive more promotions, have more
career mobility, and advance at a faster rate
than those lacking mentors. Additionally, both
male and female executives in other studies
overwhelmingly report the presence of a mentor sometime during the course of their careers (Ragins and Scandura 1994).

While mentors are important for everyone, they are particularly critical for women
seeking to break through the glass ceiling.
Influential male mentors, with preestab-
lished networks and credibility, can sponsor
their female proteges into senior management circles, and provide inside information
usually obtained in the old boy networks.
Mentors also can buffer women from adverse
forces in the organization, and help them navigate through the challenging and changing political terrain. These buffering functions were
pointed out by one interviewee:

> I think mentoring is very important for
> career advancement because you have
> somebody who is there for you, will de-
> fend you, will reinforce the decisions that
> you make with others. . . . (Mentors) help
> you understand the organization, to un-
> derstand the players, to understand the
> personalities. And they did that for me,
> but more importantly, whenever I had a
> problem, they'd stand up for me because
> they believed in me, and that's invaluable.
> It's something I could not have done for
> myself, and if I hadn't had that, I don't
> think that I could have made it because I
> do think women have different issues in

that regard, at least women who were
starting their careers 20 years ago.

> —Executive vice president, insurance
>   company

While a few women executives had female
mentors, the scarcity of women in senior management limited their supply. Yet those who
were fortunate enough to have both male and female mentors point out the differential
strengths associated with each of these key relationships. While male mentors are more influential in organizations and can provide greater
access to inner power circles, female mentors
were better able to identify and empathize with
the barriers faced by women in organizations.

Many of the interviewees recounted that
exclusionary corporate environments and
performance pressures led to erosion of self-
esteem and self-confidence during the early
career years. Mentors were viewed as instrumental for counteracting chilly corporate climates and building self-esteem. In particular,
female mentors were identified as better able
than male mentors to identify and address
self-esteem issues and concerns.

One interviewee pointed out that some
male mentors

> don't understand what you're up against.
> Or what you may be confronting, or the
> attitudes that some people, some men,
> may have, particularly a young woman
> coming into a meeting with a responsible
> job. . . . But I think that's overcome if they
> really are a good mentor, helping you un-
> derstand the male perspective and the
> male world.
>
> —Executive vice president, insurance
>   company

A key function of mentors is that they build
their protege's self-confidence and professional identity. These functions are critical
for women; many of the women in our study
reported that lack of support and isolation de-
pleted their self-esteem and self-confidence.

Because of the important role mentoring
played in their own careers, many of the senior women interviewed felt an obligation to
mentor others, especially women. Over half
of the women interviewed reported being
mentors, and nearly all of them reported
mentoring other women in their organiza-

tions. These female mentors recognize the need for mentoring as a benefit both to promising young managers and to the company. They also feel a need to give back to younger generations of women.

> The most important lesson for women . . . is to learn that they're not in competition for each other for a short list of jobs . . . it changed in my head back in the early 1980's, when I realized that was just a sexist attitude in the environment to begin with, and so (I) began mentoring in the sense of networking with other women and building a team environment with other women. . . .
> —Vice president, chemical company

This comment mirrors the finding of other empirical research, which has found no support for the idea that women become inaccessible "queen bees" once they obtain high-ranking positions in organizations.

In sum, these pioneering women relied on career strategies that were adaptive, proactive, and characterized by hard work. They attributed their success to consistently exceeding performance expectations, developing a style with which male managers feel comfortable, seeking out challenging and visible assignments, and obtaining the support of an influential mentor.

These career strategies are not independent, and may in fact build upon one another. For example, exceptional and visible job performance increases the likelihood of being selected by a mentor. Mentors, in turn, provide their proteges with coaching and visible assignments, which improves their job performance and places their proteges on the fast track to advancement (Kram 1985). By developing a managerial style with which male managers feel comfortable, these women may also have improved their chances of getting selected by a male mentor. Existing research indicates that while women are as likely as men to obtain a mentor, women need to overcome greater barriers to getting a mentor than men, and that key barriers involve the mentor's reluctance to assume a mentoring role for fear that the relationship would be misconstrued as romantic in nature (Ragins and Cotton 1991). These women may have developed the political savvy to not only recognize this barrier, but also overcome it by managing their image and the perception of others. Finally, mentors provide feedback that shapes their proteges' management style. This is particularly critical for women, who need to develop a managerial style that is not only effective, but effective for their gender. While male mentors may help female proteges develop acceptable styles, female mentors may be better suited for this task. Although most of the female executives interviewed lacked access to a female mentor, they recognized that women may be better able to share tried and true strategies for walking the fine line, and reported making it a point to share their hard-earned strategies with their female proteges.

White Noise In The Executive Suite: Divergent Perspectives On Barriers To Advancement

The executive women in these Fortune 1000 companies overcame gender-related barriers in order to break through the glass ceiling. An important question is whether their CEOs understood the barriers these women faced in their advancement. CEOs need accurate perceptions to develop effective solutions. We presented the female executives and CEOs in our survey with ten possible barriers to advancement, and asked them to select the three factors they considered to be the most significant in preventing women from advancing to the highest level of corporate leadership. What we found was both startling and revealing. Survey responses, as well as the follow-up interviews, revealed a marked gender gap in perspectives. Although the women and men in our study were all successful executives and were describing essentially the same corporate environment, they viewed this environment in different ways.

What's Holding Women Back? CEOs Blame Lack of Experience

An interesting finding in this study is the degree of consensus among male CEOs as to the key factors preventing women from advancing to corporate leadership. As shown in Figure 10.1, a decisive 82 percent point to lack of general management or line experience as the most crucial barrier holding women back. A second critical barrier, according to almost two-thirds of CEOs (64 percent), is that women have not been in the pipeline long enough—that is, the executive talent pool has included few women until recently.

In an interview, one CEO explained:

My class from business school had seven women in it, out of 650. So, there is a pipeline issue. And it'll take another five to eight years before the number of 45-year-old women ready for senior management jobs is balanced with the number of men.

However, some CEO's contend that time alone will not solve the problem. As one CEO points out:

It's not that women haven't been in the pipeline long enough; it's what they have done while they are in the pipeline.

Some CEOs attributed women's lack of experience in line management functions to women's self-selection or lack of understanding of the importance of these experiences; others see company practices as in part responsible:

I think that, without question, some women have chosen not to pursue certain tracks that, for one reason or another, might be more attractive to men. I think

that the larger reason is probably that we, the men of the organization, have built in credentials that we measure people against and, for one reason or another, that probably are biased against women.

I think many women have been held back because they haven't been prepared to make the same sacrifices as perhaps men are . . . they're not apt to move or relocate. Their families are all there.

One CEO recognized the more subtle dynamics that prevent women from obtaining key job assignments:

In the case of women, we use the lack of specific training for a job as a reason not to open the jobs to them, when we are more ready to bring men into jobs for which they are not specifically trained. That kind of discrimination or stereotyping is much subtler and more difficult to get at.

Our study also revealed a profound disparity between the kinds of experience CEOs identify as critical to advancement and the experience of most corporate women today. The majority (82 percent) of CEOs pointed to women's lack of general management/line experience with profit and loss responsibility as a key deterrent to their advancement. Only 47 percent of the female executives saw this as a critical barrier to women s advancement. Moreover, the executive women were far less likely than the male CEOs to believe that women have not been in the pipeline long

Figure 10.1
What Prevents Women from Advancing to Corporate Leadership?

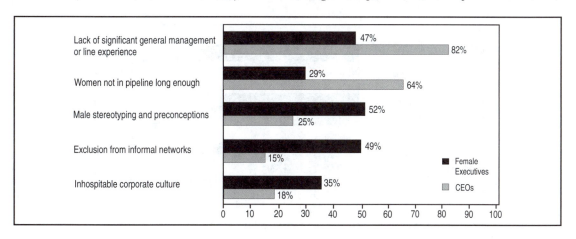

enough; only 29 percent of the women reported this as a key barrier, compared to 64 percent of the CEOs. Clearly, most of the women in our study would disagree with the argument that it is simply a matter of time until female executives catch up with their male counterparts.

Women Point to Corporate Culture

The women executives surveyed had a profoundly different view of the barriers women face in breaking the glass ceiling. The women were more than twice as likely as the CEOs to consider inhospitable work environments as a barrier to women's advancement: 52 percent of the women executives cited "male stereotyping and preconceptions of women" as a top factor holding women back, compared with 25 percent of CEOs; 49 percent of women identified "exclusion from informal networks," compared with 15 percent of CEOs; and inhospitable corporate culture was identified by 35 percent of women, but only 18 percent of CEOs.

One interviewee pointed to the tenacious nature of stereotypes by describing a situation where, despite her impressive credentials and achievements, she was still assumed to be a secretary in a business meeting:

> I was 43 years old and I was the highest ranking woman on the . . . staff, and this guy thinks I'm somebody's secretary. I

mean I was at Harvard. I was a fellow at Harvard. . . .
> —Executive vice president, transportation company

Another emphasized the exclusionary climate by her comment:

> You'd want for once in your life to walk into a room where people are talking that they continue to talk and you don't feel that you're listening in on something you're not supposed to be listening in on.
> —Vice president, high technology company

These successful female executives describe corporate cultures that are inhospitable and exclusionary, environments with white noise-constant background static that is distracting, debilitating, and a constant reality for many of these female executives, but that is often not heard by their male bosses.

In order to probe these environmental issues in more depth, our survey also included items assessing male managers' attitudes and behaviors. Again, the CEOs and executive women in our study sharply differed in their perceptions. As shown in Figure 10.2, executive women were significantly more likely than CEOs to agree or strongly agree that men have difficulty either supervising or being supervised by women.

Twice as many women executives as CEOs (40 percent versus 20 percent) believe that

Figure 10.2

Men's Attitudes Toward Women in the Workplace: Female Executives' and CEOs' Views

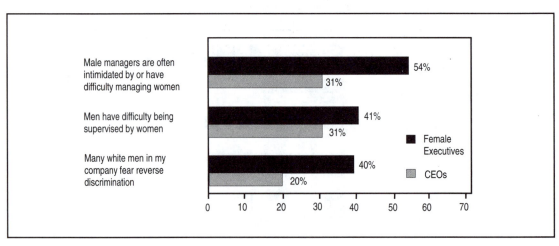

white men in their companies are concerned with reverse discrimination, presumably because of workforce diversity initiatives. To the extent that these concerns are significant, they fuel fears of a quota system and can undermine corporate efforts to achieve greater diversity in leadership.

Another striking difference in the opinions of male CEOs and female executives is the importance ascribed to politics and style. Women were more apt than men to identify women's lack of awareness of organizational politics and ineffective leadership style as factors holding women back. While these factors ranked fairly low in both executive women's and CEO's ratings, the fact that substantially more women singled them out as obstacles suggests that female executives regard the issue of cultural fit and acceptance as a greater challenge for women than do top male executives. As one female executive noted:

> To understand what was going on politically—for lack of a better word—was irreplaceable in making career progress and every bit as important as the actual assignments that I had.
>
> —Vice president, consumer products company.

One reason that male CEOs may not perceive style as being an important impediment to women's advancement is that it was not an issue for them in their own advancement. As discussed earlier, a key career strategy used by these successful female executives was the development of a managerial style that made male coworkers comfortable. It is unlikely that the CEOs in this study had to develop an adaptive style in order to make their female coworkers comfortable. This is illustrated by one CEO's comment: "I'm 56 years old and it's never happened in my career that I have reported to a woman."

Implications Of Dual Perspectives

Why would such a dramatic difference be found between the men's and women's perception of the environment they share? One interpretation of the data is that there are dual environments—one for men that is designed to foster their advancement, one for women that presents subtle, but significant obstacles to their advancement.

The CEOs in this study were logical in their approach, and viewed the problem of women's advancement in terms of what they can see and what they can count: the number of women in the pipeline and their years of experience. They have no way of understanding the corporate environment faced by their female employees because it is an environment that they do not currently experience, nor did they face in their rise to the top. As members of the majority, they were in environments designed by and for men, and presumably geared to being responsive to their needs and advancement. The problem is that CEOs are the critical change agent in most organizations, and if they do not understand the nature of the problem, it is nearly impossible for them to develop effective solutions.

The Problem Defines the Solution

The divergence in perceptions of the cause of the problem conceivably may lead to a marked divergence in proposed solutions. The CEOs viewed the major impediment to women's advancement as lack of experience and time in the pipeline. The logical solution to this barrier may be to fill the pipeline with women and then passively wait for their advancement. This pipeline approach assumes that time will take care of the problem, and that if women do not advance it is because they are unwilling or unable to do so. The burden for change therefore lies with the individual woman. The underlying assumption in the pipeline approach is that the playing field is level all the way up to the corporate suite, and it is therefore up to the individual women to perform effectively and make the right choices to obtain corporate leadership positions. The organization's role in addressing this problem is passive once there are enough women in the pipeline. Proponents of this approach are perplexed that while women are flooding into the managerial pipeline, and advancing as quickly as their male counterparts, few break through to the top leadership positions in organizations.

The female executives in our study present a very different assessment of the problem. These women sharply disagreed with the CEOs, and pointed to an exclusionary corporate culture as the primary barrier for women's advancement. In contrast to the CEOs, these women identified a playing field that was not level, but represented more of an obstacle course for women. Under this culture perspective, the problem does not lie with the individual women, but with attitudes and subtle barriers in the organization which foster an inhospitable corporate culture.

This culture perception may call for one of two solutions. The first solution is to change the corporate culture. This requires an active, planned intervention, which is clearly at odds with the pipeline approach of passively letting time handle the problem. The second solution is for the individual woman to adapt to the culture. Indeed, this is the approach that was consistently reported by these female executives. As discussed earlier, these women used career strategies that involved outperforming their male peers and developing adaptive management styles that made their male peers comfortable. While this solution may work for a select group of women who are both willing and able to adapt to an inhospitable corporate climate, it may not be an effective solution for the next generation of talented female employees aspiring to corporate leadership positions.

While this group of successful female executives adapted to inhospitable corporate cultures, this approach is definitely at odds with current perspectives on diversity in organizations and does not represent an effective, long-term solution to the problem. Diversity experts observe that organizations are most effective when active measures are taken to adapt corporate cultures to the needs of an increasingly diverse workforce, rather than placing the entire burden of change on the minority employee. Increasingly, it is recognized that by expecting minorities to adapt to the dominant culture, organizations fail to capitalize on the innovative and creative outcomes of a diverse workforce.

The view as to who is responsible for change, the individual woman or the organization, yielded contradictory results in our study. While both the CEOs (80 percent) and female executives (76 percent) strongly agreed or agreed with the statement that it is the company's responsibility to change to meet the needs of management women, 73 percent of the female executives and 61 percent of the CEOs in our study also strongly agreed or agreed with the statement that it is up to women to change to fit the corporate culture. These conflicting responses may reflect recent and incomplete shifts in attitudes regarding diversity and responsibility for organizational change.

Is the Solution Working? It Depends On Whom You Ask

It is reasonable to ask whether any of the solutions described above are working. Are these *Fortune* 1000 organizations making headway in removing promotional roadblocks and providing more opportunities for women? The answer depends on who is asked. As displayed in Figure 10.3, the CEOs were more than twice as likely as the executive women to say that opportunities for women in their companies improved greatly over the past five years. The female executives were more pessimistic about the change; fifteen percent of the women reported no change in opportunities, compared with only two percent of the CEOs. Once again, we found a sharp divergence in the perception of the same organizational environment.

Are these female executives accurate in their perceptions, or are they being overly-pessimistic in their appraisal of women's opportunities in their organizations? While it can be argued that women who break through the glass ceiling are probably best equipped to assess its density, no definitive answer to this question can be found. Existing studies reveal limited progress in women achieving corporate leadership positions. Whatever the reality, the perception that there are limited opportunities for advancement is sufficient for turnover decisions and reduced career aspirations among talented female employees. The barriers do not have to be real to be effective.

A salient finding of our study is that the majority of CEOs surveyed apparently are unaware of the corporate environment faced by

Figure 10.3
Opportunities for Women to Advance to Senior Leadership in Your Company Compared to Five Years Ago

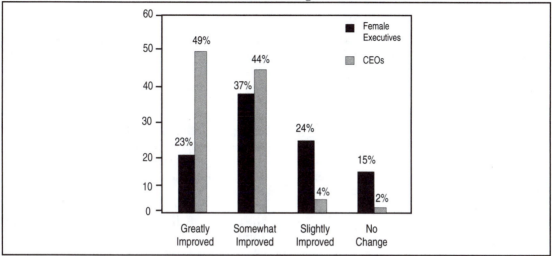

their female employees. As pointed out earlier, women were nearly twice as likely as CEOs to point to inhospitable corporate cultures as a barrier to women's advancement. CEOs, on the other hand, are more than twice as likely as women to report great improvement in the opportunities for women to advance in their corporations. How can these CEOs be so out of touch with the workplace experiences of nearly half of their workforce?

Voices From The Top: Some CEOs Get It, Others Need Work

We explored these issues further in our interviews with 20 male CEOs and found four themes underlying their perceptions of the corporate climate faced by the women in their organizations. Each theme represents a continuum on which CEOs varied, and the themes illuminated underlying assumptions that may have contributed to the differing perceptions of the CEO's and the female executives who worked for them.

Gender-blind treatment results in gender-blind outcomes. The first theme is the view that organizations need to treat men and women exactly the same. This perspective assumes a level playing field in the organization. Gender-blind treatment is therefore expected to result in gender-blind outcomes. One CEO explains:

> I think companies have to be gender-blind. Period. Whatever they do for men, they do for women. We're gender blind and that's the only thing that's going to work.

The assumption that the same career strategy is equally effective for men and women is not supported by the findings of our study; the female executives in our study attributed their success to developing a managerial style appropriate for their gender, which is clearly a gender-typed career strategy. CEOs who hold a gender-blind perspective may be reluctant to develop special career development programs aimed at helping women and other minorities navigate through the potentially non-level playing field in their organizations. . . .

Gender generalizations: All women are alike and they are all very different from men. The second theme that emerged from the CEO interviews was that CEOs varied on the extent to which they used group stereotypes to view individual women. Some saw men and women as being very different, whereas others saw them as nearly the same.

Some generalizations about gender differences had negative connotations:

Everyone has (career) slumps. I think that a greater percentage of women, when they have a slump, will look at the option of dropping out of the work force. Most men wouldn't see it as an option.

If a woman wants to be as assertive as men, she can get just as much air time. In many cases she can do better than a man. But sometimes mentally their knees buckle in an area where they are toe to toe. . . . If they want to be forceful, they are just as good.

I'd say there is a gender bias that there's less tough, aggressive women than men.

Some CEOs rejected the notion of group generalizations, and focused instead on individual differences within groups:

I find that the women in our company have the same range of ambition as the men, ranging from people who are fiercely ambitious and want to rise high and go far, to people who want to lead balanced lives and are pretty happy with what they're doing.

You can make a lot of generalizations about men and women, but when you get down to it, you've got to deal with specific people. Whether they're male or female, they don't necessarily fit the stereotype. . . . Some women we have around here aren't collaborative at all. They're extremely competitive people.

Other CEOs not only recognize individual differences, but also recognize that any gender differences in behaviors are often overshadowed by gender-neutral behaviors that emerge in response to position and responsibility:

Whether you're male or female, by the time you get to a senior management position, you've learned a different style of leadership anyway.

How do group generalizations relate to CEO perceptions of corporate climate? Existing research indicates a reciprocal relationship between group stereotyping and exclusionary corporate climates for women. Group stereotyping leads to the dual perception that all women are alike, and they are all very different from men. This perception is amplified when women are in the numerical minority (Kanter 1977). This results in a situation where men are treated on the basis of their individual characteristics, whereas women are automatically shunted into group categories, and are treated on the basis of those categories. This creates dual environments in organizations: one for women, and one for men, a distinction that is further fueled by group stereotypes. So male CEOs may assume that women do not want stretch assignments because of lack of aggressiveness or family demands, or they may place women in team leadership positions because of gender stereotypes that women are less competitive and more nurturing than men, and are therefore more likely to put their own needs aside for the good of the group. In either case, the challenge that is faced by women, but not their male counterparts, is to prove to their male colleagues that they are individuals and that they should be evaluated on the basis of their individual characteristics, rather than their group membership. In order to meet this challenge, women may expend considerable energy developing impression management strategies to project an image that runs counter to gender-role expectations.

Consciousness raising in the executive suite: The impact of personal experience. The third theme that emerged from the CEO interviews was the degree to which the CEOs were conscious of the exclusionary climate faced by their female employees. Many of the CEOs recognized that their own personal experiences influenced their awareness of gender issues, as well as issues faced by other minorities in their organizations. While most of the CEOs were white males, one CEO reflected on his own experience of being targeted for stereotyping and discrimination:

I'm Jewish. There weren't any Jewish people going into banking and there were no Jewish officers of banks. I was asked a lot, "Why are you doing this? There aren't any examples of Jews having succeeded in banking." I answered that it was because nobody had tried.

This CEO went on to relate how his background influenced his views of diversity in organizations:

People would ask, what is it like to go to school with blacks? I would think about how I would sit in class and not know the answers to questions and a black person would. So I would look at people as individuals. If you give them the same chances to perform and development experiences, you see race and religion and gender don't have much to do with success. This leads me to the conclusion that you can succeed by doing things differently.

Some CEOs observed that their early experiences interacting with competent women resulted in their casting aside gender-role stereotypes and generalizations:

Let me just say that I have been around very capable women all my working life. I certainly have never doubted the competency and capabilities of women in decision-making roles... So I have seen women all my life be very effective in very difficult situations.

I have women friends who got MBAs and have gone on to run major companies.

Other CEOs reported that they become cognizant of gender issues through direct experiences with family members, most notably, their daughters. These direct, personal experiences were instrumental in raising the CEOs' consciousness and awareness of gender issues in organizations:

I have five girls, no sons. . . . One interesting issue is my two youngest daughters, one of whom is in grad school, the other's going to start this year—they're both into women's issues. That's what they want to do as a career, work on women's issues. . . . You talk about politics. I catch it if I don't think the way they do on those issues. Those things have certainly had an impact.

I have a couple of career-minded daughters. I would like them to have the opportunity to go as far as their abilities will take them.

. . . I would stand my three daughters against most males I know and they would compete very well.

Some of the CEOs interviewed recognized that they do not automatically become sensitive to these environmental issues because it is not part of their daily experience in their organizations. These CEOs sought to increase their awareness of gender issues through experiential training. . . . Whether the experience is directly aimed at the CEO or vicariously observed through others, it generally shatters the assumption that discrimination does not exist in their organization.

The mantle for change. The final theme revealed from the CEO interviews was the CEOs' responsibility for making change occur in their organizations. The CEOs' role in the change process may involve a range of actions from actively mentoring and grooming women for high-ranking positions to providing a more flexible workplace and a corporate culture that relishes diversity. Whatever the nature of the change, for change to be effective, it must come from the top.

While many of the CEOs interviewed recognized their responsibility for taking the mantle of change, some also recognized the potential risks involved with making change happen. One CEO elaborated:

I really had to . . . take some chances in promoting women into roles that exposed them to high risk—and me as well. I had to run those risks to demonstrate that women could, in fact, handle these particular high-sensitivity, high-visibility jobs. So having done that, that's continued to open opportunities for women because there's no longer an artificial barrier to such promotions.

Other CEOs were reluctant to take the mantle of change, partly because of fears that the intervention would be viewed as an affirmative action gesture:

. . . holding managers accountable for developing women. I really dislike that. I think that could really backfire on you. I feel about that like I feel about affirmative action. People who weren't qualified were force-fed into it to match some sort of artificial goal.

Some CEOs did not take on the mantle of change because they believed that change did not need to occur. However, while these CEOs maintained that their organizations were gender-blind, they still expected women to help other women, thereby inferring that their corporate culture may not be as blind as they would like it to be.

Still other CEOs take the more benign approach that change needs to occur from a grass-roots level. Instead of active intervention, these CEOs hope that change will be initiated by women and other minorities in their organizations. Their role in the change process would therefore be to support the change, but not initiate it. However, one problem with giving the mantle for change to women and minorities is that these employees are vulnerable to backlash, and typically lack the power to sustain the change over time.

The themes that emerged from these interviews were connected. CEOs who were sensitized to the dual environments in their organizations did not assume a level playing field between the genders; they understood the exclusionary climate women face and they therefore did not advocate gender-blind policies and programs. CEOs who were sensitized to women's experiences were also more likely to emphasize individual differences between women, rather than using broad-based group generalizations to categorize their female employees. These CEOs also recognized their roles in changing the inhospitable corporate climates faced by their female employees. In short, they attempted to hear the white noise in their organizations.

Bridging The Gender Gap

How do we bridge the gender gap and sensitize CEOs to the corporate climate faced by their female employees? Most CEOs do not understand the experience of being a minority in their organization since they themselves are in the majority. However, some recognize this disparity, and that the playing field is not perceived as being level by their female employees. This understanding is often obtained by direct, personal experiences with female colleagues and family members, most notably daughters. . . .

Many organizational interventions aimed at breaking the glass ceiling that have been identified elsewhere are also supported by our study. For example, organizations need to track women into direct line experience positions with profit and loss responsibility, minimize gender bias by using objective performance appraisal systems, facilitate effective mentoring relationships, promote work/life balance by implementing flexible workplace policies, and make managers responsible for the career development and tracking of their female employees. [O]rganizations also need to address the specific career needs of midlife women by offering flexible job designs and specialized career path programs.

Our study adds one more intervention to this list: raising the consciousness of chief executive officers and other senior officers slated for those top positions. In fact, this intervention may be the key underlying factor behind effective implementation of all of the other interventions listed above; effective implementation requires top management commitment. Organizations need the support and guidance of top management if women are to break through the glass ceiling. For this to occur, the gender gap must be bridged.

Endnote

1. The response rates for the female executive and CEO samples were 36.8 percent and 33 percent. On average, the female executives were 45 years old, earned an annual salary of $248,000, and were highly educated: almost two-thirds have postgraduate degrees. Seventy-two percent of the women were married, and almost two-thirds (64 percent) have children. Only nine percent identify themselves as other than Caucasian, and these women of color earned an average annual salary of $229,000. Eight-one percent of the women were within two reporting levels of the CEO, and 44 percent report directly to the CEO or are only one level from the CEO. More than 60 percent held staff positions. The largest number held the title of vice president (54 percent) or senior vice president (19 percent); survey respondents also included a significant number of even more senior executives, such as president, executive vice president, chief financial officer and general counsel.

Selected References

Brenner, O. C., J. Tomkiewicz, and V. E. Schein. 1989. "The relationship between sex role stereotypes and requisite management characteristics revisited." *Academy of Management Journal*, 32: 662–669.

Brush, C. G. 1992. "Research on women business owners: Past trends, new perspectives and future directions." *Enterpreneurship: Theory and Practice*, 16: 5–30.

Catalyst. 1996. *Census of women corporate officers and top earners.* New York: Catalyst.

Cox, T. 1991. "The multicultural organization." *Academy of Management Executive*, 5: 34–47.

Kanter, R. M. 1977. *Men and women of the corporation.* New York: Basic Books.

Kram, K. E. 1985. *Mentoring at work.* Glenview, IL: Scott, Foresman and Company.

Phillips, J. D., and B. Reisman. 1992. "Turnover and return on investment models for family leave." In D. E. Friedman, E. Galinsky & V. Plowden (Eds.) *Parental leave and productivity: Current research*, 33–53. New York: Families and Work Institute.

Ragins, B. R., and J. Cotton. 1991. "Easier said than done: Gender differences in perceived barriers to gaining a mentor." *Academy of Management Journal*, 34: 939–951.

Ragins, B. R., and T. A. Scandura. 1994. "Gender differences in expected outcomes of mentoring relationships." *Academy of Management Journal*, 37: 957–971. Korn/Ferry International, 1993.

Food for Thought and Application Questions

1. Discuss the main discrepancies between what CEOs and female executives identify as main barriers to women executives breaking through the glass ceiling. How do you account for the differences in their views?

2. Assume you are a male CEO who wants to increase the representation of women in top echelons of his firm (so that some may eventually become CEOs). Assume, as well, that you intend to develop a long-term plan, rather than a "quick fix." Based on your reading of this article, suggest at least three strategies that could be developed to increase women's representation in top firm positions. Discuss the interrelatedness of these steps/efforts (if any), and ways that these policies can be monitored to show they are working. ✦

11

The Impact of Male Work Environments and Organizational Policies on Women's Experiences of Sexual Harassment

James E. Gruber

Since the first comprehensive analyses of sexual harassment over a decade and a half ago (Canadian Human Rights Commission [CHRC] 1983; U.S. Merit Systems Protection Board [USMSPB] 1981), researchers have developed an increasingly sophisticated and nuanced understanding of the organizational dynamics that create problems of workplace harassment and hostility for women.

... [T]his analysis will attempt to cast light on an issue that remains one of the most notable "glaring omissions" (Fitzgerald and Shullman 1993) in sexual harassment research: the impact of organizational policies and procedures for handling sexual harassment on reducing the incidence of the problem.... This analysis assumes that sexual harassment policies and procedures affect organizational climate; and it is expected that among organizations with similar occupational or workplace gender ratios those without visible, proactive program[s], will

have a higher incidence of harassment than those that have them.

Gender Dominance, Gendered Work

Numerical and normative dominance are distinct, but often interrelated, aspects of the degree of influence and control one gender has over the other. According to Acker, this "gendering" occurs as a product of at least five interacting processes: construction of divisions (e.g., labor, work space, power) along gender lines; constructions of symbols and images that articulate and reinforce these divisions; gender-based patterns and styles of interaction and communication; reflection of gender stereotypes in occupational or organizational identities (e.g., men are leaders; women are nurturers); and differential impact on women and men of the fundamental, ongoing processes "of creating and conceptualizing social structures" (1990, 146) such as rules of conduct, directives, or job evaluations. Normative male dominance occurs in a number of work contexts that vary widely in male numerical dominance from, for example, situations where a few men have superordinate status over a largely female work group (doctors/nurses, managers/secretaries) to the "male preserves" (Kimmel 1996) where women are virtually absent but highly visible.

Women in traditionally male occupations or workplaces report more experiences of sexual harassment than other women (Gutek 1985; LaFontaine and Tredeau 1986; Rubenstein 1992). . . . While women in female-traditional positions generally experience harassment due to a lack of power and/or sexualization of their work activities, women in male-traditional positions often are treated hostilely because they have infringed on male power and privilege and threaten the "production of masculinity" (Martin and Jurik 1996, 175). In a number of male-traditional positions, work identity is constructed on gendered behavior and cultural symbols of masculinity: aggression, sexual bravado, embracing dangerous or risky situations, and bonding through rituals that celebrate male superiority (Glick 1991; Martin and Jurik 1996; Stockdale 1993).

Work identities that have stereotypical images of masculinity as their basis are typically "doubly" male dominated: The male traditionality of an *occupation* creates a work culture that is an extension of male culture, and numerical dominance of the workplace by men heightens visibility of, and hostility toward, women workers who are perceived as violating male territory. Although women professionals in male-traditional fields face greater harassment than other white-collar women, they experience less severe and pervasive harassment than their blue-collar counterparts (LaFontaine and Tredeau 1986; Loy and Stewart 1984). The former appear to be better protected from harassment and hostility by virtue of norms of professionalism that stress respectful treatment of, and cooperation with, others (Gutek 1985).

The Male Preserves

While nearly half of North American women experience harassment within a two-year time period (Fitzgerald 1990; Gruber 1990), the rates are higher in the doubly male or "male culture" work environments. Sixty-four percent of women in a Department of Defense study of the total active military force (Martindale 1990) experienced one or more forms of sexual harassment.

High rates and severe forms of sexual harassment have been documented in police and security occupations as well. . . . A statewide survey of women police officers in Florida found that 62 percent had been sexually harassed (Robinson 1994). Martin (1990) reported an almost identical figure (63 percent) in her survey of five municipal police departments in different regions of the United States. . . . Women firefighters (Yoder and Aniakudo 1995) and correctional officers (Deitch and Fechner 1995; Martin and Jurik 1996) face similar problems of frequent and severe harassment.

Organizational Climate: Tolerance, Leadership, and Policies

The extent of harassment in work organizations is influenced by several factors, including environmental tolerance of harassment, the perceived commitment of organizational officials to effectively handle harassment problems, and the implementation of policies or procedures to combat such problems.

Sexualization of the work environment is significantly influenced by organizational tolerance of sexually discriminatory or offensive behaviors or materials (Hulin, Fitzgerald, and Drasgow 1996; Pryor, Giedd, and Williams 1995). Such environments may cognitively "prime" some men to perceive women as sex objects and subsequently behave in a sexist or sexually inappropriate manner (McKenzie Mohr and Zanna 1990; Pryor and Stoller 1994; Rudman, Borgida, and Robertson 1995). Women's coping behavior is also affected in sexually tolerant environments: Their responses to harassment are influenced by their perceptions of the level of risk involved in complaining about harassment, the likelihood that such complaints will be taken seriously, and the likelihood that the perpetrators will be punished (Hulin, Fitzgerald, and Drasgow 1996).

Workplace climate is also notably affected by the behavior of organizational leaders. Organizations in which leaders are perceived as proactive in addressing the problem of sexual harassment—for example, have discouraged it or spoken out against it—have fewer harassment problems than organizations in which the leadership was seen either as indifferent toward or encouraging of sexually harassing behavior (Niebuhr 1997; Pryor, LaVite, and Stoller 1993). The leadership of an organization may also affect workplace climate by implementing sexual harassment policies and procedures. . . .

The potential benefits of a concerted, multifaceted, organization-wide approach in changing organizational climate can be seen by recent outcomes in . . . the military. . . .

In the conclusion of the first comprehensive military-wide survey of sexual harassment in 1988, Martindale (1990) stated that military leaders were not adequately addressing the problem of sexual harassment. . . . The military's "zero tolerance" program was created in 1989 . . . but was not given a high funding priority until after Tailhook and other highly publicized reports of harassment (Bacon 1996) increased public and political pressure for reform. . . .

A 1995 Department of Defense (DOD) survey that used questionnaire items nearly identical to the 1988 study revealed a decline in sexual harassment from 64 percent to 55 percent. Each of eight types of harassment occurred less frequently in 1995 than in 1988, and each branch of the military showed a decline in overall levels of harassment. Also, informal reporting of harassment by targets increased fourfold (Seppa 1997).

Research Issues and Methods

This research focuses on the impact of two types of variables on women's sexual harassment experiences: the gendered aspects of women's work (normative and numerical male dominance) and the presence (or absence) of policies or procedures for dealing with problems of sexual harassment. Also, since various types of sexual harassment differ markedly in severity, we will compare the impact of gendered work activities and harassment policies and procedures on several individual and composite measures of harassment. Our work is guided by three research expectations.

Hypotheses. First, we predict that gender predominance, a composite measure of both gender composition of women's workplace contacts and the national sex ratio of occupations that the women in our sample hold, will be more strongly related to women's sexual harassment experience than each of the individual items. . . . Research over the past 15 years has provided extensive evidence of the impact of both numerical and normative male dominance on women newcomers. . . . According to [the "contact hypothesis" of Gutek, Cohen, and Konrad (1990)], sheer routine contact with members of the other sex increases sociosexual behavior and [workplace] sexualization, especially in male-majority workplaces, since men tend to sexualize interactions, irrespective of specific occupational or situational norms. On the other hand, women's visibility may be heightened in nontraditional occupations because their presence undermines both gender-based stereotypes about job competence and the routine processes men use to bond with each other (see Martin and Jurik 1996), irrespective of their numbers. The

joint relationship between workplace contact and occupational sex ratios (gender predominance) . . . helps focus our analysis on a variety of doubly male environments that include "male preserve" work situations.

Second, we predict that methods of addressing sexual harassment problems that reveal commitment by organizational leaders and attempts to actively change the work environment will yield greater success in reducing harassment than merely informing employees of the existence of organizational policies. Since the U.S. Supreme Court's decision in *Vinson v. Meritor Savings Bank* (1986) legal opinion over the past decade has argued that merely distributing or posting a generic sexual harassment policy is not sufficient to address the problem. The courts have recommended that substantial preventive efforts be made by employers in handling sexual harassment problems. . . . A very similar emphasis in Canada has paralleled U.S. policy developments since the mid-1980s (CHRC 1990). . . . Also, "hostile environment" forms of harassment were added to the law during the same time period in both countries (EEOC 1990; CHRC 1990).

On the basis of these arguments, I will compare the experiences of three groups of women: those in work environments with no policies, procedures, or training in sexual harassment; those in workplaces with only informational methods or "getting out the word" approaches such as posting a policy in the workplace or placing it in an employee handbook; and those in environments with proactive or change-oriented methods (explicit complaint procedures and training programs).

Employees without the protection of policies and procedures are predicted to have higher rates of sexual harassment than those in workplaces that have some. I predict that reductions in the percentages of women experiencing harassment will be especially noteworthy in organizations with proactive methods because they require action by organizational leaders (e.g., requiring employees to attend training sessions; creating or enlarging existing positions within the organization to handle harassment complaints), which may . . . heighten the visibility of an organization's commitment to dealing with sexual harassment. Also, proactive methods are likely to lower the perceived risks of complaining about or reporting harassment (Rudman, Borgida, and Robertson 1995) and at the same time increase the perceived costs of behaving in a sexually harassing manner.

. . . We expect proactive methods of addressing sexual harassment problems to have a greater impact than informational methods on the incidence of a wider range (i.e., personal as well as environmental forms) of sexual harassment. . . .

Sample

Telephone interviews of Canadian women who were employed or had been employed during the previous year were conducted in 1992 by researchers at a university in a large metropolitan area in eastern Ontario. A two-stage probability sampling procedure was used to develop a representative sample of women throughout Canada. Sixty-five percent of the sample completed the interviews (*n* = 1,990). The median age of the sample was 34. Nearly 70 percent were married. Most had some education beyond high school.

Measures

Sexual harassment. The interviewees were asked if they had experienced 1 or more of 11 types of "uninvited and unwanted sexual attention" in the past 12 months, based on the 1989 Inventory of Sexual Harassment (ISH): sexual assault, bribery, touching, invasions of personal space, "rumoring" or spreading sexual gossip behind the respondent's back, questioning a woman about her sex life, sexual gestures, repeated date requests, sexual categorical remarks about other women, staring, sexual jokes directed at the respondent, and sexual materials (see Gruber, Kauppinen, and Smith 1996 for a recent discussion of the ISH). Respondents who stated that they had experienced a specific form of harassment were asked two contingent questions: How many times did this (specific form) occur in the past 12 months? And how upset were you by these experiences? . . .

Four harassment variables were analyzed individually because they capture differences in type and severity (Gruber 1992): physical threat and sexual comments (personal, high severity), and sexual categorical remarks and sexual materials (environmental, low severity). . . .

Since most women experience multiple forms of sexual harassment at their workplaces (Martindale 1990; USMSPB 1981), an indicator of the overall level of harassment they have faced is a summation of all such experiences. . . .

Sexual harassment policies and procedures. The respondents were asked a series of questions about their direct knowledge of workplace polices or procedures on sexual harassment at their place of employment: official procedures for complaining about sexual harassment problems, company or union posters on harassment, company or union pamphlets, or presentations on the topic by company or union representatives. The items were combined to create variables that indicated the number and nature of such procedures/policies in the workplace. Proactive methods indicated whether the organization used approaches that modified the work environment by creating official complaint procedures for sexual harassment problems or conducting training sessions on the issue. Informational methods described whether the organization had at least alerted its employees to the issue of sexual harassment through pamphlets or posters.

Statistical and Data Analysis

Descriptive analyses were used to display the general differences in sexual harassment experiences between the categories of each independent variable [Table 11.1]. . . .

Bivariate analyses of the predictor variables revealed that each was significantly related to whether a woman had been sexually harassed in the past 12 months. . . . Specifically, women under 25 years of age (56.4 percent), unmarried women (52.2 percent), those in male-dominated occupations (53.8 percent) or workplaces (55.4 percent), and where sexual harassment policies or procedures are nonexistent (51.5 percent) experienced proportionately more harassment than women in the other respective categories.

A bivariate analysis of gender predominance and women's experiences with sexual harassment indicates that women report less harassment when they have both infrequent contact with men in their workplaces and traditionally female jobs (31 percent). On the other hand, women are most apt to be targets of harassment when their visibility in the work environment centers on gender-based status differences, that is, they have a nontraditional job in a male-dominated work environment (55 percent), or, their traditionally female job is located in a work environment that involves a high degree of contact with men (54 percent). Women whose workplace contacts are balanced between men and women experience similar rates of harassment for the occupational sex ratio categories [Table 11.2].

Regression analyses were used to determine whether predictors were significantly re-

Table 11.1
Percentages of Women Who Have Experienced Sexual Harassment by Predictors

	% (n)
Age	
Under 25	56.4 (445)**
25–39	46.2 (823)
40+	31.2 (673)
Marital status	
Not married	52.2 (605)**
Married	39.1 (1,375)
Occupational sex ratio	
Male dominated	53.8 (188)**
Majority male	46.4 (269)
Majority female	40.7 (447)
Female dominated	40.2 (1,080)
Workplace sex ratio (contact)	
Mostly men	55.4 (411)**
Equal contact	46.7 (643)
Mostly women	34.2 (905)
Sexual harassment policies/procedures	
None	51.5 (887)**
Informational	43.4 (663)
Proactive	39.6 (403)

**p < .01 based on chi-square values.

Table 11.2
Percentages of Women Experiencing Sexual Harassment by Workplace Contact and Occupational Sex Ratio

Workplace Contact	Occupational Sex Ratio			
	Male Dominated	Majority Male	Majority Female	Female Dominated
Mostly men (%)	55	52	48	54**
(n)	(78)	(67)	(71)	(194)
Equal (%)	45	48	46	45
(n)	(49)	(94)	(149)	(351)
Mostly women(%)	43	45	33	31
(n)	(63)	(103)	(225)	(514)

**p < .01 based on chi-square values.

lated either to having been sexually harassed in the last 12 months or to the total number of different types of harassment experiences during that time period. The results . . . revealed that age and workplace sex contact were the strongest predictors of experienced/last year (experienced sexual harassment in the last year). . . . Occupation sex composition was significantly related to experienced/last year and number of types experienced, although the effects were weaker than those of workplace contact. . . . [I]nformational methods was a significant predictor of both experienced/last year and number of types experienced, but its strength diminished considerably when proactive methods was introduced into the analysis of both dependent variables. Proactive methods was a significant predictor of both experienced/last year and number of types experienced.[1]

In contrast to our expectations, gender predominance was not a significant factor in predicting either dependent variable. Workplace contact was a stronger predictor of both measures of harassment than the gender composition of a woman's occupation. This suggests that sexual harassment is more generally a function of workplace dynamics than of stereotypes about occupational membership. . . . Also, providing workers with information about sexual harassment does have a modest effect on reducing its occurrence, although proactive methods are much more effective.

Discussion

The analyses present further evidence for the strength and stability of workplace sex contact or the "contact hypothesis" described and verified empirically by Gutek, Cohen, and Konrad (1990). The analyses revealed that workplace contact is not only useful in predicting whether harassment is likely to occur but also for determining which types are likely to be found. Our findings suggest strongly that *what* a woman does for a living is less important than *where* she does her job. Research studies that do not separate the what and the where are most likely concealing the substantial impact of the immediate work environment and, at the same time, overestimating the effect of gendered occupational roles. . . . Gender predominance is an important predictor of both physical threat and sexual materials. These relationships seem to capture several important aspects of women's experiences in male culture environments. First, predominantly male environments are more physically hostile and intimidating than other work environments. Women are more apt to be touched, grabbed, or stalked. Second, men are more apt to physically mark their work environments with sexually objectifying material. A descriptive analysis of these data found that in the entire sample sexual materials occurred infrequently (11 percent) compared with sexual categorical remarks (46 percent) or sexual jokes and comments (21 percent). The results in this article . . . reveal that sexual materials occur in a smaller range of work situations, specifically those where there is a high degree of male predominance.

Do sexual harassment policies and procedures work? Our answer is emphatically yes! Gruber and Smith (1995) found that women responded more assertively to unwanted sexual attention when the workplace implemented several means (e.g., policy, complaint procedure, training) for dealing with harassment problems. The present analysis revealed that men's behavior is also affected by policies and procedures. Moreover, the type of sexually harassing behavior that was affected depended on the types of strategies adopted by the workplace. The results of our analyses suggest that both informational and proactive methods are useful in curtailing harassment generally . . . and, in particu-

lar, environmental forms of sexual harassment such as denigrating sexual categorical comments about women or pornographic posters and pinups. However, merely providing employees with information about sexual harassment is not effective in deterring more serious, personal forms of harassment. In this regard, proactive strategies for dealing with harassment are effective. According to our analysis, women in workplaces with proactive strategies were less likely to be physically threatened or to be the targets of offensive sexual comments or questions.

What has not yet been established through research are the processes through which an organization's methods of addressing sexual harassment become sufficiently visible *and* credible. Even with the proliferation of policies, workshops, and training programs, it seems that some organizations achieve greater success in dealing with sexual harassment than other organizations who use similar methods. The recently reported incidents at Texaco where tape recordings of higher level managers who had participated in diversity training programs revealed that they made racist jokes and comments during a business meeting (France and Smart 1996) should alert us to both the potential and limitations of state-of-the-art training programs.

As researchers we should seek detailed information about the content and duration of various methods used to address sexual harassment. With regard to workshops or training sessions, we should ask, among other things, who did the training? How long did it last? Was there follow-up training? Was attitudinal or behavioral change assessed? Were harassers sanctioned? From a cynical viewpoint, many organizations may attempt to reduce liability from harassment suits in the 1990s through training programs in much the same way that organizations rushed to develop a sexual harassment policy in the 1980s.

Anecdotal reports by researchers and expert witnesses reveal that workshops and training programs often have high nonattendance or low participant engagement levels. Given the present level of research knowledge, it seems that the *message* of sexual harassment policies and procedures may be as

important as the *content:* What an organization does in terms of creating and implementing policies and procedures may change the
climate of the organization if these efforts are
perceived to be credible.

Note

1. The possibility that women's reporting of
their experiences of unwanted sexual attention was related to their attitudes toward sexual harassment was tested by correlating the
four types of experiences . . . with several attitudinal items: Women who get unwanted sexual attention from a man at work bring it on
themselves; men who sexually harass women
at work are basically trying to keep women in
their place; in general, women are too sensitive about unwanted sexual attention in the
workplace; and unwanted sexual attention
from men is a serious problem for working
women. The correlations were small, ranging
from .0007 to .10. It does not appear that
women report their experiences differently
because of their attitudes.

References

Acker, J. 1990. Hierarchies, jobs, bodies: a theory
of gendered organizations. *Gender and Society* 2 (4): 139–158.

Bacon, K. 1996. Department of Defense News
Briefing. 21 November.

Canadian Human Rights Commission (CHRC).
1983. *Unwanted sexual attention and sexual
harassment.* Montreal: Minister of Supply and
Services of Canada.

———. 1990. Harassment: What it is and what to
do about it. Montreal: Minister of Supply and
Services of Canada.

Deitch, C. and H. Fechner. 1995. When sexual
harassment is unwritten policy: [The] District
of Columbia Department of Corrections and
the role of the union. Paper presented at the
annual meeting of the American Sociological
Association, Washington, DC (August 20).

Equal Employment Opportunity Commission
(EEOC). 1990. Policy Guidance on Current Is-
sues of Sexual Harassment (Notice M-915-050).
Washington, DC: Government Printing Office.

Fitzgerald, L. 1990. Sexual harassment: The definition and measurement of a construct. In
Ivory power: Sexual harassment on Campus,
edited by M. Paludi. Albany: State University
of New York Press.

Fitzgerald, L. F. and S. L. Shullman. 1993. Sexual harassment: A research analysis and

agenda for the 90's. *Journal of Vocational Behavior* 42:5–29.

France, M. and T. Smart. 1996. The ugly talk on
the Texaco tape. *Business Week,* November 18,
58.

Glick, P. 1991. Trait-based and sex-based discrimination in occupational prestige, occupational
salary, and hiring. *Sex Roles* 25:351–378.

Gruber, J. E. 1990. Methodological Problems
and policy implications in sexual harassment
research. *Population Research and Policy Review* 9:235–254.

———. 1992. A typology of personal and environmental sexual harassment: Research and policy implications for the 1990's. *Sex Roles*
26:447–464.

Gruber, J., K. Kauppinen, and M. Smith. 1996.
Sexual harassment types and severity: Linking
research and policy. In *Women & work: Sexual
harassment in the workplace,* edited by M.
Stockdale. Thousand Oaks, CA: Sage.

Gruber, J. and M. Smith. 1995. Women's responses to sexual harassment: A multivariate
analysis. *Basic and Applied Social Psychology*
17:543–562.

Gutek, B. A. 1985. *Sex and the workplace: The impact of sexual behavior and harassment on
women, men and organization.* San Francisco:
Jossey-Bass.

Gutek, B. A. Cohen, and A. Konrad. 1990. Predicting social-sexual behavior at work: A contact hypothesis. *Academy of Management
Journal* 33:560–577.

Hulin, C., L. Fitzgerald, and F. Drasgow. 1996.
Organizational influences on sexual harassment. In *Women & work: Sexual harassment
in the workplace,* edited by M. Stockdale.
Thousand Oaks, CA: Sage.

Kimmel, M. 1996. Clarence, William, Iron Mike,
Tailhook, Senator Packwood, Magic . . . and
us. In *Men's lives,* edited by M. Kimmel and
M. Messner. Boston: Allyn and Bacon.

LaFontaine, E. and L. Tredeau. 1986. The frequency, sources, and correlations of sexual harassment among women in traditional male
occupations. *Sex Roles* 15:433–441.

Loy, P. and L. Stewart. 1984. The extent and the
effect of sex harassment of working women.
Sociological Focus 17:31–43.

Martin, S. 1990. *On the move: The status of
women in policing.* Washington, DC: Police
Foundation.

Martin, S. and N. Jurik. 1996. *Doing justice, doing gender.* Thousand Oaks, CA: Sage.

Martindale, M. 1990. *Sexual harassment in the
military.* 1988. Washington, DC: Manpower
Data Center, Department of Defense.

McKenzie Mohr, D., and M. Zanna. 1990. Treating women as sexual objects: Look to the (gender schematic) male who has viewed pornography. *Personality and Social Psychology Bulletin* 16:296.

Niebuhr, R. 1997. Sexual harassment in the military. In *Sexual harassment: Theory, research, and treatment.* Edited by Wm. O'Donohue. Boston: Allyn and Bacon.

Pryor, J., J. Giedd, and K. Williams. 1995. A social psychological model for predicting sexual harassment. *Journal of Social Issues* 51: 69–84.

Pryor, J., C. La Vite, and L. Stoller. 1993. A social psychological analysis of sexual harassment: The person/situation interaction. *Journal of Vocational Behavior* 42:68–81.

Pryor, J., and L. Stoller. 1994. *Sexual harassment in Florida law enforcement.* Ocala, FL: Ocala Police Department.

Robinson, G. 1994. *Sexual Harassment in Florida law enforcement.* Ocala, FL: Ocala Police Department.

Rubenstein, M. 1992. Combating sexual harassment at work. *Conditions of Work Digest* 11:285–290.

Rudman, L., E. Borgida, and B. Robertson. 1995. Suffering in silence: Procedural justice versus gender socialization issues in university sexual harassment grievance procedures. *Basic and Applied Social Psychology* 17: 519–542.

Seppa, N. 1997. Sexual harassment in the military lingers on. *APA Monitor,* May, 40–41.

Stockdale, M. 1993. The role of sexual misperceptions of women's friendliness in an emerging theory of sexual harassment. *Journal of Vocational Behavior* 42:84–101.

Stockdale, M., A. Vaux, and J. Cashin. 1995. Acknowledging sexual harassment: A test of alternative models. *Basic and Applied Social Psychology* 17:469–496.

U.S. Merit Systems Protection Board (USMSPB). 1981. *Sexual harassment in the federal workplace: Is it a problem?* Washington, DC: Government Printing Office.

Vinson vs. Meritor Savings Bank, 477 U.S. 57 (1986).

Yoder, J. and P. Aniakudo. 1995. The responses of African American women firefighters to gender harassment at work. *Sex Roles* 32:125–137.

Reprinted from: James E. Gruber, "The impact of male work environments and organizational policies on women's experiences of sexual harassment," In *Gender and Society* 12 (3) June:301–320. Copyright © 1998 by Sage Publications, Inc. Reprinted by permission.

Food for Thought and Application Questions

1. Gruber proposed that we should investigate "the content and duration of various methods used to address sexual harassment." Presume there is a training program on sexual harassment that your employer intends to have all employees attend. What would you want to know about the program to properly assess its impact? What do you need to know about the organization's experiences with sexual harassment *before the training program* in order to make an effective assessment?

2. Discuss the ways in which workplace culture can enhance or diminish the likelihood of women experiencing sexual harassment. Assess the relative importance of the role of managers and organizational policies/procedures. Given this, develop a list of suggestions for ways that women *seeking* employment can assess the workplace culture and the likelihood of difficulties regarding sexual harassment. ✦

Unit Three

Work and Family: Seeking a Balance

The breakdown of family values, increases in juvenile crime rates, declining educational achievement, teen pregnancy, latchkey children, the drug problem, and the high divorce rate are social problems that the public, politicians, the popular media, and even academicians have blamed on working women, with the suggestion that their neglect of the family has caused the variety of problems with which society now grapples. But why have working women become a popular scapegoat for so many social ills? Several reasons exist. First, sharp increases in women's employment over the last three decades of the twentieth century represent rapid social change, and rapid social change is disruptive of society, at least in the short run. It takes time for social institutions to adjust to change, and, as we will see in the selections that follow, accommodations to women's employment have been slow in coming. Relatedly, social values and individual beliefs that buttress existing social institutions also typically support the earlier status quo. The public clamor over the breakdown of family values provides a good example. Family values are not breaking down; they are simply changing in order to accommodate new family forms (e.g., single parent families, dual-worker families, gay and lesbian partnerships).

Another reason for attributing the cause of social problems to working women is re-lated to the definition of scapegoat. A scapegoat is a "safe goat"; that is, blame can be placed on a scapegoat without fear of retribution. Women, as a disadvantaged group, are relatively powerless to respond; thus, it is convenient to blame them. Yet many of the problems listed above (e.g., youth crime, declining educational achievement, teen pregnancy) are caused, by a varying degree, to economic inequality. It is difficult, however, to blame the economically advantaged for depriving others and thus contributing to social problems.

Laying the blame for social problems on women's paid work is problematic not only because women's work is seldom the cause of the problem, but also because our economy depends on women working, as do families who require the income generated by their employment. Unless unanticipated, broad-based changes in our economy occur, women will continue to work outside the home for pay. Blaming this phenomenon for social problems does little to provide solutions. A more fruitful approach to addressing these problems is to develop social arrangements that make work and family roles more compatible. This could be done by developing a vast array of workplace accommodations (e.g., flextime, on-site day care, telecommuting), the government's support and leadership in encouraging workplace changes, and by men increasing their respon-

119

sibilities in the family (with child care and domestic work). These strategies for managing the delicate balance between work and family are discussed in the selections that follow.

Working women are the ones most negatively affected by social disruption resulting from their employment and society's lack of adaptive structures to accommodate their paid work. Not only do women bear the burden of responsibility for causing social problems, they also disproportionately bear the responsibility for minimizing the disruption that results from their work. For example, regardless of how one defines or measures housework, wives still do more of it than husbands (Bianchiet al. 2000; Feree 1991; Thompson and Walker 1991). The adage that "men work from dawn to dusk, but women's work is never done" rings true today in most dual-earner families. Women work full-time outside the home and then come home to what Hochschild (1989) calls a "second shift." Drawing on previous research on time spent on household tasks, Hochschild estimated that women perform an extra month of 24-hour days of work each year. Studies show that in the mid-1990s, working wives spent an average of 19.4 hours per week on housework; husbands of working wives spent an average of 10.4 hours per week (or a ratio of nearly 2 to 1). While this was a considerable improvement in the ratio of women's to men's time given to household chores over time (the ratio in 1965 was 6 to 1), data also show that men's contribution to household chores has remained stable since 1985. By contrast, women have reduced the amount of time they spend on household chores, and this reduction accounts for the major change in the ratio of contribution to household chores (Bianchi et al. 2000).

Child care and elder care tasks are also performed disproportionately by women in dual worker families, thus exacerbating the role overload that women face. LaRossa and LaRossa (1981) found that while new fathers are willing to assist with child care tasks, they view the primary responsibility for caring for the baby as the mother's. This difference explains why mothers experience more stress in adapting to parenthood than do fathers. In addition, women's care-provider re-

sponsibilities often do not diminish significantly when the children leave the nest because that generally is the time at which aging parents and parents-in-law are in need of care. In this society, the bulk of senior care is provided informally by women relatives (Aronson 1992). As such, women are constrained with regard to employment opportunities, access to resources, and independence.

Gender gaps in housework and care giving contribute to a gender gap in marital satisfaction. Studies indicate that a fair division of family work between husbands and wives is associated with higher levels of marital satisfaction for women, and that over-burdened women are less satisfied with their marital relationship. In contrast, husbands are more satisfied with their marriages and less critical of their wives if their wives do more of the family work (Kunz Center 1998; Thompson and Walker 1991).

The burden of family work also falls disproportionately to single women. In 2003, women maintained 22 percent of the families where there were children under the age of 18. The incidence of mother-only families among blacks is especially high, with nearly 45 percent of black families headed by women. Among Hispanic households, 26 percent are headed by women (U.S. Census 2004–05). Women who head mother-only families must perform the work of two parents—breadwinning, housework, and child care—resulting in high stress levels. Furthermore, single mothers are especially likely to be blamed for the various problems surrounding today's youth; rarely does attention turn to the responsibility of the father.

Despite these actual and attributed burdens on working women, most young women anticipate combining work and family responsibilities in their future. High school seniors both preferred and expected to combine marriage, work, and children (Davey 1998), and in a four-year follow-up, three-quarters expected to work continuously—taking maternity leave rather than interrupt employment by staying out of the labor force through early child rearing (Davey 1998). College women, likewise, have a strong career orientation, but indicate they will seek jobs that provide time or flexibility for family needs (Morinaga, Frieze, and

Ferligoj 1993). Machung (1989) suggested that the expectations of young women were unrealistic given the multiple demands and lack of structures of social support to achieve a workable balance. In fact, a 2004 article in the *New York Times Magazine* focused on well-educated, high achieving women choosing to "drop out" of high demand careers in favor of caring for their families (Belkin 2003)—suggesting that some young women are realigning their expectations because of the difficulty in trying to manage the work/family balance. Indeed 2002 was the first year in which the labor force participation of married women with children, declined (by nearly 1 percent) in over 30 years (U.S. Census 2004–05).

There is some evidence, as well, that men are viewing work and family differently from the past. For example, Mince and Mahalik (1996) found men were less traditional in their attitudes about home and family and that role-sharing husbands were more likely to see their wives' interests as equal to their own.

The selections in this section address a number of issues that have emerged as families have sought a reasonable balance in the work/family arrangement. In the first article, Hochschild outlines the demands of the "second shift" experienced by most working women and the strains it imposes on marriage. Initially defined as a "women's problem," Hochschild concludes the second shift is a family problem; husbands suffer because their wives are overworked and overextended. Her analysis examines the mesh—or lack of mesh—between the way husbands and wives view their roles at home and at work as a key source of family tensions. She concludes that this tension is closely linked to men's participation in household work. The implications of this tension surrounding household responsibilities extend into issues of divorce and disinvestment in the family by both wives and husbands.

The second article, also by Hochschild, examines the pressures on dual-earner families that translate into the sense of not having "enough time," particularly for family obligations. That is, couples are in a "time bind." Parents, as she notes, seem to be putting in longer and longer hours at work. In investigating the work patterns of family members working at a company known for its "family friendly" policies, Hochschild learns about the supportive work context that seems to give relief and support from the work-like demands of the home. She suggests work is the preferred setting for a number of employees. In essence, work (the taskmaster) and home (the place of protection and relief from work) seem to have reversed their roles. The dilemma this creates for parents and partners highlight the strains on dual-earner couples, signaling the continued need for changes in social arrangements to find a workable balance between work and family.

In the third article, Stone and Lovejoy investigate the factors that influence the decision of high achieving women to leave their successful careers and become full-time stay-at-home moms. While some in the media have presented this as a "choice" to embrace traditional gender roles, Stone and Lovejoy seek to understand what factors come into play in making such a decision. Through interviews with 43 women who have left their careers to be at home full-time, they found that these women were caught between competing models of the ideal worker and the ideal parent. And while family concerns were important in their decision, work-based factors are the primary forces that influenced the decision to stay at home full-time. Husbands were an important, but secondary, factor. In the end, Stone and Lovejoy suggest that most of these women were faced with competing dilemmas that accumulated force and, after "weathering the storm" for a period of time, concluded it was best to move out of the labor force. It was usually not an easy decision, nor was it one that was ideologically anchored. Rather it was a strategy to resolve the "unrealistic expectations" to which Machung referred (1989).

In the fourth article, Blair-Loy and DeHart examine the family formation and career paths of African American female attorneys. African American female attorneys are a unique group of women who have overcome racial, gender, academic, and professional obstacles to achieve elite positions. Drawing on surveys of African American women who became lawyers in the 1950s, 1960s, and 1970s, they are able to examine the different career and family patterns corresponding with the different cohorts. The different historical/legal circumstances that corresponded with the different cohorts' entry into law also influenced career and family patterns. Blair-Loy and DeHart are able to assess whether family and marriage carry the additional "cost" of lower salaries and whether family formation and career launch patterns are similar for African American and white female attorneys. In doing so, the authors provide an informative analysis of the intersection of race with career and family patterns.

The final article in this section, by Gerson and Jacobs, reintroduces the question of Americans working longer hours and the consequences of this, particularly at a time when families are more dependent on the income that *both* parents earn. They note that while individuals work longer hours, the "time squeeze" is experienced by *families*. That squeeze is acutely felt by dual-earner families because two people are trying to manage full-time work hours along with family responsibilities. For dual-earner families, limited changes in the workplace has meant that mothers cut back on work time to be with children. At the same time, men face increasing pressures to work more because of increasingly competitive work environments. Single parent families—usually female-headed—are caught in such a time squeeze. Their earnings are likely to be lower so they must work as much as possible to support their families, but in doing so, family needs/time are likely to be compromised. Gerson and Jacobs argue that the competing pressures bring about a "time squeeze" that cannot be readily resolved through individual accommodation. Rather, adjustment must come at the level of the workplace. They discuss organizational adjustments that can ease the stress on families, noting that a number of these have been adopted in other modern societies. They propose workplace accommodations that could translate into fewer dilemmas for women who want to combine work with family, and into less of a "time squeeze" for families seeking to find a balance between work and family.

References

Aronson, J. 1992. "Women's sense of responsibility for the care of old people: 'But who else is going to do it?'" *Gender and Society*, 6: 8–20.

Belkin, Lisa. 2003. "The opt-out revolution." *The New York Times Magazine*, October 26: 42–47, 58, 85–86.

Bianchi, S. M., M. A. Milkie, L. C. Sayer, J. P. Robinson. 2000. "Is anyone doing the housework? Trends in the gender division of household labor." *Social Forces*, 79 (1): 191–228.

Davey, F. H. 1998. "Young women's expected and preferred patterns of employment and child care." *Sex Roles*, 38 (1/2): 95–102.

Feree, M. M. 1991. "Feminism and family research." In A. Booth (ed.), *Contemporary Families: Looking Forward, Looking Back*. Minneapolis: National Council of Family Relations: 103–121.

Finnigan, Annie. 2001. "The inside story: Are the 100 best as good as they say they are?" *Working Mother Magazine*. (October) WMAC, Inc.: *http://workingmother.com/oct_2001/inside_01.shtml*.

Hochschild, A. (with A. Machung). 1989. *The Second Shift*. New York: Viking Press.

Kunz Center for the Study of Work and Family. 1998. "Ohio wives still stuck with most of the housework, finds statewide survey by University of Cincinnati." June. *http://asweb.artsci.uc.edu/sociology/kunzctr/jun398.htm*.

LaRossa R., and L. Larossa. 1981. *Transition to Parenthood*. Beverly Hills, CA: Sage.

Machung, A. 1989. "Talking career, thinking job: Gender differences in careers and family expectations of Berkeley seniors." *Feminist Studies*, 15 (1): 35–58.

Mince, R. D., and J. R. Mahalik. 1996. "Gender role orientation and conflicts as predictors of family roles for men." *Sex Roles*, 34 (11–12) (June): 805–822.

Morinaga, Y., I. H. Frieze, and A. Ferligoj. 1993. "Career plans and gender role attitudes of college students in the U.S., Japan, and Slovinia." *Sex Roles*, 29 (5–6) (September): 317–335.

Thompson, L., and A. Walker. 1991. "Gender in families." In A. Booth (ed.), *Contemporary Families: Looking Forward, Looking Back*. Minneapolis: National Council on Family Relations: 275–296.

U. S. Department of Labor. 2000. *20 Facts on Women Workers*. Women's Bureau. March. *http://www.dol.gov/wb*.

U. S. Census Bureau. 2004–05. *Statistical Abstract of the United States*. Washington, DC.

Working Mother Magazine. 2001. "The 100 best companies for working mothers." (October) WMAC, Inc: *http://www.workingmother.com/oct_2001/100_best.shtml*. ✦

12
The Second Shift

Working Parents and the Revolution at Home

Arlie Russell Hochschild with Anne Machung

Chapter 1: A Speed-up in the Family

She is not the same woman in each magazine advertisement, but she is the same idea. She has that working-mother look as she strides forward, briefcase in one hand, smiling child in the other. Literally and figuratively, she is moving ahead. Her hair, if long, tosses behind her; if it is short, it sweeps back at the sides, suggesting mobility and progress. There is nothing shy or passive about her. She is confident, active, "liberated." She wears a dark tailored suit, but with a silk bow or colorful frill that says, "I'm really feminine underneath." She has made it in a man's world without sacrificing her femininity. And she has done this on her own. By some personal miracle, this image suggests, she has managed to combine what 150 years of industrialization have split wide apart—child and job, frill and suit, female culture and male.

When I showed a photograph of a supermom like this to the working mothers I talked to in the course of researching this book, many responded with an outright laugh. One daycare worker and mother of two, ages three and five, threw back her head: "Ha! They've got to be *kidding* about her. Look at me, hair a mess, nails jagged, twenty pounds overweight. Mornings, I'm getting my kids dressed, the dog fed, the lunches made, the shopping list done. That lady's got a maid." Even working mothers who did have maids couldn't imagine combining work and family in such a carefree way. "Do you know what a baby *does* to your life, the two o'clock feedings, the four o'clock feedings?" Another mother of two said: "They don't show it, but she's whistling"—she imitated a whistling woman, eyes to the sky—"so she can't hear the din." They envied the apparent ease of the woman with the flying hair, but she didn't remind them of anyone they knew.

The women I interviewed—lawyers, corporate executives, word processors, garment pattern cutters, daycare workers—and most of their husbands, too—felt differently about some issues: how right it is for a mother of young children to work a full-time job, or how much a husband should be responsible for the home. But they all agreed that it was hard to work two full-time jobs and raise young children.

How well do couples do it? The more women work outside the home, the more central this question. The number of women in paid work has risen steadily since before the turn of the century, but since 1950 the rise has been staggering. In 1950, 30 percent of American women were in the labor force; in 1986, it was 55 percent. In 1950, 28 percent of married women with children between six and seventeen worked outside the home; in 1986, it had risen to 68 percent. In 1950, 23 percent of married women with children under six worked. By 1986, it had grown to 54 percent. We don't know how many women with children under the age of one worked outside the home in 1950; it was so rare that the Bureau of Labor kept no statistics on it. Today half of such women do. Two-thirds of all mothers are now in the labor force; in fact, more mothers have paid jobs (or are actively looking for one) than non-mothers. Because of this change in women, two-job families now make up 58 percent of all married couples with children.[1]

Since an increasing number of working women have small children, we might expect an increase in part-time work. But actually, 67 percent of the mothers who work have full-time jobs—that is, thirty-five hours or more weekly. That proportion is what it was in 1959.

If more mothers of young children are stepping into full-time jobs outside the home, and if most couples can't afford household help, how much more are fathers doing at home?

As I began exploring this question I found many studies on the hours working men and women devote to housework and childcare. One national random sample of 1,243 working parents in forty-four American cities, conducted in 1965–66 by Alexander Szalai and his coworkers, for example, found that working women averaged three hours a day on housework while men averaged 17 minutes; women spent fifty minutes a day of time exclusively with their children; men spent twelve minutes. On the other side of the coin, working fathers watched television an hour longer than their working wives, and slept a half hour longer each night. A comparison of this American sample with eleven other industrial countries in Eastern and Western Europe revealed the same difference between working women and working men in those countries as well.[2] In a 1983 study of white middle-class families in greater Boston, Grace Baruch and R. C. Barnett found that working men married to working women spent only three-quarters of an hour longer each week with their kindergarten-aged children than did men married to housewives.[3]

Szalai's landmark study documented the now familiar but still alarming story of the working woman's "double day," but it left me wondering how men and women actually felt about all this. He and his coworkers studied how people used time, but not, say, how a father felt about his twelve minutes with his child, or how his wife felt about it. Szalai's study revealed the visible surface of what I discovered to be a set of deeply emotional issues: What should a man and woman contribute to the family? How appreciated does each feel? How does each respond to subtle changes in the balance of marital power? How does each develop an unconscious "gender strategy" for coping with the work at home, with marriage, and, indeed, with life itself? These were the underlying issues.

But I began with the measurable issue of time. Adding together the time it takes to do a paid job and to do housework and childcare, I averaged estimates from the major studies on time use done in the 1960s and 1970s, and discovered that women worked roughly fifteen hours longer each week than men. Over

a year, they worked an extra month of twenty-four-hour days a year. Over a dozen years, it was an extra year of twenty-four-hour days. Most women without children spend much more time than men on housework; with children, they devote more time to both housework and childcare. Just as there is a wage gap between men and women in the workplace, there is a "leisure gap" between them at home. Most women work one shift at the office or factory and a "second shift" at home.

Studies show that working mothers have higher self-esteem and get less depressed than housewives, but compared to their husbands, they're more tired and get sick more often. In Peggy Thoits's 1985 analysis of two large-scale surveys, each of about a thousand men and women, people were asked how often in the preceding week they'd experienced each of twenty-three symptoms of anxiety (such as dizziness or hallucinations). According to the researchers' criteria, working mothers were more likely than any other group to be "anxious."

In light of these studies, the image of the women with the flying hair seems like an upbeat "cover" for a grim reality, like those pictures of Soviet tractor drivers smiling radiantly into the distance as they think about the ten-year plan. The Szalai study was conducted in 1965–66. I wanted to know whether the leisure gap he found in 1965 persists, or whether it has disappeared. Since most married couples work two jobs, since more will in the future, since most wives in these couples work the extra month a year, I wanted to understand what the wife's extra month a year meant for each person, and what it does for love and marriage in an age of high divorce. . . .

Inside the Extra Month a Year

The women I interviewed seemed to be far more deeply torn between the demands of work and family than were their husbands. They talked with more animation and at greater length than their husbands about the abiding conflict between them. Busy as they were, women more often brightened at the idea of yet another interviewing session. They felt the second shift was *their* issue and most of their husbands agreed. When I telephoned one husband to arrange an interview with him, explaining that I wanted to ask him about how he managed work and family life, he replied genially, "Oh, this will *really* interest my *wife*."

It was a woman who first proposed to me the metaphor, borrowed from industrial life, of the "second shift." She strongly resisted the *idea* that homemaking was a "shift." Her family was her life and she didn't want it reduced to a job. But as she put it, "You're on duty at work. You come home, and you're on duty. Then you go back to work and you're on duty." After eight hours of adjusting insurance claims, she came home to put on the rice for dinner, care for her children, and wash laundry. Despite herself her home life *felt* like a second shift. That was the real story and that was the real problem.

Men who shared the load at home seemed just as pressed for time as their wives, and as torn between the demands of career and small children. . . . But the majority of men did not share the load at home. Some refused outright. Others refused more passively, often offering a loving shoulder to lean on, an understanding ear as their working wife faced the conflict they both saw as hers. At first it seemed to me that the problem of the second shift was hers. But I came to realize that those husbands who helped very little at home were often indirectly just as deeply affected as their wives by the need to do that work, through the resentment their wives feel toward them, and through their need to steel themselves against that resentment. Evan Holt, a warehouse furniture salesman . . . did very little housework and played with his four-year-old son, Joey, at his convenience. Juggling the demands of work with family at first seemed a problem for his wife. But Evan himself suffered enormously from the side effects of "her" problem. His wife did the second shift, but she resented it keenly, and half-consciously expressed her frustration and rage by losing interest in sex and becoming overly absorbed with Joey. One way or another, most men I talked with do suffer the severe repercussions of what I think is a transitional phase in American family life.

One reason women take a deeper interest than men in the problems of juggling work with family life is that even when husbands happily shared the hours of work, their wives felt more responsible for home and children. More women kept track of doctors' appointments and arranged for playmates to come over. More mothers than fathers worried about the tail on a child's Halloween costume or a birthday present for a school friend. They were more likely to think about their children while at work and to check in by phone with the baby-sitter.

Partly because of this, more women felt torn between one sense of urgency and another, between the need to soothe a child's fear of being left at daycare, and the need to show the boss she's "serious" at work. More women than men questioned how good they were as parents, or if they did not, they questioned why they weren't questioning it. More often than men, women alternated between living in their ambition and standing apart from it.

As masses of women have moved into the economy, families have been hit by a "speed-up" in work and family life. There is no more time in the day than there was when wives stayed home, but there is twice as much to get done. It is mainly women who absorb this "speed-up." Twenty percent of the men in my study shared housework equally. Seventy percent of men did a substantial amount (less than half but more than a third), and 10 percent did less than a third. Even when couples share more equitably in the work at home, women do two-thirds of the *daily* jobs at home, like cooking and cleaning up—jobs that fix them into a rigid routine. Most women cook dinner and most men change the oil in the family car. But, as one mother pointed out, dinner needs to be prepared every evening around six o'clock, whereas the car oil needs to be changed every six months, any day around that time, any time that day. Women do more childcare than men, and men repair more household appliances. A child needs to be tended daily while the repair of household appliances can often wait "until I have time." Men thus have more control over *when* they make their contributions than women do. They may be very busy with family chores but, like the executive who tells his secretary to "hold my calls," the man has more control over his time. The job of the working mother, like that of the secretary, is usually to "take the calls."

Another reason women may feel more strained than men is that women more often do two things at once—for example, write checks and return phone calls, vacuum and keep an eye on a three-year-old, fold laundry and think out the shopping list. Men often cook dinner or take a child to the park. Indeed, women more often juggle three spheres—job, children, and housework—while most men juggle two—job and children. For women, two activities compete with their time with children, not just one.

Beyond doing more at home, women also devote proportionately more of their time at home to housework and *proportionately* less of it to childcare. Of all the time men spend working at home, more of it goes to childcare. That is, working wives spend relatively more time "mothering the house"; husbands spend more time "mothering" the children. Since most parents prefer to tend to their children than clean house, men do more of what they'd rather do. More men than women take their children on "fun" outings to the park, the zoo, the movies. Women spend more time on maintenance, feeding and bathing children, enjoyable activities to be sure, but often less leisurely or "special" than going to the zoo. Men also do fewer of the "undesirable" household chores: fewer men than women wash toilets and scrub the bathroom.

As a result, women tend to talk more intently about being overtired, sick, and "emotionally drained." Many women I could not tear away from the topic of sleep. They talked about how much they could "get by on" . . . six and a half, seven, seven and a half, less, more. They talked about who they knew who needed more or less. Some apologized for how much sleep they needed—"I'm afraid I need eight hours of sleep"—as if eight was "too much." They talked about the effect of a change in baby-sitter, the birth of a second child, or a business trip on their child's pattern of sleep. They talked about how to avoid fully waking up when a child

called them at night, and how to get back to sleep. These women talked about sleep the way a hungry person talks about food.

All in all, if in this period of American history, the two-job family is suffering from a speed-up of work and family life, working mothers are its primary victims. . . . When a bath is crammed into a slot between 7:45 and 8:00 it was often the mother who called out, "Let's see who can take their bath the quickest!" Often a younger child will rush out, scurrying to be first in bed, while the older and wiser one stalls, resistant, sometimes resentful: "Mother is always rushing us." Sadly enough, women are more often the lightning rods for family aggressions aroused by the speed-up of work and family life. They are the "villains" in a process of which they are also the primary victims. More than the longer hours, the sleeplessness, and feeling torn, this is the saddest cost to women of the extra month a year. . . .

Chapter 2: Marriage in the Stalled Revolution

Each marriage bears the footprints of economic and cultural trends which originate far outside marriage. A rise in inflation which erodes the earning power of the male wage, an expanding service sector which opens up jobs for women, new cultural images—like the woman with the flying hair—that make the working mother seem exciting, all these changes do not simply go on *around* marriage. They occur *within* marriage, and transform it. Problems between husbands and wives, problems which seem "individual" and "marital," are often individual experiences of powerful economic and cultural shock waves that are not caused by one person or two. Quarrels that erupt . . . result mainly from a friction between faster-changing women and slower-changing men, rates of change which themselves result from the different rates at which the industrial economy has drawn men and women into itself.

There is a "his" and "hers" to the economic development of the United States. In the latter part of the nineteenth century, it was mainly men who were drawn off the farm into paid, industrial work and who changed their way of life and their identity. At that point in history, men became more different from their fathers than women became from their mothers. Today the economic arrow points at women; it is women who are being drawn into wage work, and women who are undergoing changes in their way of life and identity. Women are departing more from their mothers' and grandmothers' way of life, men are doing so less.

Both the earlier entrance of men into the industrial economy and the later entrance of women have influenced the relations *between* men and women, especially their relations within marriage. The former increase in the number of men in industrial work tended to increase the power of men, and the present growth in the number of women in such work has somewhat increased the power of women. On the whole, the entrance of men into industrial work did not destabilize the family whereas *in the absence of other change,* the rise in female employment has gone with the rise in divorce. . . .

The exodus of women into the economy has not been accompanied by a cultural understanding of marriage and work that would make this transition smooth. The workforce has changed. Women have changed. But most workplaces have remained inflexible in the face of the family demands of their workers and at home, most men have yet to really adapt to the changes in women. This strain between the change in women and the absence of change in much else leads me to speak of a "stalled revolution."

A society which did not suffer from this stall would be a society *humanely* adapted to the fact that most women work outside the home. The workplace would allow parents to work part time, to share jobs, to work flexible hours, to take parental leaves to give birth, tend a sick child, or care for a well one. As Delores Hayden has envisioned in *Redesigning the American Dream,* it would include affordable housing closer to places of work, and perhaps community-based meal and laundry services. It would include men whose notion of manhood encouraged them to be active parents and share at home. In contrast, a stalled revolution lacks social arrangements that ease life for working parents, and lacks men who share the second shift.

If women begin to do less at home because they have less time, if men do little more, if the work of raising children and tending a home requires roughly the same effort, then the questions of who does what at home and of what "needs doing" become key. Indeed, they may become a source of deep tension in the marriage. . . .

As I drove from my classes at Berkeley to the outreaching suburbs, small towns, and inner cities of the San Francisco Bay to observe and ask questions in the homes of two-job couples, and back to my own two-job marriage, my first question about who does what gave way to a series of deeper questions: What leads some working mothers to do all the work at home themselves—to pursue what I call a supermom strategy—and what leads others to press their husbands to share the responsibility and work of the home? Why do some men genuinely want to share housework and childcare, others fatalistically acquiesce, and still others actively resist?

When I sat down to compare one couple that shared the second shift with another three that didn't, many of the answers that would seem obvious—a man's greater income, his longer hours of work, the fact that his mother was a housewife or his father did little at home, his ideas about men and women—all these factors didn't really explain why some women work the extra month a year and others don't. They didn't explain why some women seemed content to work the extra month, while others were deeply unhappy about it. When I compared a couple who was sharing and happy with another couple who was sharing but miserable, it was clear that purely economic or psychological answers were not enough. . . . I felt the need to explore what I call loosely "gender strategies."

The Top and Bottom of Gender Ideology

A gender strategy is a plan of action through which a person tries to solve problems at hand, given the cultural notions of gender at play. To pursue a gender strategy, a man draws on beliefs of manhood and womanhood, beliefs that are forged in early childhood and thus anchored to deep emotions. He makes a connection between how he thinks about his manhood, what he feels about it, and what he does. It works in the same way for a woman.

A woman's gender ideology determines what sphere she *wants* to identify with (home or work) and how much power in the marriage she wants to have (less, more, or the same amount). I found three types of ideology of marital roles: traditional, transitional, and egalitarian. Even though she works, the "pure" traditional wants to identify with her activities at home (as a wife, a mother, a neighborhood mom), wants her husband to base his at work and wants less power than he. The traditional man wants the same. The "pure" egalitarian, as the type emerges here, wants to identify with the same spheres her husband does, and to have an equal amount of power in the marriage. Some want the couple to be jointly oriented to the home, others to their careers, or both of them to jointly hold some balance between the two. Between the traditional and the egalitarian is the transitional, any one of a variety of types of blending of the two. But, in contrast to the traditional, a transitional woman wants to identify with her role at work as well as at home. Unlike the egalitarian, she believes her husband should base his identity more on work than she does. A typical transitional *wants* to identify both with the caring for the home, and with helping her husband earn money, but wants her husband to focus on earning a living. A typical transitional man is all for his wife working, but expects her to take the main responsibility at home too. Most men and women I talked with were "transitional." At least, transitional ideas came out when I asked people directly what they believed.

Gender strategies. When a man tries to apply his gender ideology to the situations that face him in real life, unconsciously or not he pursues a gender strategy.[4] He outlines a course of action. He might become a "superdad"—working long hours and keeping his child up late at night to spend time with him or her. Or he might cut back his hours at work. Or he might cut back housework and spend less time with his children.

Or he might actively try to share the second shift.

The term "strategy" refers both to his plan of action and to his emotional preparations for pursuing it. For example, he may require himself to suppress his career ambitions to devote himself more to his children, or suppress his responsiveness to his children's appeals in the course of steeling himself for the struggle at work. He might harden himself to his wife's appeals, or he might be the one in the family who "lets" himself see when a child is calling out for help.

As this social revolution proceeds, the problems of the two-job family will not diminish. If anything, as more couples work two jobs these problems will increase. If we can't return to traditional marriage, and if we are not to despair of marriage altogether, it becomes vitally important to understand marriage as a magnet for the strains of the stalled revolution, and to understand gender strategies as the basic dynamic of marriage.

The Economy of Gratitude

The interplay between a man's gender ideology and a woman's implies a deeper interplay between his gratitude toward her, and hers toward him. For how a person wants to identify himself or herself influences what, in the back and forth of a marriage, will seem like a gift and what will not. If a man doesn't think it fits the kind of "man" he wants to be to have his wife earn more than he, it may become his "gift" to her to "bear it" anyway. But a man may also feel like the husband I interviewed, who said, "When my wife began earning more than me I thought I'd struck gold!" In this case his wife's salary is the gift, not his capacity to accept it "anyway." When couples struggle, it is seldom simply over who does what. Far more often, it is over the giving and receiving of gratitude. . . .

Chapter 14: Tensions in Marriage in an Age of Divorce

The two-job marriages I came to know seemed vulnerable to three types of tension. One tension was between the husband's idea of what he and his wife should do at home and work, and his wife's idea about that. This was the tension between couples whose gender strategies clashed. . . . Another existed within each person in the marriage; this was the tension between a keen desire to live an old-fashioned life—with the wife at home, the husband working—and the need to face economic hardships that made such a life impossible. . . . The third tension is more invisible, nameless, and serious: that between the importance of a family's *need* for care and the *devaluation* of the work it takes to give that care, a devaluation of the work a homemaker once did. This problem was most pronounced among upper-middle-class couples engrossed in their careers.

One Behind, One Ahead: Couples Who Clash

Two-thirds of couples in this study, most of them married for seven to ten years, shared a gender ideology. Two-thirds were *both* traditional, *both* transitional, or *both* egalitarian. But a third of the couples I talked to had important differences of feeling—especially about who should do how much work at home. (And note that couples who disagree violently don't appear in a study like mine of married couples since I eliminated couples who were currently divorced before I began.) . . .

These marital clashes reflect a broader social tension—between *faster-changing women and slower-changing men*. Because changing economic opportunities and needs influence women more powerfully than men, women differ more from their mothers than men differ from their fathers. The "female culture" has shifted more rapidly than the "male culture"; the image of the go-get-'em woman has yet to be fully matched by the image of the let's-take-care-of-the-kids-together man. More important, over the last thirty years, men's underlying feelings about taking responsibility at home have changed much less than women's feelings have changed about forging some kind of identity at work.

Perhaps because couples with dramatic schisms have been purged from the group by divorce, the "remaining" marriages I saw of this type were usually not between a man who disapproved of his wife's working and a woman who worked. They were marriages between men who were happy their wives worked but wanted them to take care of most matters at home and women who wanted more help at home.

Whether they had to or not, these wives wanted to work. Many professionally trained wives worked because they felt their work was challenging, enjoyable, or worthwhile. But even women in low level service jobs felt work gave them respect in the eyes of others, including their husband.

Tensions that arose between couples with clashing strategies often showed up in each partner's sense that he or she wasn't getting credit or appreciation for all he or she was doing, that the other wasn't grateful enough. The exchange of appreciation in these marriages became a sort of "dead letter office," thanks sent to the "wrong address." The question became: Where is my thanks? The big gift Jessica Stein offered Seth was to give up working full time. For Seth, the big gift was to give up leisure to work overtime. Their problem was not, I think, that they could not give. It was that, given their gender ideals, Seth wanted to "give" at the office, and Jessica wanted to "receive" at home—to have Seth play catch with their younger son, play piano with the older one, while she escaped to "catch up" on her career. A gift in the eyes of one was not a gift in the eyes of the other. Each felt "taken advantage of" because they differed so drastically in their frames of reference, their expectations, and ultimately in their gender strategies. In the end, each was left with a thin pile of thank-you notes. If measured not in years but in gifts exchanged, their marriage had quietly ended some time ago.

Countless other self-sacrifices—following a spouse to another city, looking after the ill parents of a spouse, paying the college tuition of a stepchild, doing with less money all around—takes on value only as they're seen through a person's cultural viewpoint, which includes his or her views about gender. Ray Judson wanted to offer Anita "the privilege of staying home." Anita couldn't accept. Peter Tanagawa wanted to offer his wife, Nina, the same. Nina appreciated the offer but not as much as Peter would have liked. Nancy Holt wanted to offer Evan the benefits of her work, her salary, participation in her work friendships, any status that might rub off, dubious rewards to Evan. It is through the different appraisals of such "gifts" that the major social revolution of our time enters the private moments that make a marriage.

The Tension of Being 'Behind the Times'

Even if this first tension between faster-changing women and slower-changing men is resolved, a second one may remain. There were families like the Delacortes whose ideas were "behind the times" in the sense that their ideals were more suited to the economic realities of the past. Both agreed on what each should do at home, and on who deserved credit for what. They had the same "exchange rate" in their marital economy of gratitude. The strain they felt was due to a clash between a traditional ideal and a thin pocketbook: the one ill-suited the other. I found this pattern more common among working-class than middle-class couples.

Their traditionalism did not mean that husbands shirked the second shift. Traditional men did slightly more at home than most transitional men. This was partly because they felt guilty they could not be the sole provider. Some husbands also cared for the house because their wives worked a different shift and they were the only one home. Traditionalism didn't stop such men from helping; it only meant they *didn't feel good* about it, that it counted as more of a favor.

The tension for traditional defenders, then, was not the second shift itself—except that they had as much trouble as anyone getting it all done. The problem was that traditional husbands hated the fact that their wives worked. And a few traditional wives felt pushed into working and hated it. Some didn't feel it was right to blame their husbands, but at the same time clung to their "right" to stay home. Like Carmen, most women tried not to "complain." But in this very effort, they were managing a conflict between their ideals—of separate sexual spheres and male rule—and the reality of their lives.

These wives wanted to seem more different and unequal than they in fact were. . . .

Women Who Become Like Traditional Men and Traditional Men Who Stay As They Are

Couples who are not affected by the first two sources of tension can still be vulnerable to a third—the assimilation of women to the values of the dominant male culture. I have focused a great deal on how much working fathers have been able to cross the "gender divide" and pitch in with work their mothers used to do at home. But the more troubling trend moves in the opposite direction. Women may be pitching in at the office with the work their *fathers* used to do, while no one does much at home. Men and women may gradually come to share the work at home more equitably, but now they may be doing altogether less of it. The latent deal between husband and wife is "I'll share, but we'll do less." A strategy of "cutting back" on the housework, the children, the marriage may be on the rise, with correspondingly reduced ideas about what people "need."

Among egalitarian couples who shared the work at home, some couples were oriented primarily toward work, both playing the "father role." Others were more oriented toward the family, both playing the "mother." The first were cutting back equally on family life; the second were cutting back equally on career.

Middle-class couples who put family first often felt at odds with the "commitment norm" in their careers, as did Adrienne and Michael Sherman. . . . Adrienne struggled against her chairman's definition of success, Michael with the hopes of his proud parents and the priorities of his colleagues. Both struggled with their own desire to make scientific discoveries and write great books. They tried to live "balanced" lives, to avoid both being "father."

Other couples, however, seemed to capitulate to a workaholism à deux, each spouse equitably granting the other the right to work long hours, and reconciling themselves to a drastically reduced conception of the emotional needs of a family. One thirty-seven-year-old woman lawyer, married to another lawyer, each of whom was trying to make partner in different firms, commented:

Our careers are important to us. Before we had children, we could work hard and play some too. We used to go out a lot together, sometimes to a different movie every night. We bicycled weekends. But when our practices got up to fifty-five hours a week and Kevin was born, we went into a stage of siege. No one tells you how a child turns your life around. For a while, there we were, just surviving, very little sleep, no sex, little talk, delight in Kevin and adrenaline. We just say hello in bed before dropping off. We're still doing this.

Although they were still doing this, it felt odd; it hadn't become normal.

To others, such a life seemed normal. For example, a thirty-two-year-old accountant married his wife with the understanding that the house "didn't matter," they could eat out, cater parties, and engage a "wonderful nanny" for the children. They were egalitarian in the limited sense that they equitably shared an aversion to anything domestic. Since the "wonderful nanny" tended the children, cleaned house, and cooked meals, this man and woman had little of the second shift to share. They had almost totally parceled out the role of mother into purchased services.

In their single-minded attention to career, these couples also focused less than others on their children. Their homes were neater; there were fewer paintings stuck to the refrigerator door, fewer toys in the hallway. The decor in the living and dining rooms was more often beige or white. The space where the children played was more clearly separated from the rest of the house. . . .

Each source of marital tension has a link back to male participation in the second shift. In the first group of marriages . . . tension focused on a clash between the husband's view of his role at home and his wife's. In the second group of marriages . . . the tension centered on finding an acceptable way for a man to do a woman's work. In the third group of marriages, the tension centered on the gap between the care a family needs to thrive and the devaluation of the work of caring for it.

The first tension could be resolved if the [husbands] of the world shared the second shift. The second tension could be resolved if the [husbands] could earn enough so the [wives] could stay home. (If husbands wanted to stay home with their children, it would resolve an as yet largely hypothetical tension, if their wives could earn enough to support them in doing so.) But these would be hollow victories indeed, if the work of raising a family becomes devalued because women have become equal to men on traditionally male terms.

Divorce and the Second Shift

Over the last thirty years in the United States, more women have gone out to work, and more have divorced. According to the sociologist William Goode, working women have a higher divorce rate than housewives in the Soviet Union, Germany, Sweden, and France. Indeed, in France, working women have twice the divorce rate of housewives. Some commentators therefore conclude that women's work *causes* divorce. As evidence of this, a recent national survey conducted by Joseph Pleck and Graham Staines found that working wives were more likely than housewives to say they wished they had married someone else and more likely to have considered divorce. But people who conclude that it is women's work that causes divorce look only at what the *women*, one-half of the couples, are doing—earning money, feeling more independent, thinking better of themselves, expecting more of men.[5]

My research suggests something else. Since *all* the wives I studied worked outside the home, the fact that they worked did not account for why some marriages were happy and others were not. What did contribute to happiness was the husband's willingness to do the work at home. Sharing the second shift improved a marriage *regardless* of what ideas either had about men's and women's roles. Whether they were traditional or egalitarian, couples were happier when the men did more housework and childcare. A national study of over a thousand married couples conducted by Ronald Kessler and James McRae also found that working wives suffered less distress if their husbands helped with the home and children.[6]

In one 1978 study, Joan Huber and Glenna Spitze asked 1,360 husbands and wives:

"Has the thought of getting a divorce from your husband (or wife) ever crossed your mind?" They found that more wives than husbands had thought about divorce (30 percent versus 22 percent) and that wives thought about it more often. How much each one earned had no effect on a spouse's thought of divorce. Nor did attitudes toward the roles of men and women. But the more housework a wife saw her husband do, the less likely she was to think of divorce. . . .

. . . Happy marriage is supported by a couple's being economically secure, by their enjoying a supportive community, and by their having compatible needs and values. But these days it may also depend more on sharing a value on the work it takes to nurture others. As the role of the homemaker is being vacated by many women, the homemaker's work has been devalued and passed on to low-paid housekeepers, baby-sitters, and daycare workers. Like an ethnic culture in danger of being swallowed up by the culture of the dominant group, the contribution of the traditional homemaker has been devalued first by men and now by more women.

In the era of a stalled revolution, one way to reverse this devaluation is for men to share in that devalued work, and thereby help to revalue it. Many working mothers are already doing all they can at home. Now it's time for men to make the move. In an age of divorce, marriage itself can be at stake.

Notes

1. U.S. Bureau of Labor Statistics, *Employment and Earnings, Characteristics of Families: First Quarter* (Washington, D.C.: U.S. Department of Labor, 1988).

2. Alexander Szalai, ed., *The Use of Time; Daily Activities of Urban and Suburban Populations in Twelve Countries* (the Hague: Mouton, 1972), p. 668, Table B. Another study found that men spent a longer time than women eating meals (Shelley Coverman, "Gender, Domestic Labor Time and Wage Inequality," *American Sociological Review* 48 [1983]:626). With regard to sleep, the pattern differs for men and women. The higher the social class of a man the more sleep he's likely to get. The higher the class of a woman, the less sleep

she's likely to get. Upper-white-collar men average 7.6 hours sleep a night. Lower-white-collar, skilled and unskilled men all averaged 7.3 hours. Upper-white-collar women average 7.1 hours of sleep; lower-white-collar workers average 7.4; skilled workers 7.0 and unskilled workers 8.1. Working wives seem to meet the demands of high-pressure careers by reducing sleep, whereas working husbands don't. For more details on the hours working men and women devote to housework and childcare, see the Appendix of *The Second Shift*.

3. Grace K. Baruch and Rosalind Barnett, "Correlates of Fathers' Participation in Family Work: A Technical Report," Working Paper no. 106 (Wellesley, Mass.: Wellesley College Center for Research on Women, 1983), pp. 80–81. Also see Kathryn E. Walker and Margaret E. Woods, *Time Use: A Measure of Household Production of Goods and Services* (Washington, D.C.: American Home Economics Association, 1976).

4. The concept of "gender strategy" is an adaptation of Ann Swidler's notion of "strategies of action." In "Culture in Action—Symbols and Strategies," *American Sociological Review* 51 (1986): 273–86, Swidler focuses on how the individual uses aspects of culture (symbols, rituals, stories) as "tools" for constructing a line of action. Here, I focus on aspects of culture that bear on our ideas of manhood and womanhood, and I focus on our emotional preparation for and the emotional consequences of our strategies.

5. See William J. Goode, "Family Disorganization," Chapter 11 in *Contemporary Social Problems*, 4th ed., Robert K. Merton and Robert Nisbet (eds.) (New York: Harcourt Brace Jovanovich, 1976). Also see Louis Roussle, *Le Divorce et les Francais*, Vol. II, "L'Experience des Divorces," Tranvautet Documents, Cahier No. 72 (Presses Universitaires de France, 1975), pp. 26–29. In many ways, the fact that wives work both benefits and stabilizes marriage. In virtually all the research on women's work, working women report themselves as happier, higher in self-esteem, and in better mental and physical health than do housewives. See Lois Hoffman and F. I. Nye, *Working Mothers* (San Francisco: Jossey Bass, 1974), p. 209. A woman's work also adds money to a marriage through the so-called dowry effect. By making a family richer, a woman's wages may protect the family from the strains of poverty associated with marital disruption. See Valerie Kincade Oppenheimer, "The Sociology of Women's Economic

Role in the Family," *American Sociological Review* 42 (1977): 387–405. D. T. Hall and F. E. Gordon, "Career Choices of Married Women," *Journal of Applied Psychology* 58 (1973): 42–48.

6. Ronald C. Kessler and James McRae, *Institute for Social Research Newsletter,* University of Michigan, 1978. See also S. S. Feldman, S. C. Nash, and B. G. Aschenbrenner, "Antecedents of Fathering," *Child Development* 54 (1983): 1628–36; M. W. Yogman, "Competence and Performance of Fathers and Infants," in A. Macfarlane, ed., *Progress in Child Health* (London: Churchill Livingston, 1983).

Food for Thought and Application Questions

1. What is the "second shift" and what does it have to do with the "stalled revolution?" Discuss the interplay between the two and their manifestation in the lives of working couples. Consider ways in which the "second shift" can be reduced for women.

2. Using the concept of the "economy of gratitude," develop a list of "traditionally wife" and "traditionally husband" tasks around the home. Assess who expects "gratitude" for doing the other's tasks. Based on your list, discuss the equality or inequality of gaining gratitude between husbands and wives. Discuss the implications of your assessment. ✦

13
The Time Bind

Arlie Russell Hochschild

An Angel of an Idea

Almost from the beginning of my stay in Spotted Deer, I could tell that the family-friendly reforms introduced with so much fanfare in 1985 were finding a curious reception. Three things seemed true. First, Amerco's workers declared on survey after survey that they were strained to the limit. Second, the company offered them policies that would allow them to cut back. Third, almost no one cut back. . . . Programs that allowed parents to work undistracted by family concerns were endlessly in demand, while policies offering shorter hours that allowed workers more free or family time languished.

To try to make sense of this paradox I began, first of all, to scrutinize the text of the policy and the results of employee surveys. Amerco defines a part-time job as one that requires thirty-five hours or less, with full or prorated benefits. A job share is a full-time position shared by two people with benefits and salary prorated. As with all attempts to change work schedules, I learned, the worker has to get the permission of a supervisor, a division head, or both. In addition, workers under union contract—a full half of Amerco's workforce including factory hands and maintenance crews—were not eligible for policies offering shorter or more flexible hours. But I discovered that among eligible employees with children thirteen and under, only 3 percent worked part time. In fact, in 1990, only 53 out of Amerco's 21,070 employees in the United States, less than one-quarter of 1 percent of its workforce, were part-timers, and less than 1 percent of Amerco's employees shared a job.

Amerco also offered its employees a program called "flexplace," which allowed work-

ers to do their work from home or some other place. One percent of employees used it. Likewise, under certain circumstances, an employee could take a temporary leave from full-time work. The standard paid parental leave for a new mother was six weeks (to be divided with the father as the couple wished). If permission was granted, a parent could then return to work part time with full benefits, to be arranged at his or her supervisor's discretion. Most new mothers took the paid weeks off, and sometimes several months more of unpaid leave, but then returned to their full-time schedules. Almost no Amerco fathers took advantage of parental leave, and no Amerco father has ever responded to the arrival of a new baby in the family by taking up a part-time work schedule.

By contrast, "flextime," a policy allowing workers to come and go early or late, or to be in other ways flexible about when they do their work, was quite popular. By 1993, a quarter of all workers—and a third of working parents—used it. In other words, of Amerco's family-friendly policies only flextime, which rearranged but did not cut back on hours of work, had any significant impact on the workplace. According to one survey, 99 percent of Amerco employees worked full time, and full-time employees averaged forty-seven hours a week. As I looked more closely at the figures I discovered some surprising things. Workers with young children actually put in more hours at work as those without children. Although a third of all parents had flexible schedules, 56 percent of employees with children regularly worked on weekends. Seventy-two percent of parents regularly worked overtime; unionized hourly workers were paid for this time (though much of their overtime was required), while salaried workers weren't. In fact, during the years I was studying Amerco, parents and nonparents alike began to work longer hours. By 1993, virtually everyone I spoke with told me they were working longer hours than they had only a few years earlier, and most agreed that Amerco was "a pretty workaholic place."

As Amerco' s experience would suggest, American working parents seem to be putting in longer and longer hours. Of workers with children aged twelve and under, only 4 percent of men, and 13 percent of women, worked less than forty hours a week.[1] According to a study by Arthur Emlen of Portland State University, whether or not a worker has a child makes remarkably little difference to his or her attendance record at work. Excluding vacation and holidays, the average employee misses nine days of work a year. The average parent of a child who is left home alone on weekdays misses fourteen and a half days a year: only five and a half days more. Fathers with young children only miss half a day more a year than fathers without children.[2]

The idea of more time for family life seems to have died, gone to heaven, and become an angel of an idea. But why? Why don't working parents, and others too, take the opportunity available to them to reduce their hours at work?

The most widely accepted explanation is that working parents simply can't afford to work shorter hours. With the median income of U.S. households in 1996 at $32,264, it is true that many workers could not pay their rent and food bills on three-quarters or half of their salaries. But notwithstanding the financial and time pressures most parents face, why do the majority not even take all of the paid vacation days due to them? Even more puzzling, why are the best-paid employees—upper-level managers and professionals—among the least interested in part-time work or job sharing?. . .

Again, if income alone determined how often or how long mothers stayed home after the birth of their babies, we would expect poorer mothers to go back to work more quickly, and richer mothers to spend more time at home. But that's not what we find. Nationwide, well-to-do new mothers are not significantly more likely to stay home with a new baby than low-income new mothers. A quarter of poor new mothers in one study returned to work after three months, but so did a third of well-to-do new mothers. . . .

In a 1995 national study, 48 percent of American working women and 61 percent of men claimed they would still want to work even if they had enough money to live as "comfortably as you would like."[3] When

asked what was "very important" to their decision to take their current job, only 35 percent of respondents in one national study said "salary/wage," whereas 55 percent mentioned "gaining new skills" as very important, and 60 percent mentioned "effect on personal/family life."[4] Money matters, of course, but other things do too.

According to a second commonly believed explanation, workers extend their hours . . . because they are afraid of being laid off. They're working scared. By fostering a climate of fear, the argument goes, many companies take away with one hand the helpful policies they lightly offer with the other.

Downsizing is a serious problem in American companies in the 1990s but there's scant evidence that employees at Amerco were working scared. During the late 1980s and early 1990s, there was very little talk of layoffs. When I asked employees whether they worked long hours because they were afraid of getting on a layoff list, virtually everyone said no. . . .

One possible explanation is that workers interested in and eligible for flexible or shorter hours don't know they can get them. . . . Yet on closer inspection, this proved not to be the case. According to a 1990 survey, most Amerco workers were aware of company policies on flextime and leaves. Women were better informed than men, and higher-level workers more so than lower-level workers. The vast majority of people I talked with knew that the company offered "good" policies and were proud to be working for such a generous company. . . .

Beyond this, studies well known to Amerco management have demonstrated the costs of not instituting such policies—in increased absenteeism and tardiness, and lowered productivity. A 1987 study conducted by the National Council for Jewish Women found that women working for family-friendly companies were sick less often, worked more on their own time, worked later into their pregnancies, and were more likely to return to work after a birth.[5] Moreover, the study found that workers who took advantage of family-friendly policies were among the best performers, and the least likely to have disciplinary problems. All in all, there is no proof that flexible hours are not in a company's long-term interest, and substantial evidence that they are. It seems that Amerco would stand to benefit by having at least some workers use its family-friendly policies.

Family Values and Reversed Worlds

If working parents are "deciding" to work full time and longer, what experiences at home and work might be influencing them to do so? When I first began the research for this book, I assumed that home was "home" and work was "work"—that each was a stationary rock beneath the moving feet of working parents. . . . However difficult family life may be at times, we usually feel family ties offer an irreplaceable connection to generations past and future. Family is our personal embrace with history.

Jobs, on the other hand, earn money that, to most of us, serves as the means to other ends. To be sure, jobs can also allow us to develop skills or friendships, and to be part of a larger work community. But we seldom envision the workplace as somewhere workers would freely choose to spend their time. If in the American imagination the family has a touch of the sacred, the realm of work seems profane. . . .

If the purpose and nature of family and work differ so drastically in our minds, it seemed reasonable to assume that people's emotional experiences of the two spheres would differ profoundly, too. In *Haven in a Heartless World*, the social historian Christopher Lasch drew a picture of family as a "haven" where workers sought refuge from the cruel world of work.[6] . . . Whatever its strains, home is where he's relaxed, most himself. At home, he feels that people know him, understand him, appreciate him for who he really is. At home, he is safe.

At work, our worker is "on call," ready to report at a moment's notice, working flat out to get back to the customer right away. He feels "like a number." If he doesn't watch out, he can take the fall for somebody else's mistakes. This, then, is Lasch's "heartless world," an image best captured long ago in Charlie Chaplin's satirical *Modern Times*. . . .

It was just such images of home and work that were challenged in one of my first interviews at Amerco. Linda Avery, a friendly thirty-eight-year-old mother of two daughters, is a shift supervisor at the Demco Plant, ten miles down the valley from Amerco headquarters. Her husband, Bill, is a technician in the same plant. Linda and Bill share the care of her sixteen-year-old daughter from a previous marriage and their two-year-old by working opposite shifts. . . .

When we first met . . . [s]he wore no makeup, and her manner was purposeful and direct. She was working overtime, and so I began by asking whether Amerco required the overtime, or whether she volunteered for it. "Oh, I put in for it," she replied with a low chuckle. But, I wondered aloud, wouldn't she and her husband like to have more time at home together, finances and company policy permitting. Linda . . . approached the question by describing her life at home:

> I walk in the door and the minute I turn the key in the lock my older daughter is there. Granted, she needs somebody to talk to about her day. . . . The baby is still up. She should have been in bed two hours ago and that upsets me. The dishes are piled in the sink. My daughter comes right up to the door and complains about anything her stepfather said or did, and she wants to talk about her job. My husband is in the other room hollering to my daughter, "Tracy, I don't ever get any time to talk to your mother, because you're always monopolizing her time before I even get a chance!" They all come at me at once.

To Linda, her home was not a place to relax. It was another workplace. Her description of the urgency of demands and the unarbitrated quarrels that awaited her homecoming contrasted with her account of arriving at her job as a shift supervisor:

> I usually come to work early just to get away from the house. I get there at 2:30 P.M., and people are there waiting. We sit. We talk. We joke. I let them know what's going on, who has to be where, what changes I've made for the shift that day. We sit there and chit-chat for five or ten minutes. There's laughing, joking, fun.

My coworkers aren't putting me down for any reason. Everything is done with humor and fun from beginning to end, though it can get stressful when a machine malfunctions.

For Linda, home had become work and work had become home. Somehow, the two worlds had been reversed. Indeed, Linda felt she could only get relief from the "work" of being at home by going to the "home" of work. As she explained,

My husband's a great help watching our baby. But as far as doing housework or even taking the baby when I'm at home, no. He figures he works five days a week; he's not going to come home and clean. But he doesn't stop to think that I work seven days a week. Why should I have to come home and do the housework without help from anybody else? My husband and I have been through this over and over again. Even if he would just pick up from the kitchen table and stack the dishes for me, that would make a big difference. He does nothing. On his weekends off, I have to provide a sitter for the baby so he can go fishing. When I have a day off, I have the baby all day long without a break. He'll help out if I'm not here, but the minute I am, all the work at home is mine.

Bill, who was fifty-six when I first met him, had three grown children from a contentious first marriage. He told me he felt he had "already put in his time" to raise them and now was at a stage of life in which he wanted to enjoy himself. Yet when he came home afternoons he had to "babysit for Linda."

. . . Today, as one of the women who make up 45 percent of the American workforce, Linda Avery, overloaded and feeling unfairly treated at home, was escaping to work, too. Nowadays, men and women both may leave unwashed dishes, unresolved quarrels, crying tots, testy teenagers, and unresponsive mates behind to arrive at work early and call out, "Hi, fellas, I'm here!"

Linda would have loved a warm welcome from her family when she returned from work, a reward for her day of labors at the plant. At a minimum, she would have liked to relax, at least for a little while. But that was hard to do because Bill, on *his* second

shift at home, would nap and watch television instead of engaging the children. The more Bill slacked off on his shift at home, the more Linda felt robbed of rest when she was there. The more anxious the children were, or the messier the house was when she walked in the door, the more Linda felt she was simply returning to the task of making up for being gone.

For his part, Bill recalled that Linda had wanted a new baby more than he had. So now that they were the parents of a small child, Bill reasoned, looking after the baby should also be more Linda's responsibility. . . .

Neither Linda nor Bill Avery wanted more time at home, not as things were arranged. Whatever images they may have carried in their heads about what family and work should be like, the Averys did not feel their actual home was a haven or that work was a heartless world.

Where did Linda feel most relaxed? She laughed more, joked more, listened to more interesting stories while on break at the factory than at home. . . . The social life that once might have surrounded her at home she now found at work. The sense of being part of a lively, larger, ongoing community—that, too, was at work. In an emergency, Linda told me, she would sacrifice everything for her family. But in the meantime, the everyday "emergencies" she most wanted to attend to, that challenged rather than exhausted her, were those she encountered at the factory. Frankly, life there was more fun.

How do Linda and Bill Avery fit into the broader picture of American family and work life? Psychologist Reed Larson and his colleagues studied the daily emotional experiences of mothers and fathers in fifty-five two-parent Chicago families with children in the fifth to eighth grades. . . . The researchers found that men and women reported a similar range of emotional states across the week. But fathers reported more "positive emotional states" at home; mothers, more positive emotional states at work. This held true for every social class. Fathers like Bill Avery relaxed more at home; while mothers like Linda Avery did more housework there. Larson suggests that "because women are constantly on call to the needs of other family members, they are less able to relax at home in the way men do."[7] Wives were typically in better moods than their husbands at home only when they were eating or engaging in "family transport." They were in worse moods when they were doing "child-related activities" or "socializing" there.[8] Men and women each felt most at ease when involved in tasks they felt less obliged to do, Larson reports. For women, this meant first shift work; for men, second.

A recent study of working mothers made another significant discovery. Problems at home tend to upset women more deeply than problems at work. The study found that women were most deeply affected by family stress—and were more likely to be made depressed or physically ill by it—even when stress at the workplace was greater. . . . However hectic their lives, women who do paid work, researchers have consistently found, feel less depressed, think better of themselves, and are more satisfied with life than women who don't do paid work.[9] . . .

In sum, then, women who work outside the home have better physical and mental health than those who do not, and not simply because healthier women go to work. Paid work, the psychologist Grace Baruch argues, "offers such benefits as challenge, control, structure, positive feedback, self esteem . . . and social ties."[10] . . .

For Linda Avery self-satisfaction, well-being, high spirits, and work were inextricably linked. It was mainly at work, she commented, that she felt really good about herself. As a supervisor, she saw her job as helping people, and those she helped appreciated her. . . .

Often relations at work seemed more manageable. . . . The plant where she worked was clean and pleasant. She knew everyone on the line she supervised. Indeed, all the workers knew each other, and some were even related by blood, marriage, or, odd as it may sound, by divorce. . . . Yet despite the common assumption that relations at work are emotionally limited, meaningful friendships often blossom. . . .

Amerco regularly reinforced the family-like ties of coworkers by holding recognition cere-

monies honoring particular workers or entire self-managed production teams. . . .

At its white-collar offices, Amerco was even more involved in shaping the emotional culture of the workplace and fostering an environment of trust and cooperation in order to bring out everyone's best. At the middle and top levels of the company, employees were invited to periodic "career development seminars" on personal relations at work. The centerpiece of Amerco's personal-relations culture was a "vision" speech that the CEO had given called "Valuing the Individual," a message repeated in speeches, memorialized in company brochures, and discussed with great seriousness throughout the upper reaches of the company. In essence, the message was a parental reminder to respect others. . . .

"Employee empowerment," "valuing diversity," and "work-family balance"—these catch phrases, too, spoke to a moral aspect of work life. Though ultimately tied to financial gain, such exhortations—and the policies that followed from them—made workers feel the company was concerned with people, not just money. . . .

In this new model of family and work life, a tired parent flees a world of unresolved quarrels and unwashed laundry for the reliable orderliness, harmony, and managed cheer of work. The emotional magnets beneath home and workplace are in the process of being reversed. In truth, there are many versions of this reversal going on, some more far-reaching than others. Some people find in work a respite from the emotional tangles at home. Others virtually marry their work, investing it with an emotional significance once reserved for family, while hesitating to trust loved ones at home. . . . Overall, this "reversal" was a predominant pattern in about a fifth of Amerco families, and an important theme in over half of them.

The Time Bind

The social world that draws a person's allegiance also imparts a pattern to time. The more attached we are to the world of work, the more its deadlines, its cycles, its pauses and interruptions shape our lives and the more family time is forced to accommodate to the pressures of work. In recent years at Amerco it has been possible to detect a change in the ways its workers view the proper use of their time: Family time, for them, has taken on an "industrial" tone.

As the social worlds of work and home reverse, working parents' experience of time in each sphere changes as well. Just how, and how much, depends on the nature of a person's job, company, and life at home. But at least for people like Timmy's parents, engineers at Amerco, it's clear that family time is succumbing to a cult of efficiency previously associated with the workplace. Meanwhile, work time, with its ever longer hours, becomes newly hospitable to sociability-periods of talking with friends on e-mail, patching up quarrels, gossiping. In this way, within the long workday of Timmy's father were great hidden pockets of inefficiency, while, in the far smaller number of waking weekday hours he spent at home, he was time conscious and efficient. Sometimes, Timmy's dad forgot the clock at work; despite himself, he kept a close eye on the clock at home.

The new rhythms of work are also linked to a new sense of self-supervision. Managers, professionals, and many workers in production teams describe feeling as if they are driving themselves ever harder at Amerco, while at home they feel themselves being driven by forces beyond their control. . . . The miracle of Amerco's engineered culture is that the company has managed to give employees, who labor according to a schedule imposed on them by others, the sense that they are still in control. This achievement has turned what might otherwise be a continual, heart-pounding, tension-provoking crisis at work into a kind of endless flow of communal problem-solving time. So Timmy's dad, for instance, lurched from one project deadline to the next at the office, but only when he came home did he feel truly pressed. He then tried to jam many necessary activities into his domestic life: a block of time for Timmy, another for Timmy's sister, another for his wife—all arranged like so many office hours, but without a secretary to control his flow of visitors and tasks. . . .

Numerous activities formerly done at home now go on outside the house as a result of domestic "outsourcing." Long ago, the basic functions of education, medical care, and economic production, once based in the home, moved out. Gradually, other realms of activity followed. For middle-class children, for instance, piano lessons, psychological counseling, tutoring, entertainment, and eating now often take place outside the home. Family time is chopped into pieces according to the amount of time each outsourced service requires—fifty minutes for a psychiatric appointment, sixty minutes for a jazzercise class. Each service begins and ends at an agreed-upon time somewhere else. This creates a certain anxiety about being "on time," because it is uncomfortable (and often costs money) when one is late, and precious time is squandered if one is early. The domestic time that remains may come to seem like filler between one appointment and another. . . .

[Some] responded to their time bind at home by trying to value and protect "quality time.". . . [Q]uality time has become a powerful symbol of the struggle against the growing pressures on time at home. It reflects the extent to which modern parents feel the flow of time running against them. Many Amerco families were fighting hard to preserve outposts of quality time, lest their relationships be stripped of meaningful time altogether.

The premise behind quality time is that the time we devote to relationships can somehow be separated from ordinary time. Relationships go on during "quantity time," of course, but then we are only passively, not actively, wholeheartedly, specializing in our emotional ties. We aren't "on." Quality time at home becomes like an office appointment. . . .

Quality time holds out the hope that scheduling intense periods of togetherness can compensate for an overall loss of time in such a way that a relationship will suffer no loss of quality. But this, too, is a way of transferring the cult of efficiency from office to home. Instead of nine hours a day with a child, we declare ourselves capable of getting the "same result" with one more intensely focused total quality hour. . . .

Feeling themselves in a time bind, most Amerco working parents wanted more time at home, protected time, time less intensely geared to the rhythms of the work world outside, time they simply did not have. They also yearned to feel different about the time they did have. But the lack of family time and the Taylorization of what little of it remained was forcing parents to do even more of a new kind of work: the emotional work necessary to repair the damage caused by time pressures at home. . . . But when children react against a speedup at home, parents have to deal with it. Children dawdle. They sulk. They ask for gifts. They tell their parents by action or word, "I don't like this." They want to be having quality time when it's a quantity time of day; they don't want quality time in the time slot parents religiously set aside for it.

Parents now increasingly find themselves in the role of domestic "time and motion" experts, and so more commonly speak of time as if it were a threatened form of personal capital they have no choice but to manage and invest, capital whose value seems to rise and fall according to forces beyond their control.

What's new here is the spread into the home of a financial manager's attitude toward time. Few people feel that they simply "sell" their time to a workplace, which then manages it for them. More feel as if they manage a temporal portfolio there themselves. But this leads them to think of time with their partners, with their children, as a commodity to be invested or withdrawn, an "it" that they wish they could purchase or earn more of in order to live a more relaxed life.[11]

Many working parents strive mightily to counter this conception of time. They want not simply more time, but a less alienating sense of time. As one Amerco working mother put it, "I love my job, I love my family, and I don't want to move to the country. But I wish I could bring some of that ease of country living home, where relationships come first." In this alternative view, time is to relationships what shelters are to families, not capital to be invested, but a habitat in which to live.

Notes

1. Galinsky, 1991. *The Corporate Reference Guide.* p. 123.
2. Arthur Emlen, "Employee Profiles: 1987 Dependent Care Survey, Selected Companies" (Portland: Oregon Regional Research Institute for Human Services, Portland State University, 1987) reported in Friedman, *Linking Work-Family Issues to the Bottom Line.* 1991. p. 13.
3. Families and Work Institute. 1995. *Women: The New Providers.* Whirlpool Foundation Study, Part 1, survey conducted by Louis Harris and Associates, Inc. (May). p. 12.
4. See Galinsky, et al. 1993. *The Changing Workplace.* p. 17.
5. Studies of Johnson & Johnson, the pharmaceutical giant, and of Fel Pro, a maker of automotive sealing products, found that family-friendly policies made workers more content and more likely to stay with their companies. See Friedman, *Linking Work-Family Issues to the Bottom Line* (1991). Pp. 47–50.
6. Christopher Lasch, *Haven in a Heartless World* (New York: Basic Books, 1977). To Lasch, what matters about the family is its privacy, its capacity to protect the individual from the "cruel world it was set up to guard against."
7. Reed Larson, Maruse Richards and Maureen Perry-Jenkins. 1994. "Divergent worlds: The daily emotional experience of mothers and fathers in the domestic and public spheres." *Journal of Personality and Social Psychology.* 67:1035
8. Larson et al., 1994. "Divergent worlds." Pp. 1039, 1040.
9. Grace Baruch, Lois Beiner, and Rosalind Barnett. 1987. "Women and Gender in Research on Work and Family Stress." *American Psychologist.* 42:130–136. Spitze, Glenna. 1988. "Women's employment and family relations: A review." *Journal of Marriage and the Family.* 50:595–618. Even when researchers take into account the fact that the depressed or less mentally fit would be less likely to find or keep a job in the first place, working women come out slightly ahead in mental health (see Rena Repetti, Karen Matthews, and Ingrid Waldron. 1989. "Employment and women's health: Effects of paid employment on women's mental and physical health." *American Psychologist.* 44:1394–1401.
10. Baruch et al., 1987. "Women and Gender in Research." p.132.
11. See Staffan Linder, 1974. *The Harried Leisure Class.* New York: Columbia University Press. Linder, an economist, argues that we assume that work time is money, and we apply this idea to leisure time. Thus a man on vacation may say to himself, "For every hour I'm on vacation, I could be earning thirty dollars!" Linden suggests that people continually substi-

tute time and "high returns" for time with "low returns." In *The Management of Time* (New York: Kend, 1987), Dale Timpe speaks of time as that which we must "audit" . . . See also Ross Webber, *Time Is Money! The Key to Managerial Success* (New York: Free Press, 1988). Furthermore, the French sociologist Pierre Bourdieu has developed the concept of "cultural capital." Like economic capital, cultural capital helps the individual progress up the social class ladder. Beliefs about time and habitual ways of handling it can also be seen as a form of cultural capital (Pierre Bourdieu, *Distinction* Cambridge, MA: Harvard University Press, 1984).

References

Baruch, Grace, Lois Biener, and Rosalind C. Barnett. 1987. "Women and gender in research on work and family stress." *American Psychologist* 42:130–136.

Bourdieu, Pierre. 1984. *Distinctions.* Cambridge, MA: Harvard University Press.

Emlen, Arthur, Paul Koren, and Dianne Louise. 1987. "Dependent care survey: Sisters of Providence." Final report. Portland, OR: Regional Research Institute for Human Services, Portland State University.

Families and Work Institute. 1995. *Women: The New Providers.* Whirlpool Foundation Study, Part One. Survey conducted by Louis Harris and Associates, Inc., May.

Friedman, Dana E. 1987. *Linking Work-Family Issues to the Bottom Line.* New York: The Conference Board.

Galinsky, Ellen, James T. Bond, and Dana E. Friedman. 1993. *The Changing Workforce: Highlights of the National Study.* New York: Families and Work Institute.

Galinsky, Ellen, Dana E. Friedman, and Carol A. Hernandez. 1991. *The Corporate Reference Guide to Work Family Programs.* New York: Families and Work Institute.

Larson, Reed, Maryse H. Richards, and Maureen Perry-Jenkins. 1994. "Divergent worlds: The daily emotional experience of mothers and fathers in the domestic and public spheres." *Journal of Personality and Social Psychology.* 67:1034–46.

Linder, Staffan. 1974. *The Harried Leisure Class.* New York: Columbia University Press.

Repetti, Rena L., Karen A. Matthews, and Ingrid Waldron. 1989. "Employment and women's health: Effects of paid employment on women's mental and physical health." *American Psychologist* 44:1394–1401.

Spitze, Glenna. 1988. "Women's employment and family relations: A review." *Journal of Marriage and the Family* 50:595–618.

Timpe, A. Dale, ed. 1987. *The Management of Time: The Art and Science of Business Management.* New York: Kend.

Webber, Ross. 1988. *Time Is Money! The Key to Managerial Success.* New York: Free Press.

Food for Thought and Application Questions

1. Discuss the factors that characterize the "time bind." What kind of family situations give rise to these characteristics? What work situations give rise to these characteristics? When we hear discussions of "family friendly" workplaces, what characteristics are being stressed? Survey various press reports on family friendly employers and list the characteristics of those organizations. Assess the extent to which these "family friendly" characteristics overlap with employment characteristics associated with the "time bind."

2. Assume you were interested in developing a policy that gave priority to the family in the "work/family" relationship. What work situations would you suggest changing, if any, in order to enhance family support and, at least indirectly, reduce the impact of the "time bind?" ✦

14

Fast-Track Women and the 'Choice' to Stay Home

Pamela Stone
Meg Lovejoy

The phenomenon of women who leave professional careers to become so-called "stay-at-home moms" has generated considerable media attention and been the subject of numerous articles, editorials, on-air commentary (Stone 1998), and a best-selling novel, *I Don't Know How She Does It* (Pearson 2002). Recent high-profile examples include Bush administration staffers Karen Hughes and Victoria Clarke. Despite larger popular interest, there is little research on this phenomenon, a paucity noted by Ann Crittenden, author of *The Price of Motherhood* (2001, 30), who characterized it as a "conspiracy of silence" borne of a "feminist and corporate taboo."

Whether or not Crittenden (2001) is correct in claiming a taboo, the specter of highly trained women who have made significant professional investments "stepping off the fast track" potentially undermines the arguments of feminist advocates for women's advancement and challenges the rationale for, and/or effectiveness of, widely publicized corporate efforts to retain and promote women. Professional women's labor force departures to "stay home" are especially highly visible because many are still tokens in their fields and firms (Kanter 1977). When they quit, their actions can signal to supervisors and colleagues alike the perception that women are not committed to work, thereby setting in motion well-known processes of statistical discrimination.

The likelihood of deleterious stereotyping and ensuing discrimination is increased by what Joan Williams (2000) has called the "choice rhetoric" used to frame women's decisions to interrupt careers. Choice rhetoric attributes women's work status to their private and personal tastes and preferences and assumes that their decisions operate outside any system of constraints. A cover story in the *New York Times Magazine* provides an especially vivid example of such an analysis. Titled "The Opt-Out Revolution," it asked "Why don't more women get to the top?" and answered "They choose not to" (Belkin 2003). In addition to Williams, a number of prominent analysts, including Susan Faludi (1991) and Rosalind Barnett (Barnett and Rivers 1996), have also challenged choice rhetoric, arguing that this portrayal of women's decisions about work and family is part of a broad backlash against feminism and gender egalitarianism.

Although the vast majority of women with professional degrees are working, they are out of the labor force at a rate roughly three times that of their male counterparts and overwhelmingly cite "family responsibilities" as the reason. In a 1993 national study of advanced-degree recipients ten years after graduation, 12.1 percent of women as compared to 4.0 percent of men in law were no longer in the labor force. Among MBAs, comparable figures were 7.8 versus 2.2 percent; and for those with an MD, the figures were 10.7 versus 3.7 percent (Baker 2002).

At the most elite echelons, there is anecdotal and accumulating evidence that these gender differentials may be even larger. Deloitte Touche, a leading professional services firm, for example, reported losing half the women in each incoming class during the five- to seven-year period from recruitment to partnership, a significantly higher rate than that seen for male recruits, until it took aggressive measures to stanch women's defections (McCracken 2000). Most of these women, moreover, were leaving the workforce, not the firm, findings echoed in studies of women graduates of leading business and professional schools. Swiss and Walker's (1993) study of the careers of women graduates of various Harvard professional schools found that about one-quarter were out of the labor force. The academy has long faced a "leaky pipeline" problem, with substantial numbers of women who have trained for scientific careers failing to pursue them (Preston 1994).

The costs of career interruption are significant (see Crittenden [2001] for an especially good summary of the research literature on this point). Individually, women bear them directly in the form of lost salary and blocked or slowed advancement. Cumulatively, interruptions account for as much as one-third of the gender gap in earnings and partly explain the relative absence of women in the upper reaches of most professions. The costs to employers of replacing departing women professionals—high-priced talent in the so-called "talent wars"—are also considerable.

Married professional women, by virtue of the privileges their jobs confer as well as the demands they entail, are subject to numerous, competing pressures on their decision to quit jobs and exit the labor force. These pressures emanate from both the workplace (Jacobs and Gerson 1998) and from the home, where expectations about parenting are shaped by an ideology of intensive mothering (Hays 1996). The facile media depiction of these women's decisions as "choices" in favor of domesticity (Williams 2000) obscures our understanding of their actions and the complex decision making leading up to them. Nor does the limited information available from national surveys offer much insight. In this article, we seek to shed light on these issues by reporting the results of a qualitative study of professional women, married with children, who made the decision to quit their jobs and interrupt their careers—at least temporarily—by leaving the labor force. The goals of the article are threefold: (1) to develop a thematic analysis of the reasons behind professional women's decision to "go home" that is grounded in their experiences, (2) to explore the implications of our findings as they shed light on choice rhetoric, and (3) to inform the development of work-family (or as they are now more often called, work-life) policies and practices.

Data and Method

Study participants (*N* = 43) were women who were formally out of the labor force (neither at work nor actively looking for work) at the time of the interview. All were married, with at least one child younger than eighteen living at home, and all had formerly been employed in professional (which includes those in male-dominated professions such as law and medicine as well as female-dominated professions such as teaching) or managerial jobs. Participants resided in seven metropolitan areas throughout the United States and were recruited through referral or "snowball" sampling, primarily through alumnae networks of highly selective colleges. We confined the study to white women because cultural traditions vary significantly regarding work and family across different racial and ethnic groups.

Interviews were semistructured and conducted by the first author in the interviewee's home or a place of her choice and typically lasted about two hours. The interviews, which were audiotaped, explored women's work and family histories and elicited a detailed accounting of how and why these women made the decision to quit, including the work-family context in which this decision was made. To protect the identities of the women interviewed, we change their names and identifying information in the results presented here.

Women in the sample ranged in age from thirty-three to fifty-six, with a median age of forty-three. On average, they had worked thirteen years prior to dropping out and had been out of the labor force six years. Typically, they had two children, with just more than a third having preschoolers at the time of interview. Across all women in the sample, the youngest child was three months and the oldest fourteen years. All but one woman in the sample had a college degree, and half had an advanced degree. Two-thirds worked in male-dominated fields such as law, business, medicine, or the sciences; approximately one-fifth worked in mixed or transitional fields such as publishing, public relations, and health and educational administration; and the remainder worked in traditionally female-dominated professions such as teaching. Their husbands also worked as professionals or managers, typically in law, medicine, or finance, or owned businesses.

Because there is so little research on this group of women, it is difficult to assess the representativeness of our sample. As highly educated women, they had deferred child-bearing, enabling most to become relatively well established in their careers. The majority worked in male-dominated professions. This may reflect a greater propensity for dropout among this group (as would plausibly be expected) or the vagaries of nonprobability sampling. As a result, we offer the caveat that our results may be more reflective of the experiences of women in male-dominated professions than of those in mixed or female-dominated professions.

Results

In the rhetoric of choice often invoked to explain why successful professional women exit the workforce, women's decisions are largely seen as an expression of their unfettered individual preferences for home and hearth over career. Our findings largely contradict this view. Approximately 90 percent of women in our sample expressed a moderate to high degree of ambivalence about the decision to quit their jobs, and for many the decision was protracted and agonizing. Claire Lott, a manager at a public utilities company, took a leave of absence from her job before finally quitting, a period during which she vacillated constantly:

> So at the end of that six months—I mean, it came down to literally the night before. What was again so hard was it was like a loss of identity. Ironically, that Sunday, after I made the decision, the sermon at church was "Loss of Identity because of Loss of Job or Loss of Spouse." That kind of clicked with me.

Quitting to "go home" was weighed against women's solid sense of identification with their careers and the heavy investments they had made in them, which for many included not only extensive work experience but postgraduate education. Women also found it hard to leave their jobs because they took pride in their professional accomplishments and derived intrinsic pleasure from their work. Nancy Yearwood, senior editor at a publishing house, voiced the difficulty

many women felt in making the decision and reflected on the variety of losses it entailed:

> I would think about like well, "How could I do this?" I mean the financial was one aspect of it, but there are other aspects. Not to minimize that, but my whole identity was work. Yes, I was a mother and a wife and whatever, but this is who I was. And I would think like about the authors, and "Oh, my God, how can I leave this author?" And then the agents and these people I'd worked with for years and my books and the house and my colleagues. I mean just on and on and on. And I really thought long—I mean I just thought for a long time about it. And I would think like, "How could I do this?"

For only five women (representing 16 percent of the sample) can the decision to step off the career track be viewed as a reflection of a relatively unconstrained choice or preference to become full-time, stay-at-home mothers. Following Faludi (1991), we call these women "new traditionalists." Like the classic traditionalists, they give full-time mothering precedence over working; however, in contrast to their earlier counterparts, they had successful and even high-powered careers in fields such as publishing, marketing, banking, and health care before starting their families. Unlike most of the women studied, they indicated that they had always planned to become full-time mothers and experienced no indecision or ambivalence in making the decision to interrupt their careers, quit their jobs, or be at home with their children. Also, unlike many of the women studied (as we will report later in the context of reasons for quitting), they made no efforts to reduce their work hours or enhance schedule flexibility to maintain their careers.

The new traditionalists were further distinguished from the other women by the value that they, and often their husbands, placed on having a full-time mother in the home, seeing own-mother care as irreplaceable in their children's lives. They often rejected unequivocally any form of child care, especially in the early years of their child's development. Vita Cornwall, who quit her job as a nonprofit executive after the birth of her first child, exemplified this perspective:

The reason [I quit] is I want them to, for better or worse, interpret my values, our values, our moral system, speak in our cadence, with our grammatical errors or proper speech. I wanted them to be our children, and I don't think we would have been able to do that with me working full-time.

As exceptions, the new traditionalists highlight the many constraints faced by the majority of women in our sample. Our analysis of women's reasons for interrupting their careers brings into focus the nature of these constraints and how they impinged on the women's "choice" to go home. The analysis revealed three major themes around which women's motivations for leaving the workforce revolved: (1) work, (2) children, and (3) husbands.

Work-Related Factors in the Decision to Quit

Work-related reasons were the most frequently cited reasons for quitting, figuring as important considerations for 86 percent of the sample. Managers and professionals are, paraphrasing Schor (1992), the most overworked Americans (Jacobs and Gerson 1998). The women in our study dwelled squarely in the world of sixty-hour workweeks and 24/7 accountability. The time bind (Hochschild 1997) was an almost taken-for-granted feature of their lives—and had been even before they had children. Typical was Nathalie Everett's description of the high-technology industry in which she had worked as a marketing manager: "The high-tech workweek is really sixty hours, not forty. Nobody works 9 to 5 anymore." Added to this, many women were employed in settings where the pace and expectations were set by men with stay-at-home wives. Meg Romano, a trader at a large investment firm, was the only woman among a group of eleven men, men about whom she said, "Every single one, their wife stayed home . . . their wives handled everything."

The amount, pace, and inflexibility of work as well as the inadequacy of reduced-hour options led many women to quit. Economic restructuring played an important role in accelerating workplace demands but also operated in other ways to influence this outcome.

Workplace Inflexibility

Upon becoming mothers, about half of the women in our sample expressed a desire to cut back on their work hours and/or to increase the flexibility of their schedules. Their efforts met with mixed results, however, as almost one-third of the sample (and 62 percent of those who had actually gone part-time) cited workplace inflexibility as a major factor in their decision to interrupt their careers. Romano's experience is illustrative. Having worked both part- and full-time over a fifteen-year period with the same firm, she took a leave of absence to attend to her child's medical problem. Ready to return to work,

I went back to talk to them about what was next, and a part-time situation presented itself in the sales area, and I got all gung-ho for that. I got all the child care arrangements in place, started interviewing people to watch the kids, and at the last minute the big boss wouldn't sign off on it. So I was like, "Alright, whatever."

Romano and others like her tried and failed, but a number who would have liked to work part- time or job share knew better than to ask. More than one-third characterized their work as "all or nothing" and viewed their options as being either working forty-plus hours per week or quitting. Maeve Turner, a federal attorney, said of workplace accommodation, "It just wasn't in their [her superiors'] realm of reality." Nancy Yearwood encountered the same phenomenon, as illustrated by her account of telling her boss that she was quitting her job in publishing after ten years with the firm:

She was kind of shocked, and she said, "Is there *anything* [emphasis added] I can do to try to get you to stay?" I did bring up to her the fact that I thought about trying to get some kind of a part-time thing, but it's just not what they need. I know what they need. They need people who are there all the time, and working like dogs. And to work part-time in my business—I think you're going to end up working more than part-time. I wasn't willing to do that. I'd already been working time and a half. I raised it [part-time work] in this conversation, I guess, just to satisfy my curiosity about it. And she basically agreed with me.

Yearwood's belief that she would "end up working more than part-time" foreshadows the most frequent complaint among those who were able to arrange part-time work: for many, the nature of their jobs and the culture of their workplaces meant that they worked part-time in name only. Women spoke repeatedly about having full-time responsibilities on a part-time schedule, of doing a "job and a half" when they were supposed to be doing half a job. Diane Childs, a nonprofit CFO, observed that "when you have young babies, they leave you alone for a while," but when the honeymoon period ended, she was asked to "take more responsibility, do more, manage more." Making it difficult to limit work hours was the fact that many of these women were the only ones in their immediate work environment who were working part-time. "[My colleagues were] putting in fifty to sixty hours a week and I was working thirty" was how Elena Toracelli, a management consultant, described her situation.

Women's inability to limit their hours on a part-time schedule meant that they felt little relief from the spillover of work into their family lives. Bettina Mason, a real estate attorney, described the dilemma she faced:

> Even though my children mean so much to me, I listen to someone who is paying me money, and I will then miss reviewing the math, reviewing the journal entry. I'll say "yes" to my employer. So then my hours were never twenty hours a week, they were much more than that—at least thirty hours a week.

In addition to feeling time pressured and emotionally torn, working part-time in jobs that were effectively full-time made many women feel inadequate. They struggled to perform to their own high standards in jobs where the demands so exceeded the time available that success was impossible. They also felt guilty, as if by working part-time they were shortchanging their employers. Mason's firm, where she described the people as "extremely nice" and the environment

as "very fast paced," had no complaints about her working part-time, but from her perspective, "Things just had to get done and two days off just was not working out," adding, "I just felt that twenty hours was not going to give them all that they needed."

Mommy Tracking and the Maternal Wall

Many of the women who worked part-time or job shared found themselves "mommy tracked," a career derailment that ultimately played a role in their decision to quit. Nancy Thomas, a marketing executive, used *Scarlet Letter*–like imagery to describe job sharing at her firm: "When you job share you have 'MOMMY' stamped in huge letters on your head." Reporting that "there were a dozen job sharers in the company and none were ever promoted," she recounted with triumph how she had finally succeeded in getting a promotion after a four-year campaign—a promotion, she observed somewhat incredulously, that "the chairman of the board of a six-thousand-person company had to approve."

Childs, the nonprofit executive, described the long-term prospects of continuing to work part-time, which eventually discouraged her from doing so:

> And I'm never going to get anywhere—you have the feeling that you just plateaued professionally because you can't take on the extra projects; you can't travel at a moment's notice; you can't stay late; you're not flexible on the Friday thing because that could mean finding someone to take your kids. You really plateau for a much longer period of time than you ever realize when you first have a baby. It's like you're going to be plateaued for thirteen to fifteen years.

Women were not only concerned about the loss of extrinsic rewards associated with the move to part-time but also bemoaned the loss of intrinsically interesting and engaging work. Toracelli, the management consultant, returned from maternity leave to a twenty-hour-a-week schedule, discovering when she did so that "I lost the vast majority of my interesting responsibilities and was really left with the more mundane modeling responsibilities that I wasn't nearly as interested in."

Many felt marginalized. Paula Trottier, a marketing executive, described how her status and authority had been eroded when she went part-time, despite having considerable seniority, and how this played directly into her decision:

> So I decided to quit, and this was a really, really big deal . . . because I never envisioned myself not working. I just felt like I would become a nobody if I quit. Well, I was sort of a nobody working too. So it was sort of, "Which nobody do you want to be?"

Economic Restructuring

The women in our sample worked in fields such as finance, marketing, professional services, law, and technology. Since the 1970s, these fields have experienced both an influx of female professionals and an economic restructuring brought about by consolidation in mature industries (e.g., finance and publishing) and extraordinarily high rates of growth in newly emerging ones (e.g., biotechnology). Reflecting this, stories of reorganization, mergers, takeovers, and rapid expansion recurred throughout our interviews, figuring prominently in the career interruptions of just less than half (42 percent) of our sample.

Speedup and disruption. Restructuring influenced women's decisions in a number of ways, most importantly by creating tremendous turbulence and speedup in the work environment, which in turn disrupted the complicated and fragile articulation of work and family that women had been able to achieve. Consolidation and rapid growth dramatically increased the scope and demands of women's jobs. Nancy Taylor's experience as an executive with a company on an aggressive acquisition binge gives a flavor of what mergers meant for the people responsible for implementing them:

> There are forty-nine hundred branches, fifteen thousand ATMs, and all of the myriad things associated with that—capital budget of maybe 260 million dollars, about seventy five people. And only five of them were in [the same city]. And that's where everything got out of control. We were scattered to the four winds. What that meant was I was traveling. I had to travel before, but this was just on a scale

like . . . [gesturing with her hands and making sounds to indicate a nuclear explosion].

Women in high-growth industries such as biotechnology faced special challenges. Lynn Hamilton, an MD who was medical director of a start-up company, recalled continuously running fax machines and a grueling schedule of nonstop travel. She reflected on this life:

> I think the punch line is, there's a reason why people that tend to be funded by venture capitalists are twenty and live on Doritos in their basement. Because the pressure's on you when you have a start-up company like this. With these kinds of guys [the venture capitalists] expecting results, it's tough to be forty, with two young children and a husband with his own job.

Changes in corporate culture. Changes brought on by restructuring also prompted women to feel a growing disenchantment with their employers, often leading them to wonder aloud, "Why am I doing this?"—ultimately a question to which they had no answer. Restructuring was frequently linked to perceptions that the corporate culture was growing more hostile to women and more value divergent. "I think each of those changes [in ownership], it just became more and more corporate" was how Nancy Yearwood described what she observed as the publishing firm where she was an editor successively merged with others. Women frequently used the word *corporate* to connote a chill in the climate toward women as a result of restructuring. Edith Hortas, a Ph.D. scientist and biotechnology executive, recounted what she called "a turning point" that occurred when her firm replaced its female CEO with a male CEO brought on to "grow" the company:

> The company turned into a big corporation. And there were people there who became extremely corporate, who took a very hard-line financial view of things. And it became a much more male-run company. It was by no means a female-run company before, but it was a very inclusive kind of company.

Manager turnover. Restructuring was often associated with rapid turnover in the managers to whom these women reported, resulting in the loss of mentors and the collapse of family-friendly work arrangements. In domino-like fashion, turnover at the top contributed to women's own turnover, which occurred via one of two processes, either by disrupting the work-family equilibrium that women had achieved or by diminishing their career prospects through the loss of an important mentor.

Because schedule flexibility and the pace of work are to some extent a function of managerial style, women often saw their work lives transformed by what they considered to be the rather arbitrary dictates of new bosses. Lisa Bernard, an executive in the health care field who worked under four senior managers in rapid succession, remarked of her last one,

> This last person [who, she pointedly noted, had a wife, nanny, and mother-in-law at home] had a different approach to how to do certain things. I remember there was one time when he sent an e-mail to me on Sunday afternoon about a meeting that was 6:30 Monday morning and was just assuming that of course I would be reading my e-mail Sunday evening at home.

Sometimes losing a boss meant losing a supportive mentor. Kate Davenport, a public relations executive, said of her experience working for a highly successful, rapidly growing high-technology firm, "I had a new boss every three weeks." One in particular she described as having been "really cool" in encouraging her efforts to combine work and family. With her last boss, however, she hit the maternal wall:

> She didn't have much patience for the whole family scene. "If you're going to choose to have kids [and Kate at this point already had three], this is as far as your career is going to go, you're derailing, you're on the mommy track now."

Children's Influence on the Decision to Quit

Seventy-two percent of the women we studied spoke of the pull of children as a factor in their decision to leave the workforce. Included among them are the five new traditionalist women in the sample. Three-quarters of women citing this reason quit when their children were in the baby or toddler years. Perhaps more surprising, a substantial number of women (32 percent)[1] who cited the pull of children were primarily compelled to leave the workforce by the needs of their older, school-aged children.

The Pull of Younger Children

Women who cited the pulls of their younger, preschool children as an important reason for taking a pause in their careers experienced these pulls in two ways.

Primacy of parental care. One-third cited their belief in the importance of one parent playing a primary caregiving role in the life of a young child. Melanie Irwin, formerly a marketing manager in a computer software company, put it this way: "I guess in my heart I didn't really want a kid raised by a nanny." Kristin Quinn, a former teacher, said, "It was hard thinking who could take care of my kid better than me." For these women, parental care in the early years was important in providing consistency and enrichment. Maeve Turner, the government attorney, reflecting on why she and her husband decided that one of them (ultimately her) would be home after the birth of their first child, emphasized the constancy of parental care:

> The kids need especially—I think the kids need routine. They need a schedule. They need—I mean, not a schedule in the hourly sense, but they need a routine. They need to know that somebody is there connected to them who cares about them.

This theme more than any others cited by the women in the study reflects traditional notions of why women choose to stay home with their children rather than combining work and family. However, the new traditionalists and the nontraditionalists spoke about this issue in different ways. The nontraditionalists typically did not see full-time, mother-only care as the optimal or necessary solution, as the new traditionalists did. In fact, among nontraditionalists citing primacy of parental care, approximately one-third asked their employers if they could return to work on a reduced schedule but were denied this option.

The emotional pull of younger children. One-quarter of the women spoke of the emotional pull of younger children as a factor in their decision. For some women, this took the form of an intense feeling of attachment and bonding with their newborn baby or young child that made the return to a full-time work schedule difficult. Lauren Quattrone, formerly a lawyer, expressed it in this way: "I was just absolutely besotted with this baby. . . . I realized that I just couldn't bear to leave him." Regina Donofrio, a senior publicist for a large media corporation, decided to return to work full-time after the birth of her first child but described the anguish she felt in coping with her competing desire to be with her baby and to maintain a much-loved career:

> Then I began the nightmare of really never feeling like I was in the right place, ever. When I was at work, I should have been at home. When I was at home, I felt guilty because I had left work a little early to see the baby, and I had maybe left some things undone.

The pull of young children was also linked to their particular developmental phase and a desire not to "miss out" on it. Helena Norton, formerly an education administrator, commented, "I just don't want to miss this part because I know it does go by so fast." Three of the women who cited the emotional pull of younger children in their decision to leave work became first-time mothers in their early forties, and for these women, the desire to be fully present in the experience of motherhood was particularly keen since they did not expect to have any more children.

Among the nontraditionalist women who cited the emotional pull of young children, 40 percent tried to reduce their hours but were denied. Among this group, both Turner and Donofrio proposed job-sharing arrangements and left flourishing careers when their proposals were rejected.

The Pull of Older Children

Older children were cited as having been a key factor in tipping the balance away from employment for one-quarter of our total sample and figured prominently for one-third of those who mentioned children as a factor in their decision to leave. Nancy Taylor echoed the sentiments of many of these women when she remarked with surprise, "It's funny. I always expected as they got older it would be easier." Instead, an increase in both the scope and complexity of the perceived needs and demands of older children relative to younger ones, as well as growing doubts about the capacities of their paid caregivers, played a role in women's career interruption.

Increased demands. Bearing in mind that the oldest child among the women we interviewed was only fourteen, women were often surprised to learn that homework started young. Diane Childs expressed an amazement shared by many:

> I don't know why this is happening, but elementary school kids get homework. These are children who can't read, who are in the first grade, and they have an assignment. And they'll be kind of sweet things, you know, "Use tally marks and count all of the pillows in your house." But if you come home from a frazzed-out day, . . . the last thing you want to do is find out that you have forty-two pillows in your house.

After-school activities added to the stress of combining work and parenting. Childs noted that, like many professional women she knows who are now at home, a precipitating factor in her departure from work was an increasing awareness of her school-aged children's needs for extracurricular enrichment and the heightened demands that this placed on her as a parent, commenting dryly, "They can't drive themselves to piano lessons."

Lack of substitutability for own care. Women's perceptions about older children's increased demands were linked to their feelings that their children had "outgrown" their paid caregivers and that they themselves were increasingly needed at this point in their children's lives. Child care arrangements that had been regarded as highly successful were reevaluated as the more sophisticated needs of older children took precedence over the simpler, more straightforward "babysitting" needs of younger children. Elena Toracelli, the management consultant, expressed the satisfaction that most felt with their caregivers when children were younger:

> I had great child care. In some ways, I think babies, if they're in a loving environment, other nonparents can fulfill their basic needs in a way that parents can too. And I liked that my kids got some tremendous socialization very early on in incredibly loving situations. And they are none the worse at all, if not the better for having been there.

As their children started entering school, however, these high-achieving women begin to question their caregivers' capacities and suitability, often comparing themselves directly with them. The premium placed on education and values transmission at this point in their children's lives served to widen the gap between themselves and their less well-educated caregivers, most of whom were from very different class, race, and ethnic backgrounds. Edith Hortas spoke of having "a sense that they were needing what I can provide and what the babysitter [her au pair] couldn't provide." Marina Isherwood, an HMO executive, elaborated this viewpoint:

> There isn't a substitute, no matter how good the child care. When they're little, the fact that someone else is doing stuff with them is fine. It wasn't the part that I loved anyway. But when they start asking you questions about values, you don't want your babysitter telling them. . . . Our children come home and they have all this homework to do, and piano lessons and this and this, and it's all a complicated schedule. And, yes, you could get an au pair to do that, to balance it all, but they're not going to necessarily teach you how to think about math. Or help you come up with mnemonic devices to memorize all of the counties in Spain or whatever.

Time and pleasure. For some women, watching their older children growing up created a heightened sense of urgency about quitting. These women saw childhood as a "little window" (as Nancy Yearwood put it) that was rapidly closing. Having worked a decade or more before quitting, many of them expressed a sense of "missing out" on their children's childhoods. Elena Toracelli

described her feelings about the desirability of being home "when you sort of realize that time's running short. Paul's eight and tomorrow is going to be eighteen, and the same thing with Amanda. It's going to be over in a blink."

Complementing this sense of urgency, these women also found older children more fun, as Toracelli's observations convey:

> I've realized within myself that I am much more stimulated by older children than I am by babies. I loved my children as babies, they were my own, . . . but I thrive more in the interaction with the level that they are at now than I did when they were infants and toddlers. They reason. They're funny. You can have conversations with them. You can plan and dream and do all kinds of great activities with them. They are much more fun now.

Among this group whose children were older, 20 percent made efforts to navigate the demands of work and family by making part-time arrangements with their employers but had their requests refused.

Husbands' Role in the Decision to Quit

The majority of the women in this study, roughly two-thirds, discussed their husbands as one of the key influences on their decision to leave the labor force. That husbands' involvement was not cited universally indicates the degree to which women perceived the work-family decision to be theirs alone to shoulder. Husbands' influence on women's decisions to quit operated through multiple channels.

Lack of husbands' help with parenting

The women in our study were married to men who worked in professional jobs much like their own, entailing long hours and extensive travel. Husbands' high octane careers effectively precluded their willingness or ability to provide help with child care or household chores. Often women did not explicitly mention their husbands' lack of support, but it was clear from their narratives that their husbands were simply not around to share much if any of the "second shift"

(Hochschild 1989) necessary to make their careers viable. Helena Norton, the educational administrator who characterized her husband as a "workaholic," described poignantly a scenario that many others took for granted:

> He was leaving early mornings; 6:00 or 6:30 before anyone was up, and then he was coming home late at night. So I felt this real emptiness, getting up in the morning to, not necessarily an empty house, because my children were there, but I did, I felt empty, and then going to bed, and he wasn't there.

Some women were more vocal in their estimation of how their husband's self-exemption from domestic labor affected their own career choices. Kristen Quinn observed about her husband, "He has always said to me, 'You can do whatever you want to do.' But he's not there to pick up any load."

Because these women had the resources to employ household help such as housekeepers, nannies, and babysitters, they rarely complained about "chore wars" occasioned by their husbands' failure to help with routine household tasks. Instead, the more profound impact of a husband's absence from the home was experienced by women in terms of his resulting inability to assist with the emotional labor of parenting. Many women were, like Helena Norton, the only parent available, and it fell to them to create a sense of family for their children. Leah Evans, a high-level medical administrator, highlighted this need when she described her decision to quit:

> So more than anything else it was just sort of what worked for the collective whole. Even though for Leah personally, I sort of feel like I'm the one who made the trade-off. Dick [her husband] certainly hasn't made any trade-off at this point and maybe eventually he will, but sort of realizing that it is a UNIT and you've got to do it [make your decision] based on what's best for the unit.

Toracelli found herself in a similar situation. Her husband's demanding career managing his own company in combination with her own near full-time work schedule meant that there was little time to create family:

> We had precious little family time, in part because, you know, here I am working like thirty hours. I have one day off, Friday, but my husband's not home Saturday and Sunday either. And so I am seven days a week, full-time, working with not too much of a break.

Another example of the "parenting vacuum" these women experienced as a result of their husbands' high-powered career came from Tricia Olsen, a former trader. Having herself once worked in the financial services industry, she was familiar with her husband's work world:

> My husband had taken a job three months earlier with a top investment bank, and we knew his life was going to go to hell because he was in the mergers and acquisitions department. So we knew that his life would be nonstop travel . . . and we decided that somebody should be home to be more attentive to the kids because now we had a second child. She was eighteen months old already, and we found that she was requiring more and more attention just because she was a child. So I decided, knowing his life was going to go to hell, we figured that somebody should be home, and that somebody was me.

Secondary Income

Despite the high-powered nature of their own careers, the majority of women in the study did not explicitly broach the idea of their husbands cutting back. Instead, they seemed to implicitly accept that their career was secondary. This perception was based to some extent on husbands' higher earnings. Approximately one-quarter of the women whose husbands played a role in their decision to quit perceived their own income, however high, as secondary to their husbands' and/or as unnecessary to family welfare. Typically, women were correct in their perceptions because they worked in lower-paying, female-dominated occupations like teaching or publishing and/or lower-paying sectors such as government; they were already working part-time at the time of their quitting; or their own high earnings were far outstripped by their husbands'. Diane Childs, who worked in the nonprofit sector, said that as a couple she and her husband did not even consider having him cut back on his career in finance, despite increasing family strains, since, as she put it, "There's too much money at stake at this point in time that I couldn't approach his earning power."

Because many of these women and their husbands are midcareer, about half mentioned promotions or other significant career achievements (such as making partner) that led to dramatic increases in their husbands' salaries during the period when they were considering the need to reorder their work lives. Marina Isherwood reported that her husband's income went up fivefold before she quit:

> And mine wasn't going up fivefold, and so the amount of contribution I was making to our household dropped significantly. And then I thought, you know, taxes, what are we really bringing in? So the economics changed.

Husband's Preference for Wife to Stay Home

About one-quarter of the women whose husbands played a role in their decision to quit indicated that their husbands communicated to them, either explicitly or implicitly, that they expected their wife to be the one to sacrifice or modify her career to accommodate family responsibilities. A minority of husbands expressed this preference in traditionalist terms. For instance, Toracelli described the role her husband's attitude played in her decision to quit in the following way:

> My husband grew up in a very traditional household. His mother was home all the time. It's an Italian household in a very traditional sense of the word where, you know, there's always sort of a warm plate of food waiting for you on the table when you get home, and he relished the idea of having that kind of person.

More often, husbands professed an egalitarian stance toward women's decisions about whether to cut back on their careers, captured in the frequent refrain, "It's your choice," while tacitly indicating discontent with their wives' working. Women seemed to take their husbands' overt statements at face value, characterizing their husbands as "supportive" while recounting narratives

that contradicted this assessment. For example, Bettina Mason described her husband in the following way:

"He has always said do what I want. He would be supportive of whatever I chose." At another point in the interview, however, she admitted that part of her reason for quitting was that her husband, who was often out of town for weeks at a time, made it clear that he resented the fact that no one was around to "pick up the slack" when she worked full-time.

Some husbands simply refused to modify their careers in the face of mounting pressure on the home front. Lynn Hamilton, the MD turned medical director, described both herself and her husband as working "these killer jobs," a situation that was creating huge stress on their marriage and family life. They earned similar incomes and had similar credentials, and he was "admiring and supportive" of her work. When Hamilton repeatedly raised the need for them to "reconfigure" their work lives, however, he was nonresponsive, and she finally realized that "he wasn't going to."

Significantly, about one-third of the women who described their husbands' implicit or explicit preference for a stay-at-home wife as a factor in their quitting were earning comparable incomes or outearning their husbands at the time of their job departure. Thus, economics was not the only factor at play in these couples' perceptions that the wife's career was secondary.

Deference to Husband's Career

Under the duress of a dual-career lifestyle, some women's decisions to quit were influenced by a perception that their husbands' careers were more important or prestigious than their own or by an unspoken agreement with their husbands that husbands' careers took precedence. Two women accommodated their husbands' careers by deciding to step off the career track when their husbands' jobs required a geographical relocation. Feeling the mounting stress of juggling family and two careers—their own and their husbands'—some women simply weighed their own careers against their husbands' and decided that theirs were more dispensable. Moira Franklin, a former engineer whose husband was in the same field as her, describes her decision to quit as influenced by her perception that her own educational credentials were less than those of her husband and that her career was not as prestigious:

> I think if I had gone to get a Ph.D., then it would have been harder to quit. But master's was kind of a half-way, you're qualified, but you're not a hotshot yet. So it's not as if I was the faculty member . . . so I think it was easier for me to quit than stick it out and torture myself a little longer.

Future Work

While this article is concerned with the forces impinging on and reasons behind the decision to interrupt careers, in the larger study of which it is a part, we also asked women about their plans to return to work in the future. Two-thirds responded that they desired to reenter the workforce and discussed their intention to return with varying degrees of specificity. Significantly, the majority of women who desired to return to work said they would prefer to do so on a part-time basis that would accommodate their ongoing family responsibilities. Despite the difficulty many had encountered in arranging a part-time schedule in their former jobs, most women who expressed interest in returning to work cited workplace flexibility as a critical feature of any future job. In fact, some women planned to switch into traditionally female-dominated fields such as teaching, in part because they perceived them to offer more flexibility than the "all-or-nothing" style of the male-dominated careers they had left behind.

Discussion

For all but a handful of the women we studied, the decision to interrupt their careers was a reluctant and complex one, reached after taking into consideration myriad factors emanating from both the workplace and the family and often after having made efforts to reduce hours or otherwise maintain employment. For these women, there was no "Eureka!" moment, no final straw, but rather the gradual accumulation of often overlapping workplace pushes and family pulls that led them to quit their jobs. Women tracked their work lives against their family lives, frequently juxtaposing the two at critical junctures, for example, a company merger coinciding with their child's first year at school. Our results can only hint at the full complexity of these unfolding processes, but they do make clear three things. First, women faced enormous constraints in making their decision. Second, work-related considerations played a significant, arguably greater, role in their decision than did those related to family. Third, children were the primary focus of family-based pulls, with husbands playing a less visible but important role.

Although women couch their decisions to quit in the language of personal choice, the reasons they give are not consistent with choice rhetoric or with the idea that they are expressing "preferences." Our results undermine the notion that women are freely choosing family over work. Inflexible and highly demanding workplaces are the major barriers to their ability to exercise discretion in any meaningful way. With the exception of the small group of women we label (following Faludi 1991) new traditionalists, the women in our study made the "choice" to be at home not out of their preference for traditional gender roles but because of their experience of gendered realities. These realities are shaped by multiple factors that include economic restructuring, workplaces that assume the male model of work, the lack of real reduced-hours options that undermines women's efforts at work-family accommodation, husbands' exemption from household parenting obligations, and the ideology of intensive mothering at home. This confluence of pressures creates a kind of "perfect storm." That so many of the women we studied "weathered the storm" for as long as they did is testimony to their work commitment, ingenuity, and tenacity in the face of significant obstacles. The fact that so many women planned to return to work is further testimony to their commitment to work and to their desire to integrate career and family.

By virtue of their professional status, women face tremendous pressures as workers; by virtue of their upper-middle-class membership, they face equally tremendous pressures as mothers. They are called on to be not only the "ideal worker" (Williams 2000) but also the "ideal parent"—a double bind from which they effectively shield their husbands, owing primarily to the latter's superior earning power as well as the ideology of husband exemption.

Our findings illustrate the mirror-image processes by which women's careers become secondary to those of their husbands, who work in equally demanding jobs. Among these couples, as women attempt to shoulder the responsibilities of work and family, they accrue cumulating disadvantages at the same time that their husbands accrue advantages by "free riding" (Folbre 2001) on their wives' relatively weaker position in the labor market as well as on their desire to create family. The ascendancy of husbands' careers is driven not simply by higher earnings but also by the construction of gendered ideologies that privilege men's work in a process Pyke (1996) has called "the ideological hegemony of the male career." She found this phenomenon to be especially characteristic of upper-middle-class families of the sort we studied. As we observed, even women with high-status jobs who earned more than their husbands deferred to their husbands' careers and were persuaded to accommodate to their husband's explicit, but more often tacit, preference for them to bear the brunt of family work.

Policy Implications

Our results highlight the importance of taking into account the perspectives of women who are no longer employed for the development of effective work-family policies by revealing the constrained context in which the majority of professional women are actually making their decision to "go home" as well as the degree to which their decisions are grounded in work, not family, considerations. The experiences of these women suggest several recommendations that would presumably not only enhance the labor force attachment of women who might otherwise leave it but improve the work and family lives of those who remain at work.

Some Good News

The results reported here suggest that while the workplace remains less than fully family friendly, there have indeed been meaningful improvements in the work-family system. Consistent with research on the provision of family benefits (Glass and Camarigg 1992), almost all the professional women in our sample had access to generous maternity leave. Very little evidence among the women we studied showed the "trailing spouse" phenomenon or the "two-person career." Strikingly, the burdens of corporate entertaining or other social supports for their husbands' high-powered careers were absent from these women's narratives. Also notably missing were mentions of sexual harassment and overtly discriminatory pay or promotion policies. If women encountered these problems, they did not appear to play a role in weakening their career attachment in favor of family.

The Family-Friendly Workplace: What Women Want

Hochschild (1997) cast doubt on the very need for work-family accommodations, arguing that workers are not interested in taking advantage of them. The struggles of the women we studied to maintain their employment, primarily through reduced hours, and their inability to obtain satisfactory part-time solutions make clear that there exists among them a strong unmet demand for increased workplace flexibility. Moreover, looking ahead to the future, the fact that they still desired part-time work and expressed a willingness to change professions if necessary to obtain it, further testifies to the strong demand for workplace flexibility and accommodation among this group. These findings underscore the importance of policy recommendations that are receiving renewed attention (e.g., Hartmann, Yoon, and Zuckerman 2000): first, to create meaningful part-time opportunities in the professions that do not penalize workers who take advantage of them; and second, to fully institutionalize these arrangements to shield them from arbitrary and individualized implementation.

The influence of children, especially school-age children, in women's decisions highlights the clash of family and occupational careers (Moen and Han 2001). Among professional women who defer childbearing, the birth of children and their entry into school and adolescence often coincides with a critical midcareer takeoff point, a period when women are assuming additional responsibilities and are poised for future earnings growth and advancement. To address this clash, worklife benefits are required beyond maternity leave to meet children's developing needs through the school years. The most progressive firms are already moving in this direction; however, broader societal-based changes might include synchronizing school and work schedules and more widespread provision of after-school programs. To overcome the reservations these women voiced about caregivers for their older children, strategies to professionalize the child care workforce via increased training and earnings are called for.

A number of the women in our study were employed by companies that were listed routinely by *Working Mother* magazine as "best places" to work (an irony not lost on some of them, but not reported to protect their identity). The professional women we studied did not work for "bad" companies; in fact, they worked for companies that are widely perceived to be highly desirable places of employment. Our analysis makes clear that to retain these women, employers must move beyond existing programmatic, human-resources-based approaches to reduce the hours of work and enhance its flexibility through work redesign.

To the extent that women disproportionately bear the burden of work speed up through the interruption, in many instances the termination, of once-flourishing careers, our results provide an additional equal-opportunity rationale for reducing work hours across the board among litigation-averse firms, in line with a strategy being developed by Joan Williams (2000) and other legal scholar/activists. They also give added impetus to reduced hours generally, as called for by the burgeoning "time movement" approach advanced by Schor (1992) and Hochschild (1997).

The striking degree to which the demands of husbands' careers cross over and influence women's decisions to interrupt their own careers underscores the importance of efforts already under way to position and implement work-family policies as gender neutral. Companies that bemoan their inability to retain highly talented professional women need to acknowledge that they are married to highly talented professional men. Not only men but employers too benefit from free riding on the coattails of women's career sacrifice. Only when both give up the free ride can women be freed from the double bind. Mounting evidence indicates that younger generations of men *are* increasingly interested in working less and devoting more time to life and family. Our results suggest that keeping work within reasonable bounds for *all* professionals and managers will be necessary to enable women in these fields to exercise their true choice, which is to maintain their careers and raise their families within the context of viable and sustained, supportive work-family structures.

Note

1. The percentages add up to slightly more than 100 percent here since there was some overlap between the categories of younger and older children. Specifically, one woman left the workforce when her youngest child was a preschooler and her oldest child was school aged and cited both types of reasons (the pull of younger and older children) as factors in her decision to quit.

References

Baker, Joe G. 2002. The influx of women into legal professions:An economic analysis. *Monthly Labor Review* 125: 14–24.

Barnett, Rosalind C., and Caryl Rivers. 1996. *She works/he works*. New York: HarperCollins.

Belkin, Lisa. 2003. The opt-out revolution. *The New York Times Magazine*, October 26, pp. 42–47, 58, 85–86.

Crittenden, Ann. 2001. *The price of motherhood*. New York: Metropolitan Books.

Faludi, Susan. 1991. *Backlash: The undeclared war against American women*. New York: Crown.

Folbre, Nancy. 2001. *The invisible heart*. New York: New Press.

Glass, Jennifer, and Valerie Camarigg. 1992. Gender, parenthood, and job-family compatibility. *American Journal of Sociology* 98: 131–51.

Hartmann, Heidi, Young-Hee Yoon, and Diana Zuckerman. 2000. *Part-time opportunities for professionals and managers: Where are they? Who uses them and why?* Washington, DC: Institute for Women's Policy Research.

Hays, Sharon. 1996. *The cultural contradictions of motherhood.* New Haven, CT: Yale University Press.

Hochschild, Arlie. 1989. *The second shift.* New York: Viking.

——. 1997. *Time bind.* New York: Metropolitan Books.

Jacobs, Jerry A., and Kathleen Gerson. 1998.Who are the overworked Americans? *Review of Social Economy* 56: 442–59.

Kanter, Rosabeth Moss. 1977. *Men and women of the corporation.* New York: Basic Books.

McCracken, Douglas M. 2000.Winning the talent war for women: Sometimes it takes a revolution. *Harvard Business Review* 78 (6): 159.

Moen, Phyllis, and Shin-Kap Han. 2001. Gendered careers: A life-course perspective. In *Working families: The transformation of the American home*, edited by R. Hertz and N. L. Marshall, 42–57. Berkeley: University of California Press.

Pearson, Allison. 2002. *I don't know how she does it.* New York: Knopf.

Preston, Anne E. 1994. Where have all the women gone? A study of exits of women from the science and engineering professions. *American Economic Review* 84: 1446–62.

Pyke, Karen. 1996. Class-based masculinities: The interdependence of gender, class, and interpersonal power. *Gender & Society* 10: 527–49.

Schor, Juliet B. 1992. *The overworked American.* New York: Basic Books.

Stone, Pamela. 1998. Media myths about labor force dropout among professional and managerial women: Bringing some facts back in. Paper presented at the annual meetings of the Eastern Sociological Society, Philadelphia, March.

Swiss, Deborah J., and Judith P. Walker. 1993. *Women and the work/family dilemma: How today's professional women are confronting the maternal wall.* New York: John Wiley.

Williams, Joan. 2000. *Unbending gender.* New York: Oxford University Press.

Reprinted from: Pamela Stone and Megan Lovejoy, "Fast-Track Women and the 'Choice' to Stay Home." In *ANNALS, AAPSS*, 596, November 2004, pp. 62–83. Copyright © 2004 by Sage Publications.

Food for Thought and Application Questions

1. Discuss the dynamics of the concept of "choice" embedded in the notion of "choice to stay home." What does "choice" appear to mean? Under what circumstances is the "choice" made to stay home for these mothers?

2. Assume you were asked to speak to a professional women's meeting about dilemmas confronting professional women who seek to combine career, marriage, and family; the potential resolutions to these dilemmas; and the implications of such resolutions. Develop a presentation that incorporates the "choice" to stay home. ✦

15

Family and Career Trajectories Among African American Female Attorneys

Mary Blair-Loy
Gretchen DeHart

This is a case study of the relationships between family and career in a sample of African American female attorneys. Black female lawyers are rare, comprising only 1.5% of all U.S. lawyers in 1990 (U.S. Department of Commerce, 1990; cf. Segal, 1983). Thus, our respondents are unusual women who circumvented racial and gender barriers to build professional careers.

African American women in elite professions are vastly understudied. There is very little previous research on how these women integrate employment and family life. Yet this is a theoretically significant group, which sheds light on how the intersection of gender, race, and class shapes work and family trajectories. African American female attorneys are survivors. They have surpassed academic and professional obstacles and have overcome racial and gender barriers to achieve elite positions. We are not studying women's chances of such attainment, nor the processes by which women are winnowed out of attorney careers. Rather, the goals of this research are to understand respondents' strategies for intertwining family and work and to see how these strategies may differ for African American female lawyers coming of age during the 1950s, 1960s, and 1970s, across a period of sharply

increasing career opportunities wrought by the civil rights and women's movements.

The study is broadly informed by a life course perspective, which sensitizes us to the intersection of people's work and family lives (e.g., Moen, 1992; O'Rand & Krecker, 1990) and to the impact of historical time on people's life trajectories (e.g., Blair-Loy, 1999; Whittier, 1995). We use a valuable data set based on a survey of over 200 African American female lawyers administered by Gwyned Simpson in 1982. The survey collected the family and work histories of Black women who launched attorney careers in the early 1950s through the early 1980s.

The data set is nonrandom. Almost 70% of the sample is under age 35, which limits the data set's usefulness for understanding middle age and later adulthood. Nevertheless, it provides detailed career histories for over 200 Black female attorneys and allows us to explore some of the complex relationships between family and work for this understudied but theoretically important group. And although the data were collected 20 years ago, they allow us to study these processes during a critical period when explicit racial and gender barriers in the workplace were beginning to fall.

Intersections: Family and Career; Race and Class

Women generally spend far more time than men personally caring for family members, and thus their work lives are often curtailed by family obligations (e.g., Gerson, 1985; Hertz, 1986; Spain & Bianchi, 1996). Some previous research has identified different patterns of integrating family and work in different race and class groupings of women in the United States. We have found numerous studies of the general population of predominately White women, some research on the general population of Black women, and some studies of predominately White professional women. However, there is very little research on African American professional women, who, due to intersections of race and class, may negotiate the demands of family and employment differently than other groups. Thus, this data set presents an

157

invaluable opportunity for studying how an understudied population of elite, African American female professionals negotiate work and family and how these processes change over time.

General (Nonelite) Populations of White and African American Women

Previous research suggests that, on average, African American women may experience different consequences of combining employment and family life than do White women. For instance, in the general, predominately White population, childbearing has been found to lower women's wages (Waldfogel, 1997). These effects of childbearing on women's wages depend on the timing of family and work events: The child wage penalty is greater when childbearing occurs during a woman's early career than if it occurs precareer or well after her career is established (Taniguchi, 1999). Korenman and Neumark (1992) and Waldfogel (1997) found that wage penalties for childbearing are smaller or nonexistent for African American women compared to White women, although Budig and England (2001) found that this racial difference exists only for mothers with more than two children. A smaller wage penalty for Black women may be due to their socialization toward and experience of being coproviders or primary breadwinners (Higginbotham & Weber, 1992). African American women have historically had higher labor force participation rates than White women, whereas African American men's labor force participation has been at lower levels than White men's (John & Shelton, 1997; Spain & Bianchi, 1996). Moreover, Black women have higher divorce rates and higher rates of never-married motherhood than White women and are more likely to raise children alone (McLanahan & Casper, 1995). Consequently, African American women may be more likely than White women to see themselves as providers and to see work and family as complementary rather than in competition (cf. Moayedi, 2000).

According to research on predominantly White women, identities of worker and mother are constructed to be separate from each other, and women are expected to give priority to family over work (Coser & Coser, 1974; Wiley, 1991). White women, of course, do combine employment and family caregiving, but in the White, middle-class culture of motherhood, these roles conflict with rather than complement one another (P. H. Collins, 1987; Hays, 1996). In contrast, African Americans understand being a "good" mother to include being a strong breadwinner and a role model who emphasizes self-reliance and independence (P. H. Collins, 1987, 1991).

Daughters can benefit from their mothers' work orientation and emphasis on independence. One study of girls in the sciences finds that African American girls are advantaged in that they are likely to have an employed mother with high educational expectations of them. Compared to White female science students, African American students date less, express more interest in school, are less likely to be oriented toward family, and tend to have more liberal sex role attitudes (Hanson, 1996).

Simpson (1984) conducted interviews as a small pretest for what would later become the survey that produced the data set this article utilizes. The African American female attorneys she interviewed support the notion that African American mothers play a critical role in daughters' work orientation. As one respondent states, "My mother was always very supportive of me . . . and was a major source of motivation in my life. . . . She said never to be limited by what other people said or what I thought couldn't happen." Another woman stressed the pressure put on her to value work over marriage: "I always expected to work. My mother always told me that I would work. . . . What was most important was to be able to support yourself and not to have to depend on anybody else."

In addition to having a strong work orientation and a culture of motherhood that sees employment as compatible with good mothering, married African American women generally enjoy more domestic support from spouses than do married White women. On average, African American men do more housework and child care than White men (although African American women still generally do the majority of this domestic work) (Broman, 1988; Hossain & Roopnarine,

1993; John & Shelton, 1997). Increased support at home may be one reason that marriage has been found to raise the earnings of African American women but not those of White women (Kilbourne, England, & Beron, 1994). Additionally, African American women are more likely to utilize extended family and friend networks for assistance with child care (P. H. Collins, 1991). A study on Black corporate managers, which includes a small sample of female managers, also emphasizes the supportiveness of family networks (Toliver, 1998). In sum, these studies suggest that family formation among African American women does not generally have the same negative effects on careers that it does among White women.

Women in Prestigious, Male-Dominated Occupations

Almost all previous research on women in prestigious, male-dominated occupations studies predominately White populations (Toliver, 1998, cited above, is an exception). This literature has documented women's attempt to time their family formation around their careers and their tendency to postpone or eschew motherhood (Blair-Loy, 2001a; Davidson & Cooper, 1992; Henning & Jardim, 1977). Below, we consider research on how women in management, in academic science departments, and in law confront the challenge of combining family with demanding professional careers.

Family responsibilities compete with the very long hours and enormous work devotion firms expect of senior managers (Blair-Loy, 2001a; Fried, 1998). High-ranking female managers are less likely to be married than women in the general population. And they tend to avoid or delay childbearing, in part because they fear motherhood will slow their career pace (Davidson & Cooper, 1992). Female managers acknowledge that taking career breaks can hurt advancement, especially if the interruptions occur before major promotions (Davidson & Cooper, 1992). In addition to time at the office, senior managers in some fields are required to spend their evenings and weekends cultivating potential clients, or rainmaking (Blair-Loy, 2001b).

Some elite, male-dominated occupations have a career structure that is even more incompatible with family responsibilities. For example, in academia and law, the first 7 to 10 years demand an intense work effort before the crucial promotion hurdle of tenure (in university departments) or partnership (in law firms) can be spanned. These careers have an "up or out" structure and are designed around the assumption that the worker has no significant family caregiving responsibilities. This prepromotion period often coincides with a woman's chief childbearing years, but starting a family then can entail substantial career risks for women (Hochschild, 1975).

Female academics in the sciences face a work culture that assumes career dedication should be all-consuming and uncompromised by family caregiving responsibilities. Yet research reveals that married women are just as productive researchers as single women and that women publish the same average number of papers whether or not they have children (Cole & Zuckerman, 1991). This lack of negative effects of marriage and motherhood on careers is probably due to the conscious strategies women use to manage career and family. For many female academics in the sciences, combining family with academic science careers is a matter of timing, a strategy of attaining tenure before having children (Cole & Zuckerman, 1991).

Similar barriers and strategies have been noted for female attorneys. The limited years with which law firm associates have to try to achieve partnership often coincide with women's chief childbearing years (Epstein, 1993; Hagan & Kay, 1995). But most law firms require enormous career dedication and long hours of their associates coming up for partner. For example, attorney associates are expected to bill high numbers of hours to clients (Harrington, 1993). Another time-consuming requirement for partnership in many firms is the lawyer's ability to make rain, or to bring in outside business (Epstein et al., 1995). Few attorneys work part-time, and those who do are stigmatized and unlikely to make partner (Epstein, Seron, Oglensky, & Saute, 1999).

Unsurprisingly, studies show that female attorneys often delay motherhood until they achieve partnership, when they think it will be less damaging to their careers (Epstein et al., 1995). Women are far less likely than men to work as law firm partners, even after controlling for human capital and family status (Hagan & Kay, 1995; Hull & Nelson, 2000). Taking a parental leave further reduces women's chances of being promoted to partner (Hagan & Kay, 1995). Work-family tension has a significant negative effect on making partner for women but not for men (Hull & Nelson, 2000). Women "intent on partnership appear to consciously avoid or postpone motherhood" (Hull & Nelson, 2000, p. 252; see also Hagan & Kay, 1995, pp. 104–105). Due to repeated delays, many female attorneys end up forgoing motherhood altogether (Cooney & Uhlenberg, 1989).

These studies of women in prestigious, male-dominated occupations all use predominately White samples. Little is known about the intersection of family formation and careers for African American professional women. In the general population, women's experience of combining family and employment is mediated by race. Unlike White women, African American women's salaries are not depressed by marriage and motherhood. If race shapes the work-family strategies of professional women in similar ways, we would expect that African American professional women can also combine work and family without negative career consequences. Thus, we hypothesize that among our respondents, married women and mothers will not have lower salaries than women without those family ties. In fact, marriage may enhance respondents' careers and be associated with higher salaries.

On the other hand, if class or the structure of elite occupations is the primary force shaping women's experience combining work and family, we would expect that African American women in prestigious occupations would use the same strategies employed by White women to limit the impact of family responsibilities on career commitment. This line of thought leads us to hypothesize that like White women in prestigious male-dominated occupations, African American professionals may delay childbearing or avoid it altogether.

A third alternative is that race and class may intersect in ways that produce as yet unanticipated ways in which African American women combine work and family. We will also examine how this process changes over time, as explicit, legal barriers to Black women's careers began to fall in the late 1960s and 1970s.

Family Formation and Careers for African American Women Across Historical Time

The life course literature has firmly established that people's life trajectories are affected by the historical period in which they live (e.g., Whittier, 1995). More specifically, periods of new labor market opportunities may affect the unfolding of women's careers (Blair-Loy, 1999).

Thus, the intersections between career and family trajectories may differ for respondents in different age cohorts. Legal and explicit workplace barriers began to be dismantled for African American women who came of age during the civil rights and women's movement. Title 7 of the Civil Rights Act of 1964 began to be enforced in the mid-1960s against race discrimination (S. Collins, 1983) and in the early 1970s against gender discrimination (Freeman, 1973). Title 9 of the Education Amendment of 1972 prohibited sex discrimination in schools receiving federal funding; this legislation contributed to the sharp rise in female enrollment in law and business schools in the 1970s (Spain & Bianchi, 1996). In their small qualitative sample of Black women, Slevin and Wingrove (1998) found that respondents who began careers in the 1960s faced less widespread and systematic gender and race discrimination than those who launched careers in the 1940s and 1950s.

In the general population, women born after World War II (baby boomers) entered the labor force after the passage of legislation prohibiting explicit sex discrimination in schools and workplaces and during a time in which liberal feminism encouraged women's labor force attachment and aspirations toward well-paid and male-dominated occupations. Baby boomers took advantage of these legal changes and gender-egalitarian ideologies. They pursued more education and worked outside the home more continuously than had older women (Spain & Bianchi, 1996).

In our sample of African American women who all became attorneys, we expect that respondents who graduated from college in the 1940s, 1950s, and early 1960s faced much more limited career opportunities in law than did younger women. We hypothesize that these older cohorts were likely to delay entry into law until more opportunities had opened up. Conversely, we anticipate that the cohort finishing college in the mid-1960s, when explicit racial discrimination in the labor force became illegal, may have seen some racial barriers dismantled. And younger African American women who graduated from college in the late 1960s through the 1970s may have seen still more barriers come down, as explicit sex discrimination at work and in education was being challenged. Thus, we hypothesize that these younger cohorts were more likely than older cohorts to attend law school and launch legal careers right after college.

We further anticipate that emerging career opportunities will affect family formation (cf. Blair-Loy, 2001a).We expect that cohorts who came of age before the mid-1960s were more likely to focus on marriage and early motherhood and to enter law at later ages. And we hypothesize that cohorts who finished college after the mid-1960s would be more likely than their older colleagues to delay or eschew marriage and childbearing and to focus immediately on establishing attorney careers.

Data

In 1982, Gwyned Simpson sent a survey to 400 African American female attorneys in large U.S. cities.[1] She constructed the survey population from names on mailing lists of African American bar associations in major cities. Two hundred thirty-eight women completed and returned the mailed questionnaires. Excluding one very old and one very young outlier, respondents graduated from law school between 1946 and 1982. Their ages ranged from 24 to 68 years old. Sixty-eight percent were under 35 years old, and 25% were between the ages of 35 and 44. The data for our analysis are based on the 203 respondents for whom we could construct complete and meaningful year-by-year career histories. To our knowledge, this is the first social scientific study written on these data, and this is the only data set with this kind of information on African American female professionals.

The data set has several advantages. It chronicles the family and work lives of a group of African American women who became attorneys across the period before, during, and after the civil rights and women's movements. Studies of African American female professionals are very rare but theoretically significant. They help us understand how race and a demanding professional career structure intersect to shape women's work and family lives. Another advantage is that the data set has detailed items from which we could construct year-by-year career histories for the 203 respondents we studied. We also have approximate dates for marriages and childbirths. Intact career histories of real people are extremely rare (cf. Blair-Loy, 1999). We use these histories to closely study the interaction of career and family formation among Black female lawyers during a critical historical period.

The data set also has some limitations. It uses a small nonprobability sample that was surveyed 18 years ago. Almost 70% of the sample is under age 35, limiting the data set's usefulness for understanding the interplay of work and family for middle-aged and older women. The data were collected at just one point in time and rely on retrospective life histories. We are appropriately cautious when interpreting quantitative results. Yet this is the only data set we know of with which to address these theoretically significant issues among a vastly understudied group.

Method

Our general approach is to use a sample of African American female attorneys as a case study in which to explore family and career trajectories. To examine these trajectories, we first extensively recoded the data into year-by-year career histories for each case. We then used optimal matching techniques to sort these individual career histories into general career patterns. Finally, we use ordinary least squares (OLS) and logistic regression to examine the relationships among variables. Given our small nonprobability data set, we interpret the results with caution. They should be investigated further in larger random data sets, should they ever become available.

Coding

We used questionnaire data to create a detailed educational and career history for each respondent. The questionnaire collected information on respondents' date of birth, dates of college and law school graduation, any jobs they held before law school, periods out of the labor market, and their professional job history from law school graduation to the present. Respondents reported the order and types of positions they had held, the organizations in which they held each position, and the number of years they worked in each position. This recoding allowed us to represent each respondent's career history as a sequence of numbers that tracked her educational and work history each year from approximately age 18 to the interview date. . . .

Findings and Discussion

Descriptive Results

The majority of respondents come from middle-class backgrounds. Fifty-six percent of respondents' fathers and 54% of their mothers had had at least some college. Approximately two thirds of respondents' fathers and mothers worked in managerial, professional, or semiprofessional occupations. Thus, respondents' parents had unusually high levels of educational and occupational attainment for the pre–civil rights era. (This finding was also reported in Segal's [1983] study of Black, predominately male lawyers.)

Previous research maintains that the high labor force participation of African American women supports daughters' career orientation. In our sample, about two thirds of respondents' mothers had managerial, professional or semiprofessional occupations. Just over half of the respondents reported that their mothers were continuously employed, whereas the remainder reported that their mothers had been employed intermittently or before childbirth. Respondents were less likely to be married or to have children than are women in the general population. Fifty-six percent were always single. Two thirds had no children, and only 25% had a child aged 19 or younger as of the survey date. Almost 70% of the sample is under age 35; some of these women may have children in the future. We now turn to models that examine relationships among respondents' family responsibilities and careers.

Intersection of Family Responsibilities and Careers

Current salary. We used OLS models to examine the effects of family responsibilities on current salaries. Consistent with the general population of employed African American women, motherhood is not associated with lower salaries for the Black attorneys in our sample. Moreover, early marriage and late marriage are both associated with higher salaries. (Also, respondents with more legal experience, those who graduated in the top 25% of their law school class, and those working in the private sector earned higher salaries.)

These findings lend support to our first hypothesis: Childbearing does not hurt and marriage helps respondents' careers, as measured by earning a higher salary. This may be in part because African American women are accustomed to seeing work and parenthood as complementary rather than as competing roles and because marriage among African Americans tends to be more egalitarian than marriage among Whites.

Sequencing. We now explore whether respondents' timing of family events were linked to typical career patterns that would accommodate (or fail to accommodate) family responsibilities. As explained in the

Method section, we used optimal matching techniques to help us locate typical career patterns. Earlier studies of predominately White women in prestigious, male-dominated occupations suggest that early marriage and early motherhood will be associated with a late professional career launch. In our sample, respondents with substantially delayed legal careers fall into one of two patterns: those with long-term previous careers and those who were long-term homemakers prior to entering law. In contrast, having no family responsibilities should be associated with having a direct career that progresses immediately from college to law school to the legal labor market.

Logistic regression models suggest that respondents do resemble elite professional White women in their sequencing of family formation and career launch. Being an early mother is more likely for women who entered law after a lengthy previous career, although this effect is no longer statistically significant when we control for age. And being an early mother is associated with the former long-term homemakers' career pattern, even net of the effects of age. These findings can be interpreted in two ways, both of which may well be true. First, second-career attorneys and former long-term homemakers took advantage of the time they had while outside the legal labor market to have children. Second, early childbearing is not easily combined with an early launch of an attorney career.

In fact, respondents with direct careers were extremely unlikely to have had children by the interview date. Although over half (117) of all respondents had direct careers, only a quarter (17) of the mothers were in direct careers. (A chi-square test shows this association to be statistically significant, p<.001.) It seems particularly difficult to combine motherhood with a legal career that has no breaks.

Logistic regression models support this notion, showing that having a direct career is associated with being childless and with being younger. However, younger age does not fully account for the likelihood that respondents in direct careers tend to be childless. The association between childlessness and having a direct career remains weakly

statistically significant even after we controlled for age. We tried restricting our analysis to the 164 respondents aged 28 and over and again found that women in direct careers were also likely to be childless. Thus, even among respondents in their late 20s and beyond, women without family responsibilities were more likely to have had direct careers. Age is negatively associated with having a direct career, suggesting that younger respondents had more opportunities than older ones to specialize immediately in a legal career.

Although we found earlier that childbearing does not directly lower salary of the African American female attorneys in the sample, respondents nonetheless shape family decisions and career trajectories around one another. Lending support to our second hypothesis, we find that respondents tend to sequence their career and family formation to minimize the potential conflict between them. Respondents tend either to have children before entering legal careers or to avoid or delay childbearing. Whatever their age at the survey date, respondents who moved directly into legal careers while they were young are especially unlikely to be mothers.

Family Formation and Careers for African American Women Across Historical Time

We now look more closely at how the timing and sequencing of family formation and career launch differs for different cohorts of respondents. The positive association between age and having initially had a lengthy nonlegal career or a long homemaking tenure and the negative association between age and having a direct career are consistent with the argument that new opportunities in law began opening up for younger cohorts of African American women.

We expected that respondents graduating from college during or after the mid-1960s would be more likely than older cohorts to have focused immediately on legal careers and to have delayed or eschewed marriage or cohabitation and motherhood. Logistic regression models lend support to these hypotheses. [Those] who turned age 22 between 1969 and 1981 were more likely than [those] who turned 22 between 1949 and

1964 to have had direct careers that progressed immediately from college to law school to the legal profession. Thus, respondents finishing college in 1969 or later were more likely than older cohorts to specialize immediately in legal careers.

These data do not allow us empirically to distinguish between age and period effects. A reasonable interpretation is that the period effect of the civil rights and women's movements may have similarly affected respondents of different ages by encouraging law careers, wherever they were in their work histories at that time. Cohorts turning age 22 in 1969 and later seemed to have more career opportunities right out of college, once some of the most blatant race- and gender-based workplace barriers had been made illegal.

These emerging opportunities for African American women also affected their family formation. Members of [younger cohorts] were more likely to be childless than were women in older cohorts, even after controlling for having a direct career. Similarly, members of [the younger cohorts] were less likely to be early mothers than were members of older cohorts, even after controlling for having a direct career.

Whether they moved directly into legal careers or took more circuitous routes, respondents who turned 22 after 1964 were more likely to delay or eschew childbearing than those who turned 22 between 1949 and 1964. These findings are consistent with our argument that among respondents who came of age after 1964, Title 7 and related legislation began to dismantle first racial and then gender barriers in employment and encouraged Black women to focus on education and work rather than on family formation while they were young. Thus, historical period can have a major impact on career and family formation, especially during periods of sharply increasing opportunities. Recall that our sample only includes women who successfully became attorneys. Possibly, women who avoided becoming young mothers during the dramatic changes of the 1960s and 1970s had more opportunity to take advantage of these new opportunities and to become professionals (and thus would be

more likely to be in our sample). Yet despite respondents' advantages, most have so far been unable or unwilling to combine a legal career with motherhood.

Although cohorts coming of age after 1964 were more likely than older cohorts to be childless at the survey date, we do not know whether they will later become mothers. But the data do indicate that 85% of childless women who moved directly from college to law school to attorney jobs do plan on having children in the future. The younger the age cohort, the more likely respondents are to plan to have children. Of the childless women in aged 36–39 at the survey date, 31% plan to have children. This percentage rises to 93% in the youngest cohort, (those aged 23–27 at the survey date).

This strategy of waiting until a later career stage to start a family resembles patterns found in previous research on predominately White, elite professional women. In our sample, childless women with direct careers have a mean age of 29 and could still have children in the future. However, many may end up not doing so, as the mean age of those who are already mothers is 31, and these mothers were far younger, on average, when their children were born. It is possible that work demands and commitments will ultimately not leave room for motherhood. Such a realization might help explain why the percentage of women who plan on having children is so much lower for third-cohort members in their late 30s than it is for younger cohorts. Yet, among childless respondents, the majority of women in direct careers and the majority of women in the three youngest cohorts express the desire to have children. They find motherhood incompatible with their careers now but hope to balance both at a later time.

Summary and Conclusion

The integration of career and family by the African American female attorneys in our sample is mediated by race and by the occupational structure of an elite, male-dominated profession. Like the general population of Black women (and in contrast to the general population of White women), male partners and children do not depress respondents' salaries. In fact, married respondents generally enjoy higher salaries than do single ones. We believe there are several reasons that family formation does not negatively affect respondents' salaries. First, our sample only includes attorneys. Women whose career goals were completely derailed by marital or parenting obligations would not be in the sample. More important, African American women generally benefit from a strong work orientation, a culture of motherhood that embraces breadwinning, and, if married, unions that tend to be more egalitarian than in the White population. These norms specific to the Black community would tend to support motherhood among committed professionals.

Another reason motherhood does not seem to depress respondents' salary is that many respondents sequence their career and family formation to minimize the conflict between them. In this way, our respondents mirrored the patterns found in previous research on predominately White, elite professional women. Sample members who began their adult lives as homemakers or in long-term jobs outside the legal profession were likely to take advantage of that time to have children. In contrast, respondents who moved directly from college to law school to legal careers have generally avoided childbearing, at least as of the survey date. Thus, the long hours and arduous demands of the legal profession constrain the family formation of White and African American women alike.

The relationships between career and family among the lawyers in our sample have changed over time. Older respondents, who came of age before the momentous-workplace opportunities forged by the civil rights and women's movements, were more likely to have had children early and to launch legal careers later, after some of the most explicit barriers to African American women's professional careers had been dismantled. In contrast, respondents who finished college after 1964 were likely as young women to immediately establish attorney careers and to postpone or eschew motherhood. Thus, the historical periods can influence work and family trajectories, especially during a rapid opening of opportunities.

African American female lawyers are still rare. Respondents in the younger cohorts are still likely to face race- and gender-based discrimination (Segal, 1983; cf. Toliver 1998). But relative to other African Americans, and even relative to many other Americans, the women in this sample enjoy some privilege. Most grew up with educated, middle-class parents, despite the fact that their parents came of age well before the civil rights movement. Respondents became highly educated and established prestigious professional careers. And they were probably more likely than many White professional women to have been raised with a culture of motherhood that accepts rather than denounces breadwinning. Despite these resources, the majority of respondents still find it difficult to combine family formation with the demands of being attorneys. Most members of the youngest cohorts hope to have children someday but are delaying motherhood for the sake of their careers.

Because this research is based on a small nonprobability sample surveyed at one point in time, these processes should be further investigated in larger, random, truly longitudinal samples. Yet these ideal samples do not yet exist. Our results are internally consistent and reasonable in terms of previous research. The findings are important for what they reveal about how an understudied but theoretically important group combines family and career over a historical period of sharply changing opportunities. For the African American female attorneys in our sample, the integration of work and family is simultaneously supported by family resources found particularly in the Black community yet constrained by the demands and structures of elite, male-dominated careers.

Note

1. Respondents were from the following cities: New York City (30%), San Francisco (21%), Washington, D.C. (26%), Chicago (10%), Atlanta (10%), and Houston (2%). Gwyned Simpson's Black Women Attorneys data set is currently archived at the Murray Research Center, Radcliffe Institute for Advanced Study at Harvard University, Cambridge, MA (producer and distributor).

References

Blair-Loy, M. (1999). Career patterns of executive women in finance: An optimal matching analysis. *American Journal of Sociology,* 104, 1346–1397.

———. (2001a). Cultural construction of family schemas: The case of female finance executives. *Gender & Society,* 15, 687–709.

———. (2001b). It's not just what you know, it's who you know: Technical knowledge, rainmaking, and gender among finance executives. *Research in the Sociology of Work,* 10, 51–83.

Broman, C. L. (1988). Household work and family life satisfaction of Blacks. *Journal of Marriage and the Family,* 50, 743–748.

Budig, M. J., & England, P. (2001). The wage penalty for motherhood. *American Sociological Review,* 66, 204–225.

Cole, J. R., & Zuckerman, H. (1991). Marriage, motherhood, and research performance in science. In H. Zuckerman, J. R. Cole, & J. T. Bruer (Eds.), *The outer circle: Women in the scientific community* (pp. 157–170). New York: Norton.

Collins, P. H. (1987). The maternal role: The meaning of motherhood in Black culture. *Sage: A Scholarly Journal on Black Women,* 4, 3–10.

———. (1991). *Black feminist thought: Knowledge, consciousness, and the politics of empowerment.* New York: Routledge.

Collins, S. (1983). The making of the Black middle class. *Social Problems,* 30, 369–382.

Cooney, T. M., & Uhlenberg, P. (1989). Family building patterns of professional women: A comparison of lawyers, physicians, and postsecondary teachers. *Journal of Marriage and the Family,* 51, 749–758.

Coser, L. A., & Coser, R. L. (1974). The housewife and her greedy family. In L. A. Coser (Ed.), *In greedy institutions* (pp. 89–100). New York: Free Press.

Davidson, M. J., & Cooper, C. L. (1992). *Shattering the glass ceiling: The woman manager.* London: Paul Chapman.

Epstein, C. F. (1993). *Women in law* (3rd ed.). Urbana: University of Illinois Press.

Epstein, C. F., Saute, R., Oglensky, B., & Gever, M. (1995). Glass ceilings and open doors: Women's advancement in the legal profession. *Fordham Law Review,* 64, 291–449.

Epstein, C. F., Seron, C., Oglensky, B., & Saute, R. (1999). *The part-time paradox.* New York and London: Routledge.

Freeman, J. (1973). The origins of the women's liberation movement. *American Journal of Sociology,* 78, 792–811.

Fried, M. (1998). *Taking time: Parental leave policy and corporate culture.* Philadelphia: Temple University Press.

Gerson, K. (1985). *Hard choices: How women decide about work, career, and motherhood.* Berkeley and Los Angeles: University of California Press.

Hagan, J., & Kay, F. (1995). *Gender in practice.* Oxford, UK: Oxford University Press.

Han, S.-K., & Moen, P. (1999). Clocking out: Temporal patterning of retirement. *American Journal of Sociology,* 105, 191–236.

Hanson, S. L. (1996). *Lost talent: Women in the sciences.* Philadelphia: Temple University Press.

Harrington, M. (1993). *Women lawyers: Rewriting the rules.* New York: Knopf.

Hays, S. (1996). *The cultural contradictions of motherhood.* New Haven and London: Yale University Press.

Hennig, M., & Jardim, A. (1977). *The managerial woman.* New York: Anchor.

Hertz, R. (1986). *More equal than others: Women and men in dual-career marriages.* Berkeley: University of California Press.

Higginbotham, E., & Weber, L. (1992). Moving up with kin and community: Upward social mobility for Black and White women. *Gender and Society,* 6, 416–440.

Hochschild, A. (1975). Inside the clockwork of male careers. In F. Howe (Ed.), *Women and the power to change* (pp. 47–80). New York: McGraw-Hill.

Hossain, Z., & Roopnarine, J. L. (1993). Division of household labor and child care in dualearner African-American families with infants. *Sex Roles,* 29, 571–583.

Hull, K. E., & Nelson, R. L. (2000.) Assimilation, choice or constraint? Testing theories of gender differences in the careers of Lawyers. *Social Forces,* 79, 229–264.

John, D., & Shelton, B. A. (1997). The production of gender among Black and Whitewomen and men: The case of household labor. *Sex Roles,* 36, 171–193.

Kilbourne, B., England, P., & Beron, K. (1994). Effects of individual, occupational, and industrial characteristics on earnings: Intersections of race and gender. *Social Forces,* 72, 1149–1176.

Korenman, S., & Neumark, D. (1992). Marriage, motherhood, and wages. *The Journal of Human Resources,* 27, 233–255.

McLanahan, S., & Casper, L. (1995). Growing diversity in the American family. In R. Farley

(Ed.), *The state of the union. America in the 1990s. Volume two: Social trends* (pp. 1–5). New York: Russell Sage.

Moayedi, R. (2000, August). *African American women and leadership.* Presented at the annual meeting of the American Sociological Association, Washington, DC.

Moen, P. (1992). *Women's two roles : A contemporary dilemma.* New York: Auburn House.

O'Rand, A., & Krecker, M. L. (1990). Concepts of the life cycle. *Annual Review of Sociology, 16,* 241–262.

Segal, G. R. (1983). *Blacks in the law: Philadelphia and the nation.* Philadelphia: University of Pennsylvania Press.

Simpson, G. (1984). The daughters of Charlotte Ray: The career development process during the exploratory and establishment stages of Black women attorneys. *Sex Roles, 11,* 113–139.

Slevin, K. F., & Wingrove, C. R. (1998). *From stumbling blocks to stepping stones: The life experiences of fifty professional African American women.* New York: New York University Press.

Spain, D., & Bianchi, S. (1996). *Balancing act: Motherhood, marriage and employment among American women.* New York: Russell Sage.

Taniguchi, H. (1999). The timing of childbearing and women's wages. *Journal of Marriage and the Family, 61,* 1008–1019.

Toliver, S. D. (1998). *Black families in corporate America.* Thousand Oaks, CA: Sage.

U.S. Department of Commerce. (1990). *Census of population and housing equal employment opportunity file* [CD ROM]. Washington, DC: Bureau of the Census.

Waldfogel, J. (1997). The effect of children on women's wages. *American Sociological Review, 62,* 209–217.

Whittier, N. (1995). *Feminist generations.* Philadelphia: Temple University Press.

Wiley, M. G. (1991). Gender, work, and stress: The potential impact of role-identity salience and commitment. *Sociological Quarterly, 32,* 495–510.

Food for Thought and Application Questions

1. In what ways do African American and white women differ with regard to experiences in combining employment and family? What are the consequences for each group's daughters? For salaries? Then discuss work-family management for *women in prestigious, male-dominated occupations.* Are these patterns replicated? What are the similarities? The differences?

2. Discuss the differences in family formation by the different age cohorts (age groups) of African-American female attorneys. What accounts for the differences found? How does this compare with white women in these same elite, male-dominated occupations? ✦

16
The Work-Home Crunch

Kathleen Gerson
Jerry A. Jacobs

More than a decade has passed since the release of *The Overworked American*, a prominent 1991 book about the decline in Americans' leisure time, and the work pace in the United States only seems to have increased. From sleep-deprived parents to professionals who believe they must put in long hours to succeed at the office, the demands of work are colliding with family responsibilities and placing a tremendous time squeeze on many Americans.

Yet beyond the apparent growth in the time that many Americans spend on the job lies a more complex story. While many Americans are working more than ever, many others are working less. What is more, finding a balance between work and other obligations seems increasingly elusive to many workers—whether or not they are actually putting in more time at work than workers in earlier generations. The increase in harried workers and hurried families is a problem that demands solutions. But before we can resolve this increasingly difficult time squeeze we must first understand its root causes.

Average Working Time and Beyond

"There aren't enough hours in the day" is an increasingly resonant refrain. To most observers, including many experts, the main culprit appears to be overwork—our jobs just take up too much of our time. Yet it is not clear that the average American is spending more time on the job. Although it may come as a surprise to those who feel overstressed, the average work week—that is, hours spent working for pay by the average employee—has hardly

changed over the past 30 years. Census Bureau interviews show, for example, that the average male worked 43.5 hours a week in 1970 and 43.1 hours a week in 2000, while the average female worked 37.1 hours in 1970 and 37.0 hours in 2000.

Why, then, do more and more Americans feel so pressed for time? The answer is that averages can be misleading. Looking only at the average experience of American workers misses key parts of the story. From the perspective of individual workers, it turns out some Americans are working more than ever, while others are finding it harder to get as much work as they need or would like. To complicate matters further, American families are now more diverse than they were in the middle of the 20th century, when male breadwinner households predominated. Many more Americans now live in dual-earner or single-parent families where all the adults work.

These two trends—the growing split of the labor force and the transformation of family life—lie at the heart of the new time dilemmas facing an increasing number of Americans. But they have not affected all workers and all families in the same way. Instead, these changes have divided Americans into those who feel squeezed between their work and the rest of their life, and those who have more time away from work than they need or would like. No one trend fits both groups.

So, who are the time-squeezed, and how do they differ from those with fewer time pressures but who may also have less work than they may want or need? To distinguish and describe the two sets of Americans, we need to look at the experiences of both individual workers and whole families. A focus on workers shows that they are increasingly divided between those who put in very long work weeks and who are concentrated in the better-paying jobs, and those who put in comparatively short work weeks, who are more likely to have fewer educational credentials and are more likely to be concentrated in the lower-paying jobs.

But the experiences of individuals does not tell the whole story. When we shift our focus to the family, it becomes clear that time squeezes are linked to the total working hours of family members in households. For this reason, two-job families and single parents face heightened challenges. Moreover, women continue to assume the lion's share of home and child care responsibilities and are thus especially likely to be squeezed for time. Changes in jobs and changes in families are putting overworked Americans and underemployed Americans on distinct paths, are separating the two-earner and single-parent households from the more traditional households, and are creating different futures for parents (especially mothers) than for workers without children at home. (On the issue of which specific schedules people work and the consequences of nonstandard shifts, see "The Economy that Never Sleeps," *Contexts,* Spring 2004.)

A Growing Divide in Individual Working Time

In 1970, almost half of all employed men and women reported working 40 hours a week. By 2000, just 2 in 5 worked these "average" hours. Instead, workers are now far more likely to put in either very long or fairly short work weeks. The share of working men putting in 50 hours or more rose from 21 percent in 1970 to almost 27 percent in 2000, while the share of working women putting in these long work weeks rose from 5 to 11 percent.

At the other end of the spectrum, more workers are also putting in shorter weeks. In 1970, for example, 5 percent of men were employed for 30 or fewer hours a week, while 9 percent worked these shortened weeks in 2000. The share of employed women spending 30 or fewer hours on the job also climbed from 16 percent to 20 percent (see Figure 16.1) In total, 13 million Americans in 2000 worked either shorter or longer work weeks than they would have if the 1970s pattern had continued.

These changes in working time are not evenly distributed across occupations. Instead, they are strongly related to the kinds of jobs people hold. Managers and professionals, as one might expect, tend to put in the longest work weeks. More than 1 in 3 men in this category now work 50 hours or more per week, compared to only 1 in 5 for men in other occupations. For women, 1 in 6 professionals and managers work these long weeks, compared to fewer than 1 in 14 for women in all other occupations. And because jobs are closely linked to education, the gap in working time between the college educated and those with fewer educational credentials has also grown since 1970.

Figure 16.1
The Percentage of Men and Women Who Put in 30 or Fewer Hours and Who Put in 50 or More Hours a Week in 1970 and 2000

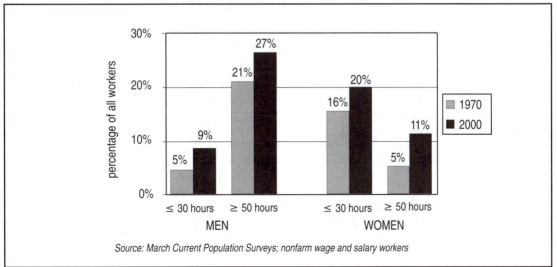

Source: March Current Population Surveys; nonfarm wage and salary workers

Thus, time at work is growing most among those Americans who are most likely to read articles and buy books about overwork in America. They may not be typical, but they are indeed working more than their peers in earlier generations. If leisure time once signaled an elite lifestyle, that no longer appears to be the case. Working relatively few hours is now more likely to be concentrated among those with less education and less elite jobs.

Workers do not necessarily prefer these new schedules. On the contrary, when workers are asked about their ideal amount of time at work, a very different picture emerges. For example, in a 1997 survey of workers conducted by the Families and Work Institute, 60 percent of both men and women responded that they would like to work less while 19 percent of men and women said that they would like to work more. Most workers—both women and men—aspire to work between 30 and 40 hours per week. Men generally express a desire to work about 38 hours a week while women would like to work about 32 hours. The small difference in the ideal working time of men and women is less significant than the shared preferences among them. However, whether their jobs require very long or comparatively short work weeks, this shared ideal does stand in sharp contrast to their job realities. As some workers are pressured to put in more time at work and others less, finding the right balance between work and the rest of life has become increasingly elusive.

Overworked Individuals or Overworked Families?

Fundamental shifts in family life exacerbate this growing division between the over- and under-worked. While most analyses of working time focus on individual workers, time squeezes are typically experienced by families, not isolated individuals. A 60-hour work week for a father means something different depending on whether the mother stays at home or also works a 60-hour week. Even a 40-hour work week can seem too long if both members of a married couple are juggling job demands with family responsibilities. And when a family depends on a single parent, the conflicts between home and

work can be even greater. Even if the length of the work week had not changed at all, the rise of families that depend on either two incomes or one parent would suffice to explain why Americans feel so pressed for time.

To understand how families experience time squeezes, we need to look at the combined working time of all family members. For example, how do married couples with two earners compare with those anchored by a sole, typically male, breadwinner? For all married couples, the work week has indeed increased from an average of about 53 hours in 1970 to 63 hours in 2000. Given that the average work week for individuals did not change, it may seem strange that the couples' family total grew so markedly. The explanation for this apparent paradox is both straightforward and crucial: married women are now far more likely to work. In 1970, half of all married-couple families had only male breadwinners. By 2000, this group had shrunk to one quarter (see Figure 16.2). In 1970, one-third of all married-couple families had two wage-earners, but three-fifths did in 2000. In fact, two-earner families are more common today than male-breadwinner families were 30 years ago.

Each type of family is also working a little more each week, but this change is relatively modest and certainly not large enough to account for the larger shift in total household working time. Two-earner families put in close to 82 working hours in 2000 compared with 78 hours in 1970. Male-breadwinner couples worked 44 hours on average in 1970 and 45 hours in 2000. The vast majority of the change in working time over the past 30 years can thus be traced to changes in the kinds of families we live in rather than to changes in how much we work. Two-earner couples work about as much today as they did 30 years ago, but there are many more of them because more wives are working.

Single parents, who are overwhelmingly mothers, are another group who are truly caught in a time squeeze. They need to work as much as possible to support their family, and they are less likely to be able to count on a partner's help in meeting their children's daily needs. Although these households are not displayed in Figure 16.2, Census Bureau

Figure 16.2
Total Hours of Work per Week for Married Couples, 1970 and 2000

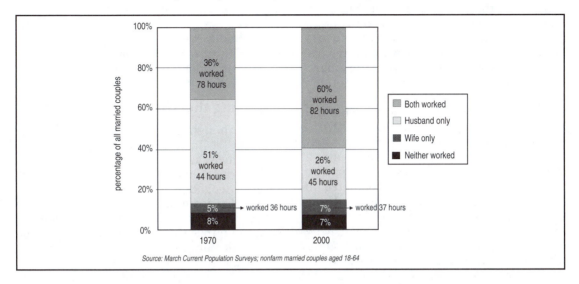

Source: March Current Population Surveys; nonfarm married couples aged 18-64

data show that women headed one-fifth of all families in 2000, twice the share of female-headed households in 1970. Even though their average work week remained unchanged at 39 hours, the lack of childcare and other support services leaves them facing time squeezes at least as sharp. Single fathers remain a much smaller group, but their ranks have also grown rapidly. Single dads work almost as much as single moms—37 hours per week in 2000. Even though this represents a drop of two hours since 1970, single fathers face time dilemmas as great as those facing single mothers. Being a single parent has always posed daunting challenges, and now there are more mothers and fathers than ever in this situation.

At the heart of these shifts is American families' growing reliance on a woman's earnings—whether or not they depend on a man's earnings as well. Women's strengthened commitment to paid employment has provided more economic resources to families and given couples more options for sharing the tasks of breadwinning and caretaking. Yet this revolution in women's work has not been complemented by an equal growth in the amount of time men spend away from the job or in the availability of organized childcare. This limited change at the work-

place and in men's lives has intensified the time pressures facing women.

Dual-Earner Parents and Working Time

The expansion of working time is especially important for families with children, where work and family demands are most likely to conflict. Indeed, there is a persisting concern that in their desire for paid work, families with two earners are shortchanging their children in time and attention. A closer look reveals that even though parents face increased time pressure, they cope with these dilemmas by cutting back on their combined joint working time when they have children at home. For example, U.S. Census data show that parents in two-income families worked 3.3 fewer hours per week than spouses in two-income families without children, a slightly wider difference than the 2.6 hours separating them in 1970. Working hours also decline as the number of children increase. Couples with one child under 18 jointly averaged 81 hours per week in 2000, while couples with three or more children averaged 78 hours. Rather than forsaking their children, employed parents are taking steps to adjust their work schedules to make more time for the rest of life.

However, it is mothers, not fathers, who are cutting back. Fathers actually work more hours when they have children at home, and their working hours increase with the number of children. Thus, the drop in joint working time among couples with children reflects less working time among mothers. Figure 16.3 shows that in 2000, mothers worked almost 4 fewer hours per week than married women without children. This gap is not substantially different than in 1970.

This pattern of mothers reducing their hours while fathers increase them creates a larger gender gap in work participation among couples with children compared to the gender gap for childless couples. However, these differences are much smaller than the once predominant pattern in which many women stopped working for pay altogether when they bore children. While the transition to raising children continues to have different consequences for women and men, the size of this difference is diminishing.

It is also important to remember that the rise in working time among couples is not concentrated among those with children at home. Though Americans continue to worry about the consequences for children when both parents go to work, the move toward more work involvement does not reflect neglect on the part of either mothers or fathers. On the contrary, employed mothers continue to spend less time at the workplace than their childless peers, while employed fathers today do not spend substantially more time at work than men who are not fathers.

Solving the Time Pressure Puzzle

Even though changes in the average working time of American workers are modest, many American families have good reason to feel overworked and time-deprived. The last several decades have witnessed the emergence of a group of workers who face very long work weeks and live in families that depend on either two incomes or one parent. And while parents are putting in less time at work than their peers without children at home, they shoulder domestic responsibilities that leave them facing clashes between work demands and family needs.

The future of family well-being and gender equality will depend on developing policies to help workers resolve the time pressures created by the widespread and deeply rooted social changes discussed above. The first step toward developing effective policy

Figure 16.3
Average Hours of Work per Week of Couples (Parents and Non-Parents)

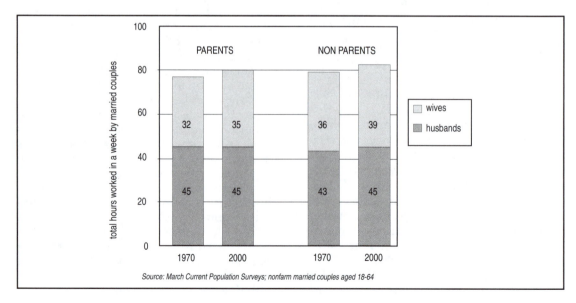

Source: March Current Population Surveys; nonfarm married couples aged 18-64

responses requires accepting the social transformations that sent women into the workplace and left Americans wishing for a balance between work and family that is difficult to achieve. Unfortunately, these changes in the lives of women and men continue to evoke ambivalence.

For example, mothers continue to face strong pressures to devote intensive time and attention to child rearing. Indeed, generally they want to, despite the rising economic and social pressure to hold a paid job as well. Even though most contemporary mothers are counted on to help support their families financially, the United States has yet to develop the child care services and flexible jobs that can help workers meet their families' needs. Whether or not mothers work outside the home, they face conflicting expectations that are difficult to meet. These social contradictions can be seen in the political push to require poor, single mothers to work at a paid job while middle-class mothers continue to be chastised for spending too much time on their jobs and away from home.

To a lesser but still important extent, fathers also face intensifying and competing pressures. Despite American families' increasing reliance on women's earnings, men face significant barriers to family involvement. Resistance from employers and co-workers continues to greet individual fathers who would like to spend less time at work to care for their children. For all the concern and attention focused on employed mothers, social policies that would help bring men more fully into the work of parenting get limited notice or support. New time squeezes can thus be better understood by comparing the large changes in women's lives with the relative lack of changes in the situation for men. The family time bind is an unbalanced one.

Even as family time has become squeezed, workers are also contending with changes in the options and expectations they face at work. Competitive workplaces appear to be creating rising pressures for some workers, especially professionals and managers, to devote an excessive amount of time to their jobs, while not offering enough work to others. In contrast to these bifurcating options, American workers increasingly express a desire to balance the important work of earning a living and caring for a new generation.

Finding solutions to these new time dilemmas will depend on developing large scale policies that recognize and address the new needs of 21st century workers and their families. As we suggest in our book, *The Time Divide*, these policies need to address the basic organization of American work and community institutions. This includes revising regulations on hours of work and providing benefit protections to more workers, moving toward the norm of a shorter work week, creating more family-supportive workplaces that offer both job flexibility and protections for employed parents, and developing a wider array of high quality, affordable child care options.

Extending protections, such as proportional benefits and overtime pay, to workers in a wider range of jobs and occupations would reduce the built-in incentives employers have to extract as much work as possible from professionals and managers while offering less work to other employees. If professionals and managers were given overtime pay for overtime work, which wage workers are now guaranteed under the Fair Labor Standards Act, the pressures on these employees to put in endless workdays might lessen. Yet, the Bush administration recently revised these rules to move more employees into the category of those ineligible for overtime pay. Similarly, if part-time workers were offered fringe benefits proportional to the hours they work (such as partial pensions), there would be fewer reasons for employers to create jobs with work weeks so short that they do not provide the economic security all families need.

Reducing the average work week to 35 hours would also reduce the pressures on workers and help them find a better work-family balance. While this goal may seem utopian, it is important to remember that the 40-hour standard also seemed unimaginably idealistic before it was adopted in the early 20th century. Other countries, most notably France, have adopted this standard without sacrificing economic well being. A shorter work week still would allow for variation in work styles and commitments, but it would also create a new cultural standard that better reflects the needs and aspirations of most contemporary workers. It would also help single parents meet their dual obligations and allow couples to fashion greater equality in their work and caretaking responsibilities.

Time at work is clearly important, but it is not the whole story. The organization of the workplace and the structure of jobs also matters, especially for those whose jobs and occupations require intensive time at work. Among those putting in very long work weeks, we find that having job flexibility and autonomy help ease the perceived strains and conflicts. The work environment, especially in the form of support from supervisors and co-workers, also makes a difference. In addition, we find that workers with access to such family-friendly options as flexible work schedules are likely to use them, while workers without such benefits would like to have them.

Flexibility and autonomy are only useful if workers feel able to use them. Women and men both express concern that making use of "family-friendly" policies, such as extended parental leaves or nonstandard working hours, may endanger their future work prospects. Social policies need to protect the rights of workers to be involved parents without incurring excessive penalties at the workplace. Most Americans spend a portion of their work lives simultaneously immersed in work for pay and in parenting. Providing greater flexibility at the workplace will help workers develop both short- and longer-term strategies for integrating work and family life. However, even basic changes in the organization of work will not suffice to meet the needs of 21st century families. We also need to join the ranks of virtually all other industrialized nations by creating widely available, high quality and affordable child care. In a world where mothers and fathers are at the workplace to stay, we need an expanded network of support to care for the next generation of workers.

These changes will not be easy to achieve. But in one form or another, they have been effectively adopted in other societies throughout the modern world. While no one policy is a cure-all, taken together they offer a comprehensive approach for creating genuine resolutions to the time pressures that confront growing numbers of American workers and their families. Ultimately, these new time dilemmas cannot be resolved by chastising workers (and, most often, mothers) for working too much. Rather, the time has come to create more flexible, family-supportive, and gender-equal workplaces and communities that complement the 21st century forms of work and family life.

Recommended Resources

Bond, James T. *Highlights of the National Study of the Changing Workforce*. New York: Families and Work Institute, 2003.

Gornick, Janet, and Marcia Meyers. *Families that Work: Policies for Reconciling Parenthood and Employment*. New York: Russell Sage Foundation, 2003.

Hays, Sharon. *The Cultural Contradictions of Motherhood*. New Haven, CT: Yale University Press, 1997.

Heymann, Jody. *The Widening Gap: Why America's Working Families Are in Jeopardy And What Can Be Done About It*. New York: Basic Books, 2000.

Jacobs, Jerry A., and Kathleen Gerson. *The Time Divide: Work, Family and Gender Inequality*. Cambridge, MA: Harvard University Press, 2004.

Schor, Juliet. *The Overworked American: The Unexpected Decline of Leisure*. New York: Basic Books, 1991.

Reprinted from: Kathleen Gerson and Jerry A. Jacobs, "The Work-Home Crunch." In *Contexts*, Vol. 3, No. 4, pp. 29–37. Copyright © 2004 by the American Sociological Association.

Food for Thought and Application Questions

1. Clarify what you consider to be the "new time dilemmas" that the authors write about.

2. The authors claim that policies that would "help bring men more fully into the work of parenting" seem to get limited support. What are some of these policies? Examine one such policy and suggest what would need to be done to (1) implement it in a work place and (2)

make it an attractive alternative to current practices (and thus help men view parenting as more attractive).

3. Interview both spouses of a dual-earner family with children at home. (Interview them separately if possible.) Ask about their job and the work/family relationship. Include questions that ask about the time demands of their job; whether or how their time at work changed with the arrival of their first child—and any subsequent children; what family activities are missed because of work; what work obligations are missed or reduced because of family obligations; how their boss reacts to or views their family obligations. Then compare the responses of both to assess how the work—home crunch is experienced and whether it differs for wives and husbands. ✦

Unit Four

Women Workers Across the Spectrum

There are over 20,000 different occupations in the United States today (U.S. Employment and Training Administration 1977) and women are employed in almost all of them (Herz and Wootton 1996). A person's location in the occupational structure is an important characteristic of their employment because occupational status is associated with job satisfaction and working conditions: earnings and other extrinsic rewards, where one lives, how one lives, personal tastes, and values. In the introduction to this text, you read that the type of work one performs is one of the most important indications to others of "who we are." It is for this reason that occupational information has been included in the U.S. decennial census since 1850 (Rothman 1987).

The structure of occupations has changed markedly since that time; technology has resulted in an increasingly complex and specialized division of labor. The broad scheme currently in use by the Bureau of Labor Statistics (BLS) for classifying occupations groups jobs on the basis of skill type, skill level, and working conditions. The composition of occupational incumbents has also changed over time, with women showing significant inroads into some traditionally male occupational groups—and very little integration into others—over the past three decades. These broad occupational catego-

ries and the percentage distributions of women working in them are presented in Table 4A; Table 4B shows women's representation in a select subset of occupations. An examination of these data show there is much variation in the percent of women employed across occupations and occupational categories. The patterns also reflect the description of occupational segregation provided in Unit Two.

Women's work experiences are affected by the type of occupation they hold, and thus vary dramatically across occupational categories. The presence of women in occupations affects the occupations as well, especially in terms of the nature of the work, how it is performed, and how others—male workers, employers, and clients—experience the occupation. The selections in this unit provide "case studies" of specific occupations, illustrating both how women are affected by their work and how they affect it.

Work experiences also have been found to vary across different racial/ethnic groups of women and by social class. The first article in this section presents a framework for understanding the range of work experiences of groups of women defined by race/ethnicity and class. Amott and Matthaei argue that race, class, and gender represent intertwining systems of domination and subordination that result in different forms, as well as

Table 4A
Employed Women by Major Occupation 2003–04 Annual Averages

Occupation	% female	% of all employed women who are in
Management, Professional, and Related Occupations	**50.3%**	**37.7%**
Management, business, and financial operations occupations	42.1	13.2
Professional and related occupations	56.1	24.5
Service Occupations	**56.8**	**19.9**
Sales and office occupations	63.9	35.0
Sales and related occupations	49.3	12.2
Office & administrative support occupations	75.9	22.8
Natural Resources, Construction and Maintenance Occupations	**4.5**	**1.0**
Farming, fishing, and forestry occupations	20.6	.3
Construction and extraction occupations	2.5	.3
Installation, maintenance, and repair occupations	4.6	.4
Production, Transportation, and Material Moving Occupations	**23.0**	**6.4**
Production occupations	30.4	4.4
Transportation and material moving occupations	14.7	1.9
Total Percent		. **100**

Source: *Women in the Labor Force: A Databook.* U.S. Department of Labor. Bureau of Labor Statistics, 2005. Tables 10, 11. *www.bls.gov/cps/wlf-databook2005.htm*.

varying degrees, of economic exploitation for women workers. Their contribution is important for two reasons. First, it represents the type of scholarship that is necessary for understanding work experiences in a pluralistic, diverse society and as, they point out, for facilitating broad-based movements against the oppressions experienced by women. Second, it shows how gender, race/ethnicity, and class can intertwine to influence the way employers might define "appropriate" job incumbents, and thus influence the workplace opportunities for women.

The remaining articles in this section focus on the experiences of women in various occupations. Managerial and professional jobs are the first occupations examined in this unit and are represented by the next four articles. These occupations are located at the top of the job hierarchy; they are high status jobs associated with relatively high levels of reward. Women's representation in these jobs is relatively high (50.3 percent) and has increased sharply over the past

three decades (BLS 2005). But it is important to note that jobs within these broad occupational categories are stratified, with women concentrated in the lower tiers of the hierarchy. Consider, for example, the profession of lawyer. There are many types of lawyers employed in commercial, governmental, charitable, and educational organizations. The highest paying positions are commonly situated in large corporate law firms in the commercial sector. These positions also are disproportionately held by men. Women, in contrast, are concentrated in government positions, small private practices, and family law—all associated with lower pay and less prestige (Harrington 1995). A similar status and sex-segregated hierarchy is found in medicine (with women in pediatrics and family medicine), management (where women cluster in low-level managerial jobs in small establishments in the service sector), and education (where women are concentrated in primary education positions

Table 4B
Women's Representation in Selected Occupations 2004–05

Occupation	% female
Chief executives	23.3%
Financial managers	56.6
Human resources managers	64.4
Management analysts	41.8
Accountants and auditors	60.5
Computer programmers	26.7
Computer software engineers	25.0
Architects, except naval	24.0
Chemical engineers	15.8
Mechanical engineers	5.8
Biological scientists	45.2
Market and survey researchers	48.2
Lawyers	29.4
Clergy	15.0
Librarians	83.0
Artists and related workers	50.7
Announcers	21.6
Editors	53.9
Pharmacists	47.0
Physicians and surgeons	29.4
Registered nurses	92.2
Emergency medical technicians and paramedics	32.7
Massage therapists	84.6
Dental assistants	96.5
Fire fighters	5.1
Police and sheriffs patrol officers	13.1
Chefs and head cooks	18.9
Bartenders	58.2
Waiters and waitresses	73.1
Child care workers	94.5
Recreation and fitness workers	64.9
Retail sales persons	50.8
Cashiers	76.1
Tellers	88.1
Customer service representatives	71.1
Carpenters	1.8
Electricians	2.1
Painters	5.8
Construction and building inspectors	12.4
Highway maintenance workers	2.7
Machinists	4.4
Printing machine operators	19.3
Bus drivers	48.2

Source: Bureau of Labor Statistics, *Women in the Labor Force: A Databook,* 2005.

(K–12 grades) and, in universities, at the assistant and associate professor levels).

The article by Parker examines the communication strategies employed by African American female senior executives to deal with problematic interactions at work. Women holding senior executive positions are relatively rare. Catalyst found that in 2002 women held approximately 16 percent of corporate officer positions in the Fortune 500 companies and that only 1.6 percent of the corporate officer positions were held by women of color (Catalyst 2002). Because African American women holding senior executive positions are rare, they work with and encounter others who have no experience with African Americans in high status positions. As a result, others may not accord them the same respect or authority that would be given to white males in the same position. African American women in these positions are challenged to establish their identity and gain the respect or authority that should be accorded to someone in their position. Parker's research presents the astute strategies they use to establish their identity and position, while maintaining effective working relationships. She also identifies working relationships where identity is less easily managed. In doing so, Parker is able to illustrate the complexities of interaction that come with the intertwining of race and gender in elite positions.

The next article by Roth focuses on gender equality in Wall Street securities firms. Those employed in Wall Street securities firms have some of the highest paying jobs in the financial professions. The jobs are client-intensive, and the rewards of work are highly compensated. Bonuses, based on performance evaluations by managers, add to the potential earnings of people in such positions. Roth's research concentrates on a cohort of business school graduates (male and female) who began careers in one of nine major securities firms on Wall Street in the early 1990s. As such, she is focusing on a set of people who are very much alike in their talents, specialty, experience, and human capital—factors that have been identified as key variables in determining earnings. These are also the factors that women have been said

to fall short on when the earnings gap is discussed. Roth's interest is in assessing gender equity in earnings. In doing so, she brings to our attention the fact that even at the top levels of earning, when all credentials appear to be equal, there is a stubborn persistence of a gender gap in pay.

Much of the research on women in high status positions has focused on white women. Significantly less research has been done on Latina women. The article by Gomez and others seeks to remedy this lack of information. Gomez et al. examine the careers of a number of Latinas who have achieved prominence and success in their professions. Through an analysis of career histories, critical decisions, personality, sources of support, culture and cultural identity, they discovered that successful Latinas often do not have a linear career path to success. Family—including extended family, teachers, and mentors—figured prominently in their careers. Career experiences varied by Hispanic subgroup, particularly as they articulated situations relating to ethnic discrimination, and they developed a repertoire of coping skills to combat the challenges they faced. Gomez et al.'s research fills an important void in the literature on Latinas, and their findings correspond with some of the issues that Amott and Matthaei discuss.

After examining high status occupations, our attention turns to the female-dominated semi-professions. Compared to the high status professions, the semi-professions are situated at a lower level in the professional hierarchy. These occupations possess many of the characteristics of "full" professions, including the requirement of specialized knowledge and training/education, but lack the power necessary to win widespread recognition as a "full profession" and the rewards associated with that status (Reiss 1955). What prevents semi-professions from achieving "full" professional status? Sociologists suggest that the major obstacle is the fact that the jobs are female-dominated. Female-dominated semi-professionals often work under the supervision of male professionals (e.g., nurses/physicians; teachers/principals), which also serves to detract from autonomous professional status (Ritzer and

Walczak 1987). The semi-professions are included in the BLS occupational category of "professional specialty." These jobs are also responsible for the reasonably high level of representation by women in the broad occupational category.

The selection by Preston presents historical data on public school teaching to explore how inferior status and wages get associated with female-dominated professions. She argues that male-dominated structures of supervision and bureaucratic control are key factors inhibiting the professionalization of teaching. Sex segregated administrative positions are described as limiting the autonomy of female teachers and preventing collective control over the profession. This selection also provides an example of the selective application of gender stereotypes in the development of job requirements. Specifically, Preston shows how gender-type traits of nurturance and high moral character became central to definitions of the "ideal" teacher.

Service occupations comprise the next category of jobs that are examined in this unit. Service occupations are the fastest growing category of occupations and encompass a wide range of areas, including health and protective services, as well as food preparation and personal care service occupations. Most jobs in this category all require some level of specialized training, though less training is required than for professional and managerial positions. Some service occupations are traditionally male-dominated, as with security and protective services. Others, like health service occupations, are traditionally female-dominated. For most of the male-dominated occupations, however, women have made significant inroads in employment. In only a few, such as firefighters and pest control workers, do women make up less than 10 percent of those employed in the occupation (BLS 2005).

Two selections in this section examine work experiences of women who have moved into security and protective services—positions that are atypical for women and where work situations do not mesh with stereotypical images of females. Security and protection occupations are those where work is more likely to be hazardous, physically demanding, and performed outdoors or in "dirty" work environments. Further, the distinguishing characteristics of these jobs reflect the "doubly male" work culture referred to by Gruber in Unit Two. Women who enter these occupations have been referred to as pioneers on the male frontier (Walshak 1981).

The selection by Yoder and Aniakudo discusses the effect of having a "double" minority status (gender and ethnicity) in the "doubly male" culture of the firehouse. Through both surveys and in-depth interviews, the authors explore issues of subordination through exclusion from information and social contact among peers. This discussion includes the co-worker hostility that undermines the cohesion necessary for effective firefighting; close supervision; the effects of tokenism; mixed relationships with black male firefighters; and relations with white female firefighters. In most cases, race is an omnipresent factor in experiences. Coping strategies by black female firefighters are discussed, as is the expectation that there is a unifying influence because of race, gender, or occupation. This article again highlights the differential work experiences of women with different social identities.

The next selection by Martin explores the importance of emotional labor in the work of police officers. Emotional labor refers to "an instrumental use of one's emotions in work or in private life" (Komarovsky 1991, 21); it includes the "act of expressing organizationally desired emotions during service interactions" (Morris and Feldman 1997, 257). Hochschild (1983) was one of the first to identify and label "emotion labor" as a dimension of work. In particular, it takes *effort* and *planning* to manage appropriate emotions on a regular basis. Learning to "be nice" or to negotiate with concern for others' feelings requires both effort and skill; that is, it is a form of labor. Yet, because of the kind of work it is (i.e., the management of *emotions*,) it is not highly valued.

As research into emotional labor expanded, more attention was paid to the "service" nature of a wide range of jobs. This approach emphasized the range of skills upon which job incumbents draw to do their work, examining closely the extent to which the management of emotion is part of the job. Two clear benefits have come from these investigations. First, it has focused on the *multiple* demands made upon occupational incumbents and the skills they draw upon in their work; in doing so, the *value* of emotional labor as work, has been enhanced. Second, the approach has been useful in identifying barriers to women's full participation and success in traditionally male occupations. In particular, even when women are in traditionally male occupations, they are often in positions where emotional labor is a larger component of their jobs. As such, their energies are directed away from the work that will help them achieve occupational or professional success (Bellas 1999).

Martin's article on police officers examines how gender affects the way in which police officers perform emotional labor. Her research highlights gender differences in "appropriate emotional responses" based on the gender of the officer and gender of the citizen with which the officer is interacting, as well as in the interaction between officers. The structure of the police organization reinforces these distinctions, while also diminishing the importance of emotional labor as a central aspect of police work. One effect is that female officers must manage a number of dilemmas surrounding the competing demands of policing-as-law-enforcement and policing-as-service. Martin's analysis shows the centrality of emotional labor in police work and argues that unless the police acknowledge its role, their effectiveness will be undermined.

The final selections in this unit focus on lower status occupations with high levels of female representation. In general, the demand for workers in these occupations is largely responsible for the large number of women employed in them. They are occupations that women can move in and out of more readily, often as a response to home life situation. At the same time, they are less well compensated and usually have no health or retirement benefits (other than social security) attached to them. As such, they are occupations in which women are most vulner-

able for meeting basic survival needs (shelter, food, clothing) for themselves and their families.

The first selection, by Rogers and Henson, focuses on "temps" or workers hired through temporary employment agencies. Rogers and Henson note that temporary workers are a growing, highly feminized, and relatively powerless group of employees. Further, the temporary work arrangement is highly gendered and makes "temps" vulnerable to unwelcome behaviors—in particular to sexual harassment. Rogers and Henson found that employers will define physical appearance as a criterion for a temp, and employment agencies will comply with the request since they are dependent on placement for their survival. Once placed, temps are instructed to defer to employers and their wishes. As such, temps are in a position where they cannot complain about sexual harassment because they will get negative ratings from the employer, and then temporary services will not place them in other jobs. The result is that sexual harassment continues in the work place, and temporary agencies do little to intervene on the temporary workers' behalf. The article highlights the vulnerability of temporary workers to sexual harassment in the workplace. In addition, it emphasizes how the link between employers and temporary agencies affirms the gendered nature of the workplace, which in turn enhances the likelihood that sexual harassment, will take place.

The article by Kang is a study of service interactions in Korean immigrant women-owned nail salons. She refers to this as "body labor," where workers provide body-related services and are required to develop emotional labor skills that correspond with the class and racial/ethnicity of customers. Kang studies nail salons that cater to three different types of clientele in three different areas of New York City. She is able to detail how emotional labor varies by clientele and location, and how the workers react to the expectations associated with the services they provide. Her study shows how different racial and class locations bring about varying forms of gendered emotional management with regard to clients, emphasizing that body work cannot be viewed only as a gendered practice, but one that must be viewed through the intersection of race, class, and gender.

In the final selection, Romero describes how gender and race/ethnicity combine to limit the job opportunities of Chicana women and lead to their clustering in domestic service work. Participant observation and interview data suggest that Chicana domestic service workers are restructuring the occupation so as to maximize its benefits (wages) and reduce its disadvantages (degrading nature). The end result is described as a transformation for domestic service workers from the role of servant to that of "expert," providing an example of how workers can have an impact on the nature of their job.

References

Bellas, Marcia. 1999. "Emotional labor in academic: The case of professors." *The Annals of the American Academy of Political and Social Science*, January: 96–110.

Bureau of Labor Statistics. 2005. *Women in the Laborforce: A Databook. www.bls.gov/cps/wlf-databook2005.htm.*

Catalyst. 2002. *Catalyst Census of Women Corporate Officers and Top Earners.* Catalyst: New York.

Harrington, M. 1995. *Women Lawyers: Rewriting the Rules.* New York: Penguin.

Herz, D. E., and B. H. Wootton. 1996. "Women in the workforce: An overview." In C. Costello and B. K. Kringold (eds.), *The American Woman 1996–1997: Where We Stand.* New York: W. W. Norton.

Hochschild, Arlie R. 1983. *The Managed Heart.* Berkeley: University of California Press.

Komarovsky, Mirra. 1991. "Reflections on feminist scholarship." *Annual Review of Sociology.* Palo Alto, CA: Annual Reviews Inc.

Morris, Andrew, and Daniel C. Feldman. 1997. "Managing emotions in the workplace." *Journal of Managerial Issues,* 9 (3): 257–75.

Reiss, A. 1955. "Occupational mobility of professional workers." *American Sociological Review,* 20: 693–700.

Ritzer, G., and D. Walczak. 1987. *Working: Conflict and Change.* Englewood Cliffs, NJ: Prentice Hall.

Rothman, R. A. 1987. *Working: Sociological Perspectives.* Englewood Cliffs, NJ: Prentice Hall.

U. S. Employment and Training Administration. 1977. *Dictionary of Occupational Titles.* Washington, D.C.: U.S. Government Printing Office.

Walshak, M. L. 1981. *Blue Collar Women: Pioneers on the Male Frontier.* Garden City, NY: Anchor Books. ✦

17
Race, Class, Gender, and Women's Works

A Conceptual Framework

Teresa L. Amott
Julie A. Matthaei

What social and economic factors determine and differentiate women's work lives? Why is it, for instance, that the work experiences of African American women are so different from those of European American women? Why have some women worked outside the home for pay, while others have provided for their families through unpaid work in the home? Why are most of the wealthy women in the United States of European descent and why are so many women of color poor? In this chapter, we lay out a basic conceptual framework for understanding differences in women's works and economic positions.

Throughout U.S. history, economic differences among women (and men) have been constructed and organized along a number of social categories. In our analysis, we focus on the three categories which we see as most central—gender, race-ethnicity, and class—with less discussion of others, such as age, sexual preference, and religion. We see these three social categories as interconnected, historical processes of domination and subordination. Thinking about gender, race-ethnicity, and class, then, necessitates thinking historically about power and economic exploitation.

There is a rich and controversial body of literature which examines the ways in which economic exploitation, ideology, and political power create and, in turn, are created by, gender, race-ethnicity, and class; we cannot do justice to the complexity of these issues here (Omi and Winant 1986; San Juan 1989; Spelman 1988; Matthaei, forthcoming). Rather, in this chapter, we develop a basic conceptual framework for thinking about the racial-ethnic histories of women's work. . . .

Gender, Race-Ethnicity, and Class Interconnected

The concepts of gender, race-ethinicity, and class are neither transhistorical nor independent. Hence, it is artificial to discuss them outside of historical time and place, and separately from one another. At the same time, without such a set of concepts, it is impossible to make sense of women's disparate economic experiences.

Gender, race-ethnicity, and class are not natural or biological categories which are unchanging over time and across cultures. Rather, these categories are socially constructed: they arise and are transformed in history, and themselves transform history. Although societies rationalize them as natural or god-given, ideas of appropriate feminine and masculine behavior vary widely across history and culture. Concepts and practices of race-ethnicity, usually justified by religion or biology, also vary over time, reflecting the politics, economics, and ideology of a particular time and in turn, reinforcing or transforming politics, economics, and ideology. For example, nineteenth-century European biologists Louis Agassiz and Count Arthur de Gobineau developed a taxonomy of race which divided humanity into separate and unequal racial species; this taxonomy was used to rationalize European colonization of Africa and Asia, and slavery in the United States (Gould 1981; Omi and Winant 1986). Class is perhaps the most historically specific category of all, clearly dependent upon the particular economic and social constellation of a society at a point in time. Still, notions of class as inherited or genetic continue to haunt us, harkening back to earlier eras in which lowly birth was thought to cause low intelligence and a predisposition to criminal activity.

Central to the historical transformation of gender, race-ethnicity, and class processes have been the struggles of subordinated groups to redefine or transcend them. For example, throughout the development of capitalism, workers' consciousness of themselves as workers and their struggles against class oppression have transformed capitalist-worker relationships, expanding workers' rights and powers. In the nineteenth century, educated white women escaped from the prevailing, domestic view of womanhood by arguing that homemaking included volunteer work, social homemaking careers, and political organizing. In the 1960s, the transformation of racial-ethnic identity into a source of solidarity and pride was essential to movements of people of color, such as the Black Power and American Indian movements.

Race-ethnicity, gender, and class are interconnected, interdetermining historical processes, rather than separate systems (Sargent 1981). This is true in two senses, which we will explore in more detail below. First, it is often difficult to determine whether an economic practice constitutes class, race, or gender oppression: for example, slavery in the U.S. South was at the same time a system of class oppression (of slaves by owners) and of racial-ethnic oppression (of Africans by Europeans). Second, a person does not experience these different processes of domination and subordination independently of one another; in philosopher Elizabeth Spelman's metaphor, gender, race-ethnicity, and class are not separate "pop-beads" on a necklace of identity. Hence, there is no generic gender oppression which is experienced by all women regardless of their race-ethnicity or class. As Spelman puts it:

> . . . in the case of much feminist thought we may get the impression that a woman's identity consists of a sum of parts neatly divisible from one another, parts defined in terms of her race, gender, class, and so on. . . . On this view of personal identity (which might also be called pop-bead metaphysics), my being a woman means the same whether I am white or black, rich or poor, French or Jamaican, Jewish or Muslim. (Spelman 1988, p. 136)

The problems of "pop-bead metaphysics" also apply to historical analysis. In our reading of history, there is no common experience of gender across race-ethnicity and class, of race-ethnicity across class and gender lines, or of class across race-ethnicity and gender.

With these caveats in mind, let us examine the processes of gender, class, and race-ethnicity, their importance in the histories of women's works, and some of the ways in which these processes have been intertwined.

Gender

Over the past 20 years, feminist theorists have developed the concept of gender as central to understanding women's lives and oppression. As we will see, while the concept of gender is invaluable, the gender process cannot be understood independently of class and race-ethnicity. Further, there is no common experience of gender oppression among women.

Gender differences in the social lives of men and women are based on, but are not the same thing as, biological differences between the sexes. Gender is rooted in societies' beliefs that the sexes are naturally distinct and opposed social beings. These beliefs are turned into self-fulfilling prophecies through sex-role socialization: the biological sexes are assigned distinct and often unequal work and political positions, and turned into socially distinct genders.

Economists view the sexual division of labor as central to the gender differentiation of the sexes. By assigning the sexes to different and complementary tasks, the sexual division of labor turns them into different and complementary genders. The work of males is at least partially, if not wholly, different from that of females, making "men" and "women" different economic and social beings. Sexual divisions of labor, not sexual difference alone, create difference and complementarity between "opposite" sexes. These differences, in turn, have been the basis for marriage in most societies.

Anthropologists have found that most societies, across historical periods, have tended to assign females to infant care and to the duties associated with raising children because of their biological ability to bear children. In contrast men usually concentrate on interfamilial activities, and gain political dominance; hence gender complementarity has usually led to political and economic dominance by men (Levi-Strauss 1971; Rosaldo 1974).

The concept of gender certainly helps us understand women's economic histories. Each racial-ethnic group has had a sexual division of labor which has barred individuals from the activities of the opposite sex. Gender processes do differentiate women's lives in many ways from those of the men in their own racial-ethnic and class group. Further, gender relations in all groups tend to assign women to the intra-familial work of child-rearing, as well as to place women in a subordinate position to the men of their class and racial-ethnic group.

But as soon as we have written these generalizations, exceptions pop into mind. Gender roles do not always correspond to sex. Some American Indian tribes allowed individuals to choose among gender roles: a female, for example, could choose a man's role, do men's work, and marry another female who lived out a woman's role. In the nineteenth century, some white females "passed" as men in order to escape the rigid mandates of gender roles. In many of these cases, women lived with and loved other women.

Even though childrearing is women's work in most societies, many women do not have children, and others do not perform their own child care or domestic work. Here, class is an especially important differentiating process. Upper-class women have been able to use their economic power to reassign some of the work of infant caretaking—sometimes even breast-feeding—to lower-class women of their own or different racial-ethnic groups. These women, in turn, may have been forced to leave their infants alone or with relatives or friends. Finally, gender complementarity has not always led to social and economic inequality; for example, many American Indian women had real control over the home and benefited from a more egalitarian sharing of power between men and women.

Since the processes of sex-role socialization are historically distinct in different times

and different cultures, they result in different conceptions of appropriate gender behavior. Both African American and Chicana girls, for instance, learn how to be women—but both must learn the specific gender roles which have developed within their racial-ethnic and class group and historical period. For example, for white middle-class homemakers in the 1950s, adherence to the concept of womanhood discouraged paid employment, while for poor black women it meant employment as domestic servants for white middle-class women. Since racial-ethnic and class domination have differentiated the experiences of women, one cannot assume, as do many feminist theorists and activists, that all women have the same experience of gender oppression—or even that they will be on the same side of a struggle, not even when some women define that struggle as "feminist."

Not only is gender differentiation and oppression not a universal experience which creates a common "women's oppression," the sexual divisions of labor and family systems of people of color have been systematically disrupted by race-ethnic and class processes. In the process of invasion and conquest, Europeans imposed their notions of male superiority on cultures with more egalitarian forms of gender relations, including many American Indian and African tribes. At the same time, European Americans were quick to abandon their notion of appropriate femininity when it conflicted with profits: for example, slave owners often assigned slave women to backbreaking labor in the fields.

Racial-ethnic and class oppression have also disrupted family life among people of color and the white working class. Europeans interfered with family relations within subordinated racial-ethnic communities through rape and forced cohabitation. Sometimes whites encouraged or forced reproduction, as when slave owners forced slave women into sexual relations. On the other hand, whites have often used their power to curtail reproduction among peoples of color, and aggressive sterilization programs were practiced against Puerto Ricans and American Indians as late as the 1970s. Beginning in the late nineteenth century, white administrators took American Indian children from their parents to "civilize" them in boarding schools where they were forbidden to speak their own languages or wear their native dress. Slave owners commonly split up slave families through sale to different and distant new owners. Nevertheless, African Americans were able to maintain strong family ties, and even augmented these with "fictive" or chosen kin (Gutman 1976). From the mid-nineteenth through the mid-twentieth centuries, many Asians were separated from their spouses or children by hiring policies and restrictions on immigration. Still, they maintained family life within these split households, and eventually succeeded in reuniting sometimes after generations. Hence, for peoples of color, having children and maintaining families have been an essential part of the struggle against racist oppression. Not surprisingly, many women of color have rejected the white women's movement's view of the family as the center of "women's oppression."

These examples reveal the limitations of gender as a single lens through which to view women's economic lives. Indeed, any attempt to understand women's experiences using gender alone cannot only cause misunderstanding, but can also interfere with the construction of broad-based movements against the oppressions experienced by women.

Race-Ethnicity

Like gender, race-ethnicity is based on a perceived physical difference and rationalized as "natural" or "god-given." But whereas gender creates difference and inequality according to biological sex, race-ethnicity differentiates individuals according to skin color or other physical features.

In all of human history, individuals have lived in societies with distinct languages, cultures, and economic institutions; these ethnic differences have been perpetuated by intermarriage within, but rarely between societies. However, ethnic differences can exist independently of a conception of race, and without a practice of racial-ethnic domination such as the Europeans practiced over the last three centuries.

Early European racist thought developed in the seventeenth and eighteenth centuries, embedded in the Christian worldview. Racial theorists argued that people of color were not descended from Adam and Eve as were whites. Later, in the nineteenth century, with the growth of Western science and its secular worldview, racial-ethnic differences and inequality were attributed directly to biology. According to the emerging scientific worldview, human beings were divided into biologically distinct and unequal races. Whites were, by nature, on top of this racial hierarchy, with the right and duty to dominate the others ("white man's burden") (Omi and Winant 1986; Cox 1959; Banton and Harwood 1975). In this racist typology, some ethnic differences—differences in language, culture, and social practices—were interpreted as racial and hence natural in origin. The different social and economic practices of societies of color were viewed by whites in the nineteenth century as "savage," in need of the "civilizing" influence of white domination. We use the term "race-ethnicity" in this book to grasp the contradictory nature of racial theories and practices, in particular the fact that those people seen as belonging to a particular "race" often lack a shared set of distinct physical characteristics, but rather share a common ethnicity or culture.

European racial theories were used to justify a set of economic and social practices which, in fact, made the "races" socially unequal. In this way, racism and the practices which embody it became self-fulfilling prophecies. Claiming that people of color were inherently inferior, whites segregated and subordinated them socially, economically, and politically. Furthermore, by preventing intermarriage between people of color and whites, whites perpetuated physical and ethnic differences as well as social and economic inequality between themselves and people of color across the generations. Although few scientists today claim that there are biological factors which create unequal races of human beings, racist practices and institutions have continued to produce both difference and inequality.

Does the concept of race-ethnicity help us understand the economic history of women in the United States? Certainly, for white racial-ethnic domination has been a central force in U.S. history. European colonization of

North America entailed the displacement and murder of the continent's indigenous peoples, rationalized by the racist view that American Indians were savage heathens. The economy of the South was based on a racial-ethnic system, in which imported Africans were forced to work for white landowning families as slaves. U.S. military expansion in the nineteenth century brought more lands under U.S. control—territories of northern Mexico (now the Southwest), the Philippines, and Puerto Rico—incorporating their peoples into the racial-ethnic hierarchy. And from the mid-nineteenth century onward, Asians were brought into Hawaii's plantation system to work for whites as semi-free laborers. In the twentieth century, racial-ethnic difference and inequality have been perpetuated by the segregation of people of color into different and inferior jobs, living conditions, schools, and political positions, and by the prohibition of intermarriage with whites in some states up until 1967.

Race-ethnicity is a key concept in understanding histories. But it is not without limitations. First, racial-ethnic processes have never operated independently of class and gender. In the previous section on gender, we saw how racial domination distorted gender and family relations among people of color. Racial domination has also been intricately linked to economic or class domination. As social scientists Michael Omi (Asian American) and Howard Winant (European American) explain, the early European arguments that people of color were without souls had direct economic meaning:

> At stake were not only the prospects for conversion, but the types of treatment to be accorded them. The expropriation of property, the denial of political rights, the introduction of slavery and other forms of coercive labor, as well as outright extermination, all presupposed a worldview which distinguished Europeans—children of God, human beings, etc.—from "others." Such a worldview was needed to explain why some should be "free" and others enslaved, why some had rights to land and property while others did not. (Omi and Winant 1986, p.58)

Indeed, many have argued that racial theories only developed after the economic process of colonization had started, as a justification for white domination of peoples of color (Cox 1959). The essentially economic nature of early racial-ethnic oppression in the United States makes it difficult to isolate whether peoples of color were subordinated in the emerging U.S. economy because of their race-ethnicity or their economic class. Whites displaced American Indians and Mexicans to obtain their land. Whites imported Africans to work as slaves and Asians to work as contract laborers. Puerto Ricans and Filipinas/os were victims of further U.S. expansionism. Race-ethnicity and class intertwined in the patterns of displacement from land, genocide, forced labor, and recruitment from the seventeenth through the twentieth centuries. While it is impossible, in our minds, to determine which came first in these instances—race-ethnicity or class—it is clear that they were intertwined and inseparable.

Privileging racial-ethnic analysis also leads one to deny the existence of class differences, both among whites and among people of color, which complicate and blur the racial-ethnic hierarchy. A racial-ethnic analysis implies that all whites are placed above all peoples of color. . . . But in fact, as European American economist Harold Baron (1975) points out, a minority of the dominated race is allowed some upward mobility and ranks economically above whites. At the same time, however, all whites have some people of color below them. For example, there are upper-class black, Chicana, and Puerto Rican women who are more economically privileged than poor white women; however, there are always people of color who are less economically privileged than the poorest white woman. Finally, class oppression operates among women of the same racial-ethnic group.

A third problem with the analysis of race domination is that such domination has not been a homogeneous process. Each subordinated racial-ethnic group has been oppressed and exploited differently by whites: for example, American Indians were killed and displaced, Africans were enslaved, and Filipinas/os and Puerto Ricans were colonized. Whites have also dominated whites; some European immigrant groups, particularly Southern and Eastern Europeans, were subjected to segregation and violence. In some cases, people of color have oppressed and exploited those in another group: some American Indian tribes had African slaves; some Mexicans and Puerto Ricans displaced and murdered Indians and had African slaves. Because of these differences, racial oppression does not automatically bring unity of peoples of color across their own racial-ethnic differences, and feminists of color are not necessarily in solidarity with one another.

To sum up, we see that, as with gender, the concept of race-ethnicity is essential to our analysis of women's works. However, divorcing this concept from gender and class, again, leads to problems in both theory and practice.

Class

Radical economists stress class as the most important category for understanding economic life. Following Marx, these economists have focused on the ways in which individuals' relationships to the production process are polarized, such that one class reaps the benefits of another class' labor (a process which Marx called "exploitation"). Struggle between the classes over the control of the production process and the distribution of its output, Marx claimed, was the key to economic history. Thus, Marx characterized different societies as involving different "modes of production," each with its own class relations. In the feudal system of medieval Europe, for example, nobles owned the land and serfs were forced to work it, giving over a portion of their product and labor to the leisured nobility. In slavery, slaveowners, by virtue of property rights in slaves, owned the product of their slaves' labor, living and enriching themselves through their exploitation of the slaves. In capitalism, the owners of the machines and factories are able to live off the labor of the workers, who own nothing but their own labor and hence are forced to work for the owners. In the century since Marx wrote, radical economists have further developed Marx's conception of class, making it into a powerful concept for understanding economies past and present.

We believe that the concepts of class and exploitation are crucial to understanding the work lives of women in early U.S. history, as well as in the modern, capitalist economy. Up through the nineteenth century, different relations organized production in different regions of the United States. The South was dominated by slave agriculture; the Northeast by emerging industrial capitalism; the Southwest (then part of Mexico) by the *hacienda* system which carried over many elements of the feudal manor into large-scale production for the market; the rural Midwest by independent family farms that produced on a small scale for the market; and the American Indian West by a variety of tribal forms centered in hunting and gathering or agriculture, many characterized by cooperative, egalitarian relations. Living within these different labor systems, and in different class positions within them, women led very different economic lives.

By the late nineteenth century, however, capitalism had become the dominant form of production, displacing artisans and other small producers along with slave plantations and tribal economies. Today, wage labor accounts for over 90 percent of employment; self employment, including family businesses, accounts for the remaining share (U.S. Bureau of the Census 1990). With the rise of capitalism, women were brought into the same labor system and polarized according to the capitalist-wage laborer hierarchy.

At the same time as the wage labor form specific to capitalism became more prevalent, capitalist class relations became more complex and less transparent. Owners of wealth (stocks and bonds) now rarely direct the production process; instead, salaried managers, who may or may not own stock in the company, take on this function. While the capitalist class may be less identifiable, it still remains a small and dominant elite. In 1996, the super-rich (the richest one-half of one percent of the households) owned 35 percent of the total wealth in our country, over 70 times the share they would have had if wealth were equally distributed. The richest tenth of all households owned 72 percent of all wealth, over seven times their fair share. This extreme concentration of wealth conveys a concentration of leisure and power over others into the hands of a small number of households, a concentration which is perpetuated through the generations by inheritance laws and customs.[1]

At the other end of the hierarchy, in 1986, the poorest 90 percent of households owned only 28 percent of total wealth, and had to send at least one household member out to work for the household's survival. Among these waged and salaried workers, a complicated hierarchy of segmented labor markets gives some workers greater earnings and power over the production process than others. Indeed, there are many disagreements over how to categorize managers, professionals, and government workers—to name only a few of the jobs which seem to fall outside the two-class model. . . .[2]

Class can be a powerful concept in understanding women's economic lives, but there are limits to class analysis if it is kept separate from race-ethnicity and gender. First, as we saw in the race section above, the class relations which characterized the early U.S. economy were also racial-ethnic and gender formations. Slave owners were white and mostly male, slaves were black. The displaced tribal economies were the societies of indigenous peoples. Independent family farmers were whites who farmed American Indian lands; they organized production in a patriarchal manner, with women and children's work defined by and subordinated to the male household head and property owner. After establishing their dominance in the pre-capitalist period, white men were able to perpetuate and institutionalize this dominance in the emerging capitalist system, particularly through the monopolization of managerial and other high-level jobs.

Second, the sexual division of labor within the family makes the determination of a woman's class complicated—determined not simply by her relationship to the production process, but also by that of her husband or father. For instance, if a woman is not in the labor force but her husband is a capitalist, then we might wish to categorize her as a member of the capitalist class. But what if that same woman worked as a personnel manager for a large corporation, or as a salesperson in

an elegant boutique? Clearly, she derives upper-class status and access to income from her husband, but she is also, in her own right, a worker. Conversely, when women lose their husbands through divorce, widowhood, or desertion, they often change their class position in a downward direction. A second gender-related economic process overlooked by class analysis is the unpaid household labor performed by women for their fathers, husbands, and children—or by other women, for pay.[3]

Third, while all workers are exploited by capitalists, they are not equally exploited, and gender and race-ethnicity play important roles in this differentiation. Men and women of the same racial-ethnic group have rarely performed the same jobs—this sex-typing and segregation is the labor market form of the sexual division of labor we studied above. Further, women of different racial-ethnic groups have rarely been employed at the same job, at least not within the same workplace or region. This racial-ethnic-typing and segregation has both reflected and reinforced the racist economic practices upon which the U.S. economy was built.

Thus, jobs in the labor force hierarchy tend to be simultaneously race-typed and gender-typed. Picture in your mind a registered nurse. Most likely, you thought of a white woman. Picture a doctor. Again, you imagined a person of a particular gender (probably a man), and a race (probably a white person). If you think of a railroad porter, it is likely that a black man comes to mind. Almost all jobs tend to be typed in such a way that stereotypes make it difficult for persons of the "wrong" race and/or gender to train for or obtain the job. Of course, there are regional and historical variations in the typing of jobs. On the West Coast, for example, Asian men performed much of the paid domestic work during the nineteenth century because women were in such short supply. In states where the African American population is very small, such as South Dakota or Vermont, domestic servants and hotel chambermaids are typically white. Nonetheless, the presence of variations in race-gender typing does not contradict the idea that jobs tend to take on racial-ethnic and gender characteristics with profound effects on the labor market opportunities of job-seekers.

The race-sex-typing of jobs makes the effects of class processes inseparable from the effects of race-ethnicity and gender. Not only is the labor market an arena of struggle in which race-ethnicity and gender, as well as class, are reproduced. In addition, the race-sex-typing of jobs has been central in determining the job structure itself. For example, secretarial work developed in the late nineteenth century as a white woman's job; hence, in contrast to the white male job of clerk which it replaced, secretarial work cast white women in the role of "office wives" to white men, and involved no path of career advancement into management.

. . . White workers, not just white capitalists, helped impose this race-ethnic hierarchy. White capitalists—wealthy landowners, railroad magnates, factory owners—imported blacks, Asians, and, later, Puerto Ricans and Mexicans as a low-wage labor supply. The entrance of these workers of color into the labor force was met with hostility and violence by both white workers and small producers such as farmers and craftsmen. Since employers used immigrant workers of color as strikebreakers or low-wage competition, white workers trying to organize for higher wages resisted this immigration. The threat of competition from workers of color and an ideology of white supremacy kept most white workers from recruiting workers of color into their emerging trade unions on equal terms. European immigrants who spoke languages other than English also faced economic and political discrimination. Thus, in an environment of nativism and racial hostility, jobs came to be increasingly segmented along racial-ethnic lines as the result of combined capitalist and worker efforts (Bonacich 1976). Furthermore, as people of different racial-ethnic groups were drawn out of the many different labor systems from which they had come into wage labor, they were also segregated within the developing labor market hierarchy.

The processes which have perpetuated the sex-typing of jobs have, for the most part, been less overt and violent. White male unions, in the late nineteenth century, fought for the passage of "protective legislation" that, by excluding women from dangerous or unhealthy jobs and from overtime work, had the effect of denying them highly paid factory jobs and confining them in lower-paying (and also hazardous) sectors such as apparel and textile manufacture. Women were also confined to low-paid, servile, or care-taking jobs by the sexual division of labor in the home, particularly married women's assignment to the unpaid work of caring for children and serving their husbands. Many employers simply refused to hire married women, with the view that their place was in the home. Domestic responsibilities also limited women's ability to compete for jobs requiring overtime or lengthy training. Professional associations and schools, dominated by white men, restricted the entry of women of all racial-ethnic groups well into the twentieth century. When individual women gained the qualifications and tried to break into jobs monopolized by men of their racial-ethnic group, or into elite, white men's jobs, they were rejected or, if hired, sabotaged, ridiculed, and racially and sexually harassed. These processes have been extremely costly to women in terms of lost wages and job opportunities. This combination of race- and sex-segregation in the labor market meant that, in general, only white men were able to earn a "family wage," adequate to support oneself and a family.

In these ways, the racial-ethnic and gender processes operating in the labor market have transposed white and male domination from pre-capitalist structures into the labor market's class hierarchy. This hierarchy can be described by grouping jobs into different labor market sectors or segments: "primary," "secondary," and "underground." The primary labor market—which has been monopolized by white men—offers high salaries, steady employment, and upward mobility. Its upper tier consists of white-collar salaried or self-employed workers with high status, autonomy, and, often, supervisory capacity. Wealth increases access to this sector, since it purchases elite education and provides helpful job connections. . . .

The lower tier of the primary sector, which still yields high earnings but involves less autonomy, contains many unionized blue-collar jobs. White working-class men have used union practices, mob violence, and intimidation to monopolize these jobs. By World War II, however, new ideologies of worker solidarity, embodied in the mass industrial unions, began to overcome the resistance of white male workers to the employment of people of color and white women in these jobs.

In contrast to both these primary tiers, the secondary sector offers low wages, few or no benefits, little opportunity for advancement, and unstable employment. People of color and most white women have been concentrated in the secondary sector jobs, where work is often part-time, temporary, or seasonal, and pay does not rise with increasing education or experience. Jobs in both tiers of the primary labor market have generally yielded family wages, earnings high enough to support a wife and children who are not in the labor force for pay. Men of color in the secondary sector have not been able to earn enough to support their families, and women of color have therefore participated in wage labor to a much higher degree than white women whose husbands held primary sector jobs.

Outside of the formal labor market is the underground sector, where the most marginalized labor force groups, including many people of color, earn their living from illegal or quasi-legal work. This sector contains a great variety of jobs, including drug trafficking, crime, prostitution, work done by undocumented workers, and sweatshop work which violates labor standards such as minimum wages and job safety regulations.

White women and people of color have waged successful battles to gain admittance to occupations from which they once were barred. Union organizing has succeeded in raising jobs out of the secondary sector by providing higher wages, fringe benefits, a seniority system, and protection from arbitrary firing for workers. Similarly, the boundaries of the underground economy have been changed by struggles to legalize or make illegal acts such as drug use and prostitution—for example, by women's successful struggle to prohibit the sale of alcohol dur-

ing the early twentieth century—as well as by immigration and labor laws.

Conclusion

Women throughout the United States have not experienced a common oppression as women. The processes of gender, race-ethnicity, and class—intrinsically interconnected—have been central forces determining and differentiating women's work lives in U.S. history. Thus, while the explanatory power of each concept—gender, race-ethnicity, and class—is, in itself, limited, together they form a basis for understanding women's work. . . .

Notes

1. This represents an increase for the top 0.5 percent, from 25.4 percent of total wealth 20 years ago; 20 years ago, the poorest 90 percent of all households had 34.9 percent of all wealth, 6.7 percentage points more than they have presently. There has been a controversy over these numbers; after these data, collected by the Federal Research Board, were publicized by the Joint Economic Committee of Congress, the Federal Reserve claimed that a mistake had been made in the original survey, and that actually there had been no increase in the share of wealth held by the top 0.5 percent. See "Scandal at the Fed? Doctoring the Numbers on Wealth Concentration," *Dollars and Sense*, No. 125 (April 1987):10.

2. For good discussions of this process, see David Gordon, Richard Edwards, Michael Reich, eds., *Segmented Work, Divided Workers: The Historical Transformation of Labor in the United States* (New York: Cambridge University Press, 1982); and Eric Wright, "Class Boundaries and Contradictory Class Locations," in *Classes, Power, and Conflict*, ed. Anthony Giddens (Berkeley: University of California Press, 1982):112-129.

3. Marxist-feminists did attempt to analyze this work as "domestic labor" in a theoretical debate in the 1970s; for a review of this debate, see Wally Seccombe, "Reflections on the Domestic Labor Debate and Prospects for Marxist-Feminist Synthesis," in *The Politics of Diversity*, ed. Robert Hamilton and Michele Barrett (Canada: Book Center Inc., 1986). Some claim that the household is part of a different mode of production which coexists with capitalism; see Harriet Fraad, Stephen Resnick, and Richard Wolff, "For Every

Knight in Shining Armor, There's a Castle Waiting to Be Cleaned: A Marxist-Feminist Analysis of the Household," *Rethinking Marxism* 2 (Winter 1989):10–69; and the comments by Julie Matthaei, Zillah Eisenstein, Kim Lane Scheppele, Nancy Folbre, Heidi Hartmann, and Stephanie Coontz in the same issue.

References

Banton, M. and J. Harwood. 1975. *The Race Concept.* Ch. 1. New York: Praeger.

Baron, H. 1975. "Racial domination in advanced capitalism: A theory of nationalism and divisions in the labor market." In R. Edwards, M. Reich, and D. Gordon (eds.), *Labor Market Segmentation.* Lexington, MA: D. C. Heath and Company.

Bonacich, Edna. 1976. "Advanced Capitalism and Black/White Race Relations in the United States: A Split Labor Market Interpretation," *American Sociological Review* 41(Feb): 34–51.

Cox, O. C. 1959. *Class, Caste and Race: A Study in Social Dynamics.* New York: Monthly Review Press.

Ferguson, A. 1983. "On conceiving motherhood and sexuality: A feminist materialist approach." In J. Treblicot (ed.), *Mothering: Essays in Feminist Theory.* Totowa, NJ: Rowman and Allanheld.

Gould, S. J. 1981. *The Mismeasure of Man.* New York: W. W. Norton and Company:42–51.

Gutman, H. 1976. *The Black Family in Slavery and Freedom, 1750–1925.* New York: Pantheon Books.

Hodges, J. et al. 1975. *The Cultural Bases of Racism and Group Oppression.* Berkeley: Two Riders Press.

Levi-Strauss, C. 1971. "The family." In A. Skolnick and J. Skolnick (eds.), *The Family in Transition.* Boston: Little Brown.

Matthaei, J. forthcoming. "Marxist contributions to radical economics." In S. Feiner and B. Roberts (eds.), *Radical Economics.* Norwell, MA: Kluwer-Nijhoff.

Omi, M. and H. Winant. 1986. *Racial Formation in the United States: From the 1960s to the 1980s.* New York: Routledge & Kegan Paul.

Rosaldo, M. Z. 1974. "Women, culture, and society: A theoretical overview." In M. Rosaldo and L. Lamphere (eds.), *Woman, Culture, and Society.* Stanford: Stanford University Press.

San Juan, E. 1989. "Problems in one Marxist project of theorizing race." In *Rethinking Marxism*, 2 (Summer):58–80.

Sargent, L. (ed.) 1981. *Women and Revolution.* Boston: South End Press.

Spelman, E. V. 1988. *Inessential Woman: Problems of Exclusion in Feminist Thought.* Boston: Beacon Press.

U.S. Bureau of the Census. 1990. *Statistical Abstract of the United States: 1990.* Washington, D.C.:GPO:386.

Food for Thought and Application Questions

1. Select any two of the following racial/ethnic groups: African Americans, American Indians, Chinese Americans, Filipinos, Japanese Americans, Mexican Americans, Puerto Ricans, and Anglos/Whites. Collect information on the labor-force participation rates and average earnings for women in the two groups you selected. How have racial/ethnic processes operated to create any differences you find in work experiences between the two groups? (In order to answer this, you should read about the economic history of the groups you selected. The book this chapter was excerpted from is one good source; the sources cited in the bibliography for this chapter provide others. You may also find useful information in textbooks on race and ethnic relations.)

2. In your opinion, has gender, race/ethnicity, or class had the most impact on your work aspirations and experiences? Ask the same question to people from different racial/ethnic and class groups. Also ask a member of the opposite sex. Are their responses similar to yours? Do any patterns begin to emerge in the responses you receive? ✦

18

Negotiating Identity in Raced and Gendered Workplace Interactions

The Use of Strategic Communication by African American Women Senior Executives Within Dominant Culture Organizations

Patricia S. Parker

An interview published in *Essence* magazine dubbed U. S. national security advisor, Condolleeza Rice, as "The Most Powerful Woman in the World" (Wilkerson, 2002). In that article, Rice detailed a recent encounter with a sales clerk in a jewelry store, in which the clerk ignored her request to see the "nicer jewelry." As Rice persisted in her request, the sales clerk, "turned and said something . . . 'Black trash' or something like that." To which Rice reportedly responded, "Let's get one thing clear. If you could afford anything in here, you wouldn't be behind this counter. So I strongly suggest you do your job." Rice went on to say, "It's something that's happened to every Black person at some point in time. . . . My view is you just don't let that sort of thing go at all" (Wilkerson, 2002, p. 154).

The above description of a brief encounter between national security adviser Condolleeza Rice and a jewelry store sales clerk points to the central issues that form the basis of this article. First, the negotiation of identity is an ongoing endeavor for African American women, even (or perhaps especially) when they have attained positions of power. Second, identity negotiation is an interactive process in which much can be learned about African American women's agency (i.e., "not letting that sort of thing go") in raced and gendered workplace encounters.

Organizations are gendered and raced to the extent that power relations are patterned through taken-for-granted, often hidden, assumptions about gender and race (see Acker, 1990) that are embedded in organizational discourses and that privilege the experiences and interests of the dominant racial and gender group (White middle class men). Race and gender conflicts are inevitable as non-dominant culture interests and experiences are suppressed, devalued, and muted (Orbe, 1998) through organizational discourses that privilege dominant culture interests and experiences. This article examines how members of one non-majority group, African American women senior executives, define constraining aspects of interaction within dominant organizational cultures and create communicative strategies for resisting and changing those interaction contexts and for negotiating their identities as Black women.

The workplace interactions of African American women senior executives provide a particularly good case for exploring identity negotiation within gendered and raced organizational contexts. Executive leadership represents an interaction context in which dominant culture norms and values regarding gender and race take on high symbolic importance (Biggart & Hamilton, 1984). Dominant culture organizational members come to expect leaders to look, act, and think in ways consistent with the socially constructed meanings of "organizational leader" and "leadership." Traditionally, those meanings have been in conflict with stereotypical assumptions about African American women (Parker, 2001).

Standpoints and Identity Negotiation

In this article, I examine those interaction encounters within dominant culture organizations which African American women executives perceive as problematic. I use standpoint analysis (Harstock, 1987) as a way of discovering how those encounters are defined, and what the women do as active agents to manage their identities, as they resist, subvert or otherwise respond strategically to perceived problematic encounters. Standpoint epistemology encourages research that explores the practices of people who, in their everyday interactions, "take up resistance and struggle . . . producing knowledge that extends and expands their and our grasp of how things are put together and hence their and our ability to organize and act effectively" (Smith, 1987, p. 96). Broadly defined, a standpoint analysis offers insights into how a person's location within culture shapes her or his life. It emphasizes how gender and race position individuals in society, how that position or standpoint guides what she or he knows, feels, and does, and directs a person's understanding of social life as a whole (Wood, 1998).

The process through which persons develop standpoints can be understood as an ongoing process of self-definition. Indeed, Collins (1990) asserts that standpoints must be self-defined. Similarly, Bullis and Stout (2001) emphasize that standpoints are "achieved through reflexive struggle" (p. 58). Conceptually, developing standpoints is very much related to a communication view of identity negotiation in that both emphasize processes of self-definition. Jackson (1999) describes identity as "a code for being, providing a capsule for understanding how one defines oneself and one's place in a community of interactants. One's ability to define self (i.e. identity) predetermines conduct; consequently, who one thinks he or she is relates to what one thinks one should be doing" (p. 60). It is within that interaction space that the present analysis is centered—where an African American woman executive in a dominant culture organization determines who she thinks she is and

what she should be doing in response to problematic workplace encounters.

Method

This research is part of a larger study that focused on the leadership socialization, strategic communication and leadership approaches of 15 African American women who held executive positions within dominant culture organizations (Parker, 1997). The data analysis for the strategic communication portion of that study is reported in this article.

Participants

The participants were 15 African American women executives, including 13 in senior management positions and two in upper-middle management. The participants were chosen based on the following sampling criteria: (a) they were employed at a dominant culture organization at the time of the study; (b) they were at the level of director or above; (c) they had line responsibility; and (d) they had supervisory responsibilities. These criteria are consistent with those used by other researchers interested in executive management by women (e.g., Mainiero, 1994). Because of funding limitations, sampling was limited to the western, southern, and southeastern regions of the United States. The final sample consisted of fifteen African American women executives who were interviewed in five states and in Washington, DC. Six executives worked at organizations in the southern region of the United States (Arkansas, Louisiana, Tennessee), six were in the southeast (Georgia and Washington, D. C.), and three were in the Pacific southwest (California).

In addition to regional diversity, participants varied in terms of socioeconomic backgrounds, age, and tenure, as well as organizational industry and type. The industries represented in the sample were insurance, communications, education, and state and federal government. Seven of the women worked in private corporations and eight were employed at public organizations.

Data Collection

Data for this portion of the study were collected through face-to-face interviews with each executive. Interviews followed semistructured interview protocols based on topics related to the research questions. Because I was interested in understanding the women's interpretations of their everyday workplace interactions, the questions were designed to solicit descriptions of the executives in interaction with coworkers, subordinates, and clients. Most interviews lasted about one hour; they ranged from 45 minutes to two and one-half hours. The interviews were tape recorded and transcribed. I used field notes to record descriptions of organizational contexts and to document my preliminary analyses and responses to the data.

Results

The research questions that guided the study were: Within dominant culture organizations, (1) What do African American women executives describe as salient challenges in their workplace interactions? And (2) What communication strategies do African American women executives use to adapt to, resist, or reconstruct perceived challenges in their workplace interactions? With regard to research question one, two interaction contexts emerged as salient in the executives' narratives: (a) interacting with their White male colleagues, and (b) interacting with other African Americans. Regarding research question two, data analysis revealed a combination of direct and indirect or avoidance strategies that the executives used to adapt to, resist, or transform perceived challenges in their workplace interactions (see Table 18.1).

Problematic Interactions with White Male Colleagues

The data revealed three salient challenges related to the executives' interaction with their White male colleagues in upper and senior management: (a) experiencing direct interpersonal conflict with their White male colleagues; (b) encountering attempts at subordination through perceived exclusionary practices; and (c) having their ideas co-opted or ignored in meetings (see Table 18.1). Underlying each of these instances were the perceptions that their colleagues were operating on misguided assumptions that simply needed to be set straight. This was especially apparent in the executives' descriptions of direct interpersonal conflict with their White male peers.

Table 18.1
African American Women Executives' Communication Strategies for Managing Raced and Gendered Interactions within Dominant Culture Organizations

Interaction Contexts	Communication Strategies and Tactics
Interacting With White Male Colleagues	
1. Experiencing interpersonal conflict	Indirect: Unassertive communication in initial encounters "Model" excellence Direct: Face-to-face negotiation
2. Having ideas co-opted or ignored during meetings	Avoidance: Build reputation for "toughness" Indirect: Use of humor to co-opt gender bias Direct: Face-to-face negotiation
3. Being excluded from communication networks	Direct: Confront excluding behavior Develop ties with "insider" Indirect: Recreate networks
Interacting with Other African Americans	
1. Perceived unmet expectations	
2. Personal attacks	Indirect: Focus on issue at hand Avoidance

Interpersonal conflict. Several instances emerged in the data related to direct interpersonal conflict between the executive and their White male colleagues. Interpersonal conflict is defined here as an expressed struggle between two parties who perceive incompatible goals (Wilmot & Hocker, 1998). In each of the instances, it was the executive who was instrumental in expressing the struggle, including identifying and defining her perceptions of the salient elements of the conflict. One executive's account reveals how this process unfolds:

> There has been one [White male member of the senior management team] that we had to find a comfort level with one another, and that was probably gender and race-based. But we found it and work extremely well together, and probably work more closely than any of the members of the group, probably get along better than any others. [Before that] we had some difficult moments. . . . I began getting the sense that he was making decisions that were sending the wrong message as to how we worked together and who was doing what—as if we were on different levels. And we had to get that straight.

In this instance, getting it "straight" involved getting out in the open issues the executive felt were unspoken assumptions her colleague was making. She describes the face-to-face encounter in which she began the process of setting things straight:

> I said to him . . . in so many words, that my sense was he did not have any experience working with Black women in a professional capacity on the same level as he. And I felt like he had to get used to it and had to learn that we were both doing the same thing and at the same level. But he didn't agree. He said he certainly did not intentionally, and I believe this, he was not intentionally doing anything to send the wrong messages. But again, you know, I don't think he realized the messages that he was sending.

A common theme among all the accounts of interpersonal conflict was that the perceived struggle was caused by unintended or taken for granted assumptions on the part of their White male colleague. The executives used words and phrases such as "ignorance" (in the non-pejorative sense), and "force of habit" to characterize what they perceived as their White male colleagues' tendency to cause unintentional conflict. The following is a typical account of this perception:

> [A White male coworker in management] would send voice mail to his old boys network, which were a couple of guys who had been around for years and years, and send them to the meeting, or send them the information, and leave me out of the loop. And I would go back and [he'd] say, "Oh no. I didn't mean to do that. I'm sorry. I screwed up." OK. And he swore that it was an oversight and that he would fix it. . . . And he would correct himself for a month or so. And then he would slip right back. And I think it was something that was difficult for him to control, I mean, it was an old habit, you know, it was hard for him to break. And I think that's why he's, you know, he's not in [that position any longer] ... because he didn't break that. Because I think our business is looking to try to gain the best experience, the best expertise, and use everybody in the organization.

The executives' strategic responses to instances of interpersonal conflict included a combination of direct and indirect or avoidance strategies (see Table 18.1), and reflected this understanding that their colleagues may be unaware that there was an actual conflict. An example of an indirect strategy is the case of one executive who said that in initial encounters with her White male colleagues, she sometimes alters her communication in ways that will not be perceived as threatening:

> So I try not to be overly assertive. I try to, I guess, conform to their perceptions of a female in that I ask very gingerly things that I want done. I am not as direct as I might be . . . if I wasn't aware of their problems with the fact that I'm the first female they have ever had to deal with that way. I take that approach first, you know. Let's work on this. Whenever I have to be direct, then I am.

From the point of view of this executive, varying her strategic communication was a way of transforming a potentially constraining situation into a more workable one. Although she reported that being more direct was her preferred communication style, the executive was willing to use a more indirect style to accommodate her colleague's initial point of view. She was in essence recreating a space for her voice to be heard.

Another executive said she actually favored avoidance and indirect strategies, which she has honed over time to deal with race and gender issues. Rather than engaging her White male colleagues about unfair treatment based on what she sees as their dominant culture privileges, she "models excellence."

> What I focus on is results. From the time I was a sales rep through all of my management jobs, whether I directly had sales measurements or whatever the measure of quality was, I always assumed that I would never be allowed to do less than almost perfect. I had a conversation recently with my boss's boss, who is a White female, and we've known each other for ten years. I said, "You see, I have never felt from the first day I came to [this organization] that I could do anything less than almost perfect." I said, "The things that my White counterpart V. P.'s are forgiven for, like not making their profit numbers or not making their customer numbers or not gaining market share, I don't think I would ever have been allowed."

The most commonly reported strategic approach was face-to-face negotiation. In the following passage, one executive describes how she used a direct cooperative approach with a White male coworker who had been making decisions without coordinating with her first, which was the established procedure:

> [W]e had several conversations. And I think we had conversations with friends of ours [that we had in common] . . . and because we both knew that each of the other of us had good intentions, were looking toward the same goal, it enabled us probably more easily to find that comfort level. And, I mean, he said very clearly and very directly, "I really am not intending to do anything like that. I would never do anything like that. I don't want to do that. . . ." And so he is now, I think, as a result of our conversations very conscious of it and I think he'll go to his next workplace

and in a similar situation be very . . . know that he needs to think about it, and will think about it. So it has been a good experience for both of us. It's worked out fine. So we get along fabulously now.

Having ideas co-opted or ignored in meetings. Another salient element in the women's accounts related to their interactions with their White male colleagues during meetings. All of the women who gave accounts of this challenge made observations about their perceptions that their colleagues "talked for the sake of talking" or "liked to hear themselves talk." The following account is a typical scenario:

> You will sit in a meeting or be on a conference call, and the White males will be talking loud and aggressively, and they like to hear each other talk. You can say something, and get no attention. They will say something, restate [what you said] (not as clearly as you did, by the way) and all of a sudden it's a good idea.

The executives perceived that this tendency to "talk for the sake of talking" sometimes contributed to a conversational pattern that led to their being ignored or excluded. One executive described an encounter involving herself and seven of her peers, all White men, who met for regular executive strategy meetings.

> I started to notice in that forum, when I would speak . . . they would just kind of politely say, "Oh. That's nice." And then they would just go back to what they [had been talking about]. . . . And so, a couple of meetings like that and I decided, "Hey, I'm going to have to do something about this because I can't just keep showing up here and not having an impact and really being ignored."

As with the instances of interpersonal conflict, the executives reported that their colleagues appeared not to be aware that what they saw as "normal" behavior was perceived by the executives as ignoring or co-opting their ideas. The data revealed avoidance, indirect and direct strategies for handling this challenge. One executive reported using avoidance as a primary strategy, the main tactic being to establish over time a reputation for toughness:

I don't offer them [White male cowork-ers] the ideas. I listen. Another thing is, and it takes time, over time, you establish your reputation . . . [People in the organ-ization have learned], "She's tough. Don't cross her. And you better have your act to-gether." I have spent my life, my educa-tional experience building my skills. I have spent twenty-two years with this company building my skills. And I am very competitive. And I am not at all go-ing to hide that under a barrel. I don't jump up and down. . . . In fact, in meet-ings, very often, I'm very quiet. But it's in-teresting. . . . before the end of the meet-ing, the senior guys in the room will always ask me, "What do you think?" . . . "Do you think that's going to work?" . . . And they know . . . the deal is, if I don't buy it and I'm going to sell it to the executives, it ain't going to work. I think I'm really clear that I'm qualified. I never force any-thing. So how do you compete? You can't compete on the rhetoric.

An indirect tactic for getting one's voice heard in meetings is to use humor, as de-scribed below:

Sometimes if possible, I'll be humorous, and, and, you know, insert myself and say listen you guys just are not listening. Lis-ten, this is your mother speaking, this is a woman's voice, you know, just kind of making light of it.

The majority of the women with reports in this category said they used a direct strategy for handling co-workers who co-opt or ig-nore their ideas in meetings. The primary tactic is face-to-face confrontation. The ex-ecutive mentioned above who realized, "Hey. I'm going to have to do something about this because I can't just keep showing up here and not having an impact and really being ig-nored," provides an excellent example of the direct confrontation approach. This execu-tive devised a strategy for getting her voice heard at meetings with her seven White male colleagues:

And so [for our next meeting] we went to the training center . . . [for a special exec-utive meeting], and the guy that was lead-ing it, I made sure that I sat next to him. We were at a rectangular-shaped table; he was at the head of the table, and I sat to

his right. I wanted to be right close to [the person in charge of the meeting] So we're having the meeting, and the guys are just . . . they just love to hear themselves talk, you know. You can just tell. It didn't mat-ter too much what they were saying as long as they each talked. And one would make a point, and somebody else would have to reiterate it in their own words, and a lot of that going on. Not a lot of fa-cilitation . . . you know. Well, in any event, I sort of took my time, the only female . . . at the table, and we got to some area that I thought, in my mind, I said, "I know this is a good idea. I mean, I'm gonna throw this one out because this is good." Threw it out there, and true to form. . . , [the per-son] who was leading the meeting, when I said what I had to say, he kind of said, "Oh. That's a thought." And then moved on, and I just touched his arm, and I said, "does that mean that we're not going to consider what I just said?" He said, "Oh. No." And you know what. . . , this is the truth, he said, "No. You know, that really did have a lot of merit, and I can see how that'd work." And all of those guys jumped in, and they all said it was good, and they all . . . for some reason they just didn't want to acknowledge it. . . . And af-ter that, they voted for me Employee of the Month. I was just their best girlfriend, you know. . . . And so I won them over in that split . . . you know, it was probably two minutes . . . and that was it.

Another executive advised that one must gauge when it is appropriate to use a direct or an indirect strategy to be heard in meet-ings.

A lot of times, you know, if you don't bang on the table which I, I can do that, you know, I have done that. But, when you bang on the table, very often what they hear is the bang and not what you have to say, so I, I strategically pick the times when I might bang on the table. But, and I have had to do that in the past. I haven't done it recently, but for the most part that happens at a time when usually conversa-tion is very heated, people are talking back and forth, and the person that I want to hear what I want to say is not lis-tening. And, I'll just say, look I'm trying to give you some information here, can I have the floor. I mean, I literally will say that if I have to because I think, you know, it's important enough for me to be heard. I would definitely choose the time I do that because you can overdo that strategy. The confrontation, I think is very effective, but it can not be a usual style or people will come to discount your confrontations.

Being excluded from important networks. The final challenge related to interacting with their White male colleagues reported by the executives was being excluded from important networks. One executive describes this challenge succinctly:

> I was working for a gentleman that promoted me to district [level], so I have some loyalty to him, but he still has his, you know old network of guys around him. He has this club of guys that are *his guys* and you know they are *his guys*. And I think that has an influence on, you know, your thought pattern—has an influence on how you act. You have to send three or four memos, where they send no memo. You send a memo and three voice mails to make sure you are even heard.

To handle the obstacle of being excluded from informal organizational networks, the executives identified a set of strategic communication behaviors that are mostly indirect, or contain elements of both indirect and direct strategies. For example, some women who reported being excluded from information networks created other networks or obtained at least one contact within the network to obtain information. For instance, one executive said that she had her own style of informal networking that worked better for her than her White male peers' networking on the golf course:

> I think for me, the way I managed was, you know, it was right for me. You know, if I really wanted something from you, I'd call you and say come over to my office and let's have lunch. And then what I would do is I'd send out for lunch and we'd have lunch at my office and then, we'd talk about what I wanted to talk about.

Other executives emphasized the importance of direct communication strategies that utilize White male mentors within the dominant cultural system. One executive said that her main strategy was to find one

person to use as a sounding board and to get informal information that she might not receive otherwise. She said that she has gained several such mentors throughout her career through a process of "observing people over time to see how receptive they are to you." Similarly, another executive described how she put this process into practice:

> I had White male mentors who held positions of power in the community, who were the best [at networking]. [I learned from them] by observation. I watched how they worked with other people. How they worked with the [nationally prominent politicians from the state] to get grants for the city. How they talked to people, and what they used, the networking they used to get things done. And it works.

Finally, one executive said she used both direct and indirect tactics to deal with the challenge of being excluded from communication networks. Like the other executives, she formed her own networks for getting information, yet she also brought attention to the fact that she was being excluded from important communication networks. However, she noted that the more direct tactics failed to have any long-term effects for changing the exclusionary practices.

Problematic Interactions with Other African Americans

The data revealed two salient challenges related to the executives' interaction with other African Americans both inside and outside the organization: (a) direct conflict based upon perceived unmet expectations about the executive's behavior toward African Americans; and (b) personal attacks on the executive's character through direct and indirect channels (see Table 18.1). As with the challenges related to interacting with their White male colleagues, underlying each of these instances of conflict with other African Americans were the perceptions of misguided assumptions. However, the executives' strategic responses to these instances of conflict were, in some ways, in stark contrast to those used with their White male colleagues.

One challenge the executives reported was direct conflict based upon perceived unmet expectations about the executive's behavior toward African Americans in general. In the following example, an executive described a conversation she had with an African American city official who wanted assistance from the large government agency she directs:

> One of the things he said was, "I saw your name in the paper, and I thought that once we got a Black person in government that we could get some help." And I said, "Okay, tell me your problem, let me look into it." So he started to tell me [that they needed a new system]. And I said, let me see what we've done, and I'll see what we can do to help you, and I'll call you back. So I did, and I called him back. And I told him, we already did a [system] for you, and I explained that we install [systems], we don't maintain [systems]. And I said, "At the time [your system was installed], you were told you need to hire an engineer, you need to monitor the quality of your [system]." And he said (and these were his exact words), "We need to help each other." And I said to him, "We need to help each other to help ourselves. We can't continue putting government money into a project that you're not going to maintain. And it doesn't matter whether I'm helping you, or helping Joe Blow. I would expect the same thing from you that I would expect from someone else. . . ." Eventually, we agreed to renovate the [system] he had, and he agreed to tax people to hire an engineer.

Other examples of conflict based on unmet expectations related to interaction between the executives and their African American coworkers. In these instances, however, it was sometimes the executive whose expectations were unmet. One executive experienced conflict with an African American man who had been passed over for the senior-level position for which she was hired. She reasoned that their conflict was related in some ways to the fact that prior to her being hired as a senior executive, he "had been *the* Black person in upper management," and that he felt somewhat threatened by her presence. After the man brought a lawsuit against the organization, the executive said she felt somewhat uneasy about their relationship:

> "I think, that I might have been more understanding of the decision to bring a lawsuit if it had been someone White as opposed to it being someone Black. Because I do have this perception that you just don't do things like that to someone of the same race because you don't want to bring anyone down."

The second reported challenge for dealing with African Americans related to interpersonal conflict that involved personal attacks on the executive's character. One executive says she has experienced conflict with African Americans that seemed to be related to her position of visibility:

> I've got somebody who's been negative toward me and they're Black, and I think there is more maliciousness than if it's a White person. With a White person, you got the racial thing, you expect that; [But with African Americans] I'm not sure where they're coming from. And of course, I'm in a position where there is visibility and there's always stuff going on, and there's going to be more discussion and talk and, indeed, jealousy.

The women who described challenges related to their interaction with other African Americans expressed some ambivalence in dealing with this issue. Although they seemed convinced that the nature of the interaction should be different, their strategies for changing the interaction were indirect (see Table 18.1). For instance, in the example involving the Black government official, the executive said she was "affronted" by his expectation that she should "compromise" her position as director of the agency. Yet the strategy she used in the conflict was avoidance. She focused on the issue at hand, rather than the target person's unmet expectations regarding his perceptions of the executive's duty to the Black community.

Another executive reporting a conflict with an African American female coworker recommended avoidance as a strategy for dealing with intra-racial conflict:

> If they're in my way, and are gonna harm me, then I just kind of like go around. You know, I don't think you want to go about looking for conflict. And you know how you see people that will say, you know, I'm

taking this issue on. Well, I've got enough issues with all the other stuff in my life to not look for a fight and try to battle something out.

In summary, the results of this study represent one current interpretation of negotiating identity within dominant organizational culture, grounded in the experiences of African American women executives. In the next section, I discuss how these findings contribute to our understanding of identity negotiation within raced and gendered workplace interactions.

Negotiating Identity Within Raced and Gendered Workplace Interactions

This research examined how African American women executives used strategic communication in response to interaction encounters they perceived as problematic or challenging within dominant culture organizations. Standpoint epistemology (Hartsock, 1987; Collins, 1990) was used as a framework for analysis. Two important epistemological goals of standpoint theory are: (1) to encourage research that empowers women to speak their own voices, about their own experiences from marginalized positions in social relations; and (2) to expose everyday acts of oppression and resistance. Consistent with these goals, this study gives voice to one particular perspective on oppression and resistance within dominant culture organizations—that of African American women executives. Black women's standpoints historically have been excluded or devalued in theorizing about organizational communication in general and women's leadership in particular (Parker, 2001). Findings from these women's narratives contribute to our understanding of how non-majority organizational members define constraining aspects of interaction and how power interacts with race and gender to structure conflict in dominant culture organizations, and how non-majority members create strategies for finding their voice within dominant culture organizations.

Defining Constraints on Interaction within Dominant Culture Organization

The findings of this study reinforce the idea that, in addition to promoting the recognition of similarities among the responses to oppressive organizational practices, researchers and practitioners should acknowledge the diversity within and among nondominant group organizational members (Orbe, 1998). Each of the African American women executives in this study reported that they believed there existed, or there was the potential for, differential treatment based on gender and race in their respective organizations. Also, all of the women emphasized their confidence in themselves as Black women within predominantly White and male environments. However, there were differences in the women's interpretations of how race and gender influenced their interactions. About half of the women seemed compelled to engage in complex analyses to determine if race or gender are salient in a particular encounter they might have in their daily work lives (King, 1990). These women seemed to employ a type of self-surveillance in which they maintained a heightened awareness of their visibility as Black women. One executive commented:

> I am very clear about what White Americans think of me, and what [people in this organization] think of me, and what corporate America thinks. So every day, I go about proving that ain't so. I approach it like . . . "I know that you think I am supposed to be cleaning your house. I'm better educated than you are. I am more articulate than you are. I surely have demonstrated results better, and I'm twice as smart. So, I'm not going to clean your house."

For the women who maintained a heightened awareness of race and gender constraints on interaction, their subjectivity as Black women was an ever-present source for framing the context of interaction and deciding on a course of action, whether it was to resist, subvert, or otherwise transform the interaction context.

The remaining women seemed to equate analyzing the impacts of race and gender to a type of "mind game" which they had no time to play as they went about the business of executive leadership. For these women, their visibility as Black women in a predominantly White environment was a rather obvious fact that required no complicated analytical attention. Their focus was on controlling how they interpreted or framed specific interaction contexts in which they were involved. One executive commented that throughout her career, which is in the White male-dominated medical field, she had always focused on her goals for achievement and doing God's work and simply has not had time to attend to what others might have been thinking. For these women, it seemed important to downplay, ignore, or even deny race and gender as a constraint on their behavior in organizations. The underlying assumption for these women seemed to be that if a dominant culture group member had a problem with them as Black women, it was that person's problem, not theirs.

The women's diverse perspectives about the impacts of race and gender on their interactions can be understood as attempts to "make sense" of their experiences within dominant culture organizations. Weick (1979) conceptualizes sense making as a process of enactment in which organizational members create their interaction environments through meaningful patterns of attention, action, and interaction. For non-majority organizational members, this sense-making process may be related to a person's preferred communication orientation, relative to interacting with the dominant culture. In his co-cultural theory of communication, Orbe (1998) identifies nine such orientations on a continuum of nonassertive, assertive, and aggressive communication approaches, associated with three possible outcomes, assimilation, accommodation, and, separation. Briefly, assimilation involves attempts to eliminate cultural differences, including the loss of any distinctive characteristics, to fit in with the dominant culture. Accommodation refers to attempts to change the organizational culture so that many cultural experiences are reflected in it. Separation involves rejecting the notion of forming a common bond with dominant group members or members of other groups. The nine communication orientations range from nonassertive assimila-

tion to aggressive separation. Orbe argues that co-cultural group members (i.e., people of color, women, gay/ lesbian/bisexuals, persons with different abilities) enact one or more of these nine orientations in their interactions within dominant culture organizations.

In applying Orbe's (1998) typology to the present study, the diversity in the women's interpretations of dominant culture constraints seems to coincide generally with the differences between the *assertive separation* and the *assertive accommodation* orientations. Practices associated with the assertive separation mode include *exemplifying strength* (promoting recognition of strengths) and *embracing stereotypes* (applying a negotiated reading to dominant group perceptions). These assertive separation practices corroborate the perspective of women who emphasized a heightened awareness of their presence as Black women in defining problematic encounters. Assertive accommodation practices include *communicating self* (interacting in an authentic, open, and genuine manner), *intra-group networking* (identifying and working with other co-cultural groups), *using liaisons* (identifying specific dominant group members trusted for support, guidance, and assistance), and *educating others* (enlightening dominant group members of co-cultural norms and values). These practices coincide generally with the perspective of women in the study who were not overly concerned with the perceptions of dominant group members.

It is important to note that because the women in this study hold positions of power within dominant culture organizations, the consequences of using a particular orientation may be different for persons who are not in positions of power. For example, Orbe (1998) argues that an assertive separation orientation must be enacted without access to most of the organizational resources controlled by dominant group members, and that outsider positioning (e.g., being perceived as *anti-dominant group*) reduces the ability of co-cultural group members to influence decisions made outside their specific communities. However, women of power would presumably be positioned to circumvent these limitations.

Power, Race, and Gender in Interaction Contexts

The findings of this study provide insights about how power interacts with race and gender to structure conflict in dominant culture organizations. Among the executives who reported conflicts with their White male colleagues, there were no instances in which the executives reported having significant interpersonal conflict with their bosses (all of whom were White men). Rather, the conflicts involved their White male peers, and in fewer cases, their White male subordinates. One interpretation of this finding is that the power-relationships among coworkers are not well-defined in the formal organizational structure, as are the superior-subordinate relationships. Therefore, it is more likely that the sites of negotiating power and identity issues in complex organizations in general would occur at the coworker interaction level as organizational members work out the terms of their participation (Stohl and Cheney, 2001). However, the executives' narratives revealed how race and gender make this negotiation more complex. As dominant culture values influenced the informal rhetorical context (e.g., who should speak to whom, about what content, under what circumstances), many of the women engaged in complex self reflection and intellectual work to analyze, define, and develop strategies in response to their rhetorical environments. Significantly, their White male colleagues, unaware of how their own discourses might be perceived as contributing to creating the conflict, were positioned to avoid such self reflection and intellectual work. That is, as part of the dominant culture, they were positioned to see their actions as normative with little reason to challenge the taken-for-granted ways of doing things.

Kanter's (1977) theory of numerical imbalance (e.g., the effects of tokenism), and the extension of that theory by Fairhurst and Snavely (1983), provide another interpretation of these findings relative to power, race, and gender. According to Kanter (1977), individuals are deemed tokens when they enter a job environment in which their social category (e.g., sex or race) historically has been numerically scarce and rare to a given occupation, as was the case of the women in this study. She theorizes that interaction among tokens and dominants is guided by certain perceptual tendencies that create token dynamics that, in turn, generate typical token responses, such as overachieving and playing limited and caricatured roles. Expanding Kanter's work, Fairhurst and Snavely (1983) argue that token status, when enhanced by the attainment of power, causes tokens to be perceived more complexly by majority members and empowers tokens to behave *strategically*. This suggests that the executives' visibility as Black women, enhanced by their positions of authority, empowered them to challenge (through direct and indirect means) perceived constraints in their interaction with White male colleagues.

Another contribution of this study relates to how power, race, and gender structured the reported conflicts between the executives and other African Americans both inside and outside the organization. Interactions among African Americans within dominant culture organizations can be understood within a socio-historical context that gave rise to an emphasis on racial solidarity as one response to oppressive structures in U.S. American society. From that vantage point, race can be seen as a way of structuring interactions between and among African Americans in dominant culture organizations, forcing them into the dualistic discourses of Black nationalism or assimilationism, or being Black-identified or White-identified. In the reported instances of intra-racial conflict, the women expressed a degree of ambivalence about their strategies for managing the conflict. On the one hand they seemed compelled to define the conflict in terms of their own expectations about race relations. On the other hand, unlike the direct approaches used with their White male colleagues, they seemed reluctant to act in ways that would directly articulate their perceptions of race relations with other African Americans. This ambivalence can be interpreted as indicative of an ongoing process among African Americans in general and African American women in particular, for rearticulating the basis for collective bonding.

Finding a Voice within Dominant Culture Organizations

Finally, these results shed light on how non-majority organizational members, particularly women, negotiate meaning, identity, and power to find a voice within dominant culture organizations (Houston & Kramarae, 1991). Hirschman (1970) conceptualizes voice as one of three behavioral responses to an objectionable state of affairs, the other two being exit and loyalty. He defines voice as any attempt at all to change, rather than to escape from, an objectionable state of affairs. While the women in this study differed in the ways in which they found their voice in a particular interaction context—whether through direct, indirect, or avoidance strategies—common among the women's narratives was an emphasis on their identity as Black women. That is, they started from the standpoint of being self-defined and confident as Black women (Collins, 1990).

The African American women executives' strategic responses to problematic encounters within the dominant culture can be seen as a way transforming organizational structures to be more inclusive of them as executive leaders. Their presence as Black women in positions of authority represents a contradiction to the normative meanings for "organizational leader" as White and male. The different, and sometimes seemingly conflicting, communication strategies enacted by the executives can be understood as attempts to "un-fix" these meanings. Aspects of the formal structure, such as meetings and cross-functional networks, became sites for negotiating informal power relationships in which the women asserted their identity as Black women, as executive leaders, and as legitimate members of the organization.

Conclusion

The results of this study indicate that it is not enough to know that racism exists or that gender discrimination persists in complex organizational systems. What is needed, and what a focus on identity negotiation provides, is an understanding of how people create those systems through their everyday interactions and how people transform them.

As Fine (1994) emphasizes, following Bhavnani (1992), it is important to analyze "not just the decontextualized voices of Others, but the very structures, ideologies, contexts, and practices that constitute Othering" (p. 70). The present study brought to light practices that can be seen as constituting "Othering" as revealed in the African American women executives' perceptions of exclusionary and oppressive tactics by their White male colleagues and by their African American colleagues and clients. More research is needed that takes into account the dual role of social actors to both create and transform intercultural social systems (c.f., Allen 2000; Houston & Kramarae, 1991; Jackson, 1999).

References

Acker, J. (1990). Hierarchies, jobs, bodies: A theory of gendered organizations. *Gender & Society*, 4, 139–158.

Allen, B. J. (2000). "Learning the ropes": A Black feminist standpoint analysis. In P. Buzzanell, (Ed.), *Rethinking organizational & managerial communication from feminist perspectives*, (177–208). Thousand Oaks: Sage.

Bhavnani, K. (1992). Talking racism and editing women's studies. In D. Richardson & V. Robinson (Eds.), *Thinking feminist* (pp. 27–48). New York: Guilford.

Biggart, N. W., & Hamilton, G. G. (1984). The power of obedience. *Administrative Science Quarterly*, 29 (4), 540–549.

Bullis, C., & Stout, K. R. (2000). Organizational socialization: A feminist standpoint approach. In P. Buzzanell, (Ed.), *Rethinking organizational & managerial communication from feminist perspectives* (pp. 47–75). Thousand Oaks: Sage.

Collins, P. H. (1990). *Black feminist thought: Knowledge, consciousness, and the politics of empowerment*. Boston: Unwin Hyman.

Fairhurst, G. T., & Snavely, B. K. (1983). Majority and token minority group relationships: Power acquisition and communication. *Academy of Management Review*, 8, 292300.

Fine, M. (1994). Working the hyphens: Reinventing self and other in qualitative research. In N. K. Denzin & Y. S. Lincoln (Eds.), *Handbook of qualitative research* (pp. 70–82). Thousand Oaks, CA: Sage.

Hartsock, N. (1987). The feminist standpoint: Developing the ground for a specifically feminist historical materialism. In S. Harding (Ed.),

Feminism & methodology. (pp., 157–180). Milton Keynes: Open University Press.

hooks, b. (1990). *Yearning: Race, gender, and cultural politics.* Boston: South End.

Hirschman, A. (1970). *Exit, voice, and loyalty.* Cambridge, MA: Harvard University Press.

Houston, M. & Kramarae, C. (1991). Speaking from silence: Methods of silencing and resistance. *Discourse & Society,* 2, 387–399.

Jackson II, R. L. (1999). *The negotiation of cultural identity: Perceptions of European Americans and African Americans.* Westport, Connecticut: Praeger.

Kanter, R. M. (1977). *Men and women of the corporation.* New York: Basic Books.

King, D. K. (1990). Multiple jeopardy, multiple consciousness: The context of a Black feminist ideology. In M. R. Malson, E. Mudimbe-Boyi, J. F. O'Barr, & M. Wyer, (Eds.) *Black women in America: Social science perspectives.* Chicago: University of Chicago Press.

Mainiero, L. (1994). Getting anointed for advancement: The case of executive women. *The Academy of Management Executive,* 8, 53–68.

Orbe, M. P. (1998). *Constructing co-cultural theory: An explication of culture, power, and communication.* Thousand Oaks, CA: Sage.

——. (1998). An outsider within perspective to organizational communication: Explicating the communicative practices of co-cultural group members. *Management Communication Quarterly,* 19 (2), 230–279.

Parker, P. S. (1997). African American women executives within dominant culture organizations: An examination of leadership socialization, communication strategies, and leadership behavior. Unpublished Doctoral Dissertation, The University of Texas at Austin. (University Microfilms Number 9802988).

Parker, P. S. (2001.). African American women executives within dominant culture organizations: (Re)conceptualizing notions of instrumentality and collaboration. *Management Communication Quarterly,* 15, 1, 42–82.

Smith, D. (1987). *The everyday world as problematic: A feminist sociology.* Boston: Northeastern University Press.

Stohl, C., & Cheney, G. (2001). Participatory processes/paradoxical practices: Communication and the dilemmas of organizational democracy. *Management Communication Quarterly,* 14, 349–407.

Weick, K. (1979). *The social psychology of organizing,* 2nd. edition. Reading, MA: Addison-Wesley.

Wilkerson, I. (2002, February). The most powerful woman in the world. *Essence* 32 (10), 114–162.

Wilmot, W. & Hocker, J. (1998). *Interpersonal conflict.* New York: McGraw-Hill.

Wood, J. T. (1998). *Gendered lives: Communication, gender and culture* (2nd ed.). Belmont, CA: Wadsworth.

Reprinted from: Patricia S. Parker, "Negotiating Identity in Raced and Gendered Workplace Interactions: The Use of Strategic Communication by African American Women Senior Executives Within Dominant Culture Organizations." In *Communication Quarterly,* Vol. 50, No. 3, pp. 251–268. Copyright © 2002 by Taylor & Francis, Inc. Reproduced by permission of Taylor & Francis, Inc., *http://www.taylorandfrancis.com.*

Food for Thought and Application Questions

1. Explain why "negotiating identity" is an issue that confronts African American women in positions of power. What is the context that makes identity problematic?

2. Elaborate on the different strategies that were used to establish one's authority and identity by African American women and the different contexts in which these have been found to be successful. What, if any, situations were more difficult to deal with or resulted in identity management being basically unresolved?

3. Develop a series of skits or training modules that can be used to show students the roles or positions that African American women encounter in high powered positions and the strategies that can be used to resolve these issues of identity. Create three or four different situations that present problems in identity management in order to represent the range of situations encountered. ✦

19
Selling Women Short

A Research Note on Gender Differences in Compensation on Wall Street

Louise Marie Roth

Studies of gender inequality in earnings debate the importance of discrimination, once the effects of productivity-related characteristics and sex segregation have been taken into account. Previous research has demonstrated that human capital variables together account for 30% to 50% of the gender gap in pay (Blau & Ferber 1992; Jacobs 1989; Kilbourne et al. 1994; Marini 1989), while much of the remaining gap has long been credited to sex segregation of the labor force by occupation, organization, and specific job (Bird 1996; Blau & Ferber 1992; Dixon & Seron 1995; England 1992; Guthrie & Roth 1999; Reskin & Roos 1990; Tanner et al. 1999). Many scholars also argue that residual discrimination against women contributes to the maintenance of gender inequality, even after human capital and segregation have been controlled (Bartlett & Miller 1988; Rosenberg, Perlstadt & Phillips 1993; Sokoloff 1988). However, some recent quantitative research has suggested that there is no gender gap in earnings for recent hires within some occupations, once all forms of segregation are controlled (Morgan 1998; Petersen & Morgan 1995). In other words, controlling for cohort, for educational preparation, and for segregation by organization and job, there may be few, if any, gender differences in pay. Using data on securities professionals, this article analyzes gender differences in compensation within an elite, male-dominated occupation and examines whether such dif-ferences can be attributed to human capital or to segregation by job.

A notable example testing for gender inequality in a male-dominated occupation is Morgan's (1998) study of multiple cohorts of engineers, which found no significant gender differences in earnings within the most recent cohorts. Her findings are provocative, because the sex composition of engineering is more male-dominated than that of most other professions, and many have theorized that sex discrimination is most likely in contexts that are numerically dominated by men (Gutek & Morash 1982; Kanter 1977; Yoder 1994). Accordingly, Morgan's finding of statistical equity in earnings among recent cohorts of engineers raises the question of whether similar processes may operate in other equally male-dominated professions. However, Morgan explicitly recognized that her findings might not be generalizable to other professional contexts (Morgan 1998). In this article, I present rich and unique data that challenge the generalization of Morgan's findings by revealing a substantial gender gap in compensation among recent cohorts in another male-dominated profession.

Theoretically, differences across organizational and professional contexts seem likely. Different industries and types of organizations use a variety of methods and mechanisms to determine pay rates. Market-driven demands for particular professional skills influence pay rates, and institutional norms affect starting salaries, promotions, raises, and bonuses within occupations. Thus, both markets and institutional forces shape internal and external labor markets and the relative rewards offered to workers in various occupations. These processes lead to a great variation in pay scales across occupations (Bridges & Villemez 1991). The degree of gender inequality in different professions and different organizations is also likely to vary, rather than corresponding directly to productivity-related inputs such as human capital characteristics. For example, in state government jobs, Bridges and Nelson (1989) found gender inequality in pay that was based partly on institutional norms and partly on market efficiency considerations. Discretion, subjectivity, custom, and "bureaucratic politics" strongly influence pay scales, even when organizations refer to market mechanisms as a justification for pay differentials (Bridges & Nelson 1989). Thus, the processes that might create gender equity in some settings and inequity in others interact with institutional mechanisms within organizational contexts. These contexts vary in many features, including criteria for performance evaluation and compensation, governance structures, organizational climate, and flat versus hierarchical firm structures. Also, there may be considerable variation across organizational fields in the quality and quantity of interpersonal interactions both within and outside the employer organization, such as team structures, internal chains of accountability, allocation of responsibility, access to client accounts, and the conventions of client relationships. Variation by institutional context is likely to produce different consequences for gender equality, regardless of the proportion of females in an occupation.

In this research, data from a cohort sample of Wall Street professionals permit an assessment of gender inequality in a particularly male-dominated professional context that differs institutionally from engineering. The cohort began careers on Wall Street in the 1990s. The industry's high demand for skilled labor with master of business administration (MBA) credentials, fueled by the bull market of the mid- to late 1990s, could have created a more open opportunity structure for women at that time than in other historical periods (SIA Research Department 1998). In this context, women on Wall Street might be well positioned to gain income equality with their male peers. However, the institutional context of finance is unique in ways that may contribute to the persistence of gender inequality.

First, most of the highest-paying jobs in financial professions tend to be very client-intensive, and a majority of high-paying clients are male-dominated corporations. The nature and amount of client interaction may contribute to differences in the gender gap in income, especially if client preferences for homophily and certain types of client-entertaining activities advantage male workers (Blair-Loy 2001b; Roth n.d.). For example, in personal interviews, female respondents referred to strip clubs or "girlie bars," cigar smoking, and elk hunting as client-entertaining activities in which their presence was unwelcome and that harmed their ability to develop solid client relationships. In this industry, women in corporate finance or sales and trading may have difficulties establishing high-profile client relationships or gaining access to lucrative accounts, contributing to many women's lower compensation vis-à-vis their male peers (Blair-Loy 2001b; Roth n.d.).

Second, securities firms are formally flat, with a small number of hierarchical levels, in comparison to hierarchical organizations where salary follows level and seniority within a bureaucratic structure. As a result, Wall Street has a rather unusual institutionalized compensation structure. In an effort to reward employees on the basis of their performance, Wall Street firms compensate most of their employees with variable year-end bonuses that permit and justify wide variation in total income among workers at the same level and in the same job. Firm revenues are divided among "groups" specializing in particular types of financial function or client industry. Within each group, employees are ranked relative to others at the same level on the basis of performance evaluations, and managers allocate bonuses that are based on these rankings.[1] These compensation practices permit differences in total compensation for employees *in the same job* and also allow for much managerial discretion over interemployee differences within each work group. In personal interviews, female securities professionals often claimed that managerial discretion produced gender-biased compensation outcomes. These industry-specific practices may also lead us to anticipate how this context produces dramatically different results for recent female entrants in the securities industry than Morgan (1998) found among her sample of engineers. Thus, the gender gap in earnings within occupations may not follow a pattern of disappearance over time across industries but may vary widely across institutional contexts.

In this article, I investigate gender inequality in compensation among elite business school graduates who entered Wall Street securities firms during a three-year period immediately before Wall Street's longest bull market in history (*Wall Street Journal*, 15 December 1998, pp. C1, C25). I employ a three-year cohort sample that was carefully chosen to control for human capital, organizational prestige, and market conditions. In light of the institutional and organizational context of the securities industry, I hypothesize that gender inequality will persist on Wall Street even when men and women hold identical jobs.

Research Design

Data

The data come from a cohort of business school graduates who began their careers in one of nine major Wall Street securities firms in the early 1990s. I randomly selected 44 women and 32 men from placement reports and alumni information for the years 1991–93 from five elite graduate programs in finance. Those respondents who remained in the industry would have passed their first promotion and should have been at the vice president rank or higher at the time of the data collection. Only those respondents who were employed and paid in the securities industry in 1997 were included, eliminating 3 male respondents who had moved into other industries. The remaining sample contains 73 cases.

In MBA programs nationally, women represent approximately 25–30% of all graduates (*Guide to Business Schools* 1996). Among the individuals whose names were obtained through the business schools in this study, women constituted 19.8% of the graduates who entered Wall Street securities firms upon graduating. The five graduate schools of business contained 621 graduates who entered major Wall Street firms during the three years included in the sample. All graduates who started their careers in nine major Wall Street firms as defined by Eccles and Crane (1988) were eligible for inclusion in the study. These firms are the largest securities firms in a highly concentrated industry, which has become increasingly consolidated over time (SIA Research Department 1998). To obtain comparable samples of men and women, I separated all eligible respondents' names by gender to create lists of 498 men and 123 women and selected separate subsamples using a random numbers table.

After the disqualification of 3 men who had exited financial services before the end of 1997, the sample contains 44 women and 29 men. In-depth interviews about their career histories and total compensation for 1997 were conducted in 1998 and 1999. The interviews lasted an average of one hour.

While the sample size is modest, this business school cohort sample has several advantages. First, it controls for important human capital variables, market conditions, and organizational prestige. Elite MBA programs are mediating institutions that control for the most important educational credential for a career on Wall Street and, to a great extent, for class background. In addition, these programs filter for previous educational and work experience and for performance on the GMAT. This sample of respondents who entered a small set of organizations with comparable prestige within a single industry during a short period of time also largely controls for variation in market conditions and organizational market position. These controls that were built into the sampling strategy permitted an assessment of gender differences among very comparable men and women from a recent cohort of financial service professionals whose labor was in high demand in the late 1990s. Second, the sample was able to be drawn without the involvement of the firms themselves. Gaining the cooperation of even one of these highly secretive organizations would have been extremely difficult. Moreover, a firm-generated sample would likely have contained less variation in areas of financial services, and respondents might have been less candid if they believed that their employer could have access to the data.

Compensation: The Dependent Variable

The outcome of interest for this analysis is total compensation in 1997. Possibly more than other industries, Wall Street is driven by compensation as a measure of success. As a baseline for this population, a survey of executive recruiters specializing in the securities industry indicated that the median total annual compensation in 1997 for the business school class of 1991 was $635,000; for the class of 1992, $540,000; and for the class of 1993, $430,000 (Horowitz & Copulsky 1998). It is revealing that this survey indicated that "low range" Wall Street professionals who had graduated in 1993, most of whom were approximately 30 years old at the time of the survey, earned $300,000 in 1997. This amount is more than twice the $128,521 cutoff for the 95th percentile of household income in the U.S. for the same year (U.S. Bureau of the Census 1998), illustrating the degree to which this population represents an economic elite. While some respondents bemoaned the emphasis on money, all Wall Street professionals had a strong sense that their compensation was an indicator of their success and their value as professionals. This orientation suggests that earnings are an appropriate outcome to analyze and a proxy measure for success in the industry.

In the current study, respondents were asked to check the appropriate box on an income scale for their total compensation in 1997. Five respondents (three women and two men) refused to disclose their compensation and are omitted from the analysis. For all other respondents, income in dollars is coded as the midpoint of the range indicated unless the respondent gave an exact income amount, in which case that number is used instead. For respondents earning more than $1,000,000, income is coded as $1,100,000.

Control Variables

Control variables include background characteristics, human capital other than the MBA degree, rank in the industry, area of finance, and whether the respondent still worked for one of the original nine Wall Street firms at the time of the 1997 bonus payment. Measures of background characteristics include family status dummy variables for whether a respondent was married or had children at the time of the interview. However, only seven respondents were not white, among whom one was African American and the remaining six were of Asian descent. Three variables capture rank within the industry, indicating whether respondents were below the vice president level, at the vice president level, or above the vice president level.

The sample holds constant the most important educational human capital, since all respondents have a prestigious MBA degree and similar years of experience in the industry after graduating. Several additional human capital control variables are also included. I include a dummy variable for having an undergraduate major in economics, finance, or accounting because these majors may offer skills relevant to careers on Wall Street.

An important control variable is the natural logarithm of the estimated number of hours worked per week. The respondent defined his or her average weekly hours, which acts as a measure of work effort and work commitment.

Research on gender and labor markets suggests that sex segregation by function is also likely to lead to gender differences in earnings. Consequently, variables were included for the various functions of financial services: corporate finance, public finance, sales and trading, equity research, and asset management. Finally, continuing to work for one of the original nine Wall Street firms is expected to affect career processes positively. Respondents who had moved into securities firms outside the nine selected for initial inclusion in the study typically categorized themselves as "doing the same thing" as they had before. These respondents entered smaller investment banks or commercial banks. So an indicator variable for firm tier is included.

Results

Table 19.1 presents descriptive statistics for all variables that were tested for the entire sample and separately by gender, as well as the t-test for difference of means by gender. The descriptive statistics illuminate several trends in the overall sample. Men and women had comparable human capital in terms of undergraduate achievement and work experience in an investment bank before and during business school, as one would expect given the sample design. There are no statistically significant gender differences for grade point average, economics-related major, mathematics/engineering major, previous experience as analysts or summer associates, or self-reported hours. This suggests that these men and women bring very similar characteristics to the labor market.

The difference between genders by functional area is statistically significant, implying sex segregation within the securities industry. Women are more likely to work in public finance or equity research. In fact, no men in the sample worked in public finance. Personal interviews indicated that sex segregation within the securities industry constituted an important source of gender disparity and that men and women were sifted into different career paths at various points in their careers. This finding suggests that sex segregation by job within Wall Street may account for some of the gender difference in earnings.

With respect to compensation, women in the sample earned 60.5% as much as their male peers from graduate business school. That figure compares unfavorably with the earnings inequality ratio for the labor force as a whole, calculated at approximately 75% for the same year (U.S. Bureau of the Census 1998). These men are earning 165% of their female counterparts' compensation a mere four to seven years after completing business school. Furthermore, the raw numbers reveal the magnitude of gender inequality even more powerfully. The gender *difference* in average compensation among financial professionals was an astounding $223,368. Examination of the zero-order correlation of gender and compensation reveals that gender alone explains approximately 18% of the variance in income ($r = -.43$).

These descriptive statistics demonstrate that, on average, women's relative compensation suffers in comparison to that of their male peers in this industry. Can other variables explain part of this gender gap among comparable men and women in the same occupation? Ordinary least-squares (OLS) regression models were used to explore effects on total compensation for 1997.

[In the first analysis], background characteristics such as gender, marital status, and parental status and human capital characteristics such as undergraduate major and hours worked per week explain approximately 41% of the variance in total compensation. Marital status and parental status have no significant effects in multivariate models. [While] hours per week has a significant and positive effect on compensation, such that each additional estimated weekly hour increases annual compensation by approximately 5.3%. Gender has a strong negative effect that is statistically significant. According to this model, women earn 39% less than men with the same background and family status characteristics). This model reveals that the supply-side characteristics of financial professionals, including the human capital controls built into the sample, cannot account for gender inequality in earnings on Wall Street.

[The second analysis] controls for background characteristics, human capital, and the structural variables of functional area segregation and continued employment in a top firm. This model explains about 54% of the variance in total compensation, which improves upon model 1 by 20%. Gender is statistically significant and negative, with women earning approximately 29% less than comparable male peers in similar organizations and the same functions. The effect of estimated weekly hours is not significant in this model ($p = .07$). In terms of area effects, employees in corporate finance earn approximately 173% more than peers in support functions, and professionals in sales or trading earn approximately 210% as much as those in support functions. These areas were also the most male-dominated. The fitted model for the gender gap, holding all other variables constant at their means, is presented graphically in Figure 19.1. Figure 19.1 illustrates that women earn lower compensation for each hour they work, in comparison with men who bring identical characteristics to the job and who work in the same areas and organizations at the same rank.

Contrary to Morgan's (1998) findings for engineers, recent cohorts of men and women on Wall Street experience inequality in compensation, independent of human capital and background characteristics and independent of segregation by area, rank, or organization.

Table 19.1
Descriptive Statistics—Means and Standard Errors

	All Cases	Men	Women	T-value for Difference
Married	.60 (.06)	.70 (.09)	.54 (.08)	1.40
Children	.43 (.06)	.56 (.10)	.34 (.08)	1.76
White	.10 (.04)	.04 (.04)	.15 (.06)	−1.63
GPA	3.41 (.04)	3.42 (.06)	3.41 (.06)	.10
Economics/finance/ accounting major	.56 (.06)	.44 (.10)	.63 (.08)	−1.55
Mathematics/engineering major	.21 (.05)	.26 (.09)	.17 (.06)	.88
Previous experience	.54 (.06)	.59 (.10)	.51 (.08)	.64
Hours per week	61.62 (1.30)	64.26 (2.18)	59.88 (1.58)	1.67
Corporate finance	.37 (.06)	.48 (.10)	.29 (.07)	1.55
Public finance	.06 (.03)	.00 (.00)	.09 (.05)	−2.08*
Sales and trading	.15 (.04)	.15 (.07)	.15 (.06)	−.02
Equity research	.18 (.05)	.07 (.05)	.24 (.07)	−2.00*
Asset management	.15 (.04)	.19 (.08)	.12 (.05)	.71
Below vice president	.29 (.06)	.15 (.07)	.39 (.08)	−2.33*
Vice president	.59 (.06)	.59 (.10)	.59 (.08)	.06
Above vice president	.12 (.04)	.26 (.09)	.02 (.02)	2.63*
Top firm in 1997	.82 (.05)	.89 (.06)	.78 (.07)	1.21
Total 1997 earnings ($)	431,434 (30,453)	566,111 (50,887)	342,743 (31,189)	3.96***
N	73	27	41	

Note: Numbers in parentheses are standard errors. All numbers rounded to two decimal places.
*p < .05 *** p <.001 (two-tailed)

Figure 19.1
Fitted Full Model of Gender Differences by Hours Worked per Week

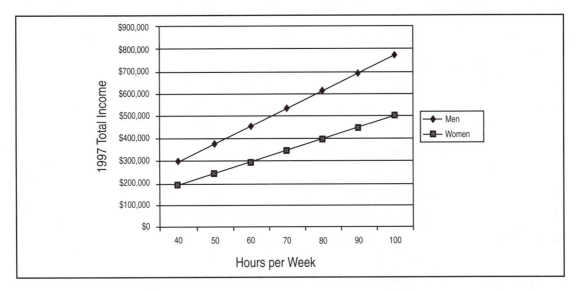

Conclusion

This article addresses the question of whether gender equity within jobs occurs among elite securities workers. While it is possible that recent hires in some male dominated professions may have obtained gender equity in pay, as Morgan (1998) found in her sample of engineers, a gender gap persists in other institutional contexts such as the securities industry. Thus, the earnings penalty may differ by professions, and the evidence in this particular case suggests that the gender wage penalty is quite substantial in some occupational settings, even in comparison to similarly male-dominated fields. In this sample, women on Wall Street earn less than men at the same rank, with the same credentials, and in the same organizations. While internal segregation of the securities industry may explain some of this difference, female respondents also earned less than their male peers in the same financial functions. A consistent and statistically significant negative effect of gender on compensation suggests that some form of residual discrimination shapes earnings disparities among comparable individuals on Wall Street. These data challenge hypotheses that gender inequality is a result strictly of individual differences in human capital or the structural impact of sex segregation.

The institutional practices of the securities industry may help explain how inequality can persist in this male-dominated occupational context. Patterns of gender inequality may also exhibit cohort effects in this context, as Morgan (1998) found for engineers. Blair-Loy (1999, 2001 a-b) has analyzed cohort differences among women in financial services, finding that women experienced differences in their encounters with discrimination, abilities to combine work and family, and difficulties generating clients that depend on their entering cohort. To further assess the arguments of Morgan and others, future research might similarly compare men and women across cohorts of securities workers while accounting for this industry's institutional characteristics.

The findings presented here contribute to the literature on gender inequality in the professions both methodologically and theoretically and also raise several new directions for inquiry. First, methodologically, this research contributes to the study of elite occupations through its sample design. The graduate business schools provided a sampling frame that controlled for most relevant human capital and, consequently, permitted a relatively small sample to provide powerful results. Careful sampling improves researchers' ability to use a smaller sample to obtain both qualitative and quantitative results while maximizing the comparability of respondents.

Theoretically, differences in the organization of elite occupations and the industries in which they exercise their expertise must be incorporated into constructions of gender differences in occupational outcomes. It is obvious that, while some research has revealed the importance of numerical proportions within organizational settings (Kanter 1977), the percentage of males in a profession cannot explain differences between the results for finance found here and Morgan's (1998) findings for engineers. These professions are both highly male dominated, and women's entrance into them occurred during the same historical period. Yet while gender equity may have emerged in engineering, gender inequality persists in finance, and the gap is particularly large in both percentage and absolute terms. Attention to profession-specific pay determination procedures, including institutional understandings of market mechanisms, may provide a key to theorizing how inequality occurs and how it varies in magnitude from one profession to another. Future research should aim to make qualitative comparisons between the institutional structures of different professions.

Notes

1. In sales and trading, it is easier to trace revenues to individuals, and bonuses are often commission-based. As a result, access to accounts represents a larger source of variation than managerial discretion over actual year-end compensation, although some sales and trading professionals are also paid on this more discretionary bonus system. In investment banking, teams of bankers generate revenues, making the bonus determination process more subjective. Similarly, research analysts have more indirect influences on revenues, and their just allocation is necessarily more subjective as well (Roth n.d. a). However, the institutional compensation-setting structures examined in this article tended to be relatively uniform within firms. These firms had quite elaborate organizational procedures for performance re-

views that they applied firm-wide. The effectiveness of these structures depended on the degree to which performance could be objectively assessed, which varied across areas.

References

Bartlett, Robin L., and Timothy I. Miller. 1988. "Executive Earnings by Gender: A Case Study." *Social Science Quarterly* 69: 892–909.

Becker, Gary. 1964. *Human Capital: A Theoretical and Empirical Analysis with Special Reference to Education.* National Bureau of Economic Research.

Bielby, William T., and James N. Baron. 1984. "A Woman's Place Is with Other Women: Sex Segregation within Organizations." Pp. 27–55 in *Sex Segregation in the Workplace: Trends, Explanations, Remedies,* edited by Barbara E Reskin. National Academy Press.

Bird, Chloe E. 1996. "An Analysis of Gender Differences in Income among Dentists, Physicians, and Veterinarians in 1987." *Research in the Sociology of Health Care* 13, pt. A: 31–61.

Blair-Loy, Mary F. 1999. "Career Patterns of Executive Women in Finance: An Optimal Matching Analysis." *American Journal of Sociology* 104: 1346–97.

———. 2001a. "Cultural Constructions of Family Schemas: The Case of Women Finance Executives." *Gender and Society* 15: 687–709.

———. 2001b. "It's Not Just What You Know, It's Who You Know: Technical Knowledge, Rainmaking, and Gender among Finance Executives" *Research in the Sociology of Work* 10: 51–83.

Blau, Francine D., and Marianne A. Ferber. 1992. *The Economics of Women, Men, and Work.* 2d ed. Prentice-Hall.

Bridges, William P., and Robert L. Nelson. 1989. "Markets in Hierarchies: Organizational and Market Influences on Gender Inequality in a State Pay System." *American Journal of Sociology* 95: 616–58.

Bridges, William P., and Wayne J. Villemez. 1991. "Employment Relations and the Labor Market: Integrating Institutional and Market Perspectives." *American Sociological Review* 56: 748–64.

Dixon, Jo, and Carroll Seron. 1995. "Stratification in the Legal Profession: Sex, Sector, and Salary." *Law and Society Review* 29: 381–412.

Eccles, Robert G., and Dwight B. Crane. 1988. *Doing Deals: Investment Banks at Work.* Harvard Business School Press.

England, Paula. 1992. *Comparable Worth: Theories and Evidence.* Aldine de Gruyter.

Gutek, Barbara, and Bruce Morash. 1982. "Sex Ratios, Sex-Role Spillover, and Sexual Harassment of Women at Work." *Journal of Social Issues* 38: 55–74.

Guthrie, Douglas, and Louise Marie Roth. 1999. "The State, Courts, and Equal Opportunities for Female CEOs in U.S. Organizations: Specifying Institutional Mechanisms." *Social Forces* 78: 511–42.

Horowitz, Jed, and Erica Copulsky. 1998. "Putting on the Brakes." *Investment Dealers' Digest,* May 11, pp. 20–27.

Jacobs, Jerry A. 1989. *Revolving Doors: Sex Segregation and Women's Careers.* Stanford University Press.

Kanter, Rosabeth Moss. 1977. *Men and Women of the Corporation.* Basic Books.

Kilbourne, Barbara, Paula England, George Farkas, Kurt Beron, and Dorothea Weir. 1994, "Returns to Skill, Compensating Differentials, and Gender Bias: Effects of Occupational Characteristics on the Wages of White Women and Men." *American Journal of Sociology* 100: 689–719.

Marini, Margaret Mooney. 1989. "Sex Differences in Earnings in the United States." *Annual Review of Sociology* 15: 343–80.

Morgan, Laurie. 1998. "Glass Ceiling Effect or Cohort Effect? A Longitudinal Study of the Gender Earnings Gap for Engineers, 1982 to 1989." *American Sociological Review* 63: 479–83.

Petersen, Trond, and Laurie A. Morgan. 1995. "Separate and Unequal: Occupation-Establishment Sex Segregation and the Gender Wage Gap." *American Journal of Sociology* 101: 329–65.

Reskin, Barbara F., and Patricia A. Roos, 1990. *Job Queues, Gender Queues: Explaining Women's Inroads into Male Occupations.* Temple University Press.

Rosenberg, Janet, Harry Perlstadt, and William R.F. Phillips. 1993. "Now That We Are Here: Discrimination, Disparagement, and Harassment at Work and the Experience of Women Lawyers." *Gender and Society* 7: 415–33.

Roth, Louise Marie. "Bringing Clients Back In: Homophily Preferences and Inequality on Wall Street." Unpublished manuscript.

Securities Industry Association (SIA) Research Department. 1998. *1998 Securities Industry Factbook.* Edited by Grace Toto and George Monahan. Securities Industry Association.

Sokoloff, Natalie J. 1988. "Evaluating Gains and Losses by Black and White Women and Men in the Professions, 1960–1980." *Social Problems* 35: 36–53.

Tanner, Julian, Rhonda Cockerill, Jan Barnsley, and A. Paul Williams. 1999. "Gender and Income in Pharmacy: Human Capital and Gender Stratification Theories Revisited." *British Journal of Sociology* 50: 197–17.

U. S. Bureau of the Census. 1998. "Historical Income Tables—People." *March Current Population Survey.* Government Printing Office.

Yoder, Janice D. 1994. "Looking beyond Numbers: The Effects of Gender Status, Job Prestige, and Occupational Gender-Typing on Tokenism Processes." *Social Psychology Quarterly* 57: 150–59.

Food for Thought and Application Questions

1. Discuss the different organizational and professional factors that can account for different levels of pay (compensation) among professionals. Explain how the author attempts to control these influences so that she can effectively assess gender differences in compensation among Wall Street securities professionals.

2. When examining male and female compensation in the security industry, what are the primary differences between the males and females sampled (see Table 19.1)? To what extent do they differ in human capital factors? In professional specialization? To what extent do family/marital status factors influence the level of compensation? How do *you* explain differences in the compensation received by the males and females in the study? ✦

20

Voces Abriendo Caminos (Voices Forging Paths)

A Qualitative Study of the Career Development of Notable Latinas

Maria J. Gomez
Ruth E. Fassinger
Joann Prosser
Kathleen Cooke
Brenda Mejia
Jeanette Luna

The women's career development literature has expanded in the past 3 decades (Fitzgerald, Fassinger, & Betz, 1995; Phillips & Imhoff, 1997), with growing focus on the career development of women of color (e.g., Bingham & Ward, 1994; Byars & Hackett, 1998). However, research on the career development of Latinas,[1] in particular, is practically nonexistent (Arbona, 1995). Latinas comprise one of the fastest growing groups of women working outside the home in the United States (U.S. Department of Labor—Women's Bureau, 1997); in 1997, there were 5.5 million Latinas in the U.S. labor force, with projections of a 43% increase in the Latina workforce by the year 2005 (U.S. Census Bureau, 1998). . . . Because Latinas have potential to make important contributions to the U.S. workforce, models of career development that explicitly address the Latina experience need to be articulated (Bingham & Ward, 1994). . . . [T]he present study used a qualitative research methodol-

ogy to develop a theoretical framework explicating the career development of 20 notable Latinas in the United States.

The present study included contextual and cultural variables in addition to personal variables and incorporated the family-work interface (Arbona, 1995; Phillips & Imhoff, 1997). *Contextual variables* take into account macro- and microenvironmental factors that limit or facilitate vocational behaviors and aid in understanding the particular social and political context in which participants operate (Morrow & Smith, 2000). These factors may include social movements, economic trends, and public policies (Poole & Langan-Fox, 1997); gender and racial-ethnic discrimination (Fitzgerald et al., 1995); assistance with or barriers to education (DeLeon, 1996); social support (Gutierres, Saenz, & Green, 1994); availability of mentors and role models (Gutierres et al., 1994); and socioeconomic status (Fassinger, [2001]). An individual's culture influences vocational behavior by providing a set of assumptions, values, and world views implicitly used to determine actions (Carter & Cook, 1992). *Cultural variables* are critical to understanding career development and may include cultural assumptions and world view (Carter & Cook, 1992), gender stereotypes (Fitzgerald et al., 1995), the role of the family (Fouad, 1995), and cultural identity processes such as acculturation level, ethnic identity, and race (Arbona, 1995). *Personal variables* encompass an individual's unique characteristics. The literature consistently has suggested, for example, that self-efficacy (Bandura, 1989) and instrumentality (Betz, 1995) are important personal variables in women's career development. Several authors also have suggested investigating the interface between family and work and the balancing of multiple roles and responsibilities demanded of women (e.g., Betz, 1995; Phillips & Imhoff, 1997). . . .

In the present study, we interviewed notable Latinas—women whose contributions on the local, national, or international level have been identified as having a visible impact in their respective occupational fields, communities, or society-at-large. Studying women who have achieved in their fields despite challenges they may have encountered can aid in identifying successful career strategies in order to facilitate healthy career development in diverse women (Richie et al., 1997).

Method

Research Team

. . . [T]he present study was conducted in 1995–1996 by a research team consisting of the primary researcher, a 31-year-old Latina graduate student in counseling psychology; a 26-year-old Eurasian female graduate student in counseling psychology; two Latina undergraduate students (ages 22 and 20); two White females (both age 22), who had recently graduated with bachelor's degrees in psychology; and the faculty advisor, a 43-year-old, White woman with a PhD in counseling psychology who served as the auditor of the investigation. An auditor was used to increase the dependability and confirmability of the data analysis (Lincoln & Guba, 1985) and therefore increase the emergent theory's trustworthiness, the qualitative counterpart to the quantitative concepts of reliability and validity (Miles & Huberman, 1994). . . .

Participants

The participants in the present study were 20 notable Latinas in the United States, recognized by a panel of eight distinguished Hispanic American women who published a biographical directory of 275 notable Latinas in the United States. Sixty-three potential participants were selected for demographic diversity (age, occupation, Latina subgroup (e.g., Mexican, Puerto Rican, Cuban], socioeconomic status, immigration status, and educational level), with contact information available for only 52 of these women. Because of financial and logistical constraints [e.g., geographic location), the list was further narrowed to 39 women who were invited to participate; of the 39, 9 did not respond, 7 declined participation, and 3 agreed to participate but could not be accommodated, leaving 20 women who participated in the study. The participants' collective contributions included being leaders in their occupational fields and professional organizations; being appointed to influen-

tial positions in government and private industry; being the recipients of prestigious awards, prizes, grants, and fellowships; being frequently invited speakers at professional meetings; and being members of important executive and professional boards.

Ages of the participants ranged from 34–60 years (averaging late 40s), and their occupations represented 10 areas: arts (director-choreographer, artist-educator, visual artist); business (CEO, business owner, entrepreneur, public relations consultant); economics (economist); education (educator, college president); government and politics (elected public official, political nonprofit executive); journalism (journalist, publisher); law (judge, lawyer); science (scientist, engineer); and social science (psychologist, social activist, organization vice president). Eleven women (55%) were Chicana or Mexicans, four (20%) were Puerto Rican, two (10%) were South American, two (10%) were Cuban, and one (5%) was Mexican-Puerto Rican; these percentages are similar to those of Latino subgroups in the U.S. (U.S. Census Bureau, 1998). There were three distinct patterns of immigration: 12 (60%) of the women were born in the continental United States, 5 (25%) were born outside the United States, and 3 (15%) were born in Puerto Rico. Of those women who immigrated, the mean age of immigration was 13 years of age (SD = 10).

. . . [Their] childhood socioeconomic status was lower-middle class, and upper class, as adults. The average educational level was 18 years of education (SD = 3) or the equivalent of a master's degree and ranged from 12 years (high school) to 25 years of educational attainment (PhD plus two master's degrees). In terms of relationships, one woman (5%) identified as bisexual, the remaining 19 (95%) identified as heterosexual, and none self-reported as lesbian. Twelve women (60%) currently had a spouse or partner, six (30%) were divorced or had been in a long-term committed relationship, and two (10%) had never had a serious relationship. Of the 12 women who were in a committed relationship, 6 (30%) were married to an Anglo American, 5 (25%) to a Latino, and 1 (5%) to an African American. More than half of the women, 11 (55%), had children; the number of children ranged from 1–4, with an average of 2.5 (*SD* = 1.0). At the time of the interview, seven of the women had children living at home, one woman lived with her children and her parents, and three women lived with their mothers.

Instruments

Data collection consisted of an in-depth, semistructured interview and a brief demographic questionnaire administered at the end of the interview. The interview protocol . . . included the following: (a) career path (current position, likes and dislikes about job, career path, educational experiences, background influences on beliefs about career success); (b) professional stress (work-related problems and ways of handling them, handling stress over time, relation to stress in personal life); (c) external challenges and limitations to achievement (obstacles encountered and effects on career, presence or absence of women and Latinas in field); (d) success and failure (definition of, perceptions of responsibility, internal beliefs about capabilities and achievements); (e) background and current influences (family of origin, spouses or partners, colleagues, friends, community, culture, and temperament-personality); (f) family-work interface (challenges and handling of family and work); (g) cultural identity (definition and development of, influence on career path); (h) career and life satisfaction and summary (what would one change if living life over, other information participant judged important). Congruent with qualitative methodology, the interview questions were open-ended to allow new constructs to emerge that might be limited by a more restricted interview structure.

Procedure

Initial contact with potential participants was made by letter and was followed up twice by telephone calls or letters. Interviews were conducted in locations chosen by participants and occurred in Washington DC, New York City, Los Angeles, San Francisco, Denver, and Chicago. The interviewer was the primary researcher, a bilingual Latina with 5 years of experience conducting assessment and counseling interviews. . . .

Results

Overview of Emergent Model

The emergent model explicating the career development of the 20 participants is presented in Figure 20.1. The model is represented as a series of reciprocally interactive and pervious concentric circles in which the women's concept of Self, using Culture, Family, and Personal Background factors as an interpretive lens, operates and acts within an immediate context, which in turn is shaped by Sociopolitical Conditions; as the Self interacts with her immediate context, her actions have consequences that forge a Career-Life Path, changing her immediate context and, therefore, the social and political conditions in which she lives and works. . . .

Core Category: Career-Life Path

In grounded theory, the core category or central construct narrates the main story of the study and encompasses all other categories (Strauss & Corbin, 1998). In the present study, the core category is the Career-Life Path, and it is created by the interaction of the four constructs titled Self, Culture-Family-Personal Background, Immediate Context, and Sociopolitical Conditions. The Career-Life Path describes the actions of the Self and the ensuing consequences on herself and the environment; thus, the Career-Life Path is represented in Figure 20.1 as an arrow beginning at the Self, moving outward through the varying layers of influence, and returning to the Self. . . .

The career paths of the women in this sample tended to be unplanned and nonlinear. Most women attributed their career trajectory to serendipity or a created, encountered, or offered opportunity. Typically, they described their career path as a "mix of hard work and luck" (judge), with "luck being where opportunity and readiness meet" (lawyer). Usually, they expressed an analysis similar to that of the following participants: "I fell into my career. It was not something I planned" (psychologist) and it did not follow "one particular path" (organization vice president). Most women located their unplanned careers through lack of exposure, information, or opportunity, as voiced by the entrepreneur: "The difficulty we have is not lack of ability or aptitude, it's been lack of opportunity. I believe all great careers are not planned, particularly for women". . . .

Personal Characteristics

The women in the study described themselves as passionate, tenacious, persistent, curious, flexible, and highly committed to their values and work. All participants felt a strong need to achieve their best in any situation, having a strong work ethic and often working "twice as hard" (judge) to prove themselves in the face of sexism and racism. The majority

expressed a strong belief in their ability to succeed in their professional field and judged themselves according to internal rather than external standards of success, as exemplified by the scientist, who said, "Internally, success is feeling that as an individual I have contributed. That validation gives your whole life flavor that makes you happy to be alive." Most women remembered having strong beliefs about their capabilities all their lives, crediting their parents for instilling high self-esteem. For a few, however, belief-in-self developed slowly, as mentors and significant others encouraged them and as they were reinforced by

Figure 20.1
Emergent Theoretical Model of the Career Development of Notable Latinas

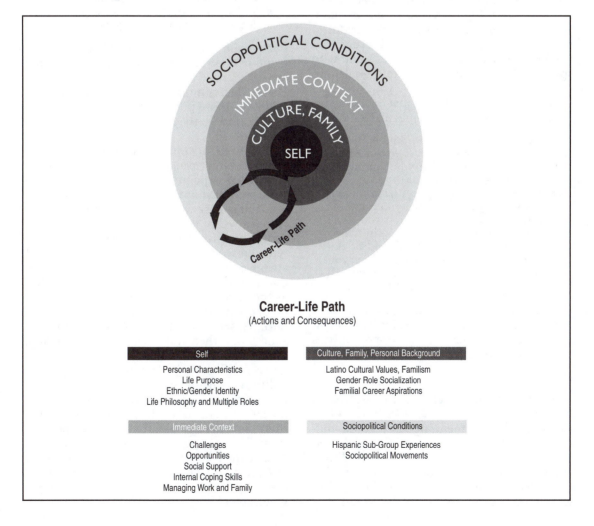

Career-Life Path
(Actions and Consequences)

Self	Culture, Family, Personal Background
Personal Characteristics Life Purpose Ethnic/Gender Identity Life Philosophy and Multiple Roles	Latino Cultural Values, Familism Gender Role Socialization Familial Career Aspirations
Immediate Context	Sociopolitical Conditions
Challenges Opportunities Social Support Internal Coping Skills Managing Work and Family	Hispanic Sub-Group Experiences Sociopolitical Movements

successful work experiences. The women saw themselves as "agents of our own destiny" (scientist), were passionate about their work, and measured success by career fulfillment: "I get to work every day in what I believe in. I don't go to the factory like my dad did for 35 years doing a job that was no choice. Definitely, that is my bottom line success" (visual artist).

Life Purpose

The women's careers seemed motivated by the desire to fulfill a particular calling or life conviction. For some, their passion was to their work specifically (e.g., space science, dance, education, art), whereas for others the purpose was either to survive (emotionally, economically), to prove to themselves and others that they could succeed, or to achieve a certain lifestyle (e.g., not be poor, to be an integrated person). The predominant motivator was to make a difference, as exemplified by the college president who spoke of "commitment to certain goals and values, to how you want to live your life . . . to stand up for something, not just to make a lot of money." Similarly, the visual artist noted:

> You've been given this gift, and with that gift comes responsibility . . . you must figure out a way to go back to your communities and solve the problems of those communities in the 21st century . . . I think that one has to understand what you get back. You never live a day in which you don't know the value of your life . . . in which you are not sure what you should be doing. You never live a moment in which you are not clear who is being affected. All those things are the values of this work.

Although several women knew their life calling as children (e.g., artists, scientists), most discovered their passion as opportunities developed in young adulthood.

Cultural Identity

Most participants viewed themselves as bicultural, with a few describing themselves as multicultural, meaning they could maneuver in both Anglo American and Hispanic culture, and they often behaved differently in each world: "There is a way in which I am when I live at home, behind the doors with my husband, and there's a way that I am outside, in my office" (journalist). Some, like the engineer, felt they were "becoming one of them [Anglos] to survive. And it is not that it is bad. It is that it's different." Although most felt at ease in both Anglo and Hispanic worlds, a few felt more Hispanic- or Anglo-identified, reflected in their choice of career and home location. For example, those who were Hispanic-identified tended to work and/or live in the Hispanic community, as the entrepreneur explained:

> This business is located here because this is the Hispanic community. I could locate this business anywhere, but I choose to be here, because I think it is a statement not just to the community [but] to the people we do business with. We force them to come down to the Latino west side. . . . I feel that I have accomplished success in changing people's attitudes.

Participants who were Anglo-identified felt some connection to Latino culture, but did not have a need to be directly connected to the Hispanic community, whereas bicultural individuals more purposefully and directly incorporated both cultures into their work and lives.

Although most participants viewed themselves as bicultural, their ease with this identity varied depending on their families' cultural and ethnic ideology. The few women who felt at ease with their bicultural identity were raised in families that valued and promoted biculturalism. However, the majority, who viewed biculturalism as a constant struggle, had been raised in families that requested adherence to Latino cultural values, as the educator described, "I went through a lot of turmoil with that, especially when your parents send you to a private Anglo girls school and then want you to act Mexicana, which you can't, and there are some times when I still have difficulty." Often, the bicultural struggle was described as the need to "straddle both worlds" (public relations consultant) while feeling "I am from here, there, nowhere" (scientist), and the perception of remaining an outsider was common: "I have the vocabulary so I can operate in the outside world without a problem, but it's not the place where I feel most comfortable, where I feel best" (journalist).

A common sentiment expressed by many of the Chicana participants in the sample was that their professional and economic success was suspect to the Mexican American community because it was assumed that they had "sold out" (publisher) to achieve. This cultural judgment often made them feel embarrassed and guilty that they had financial and professional success. A participant suggested this judgment is due to Mexicanos' cultural emphasis on being humble and not taking advantage of others. This was not a salient issue for the non-Mexican American women in the sample.

Gender Identity

Frequently, gender and ethnic identity were intertwined and interconnected. With few exceptions, the participants were raised in traditional gender roles, but as they encountered Anglo culture, their gender identity began to shift, as the organization vice president described:

> When I was growing up I had the sense that to become more Anglo was probably to leave. It was almost like a departure from the kind of traditional culture in which I grew up . . . to become a more traditional woman. . . . But I wanted to go find out what the world was all about.

Several of the women saw their American female side as being "very independent, determined, outspoken, feminist. I do what I want" (journalist), whereas their Latina side was "obedient, virginal, extremely feminine, motherly, respecting authority" (journalist). As adults, most women felt they faced a double jeopardy because they were women and Latina, facing sexism not only in majority culture but within the Latino community as well, as the artist-educator noted, "On the onset of defining myself culturally, it was around ethnic issues, but very soon within that it became defined by gender issues." A few of the participants rejected Hispanic men as spouses because they feared the men were too ensconced in traditional gender roles to be supportive, whereas those who were married to Latino men described them as nontraditional.

Life Philosophy and Multiple Roles

Being in leadership positions where they could create change, all participants voiced a strong sense of responsibility toward others; the majority dedicated and committed themselves to being mentors and role models, attempting to create new opportunities for those who followed. They usually gave credit to their family and culture for teaching them "the critical core value of responsibility towards community and family" (psychologist). For many, their family was "the center and the foundation" (elected public official). The women's defined sense of self, their need to pursue a life passion, their strong cultural and gender identity, and their commitment to their communities and family resulted in a self-concept that was multifaceted and required the women to maintain multiple roles: At work, in addition to their job titles, the participants were mentors, lecturers, community advocates, consultants, board members, and leaders in professional organizations; in their communities many were organizers, Sunday school teachers, deacons, mentors, role models, and public speakers; and at home they were spouses, mothers, *comadres* (godmothers), and family members. Their multifaceted self-concept required them continually to make career and life choices that would fulfill responsibilities within their many roles (role management is described below). . . .

Latino Cultural Values and Familism

The participants' families typically valued a strong collective identity, wherein all was shared and each person had responsibility toward the well being of the family and community, values carried into adulthood by most women in the sample. As the elected public official described: "In my family there was never any 'yours,' it was 'ours' . . . if everybody had to mop toilets to do it [get her through law school], we were all going to do it." The centrality of family, or familism, was also valued highly. This meant that family was the first line of support, they were in constant communication, and there was deference to parents and elders, as the journalist noted, "Before I do anything, I think about my parents. That was something that was just inculcated." As adults, the women relied heavily on their extended and immediate family for support: "When all else fails you, they're gonna be there and they're gonna love you" (elected public official).

Gender Role Socialization

Most of the women felt that they had received mixed messages about gender roles. On one hand, their parents adhered to strict gender roles, where, as the journalist described, women were expected to be "virginal, motherly, definitely obedient. *O sea* (I mean), respecting authority, putting family first, putting the care of your brothers and sisters and your parents before anything else." Women were expected to marry and have children because motherhood was highly valued, as the educator remembered from a conversation with her mother.

> *'Pero no estas completes.' Dije, '¿Que, me falta mama?' Dise 'un hijo.'* ('But you are not complete.' And I said, 'What am I missing Mother?' and she said, 'A son.') ... Before my father died, he said, 'If you really want to make me happy, you can walk in with a son.'

On the other hand, the majority of the women had strong female role models who behaved differently than expected. The participants' mothers were labor union organizers, business women, teachers, professional women, and single parents in an era during which few Latina mothers were unwed. In addition, full-time mothers were community activists, church leaders, organizers, and board members. In general, the women in the sample ignored restricting messages about gender roles and, instead, chose to internalize the behaviors and actions of mothers, grandmothers, and teacher-nuns who were persistent, strong, resilient, disciplined, and leaders in their communities. The public relations consultant recalls:

> My mother would always share [verbally agree] with my father [about] traditional things that you were supposed to do with women. But on the other hand that's not how she behaved. She worked, she was the head of the family ... so even though she would tell me one thing, I was watching something else.

Familial Career Aspirations

From their respective families the women received mixed messages about what they could aspire to be in the world. Typically, parents espoused education as the key to a better life, and several of the women (e.g., scientist, artist-educator, elected public official, journalist) were encouraged by parents to pursue their desired career. The majority of the women felt encouraged to be intelligent, do well in school, do "110%" (educator), received "huge doses of self-esteem" (entrepreneur), and grew up believing in themselves. The exceptions were three women who received negative messages from parents; however, all three had other people in their lives (e.g., sisters, teacher-nuns) who provided nurturing and support.

Nevertheless, despite positive messages, most participants were encouraged to excel within limited and traditional boundaries. The words of the women suggested that parents' limited career aspirations were often shaped and guided by financial concerns, an understanding of a Latina's place in society, cultural norms (e.g., familism), and strict gender roles. For example, some parents did not want their children to struggle like they had, so they encouraged their children to prepare themselves through education to achieve practical, concrete, and female "appropriate" jobs such as teaching or secretarial work. Other parents did not want their daughters to have false dreams given the limited opportunities for Latinas at that time and, therefore, did not encourage their daughters to be anything more than a secretary; the journalist, for example, never expected to pursue a career because of believing that "I'm just a little Mexican." Some parents were wedded to strict gender roles and prohibited their daughters from entering certain careers, such as law or medicine, because, as the judge's father said, "You would be taking the job of a man who has to provide for his family." Because of the strong sense of familism in Latino culture, some parents had difficulty in allowing their daughters to leave the family and community to pursue a career, and in the case of the engineer, even tried to sabotage her departure:

The day I left, everyone started crying, screaming. They couldn't take me to the airport. So I called my girlfriends . . . when I went to the airport in San Juan, they called me that my father was feeling bad. 'Come back. He is probably having a heart attack.' They were probably lying for me to come back. But I did not. I said, 'No . . . I am not going back.' So I had to make a big decision. And I did it. And thank God, I haven't regretted it.

Thus, the women in this sample generally were either discouraged or not strongly encouraged to have careers or were pressured to pursue careers that were traditional for women. . . .

Distinct Hispanic Subgroup Experience

The sociopolitical climate deeply influenced occupational barriers, opportunities, motivations, self-identity, and careers of participants and varied depending on the women's social and political location within the U.S. There tended to be three distinct experiences: (a) those who immigrated to the continental U.S. from Cuba or South America; (b) those who were second-generation Puerto Ricans; and (c) those who were Mexican Americans born in the continental U.S. Those who immigrated to the U.S. from Cuba or South America came for economic betterment and had the "immigration mentality" (psychologist) wherein the goal was to survive: "I was not in the business of making dreams come true but of surviving" (economist). In contrast, the two women who immigrated in pursuit of opportunities other than economics were motivated by dreams rather than by survival, as the scientist attests: "When I came to the U.S., I was 15 years old . . . a dream come true . . . an opportunity to do that [pursue technical career] more freely." Although the immigrant women's motivations were different, their attitudes exhibited similarity—they were grateful to be in the U.S. and to have opportunities not available in their country of origin. The focus on opportunities not available within their own countries may help to explain why these women were less apt to articulate racial-ethnic discrimination rather than gender discrimination.

The Puerto Rican and Mexican American women reported a different experience. Because of their ability to move easily between Puerto Rico and the mainland, the Puerto Rican women in the sample tended to be raised viewing biculturalism as an asset rather than as a hindrance. As the public elected official stated: "My parents taught us that you could be two cultures and know two languages and still be very proud of both, and that has been an incredible experience." In contrast, the Mexican American women, born into an oppressed group with a long history of colonial domination by the U.S. government, experienced the effects of oppression early on: "I think it's an artifact of colonialism that we don't like ourselves very much" (artist-educator). Despite being second- to fifth-generation American, the Mexican American women in this sample felt they constantly had to assert their right to equal citizenship. The publisher voiced the Mexican Americans' collective historical struggle as follows:

> My first ancestor's family was from [area in U.S.] 500 years ago. My family was here before it became American territory. So, to tell me that I'm a foreigner, I'm not. Or that my allegiance should be anywhere else, where? Or that I'm recently off the plane, off the boat, off anything, isn't true.

Generally it was the Mexican American women in this sample who voiced racism and sexism equally as influences in their lives, perhaps because of the historically oppressive sociopolitical conditions experienced by this Latina subgroup.

Sociopolitical Movements

Because of the large age range in the sample, it was possible to explore how the social and political climate of the decades between 1940 and 1970 influenced these women's identities and career paths. Latinas raised in the 1940s and 1950s, prior to the civil rights movements of the 1960s–1970s, described their upbringing as traditional and conformist. As expected, they married and had children at a young age. However, as the civil rights movements emerged, including Black Civil Rights, Chicano-La Raza, and Women's

Liberation, these women began to change and take advantage of the rights and career opportunities won by such movements. The publisher describes her transformation from traditional housewife to assertive businesswoman:

> You start out being this traditional mother, housewife, *wife*. And it's almost having a second-class status as far as decision making is concerned in a family unit . . . the traditional kinds of things that people who grew up in the 50s believed. . . . As you get older you either let it overwhelm you or you start developing a personality of your own; the ability to be forceful, confrontational. Women of my generation didn't like confrontation. . . . Then my children were older, I wasn't so tied to the apron strings. So I had a little more freedom. I think I associated with women who were a little bit more assertive. . . . So that was an awakening too.

Most women benefited from the new career opportunities brought on by the civil and women's rights movements, as the CEO business owner explained, "Had it not been for the affirmative action program I never would have gotten on . . . it wasn't like they gave me anything, all they did was open the door to me that had been closed before."

For the Mexican American women who came of age in the 1960s and 1970s, the Chicano-La Raza movement became "the defining ethic . . . it was what made you able to do things that people before us and people after us haven't been able to do" (artist-educator). The Chicano movement directly influenced the Mexican American women's career paths by providing empowerment, new career aspirations, and opportunities: "If you're Hispanic and you're from the Southwest it's [Southwest Voters is] an important organization for raising our consciousness and Latino politics and empowerment . . . I got swept up in all of that Chicano power. And that's how my interest in politics began" (political nonprofit executive). In addition, the Chicano movement became an integral aspect of the Mexican American women's cultural identity: "And then I see myself within the larger community of Chicanos here, and went through that whole movement with them. I'm

a *movimiento* [Chicano movement] girl" (visual artist). Above all, the Chicano movement provided hope, empowerment, new career aspirations, and opportunities not encountered before by Mexican American women:

> It [Chicano movement) came at the right moment of salvation, where you have finally realized how racist and how exclusionary and how marginalized you really were, and there was no hope for ever changing that, and then this moment came and everything changed. And then all of a sudden you discovered you weren't the only one, there was [sic] all these people who were similar to you, artistic, creative, from big families, working-class, pissed off, and you were all together, and you could figure out what to do. (artist-educator)

It was primarily the Mexican American women who acknowledged the impact of the civil rights movements on their lives, perhaps because of dramatic changes in their sociopolitical conditions as a result of those movements, again highlighting the interaction between the contextual and the personal in forging the Career-Life Path. . . .

Challenges

The most salient challenges encountered by the women in this sample included discrimination because of ethnicity (racism) and gender (sexism), financial deterrents, and for some women, health problems and internal conflicts.

Racism. The majority of the women reported experiencing both overt and covert forms of discrimination throughout their lives, in both educational settings and at work. For those who attended public or Catholic primary and secondary schools in the continental U.S., their experience embodied a mixture ranging from discouragement and institutionalized racism to an environment in which they were neither supported nor discouraged to crucial encouragement from at least one teacher, parent, or sister. Institutionalized racism consisted of teachers and school counselors who actively discouraged many of the women from pursuing college and suggested factory work or trade school instead. The elected public official gave one of many examples:

> My counselor in high school did not encourage me to go to college, she thought I should go to vocational training. . . . I never received any [career] counseling because people thought as a Hispanic female I just would not go to college. Purely by chance I found out on my own.

In the workplace, participants reported often being ignored in meetings, and many had to contend with the assumption that they maintained their position because of affirmative action rather than because of ability. Some organizations exhibited liberal racism, as described by the journalist: "It was kind of like you're strange, you're exotic, extraterrestrial. We need to grab you because if we let you go there's not going to be any more of you." However, two women acknowledged experiencing little racism because of their White phenotype and American-sounding English. These women were aware of "fitting in" and, therefore, dodged ethnic discrimination.

Sexism. In addition to racism, the majority of the women described numerous incidents of sexism. The strict female gender socialization of Latina culture initially limited career aspirations for many of the participants. In addition, throughout their careers most women reported sexual harassment and gender discrimination from men and women. As the economist stated, "It was a kiss of death every time I came to deal with a woman in a senior position." Sexism was manifested by attitudes and behaviors, such as encountering lack of confidence in their abilities, being ignored in meetings, being passed for important positions, men "tend[ing] not to take me seriously" (judge), and being accused of being "hysterical" (lawyer) and "out of control" (elected public official). As with racism, sexism was overt as well as subtle. The CEO business owner described her early years as a police officer:

> There was not so much a concerted effort but a kind of informal effort to make sure that women were never placed in a position where they would really be a threat to anybody else's position or advancement. . . . So very early in my career I saw that. Even though I had gotten my foot in

the door, that was as far as I was going to go.

It is difficult to assess from these women's stories to what extent discrimination encountered was because of gender rather than ethnicity and vice versa because the two usually were intertwined. As the nonprofit executive and the psychologist explained: "Being an Hispanic, being a woman, and then being an Hispanic woman, a lot of doors are closed to you." However, most participants stated that being a woman was the primary limitation in their career.

Financial deterrents. Socioeconomic status tended to influence the participants' educational trajectories and career paths such that those who could afford college went, whereas those who struggled financially did one of the following (a) attended college because they worked two or three jobs concurrently (e.g., the public elected official worked a factory night shift throughout college and graduate school), received scholarships, and were awarded financial aid; (b) disrupted their educational path; or (c) abandoned higher education altogether. For example, a few of the women interrupted their studies to provide for their families: "I was actually pulled out of school between my junior and senior year for a year, and worked to help support the family when both my mom and dad were ill" (CEO business owner). Some of the women initially attended community colleges because that was the expectation for Latinos and the sole institution they could afford. A few of these women never completed a college degree because of financial difficulties. However, those who were middle class and had less economic barriers could afford the education and career of their choice: "I was lucky to have him [husband] put me through school . . . I've never had to work and go to school at the same time, which is a tremendous advantage" (organization vice president). For a few women, their career path was initially defined by economic survival rather than by interest or choice. The social activist exemplifies this course: "I tried to stay in school to get that degree but I couldn't, I had to drop out. I could not keep up with all the emotional, economical things

that my children and I were going through."
However, once she had economic stability by
accepting a job outside her chosen profession, she was able to reignite her career.

Also apparent in this sample was the interaction of cultural values and socioeconomic
level (recall the Mexican American women's
reports of their success being viewed in the
Mexican community as selling out or as
somehow taking advantage of others) and
the deep and lasting influence of childhood
socioeconomic status in one's own perceptions of current success. The artist-educator
perhaps best articulated this:

> I've never had a sense of this protection or
> stability of the middle class. I always be-
> lieved that in a given moment if I'm
> standing on the wrong corner, I could be
> thrown in a van with a bunch of other
> people. You know, my English might save
> me, because they would think I wasn't
> [Mexican], but I don't ever feel totally re-
> ally safe about those issues.

Health problems and internal conflicts.
In addition to racism, sexism, and financial
deterrents, most women encountered hinder-
ing policies and bureaucratic problems
within their organizations. A few women had
severe health problems and attributed deteriorating physical health to stress, rage over
discrimination, and lack of rest. Finally, a few
struggled with internal conflicts around issues of self-esteem, histories of abuse, and
cultural identity. These internal struggles per-
meated their lives, but did not stop them from
achieving and persevering.

Opportunities

Despite multiple challenges and barriers,
all the women in this sample reported either
having or creating the opportunities which
sparked their careers. Analysis of the women's
words revealed two conditions. The first suggested that the women tended to be offered opportunities and they quickly seized them.
These were occasions for educational or professional advancement, such as the financial
and emotional support to pursue higher education, a position opening, or obtaining an important contract. Opportunities usually were
provided by a teacher or mentor or came as a
result of equal employment opportunity legis-

lation. In the second scenario, if opportunities
were not available, the women created them
by working "two times as hard" as their colleagues (judge), opening doors by taking risks,
and seeking out mentors, and networks in
which crucial career opportunities could be
provided.

Social Support

All the women in this sample recognized and
paid tribute to the social support they received
throughout their lives. In general, current social support encompassed communities or networks of women who were Anglo, Chicana, or
feminist; extended, nuclear, or current immediate family members who served as "my
rootedness in the world" (organization vice
president); coworkers; professional organizations; teachers, mentors and role models; and
spouses. Typically, the women spoke of one individual who was central in their lives or crucial to their career development. More often
than not this person was a teacher, mentor,
role model, mother, or spouse who fostered
their educational, professional, and personal
development.

Teachers. Despite barriers to education
described above, the majority of participants
encountered one teacher who made a difference. For example, the primary reason the
public relations consultant attended a 4-year
college, despite having been discouraged by
her school counselor from applying, was because her English teacher offered to help
with the application process. Participants
who attended Catholic schools (e.g., judge,
educator) perceived their teacher-nuns as
"very bright, very smart, very independent
women" (judge), who acted as role models
and counteracted traditional gender roles.
Participants reported the presence of professors and advisors in college who nurtured
their intellect and provided career information and advice. For many of the women in
this sample, one teacher made a tremendous
difference in their life.

Mentors and role models. Mentors were
salient in the lives of these women, because
of either their presence or absence. Eleven of
the women lacked mentors early in their careers and had to launch their careers alone
using optimism, tenacity, perseverance, and

hard work. Most women identified at least one mentor, whom they had found later in their careers. Mentors were individuals (e.g., professional colleagues, spouses, friends) or members of professional organizations (e.g., Hispanic professional groups, feminist organizations) who promoted their development in terms of offering opportunities, providing information known only to those in the "old boy's network" (educator), giving emotional support, and boosting self-confidence.

Role models also were crucial to these women. The elected public official expressed the common sentiment:

> All of a sudden I was in an environment where there were women in power positions. If you see them it becomes very important. I didn't have that growing up. It made a big difference to know, that not only can you achieve it, but you can go further.

As previously mentioned, several of the participants viewed their mothers as role models who behaved outside traditional gender stereotypes. However, lacking Latina-Latino professional role models, many of the participants sought role models across profession, ethnicity, race, gender, and age. For example, the engineer and the scientist used as role models historic figures and events, such as Galileo and the televised moon landing; others saw male politicians and movement leaders, such as Cesar Chavez, as role models.

Spouses. The 12 women who had spouses described their spouse as their most important source of support. The women tended to rely on their husbands (none of the women was partnered with a woman at the time) for both emotional and practical sustenance. Emotionally, their husbands were encouraging, their "staunchest supporter" (CEO business owner), and a balancing force in the participants' lives. Out of the 12 husbands, 4 were described as equally sharing household responsibility, whereas 7 of the spouses took on nontraditional male roles to champion their wives' careers. Regardless of ethnicity or race, the nontraditional husbands were the primary caretakers of home and children. They did a great deal of housework, were the parent-on-call, often chose to work

at home as consultants, were the primary liaison to their children's schools, and took care of extended family. Given traditional gender roles in Latino culture, the women felt blessed to have found their spouses. The college president described her husband's transformation as follows:

> My husband is very much a Latin male. If there were letters from school, a teacher to be seen, it was my job. Before I took this job, he never even bought a handkerchief by himself. But he assumed many of those responsibilities when I took the new job. He changed his life. . . . Today my husband runs his own consulting firm. He now defines his hours of work so he has more flexibility to attend family related activities.

Many of the women reported benefttting from more relaxed gender roles brought about by the feminist movement. As the scientist said of her husband, "I was lucky to be able to find somebody like that. In the past unfortunately there was no option. It was always the woman who had to be part-time teacher. I wasn't going to do that." Four out of the seven participants who were previously married or partnered left the relationship in part because the partner was unsupportive of her career aspirations. Those with spouses generally asserted that "I couldn't have done it without his support" (lawyer).

Coping Skills

In addition to social support, the women in the sample articulated strong coping skills, which they used in their immediate contexts to combat the myriad challenges they faced. The most salient internal coping skills were cognitive refraining, achieving and maintaining an appropriate perspective, religion and spirituality, denial, humor, acculturating to corporate culture, and self-soothing talk. Despite numerous difficulties and barriers encountered throughout their careers, the participants successfully and consistently used cognitive refraining to reconceptualize potential negative events into positive ones. For example, barriers were viewed as challenges: "I see a door closed, I open it" (director-choreographer-dancer); failures were "mistakes that are your next solutions" (artist-educator); and apparent disadvantages, such as age, gender or ethnicity, were made into advantages:

> Think twice about stereotypes and you can turn them around. . . . I stopped fighting them a long time ago. . . . Like not being taken seriously, that has enormous advantages, and you can choose to get angry and aggravated, or you can use it instead to infiltrate your position. There's nothing better than somebody who doesn't take you seriously to have all the guards down. You just cannot let it get under your skin. (economist)

Most participants were able to appropriately label sexism and racism rather than internalize culpability. When confronted with discrimination, some participants used "humor to disarm" (artist educator), whereas the older participants consciously used denial as a strategy:

> Contrary to what people in your generation might think, there were days when it [discrimination] was so bad, it was not even an issue. . . . You don't have to spend time worrying about it. You just go on with life. Some people have a limp, others are women. . . . I pushed it out of my head. (economist)

Many of the women purposely dressed conservatively and tried to match men's interpersonal style by being reasonable, keeping their voice down, and "not acting hysterical and emotional" (journalist). Other participants curbed their predisposition to close physical contact by refraining from hugging and kissing while greeting coworkers and by maintaining more physical distance. In difficult times, several women used self-soothing talk, such as "This too shall pass" (public relations consultant) and "You don't die from bad times, you just keep resprouting" (elected public official). To reach and maintain a balanced lifestyle, the women reported that they set limits at work, "turn off work" (CEO business owner), use time-management techniques, exercise, eat well, and participate in leisure activities such as sports, reading, and the arts. For several of the women, religion and spirituality provided a balancing force:

"[Religion] is an umbrella. . . . It is the source of internal peace, essentially. That's really where my ultimate reckoning is and the rest of the world keeps going" (economist). In addition, participants reported using solitude, psychotherapy, introspection, massage, acupuncture, and meditation as ways of turning inward to recharge and regenerate, tapping into their core self, which is based on optimism, service, resilience, passion, and a strong belief in themselves and their ability to succeed. The scientist captured the abiding optimism in her statement:

> I'm always full of optimism and I think that, like in Spanish we say 'no hay mal que por bien no venga' (there is no bad from which good cannot come). There is something good even from the worst situations that can come to your life, it's just that sometimes you have to look harder for them.

Managing Family and Work

Most participants reported that managing family and work responsibilities was an enormous challenge, particularly for the 10 participants who had children living at home or elderly parents and other family members for whom they cared. Typically the women acknowledged that managing work and family was not a balance, but a "juggling act" (economist) that caused "a continued source of stress" (economist). As the publisher stated, "I don't know that they [work and family] can ever be balanced. It's always going to be weighted on one side or the other." Most women experienced guilt, as they realized they could not be "a hundred percent every day in all roles" (lawyer), and acknowledged that "it is extraordinarily difficult to have two people in two frenetic careers and have children" (lawyer).

Typically, the participants managed work and family responsibilities by making life choices which either favored their careers (e.g., missing the school play to attend a meeting) or placed their career plans on hold while tending to family matters (e.g., taking care of elderly parents or young children). For example, before embarking on demanding careers, five of the women simply held jobs until their children had grown. As the entrepreneur stated, "you can have it all, you just can't have it all at the same time. So you have to make choices."

Another strategy for managing the work-family interface was to create partnerships with spouses such that each took turns as the primary caretaker while the other pursued a high-profile career, or, for six of the women with young children, to allow highly supportive spouses to take on the role of primary caretaker. The college president, for example, stated, "We supported my husband's career when we were first married. I took care of the kids and the house and everything. When I got the position of college president, it was his turn."

A third strategy used by participants for managing work and family was to include family members in their careers. Four women in the sample worked closely with family members, making the work a family commitment, whereas five women consistently brought their children to work (e.g., the lawyer breast-fed in her office) or included immediate family members in important work events. In the face of a challenge, several women developed a family-involved-in-work model, which created new opportunities for themselves and their family members. Thus, participants attempted to manage the family-work interface by making lifestyle choices, creating nontraditional partnerships with spouses, and including family in their work.

Summary

The participants' stories suggest that their unplanned and nonlinear career paths resulted from the confluence of challenges (e.g., discrimination because of culture, race, and gender; strict gender roles and mixed messages regarding careers; financial obstacles; and family responsibilities), opportunities (either provided or created), and social support (from spouses, family, mentors, role models) encountered by the women, yet shaped by their Self, which included passion, perseverance, optimism, and commitment. Thus, the Career-Life Path of the 20 participants can best be described as an implementation of the Self within an Immediate Context, such that

both have been influenced by Culture and Family Background and Sociopolitical Conditions. Most women described themselves as bicultural and felt a strong sense of responsibility toward their family and others, values that seem to have originated in Latino culture. When confronting challenges, the participants used social support networks and cognitive reframing to maintain a balanced perspective, the most noteworthy example being their ability to reframe negative events into positive ones. When doors closed, they opened new ones, forging a nonlinear Career-Life Path sculpted by an ardent sense of Self.

Discussion

Comparison of Results to Existing Literature

The career development model articulated in the present investigation is congruent with the Richie et al. (1997) and Poole and Langan-Fox (1997) models. All three are dynamic, fluid, interactive person-environment models of women's career development that take into account personal characteristics, beliefs about self, personal background, and social, cultural, and contextual variables. All three models point out that women's careers are filled with career-life choices that lead to negotiation and compromise, often rendering nonlinear and unplanned career paths.

The results of the present investigation, along with a growing body of literature (e.g., Poole & Langan-Fox, 1997; Reddin, 1997; Richie et al., 1997), suggest an emerging profile for the high-achieving, professional woman. In all studies, the high-achieving women were passionate, tenacious, demonstrated strong career self-efficacy, and had an inner conviction that included effective coping skills, internal motivation, career persistence, and high instrumentality. When confronted with challenges and potential barriers, high-achieving women used similar support systems such as mentors, networks of women, role models, family, and spouses. They reframed obstacles as advantages or ignored potential barriers.

The differences between the women in the present investigation and those in the Richie et al. (1997) and Poole and Langan-Fox (1997) studies lie in the particulars of the women's backgrounds and contextual factors. The Latina participants in this study experienced challenges, barriers, and support systems particular to their Latina cultural background. For Latinas, for example, family was both a strong support system and a potential barrier. Because family is so central in Latina culture, the women in the present investigation frequently relied heavily on their extended families for support, as some authors (e.g., Carter & Cook, 1992; DeLeon, 1996) have suggested. However, many of the women also felt constrained by the cultural norms of the family and felt enormous conflict when forced to choose between their families and career opportunities. In addition, the Latinas in the present investigation appeared to have been raised with stricter gender roles than those reported by the women in other studies (Poole & Langan-Fox, 1997; Reddin, 1997; Richie et al., 1997), suggesting that Latinas may have a stronger degree of female gender role traditionality to overcome in their paths toward achievement. An important finding is that most women in our study, despite traditional gender socialization, found nontraditional role models in their mothers or teachers, suggesting that providing diverse female role models for women of color can have a positive and lasting impact on career development (Fassinger, [2001]).

The struggle inherent in being a "minority within a minority," the development of a bicultural identity to navigate two cultures successfully, and the guilt and preoccupation with not appearing to "sell out" to White America also were unique for Latinas and add another layer of complexity and stress to their lives, as other authors have suggested (e.g., Arbona, 1995; Bingham & Ward, 1994). Finally, the ethnohistorical location of the notable Latinas in the present investigation presented unique barriers, opportunities, and support systems including discrimination due to ethnicity in the educational system and work, salient differences for the various Latina subgroups in terms of career aspirations and selfconcept, and the support of the Chicano movement for many of the

Mexican American women. These differences have been suggested in the career development literature on women of color (e.g., Arbona, 1995; Byars & Hackett, 1998) and are important to note when creating research, policy, and career interventions for Latinas.

However, several results from the present investigation may be applicable not only to Latinas and women of color but to all women. The career-life paths of the participants in the present study were nonlinear and often were influenced by serendipitous events, similar to findings of Betsworth and Hansen (1996). Many women felt their careers were shaped by their being extremely prepared when opportunities appeared, suggesting that Latinas and other women should be encouraged to prepare themselves as thoroughly for unplanned events. . . .

As reported in the literature (Poole & Langan-Fox, 1997; Richie et al., 1997) and found in the present study, managing family and career was a juggling act that caused constant stress; the participants often expressed feeling unsuccessful at managing work and family because attending to one involved neglecting the other. As Gilbert (1994) suggested, what appeared to be most effective for participants' management of career and family responsibilities was having a supportive spouse who could share or assume the role of the family's primary caretaker. Another way in which the participants managed work and family was by making their work a family affair, ably combining their strong value of familism with a demanding career. Perhaps we can learn from Latinas how to blend, rather than segregate, family and work responsibilities, adding another option for managing the family-work interface that other groups may not have considered (Fassinger & O'Brien, 2000).

The career self-efficacy of the women in the present sample appeared to be very high, a finding that adds to the existing research (e.g., Byars & Hackett, 1998; Richie et al., 1997), suggesting that self-efficacy is a particularly salient variable in the career development of women. The present study suggests that verbal persuasion (e.g., from parents, teachers, and mentors), vicarious learning (e.g., from role models, mother), physiological and affective states (e.g., using bicultural behaviors and soothing self-talk as coping strategies against racism and sexism), and performance accomplishments (e.g., having opportunities, succeeding at work) strongly influenced the career self-efficacy of many Latinas. In addition, the present investigation found support for the idea that environmental factors affect self-efficacy in diverse populations. For example, the ethnohistorical location of the Latina participants in the U.S. appeared to influence their motivations, career aspirations, and self-efficacy. Also, political movements such as the Chicano and Women's rights movements offered the participants both verbal persuasion (encouragement) and new opportunities for performance accomplishments, perhaps contributing to increased career self-efficacy in participants. . . .

Finally, the most successful personal characteristics and coping strategies documented in the literature (Poole & Langan-Fox, 1997; Richie et al., 1997) and practiced by this study's participants should be fostered. These characteristics include tenacity and persistence; flexibility; creativity; reframing and redefining challenges, barriers, or mistakes; maintaining a balanced perspective by understanding how racism and sexism may affect career-related behavior; developing support networks congruent with personal style, values, and culture; and developing bicultural skills where applicable.

The emergent theory in the present study adds to the understanding of women's career development by highlighting the importance of ethnohistorical relationships between person and environment, the influence of immigration experience and sociopolitical movements, the importance of analyzing data by Latina subgroup, and the salience of culture in Latina career development. These additions to a model of women's career development are important because, as Carter and Cook (1992) suggested, it is impossible to fully understand the career development of people of color without understanding the sociopolitical history and location of individuals in society. Despite some differences rooted in culture, the Richie et al. (1997) and Poole and Langan-Fox

(1997) models and the emergent theory in the present study add to the growing consensus in the women's career development literature that personal characteristics and identities, sociocultural and sociopolitical conditions, immediate contextual factors, and the family-work interface are important constructs in the career development of women.

Note

1. The terms Latina and Hispanic are used interchangeably throughout this article. Latin-Hispanic women are those living in the United States whose cultural and ethnic heritage originates from the varying mixtures of Spanish, indigenous, and African cultures in the southwest United States, Mexico, the Caribbean, Central America, and South America.

References
Arbona, C. (1995). Theory and research on racial and ethnic minorities: Hispanic Americans. In F. T. L. Leong (Ed.), *Career development and vocational behavior of racial and ethnic minorities* (pp. 37–66). Mahwah, NJ: Erlbaum.

Bandura, A. (1989). Human agency in social cognitive theory. *American Psychologist, 44,* 1175–1184.

Betsworth, D. G., & Hansen, J. C. (1996). The categorization of serendipitous career development events. *Journal of Career Assessment, 4,* 91–98.

Betz, N. E. (1995). Basic issues and concepts in career counseling for women. In W. B. Walsh & S. H. Osipow (Eds.), *Career counseling for women* (pp. 1–41). Hillsdale, NJ: Erlbaum.

Bingham, R. P., & Ward, C. M. (1994). Career counseling with ethnic minority women. In W. B. Walsh & S. H. Osipow (Eds.), *Career counseling for women* (pp. 165–195). Hillsdale, NJ: Erlbaum.

Byars, A. M., & Hackett, G. (1998). Applications of social cognitive theory to the career development of women of color. *Applied and Preventive Psychology, 7,* 255–267.

Carter, R. T., & Cook, D. A. (1992). A culturally relevant perspective for understanding the career paths of visible racial/ethnic group people. In Z. Leibowitz & D. Lea (Eds.), *Adult career development* (pp. 192–217). Alexandria, VA: National Career Development Association.

DeLeon, B. (1996). Career development of Hispanic adolescent girls. In B. J. R. Leadbeater & N. Way (Eds.), *Urban girls: Resisting stereo-*

types, creating identities (pp. 380–398). New York: New York University Press.

Fassinger, R. E. ([2001]). Diversity at work: Research issues in vocational development. In D. Pope-Davis & H. Coleman (Eds.), *The intersection of race, class, and gender in multicultural counseling* (pp. 267–288). Thousand Oaks, CA: Sage.

Fitzgerald, L. F., Fassinger, R. E., & Betz, N. E. (1995). Theoretical advances in the study of women's career development. In W. B. Walsh & S. H. Osipow (Eds.), *Handbook of vocational psychology* (pp. 67–109). Hillsdale, NJ: Erlbaum.

Fouad, N. A. (1995). Career behavior of Hispanics: Assessment and career interventions. In F. T. L. Leong (Ed.), *Career development and vocational behavior of racial and ethnic minorities* (pp. 165–192). Mahwah, NJ: Erlbaum.

Gilbert, L. A. (1994). Current persperctives on dual-career families. *Current Directions in Psychological Science, 3,* 101–104.

Gutierres, S. E., Saenz, D. S., & Green, B. L. (1994). Job stress and health outcomes among White and Hispanic employees: A test of the person-environment fit model. In G. P. Keita & J. J. Hurrell Jr. (Eds.), *Job stress in a changing workforce: Investigating gender, diversity, and family issues* (pp. 107–125). Washington, DC: American Psychological Association.

Lincoln, Y. S., & Guba, G. S. (1985). *Naturalistic inquiry.* Beverly Hills, CA: Sage.

Miles, M. B., & Huberman, A. M. (1994). *Qualitative data analysis: An expanded sourcebook* (2nd ed.). Thousand Oaks, CA: Sage.

Morrow, S. L., & Smith, M. L. (2000). Qualitative research for counseling psychology. In S. D. Brown & R. W. Lent (Eds.), *Handbook of counseling psychology* (3rd ed., pp. 199–230). New York: Wiley.

Phillips, S. D., & Imhoff, A. R. (1997). Women and career development: A decade of research. *Annual Review of Psychology, 48,* 31–59.

Poole, M. E., & Langan-Fox, J. (1997). Australian women and careers: Psychological and contextual influences over the life course. Melbourne, Victoria, Australia: Cambridge University Press.

Reddin, J. (1997). High-achieving women: Career development patterns. In H. S. Farmer (Ed.), *Diversity and women's career development: From adolescence to adulthood* (pp. 95–126). Thousand Oaks, CA: Sage.

Richie, B. S., Fassinger, R. E., Linn, S. G., Johnson, J., Prosser, J., & Robinson, S. (1997). Persistence, connection, and passion: A qualitative study of the career development of highly achieving African-American, Black, and White women. *Journal of Counseling Psychology, 44,* 133–148.

Strauss, A. L., & Corbin, J. (1998). *Basics of qualitative research: Techniques and procedures for developing grounded theory* (2nd ed.). Newbury Park, CA: Sage.

U.S. Census Bureau. (1998). *Statistical abstract of the United States: 1998.* Washington, DC: Author.

U.S. Department of Labor—Women's Bureau. (1997, February). Women of Hispanic origin in the labor force (No. 97–2). Washington, DC: Author.

Reprinted from: Maria J. Gomez, Ruth E. Fassinger, Joann Prosser, Kathleen Cooke, Brenda Mejia, and Jeanette Luna, "Voces Abriendo Caminos (Voices Forging Paths): A Qualitative Study of the Career Development of Notable Latinas." In *Journal of Counseling Psychology*, Vol. 48, No. 3, pp. 286–300. Copyright © 2001 by the American Psychological Association, Inc.

Food for Thought and Application Questions

1. Discuss what you consider to be the primary personal and cultural factors that characterize pathways to success for these Latina women. What factors are not so uniformly shared by these women? How does this vary by Hispanic subgroup, and with what consequences?

2. What are the main challenges these women faced as they progressed through their careers? What strategies do they use to overcome or rise above these challenges?

3. Assume you are to address a campus group of Latina women about career issues and challenges. Based on your reading, what issues would you include in your presentation and why? ✦

21

Gender and the Formation of a Women's Profession

The Case of Public School Teaching

Jo Anne Preston

Despite the burgeoning literature on gender and occupations, little attention has been given to the influence of gender in the formation of professions. For almost half a century sociologists have recognized differences between predominantly female professions and predominantly male professions, but most theoretical and empirical considerations of the professionalization process have failed to account for the development of these differences. Without examining the influence of gender in the formation of professions, sociologists have difficulty explaining how inferior status and wages have become associated with female professions. Employing historical data, this chapter seeks to demonstrate how gender affects professionalization of teaching. Evidence from 19th-century school records reveals that the development of gender distinctions in wages, in authority, and in cultural representation was an essential part of professionalization of teaching. Carr-Saunders and Wilson (1933) first identified common characteristics of predominantly female professions when they developed the category *semiprofessions* to include all major women's professions. Following Carr-Saunders and Wilson's conceptualization, Simpson and Simpson (1969) recognized that women's professions have been governed by more extensive bureaucratic structures than men's professions. Working within a functionalist framework, they proposed that women workers needed greater bureaucratic control due to their lesser commitment to work. Simpson and Simpson also postulated that a woman's concern for her duties outside the workplace induced her to submit more readily to authority. Gender, in this formulation, has an impact on professionalization by calling forth extensive bureaucratic structures. Although correctly identifying bureaucracy as characteristic of many women's professions, Simpson and Simpson failed to recognize another gender dimension of this development: Men control and often completely make up the bureaucratic structures that govern female professionals.

More recent theoretical considerations of professionalization, eschewing simple ahistorical trait-based views, stress the importance of locating professionalization within its historical period and in reference to external processes. Most, however, do not accord gender much significance. Johnson (1972) conceptualizes professionalization as a process transformed by the growth of the state but ignores the influence of gender in this transformation. He defines professionalization as a process that results in control over an occupation without examining how gender affects that control. Larson (1977), arguing that professions developed as part of the evolution of late-18th-century and 19th-century capitalism, emphasizes the historically bound character of professions as they are locked into broader structural and historical processes. Although she discusses how a category of supervisors was created as a result of the bureaucratization of teaching, she fails to recognize that most of these newly created supervisory positions were filled by men whereas women remained the vast majority of classroom teachers. These gender distinctions, with their attendant wage and power differences, constituted an integral part of the professionalization of teaching.

Abbott (1988) calls for an ecological perspective, viewing professions as a system of continuous, historically located struggles over jurisdictions. In his historical analysis, he concludes that gender had limited significance in the formation of professions. He considers that in cases of occupational transformation gender acts only as a following variable. Like Larson, he discusses the emergence of school supervisors with professionalization without recognizing the importance of the growing number of female teachers to the creation of supervisory positions. The increase in female teachers may not have followed bureaucratization as he suggests; rather, bureaucratic structures may have arisen during and after the increased employment of female teachers. Historical evidence shows that the development of male-dominated bureaucratic structures in New England teaching occurred during the feminization of teaching.

Not all contemporary considerations of professionalization have ignored or minimized the importance of gender. In the last decade two English sociologists, Hearn and Witz, independently proposed models to explain the relationship of gender and professionalization. Hearn (1982) formulated a model for gendered professionalization that places the process within a patriarchal society. Based both on a stage theory of professionalization and the conception of female professions as semiprofessions, his model proposes that occupations achieve full professionalization only when they are completely dominated by men; that is, so long as women make up the rank and file in teaching, nursing, social work, and public librarianship, these occupations will be denied many of the benefits accruing to male professions. As men increase their participation in semiprofessions, Hearn forecasts that they will gain more control until, when men compose the entire workforce, a semiprofession becomes a full profession. In his model, the process of professionalization is equated with process of achieving male hegemony. His analysis, however, conflates patriarchal power and professional power, denying women the possibility of achieving professional power. More problematic is his view of semiprofessions as on a continuum with full professions and eventually becoming entirely composed of men. The historical studies of women's professions, such as

nursing (Melosh 1982) and public librarianship (Garrison 1979), reveal no such trend. In teaching, the labor force has remained predominantly female since [1890] (Oppenheimer, 1970).

In contrast, Witz (1990, 1992) views professionalization as a process that is profoundly altered by the dynamics of gender relations. Using a neo-Weberian framework, she argues for a model of gendered closure strategies in which men as a dominant social collectivity seek to exclude or to control women who, in turn, respond either by challenging the male monopoly of an occupation or by creating a related, exclusively female occupation. Closure practices—exclusionary, inclusionary, demarcationary, and dual—have gendered dimensions. Gendered agents choose specific closure strategies and bring gender-determined differential power to bear upon specific professionalization projects. Male doctors, for example, choose to exclude women from medicine by employing their greater power over credentialing institutions and the state. Female nurses and midwives, on the other hand, engage in a dual closure strategy which contains both usurpationary and exclusionary activities; they resist domination from male doctors and, at the same time, restrict entry to their own professions. Gendered agents, therefore, can construct women's professions through dual closure strategies. Although Witz's model may explain the development of medical professions, it is less revealing in the case of school teaching, in which state officials have always prevailed and teachers have had little success in influencing the social construction of their profession.

Borrowing from Witz's conception of gendered agents, however, this chapter considers the actions of those gendered agents who influenced the professionalization of teaching, chiefly school reformers Horace Mann and Henry Bernard. In addition to considering the influence of these gendered agents and rather than simply confining their influence to closure strategies, it recognizes that gender "is present in the processes, practices, images and ideologies, and distributions of power" (Acker 1992, p. 567). According to Acker, gender is "the patterning of difference and domination through distinctions between men and women that is integral to many social processes" (p. 565). I argue, therefore, that gender is integral to the process of professionalization. Thus gender, as a part of the process of professionalization, affects both the dynamics and the outcome of the process in a variety of ways. This study employs this broader conceptualization of gender.

The definition of professions and professionalization is more problematic, with little consensus among sociologists. Abbott (1988) defines professions as "exclusive occupational groups applying somewhat abstract knowledge to particular cases" (p. 8). He explains that he arrives at this conceptualization because of its relevance to answering his theoretical questions on how professions control skill and knowledge in relation to one another. The process of professional development of any occupation, he demonstrates, is influenced by jurisdictional conflicts. Abbott proposes that professionalization theory should focus on work rather than the structure of occupations. This study focuses on how gender influences the development, structural as well as ideological, of one profession; my conceptualization of professionalization follows from those theoretical formulations that concentrate more extensively on these changes within an occupation. This chapter considers professionalization as a process that can result in the development of bureaucracy (Larson 1977), in the evolution of cultural legitimation (Bledstein 1976), in the establishment of formal training and credentialing with the related raise in material rewards (Wilensky 1964), and in changes in workers' autonomy and control over their occupation (Johnson 1972).

Using these formulations, this study examines the case of the professionalization of teaching in 19th-century Massachusetts. In the United States, school teaching became professionalized first in Massachusetts, which later served as the model for other states. Over the course of the 19th century, driven by the same social and economic forces that professionalized law and medicine (Larson [1977]; Starr 1982), it evolved from an undesirable occupation to a more highly regarded profession, experiencing all the changes enu-

merated above. At the beginning of the century, teaching was a low-status, low-paid occupation demanding little expertise or training. By the end of the century, it was a higher-paid, higher-status profession governed by bureaucratic structures and requiring education in teacher-training colleges and additional formal credentials. Each of these changes was affected by another important transformation in teaching, feminization. As teaching became increasing[ly] female through the first half of the century, the changes wrought by professionalization were shaped by the increasing presence of women in the classroom. In the second half of the century, when women composed the vast majority of teachers, gender had even a more powerful impact on workers' control over the profession and workers' autonomy.

I have analyzed the causes of feminization of teaching in New England extensively elsewhere and will not discuss them here at length. My empirical work has demonstrated that the transformation of teaching from a male occupation to a female occupation was a process that took more than 200 years and was finally completed in the 19th century with structural and ideological changes in teaching, both driven by the school reform movement (Preston 1982, 1989, 1993). The new hierarchical job segregation by sex, increased supervision, and a female representation of the ideal teacher all reduced the prejudice against female teachers, the greatest impediment to feminization. Strober and Landford (1986), analyzing 19th-century quantitative school data in six states for the years 1850–1880, also found that feminization was associated with structural changes in teaching. Specifically, they found higher percentages of female teachers in counties where teaching was formalized, where it was calculated by length of the school year and teachers per school, and where women's earning were a small fraction of men's. These changes were also developments in the professionalization of teaching and as such were, in turn, extensively transformed by the increase in female teachers. In related work, Strober and Tyack (1980) identified the development of sex-segregated, male-dominated bureaucratic structures in schooling. Empirical evidence from the history of teaching cited below demonstrates that these sex-segregated bureaucratic structures arose with professionalization and increased the gender gap in absolute wages.

In the following sections, the chapter presents some empirical evidence from the history of teaching demonstrating the impact of gender on professionalization. The evidence reveals that professionalization, rather than being a gender neutral process, was profoundly influenced by gender. The first section explores changes in teachers' autonomy. Freidson (1986), who considers an increase in autonomy critical to professionalization, defines autonomy as "the right to use discretion and judgment in the performance of their work" (p. 184). Similarly, Jaffe (1989) measured autonomy by "the extent to which employees exercise self-direction and discretion over the execution of their jobs" (p. 381). Others define autonomy as the absence of supervision imposed on the worker. For example, Forsyth and Danisiewicz (1985) conceptualize professional autonomy as a phenomenon "manifested by freedom from the client and employing organizations" (p. 61). To explore the various dimensions of autonomy, this section employs these definitions to examine 19th-century changes in teachers' capacity for self-direction and the degree to which they have control over their work.

The second section presents historical data on the changes in teachers' control over their occupation during professionalization. Johnson (1972) defined a profession as "not an occupation but a way to control an occupation" (p. 45). In contrast, as teaching evolved from a male occupation to a female profession, male administrators assumed more control over recruitment, licensing, and training. Despite the efforts of male and female teachers and prominent female educators, the male leaders of the school reform movement gradually transferred teacher training from female academies to state-dominated normal schools and successfully lobbied for greater state control over credentialing teachers.

The third section of this chapter discusses changes in wages during professionalization. During professionalization wages rose for both men and women teachers. Although not extensively discussed in the work

and occupations literature, professionalization customarily elevates financial rewards by creating an elite occupation. Despite feminization, which is associated with declining wages (Reskin and Roos 1990), professionalization caused teachers' wages to rise. More significantly, the gender difference in absolute wages of teachers also increased, with men benefiting more economically from professionalization than did women. The causes of the gender gap in wages are not well-explained by neoclassical economic theories; the problems with these approaches are extensively discussed elsewhere (Marini 1989; Stevenson 1988), and they will not be reviewed here. In spite of the failure of various theoretical approaches to fully account for the gender gap in wages, empirical studies have found a relationship between the gender gap in wages and job segregation by sex (Bielby and Baron 1984; Treiman and Hartmann 1981). Data presented in this section suggest that the increase in the gender gap in teachers' wages was caused, in part, by the creation of sex-segregated bureaucratic structures.

Gender, however, was not expressed solely by structures. A specific cultural representation of the female schoolteacher evolved during professionalization of school teaching, and this representation had a direct effect upon the process. Professions acquire sex-specific ideologies, like all occupations, as they are socially constructed, and these constructions are informed by gender ideology—that is, a set of ideas that consider either men or women better suited to do the work required of an occupation because of their supposed innate qualities. Milkman (1987) identifies these ideas as the "idiom" of an occupation. Although the idiom of every female profession prescribes that women are best suited for that type of work, the content of each idiom is idiosyncratic and not necessarily related to women's domestic roles (Crompton 1987; Milkman 1987); neither is it always shared by the professional workers themselves (Preston 1989, 1993). The construction of the idiom may well be part of image building during the professionalization process and may act to limit the aspirations of the female professionals

(Forsyth and Danisiewicz 1985; Hearn 1982). Ideology is crucial to the professionalization of occupations because professions need cultural legitimation (Bledstein 1976). As part of that legitimation process, the public must be convinced that the service rendered is "essential, exclusive, and complex" (Forsyth and Danisiewicz 1985, p. 64). They must view the professional worker as competent to perform the professional service. Section four examines the evolution of a gendered professional image of the school teacher.

The final section of this chapter discusses the findings of limited autonomy and control over the occupation, gendered bureaucratic structures, increased gender gap in wages, and sex-typed ideology. It then speculates on the implication of these findings in light of current understandings of professions and professionalization.

Autonomy in the Teaching Profession

The autonomy of the teacher, whether measured by capacity for self-direction or by degree of control over the work process, declined over the course of the 19th century. In the 18th century, when the occupation was predominantly male, little supervision was exercised over Massachusetts teachers. Teachers' diaries and correspondence reveal that teachers could open and close their schools as their needs dictated. Thomas Robbins, teaching in Torringford in 1798, felt entitled to close his school when he had a pain in his jaw (Tarbox 1886–1887). After he heard of a disturbance in Cambridge in 1775, Scituate schoolmaster Paul Litchfield (1881–1882) closed his school for two and one half days to check on his rooms at Harvard. Earlier in the same week he chose to miss one morning of school because of "rainey weather." Likewise, female teachers had some control over their schedules. Elizabeth Bancroft, a teacher in Groton, freely dismissed her school for funerals and barn raisings during her 1773 summer session (Bancroft, 1793–1799). In these accounts, use of the term *schoolkeeping* rather than *school teaching* indicates the control 18th-century teachers had over their workplace.

From the second decade of the 19th century, when feminization of the winter session began, changes in schooling increased the supervision of teachers. Towns had traditionally reserved the winter sessions, usually equivalent to the summer sessions in length and content, for male teachers while appointing only women to summer session schools. As towns began to hire women for winter session positions, they directed male supervisors to assume more control over schoolteachers' work, curtailing their freedom to execute their job as they chose. The timing of the increase in supervision, coincident with the feminization of the winter sessions, suggests that the state and towns perceived a need to assume more control over an increasingly female workforce. The frequency and character of the selectmen's visits changed in the 1820s with the passage of state legislation granting more powers to the selectmen and requiring more stringent supervision of teachers. The Massachusetts acts of 1826 and 1827 conferred on local school committees, which comprised male leaders of the community, powers to appoint and certify teachers, to visit and inspect the classroom work of the teacher, to direct and supervise the teacher's work, and to select textbooks. Authority to certify and appoint gave the committee the power to decide what personal qualifications and training made an applicant an acceptable teacher. Selection of textbooks allowed the committee to influence the curriculum but not yet the course of study or teaching methods, changes which were to come later (Suzzallo 1906). More importantly, the school committee now had general charge and "superintendence" over the teachers' work. To assure that the school committeemen carried out their new function, the 1826 and 1827 acts stipulated that they visit the classroom once a month without advance notice to observe the teacher and question the students. Superintendence of the teacher, therefore, increased the control of the administrators, all men, over the standards of teaching and, consequently, diminished teachers' autonomy.

The new superintendence of the teachers is well described by a Massachusetts teacher writing home in 1826:

Dear Achsah,

. . . I am almost tired to death. . . . I have engaged a school. . . . Oh I have been brought under the most rigid laws this season than I ever was in New York State. The Legislature of this state has adopted a new system in regard to public schools. This is that each town choose a committee of five or more to superintend the schools in town . . . that is to process the teacher, select the books and direct the studies and everything concerning the schools. No teacher is entitled to their pay unless they are examined by the committee. . . . They also visit the school the first or second week after commencement and give the teacher notice before coming after that once a month without previous notice to the teacher until the last week when they are there to let them know they are coming. . . . I have been under their contract since the first of May when I went before them for inspection since then they have visited my school six times—sometimes one at a time, sometimes two or more just as they choose but thank fortune I am almost done with them a week from Monday comes my exam on Tuesday I close my school and I think I shall rejoice if I ever did [school] has almost worn me out. . . . It has made my fat checks look rather hollow. (Brammer 1826)

In addition to reporting the changes in Massachusetts school laws, Electa Snow's account also illustrates the resentment generated by the selectmen's expanded authority over teachers' work.

By the 1830s, Massachusetts towns hired male teachers in the winter to supervise female teachers, thereby seeking to lessen their residents' resistance to hiring female teachers for the exclusively male-taught winter session. Towns, for example, often consolidated two district schools during the winter session, assigned the younger students to a female teacher and the older students to a male teacher, and placed "the whole school" under the male teacher (Massachusetts school reports, 1833–1834). These districts often referred to the man as teacher and the woman as assistant teacher. The town of Sunderland, for example, reported that it incorporated

two female teachers into the winter session schools as follows:

> District No. 3 and 4 lying near each other unite and in winter have a central school attended by the scholars in each district over ten years of age. This school is taught by a man. Those under ten attend schools in each district taught by a woman. (Massachusetts School Reports 1833–1834)

Sunderland then granted the male teacher authority over the female teachers. Restructuring schooling along gender lines thus maintained male dominance of the winter sessions.

The subsequent proliferation of managerial positions, which accompanied professionalization, further constrained teachers' autonomy. Towns evolved a structure of control and supervision that included a school committee, a superintendent, and one or more principals, all of whom were male, with the exception of principals of female high schools. The most developed of these systems were the fully bureaucratized school systems of cities and large towns. In the bureaucratizing urban school systems that developed with professionalization, full-time administrators, all male, supervised teachers, who were primarily female. In addition, grammar masters began to supervise female assistant teachers.

As shown in Table 21.1, Boston in 1852 hired 37 male grammar schoolmasters and submasters to supervise 138 female "assistants." In 1866, the Boston School Committee also extended the powers of the grammar masters to include overseeing the primary mistresses in their respective districts. In 1875, new legislation abolished the school committee, created a school board of 24 members, added six new supervisors, and formed a board of supervisors to be chaired by the superintendent (Katz 1987)—actions that definitively placed most of the power in the superintendent's office. Table 21.2 shows the new configuration of hierarchy in the Boston schools. Female and male teachers were segregated not only by job title but also increasingly by the degree of autonomy conferred by the title. By 1876, 48 men held administrative posts as principals whereas one woman occupied the recently created position of assistant principal of the normal school, an institution attended by a majority of female students. Other female positions in the primary, grammar, and high schools had been divided into first, second, third, and fourth assistants. Boston now gave all women the rank of assistant—assistant principal; first, second, and third assistant in the high schools; normal school assistant; first, second, and third assistant in the grammar schools; and fourth assistant in the primary schools. Gone were the female positions that implied some independence, such as head assistant or primary mistress. All of these changes in job titles accompanied the increase in supervision and the resulting decline in autonomy experienced by teachers. Significantly, the erosion of autonomy was greater among female teachers.

In these bureaucratized school systems, the resident principal and various members of the school committee made frequent, unannounced visits to each classroom to assess the progress of the teacher by examining the

Table 21.1
Hierarchy and Annual Wages of Boston Teaching Positions by Sex, 1852

Position	Number	Wages
Male (*N* = 82)		
Supervisory		
Superintendent	1	$2,500
High School		
Masters	2	$2,400
Submasters	3	$1,500
Ushers	5	$800–$1,200
Grammar Schools		
Grammar masters	23	$1,500
Writing masters	5	$1,500
Submasters	9	$1,000
Ushers	13	$800
Female (*N* = 315)		
Grammar Schools		
Head assistants	3	$400
Assistants	135	$250–$300
Primary Schools		
Primary mistresses	177	$300

Source: Report on the Boston Schools, 1852; Massachusetts State School Returns, 1851–1852.

students. These evaluations were more extensive than those of the 1820s. In her diary, Lynn, Massachusetts, school teacher Mary Mudge (1854) described one visit as follows:

> Dr. Callaupe and Mr. Ambler into the school this P.M. . . . Heard the 1st class read . . . asked many questions not in their lesson. Harriet Brown got confused and could not spell Alcohol. 2nd class read "The Father" . . . did very well in reading and spelling. 1st class in Colburns recited on division of mixed numbers . . . 1st Class in Geography did well but could not tell what year Greenland was discovered. Dr. [Callaupe] made a few remarks; . . . said he had been well pleased . . . they did well in Geography and Arithmetic and would be excellent readers if they kept their voices up at the comma.

Although female teachers privately lamented the encroachment on their work by the extended, intrusive classroom visits of supervisors, the historical record reveals no direct opposition. Finding no meaningful means of protest, female and male teachers' most common recourse was to seek alternative employment. Men sought and gained employment in the emerging exclusively male professions of law and medicine. Women, more limited in their options, moved from teaching job to teaching job in search of more suitable employment. For example, in the mid-19th century, Massachusetts school teacher Aurelia Smith, constantly dissatisfied with her work, taught in five towns during her 6-year teaching career. Work biographies of 19th-century Mount Holyoke graduates show that female teachers continually moved from one teaching position to another (Preston 1982).

Even more central to workers' autonomy is the capacity to determine how the work is done. In 18th-century Massachusetts, pedagogy, the method of teaching, remained primitive. Teachers developed what teaching methods they had idiosyncratically. Although they frequently followed a series of texts, teachers could choose the lessons or recitation exercises. Supervisors rarely imposed a method of teaching. Most 18th-century teachers taught alone in one-room schoolhouses; supervision consisted of occasional visits by one or more town selectmen.

Because the average selectman had less education than the teacher, he usually concerned himself only with decorum and the physical appearance of the classroom (Suzzallo 1906). Teachers had control over how teaching was done and over other conditions of their work.

Nineteenth-century male administrators, at more elevated positions, began to assume responsibility for developing teaching methods. The science of pedagogy was almost nonexistent in Massachusetts until the first decades of the 19th century, when Horace Mann and other leaders of school reform began to advocate teaching methods. Mann's second annual report (1838) included a treatise on methods of instruction. But even before Mann published his directives, Samuel Hall (1829), founder of the first teacher-training institution in America, published his *Lectures on Schoolkeeping*. In his lectures, he spelled out the teacher's appropriate presentation of lessons, the proper curriculum to be taught in each type of school, and the correct relationship between the teacher and the student. Such instructions, when followed, may have improved teachers' performance in the classroom. From the standpoint of the autonomy of the worker, however, teaching methods imposed by managers reduced teachers' control over the work process. Later developments in curriculum reform further restricted teachers' decision making in the formulation of the content and methods of teaching (Apple 1986). Consequently, the mid- to late-19th-century teacher became less autonomous as a result of the professionalization of teaching.

Thus changes in the structure and content of teaching during the professionalization of the occupation curtailed the professional workers' control over their work. Significantly, I argue, the professional workers were increasingly women. Because 19th-century women's low social status and subordination to men in all other aspects of their lives allowed school reformers to create male-dominated bureaucratic structures to control female teachers and because women's limited employment opportunities curtailed their options, teaching evolved as a profession that was structured by a sex-segregated system of hierarchical control and supervision. This hi-erarchical restructuring of teaching permitted reformers to achieve their goal of making schooling a more influential social institution without granting power to the growing number of female teachers. Gender, then, rather than having an influence after the fact, determined important and enduring characteristics of the teaching profession. These changes are in contrast to those occurring in the 19th century male occupations of law and medicine. The professionalization of these occupations resulted in greater power for the individual worker and for the profession in general (Larson 1977; Starr 1982). The much more limited autonomy of the teachers resembled that experienced by workers in other female professions. For example, the development of managerial positions primarily held by men can also be found in the professionalization of librarianship (Garrison 1979). Although nursing did not develop a male-dominated managerial structure, control was exercised by a related male profession—that of medicine (Hearn 1982; Witz 1990).

Control Over the Teaching Profession

Teachers never achieved control over the development of their emerging profession. During the course of professionalization, the state took over the responsibility of training teachers, denying teachers authority over the training of the new members of their profession. This further constraint on female teachers' autonomy came about as state-financed and state-controlled normal schools replaced the female academies as the educators of teachers. Normal schools, first established in the late 1830s, became the primary institution for teacher training by the end of the Civil War. The state legislature also mandated criteria for certification and employment (Woody 1929).

Female academies were first established in New England in the 18th century and proliferated during the antebellum period. Most academies were not specifically aimed at training women to become teachers; rather, they were devoted to educating young women in liberal arts, science, and religion. Many academy founders explicitly saw themselves as committed to improving the situation of women, who were barred from studying at men's colleges (Woody 1929). Some academies even conferred explicitly female degrees. The Springfield Female Collegiate Institute, for example, awarded an M.E.L., or Mistress of English Literature, an L.B.A., or Lady Baccalaureate, and an M.L.A., or Mistress of Liberal Arts (Springfield Female Collegiate Institute 1860–1861).

Less concerned with intellectual development, the curriculum at normal schools prescribed methods of teaching developed by male administrators. When the first normal school was established in 1839, female academies were the main educators of female teachers. By 1860, with the founding in Massachusetts of five more normal schools, school committees—with the encouragement of the state legislature—hired normal school graduates over female academy graduates (Magnum 1928). Increasingly, more teachers prepared for their work at normal schools with their state-mandated course of study rather than at female academies. Because normal schools emphasized methods and most female academies taught only subject matter, leaving choice of method to the prospective teacher, the transition from female academies to normal schools gave the state control over the training of new workers.

The state also usurped any power teachers may have possessed over recruitment and standards of the profession. By passing legislation requiring training in state-run normal schools and setting criteria for certification, the state, rather than a professional organization, assumed control of entry to the profession. Town school committees still retained the power to hire teachers; these committees, however, were directly influenced by the voters—not by teachers' associations. How voters conceived of the proper role of the teacher in any particular historical period can further dictate what the school committee sets as professional standards (Freidson 1986).

Teachers made repeated unavailing efforts to influence the development of teaching. In 1830, 45 men met in Topsfield to form the Essex County Teachers' Association, whose express purpose was "the improvement of teach-

ers and the system of education generally." By the 1850s, the organization allowed women to attend their lectures but reserved all policy making to male members. In its first 3 decades, the organization sponsored lectures on timely educational issues, petitioned Congress for federal support of education, and established a fund to aid disabled teachers. It expressed its dissatisfaction with the current system of supervising teachers through published essays in *The Massachusetts Teacher*. Unfortunately, the association's recommendations on this issue and other matters were spurned by state officials. Norfolk County also formed an all-male teachers' association in 1830 for "mutual improvement, with reference to professional duties." It too failed to shape the profession. Later teachers' organizations, such as the American Institute for Instruction, an organization also dominated by men, suffered a similar fate (Messerli 1972).

Promoters of female education were also enthusiastic supporters of the professionalization of teaching, perceiving it as a way of increasing the status and wages of female teachers and ultimately elevating them to a position equal to that of male professionals. Prominent educators Catherine Beecher and Emma Willard advocated professional status for female teachers (Lutz 1964; Sklar 1973). Catherine Beecher (1851), for example, argued for upgrading teaching to a "profession for women, as honorable and lucrative for her as the legal, medical, and theological professions are for men" (p. 79). Rather than establishing separate teacher-training schools run by the state, Beecher recommended adding teaching departments to already existing female academies (Beecher 1835). Correspondence of female teachers describes similar aspirations for their new profession (Preston 1989). These women, however, lacked the power to control the development of the profession. It was the school reformers and the state legislatures with their greater political power who ultimately determined its shape and content. Teachers became the objects of school reform: Having found no effective means of gaining political influence, they were excluded from active participation.

Furthermore, with the development of bureaucratic structures during professionalization, male administrators directly oversaw the implementation of state- or local-mandated educational policy. As managers, they had decision-making power over the formulation of classroom instruction. Frequent supervision of classroom instruction ensured that certain pedagogical techniques were followed. Formal and impromptu oral examinations of students, as in the case cited in Mary Mudge's diary, guaranteed that teachers adhered to certain curricular directives. By 1880, the very content of teaching became determined and enforced by male administrators, not teachers, the vast majority of whom were now women.

Professionalization and the Gender Gap in Wages

Massachusetts teachers' wages rose from 1840 until the end of the century. Yet many studies of feminized occupations find that wages decline (Reskin and Roos 1990). Thus, in teaching, the effects of professionalization must have outweighed those of feminization. When broken down by sex, however, the data show that men benefited more from professionalization than did women. The average monthly wages of Massachusetts teachers from 1840 to 1870, inclusive of board, are presented in Table 21.3. Men's wages rose from $33.08 in 1840 to $74.24 in 1870, whereas women's wages rose from $12.75 in 1840 to only $30.24 in 1870. The gender difference in absolute wages grew from $20.33 to $44. Relative wages, however, remained nearly the same; women continued to make approximately 40 percent of what male teachers earned.

Towns exploited the gender gap in pay to contain the cost of the wage bill. By hiring female teachers, they could raise teachers wages without significantly increasing the school budget. If, for example, a town hired three male teachers and one female teacher in 1840 at the respective average wages, the cost of wages would be $111.99. By hiring one female to replace one male teacher in 1850, at the average wages paid for that year, the town expense for teachers' wages would be only $98.62. In 1860, if the same town replaced one more male teacher with a female teacher, paying the higher average wage, the cost to the town would be $110.50, less than the 1840 figure. Thus feminization contained or even lowered the total cost of wages to the towns, even as professionalization increased the wages of both male and female teachers.

Even with the gender gap in wages, 19th century women sought teaching positions. Although female teachers continued to earn less than male teachers, increasingly they earned more than other categories of female workers. In 1840, textile corporations in Massachusetts paid female operatives approximately the same wages as Massachusetts towns paid female teachers. After 1840, female teachers' wages rose while female textile workers' wages plummeted; by 1960 female teachers earned twice the wages of millgirls (Gitelman 1967). Other women's occupations, such as shoe binder, seamstress, tailoress, and domestic service, paid even less than factory work (Abbott 1910). In comparison to other forms of employment available to women, school teaching, despite the gender gap in pay, represented a remunerative opportunity (Carter 1986).

Although women schoolteachers were relatively well paid, the gendered wage differential still denied women the full advantages of professionalization. Towns that were willing to pay higher wages for professional workers paid more to male teachers. Data from local school reports indicate that the greater gender gap may be related to the establishment of hierarchical structures during professionalization. In bureaucratized school systems, where qualifications for teachers were the most stringent, school committees hired men as supervisors of female teachers. Men not only held different jobs from female teachers but ones that were regarded as clearly superior and that paid higher wages. The wage structure in the Boston school system in 1852, for example, indicates a clear relationship between hierarchical structure and the gender gap in earnings: Men hold all the higher-paying, supervisory positions and women predominate in the lower-paying teaching positions (see Table 21.1). With the increased number of supervisory positions, all filled by men, and the greater preponderance of female teachers in lower-level teaching positions in 1876, the gender gap widened. In 1852, the average male wage was $1,134 and the average female wage, $290. In 1876, the average male wage rose to $2,654 while the average female wage increased to only $840 (see Table 21.3).

Even in those towns that did not report by job title a special supervisory role for men, male teachers may have acted as supervisors to female assistant teachers, a practice discussed earlier and a rationale for differential pay. To further complicate matters, some

---

Table 21.2
Hierarchy and Annual Wages of Boston Teaching Positions by Sex, 1876

Position	Number	Wages
Male (*N* = 124)		
Supervisory		
Superintendent	1	$4,500
Supervisor	6	$4,000
Principal	48[a]	(wages for teaching rank)
High schools		
Master	40	$1,700–$4,000
Submaster		
Usher		
Grammar schools		
Master	87	$1,700–$3,200
Submaster		
Usher		
Female (*N* = 962)		
High schools		
Assistant principal; first, second, and third assistant; normal school assistant	46	$1,000–$2,000
Grammar schools		
First, second, and third assistant	493	$600–$1,200
Primary schools		
Fourth assistant	423	$600–$800

[a]Principals are also enumerated in high school and grammar schoolmaster categories.
Source: City of Boston Abstract of Semi-Annual Returns, January 31, 1876.

---

towns routinely included the wages of their male principals and superintendents in their calculations of the average male teacher wage, thus inflating the wage of regular male teachers (Preston 1982). Much of the gender gap in wages, therefore, may be accounted for by the assignment of supervisory tasks to male teachers, a practice which became widespread during professionalization.

The wage differential was not wholly due to men's supervisory positions in teaching, however. Evidence from antebellum Massachusetts shows that where the professionalization and feminization of teaching had yet to have much impact, male teachers, segregated from female teachers only by the season in which they taught, earned higher wages. In 10 towns that continued under the district system, male teachers, all of whom taught in the winter season, earned on average higher wages than did female teachers—almost all of whom taught in the summer session. Because most towns did not hire female teachers for the winter session and because each male teacher taught alone in a one-room district school, the male teachers could not have been supervisors. Female teachers who taught in the winter session made on average more than females teaching in the summer but less than their male counterparts. The higher wage for female teachers may have been due to their participation in the winter session, which was considered "men's work."

Prevailing attitudes toward women workers may also have contributed to women's lower wages. Many state and local school officials announced in their annual reports their intention of paying female teachers, yet to be hired, lower wages than male teachers. School reformer Henry Bernard, for example, argued that "a female teacher could be hired for twelve weeks for the same price as hiring a male teacher for five weeks" (Rhode Island Board of Education 1846, p. 144). Massachusetts town school reports are replete with remarks on the economic advantages of hiring female teachers. Gardner reported "Females may be procured for sixteen dollars per month . . . males [for] . . . twenty dollars a month" (Massachusetts Board of Education 1845, p. 128). Northbridge stated that "A female might be employed . . . at an expense of nearly one half a male" (Massachusetts Board of Education 1845, p. 150). The savings realized by paying female teachers less than males for the winter session, Ashburnham calculated, "would hire a competent man for six months" (Massachusetts Board of Education 1840–1841, p. 85). Significantly, the wage was determined by the gender of the worker, because no other differences between the two workers were known to the school committeemen. This evidence suggests that women's work was devalued independent of its structural position in the occupation. Moreover, it shows that jobs became female jobs as women were hired for them; that is, a teaching job acquired a woman's wage as women were hired.

The absolute wage gap between male and female teachers increased over the 19th century. As shown in Table 21.3, male teachers earned on average $21.33 a month more than female teachers in 1840 and by 1870, male teachers earned on average $44.00 a month more than female teachers. Many of the male workers in this category were administrators, and by 1870 their numbers had increased, a possible cause for the widening [of] the gender gap in absolute wages. The further development of hierarchical structures in teaching, then, may have been the cause of the change in absolute wages.

Centralized, bureaucratic school systems also created the conditions for collective action. In the Lynn school system, female teachers organized to improve their wages. In 1854, Lynn schoolteacher Mary Mudge recorded the

following in her diary: "about 8 ½ o'clock Miss Row, Miss Nickerson, Cook, and Dodge called to get me to sign a petition to have the Female Teachers' salaries raised. Called with them on Misses Newhall, Neal and Anna. They all signed." Their campaign was unsuccessful. Lynn schools records report no increase in female wages in the next year (Lynn [MA] School Committee 1855). An examination of 92 female teachers' writings revealed no other collective endeavor to improve wages (Preston 1993). As discussed above, most female teachers strove to improve their situation by seeking alternative employment.

Undeterred by female teachers' complaints or brief tenure, school committees continued to appoint male supervisors at superior wages. Thus, the material gains from the professionalization of teaching continued to affect male and female workers differently. Higher-paying supervisory positions for men amplified the existing gender gap in wages caused by sex segregation by season and by discriminatory attitudes. These attitudes were strengthened by the association of gender ideology with the newly constructed jobs within teaching, a development that also influenced the creation of a gendered image of the professional teacher.

Professionalization and the Cultural Representation of the Female Schoolteacher

During the professionalization of school teaching, Horace Mann, Henry Bernard, and other school reformers created a representa-

Table 21.3
Average Monthly Wages (Inclusive of Board) of Massachusetts Teachers, by Sex, 1840–1880

Year	1839–40	1849–50	1859–60	1869–70
Males	$33.08	$34.89	$50.56	$74.24
Females	$12.75	$14.42	$19.98	$30.24
Female wages as percent of male wages	39%	41%	40%	41%

Source: Massachusetts Board of Education, 1839–1870.

tion of the ideal professional teacher to per-suade towns to increase the wages and status of female teachers. Like other aspects of the professionalization process, this cultural representation was gendered; the conception of the professional teacher as female constituted an integral part of the social construction of the profession. The reformers argued that women possessed gender-specific characteristics that enabled them to do the work required of professional teachers: that the characteristics attributed to women in the 19th century, qualities of nurturance and moral rectitude, gave women a special expertise in teaching.

The school reformers, all men, actively created and propagated a new cultural representation of the female teacher that later became firmly implanted in the educational and popular literature of the second half of the 19th century. The ideology of woman's domestic sphere, ideas that emerged with the advent of industrial capitalism, furnished the basis for this new representation. Both reformers and female advocates of women's education—Catherine Beecher, Mary Lyons, and Emma Willard—borrowed selectively from this dominant ideology to argue that the ideal teacher must be a woman. Catherine Beecher strove for 40 years to advance the cause of women by advocating that women's domestic duties necessitated improving female education and hiring women as public school teachers (Sklar 1973). Because women lacked access to political power, especially within the male-dominated state administration, the view of the female teacher promoted by Beecher and other female educators, one that stressed a capacity for intellectual achievement and merited high wages, failed to predominate. Instead, the representation provided by the reformers, which attributed to women a lack of interest in wages and little intellectual ability, became the 19th-century cultural image of the female schoolteacher.

The school reformers had one primary goal: They sought to create a school system that would socialize students to the changing requirements of work in industrial society by instilling habits of obedience and respect for authority (Bowles and Gintis 1976; Katz 1971). Whether school reform created an appropri-

ate workforce for New England factories, or more generally quelled social disorder by producing more obedient citizens, the school reformers' rhetoric leaves no doubt that they perceived a new school system as critical to the smooth transition from an agricultural to an industrial society. In achieving this goal, the reformers concluded that professional female teachers were essential. To promote public acceptance of women as professional teachers and to encourage school committees to hire them, the school reformers created a new conception of the female teacher, which they propagated by using lectures, essays, and reports widely disseminated throughout New England (Preston 1989, 1993).

Four supposedly innate qualities of 19th-century women made them the appropriate teachers for the new school system: high moral character, disregard for material gain, limited intellectual capacity, and a natural love of children. The first quality, high moral character, was congruent with their mission to instill in children appropriate values. Horace Mann, the most eminent of the school reformers, argued in his numerous essays and lectures that female teachers were more qualified to teach because "by nature" they possessed purer morals (Massachusetts Board of Education 1841). Another school reformer, Henry Bernard, proclaimed that women were ideal teachers because, among "their peculiar talents," were "purer morals" (in Rhode Island Board of Education 1845, p.11). Drawing on this supposed natural quality of women, the reformers hoped to reduce the use of corporal punishment in the schools, substituting instead moral control. They advocated that "moral influence should be substituted, as far as possible, in place of mere coercion" and that "it must follow that women are, in most respects, preeminently qualified to administer such a discipline" (Bernard in Rhode Island Board of Education 1852, p. 6). School reformers, then, sought to persuade the 19th-century public that purer morals, as assumed characteristics of women, uniquely qualified them to assume professional positions in the new school systems.

School reformers also ascribed to 19th century women a lack of ambition, especially for financial gain. Mann first proposed this self-serving belief in the 1841 school report: "As a class, they [women] never look forward as young men invariably do, . . . to build up a fortune for themselves; and hence the sphere of hope and of effort is narrower, . . . and the whole forces of the mind are more readily concentrated upon present duties." He cited this as one of the characteristics that make "females incomparably better teachers for young children than males" (Massachusetts Board of Education 1841, p. 45). Although this quality is consistent with moral purity, it contradicts the notion of the monetary value of expert labor. Here one must consider that the development of professional ideology, as a part of the professionalization process, is gendered: Among the emerging 19th-century professions, the desire for financial remuneration consistent with the value of their expert knowledge is acceptable for male professionals in law and medicine, but not for female professionals in teaching and nursing. As part of the professionalization of teaching, school reformers represented female teachers as morally pure, self-sacrificing professional workers. Accordingly, towns could pay female teachers low wages and still regard them as professionals.

Third, school reformers argued that female teachers, like all women, had limited capacity and interest in intellectual endeavors. Since the colonial period, the predominant view was that women had little intellectual capacity. Contrary to popular thinking, the reformers asserted that women did have enough mental ability to teach school, but they did not go so far as to claim that women's intellect was equal to men's. Women, "although deficient in natural brilliance and literary attainments," could acquire enough knowledge to teach children (Rust in New Hampshire Board of Education 1848 p. 8). Their lack of intelligence was compensated for by other qualities. In the "female character there is always a preponderance of affection over intellect," which, reasoned Mann, "made the female . . . the guide and guardian of young children" (Massachusetts Board of Education 1842 p. 9). The limited intellectual abilities ascribed to female schoolteachers were sufficient for

teaching. Their claim to expert knowledge, however, lay not in their intellect but in their unique relationship to children.

Women's "natural" association with children proved the most compelling reason for school committees to consider women the ideal teachers. Transformations in 19th-century gender ideology prescribed a more intense relationship between mother and child. Elaborating on this new conception of motherhood, school reformers extolled the special ability of women to teach children: "Women's stronger parental impulse makes the society of children delightful [for them], and turns duty into pleasure" (Mann in Massachusetts Board of Education 1841 p. 45); "The influence of the mother on the young mind is far greater than even the father" (Cembe in Rhode Island Board of Education 1853, p. 87); "Heaven has plainly appointed females as the natural instructors of young children, and endowed them with those qualities of mind and disposition . . . a greater measure of the gentleness so winning and grateful to the feelings of a child, and of . . . patient forbearance" (Bernard in Connecticut Board of Education 1840, p. 6). This special relationship extended to the ability to control children "by the silken cord of affection, [which has] led many a stubborn will, and wild ungovernable impulse into habits of obedience and study" (Bernard in Connecticut Board of Education 1840, p. 7). Drawing on the dominant gender ideology of the mid-19th century, the school reformers portrayed female teachers as possessing unique talents enabling them to become superior teachers. These talents were not acquired through rigorous professional training; they were bestowed on women "by nature."

My examination of 92 female teachers' correspondence found that these 19th-century women held different self-conceptions (Preston 1993). Their correspondence is replete with discussions of wages. Instead of eschewing the material rewards of teaching as claimed by Mann, Massachusetts women constantly bargained for better wages and, if the school committee was unyielding, sought better-paying teaching positions. Female teachers, rather than limiting their intellectual goals, read poetry, studied foreign languages, attended public lectures, and wrote compositions. Although the women concerned themselves with moral questions, especially as related to religious doctrine, they did not conceive of moral behavior as a means of managing unruly children. Spurning "moral suasion," female teachers maintained discipline by employing various forms of corporal punishment. Although some demonstrated affection and concern for their students, many others, shocked by their first contact with the bedraggled and underfed children who populated 19th-century public schools, expressed disapproval and disdain.

In spite of female teachers' self-conceptions, the four qualities of the ideal 19th-century schoolteacher—moral rectitude, limited intellectual ambition, disregard for material gains, and a natural love of children—constituted the popular cultural representation. All were derived from the prevailing mid-19th-century gender ideology, which postulated separate spheres for men and women. Because this ideology consigned male and female qualities to mutually exclusive categories, only women could fulfill the social ideal of the professional teacher. The evolution of this social ideal of the professional worker was, therefore, necessarily a gendered process.

Once in place, the cultural representation of the ideal worker is difficult to modify and hence acts as a conservative force upon an occupation (Milkman 1987). In the present case, it principally affects the actions and attitudes of the employers and the public, although, as stated before, not the female schoolteachers themselves (Preston 1989). This incorporation of a certain conception of the female teacher in the social construction of the teaching profession offers a compelling explanation for the persistence of sex-typing in teaching. Moreover, it may account for why certain negative characteristics of teaching—low wages, limited intellectual content, restricted upward mobility—are so resistant to change.

Conclusions

Gender influenced historically specific changes in teaching during the process of its professionalization, including sex-segregated structures of supervision and bureaucratic control. These structures allowed male administrators and state legislatures to curtail the autonomy of female teachers and limit their collective control over the teaching profession. By examining changes in wage levels, one finds that whereas professionalization raised the wages of both male and female workers, men benefited more from the increase. The gender gap in teachers' pay was associated with sex-segregated hierarchical structures and job location, and with discriminatory attitudes. Finally, the chapter identifies and discusses four qualities of the ideal professional schoolteacher and shows how the evolution of this ideal, based on 19th-century gender ideology, specified that women would make the best professional teachers.

The evidence presented shows that men came to dominate teaching during professionalization—a finding that confirms the models proposed by both Hearn and Witz. Other findings of this investigation are not accounted for in either model. Witz (1992) ignores the influence of gender ideology. Hearn (1982), although acknowledging the importance of gender ideology, limits its power to persuading women to enter a women's profession—a contention that has been contradicted by empirical studies (Preston 1989, 1993). Moreover, Hearn attributes the content of gender ideology to women's domestic roles, an assertion disputed by Milkman's study of the electrical and automobile industries (1987). Both ignore the gendered effect professionalization has on wages. Witz accords women's actions the power of usurping a portion of a profession from men while, through closure, also denying entry to other workers. Hearn disregards the agency of women in professionalization. In 19th-century Massachusetts, women attempted to shape teaching so it would be a profession equal to men's; their efforts, however, were overpowered by those of male state officials. A complete model of gendered professionalization should therefore consider how gender affects wages, professional ideology, and actions of agents.

Even without a comprehensive model, the empirical findings of this investigation support the proposition that professionalization is a gendered process: that occupations in the process of becoming female professions undergo unique changes that in time may differentiate them from male professions. The transformations occurring in the teaching occupation during professionalization included formation of male-dominated bureaucratic structures restricting autonomy, wage restructuring leading to greater gender differences in absolute wages while increasing wages overall, and the creation of a cultural representation of the female teacher. The evidence suggests that female professions may not be occupations in a state of arrested development, stalled on the road to full professionalization, as the category semiprofessions implies; rather, they may be in many respects qualitatively different from male professions, acquiring these differences during the process of professionalization.

The generality of this interpretation will remain unclear until the results of investigations on the influence of gender on professionalization of other occupations can be assessed. Furthermore, comparative data based on historical studies will enable sociologists to determine if the social construction of all female professions differs from that of male professions. Such findings would have important theoretical implications for the sociology of the professions because they would indicate that current conceptions of a profession and of professionalization should be revised to consider gender as constitutive of the process.

References

Abbott, A. 1988. *The System of Professions.* Chicago: The University of Chicago Press.

Abbott, E. 1910. *Women in Industry: A Study in American Economic History.* New York: Appleton.

Acker, J. 1992. "From sex roles to gendered institutions." *Contemporary Sociology,* 21(5):565–569.

Apple, M. W. 1986. *Teachers and Texts: A Political Economy of Class and Gender Relations in Education.* New York: Routledge and Kegan Paul.

Bancroft, E. 1793–1799. *Diary.* Boston: Massachusetts Historical Society.

Beecher, C. 1835. *Essay on the Education of Female Teachers.* New York: Van Nostrand & Dwight.

———. 1851. *True Remedies for the Wrongs of Women.* Boston: Phillips, Sampson.

Bielby, W. T. and J. N. Baron. 1984. "A woman's place is with other women: Sex segregation within firms." In B. F. Reskin (Ed.), *Sex Segregation in the Workplace: Trends, Explanations, Remedies.* Washington, DC: National Academy Press:27–55.

Bledstein, B. J. 1976. *The Culture of Professionalism.* New York: W. W. Norton.

Bowles, S., and H. Gintis. 1976. *Schooling in Capitalist America: Educational Reform and the Contradictions of Economic Life.* New York: Basic Books.

Brammer, E. S. 1826. *Correspondence, 1818–1838.* Berkeley: Bancroft Library. University of California.

Carr-Saunders, A. M., and P. A. Wilson. 1933. *The Professions.* Oxford: Oxford University Press.

Carter, S. B. 1986. "Occupational segregation, teachers' wages and American economic growth." *Journal of Economic History,* 46(2):373–383.

Connecticut Board of Education. 1837–1860. *Connecticut School Reports.* Hartford: Author.

Crompton, R. 1987. "Gender, status, and professionalism." *Sociology,* 21(3):413–428.

Essex County Teachers' Association. 1830. *Journal, 1830–1888.* Salem, MA: James Duncan Phillips Library, Peabody and Essex Institute.

Forsyth, P. B. and T. J. Danisiewicz. 1985. "Toward a theory of professionalization." *Work and Occupations,* 12(5):59–76.

Freidson, E. 1986. *Professional Powers: A Study of the Institutionalization of Formal Knowledge.* Chicago: University of Chicago Press.

Garrison, D. 1979. *Apostles of Culture: The Public Librarian and American Society, 1876–1920.* New York: Free Press.

Gitelman, H. M. 1967. "The Waltham system and the coming of the Irish." *Labor History,* 8:227–253.

Hall, S. R. 1829. *Lectures on Schoolkeeping.* Unpublished manuscript, Boston.

Hearn, J. 1982. "Notes on patriarchy, professionalization and the semi-professions." *Sociology,* 16(2):184–202.

Jaffe, D. 1989. "Gender inequality in the workplace: Autonomy and authority." *Social Science Quarterly,* 70(2):375–390.

Johnson, T. J. 1972. *Professions and Power.* London: Macmillan.

Kanter, R. 1976. "The impact of hierarchical structures on the work behavior of women and men." *Social Problems,* 23:415–430.

Katz, M. B. 1971. *Class, Bureaucracy and Schools: The Illusion of Educational Change in America.* New York: Praeger.

——. 1987. *Reconstructing American Education.* Cambridge, MA: Harvard University Press.

Larson, M. S. 1977. *The Rise of Professionalism.* Berkeley: University of California Press.

Litchfield, P. 1881–1882. Diary July 1 to March 23, 1775, Massachusetts Historical Society. *Proceedings of the Massachusetts Historical Society,* 19:376–379.

Lutz, A. 1964. *Emma Willard: Pioneer Educator of American Women.* Boston: Beacon.

Lynn [MA] School Committee. 1855. *City of Lynn School Report.* Lynn, MA: Author.

Magnum, U. L. 1928. *The American Normal School: Its Rise and Development in Massachusetts.* Baltimore: Warweek & York.

Marini, M. M. 1989. "Sex differences in earnings in the United States." *Annual Review [of] Sociology,* 15:343-380.

Massachusetts Board of Education. 1839–1880. *Massachusetts School Reports.* Boston: Author.

Massachusetts School Reports. 1833–1834. Manuscripts, 1830–39. Boston: Massachusetts State Library, Special Collections.

Melosh, B. 1982. *The Physicians' Hand.* Philadelphia: Temple University Press.

Messerli, J. 1972. *Horace Mann: A Biography.* New York: Knopf.

Milkman, R. 1987. *Gender at Work: The Dynamics of Job Segregation by Sex During World War II.* Urbana: University of Illinois Press.

Mudge, M. 1854. *Diary.* Cambridge, MA: Schlesinger Library, Radcliffe College.

New Hampshire Board of Education. 1848–1867. *New Hampshire School Reports.* Concord: Author.

Oppenheimer, V. K. 1970. *The Female Labor Force in the United States* (Population Monograph Series No. 5). Berkeley: University of California Press.

Preston, J. A. 1982. *Feminization of an Occupation: Teaching Becomes Women's Work in Nineteenth-Century New England.* Unpublished doctoral dissertation, Brandeis University.

——. 1989. "Female aspiration and male ideology: School teaching in nineteenth-century New England." In A. Angerman (Ed.), *Current Issues in Women's History.* London: Routledge:171–182.

——. 1993. December. "Domestic ideology, school reformers, and female teachers: Teaching becomes women's work in nineteenth-century New England." *New England Quarterly*:531–561.

Reskin, B. and P. Roos. 1990. *Job Queues and Gender Queues: Explaining Women's Inroads Into Male Occupations.* Philadelphia: Temple University Press.

Rhode Island Board of Education. 1845–1860. *Rhode Island School Reports.* Providence: Author.

Simpson, R. L. and I. H. Simpson. 1969. "Women and bureaucracy in the semi-professions." In A. Etzioni (Ed.), *The Semi-Professions and Their Organization: Teachers, Nurses, Social Workers.* New York: Free Press:196–265.

Sklar, K. K. 1973. *Catherine Beecher: A Study in American Domesticity.* New York: W. W. Norton.

Springfield Female Collegiate Institute. 1860–1861. *Catalogue.* Cambridge, MA: Special collections, Gutman Library, Harvard University.

Starr, P. 1982. *The Social Transformation of Medicine.* New York: Basic Books.

Stevenson, M. H. 1988. "Some economic approaches to the persistence of wage differences between men and women." In A. H. Stromberg and S. Harkness (Eds.), *Women Working: Theories and Facts in Perspective.* Mountain View, CA: Mayfield:87–100.

Strober, M. H. and A. G. Landford. 1986. "The feminization of public school teaching: Cross-sectional analysis, 1850–1880." *Signs: Journal of Women in Culture and Society,* 11(2):212–235.

Strober, M. and D. Tyack. 1980. "Why do women teach and men manage? A report on research on schools." *Signs: Journal of Women in Culture and Society,* 5(3):494–503.

Suzzallo, H. 1906. *The Rise of Local School Supervision in Massachusetts.* New York: Columbia University Press.

Tarbox, I. N. (Ed.). 1886–1887. *Diary of Thomas Robbins.* Boston: Connecticut Historical Society.

Treiman, D. and H. Hartmann (Eds.). 1981. *Women, Work, and Wages: Equal Pay for Jobs of Equal Value.* Washington, DC: National Academy of Sciences.

Wilensky, H. L. 1964. "The professionalization of everyone?" *American Journal of Sociology,* 70:137–158.

Witz, A. 1990. "Patriarchy and professions: The gendered politics of occupational closure." *Sociology,* 24(4):675–690.

Witz, A. 1992. *Professions and Patriarchy.* London: Routledge.

Woody, T. 1929. *Women's Education in the United States.* New York: Octagon Press.

Reprinted from: Jo Anne Preston, "Gender and the Formation of a Woman's Profession." In Jerry Jacobs (ed.), *Gender Inequality at Work*, pp. 379–407. Copyright © 1995 by Sage Publications, Inc. Reprinted by permission.

Food for Thought and Application Questions

1. Select a female-dominated semi-profession other than teaching (e.g., librarian, social worker, registered nurse). First, locate recent data on the percent female in the job category you selected. (The *Statistical Abstract of the United States* is a good source.) Then describe the cultural representation of the "ideal" professional in this job category. Does this cultural representation consist of gender-linked traits? Discuss. Do you think the cultural representation you described influences the percent female in the occupation?

2. Preston argues that male-dominated bureaucratic structures developed in the nineteenth century to limit the autonomy and professional status of public school teachers. Do these male-dominated bureaucratic structures still exist? In order to answer this question, you must collect information on women's representation in educational administration. One way to find the information you will need is to collect data from sources such as the U.S. Department of Education on the percentages of women who are principals, superintendents, members of school boards, and so forth. Another option is to gather data on your local school district. This may require that you interview an employee of the district. ✦

22

'Outsider Within' the Firehouse

Subordination and Difference in the Social Interactions of African American Women Firefighters

Janice D. Yoder
Patricia Aniakudo

Early feminist theory described woman as "other" in contrast to a normative man (de Beauvoir 1952). Two critical assumptions are implicit in this conceptualization: first, that women and men are homogeneous groups, and second, that differences between the two mutually exclusive groups are accounted for by gender alone. Subsequent feminist theorists and researchers have challenged both assumptions by arguing for a more complex approach to recognizing and understanding differences among women based on race/ethnicity, class, sexual orientation, and so on (e.g., see Andersen and Hill Collins 1995; Moraga and Anzaldua 1981). Spelman (1988) argued that there is no raceless, classless, generic woman. This was illustrated empirically by Landrine (1985), who documented that stereotypes of a presumably generic woman actually reflect assumptions about the target's race (White) and class (middle).

Given the diversity of women (and men), the study of difference has moved beyond simple comparisons of women and men to a more complex, nuanced view. Focusing on race and gender, a few theorists have regarded these as distinct and additive statuses such that, within American society, while women are subordinated on one count (gen-

der) in contrast to African American women, who are doubly jeopardized (Wan-Ping Pak, Dion, and Dion 1991) or paradoxically advantaged (Fuchs Epstein 1973). This perspective implies that race and gender can be separated and that the gender portion is shared similarly by all women. . . .

In contrast, West and Fenstermaker (1995) describe an ethnomethodological perspective to "doing difference" that conceptualizes gender, race, and class as omnirelevant and as working simultaneously to organize women's lives. Although gender, race, and class take on varying degrees of salience within different social contexts, West and Fenstermaker (1995) argue that each is potentially omnirelevant such that all social exchanges are affected to some degree by the confluence of all three. For example, gender may be especially salient when a lone woman works in a group of men of the same race and class, yet her race and class help shape her gender enactments and the expectations of others. . . . [I]f this lone woman is African American (and even if her colleagues share her race), a possible expectation may be that she is strong and self-reliant (Hurtado 1989). Thus, gender cannot be enacted separately from race and class, even though it may be the obvious differentiating factor in a specific social context.

The purpose of this study is to explore the omnirelevance, inseparability, and confluence of gender and race in the social workplace interactions of African American women firefighters. These interactions will be probed for evidence of subordination, difference, and the intertwining of race and gender, drawing on theory and research from two interrelated strands of work.

The first strand explores subordination by conceptualizing race and gender as status variables (Berger et al. 1977) constructed through social exchanges (West and Fenstermaker 1995) such that African American women are subordinated in an occupation that is dominated and defined by white men. Hill Collins (1986) captures the marginalization of African American women in white male-dominated groups by describing them as "outsiders within" who ultimately offer an alternative vision by sharing their personal and cultural biographies. . . . The stories of outsiders within can tell us both about their own experiences and about aspects of group functioning that pass unnoticed by those immersed in the setting. Thus, the experiences of African American women firefighters in this study will inform us both about their marginalized position and about the intimate day-to-day workings of a nontraditional work setting.

Examining the perspective of the outsider within, Hurtado (1989) theorizes that African American women's subordination will be experienced as exclusion in contrast to white women. . . . Documentation of the exclusion of African American women as a means of subordination was provided by Martin (1994), who examined the social-work relations of African American policewomen. Martin (1994, 390) enumerated the forms their exclusion took: "They faced insufficient instruction, co-worker hostility, and the 'silent treatment'; . . . close and punitive supervision; exposure to danger and lack of backup; and paternalistic overprotection [stereotyping]." Each of these will be explored with our sample of African American women firefighters.

A second strand of relevant theory and research, focused on work group composition and differences among coworkers, provides a basis from which we can explore ongoing group processes—in this study, from the vantage of the outsider within. Early tokenism theory (Moss Kanter 1977) conceptualized marginalization as one consequence of token difference, defined as proportional under-representation (less than 15 percent) in a skewed work group. Token difference originally was defined by Moss Kanter (1977) as using any categorizing factor, but most empirical work used gender as the defining difference between tokens and dominants. Although Moss Kanter (1977) speculated that tokenism processes would occur for any underrepresented group, including white men, recent reviews concluded that tokenism processes are not gender neutral (Yoder 1991; Zimmer 1988). . . . [W]e propose that tokenism theorists and researchers consider the intertwining of differences in work group composition, such as tokens who differ from their coworkers along both racial and gender lines (cf. Dugger

1988; Gooley 1989; King 1988; Marynick Palmer 1983; Reid 1988; Segura 1992; Spelman 1988; Thorton Dill 1983).

What results is a more expansive exploration of tokenism processes. While prior research was confined to exploring differences between token women and dominant men in male-dominated work settings, we propose that theorists and researchers consider multiple intertwining differences (and similarities) between tokens and dominants. This becomes most obvious in the case of African American women in white male-dominated occupations. Analyses can no longer be confined to differences between presumably generic (white?) women and generic (white?) men. Rather, explorations of work group interactions encompass the relations of African American women with white men, African American men, and white women coworkers. In this article, token difference will be examined from the vantage point of African American women themselves across these three relations.

Professional firefighting is an especially fertile area in which to study social interaction. Firefighters rely heavily on team cohesiveness and support, often in life and death situations. Social exchanges are intensified by the demands of shift work—units spend 24 hours or longer together in shared quarters. . . .

Furthermore, professional firefighting has a long history of discriminatory access, assignment, and assessment. Although women have long served as volunteer firefighters, the first woman career firefighter was hired in 1974 (Women in the Fire Service 1991) at a time when the occupation itself was moving toward greater professionalization and integrating men of color (McCarl 1985). In a 1990 survey of 356 career women firefighters, fully 16 percent reported that they gained entry to the fire service as the result of a successful equal employment opportunity complaint (Armstrong et al. 1993). . . . More than 95 percent of all workers in fire protection nationwide are men; 83 percent are white (*American Statistical Index* 1992). It is estimated that there are more than 3,000 women in the fire service nationwide, and 11 percent of these are African American (Armstrong et al. 1993).

Research Participants and Design

Because we know of no comprehensive (or even rudimentary) list of career women firefighters nationwide, we began our search for African American women firefighters at the 1992 meetings of the International Association of Black Professional Firefighters (IABPFF), a loosely organized group of mostly Black male firefighters. With the help of the head of the women's caucus within the IABPFF and a handful of attendees at these meetings, we started with a list of 15 names of African American women firefighters. From these beginnings and by using snow-ball sampling, we generated a list of 48 Black women across all regions of the United States who work in a range of small to large metropolitan firehouses. Of these 48 women, 24 (50 percent) returned an hour-long survey (a respectable return rate for African American women) (Weber Cannon, Higginbotham, and Leung 1988); 22 of the 24 engaged in an hour-long phone interview.

The median age of these African American women firefighters was 32 years (range = 26–42), and their median length of service was more than 5 years (range = 1–16). Regarding their family arrangements, 12 percent were married, 42 percent were divorced or separated, 38 percent were never married, and 52 percent had children. Finally, the majority (74 percent) were gender-defined tokens (less than 15 percent women), and 46 percent were the first woman in their firehouse.[1]

Black women averaged 14.87 weeks of firefighting training. Three were high school graduates, 14 (58 percent) had some college, and 7 (29 percent) held B.A.s or more. One-third of the Black women worked in white-dominated houses of more than 65 percent Whites, half worked with balanced numbers of Whites (36–65 percent), and the remaining 4 (17 percent) worked in Black-dominated houses of less than 35 percent Whites (28–35 percent). Although 71 percent of the Black women were not the first African American in their firehouse, only three worked with another Black woman.[2]

In collaboration with two African American women firefighters, we developed a 20-page mail survey that included demographic information and items exploring differential treatment, sexual harassment, work group race and gender composition, tokenism outcomes, mentoring relations, beliefs about affirmative action, and ratings of chilly climate focused on both race and gender. Participants were paid $35 for completing both the survey and interview. Upon return of the survey, 22 hour-long phone interviews were conducted by the second author, who is African American, has a sister who is a firefighter, and did preliminary field observation of the daily routines of firefighters before interviewing.

The interview schedule consisted of three questions that were given to the Black women interviewees prior to the prearranged phone call. (1) "What influenced you to become a firefighter?" was included as an icebreaker. (2) "Have you ever been treated differently because you are Black or a woman?" was included to parallel its use by prior researchers (Brooks and Perot 1991; Essed 1991; Rosenberg, Perlstadt, and Phillips 1993) to sensitively elicit reports of racial discrimination. (3) "Do you know of any rumors that have circulated about you as a firefighter?" was asked because prior research with firefighters (Gruber 1992; McCarl 1985) identified rumors as a way to embellish or diminish a firefighter's reputation on a team. Respondents voluntarily spent the most time responding to the second question.

Firehouse Interaction

Three global themes emerged from our analysis of African American women firefighters' responses: (1) subordination through exclusion, (2) a more encompassing definition of difference, and (3) the omnirelevance, inseparability, and confluence of race and gender.

Subordination Through Exclusion

Paralleling the findings of Martin (1994) with policewomen, the subordination of African American women firefighters was expressed throughout these women's stories in examples of insufficient instruction, coworker hostility, silence, close supervision, lack of support, and stereotyping and differential treatment.

Insufficient instruction. An undercurrent of colleagues' animus was exposed in several accounts of training by Black women firefighters. Several recounted examples of training exercises that they alone endured. The Black woman with the least amount of formal training in our sample (only six weeks) described how she was duped into chopping down a live tree under the pretext of testing her ability to swing an ax. A Californian reported that she filed a grievance when the shelf, onto which she had been trained to hoist a hose, grew five inches before her formal testing. A third Black woman described how, when she naively asked a senior white male colleague for help with a leaking air pack, she received no constructive instruction, was subsequently written up for presumed negligence, and was referred for additional training. She recalls thinking:

> I can't go ask for help unless it gets written up that something was wrong. You know, so I really don't know how I can trust you guys.

Coworker hostility. The message that underlied the above training experiences was one of hostility. All too often, no attempt was made to cloak coworkers' disdain. A 16-year veteran vividly recalled her first encounter with her white male captain:

> The first day I came on, the first day I was in the field, the guy told me he didn't like me. And then he said: "I'm gonna tell you why I don't like you. Number one, I don't like you cuz you're Black. And number two, cuz you're a woman." And that was all he said. He walked away.

Such blatant confrontations were not isolated incidents but rather appeared across many interviews with Black women:

> I've been told a number of times that I'll never make it [in a firehouse of four Black men and two white men].

> They [nine white men and seven Black men] let me know: "You don't belong here, but since you're here, just stay out of the way. We get a fire, I don't want you touching nothing. I don't want you doing nothing. Just stay out of the way."

[After a few minutes in the bathroom of a firehouse with five white men and seven Black men, a woman reported hearing]: "We don't need no woman over here. I told y'all we don't need no woman in here. We don't have no space for a woman. She's in the restroom 20 minutes!"

> They [six white men] kept telling me that I shouldn't be here, that I was taking up a man's job.

> The majority of the guys, like I said, make it highly known that they do not want women on the job. . . . It's been, you know, stated to me directly to my face that I shouldn't be here. You know, just for the simple fact that I am a woman, and God forbid that I'm a Black female.

Three Black women reported that peers sought transfers to avoid being paired with them. Another described a white male captain who "fought tooth and nail to make sure I was not gonna get on his shift." A fifth Black woman described notes she would find on her bed in a firehouse with three white men and four Black men: "You're not going to sleep because this spot is reserved for someone else." A sixth Black woman claimed that she was denied materials for a promotion exam that she directly requested and had seen being shared among her colleagues. A seventh Black woman in a firehouse of nine white men, one Black man, one other Black woman, and one other man was literally left sleeping at the station "because they want to see me fail, you know."

Silence. The "silent treatment" is another expression of enmity keenly felt by firefighters. A 40-year-old woman in an Eastern metropolitan area, who was the first woman and the first African American in her firehouse, which now included four Black men and three white men, described the persistence of silence:

> No one really talked to me. It was difficult the first, I'd say, six months, because I was basically alone. I'd walk in and everything would get quiet. I'd go to eat; everybody leaves the room. Once they saw I was not going anywhere and I was there

to stay, slowly guys started coming around, you know, talking. As I said, I've been on the job now seven years, and there're still guys that don't talk to me. They speak and that's it. Haven't really accepted the fact that yes, we do have women on the department.

There is some evidence that what started as imposed exclusion became self-sustaining. Many of these women's stories of silence began on their first day of work. Years later, these women seem to have excluded themselves so that one could easily look at these women now and blame them for failing to interact with their colleagues. For one firefighter, the initial message from nine white men and seven Black men was clear: "You don't belong here, but since you're here, just stay out of the way." Ten years later she says, "Now, like I said, I stay to myself as much as I possibly can."

Close supervision. The close and often punitive supervision of Black women firefighters was captured well by a 12-year veteran serving in a firehouse of five white men and two Black men. She describes the alleged practice of "pencil whipping":

> It was a process of what they call being "pencil whipped." Where if they keep writing enough damaging information about you, then it will give them justifiable reason to say. . . . "We've tried and train her. We've tried to do this, and she's just not going to be able to handle this job."

Repeatedly, these women complained that they were closely observed, held to the letter rather than the spirit of rules and regulations, and quickly and needlessly chastised for their failings. A driver (in a small firehouse of three white men and one Black man) was forced by her white male captain to recertify after skidding into a pole during an ice storm, while a male colleague was absolved of blame for accidentally killing an elderly pedestrian crossing a street. Others recounted the following:

> I was always written up for whatever I did. He's [a white male lieutenant] writing up forms when he feels that you're doing badly, but when he feels you're doing well, he's not writing up reports.

A man can make a mistake and it will be covered up or will not be discussed . . . [for me,] they try to make things out of nothing. It's always something out of nothing.

> He [a white male captain] just decided to take it out on me by using the rules and regulations.

Although no firefighter told a story of being physically endangered by colleagues, few felt supported. Most felt that they were given assignments designed to discourage them, that coworkers subtly questioned their competence, and that accommodations were seemingly made for white women but not for Black women. Two Black women interpreted their assignments to blatantly racist areas of large metropolitan cities as a signal to quit. Others viewed assignments to firehouses dominated by white men as attempts to isolate and discourage them:

> It just seems to me too coincidental that I would be sent to a house [of nine white men and four Black men] where problems were, you know, hatred. I mean hatred.

Lack of support. Lack of backup from colleagues appeared in gestures that subtly raised questions about the competence of these Black women firefighters. Although most (75 percent) felt that affirmative action facilitated their hiring, none reported that this undermined their own feelings of competence. In contrast, fully 79 percent of Black women felt that others believed that [affirmative] action influenced their hiring, and the majority (58 percent) believed that this fueled uncertainties in other firefighters about the women's competence. As a firefighter of nine years who was the first African American in her house described,

> They felt that I had been given special preference to get onto the job. And those were the types of rumors that I heard as time went on: that I was hired because I was a Black woman, that I could not perform.

The repeated challenge for many Black women was to "prove myself." They felt pressured to prove their physical prowess, knowledge of firefighting, and commitment to the cohesiveness of the team. No one "proof" ever seemed sufficient, nor was it generally recognized:

> Every time I have to go out someplace I have to prove myself just because I'm a woman . . . no matter, you know, how many times you go out and you do a great job and you do everything right . . . but that one time, that one time that you have a slight little problem or you need just a little bit of help or something might go wrong on your end, that's what they're gonna remember you for, not all the good things that you did, just that one bad thing. You know, and they're going to build on that.

Many Black women noted dissatisfaction with sleeping and bathroom facilities (54 percent) and the sizing of gear (54 percent). Yet, African American women felt that progress in each of these areas came more readily when white women appeared on the scene:

> The first [restroom] facility that was built wasn't done until 1987, and it was done in a firehouse that had only white females.

> When white females started coming on the department in great numbers, all of a sudden sexual harassment classes were given; women's clothes were purchased.

Stereotyping and differential treatment. Almost all women (92 percent) felt that they were treated differently than other firefighters because they were women; none reported that this difference was positive. Not surprisingly, similarly high proportions of Black women (96 percent) noted differential treatment based on race; again, none regarded this difference positively.

The influence of race and gender on the stereotyping of Black women was evident in how stereotyping was expressed. In contrast to prior research with white women who coped with stereotypic paternalistic overprotection (Martin 1994; Yoder, Adams, and Prince 1983) and sexualization (MacCorquodale and Jensen 1993; Tallichet 1995), Black women firefighters dealt with denigrating stereotypes of themselves as welfare recipients and "beasts of burden" (Thornton Dill 1979).

I am a woman, and God forbid, I'm a Black female. . . . [Others in her firehouse of eight white men and one other man said]: "You're taking a spot away from, you know, some white male who has a family. A white male who needs this job" . . . So just because I'm a Black female, I don't need this job? So in other words you're telling me that I should be on welfare and I should fit into that stereotype. . . . I should be at home, you know, having babies, and let some man have this position.

> I would end up with more chores than another female would. And she would happen to be white there. And . . . the [white male] lieutenant would assign me to carry heavier things.

Token Difference

When subordinated difference is defined along interlocking lines, contrasts multiply such that African American women experience strained relationships with at least three distinct groups of differing statuses: white men, Black men, and white women. Each is explored within our data from the perspective of Black women as outsiders within.

Relations with white men. Although Black women tended to work in racially integrated firehouses, the majority of Black women (71 percent) worked with at least 50 percent white men (median = 57 percent, range = 28–86 percent). Examining a composite measure of work group atmosphere developed within the tokenism literature (Yoder [1991]), Black women reported that overall work relations were less favorable as the proportion of white men in their firehouse increased ($r = -.49$, $p < .05$). Specifically, as the percentage of white men increased, Black women reported less encouragement from team members to seek promotion ($r = -.61$, $p < .01$), less favorable expected reactions from team members to their own promotion ($r = -.63$, $p < .01$), less discussion of general topics with teammates ($r = -.46$, $p < .05$), less acceptance as a colleague ($r = -.57$, $p < .01$), less acceptance by coworkers' families ($r = -.42$, $p < .05$), and less leisure time spent with peers ($r = -.47$, $p < .05$). Similarly, Black women felt that their own competent work was more likely to be ignored in the presence of greater numbers of white men ($r = .59$, $p < .01$). Although there was no relationship between the proportion of white men in the firehouse and both chilly climate toward women ($r = .33$, n.s.) and incidents of sexual harassment ($r = .04$, n.s.), Black women did note a negative association between more white men and heightened chilly climate toward Blacks ($r = .61$, $p < .01$).[3] In sum, then, these correlations paint a picture of increasingly strained relations between Black women and white men as the representation of the latter increases.

Relations with Black men. African American women firefighters' relationships with Black men typically were mixed. Most of our Black women interviewees reported having at least some supportive relationships with their Black male colleagues. Of the 19 (79 percent) noting in the survey that they had a mentor, 15 were mentored by Black men,[4] and all described these mentors as very helpful to them both personally ($M = 6.42$, SD $= 1.22$) and professionally ($M = 6.74$, SD $= .56$) on 7-point Likert scales. Black women noted that Black men broke the racial ground for them. As one woman in a Southern department with a solid Black representation of four Black men (and two white women) noted,

I think that the Black men that were there, they had to struggle because they made it possible for us to come on.

Black women firefighters described two scenarios involving their interactions and Black men's interactions with white men. In the first, Black men served as intermediaries between Black women and white men. Black women reported that some Black men seemingly traded on their commonality with both Black women and white men and thus mediated between them. For example, a sole Black woman (on a team with four Black men and nine white men) recounted that a Black male colleague warned his white coworker:

"You know what? You guys are gonna keep pushing her, and one day, you're gonna find yourself out of a job because she's gonna file harassment charges." And he said, "You see that book she's keeping? Don't think your name is not in there."

In the second scenario, Black women perceived that male bonding was achieved at the expense of Black women. Black women felt that their inclusion may have helped to reduce the gap between Black and white men who became united, to some degree, by virtue of their shared gender and opposition to women firefighters. The same woman who spoke of a Black male defender immediately above and who was in a large Midwestern department summed this up:

Before women came on this job ... the big picture was white and Black, and you have some Hispanic. And, that was it. ... That's the big picture. Before we came on the job, the Blacks were having a lot of trouble. Now the women are on the job, the white guys say, "Come on, guys. We're all one now. Look at those women. They aren't, you know, they can't do this. Look at that." And you got some of the Black guys believing this. You got some of them believing that women don't belong on the job. Of course, you will find some who don't, but then you will find a lot of men who do.

Overall, from the perspective of African American women, relations of Black women with Black men reflected their relative positions within a race-gender power hierarchy:

Black men [seven Black men with five white men] on the fire department . . . have been the underdogs . . . for so long. Now there's a group of people under them who they consider the underdogs . . . the Black woman. . . . And you know how it is; I explained it to the children: how the big brother gets picked on, how he picks on the little brother, and the little brother to the baby . . . it's that kind of effect.

Relations with white women. Given that firefighting is a highly skewed, male-dominated occupation, it is rare for women to work together in the same firehouse, and only 1 of the 24 women in our sample worked directly with a white woman firefighter. However, African American women firefighters did encounter white women in positions related to firefighting (e.g., dispatchers and paramedics), in training programs, and across companies. Reports about these relationships describe divisions among women, separated by race, that have been documented elsewhere (Giddings 1984; hooks 1984; Martin 1994; Poster 1995).

The impact of others' racism on the formation of relationships between Black and white women was illustrated in the following anecdote from a lone woman firefighter of three years:

> I can tell you about the first day I walked into my firehouse. Here I am a Black woman, the first woman in the firehouse. . . . Just being there, being the first woman, I was treated a lot differently than anybody else. We have a white woman who's on the ambulance, and she's been there, and they never spoke to her before. She would bring things into the firehouse, like pies or cookies or things she'd make at home. They would never eat them. They wouldn't even talk to her. As soon as they knew I was coming, and I walked in the door, all of a sudden they're talking to her and they really don't have a lot of conversation with me. And I worked with them on the same apparatus, and she's on something totally different. I mean, I felt that was a blow right here. I really did. And I never really found out, I didn't know if it was just me thinking that or what, but the guys, some of the Black guys on the job, told me . . . "That's the way it is."

Although the Black woman who told this story recognized that her problems with this white woman began with the sexism of her male colleagues, it was race that drove a wedge between these women and that co-opted the white woman in the eyes of our Black respondent.

A second reason women can be divided along racial lines is because white women are perceived by African American women to be co-opted by white men who share their race. Two stories from our interviews with Black women illustrate this point clearly. First, a 29-year-old firefighter described her 14 weeks of training:

> In the academy, I had a friend. Her name was [Jane]. And, we used to be really tight. White girl. We were really tight. Because I don't have anything against being white or anything else. And we were good friends until all of a sudden a white guy

tells her to be snooping around, because there was four Black women in our class, and one white woman. And we all participated; we all went out to drink together, to eat together, whatever. We baked for each other. But in the academy, they told her to find out if we had any information on a test. For her to be snooping through our stuff. And one of the girls caught her doing that. So then all of a sudden, she was accepted by a white peer group, and she no longer needed us. And everything changed. But before that, we were like really good friends. It was so weird.

Second, a 10-year veteran talked about promotion exams:

> On the first test we took, only Black women were taken because we were the ones who had the most seniority. The second test, there was a couple of white women that did take the test. . . . We kept hearing things about this one particular girl. They were calling her, believe it or not, they were calling her their "great white hope." They grilled her . . . now of course this is just rumor, but she got a lot of study material that wasn't available to everyone else.

Both anecdotes illustrate how Black women believe that white women's race can serve simultaneously to unify them with white men, however tenuously, and to separate them from Black women.

The Intertwining of Race and Gender

The omnirelevance and inseparability of racism and sexism in constructing the forms of Black women firefighters' exclusion and token difference appear throughout the descriptions of social interactions presented here. Although a few quotations from African American women realistically could be attributed to white women, most cannot. Race is either clearly noted as a contributor to the point being made by the interviewee, or it hovers in the background as a subtle but omnirelevant influence (West and Fenstermaker 1995).

The inseparability and confluence of race and gender for Black women became blatantly clear in our interviews when we asked women to indicate whether the incidents of differential treatment they had just described were attributable to their race or gender. Almost universally, these women rejected our assignment, claiming instead that such a distinction was artificial:

> It's hard to say whether it was just specifically because I was Black. With it being a double edge: being Black and being female [in a firehouse with all (six) white men].

> But I don't know if I had been white, would the situation [have] been any different? I don't know. Only because I got the same treatment from both sides. I wasn't just one of the group [of four Black men and two white men].

> Being a Black female . . . it was like two things that needed to be proven [to two Black men and five white men].

> We just seem to be the lowest on the totem pole when it comes to any type of support on this job [from four Black men and nine white men].

The same sentiments, expressed almost verbatim, appeared in Martin's (1994, 393) interviews with Black women police officers:

> Sometimes I couldn't tell if what I faced was racial or sexual or both. The Black female is the last one on the totem pole in the department, so if things are okay you thank God for that.

Our sense is that more was happening here than the confounding of race and gender as underlying causes of the events reported. The question itself seemed foreign to our respondents, as if we were trying to impose a distinction they simply did not share. Only one woman describing the incident in which she was required to recertify as a driver after a minor accident attributed her experience exclusively to her gender. All other responses described events in terms of being Black and being a woman. The assignment to distinguish between the two was ignored.

Conclusion and Implications

Research with African American women firefighters highlights patterns of social interaction that involve subordination, token difference, and the intertwining of race and gen-

der. A series of processes—including insufficient, unnecessary, and hypercritical training; open and subtle coworker hostility; silence; exacting supervision; lack of support; and demeaning stereotyping with negative treatment—combine to send a clear message of exclusion to Black women firefighters.

Noting these women's vantage as outsiders within (Hill Collins 1986), their stories suggest that the persistence of exclusion makes their withdrawal from their coworkers ultimately self-sustaining. Only from the perspective of African American women themselves can we see that what now appears to be the rejection of the group by the Black women is instead a coping strategy to deal with repeated past experiences of subordination through exclusion. . . . As Baca Zinn et al. (1986) sagely note, misinterpretations, such as the alleged positive status afforded Black women professionals as affirmative action double-counts (Fuchs Epstein 1973), "double jeopardy," and firefighters' self-exclusion, are formulated and promulgated only by those uninformed and unresponsive to the perspective of outsiders within. One valuable use of the present data is to provide this outsiders' perspective.

Unlike many studies of token difference, we defined difference along both racial and gender lines by considering Black women's relations with white men, Black men, and white women. Although African American women's relations with white men predictably are strained, and although this strain is reduced somewhat with the inclusion of coworkers other than white men, the presence of Black men is in no way a panacea for African American women. Black men may provide mentoring to Black women, but they also may contribute to their exclusion, at least from the perspective of Black women. Furthermore, although most of the direct agents of discriminatory treatment identified by Black women were white men, the mere presence of Black men, even as a proportional majority, did not seem to discourage hostile behavior from white men, especially when the white male transgressors were in positions of higher rank. Similarly, African American women report that contact with white women does not automatically lead to gendered solidarity. These data, along with other studies (e.g., South et al. 1982), argue that more than number balancing must be done to reduce the negative impact of token proportions. . . .

The stories of these African American women challenge the extensive literatures on subordination and token difference that have relied on comparisons of presumably generic women with presumably generic men. Subordination does not take the form of protection, co-optation, and sexualization, as has been documented with white women vis-à-vis white men. Nor are token processes limited to relations between white women and white men (or even between African American women and white men). These findings not only call into question the generalizability of prior findings that have been blind to race or that have presumably controlled for race by holding it constant but also raise questions about the ways in which being white reflects racial influences in and of itself (Frankenberg 1993; Roman 1993).

Such analyses pave the way for future research to openly and systematically explore the impact of the privileges afforded by whiteness in a Eurocentric society (McIntosh 1992). Studies of subordination and token difference must be revisited with these considerations in mind. For example, African American women believe that white women and Black men can parlay their race and gender, respectively, to gain some acceptance, however tenuous, with dominant white men. Empirical data are needed to confirm if these perceptions accurately reflect the privileges afforded whiteness and maleness in American society and to detail how each affects our understanding of gendered relations.

Considering the present findings as they relate to strategies for social change, these African American women's stories support the idea that there are no "automatic concepts of connection" (Jordon 1985, 46) linking Black women with Black men and Black women with white women. It is paradoxical that solidarity must be forged with an unwavering recognition of difference (Lorber 1994; Lorde 1992). Furthermore, our analyses suggest that social change aimed at countering discrimination based on subordinated gender or subordinated race alone will continue to exclude Black women or, worse yet, use them as pawns in a competition for redress (Martin 1994). In addition, it will continue to perpetuate the false sense that only people of color experience race and only women of all colors experience gender, when in fact we all experience gender and race (as well as class, physical ability, sexual orientation, etc.) throughout our working and personal lives (Spelman 1988; West and Fenstermaker 1995). When Black women hastily are grouped with white women as women or with Black men as Blacks, and when Black women are not heeded as outsiders within, we believe that the subordination and token difference illustrated here will remain unchallenged.

Notes

1. These patterns for African American women parallel those for both a sample of 356 women responding to a survey sent to 1,300 women firefighters from Women in the Fire Service (WFS) (Armstrong et al. 1993), 91 percent of whom were white. . . .

2. Our sample of African American women differed from our white sample along these three dimensions. White women averaged less training. . . . All white women had at least some college, and 51 percent held at least a B.A. . . . White women tended to work in settings with more whites: 54 percent worked only with whites; all but one worked with at least 65 percent whites . . . and 41 percent worked with at least one other white woman.

Although the above identifies some likely differences between Black and white women involving training, education, and racial composition of their firehouses, all firefighters used in these comparisons have voluntarily joined organizations emphasizing gender (e.g., WFS) or race (e.g., IABPFF). This differentiates them from the majority of women firefighters. Our sense is that many Black women feel that they are not well represented by either organization. . . . In addition, not one African American woman responded to our call for volunteers sent to the 1,050 members (about 750 of whom are women in the fire service) of WFS through their monthly newsletter. Thus, we speculate that the African American women in our sample, generated mainly through IABPFF contacts and all but one of whom are members of the IABPFF, have strong racial identities that motivate them to join a racially focused organization. Thus, race may be an especially salient component in their experiences.

3. Twenty-four items on the Working Environment Scale (Stokes, Riger, and Sullivan [1993]) focused on both gender and racial climate. The composite or racial items summed agreement on five items: increasing number of minorities will lead to reverse discrimination, people treat minorities equally (reverse coded), racially demeaning joking would be criticized (reverse coded), racial discrimination is a big problem here, and those who complain about racial discrimination are not supported. Seven behavioral indicators of sexual harassment, defined by the U.S. Merit Systems Protection Board (1987), were used to measure incidence.

4. Two were mentored by white men and the remaining two by other Black women.

References

American Statistical Index. 1992. Bethesda, MD: Congressional Information Services.

Andersen, Margaret L. and Patricia Hill Collins. 1995. "Preface." In *Race, Class and Gender: An Anthology,* edited by Margaret L. Andersen and Patricia Hill Collins. Belmont, CA: Wadsworth.

Armstrong, Dee S., Brenda Berkman, Terese M. Floren, and Linda F. Willing. 1993. *The Changing Face of the Fire Service: A Handbook on Women in Firefighting.* Washington. D.C.: U.S. Fire Administration.

Berger, Joseph, M. Hamit Fisek, Roben Z. Norman, and Morris Zelditch, Jr. 1977. *Status Characteristics in Social Interaction: An Expectation Status Approach.* New York: Elsevier.

Brooks, Linda, and Annette R. Perot. 1991. "Reporting sexual harassment: Exploring a predictive model." *Psychology of Women Quarterly* 15, 31–47.

Cannon, Lynn Weber, Elizabeth Higginbotham, and Marianne L. A. Leung. 1988. "Race and class: Bias in qualitative research on women." *Gender & Society* 2:449–62.

Collins, Patricia Hill. 1986. "Learning from the outsider within: The sociological significance of Black feminist thought." *Social Problems* 33,514–532.

de Beauvoir, Simone. 1952. *The Second Sex.* Translated by H. M. Parshley. New York: Knopf.

Dill, Bonnie Thornton. 1979. "The dialectics of Black womanhood." *Signs: Journal of Women in Culture and Society* 4:543–55.

——. 1983. "Race, class and gender: Prospects for an all-inclusive sisterhood." *Feminist Studies* 9:131–50.

Dugger, Karen. 1988. "Social location and gender-role attitudes: A comparison of Black and white women." *Gender & Society* 2, 425–48.

Epstein, Cynthia Fuchs. 1973. "Positive effects of the double negative: Explaining the success of Black professional women." In *Changing Women in a Changing Society,* edited by Joan Huber. Chicago: University of Chicago Press.

Essed, Philomena. 1991. *Understanding Everyday Racism: An Interdisciplinary Theory.* Newbury Park, CA: Sage.

Frankenberg, Ruth. 1993. *White Women, Race Matters: The Social Construction of Whiteness.* Minneapolis: University or Minnesota Press.

Giddings, Paula. 1984. *When and Where I Enter: The Impact of Black Women on Race and Sex in America.* New York: Morrow.

Gooley, Ruby Lee. 1989. "The role of Black women in social change." *Western Journal of Black Studies* 13:165–72.

Gruber, James E. 1992. "A typology of personal and environmental sexual harassment: Research and policy implications for the 1990s." *Sex Roles* 26:447–64.

hooks, bell. 1984. *Feminist Theory: From Margin to Center.* Boston: South End.

Hurtado, Aida. 1989. "Relating to privilege: Seduction and rejection in the subordination of white women and women of color." *Signs: Journal of Women in Culture and Society* 14:833–55.

Jordon, June. 1985. "Report from the Bahamas." In *On Call: Political Essays.* Boston: South End.

Kanter, Rosabeth Moss. 1977. *Men and Women of the Corporation.* New York: Basic Books.

King, Deborah K. 1988. "Multiple jeopardy, multiple consciousness: The context of a Black feminist ideology." *Signs: Journal of Women in Culture and Society* 14:42–72.

Landrine, Hope. 1985. Race × class stereotypes of women. *Sex Roles* 13:65–76.

Lorber, Judith. 1994. *Paradoxes of Gender.* New Haven, CT: Yale University Press.

Lorde, Audre. 1992. "Age, race, class, and sex: Women redefining difference." In *Race, Class, and Gender: An Anthology,* edited by Margaret L. Andersen and Patricia Hill Collins. Belmont, CA: Wadsworth.

MacCorquodale, Patricia, and Gary Jensen. 1993. "Women in the law: Partners or tokens?" *Gender & Society* 7:582–93.

Martin, Susan E. 1994. "'Outsider within' the station house: The impact of race and gender on Black women police." *Social Problems* 41:383–400.

McCarl, Robert. 1985. *The District of Columbia Fire Fighters Project: A Case Study of Occupational Folklife*. Washington, D.C.: Smithsonian Institution Press.

McIntosh, Peggy. 1992. "White privilege and male privilege: A personal account of coming to see correspondences through work in women's studies." In *Race, Class, and Gender: An Anthology*, edited by Margaret L. Andersen and Patricia Hill Collins. Belmont, CA: Wadsworth.

Moraga, Cherrie, and Gloria Anzaldua, eds. 1981. *This Bridge Called My Back: Writings by Radical Women of Color*. Watertown, MA: Persephone.

Nkomo, Stella M. 1992. "The emperor has no clothes: Rewriting race in organizations." *Academy of Management Review* 17:487–513.

Pak, Anita Wan-Ping, Kenneth L. Dion, and Karen K. Dion. 1991. "Social psychological correlates of experienced discrimination: Test of the double jeopardy hypothesis." *International Journal of Intercultural Relations* 15:243–54.

Palmer, Phyllis Marynick. 1983. "While women, Black women: The dualism of female identity and experience in the United States." *Feminist Studies* 9:151–70.

Poster, Winifred R. 1995. "The challenges and promises of class and racial diversity in the women's movement: A study of two women's organizations." *Gender & Society* 9, 659–79.

Reid, Pamela T. 1988. "Racism and sexism: Comparison and contrast." In *Eliminating racism: Profiles in Controversy*, edited by Phyllis A. Katz and Dalmus A. Taylor. New York: Plenum.

Roman, Leslie G. 1993. "White is a color! White defensiveness, postmodernism, and anti-racist pedagogy." In *Race Identity and Representation in Education*, edited by Cameron McCarlhy and Warren Crichlow. New York: Routledge & Kegan Paul.

Rosenberg, Janet, Harry Perlstadt, and William R. Phillips. 1993. "Now that we are here: Discrimination, disparagement, and harassment at work and the experience of women lawyers." *Gender & Society* 7:415–33.

Segura, Denise A. 1992. "Chicanas in white-collar jobs: You have to prove yourself more." *Sociological Perspectives* 35:163–82.

South, Scott J., Charles W. Bonjean, William T. Markham, and Judy Corder. 1982. "Social structure and intergroup interaction: Men and women of the federal bureaucracy." *American Sociological Review* 47:587–99.

Spelman, Elizabeth V. 1988. *Inessential Woman: Problems of Exclusion in Feminist Thought*. Boston: Beacon.

Stokes, Joseph, Stephanie Riger, and Megan Sullivan. 1993. "Measuring perceptions of the working environment for women in corporate settings." *Psychology of Women Quarterly* 19:533–50.

Tallichet, Suzanne E. 1995. "Gendered relations in the mines and the division of labor underground." *Gender & Society* 9:697–711.

U.S. Merit Systems Protection Board. 1987. *Sexual Harassment of Federal Workers: An Update*. Washington, D.C.: Government Printing Office.

West, Candace, and Sarah Fenstermaker. 1995. "Doing difference." *Gender & Society* 9:8–37.

Women in the Fire Service. 1991. Brochure. [Available from WFS, P.O. Box 5446, Madison, WI 53705]

Yoder, Janice D. 1991. "Rethinking tokenism: Looking beyond numbers." *Gender & Society* 5:178–92.

Yoder, Janice D., Jerome Adams, and Howard T. Prince. 1983. "The price of a token." *Journal of Political and Military Sociology* 11:325–37.

Zimmer, Lynn. 1988. "Tokenism and women in the workplace: The limits of gender-neutral theory." *Social Problems* 35:64–77.

Zinn, Maxine Baca, Lynn Weber Cannon, Elizabeth Higginbotham, and Bonnie Thorton Dill. 1986. "The costs of exclusionary practices in women's studies." *Signs: Journal of Women in Culture and Society* 11:290–303.

Food for Thought and Application Questions

1. This article suggests that race and gender *cannot* be separated as they relate to the experiences of the women studied. Yet most research attempts to separate these effects. Discuss the implications of our *not* separating them when we approach research issues? Does this mean that gender is not a master status independent of race? . . . that race is not a

master status independent of gender? Discuss the advantages and disadvantages of taking such a position in approaching research.

2. Yoder and Aniakudo found that African American female firefighters had experiences similar to those of the African American female police officers studied by Martin. What occupational circumstances might account for their similarity? With what other occupations might you find these results replicated? Why do you think this? How might you find out? ✦

23

Police Force or Police Service?

Gender and Emotional Labor

Susan Ehrlich Martin

Police work involves extensive emotional labor since it requires the officer "to induce or suppress feelings in order to sustain the outward countenance that produces the proper state of mind in others" (Hochschild 1983, 7). To be effective, officers must control both their own feelings and the emotional displays of citizens. The importance, skills, and scope demanded of police in performing emotional labor often are overlooked or downplayed by both the police and the public for two closely linked reasons. First, policing has been defined in terms of fighting crime or catching criminals, although it involves a far wider variety of tasks. Second, the occupation has long been dominated by men and closely associated with the stereotypical inexpressive masculinity of Sergeant Friday, although women have served as sworn officers since 1910 and been on street patrol since 1972. Despite the professional (that is, unemotional) image that the police have cultivated, the activities and incidents that police encounter often arouse deep emotions in themselves and the citizens with whom they come into contact. A cop's failure to manage these emotions may have high costs, as illustrated by the disturbance ensuing from officers' lack of self-restraint in their interaction with Rodney King in Los Angeles, California.

This article explores the feeling and display rules that regulate emotional expression in police work, the ways these are made masculine, and how this affects occupational and organizational norms. Norms regarding emotional labor vary across police interactions with both coworkers and the public and are affected by the gender of the officer and of the person the officer encounters. Although policing is a traditionally male job, it requires frequent performance of emotional labor affecting both the hard and soft emotions (Price 1996). Since these, in turn, are associated, respectively, with masculinity and femininity, this article explores how gender contributes to the apparent division of emotional labor in policing.

Emotional Labor: Definitions and Theoretical Issues

Emotions are feelings that people experience, interpret, reflect on, express, and manage (Thoits 1989; Mills and Kleinman 1988). They arise through social interaction; are influenced by social, cultural, interpersonal, and situational conditions; and are managed by workers along with physical and mental labor on the job.

Workers do emotional labor (that is, manage feelings to create a publicly observable display) on the job. Hochschild (1983) emphasized how employees are required to manage their own feelings in order to create displays that affect others in desired ways.... For example, Fineman (1993) observed:

> Many professional workers . . . are . . . paid for their skill in emotion management. They are to look serious, understanding, controlled, cool, empathetic and so forth with clients or patients. . . . Benign detachment disguises, and defends against, any private feelings of pain, despair, fear, attraction, revulsion or love; feelings which would otherwise interfere with the professional relationship. (19)

As this statement suggests, there are organizational norms governing both the appropriate expression and the suppression or management of emotions. The work of supervisors and professionals includes serving as emotional managers and enforcing the feeling rules associated with subordinates' roles. Feeling rules are norms regarding what emotions should be experienced by workers. In contrast, display rules are norms guiding which emotions ought to be publicly expressed and how; thus these norms are observable.

Both feeling rules and display rules are essential parts of the broader occupational and organizational work cultures in which they are embedded (Van Maanen and Kunda 1989). . . . Occupations and organizations create myths, stage-manage events like award ceremonies and retirement parties, and use occasions such as police funerals to ritually handle emotion, support a collective identity, and reinforce organizational values and bonds.

Organizations also exercise cultural control through recruitment, selection, socialization, and supervisory practices. Potential employees are screened not only on skills but for temperamental fit with the emotional demands of the job. Through socialization, individuals learn the rules regarding the content, intensity, and variety of emotions demanded in performing their work role; once these are internalized, the work and desire for success provide incentive for conforming with display rules. When display rules are not congruent with workers' inner feelings, organizations manage those emotionally dissonant feelings through monitoring, rewards (for example, raises and promotions), inculcating psychological defense mechanisms, and occasional punishments (such as transfers and terminations) (Sutton 1991). . . .

Ritualized expression of emotion also may be part of the informal culture of occupations or work groups. Opportunities for venting may occur in backstage areas of the work site such as the locker room or nursing station, or in offstage areas such as a local bar or parking lot where workers socialize together after work.

In sum, jobs that involve emotional labor require contact with other workers or customers; the use of skills and the performance of tasks and activities that are associated with the expression of an emotion by the employee or its suppression through self-management; and production of an emotional state in another person. Emotional displays are shaped by employers through their control of selection, training, supervision, and rituals; by occupational cultures and informal work groups through their norms regulating emotional expression; and by the im-

mediate situation, setting, and feedback as an interaction unfolds.

Jobs also vary in the amount of emotional labor and the type of emotion they require or permit employees to express. These variations are related to the gender of the worker and the gendered stereotype of the job. In brief, service workers, who are primarily women, are expected to display soft emotions such as nurturance; professionals and others in jobs dominated by men are expected to display no emotion or to manage emotional displays that revolve around anger and implied threats in order to induce fear and compliance in others (Hochschild 1983; Pierce 1995; Sutton 1991; Wharton 1996). At the same time, because gender assumptions transfer from the workers to their jobs, workers simultaneously construct, or do, gender through their work, and the culturally shaped gender designations of work activities are reinterpreted in ways that support the jobholders' gender identities (Leidner 1991).

Emotional Labor, Gender, and Police Work

There is a wide gap between the work that the police actually do and the public image of policing, which is associated with crime fighting and stereotyped as masculine. Police not only enforce the law and arrest offenders; they also are responsible for preventing crime, protecting life and property, maintaining peace and public order, and providing a wide range of services to citizens 24 hours a day. Across these tasks, an essential part of policing is taking charge of situations. . . .

While most calls to the police do not clearly refer to a crime or result in invocation of officers' legal powers, most incident[s] do deal with an element of latent conflict and the potential ingredients of a criminal offense (Reiner 1992). This enables an officer to interpret an event either as a conflict requiring an aggressive response or as an interpersonal dispute requiring informal conflict resolution. Since the character of the incident often is in the eye of the beholder, policing becomes a site for competing ways of doing gender.

Aggressive crime fighting is viewed by both police and the public as real police work and is visible, valued, and rewarded. The association of catching criminals with danger and bravery is what marks police work as "men's work."

In reality, however, much of police work is dirty, insignificant, boring, or unpleasant. Most calls involve a request for service or order-maintenance tasks (Brown 1981) and involve officers interacting with people at their worst—when they have been victimized, are injured or helpless, or are guilty and seeking escape. This means officers must restore order in volatile situations and use interpersonal skills to gain citizen compliance.

The unique combination of occupational activities and unpredictable threats to their safety also has led to a set of attitudes and behaviors characteristic of police termed the "working personality" (Skolnick 1966). Cops tend to be suspicious of and isolated from the public, which fears them and which they view as hostile. . . . The informal norms of this work culture include the expectations that an officer will remain silent about others' illicit behavior, will provide physical backup to other officers, and will punish displays of disrespect for the police (Westley 1970). In addition, they include a norm of emotional self-management. . . .

The solidarity of the homogeneous group of white working-class men who previously composed police forces has eroded over the past 25 years due to both the recruitment of many female and ethnic-minority male officers and an organizational shift in focus from detached crime fighting to community policing. These changes have, among other things, feminized policing and have met resistance from many male rank-and-file officers who still believe women are unfit to handle the work either physically or emotionally (Martin 1980) and whose informal culture continues to demand that women officers adopt, "'male characteristics' to achieve even a limited social acceptability" (Young 1991, 193). . . .

The norms of the department and of the informal culture demand that police officers severely limit expression of emotions. Even talking about pain, guilt, or fear is rare since officers who reveal their feelings to other officers may be viewed as weak or inadequate. Nevertheless, there are variations in the amount of emotional labor and emotion management performed by officers that are related to the immediate situation, its interactional demands, and the role of the citizen as victim, suspect, or third part in that interaction. . . . In interactions with both citizens and fellow police, the gender of the officer and the gender of the other participants affect interactional norms, including those related to emotion work, and which emotion is evoked.

Doing Gender and Emotional Labor in Police Work

Officers do emotional labor in their encounters with citizens that are affected by the gender of the participants. They also do emotional labor in their backstage interactions with other officers. This section looks at the ways gender affects officers' performance of emotional labor.

Gendered and Police-Citizen Encounters

. . . Since a key element of policing—gaining and maintaining control of situations—remains associated with manhood, male officers do gender along with doing dominance. For women officers, however, this means finding ways to take control while dealing with uncertainties arising from citizens' assumptions (for example, that women are nicer or more emotional), the unfolding situation itself, occasional challenges to their authority, and their own emotional reactions to citizens' behavior (Martin and Jurik 1996). . . . In addition to gendered scripts in police work related to the definition of the encounter and the citizen . . . the gender of the officer and the citizen affects their expectations and behaviors and poses specific management problems (Martin and Jurik 1996). Each of these four combinations of gender and social category will be examined.

Male officer, male citizen. As officers, male police have status superiority over male citizens, who are obligated to defer and comply. As men, however, both may draw on masculinity as an interactional resource, thereby implying a reduction in social distance. . . . If a man displays inappropriate emotions, tactics for getting him to express appropriate emotions include rationalizing the other's emotion, offering alternative solutions, ignoring him, or not acknowledging his emotional expression (Price 1996). For example, to get a man to stop cursing the officer may assert, "Pull yourself together," saying, in effect, "Act like a man (that is, exercise self-control) and I won't have to exert my authority as an officer to overpower you." . . . Similarly, with male victims, the invocation of shared masculine norms of emotional self-control permits the officer to limit the emotion labor (that is, expressions of compassion, sympathy, or support) demanded of him in the interaction. Thus, drawing on shared manhood is an effective control technique used [in] some situations by male officers. . . .

For detectives (who are usually men), the most rewarding part of their work is handling criminals (who are mostly men). . . . Criminals do not make detectives' jobs easy; they curse, refuse to talk, and sometimes cry. Detectives deal with criminals' emotional outbursts by discounting their expressive displays as feigned "strategic interaction" (Goffman 1969). They may finagle information out of a criminal by getting him or her to boast about a crime, hinting at leniency, or employing "strategic friendliness" (Pierce 1995). By interpreting the emotional labor they do with criminals as "higher status mental work," detectives are able to enjoy it as a challenging intellectual game (Stenross and Kleinman 1989).

Male officer, female citizen. Male officers' double-status superiority over female citizens enables the men to gain control by choosing to use the authority of their office or the authority of their gender. They can do gender by, for example, seeking compliance from "shrill" (that is, verbally abusive) female citizens by asserting, "Act like a lady (that is, behave in a calm, dignified manner) and I will treat you like one." . . . If this gender-based strategy works, the officer maintains control while enhancing his sense of manly generosity. . . .

Interactions with female victims that require displays of support, compassion, or empathy, however, create emotional demands that many men seek to avoid. Men's discomfort arises both because of the emotional hardness they have developed in response to their continual work exposure to the worst in humanity and because of the norms of emotional reserve included in their definition of masculinity. Victims of rape and domestic violence, for example, often have criticized police for their demeanor when they seek "just the facts, ma'am," or show outright insensitivity to victims' complaints. . . .

Many police recognize that the victims' pain is genuine, but they feel powerless in dealing with emotional outbursts (Stenross and Kleinman 1989) and regard providing emotional support as low-status women's work (Hunt 1984); others fail to feel sympathy because what is traumatic for the victim is routine for the officer. Their emotionality aside, victims can be troublesome to police in other ways. Even when an officer spends a great deal of time with a victim, the latter may complain of police inefficiency despite the absence of leads to solve the case, try to tell the officer or detective what to do, hound him or her with ideas and leads to follow up, fail to show up in court, and even be ungrateful when his or her property is returned. Thus, despite sympathy for the victim's plight, victims are an emotional burden for police.

Female officer, male citizen. Interactions between female officers and male citizens are problematic because men defer to the office but may resist being controlled by or deferential to a woman. Women police usually are given deference either out of gender-blind respect for the uniform or a sense of chivalry that enhances a male citizen's sense of self. . . . Still, given women's physical disadvantage, female officers must find alternative ways to control situations when they encounter male citizens' resistance.

Women officers generally ignore sexist or sexual comments that intrude on but do not alter the outcome of an interaction. In dealing with offenders, some women draw on citizens' stereotypes, including the fear that women are "trigger happy" or are emotional in the face of danger (Martin 1980). . . .

Women's situational control strategies include a variety of verbal and nonverbal cues involving use of their voice, appearance, facial expression, and body postures to convey that they are to be taken seriously regardless of their physical stature. This often requires changing habits such as learning not to smile and how to literally "stand up to people" (Martin 1980).

Female officer, female citizen. Female officers get both greater cooperation and more resistance from women citizens than do male officers. They may draw on their common female status to reduce social distance and gain cooperation, particularly from women victims who refuse to talk to male officers. But female officers also revoke the special consideration given to female citizens by chivalrous male officers and, for that reason, may need to control a female citizen angered at not being able to flirt or manipulate her way out of a situation.

Effective officers of both genders are flexible, able to use both the crime-fighter script (associated with masculinity) and the service script (associated with femininity) to gain and maintain emotional control of situations and thereby physical control. By accurately reading the citizen's emotional state and responding to it, they use all the interpersonal resources available to them, actively seeking control by appealing both to gender-appropriate behavior and to the citizen's respect for the officer's authority. They use the citizen's expectations and values to their advantage, do gender so as to simultaneously diminish social distance and maintain control, often by invoking gendered familial roles (such as the role of mother or big brother), and limit reliance on the authority of the badge and the tools of policing. Ineffective officers either too rigidly rely on their formal authority, enact only the crime-fighting aspects of policing, and fail to provide emotional support to citizens when it is needed or, conversely, provide service and support to citizens but are unable to deal with defiance and back off from challenges.

The Link Between Emotional Labor and Policing Assignments

There is a close association between the emotional demands of various policing assignments and the status of those assignments. Most desirable are assignments that involve organizational functions most closely aligned with what is thought of as real policing (that is, fighting crime) and that emphasize control of the hard emotions. . . . [C]aring assignments that demand control of the soft emotions (for example, missing-persons cases and victim services) or make limited emotional demands (such as work at a training academy and administrative assignments) tend to be devalued as feminized, judged as appropriate for women officers, and regarded as assignments in which women tend to be overrepresented (Martin 1990). Similarly, within patrol work, women officers are especially valued in domestic disputes since they are believed to be better able than men to calm an angry man, understand him, and prevent violence (Kennedy and Homant 1983).

Police Organizations, Gender, and Strategies for Discharging Emotions

Police organizations manage officers' emotions through a number of mechanisms, including selection, socialization, supervision, reward systems, and ritual or ceremony. These indicate occupational norms and provide emotion management techniques.

Selection, socialization, and gender. All police departments carefully screen applicants. One important selection criterion is emotional stability. Candidates usually undergo extensive background investigations, psychological testing . . . and an interview with a psychologist (Scrivner 1994).

Socialization occurs in several phases, each of which teaches alternative ways to manage feelings. In the police academy, rookies learn that professional behavior and demeanor include the repression of emotional displays. This is conveyed largely through instructors' war stories that emphasize the importance of solidarity, teamwork, toughness, and stoicism in the face of pain. They also stress the importance of viewing the public in a detached manner and the belief that both hard and soft emotions are an occupational weakness in performing their duties (Pogrebin and Poole 1995).

On the street, rookies first work under supervision of a training officer. Through observation, instruction, experience, and correction, they become increasingly aware of their isolation from the community, and they develop verbal and nonverbal skills in managing situations. The primary concern in the early weeks is how the rookie handles the "hot" call (an in-progress crime or officer in trouble). Such calls constitute a behavioral test. To pass, the recruit must show willingness to share the risks of police work.

Policing norms reinforce the wider norms that men must hide fear in frightening situations and take action or face humiliation for failure to "act like a man." Women, in contrast, are permitted a greater range of self-expression and are expected to show fear. They are allowed to cry and seek exemption from duties felt to be too difficult or frightening, and they even are encouraged to be helpless. If they accept this paternalistic bargain, however, they fail to meet the occupational expectations of officers. Thus new women officers must adopt new patterns of behavior and simultaneously ignore the "double messages" and double standards for male and female competence and emotional displays on the job (Martin and Jurik 1996).

Women also must learn new behavior regarding verbal, facial, and bodily displays that convey their authority to citizens. This includes learning not to smile (smiling may cool a situation but signals deference, so usually is inappropriate) and to avoid postures that indicate hesitation or unreadiness to act.

Officers also need to learn techniques for dampening their own anger or annoyance at citizens' comments or taunts. Both male and female officers maintain calm by "thinking of the source" (that is, reminding themselves that the citizen in question is immature, ignorant, or unworthy of a rejoinder) and thus remain "above it all" (Martin 1980, 172).

Mechanisms for coping. Emotions remain, and undesirable feelings need to be discharged. Organizational mechanisms that help officers deal with work-related emotional stresses include psychological counseling services (including mandatory counseling for officers involved in a shooting) (Scrivner 1994) and elaborate rituals and ceremonies related to the death of an officer on duty that facilitate collective coping with stressful or tragic events.

The informal culture permits coping with emotions that must be repressed on the job through humor, and displacement of emotional energy through physical and social activity. However, gendered norms for expressing feelings may lead to differences in the activities that are acceptable for men and women officers.

To conform with the demands of masculinity, the men mask their feelings of affection for and dependency on each other. @EX = They guard themselves from the emotionally wrenching situations they face with slogans like "don't let it get to you" and seek acceptable manly outlets such as heavy drinking, cursing, sexual exploits, fast driving, and other dangerous sports, and displacing anger onto others (Martin 1980, 97).

The presence of women threatens to expose the activities that men use to deal with emotions and so magnifies men's fear of losing self-control. At the same time, because men often find it easier to express emotions to a woman than to another man, they frequently cast women into the stereotypical role of "nurturant mother." Such women face the dilemma that they are "thrust into the role of emotional specialist, and then criticized for being emotional" (Martin 1980, 152).

. . . [B]oth male and female officers believe that socializing and drinking together promote feelings of group unity, trust, and camaraderie. In addition, alcohol is widely used to relieve stress. Thus drinking serves two distinct but important functions in the police culture: as a social lubricant involved in bonding rituals and as a stress reliever. However, while heavy drinking and the ability to hold one's liquor are ways of enhancing masculinity, women who drink heavily fail to meet the social ideals of feminine behavior. Because of this defeminization, women officers risk criticism if they seek acceptance by conforming to the drinking norms for releasing work-related tensions and are the subjects of contempt rather than admiration for sexual behavior similar to that of male officers.

Conclusion

Policing makes great emotional demands on officers, who are required to deal with a wide variety of situations involving people in crisis while maintaining order, providing service, and controlling crime. Even more than bravery and physical strength (qualities associated with masculinity), the work demands communication and human relations skills that often are both unrecognized and undervalued by police managers and officers themselves. This occurs, in large part, because these skills are associated with femininity. Nevertheless, both masculine- and feminine-typed skills are essential for officers to be effective. They must have a command presence that enables them to act decisively to maintain control in volatile situations, and they must have the ability to actively listen and talk to people.

Women entering policing still encounter gender-related dilemmas in coping with norms related to emotional labor. On the street, they must not be too emotional in responding to volatile situations; yet the woman who conforms to emotional display rules of policing (that is, is inexpressive) is regarded as unfeminine. In informal interaction with other officers, women are cast into the mother or confidante role, expected to be supportive of a man's emotional venting, but criticized for expressing similar feelings. In addition, their opportunities to participate in social activities through which other officers discharge emotional stresses are limited, and, when they join in, they are criticized for acting like men. Despite changes in the number of women and minority men officers and in departmental policies and practices over the past two decades, the informal police culture has remained resistant to changing the definition of the core aspects of the work. Thus the police continue to emphasize that they constitute a police force and downplay the fact that they also comprise a police service.

References

Brown, Jennifer and Jennifer Grover. 1998. Stress and the Woman Sergeant. *Police Journal* 71:47–54.

Brown, Michael K. 1981. *Working the Street: Police Discretion and the Dilemmas of Reform.* New York: Russell Sage Foundation.

Fineman, Stephen. 1993. Organizations as Emotional Arenas. In *Emotion in Organizations,* ed. S. Fineman. Newbury Park, CA: Sage.

Goffman, Erving. 1969. *Strategic Interaction.* Philadelphia: University of Pennsylvania Press.

Hochschild, Arlie Russell. 1983. *The Managed Heart: Commercialization of Human Feeling.* Berkeley: University of California Press.

Hunt, Jennifer. 1984. The Development of Rapport Through Negotiation of Gender in Field Work Among Police. *Human Organization* 43:283–296.

Kennedy, David and R. Homant. 1983. Attitudes of Abused Women Toward Male and Female Police. *Criminal Justice and Behavior* 10:391–405.

Leidner, Robin. 1991. Serving Hamburgers and Selling Insurance: Gender, Work, and Identity in Interactive Service Jobs. *Gender & Society* 5(2):154–177.

Martin, Susan E. 1980. *"Breaking and Entering": Policewomen on Patrol.* Berkeley: University of California Press.

——. 1990. *On the Move: The Status of Women in Policing.* Washington, DC: Police Foundation.

Martin, Susan E. and Nancy C. Jurik. 1996. *Doing Justice, Doing Gender: Women in Law and Criminal Justice Occupations.* Thousand Oaks, CA: Sage.

Mills, Trudy and Sherryl Kleinman. 1988. Emotions, Reflexivity, and Action: An Interactionist Analysis. *Social Forces* 66:1009–1027.

Pierce, Jennifer L. 1995. *Gender Trials: Emotional Lives in Contemporary Law Firms.* Berkeley: University of California Press.

Pogrebin, Mark R. and Eric D. Poole. 1995. Emotion Management: A Study of Police Response to Tragic Events. *Social Perspectives on Emotion.* Vol. 3. Greenwich, CT: JAI.

Price, Jammie. 1996. Doing Gender: Men and Emotion. Paper presented at the annual meeting of the American Sociological Association.

Reiner, Robert. 1992. Police Research in the United Kingdom. In *Modern Policing,* ed. M. Tonry and N. Morris. Chicago: University of Chicago Press.

Scrivner, Ellen. 1994. *The Role of Police Psychology in Controlling Excessive Force.* Washington, DC: Department of Justice.

Skolnick, Jerome. 1966. *Justice Without Trial.* New York: John Wiley.

Stenross, Barbara and Sherryl Kleinman. 1989. The Highs and Lows of Emotional Labor: Detectives' Encounters with Criminals and Victims. *Journal of Contemporary Ethnography* 17(4):435–452.

Sutton, Robert I. 1991. Maintaining Norms about Expressed Emotions: The Case of Bill Collectors. *Administrative Science Quarterly* 36(June):245–268.

Thoits, Peggy A. 1989. The Sociology of Emotions. *Annual Review of Sociology* 15:317–342.

Van Maanen, John and Gideon Kunda. 1989. "Real Feelings": Emotional Expression and Organizational Culture. In *Research in Organizational Behavior,* ed. Barry M. Staw and L. L. Cummings. Vol. 11. Greenwich, CT: JAI Press.

Westley, William. 1970. *Violence and the Police.* Cambridge, MA: MIT Press.

Wharton, Carol S. 1996. Making People Feel Good: Workers' Constructions of Meaning in Interactive Service Jobs. *Qualitative Sociology* 19:217–233.

Young, Malcolm. 1991. *An Inside Job: Policing and Police Culture in Britain.* Oxford: Clarendon.

Food for Thought and Application Questions

1. What is "emotional labor" and why is it an important aspect of work? How is it rewarded in police work? How is it different from "traditional" approaches in police work? What kind of dilemma does each type of work activity present to female officers? Why?

2. What occupations, in addition to that of police officer, are characterized by "male" qualities, but where actual work practices require some combination of traditionally defined "masculine" behaviors and emotional labor? Discuss how these might be similar to police work in terms of the way people do their work. What things might differ with regard to emotional labor demands?

3. Interview a male and a female police officer about their work. Describe a situation that requires a lot of emotional labor and ask about how they manage such an encounter. Describe a second encounter that does not appear to require much emotional labor and ask about how they would manage that. Compare responses to the situations. Do male and female officers differ in responses? How do you account for the similarity or differences? How similar are their responses to the material covered in the article? ✦

24

'Hey, Why Don't You Wear a Shorter Skirt?'

Structural Vulnerability and the Organization of Sexual Harassment in Temporary Clerical Employment

Jackie Krasas Rogers
Kevin D. Henson

Sexual Harassment in the Workplace

A large portion of the social research devoted to sexual harassment has focused on documenting the extent of sexual harassment: what percentage of women are sexually harassed (MacKinnon 1979); which women are sexually harassed and in what jobs (Carothers and Crull 1984); and who are the harassers (Gruber and Bjorn 1982; Gutek 1985). Other research categorizes types of sexual harassment (Fitzgerald 1990; MacKinnon 1979), delineates responses to sexual harassment (Gruber 1989; Maypole 1986), determines who labels which experiences as sexual harassment (Giuffre and Williams 1994; Schneider 1982), and asks the question "What factors contribute to sexual harassment?" Answers to this question have included sex-role spillover (Gutek 1985; Ragins and Scandura 1995), patriarchy (MacKinnon 1979), and compulsory heterosexuality (Giuffre and Williams 1994; Schneider 1982, 1985).

Gutek (1985) describes sexual harassment as a result of the inappropriate spill-over of gender roles to the work environment. Sex-role spillover theory, while still widely employed in some fields such as social psychology, assumes that organizations are gender-neutral, asexual environments; gender and sexuality are "smuggled" into organizations by gendered workers. Women workers, in this light, are seen as women first, workers second. In female-dominated jobs, feminine role attributes such as nurturance and (hetero)sexuality spillover into the workplace. When combined with a workplace that emphasizes sexuality, men who interact with women in female-dominated jobs take on the sexual aggressor role, and the result is often sexual harassment.

There are several problems with spillover theory, most of which derive from critiques of sex-role theory in general (Connell 1987; Segal 1990). A sex role is conceptualized as something that exists outside work, a characteristic of individuals, and spills over inappropriately to the workplace. Therefore, sexual harassment is a matter of unprofessional or inappropriate behavior of individuals in the workplace. Organizational responsibility for sexual harassment, then, extends only to punishing the occasional harasser. Consequently, sex-role spillover theory identifies the sex ratio of an occupation as a key contributing factor; jobs that are highly sex segregated are fertile ground for sexual harassment.

However, gender and sexuality construct and are constructed by work relations (see, for example, Acker 1990; Hall 1993; Hochschild 1983; Lorber 1994; Pierce 1995). . . . Schneider (1982, 1985) notes how workers are obligated to enact female receptivity to heterosexual advances, which, in conjunction with their relative lack of power in the work context, creates sexual harassment. . . . A fruitful analysis would use a labor process theory approach to gendered organizations (see West 1990) including a systematic analysis of power and control in the employment relationship as it derives from and results in gender inequality.

In this light, sexual harassment is about the control of women workers, of women as workers and workers as women. Sexual harassment is about particular constructions of gender, especially organizational imperatives to "do gender" in a particular manner

(Lorber 1994; West and Zimmerman 1987). Many have implicitly if not explicitly recognized the role of asymmetrical power relations in creating sexual harassment (Fiske and Glicke 1995; Gutek 1985; MacKinnon 1979).

This research explores a form of employment that ties together these themes. Temporary workers are a growing, highly feminized, and relatively powerless group in today's workplace. In the office, temporary workers are often treated as nonpersons, as passive recipients of orders (Henson 1996; Rogers 1995b), much like wait persons or even children. They find themselves interactionally invisible as they do inconspicuous work in conspicuous places, such as filing for hours in a busy hallway (Rogers 1995b). In addition, temporary workers are generally considered to hold the lowest rank in the office, as they are given work and orders by supervisors and coworkers alike. In fact, it is not unusual for permanent coworkers to participate in "dumping" undesirable work on temporary employees (Henson 1996; Rogers forthcoming).

While their low status leaves temporary workers open for many types of workplace abuse, the transitory nature of much temporary work further intensifies this vulnerability. Temporary workers report that people seldom remember their names (referring to them simply as "the temp"), isolate them from office sociability, and often treat them as a piece of furniture (Henson 1996; Rogers 1995b). Thus, temporary workers are objectified and stripped of their personhood, paving the way for poor treatment, including sexual harassment.

Understanding the interplay of gender, sexuality, and power as it relates to the organization of temporary work will enable us to gain a better understanding of some of the shortcomings in theories of sexual harassment. We address the sexual harassment of these workers and attempt to locate structural influences that affect their workplace experience as well as their opportunities for resistance. . . .

It is our contention that temporary work arrangements create an environment that both fosters and tolerates sexual harassment, fre-

quently punishing the harassed rather than the harasser even to a greater extent than in traditional employment relationships. . . . [I]f we consider that temporaries are likely to have the lowest status in an office (virtually everyone is superior to a temporary worker) and to work in a largely female occupation (63 percent of all temporary workers are clerical), it is conceivable that they would be even more likely to be harassed than permanent workers.

Method

This research is based on in-depth interviews and extensive participant observation from two broader studies on temporary clerical work. One of the studies was conducted in Chicago in 1990–91, while the other was conducted in Los Angeles; in 1993–94. In these studies, the subject of sexual harassment was not initially included in the interview guides; both researchers, however, found it to be of concern to the interview subjects. As a research focus, sexual harassment was emergent from the data and gained in importance throughout the course of the research process. In both studies, the researcher questioned the interview subjects about their relationships with coworkers. For example, general questions such as "Who did you work with and what were those relationships like?" elicited stories of sexual harassment. . . . [A]pproximately 40 percent of the respondents found it troublesome enough to mention without being prompted to do so. It is likely that more direct questioning would have uncovered even more sexual harassment.

Together, these two studies yielded 68 in-depth interviews (35 in Chicago and 33 in Los Angeles) ranging from one to three hours in length. Interview subjects included temporary agency personnel and client company representatives, but the majority were temporary clerical workers. All interviews were tape-recorded, transcribed, coded, and analyzed. All names indicated in the body of this article are pseudonyms.

. . . Collectively, the interview subjects had worked in over 40 temporary agencies, with individual tenure in temporary employment ranging from a few months to over 10 years. The data represent a diverse group of African

American, Latino, Asian American, and white men and women ranging in age from 20 to 60 years old. . . .

Gendered Worker in a Gendered Job

The clerical sector of temporary employment, like the general full-time clerical sector, is predominantly composed of women (Bureau of Labor Statistics [BLS] 1995; Howe 1986). Historically, this association of temporary work with women's work was reflected in the common inclusion of the infantilizing term *girl* in the names of the earliest temporary agencies (e.g., Kelly Girl, Western Girl, Right Girl). While temporary agencies have formally modernized their names (i.e., Kelly Girl became Kelly Services), the continued popular usage of the outdated names accurately reflects the gendered composition of the temporary workforce. Although more men have been seeking employment through temporary agencies, particularly as industrial temporary workers (Parker 1994), they still make up a relatively small proportion of the clerical temporary workforce. Indeed, a recent survey by the National Association of Temporary Services (1992) estimated that 80 percent of member agency temporaries were women; Belous (1989) estimated that more than 64 percent of the entire temporary workforce are women, and more than 20 percent of the temporary workforce is Black. Furthermore, a recent government survey concluded that "Workers paid by temporary agencies were more likely than workers in traditional arrangements to be women, young, and black" (BLS 1995, 4).

In fact, the gender composition of the temporary workforce leads to the expectation, often the assumption, that temporary workers (as secretaries) are women; the job, in other words, is gendered. . . . Furthermore, the feminized nature of the work is particularly highlighted when others fail to even recognize a male temporary as the secretary, mistaking him for someone with higher organizational status. . . .

The feminized nature of the job, shaped in part by sexualized cultural images of temporary workers, actually requires temporary workers to enact a particular construction of femaleness as part of the job. In addition, temporary agencies' demands for particular physical presentations and requirements for doing deference further highlight the gendered, racialized, and sexualized nature of temporary work.

Doing Difference

West and Fenstermaker (1995) invoke the concept of *doing difference* to explain the production of social inequalities; some of their critics argue that the notion of doing difference, with its emphasis on interaction, obfuscates power relations and relegates structures of inequality to the realm of performance (Collins 1995). . . . We attempt here to forge some of these links through an empirical examination of the structures of inequality in temporary employment and the ways in which temporary workers' interactions are shaped by the gendered expectations of their clients, their agencies, and even themselves.

Although temporary agencies are legally required to operate under equal opportunity employer legislation (i.e., to hire workers without regard to race, sex, or age), temporaries are nevertheless often hired or placed for personal characteristics other than their jobs skills. Even some of the more specific and egregious requests (e.g., for a young, blond woman with great legs) are often honored. One temporary worker overheard the following exchange:

> One guy had gone through like five secretaries in that year and he had temps, different temps, every couple of weeks. And the office manager asked him if he wanted that temp back the following week because she had to contact the agency to arrange it. And I remember he looked out of his office and kind of looked at her legs and [said], "No, she's kind of on the heavy side." So that was it. (Ludy Martinez, 36-year-old Filipina American)

The temporary industry reinforces this emphasis on physical appearance. A 1986 study of the temporary industry reported a disproportionate emphasis on temporaries' physical appearance or "femininity"; a receptionist at one temporary agency reported filing "evaluation cards of temporary worker applicants that had comments like 'homely' and 'stunning' written on them with virtually no mention of office skills" (National Association of Working Women 1986, 28). Occasionally, as in an incident that Helen Weinberg described, clients assert their right to control a temporary's personal appearance by filing a formal complaint with the agency. The agency then "counsels" the errant temporary about her or his appearance (or removes her or him from the job):

> And you're expected to dress like Christie Brinkley! Oh, it's ridiculous. I wear nice clean clothes. I'm clean. My body is clean. I have good breath. I mean, I try to look as good as I possibly can. So I get a call from the temp agency at home at seven thirty at night. . . . I was just mortified. Like, "What is it?!" I felt like I was on death row for temps! So she says, "Well, it seems that you're not dressing professionally enough. Laura gave me a call." And of course I feel horrible. (Helen Weinberg, 24-year-old white woman)

The demands for a particular gendered (even sexy) physical presentation are not freely chosen based on the personal tastes of the temporary worker; rather, they are recognized as a right of the employer (see also Hall 1993; Paules 1991).

The depoliticized managerial prerogative to control the appearance of temporary workers can also be used to justify racial bias in placing temporary workers.

> Nine out of ten times it's a little blond girl with colored eyes. Or somebody with an English accent. Nobody overweight. And if it's a person of color, she's gotta be drop-dead gorgeous. Not just pretty—drop-dead gorgeous. (Regina Mason, 44-year-old Latina)

"Gorgeous" women of color (those beautiful enough to be receptionists) must conform to white notions of female beauty.

Clients and temporary help service personnel also employ racialized notions about workers' capabilities: "articulate" workers are white. This racial logic (Hossfeld 1990) reproduces and naturalizes racial inequality.

> I think "articulate" is a code word [for racial preference] that you can't ever really get called on. You can't say, "Oh you were discriminating." You were just telling them what you need. It's kind of a fine line. There's a lot of clients who are like that. Especially a lot for reception people. (Sonja Griffin, 31-year-old white woman)

Closely related is the tendency to assign back-office temporary assignments to women of color. This arrangement shapes interaction and then uses those very interactions to justify the view that people of color cannot "do" front-office work (i.e., white, middle-class sociability).

> But there was one Black woman in our group. And she was sent to like way in the back room on some top floor. Which was not like the corporate floor or whatever. She was put in the back. And she said she gets a lot of crappy . . . gets asked to do things that she doesn't think other people would be asked to do. I was put up front. . . . And then there was a very large white woman who was there. And she, too, was sort of hidden in the back so people wouldn't see her. I'm no beauty queen. But they put me in front, I guess, because I was the white woman. (Helen Weinberg, 24-year-old white woman)

It quickly becomes apparent that the type of femininity one must do in temporary work is white, middle-class, heterosexual femininity. While certain exceptions are made, it is nearly impossible to do this brand of femininity if you are a woman of color. The consequences of the gendered/raced/classed organization of temporary work are a lower paid, back-office job or no job.

Men pose an especially interesting case concerning the gendered nature of temporary work. Their presence in female-dominated work has the potential to disrupt gender categories because men who are temporaries fail to live up to normative conceptions of masculinity by not having a "real job." Therefore, they risk gender assessment. One accommodation that underscores the gendered nature of temporary work is the popular construction of male temporaries as gay, which neither disrupts the essential nature of gender for the observer nor challenges the dominant/subordinate statuses of male/female. Male temporary workers, heterosexual and gay, were very aware of this construction. . . . As with other men who cross over into women's work (see also Pringle 1988; Williams 1989, 1995), male temporaries risk their status as "real" (or at least heterosexual) men. In everyday practice, these gender crossings are assumed to say more about the essential nature of the individual men than the gendered organization of the work.

Male temporary workers' individual failings, when faced with the gender assessment of others, do not stop with questioning their sexual orientation. In addition, their drive, motivation, and competence for (male) career success may be questioned—that is, these are dead-end jobs that no "self-respecting" man would accept. Ironically, the dead-end nature of these jobs is rarely seen as problematic for women.

> I think men get a little less respect if they're temping. There's that expectation that they should be like career oriented and like moving up in the world and being a businessman and moving himself forward in business. Where women can do that but it's not an expectation. And so I think that, I think that's where that Kelly Girl image, that temporaries are women, is. I have noticed that there is a certain amount, looking down upon. I think that's true of temps in general. They're somewhat looked down upon. I think the men maybe more. (Albert Baxter, 31-year-old white man)

The discussions of male temporaries' masculinity highlight the gendered nature of the work as they struggle with maintaining masculinity in an organizational environment that requires doing femininity.

Doing Deference

Doing deference is a special case of doing gender that demonstrates how organizational imperatives shape interaction that becomes essentialized. Temporaries, like many women workers, . . . are also expected to enact a submissive, deferential, even solicitous stance toward management, coworkers, and clients (Henson 1996). Indeed, temporary agencies demanded that their workers adopt a pleasing demeanor while on the client company's premises. Thus, the proper enactment of gender (even an institutionalized *job flirt* [see Hall 1993]) was conflated with proper job performance and monitored by the temporary agency.

Temporaries, like many service workers, were expected to smile whether or not they were particularly happy. . . . Indeed, temporary workers at an agency that one of the researchers worked through were instructed to think of themselves as guests rather than laborers engaged in a primarily economic transaction: "Try to remember that you are a guest in each new office and must always observe the basic rules of etiquette" (Welcome to Right Temporaries, Inc. 1989). Drawing on their personal knowledge of behavior appropriate to a well-behaved guest, temporaries were reminded that a polite guest neither challenges nor otherwise risks offending his or her host.

This guest metaphor, however, also enforces passivity by rendering any complaining or self-assertion by temporary workers on assignment as inappropriate: "Please do . . . observe the hours, procedures, and work methods of the customers without criticism" (Welcome to Right Temporaries, Inc. 1989). As the commercial nature of the relationship is obscured by the personal relations fiction, criticisms of the work, including those about abusive or disrespectful treatment, are defined as illegitimate. . . .

Being on one's best behavior, or doing good work, may be interpreted as responding to flirtatious behavior on the job, to perform a kind of job flirt (Hall 1993; MacKinnon 1979). . . . Mary LeMoine described putting up with the "flirtatious" (even harassing) behavior of a client on the job to be gracious:

> And then on the phone I've had men ask me out after talking to me. I'm a temporary. And they start talking to me. They start these entire conversations. I had one man at the bank offer to fly me to San Diego to spend the weekend with him. . . . I felt very bad about that because in my normal situation . . . if someone called me at school and did that, if someone called

me at home and did that . . . I wouldn't talk to you. You know, you have no place doing this to me. *[So why didn't you say that there?]* Because it was a bank. *Because it was my job.* And when I got home I felt very bad about it. I should have just said that anyway. I just kind of ignored it. And I don't think I handled it as well as I should have. (Mary LeMoine, 27-year-old white woman; emphasis added)

Temporary workers, in an effort to conform to the requirements of doing deference, may accept treatment on the job that they would not tolerate in another context.

The extent to which deference was conflated with proper job performance is highlighted by the negative reactions of male temporaries to these demands for subservience and its implicit threat to their sense of masculinity.

It's a manly thing to be in charge. And men should want to be, supposedly in charge and delegating things. If you're a man and you're being delegated to, it somehow makes you less manly. You know what I'm saying? Whereas it seems to be okay for the person delegating to women. They seem to be okay with that relationship. And the women, maybe they're just projecting that to get by. It seems that they're more okay with that than men are. I guess I'm saying that it makes me feel less of the manly kind of qualities, like I'm in charge, you know. And men should be like takin' meetings and barking orders instead of just being subservient. (Harold Koenig, 29-year-old heterosexual white man)

Similarly, one of the authors discovered the required nature of deference when he refused to adopt a submissive demeanor and was removed from an assignment despite adequate completion of the formal work (see Henson 1996). . . .

Reviewing how the organization of temporary work operates in the daily work lives of temporaries provides us with the opportunity to evaluate the usefulness of sex-role spillover theories. In these examples, gendered (or sexualized) work behavior is not something temporaries freely choose to enact based on their own tastes and preferences. Rather, the low status of temporaries (as secretaries, but lower

than secretaries) and the expectations of temporary agencies and clients (which quickly become job requirements) help shape temporary workers' interactions in such a way that their gender (and sexuality) is prominently featured as an aspect of the work. The emphasis placed on temporary workers' physical presentation as well as requirements for doing deference coincides with a particular construction of gender, including heterosexuality and whiteness.

. . . The organization of temporary work, in other words, helps create the gendered workplace. This theoretical stance resonates closely with the gendered organization perspective holding that gender is not something that comes from outside organizations but is constructed and reproduced within them (Acker 1990; Ferguson 1984; Lorber 1994; Williams 1995). Therefore, gendered work behavior (even that which results in sexual harassment) should be understood as constructed within and by gendered workplaces rather than the result of inappropriate sex-role spillover.

. . . We now turn to an analysis of the factors that constrain temporary workers in reporting sexual harassment and the range of temporary workers' responses to sexual harassment.

Factors That Constrain Reporting: The Organization of Vulnerability

The organization of temporary work has a tremendous impact on the extent to which temporary workers find opportunities for resistance. Chief among the organizational constraints are the institutionalization and magnification of asymmetrical power relationships between the agency, client, and temporary worker. These asymmetrical power relationships are exacerbated for temporary workers by the fear of downtime (i.e., inadequate income) and uncertainty about the actual scheduling practices of their agencies.

As employers, most temporary agencies tell their workers to report any kind of problem (such as sexual harassment) to the agency rather than handle it at the work site. At first glance this would seem to benefit the temporary workers, and indeed there is that potential. However, temporary agencies are also supposed to represent the interests of their (paying) clients. One Los Angeles agency counselor, in fact, portrayed these relationships as completely "equal" and "fair": "You have an . . . allegiance not only to the person who's paying you, but you have an allegiance as a responsibility for the applicant that you're sending out" (Sandy Mathers, 28-year-old African American woman).

However, even the agencies themselves recognize that their "natural" alignment is with the client rather than the worker. . . . [A] temporary agency counselor who reported "going to bat" for his temporary felt constrained by the need to maintain client relationships: "But you have to be very careful. This one [incident], I didn't lose a client, but there's been others where you do lose a client" (Manny Avila, 28-year-old Latino). It is almost always easier to replace a complaining temporary worker than an offended client. Therefore, in almost all conflictual circumstances, the client company is favored. . . . Temporary workers are often very much aware of where their agency's interests lie and their own ultimate dispensability: "You don't have an alliance. If you're a temp you don't have an alliance. And I'm afraid if I complain [to my agency], they'll just throw me off the assignment" (Cindy Carson, 38-year-old white woman).

The agency and the client have tremendous power to determine the terms of work, and the relationship ranges from asymmetrical to unilateral. For example, while client companies enjoy staffing flexibility, terminating the assignment at will and often without notice, individual workers are often at the mercy of both their agency and client assignment supervisors (Henson 1996; Rogers 1995a). Neither the company nor the agency need justify these work schedule changes to temporary workers. In some cases temporaries are replaced rather than just having the assignment cut short. They are seldom advised of the reason for such decisions and may, in fact, not even know that they were replaced.

Temporaries, then, willing and eager to work, often find themselves with time off instead, time off that can be financially cata-

strophic. This uncertain environment led temporaries to believe that any transgression they committed against their agency, including complaining about abusive treatment, would result in punishment—primarily work deprivation.

> I should have vocalized that [displeasure] more, but I didn't feel like I was really in a position to even say that. Because underneath it all is, if they get pissed at you, they can just not give you work and say, "Oh there's no jobs." (Don Birch, 24-year-old white man)

Temporary workers' fears regarding loss of access to work assignments were not mere paranoia. As we discovered, some temporary agencies do keep records of temporaries who declined assignments to better "direct" work flow. Indeed, one agency counselor said that she gave her temporary workers only "one strike" before they were no longer considered for assignments. The definition of a strike was considerably broad including lateness, asking for higher wages, or complaining about an assignment. More than one agency counselor said that they would not send out any "prima donnas," and this was defined as people who had complaints about any aspect of the job. . . .

. . . It was not uncommon for temporaries to report tolerating offensive jokes and patently hostile environments to maintain their "steady" assignments:

> I didn't walk out on it and I wish I would have. I was really strapped for money. And that was the office where everybody smoked. And everybody was like, I don't know how to put it . . . constantly making like racial jokes, sexist jokes. There was this guy who was like just this really sleazy sales guy. Like a stereotype. He wore like a plaid suit and slicked-back hair. He smoked a cigar. Hairbrush mustache. And he would come over and he'd just be so rude and so sexist. . . . And I was like, "Oh this is horrible! This is so humiliating! I can't take it anymore." But I stayed . . . I had to. Two weeks. It was a drag. (Pamela O'Connor, 26-year-old white woman)

Regardless of how unpleasant, any work is often better than no work at all to a temporary worker at the limits of his or her budget and without access to traditional social safety nets (e.g., unemployment benefits). As marginal workers with an unsteady flow of income from one week to the next, temporary workers feel financial constraints keenly and make decisions regarding their reactions to harassment in light of those constraints. Any behavior that has the real or perceived potential to displease the agency, including reporting legitimate problems with the assignment, is seen as putting the temporary's future prospects for work in jeopardy.

In this context, it is evident that the reporting of any difficulties, like sexual harassment, can work against a temporary worker's economic interests. . . .

Dilemmas of Resistance

Not surprisingly, most women do not report incidents of sexual harassment. Sexual harassment research has suggested a response matrix or continuum (Gruber 1989; Maypole 1986) including four major types: avoidance, diffusion, negotiation, and confrontation.

. . . This research draws on an institutional understanding of women's responses to sexual harassment, but more specifically, it examines how a particular organization of work configures power relations to the detriment of sexual harassment victims. Thus, we view the range of responses to sexual harassment as they are shaped by organizational constraints rather than as individual strategies or coping behaviors.

Complain to the Agency

Temporaries are instructed to bring any work-related problems, including sexual harassment, to the attention of their agency rather than the client company. The position of the agency, however, makes bringing complaints directly to the temporary counselors a risky move. Agencies' responses can range from support to passive complicity and even overt complicity:

They flirt with the applicant . . . oh . . . sexual harassment. I've had applicants call me in tears saying, "This man won't leave

me alone. I don't know what to do. He's lookin' down my blouse. He wants to sit next to me and show me how to use the phone. I don't know what to do." Yeah, and it's difficult to say, "Well, grab your purse and leave." Because then your client's calling you and saying, "How dare you." [What do you tell them?] It all depends. It all depends. (Sandy Mathers, 28-year-old African American woman)

Agency representatives often infantilize the workers (Rogers 1995a), diminishing the significance of their complaints, their capability to read situations correctly, and their ability to take constructive action. They are seen as hysterical, overreacting, or oversensitive women. . . .

Most temporary workers are keenly aware (or suspect) that their complaints will not be successfully mediated or dealt with by temporary agencies. Even if they have not experienced it directly, many temporaries are able to relay stories about those they know who were not supported by their agency.

With the allegiance of the agency more closely aligned with the client than the temporary worker, . . . [w]hen they recast sexual harassment as flirting or a minor nuisance, they are clearly acting in the interests of their clients. The organization of the relationship among temporaries, clients, and agencies provides the impetus to downplay sexual harassment.

Confront the Harasser

The most direct, but least used, avenue of recourse that the women we interviewed followed was to confront the harasser. Although only one woman reported this type of resistance, it is important to note because she was able to use her position as a higher paying executive temporary secretary as well as her personal connections to the temporary agency to her benefit:

I know one instance I had to tell the guy, "If you do that to me again, not only will your wife and human resources know, but I think I will have to tell the chairman." . . . I told the guy I was gonna tell his wife because she and I had become quite chatty friends on the phone. (Ludy Martinez, 36-year-old Filipina American)

In this case, the harassment stopped before the assignment ended. . . . Ludy was partly successful because this was a longer term executive secretarial assignment in which she had the opportunity to get to know her supervisor's wife and was able to use that relationship as a threat. Such opportunities for resistance are less likely to occur in the lower paying filing or data entry positions in which temporaries are more isolated. Even more important, at this assignment, Ludy was working through an agency managed and owned by a personal friend. This personal connection gave her more assurance that if she were to make a complaint, she would not be risking her job and the complaint would be taken seriously. However, Ludy's situation is unique, and as the exception, her experience further demonstrates the unequal alignment of power in temporary employment.

Ignore the Harasser

The most common response of temporaries to sexual harassment, like other women workers, was to ignore the harasser, take no action at all, and put up with it (Gruber 1989; Schneider 1991). For example, Kara Wallace and Pamela O'Connor described experiencing patently offensive workplace behavior that many would define as hostile environment sexual harassment, yet they chose to reframe it as "nothing major":

> Well, nobody actually physically . . . sexual harassment like that. But I would always bump into, "Honey, Baby, Sweetheart." And that place that the sleazy sales guy was . . . he would like come over and tell me dirty jokes and stuff. And I was like, "My life sucks" at that point. (Pamela O'Connor, 26-year-old white woman)

Particularly with verbal or hostile environment harassment, temporary workers were likely to ignore the harassment or fail to label it as sexual harassment at all.

Temporary workers who ignored the sexual harassment frequently explained their response (or lack thereof) in terms of the transitory nature of the work. In other words, while they noted that their temporary status may have contributed to or fostered the harassment, they also ignored it because "it's

only temporary." The time required to file a complaint and procedurally follow through on it would exceed the time of the assignment:

> He'd say, "Hey, why don't you wear a shorter skirt and that would make it more interesting for us." And then later he offered me breakfast . . . and some other things. And I thought, you know, I just don't think this is the way I want to go. And it's because you're a temp. (Cheryl Hansen, 23-year-old white woman)

> There has been the usual harassment type stuff that they figure it's a temp. She'll be gone next week. And I didn't make the typical woman-type fuss . . . and that was due to temping more than anything else. . . . It wasn't worth my time filing a complaint anymore because I was a temp and I was gonna be out of there and could refuse to work for that man and everything. (Ludy Martinez, 36-year-old Filipina American)

By focusing on the short duration of the assignment, temporary workers down-play the meaning of sexual harassment. The result is that none of the women we interviewed filed a formal complaint about the sexual harassment they experienced on their assignments. These women's status as temporary seemed to work against filing a formal complaint. They felt that people would see them as making a big deal out of nothing or making the "typical woman-type fuss"; after all, it's only temporary.

While this strategy may help individual temporaries in individual situations, when we consider that several of our interview subjects were sexually harassed on a number of assignments, this strategy seldom works in the long run. . . . Being sexually harassed seems to be a routine part of being a temporary worker. Furthermore, chronic harassers have easy access to a supply of potential victims in the event the person they are harassing decides to leave the assignment.

Abandon the Assignment or Agency

One way that temporaries have resisted abusive treatment, including sexual harassment, is by finding an "acceptable" reason to leave or not renew a particular assignment.

For instance, several of our subjects acknowledged that once they had a difficult assignment, they turned down further assignments at that company. . . . A second acceptable reason for refusing work was that they had something else to do other than work that week. Here, temporary workers play on the misconception that most temporaries are seeking flexible hours to combine either work and family or work and some other interest. . . . These strategies, however, can have serious financial repercussions for temporary workers who, contrary to industry propaganda, are unlikely to be working for pin money (Henson 1996; Martella 1991; Parker 1994). Furthermore, an unfortunate side effect of co-opting the flexibility myth is that it perpetuates the misconception.

Another avenue of recourse is for the temporary worker to move to another agency. . . . This strategy seems to be reserved for extreme circumstances because leaving one agency may require developing relationships with new agencies (Henson 1996; Rogers 1995a). . . . Once the switch is made, there is no guarantee that problems will not arise with the new agency since the structure of the relationships between temporary worker, agency, and client favors the link between the agency and the client.

Conclusions and Suggestions

Temporary clerical work is a highly feminized and disempowering form of employment. The low status, depersonalization, and objectification of temporary workers fosters an environment in which poor treatment including sexual harassment is likely. The gendered (raced, classed, and even heterosexualized) organization of the work is highlighted in numerous ways. . . . Therefore, the metaphor of doing gender (or race or class) can speak to oppression and exploitation when combined with a gendered organizations approach. Similarly, sexual harassment can now be seen as an outgrowth of the organization of work rather than merely the result of individual actions or even sex-role spillover in the workplace.

Possibilities for resistance to sexual harassment are severely constrained (although not eliminated) as temporary clerical work shifts more power to the employers. Judith Lorber (1994) notes that economically marginal women and men cannot be the ones to solve the problem of constant sexual harassment. The temporary employment relationship creates marginal workers as it aligns the agencies' interests with the clients' interests while pushing the demands and rights of the worker into the background. In this environment, proving harassment, damages, or even that the agency had knowledge of the harassment becomes quite difficult. Many workers tolerate harassment or other abuses rather than risk losing access to future assignments and income through the agency.

. . . Temporaries must be provided with more power, either through industry regulation or worker-owned agencies, to address sexual harassment problems without fearing economic reprisals. Yet, this would not eliminate sexual harassment from temporaries' workplaces. Organizational imperatives to do gender contribute to the problems of sexual harassment, and at the same time, they naturalize and solidify inequalities.

References

Acker, Joan. 1990. "Hierarchies, jobs, bodies: A theory of gendered organizations." *Gender & Society* 4:139–58.

Belous, Richard S. 1989. *The contingent economy: The growth of the temporary. part-time and subcontracted workforce.* Washington. DC: National Planning Association.

Bureau of Labor Statistics (BLS). 1995. *Handbook of labor statistics.* Washington, DC: U.S. Government Printing Office.

Carothers, Suzanne C., and Peggy Crull. 1984. "Contrasting sexual harassment in female- and male-dominated occupations." In *My Troubles Are Going to Have Trouble With Me*, edited by Karen Brodkin Sacks and Dorothy Remy. New Brunswick, NJ: Rutgers University Press.

Collins, Patricia Hill. 1995. Symposium on West and Fenstermaker's "Doing Difference." *Gender & Society* 4:491–4.

Connell, R. W. 1987. *Gender and Power.* Stanford, CA: Stanford University Press.

Ferguson, Kathy E. 1984. *The Feminist Case Against Bureaucracy.* Philadelphia: Temple University Press.

Fiske, Susan T., and Peter Glicke. 1995. "Ambivalence and stereotypes cause sexual harassment: A theory with implications for organizational change." *Journal of Social Issues* 1:97–115.

Fitzgerald, L. F. 1990. "Sexual harassment: The definition and measurement of a construct." In *Ivory power: Sexual Harassment on Campus,* edited by M. A. Paludi. Albany: State University of New York Press.

Giuffre, Patti A., and Christine Williams. 1994. "Boundary lines: Labeling sexual harassment in restaurants." *Gender &. Society* 8:378–401.

Gruber, James E. 1989. "How women handle sexual harassment: A literature review." *Sociology and Social Research* 74 (October):3–7.

Gruber, James E., and Lars Bjorn. 1982. "Blue collar blues: The sexual harassment of women autoworkers." *Work and Occupations* 9:271–98.

Gutek, Barbara. 1985. *Sex and the Workplace: The Impact of Sexual Behavior and Harassment on Women, Men, and Organizations.* San Francisco: Jossey-Bass.

Hall, Elaine I. 1993. "Smiling, deferring, and flirting: Doing gender by giving 'good service.'" *Work and Occupations* 20:452–71.

Henson, Kevin D. 1996. *Just a Temp.* Philadelphia: Temple University Press.

Hochschild, Arlie Russell. 1983. *The Managed Heart: Commercialization of Human Feeling.* Berkeley: University of California Press.

Hossfeld, Karen. 1990. "Their logic against them: Contradictions in sex, race, and class in Silicon Valley." In *Women Workers and Global Restructuring,* edited by Kathryn Ward. Ithaca, NY: ILR.

Howe, Wayne I. 1986. "Temporary help workers: Who they are, what jobs they hold?" *Monthly Labor Review* 109 (November): 45–7.

Lorber, Judith. 1994. *Paradoxes of Gender.* New Haven, CT: Yale University Press.

MacKinnon, Catharine A. 1979. *Sexual Harassment of Working Women: A Case of Sex Discrimination.* New Haven and London: Yale University Press.

——1987. *Feminism Unmodified: Discourses on Life and Law.* Cambridge, MA: Harvard University Press.

Martella, Maureen. 1991. *Just a Temp: Expectations and Experiences of Women Clerical Temporary Workers.* Washington, DC: U.S. Department of Labor Women's Bureau.

Maypole, D. 1986. "Sexual harassment of social workers at work: Injustice within?" *Social Work* 31 (1):29–34.

National Association of Temporary Services. 1992. *Report on the Temporary Help Services Industry.* Alexandria, VA: DRI/McGraw Hill.

National Association of Working Women. 1986. *Working at the Margins: Part-Time and Temporary Workers in the United States.* Cleveland, OH: National Association of Working Women.

Parker, Robert E. 1994. *Flesh Peddlers and Warm Bodies: The Temporary Help Industry and its Workers.* New Brunswick, NJ: Rutgers University Press.

Paules, Greta Foff. 1991. *Dishing it Out: Power and Resistance Among Waitresses in a New Jersey Restaurant.* Philadelphia: Temple University Press.

Pierce, Jennifer. 1995. *Gender Trials: Emotional Lives in Contemporary Law Firms.* Berkeley: University of California Press.

Pringle, Rosemary. 1988. *Secretaries Talk: Sexuality, Power, and Work.* New York: Verso.

Ragins, Belle Rose, and Teri A. Scandura. 1995. "Antecedents and work-related correlates of reported sexual harassment: An empirical investigation of competing hypotheses." *Sex Roles* 718:429–55.

Right Temporaries, Inc. 1989. Welcome to Right Temporaries, Inc. Organizational brochure. Chicago.

Rogers, Jackie Krasas. 1995a. It's only temporary?: The reproduction of race and gender inequality in temporary clerical employment. Ph.D. diss., University of Southern California, Los Angeles.

——. 1995b. "Just a temp: Experience and structure of alienation in temporary clerical employment." *Work and Occupations* 2:137–66.

——. Forthcoming. "Deskilled and devalued: Changes in the labor process in temporary clerical work." In *Rethinking the Labor Process,* edited by M. Wardell, P. Meiksins, and T. Steiger. Albany: State University of New York Press.

Schneider, Beth E. 1982. "Consciousness about sexual harassment among heterosexual and lesbian women workers." *Journal of Social Issues* 38(4): 75–98.

——. 1985. "Approaches, assaults, attractions, affairs: Policy implications of the sexualization of the workplace." *Population Research and Policy Review* 4:93–113.

——. 1991. "Put up and shut up: Workplace sexual assaults." *Gender & Society* 5:533–48.

Segal, Lynne. 1990. *Slow Motion: Changing Men, Changing Masculinities.* New Brunswick, NJ: Rutgers University Press.

West, Candace, and Sarah Fensternlaker. 1995. "Doing Difference." *Gender & Society* 1:8–37.

West, Candace, and Don H. Zimmennan. 1987. "Doing Gender." *Gender & Society* 1:125–51.

West, Jackie. 1990. "Gender and the labor process." In *Labor Process Theory,* edited by D.

Knights and H. Willrnott. London; Macmillan.

Williams, Christine. 1989. *Gender Differences at Work: Women and Men in Nontraditional Occupations.* Berkeley: University of California Press.

——. 1995. *Still a Man's World: Men Who Do Women's Work.* Berkeley: University of California Press.

Food for Thought and Application Questions

1. List the characteristics of temporary jobs that make women who work in these jobs vulnerable to sexual harassment. How does this information challenge the argument that sexual harassment is the result of "sex-role spillover"? What are the assumptions about the cause or source of harassing behavior that the "sex-role spillover" position makes? How does this differ from the authors' approach?

2. Rogers and Henson argue that temporary agencies have a role in perpetuating the practice of harassment that temporary workers face. Why is this so? Assume you wanted to develop a policy (or policies) that would be directed toward reducing the incidence of harassment of temporary workers. What policy (or policies) would you suggest? Why? Explain how each policy you suggest responds to changing one of the aggravating conditions that leads to harassment. ✦

25

The Managed Hand

The Commercialization of Bodies and Emotions in Korean Immigrant-Owned Nail Salons

Miliann Kang

The title of Hochschild's (1983) ground-breaking study of emotional labor, *The Managed Heart,* provides a rich metaphor for the control and commercialization of human feeling in service interactions. The title of this article, "The Managed Hand," plays on Hochschild's to capture the commercialization of both human feelings and bodies and to introduce the concept of body labor, the provision of body-related services and the management of feelings that accompanies it. By focusing on the case study of Korean immigrant manicurists and their relations with racially and socioeconomically diverse female customers in New York City nail salons, I broaden the study of emotional labor to illuminate its neglected embodied dimensions and to examine the intersections of gender, race, and class in its performance.

The past decade has witnessed a turn toward "Bringing Bodies Back In" (Frank 1990) to theory and research in sociology and feminist scholarship. What can be gained by "bringing the body back in" to the study of emotional labor and, more broadly, of gendered work? What are the dimensions of body labor, and what factors explain the variation in the quality and quantity of its performance? An embodied perspective on gendered work highlights the feminization of the body-related service sector and the proliferation of intricate practices of enhancing the appearance of the female body. A race, gender, and class perspective highlights the increasing role of working-class immigrant women in filling body-related service jobs and the racialized meanings that shape the processes of emotional management among service workers.

This study compares nail salons in three racially and socioeconomically diverse settings, employing participant observation and in-depth interviews ($N = 62$) in the tradition of feminist ethnography and the extended case method. After providing a brief overview of the case study of Korean-owned nail salons in New York City, the data presentation maps out the physical and emotional dimensions of body labor in three different nail salons and explains patterns of variation according to the race and class of the clientele and neighborhood.

In addition to contributing original empirical research on Korean immigrant women's work in the new and expanding niches of body service work, this article broadens the scholarship on emotional labor by addressing its performance by racial-ethnic and immigrant women in the global service economy. It demonstrates how the gendered processes of physical and emotional labor in nail salon work are seeped with race and class meanings that reinforce broader structures of inequality and ideologies of difference between women.

Theoretical Framework

Emotional Labor in Body Service Work: Race, Gender, and Class Intersections

Work on the body requires not only physical labor but extensive emotional management, or what Hochschild's (1983) seminal work describes as emotional labor. The concept of body labor makes two important contributions to the study of emotional labor: (1) It explores the embodied dimensions of emotional labor and (2) it investigates the intersections of race, gender, and class in shaping its performance. By bringing together an embodied analysis of emotional labor with an integrative race, gender, and class perspective, I show how this case study of nail salon work retheorizes emotional labor to have greater applicability to gendered occupations dominated by racialized immigrant women.

Building on Hochschild's (1983) work, studies of emotional labor have illuminated the increasing prevalence of emotional management in specific occupations and industries, the gendered composition of the emotional labor force, wage discrimination, burnout, and other occupational health issues (Hall 1993; Leidner 1999; Lively 2000; Wharton 1999). Steinberg and Figart (1999) provide a comprehensive overview of the field that examines both qualitative case studies of the contours of emotional labor in specific work sites and quantitative investigations of its prevalence and its impact on job satisfaction and compensation. Despite the many dimensions of emotional labor that have been addressed by feminist scholars, the body-related contours of emotional labor as it is manifested in low-wage service work dominated by racial-ethnic women, particularly in the beauty industry, have yet to be examined in depth....

In addition to neglecting emotional work in body service jobs, the literature on emotional labor has framed the processes of interactive service work primarily through a gender lens and paid less attention to the crosscutting influences of gender, race, and class. Russsell Hochschild's original case study of flight attendants and subsequent applications to other female-dominated occupations have emphasized the gendered employment experiences of native-born white women as paralegals (Pierce 1995), nannies and au pairs (Macdonald 1996), fast food and insurance sales workers (Leidner 1993), and police officers (Schmitt and Yancey Martin 1999). My research expands this work not only in its empirical focus on immigrant women of color doing gendered, emotional labor but through the theoretical framework of race, gender, and class as "interactive systems" and "interlocking categories of experience" (Anderson and Hill Collins 2001, xii). This framework critiques additive models that append race and class to the experiences of white middle-class women and instead highlights the simultaneity and reciprocity of race, gender, and class in patterns of social relations and in the lives of individuals (Baca Zinn 1989; Hill Collins 1991; hooks 1981; Hurtado 1989; Nakano Glenn 1992; Ngan-Ling Chow 1994). Thus, I demonstrate that different expectations or "feeling

rules" (Hochschild 1983, x) shape the performance of emotional labor by women according to the racial and class context.

Drawing from Hochschild's (1983) definition of emotional labor, I incorporate this intersectional analysis to define important parallels and distinctions between the concepts of body labor and emotional labor. First, Hochschild's definition of emotional labor focuses on a particular form that "requires one to induce or suppress feeling in order to sustain the outward countenance that produces the proper state of mind in others—in this case, the sense of being cared for in a convivial and safe place" (1983, 7). While Hochschild develops this definition in reference to the specific case of flight attendants and the feeling rules that govern their work, this kind of caring, attentive service has become a widely generalized definition, rather than being regarded as one particular form of emotional labor performed by mostly white, middle-class women largely for the benefit of white, middle- and upperclass men. Korean-owned nail salons thus serve as a contrasting site to explore other forms of emotional labor that emerge in work sites that are differently gendered, differently racialized, and differently classed. The patterns of emotional labor described in this study can illuminate similar sites in which emotional labor involves women serving women (as opposed to mainly women serving men), and is not necessarily governed by the social feeling rules of white, middle-class America.

Furthermore, while Hochschild and other scholars of emotional labor have examined certain embodied aspects of emotional labor concerned with gendered bodily display, ranging from control of weight to smiles, this study highlights emotional management regarding bodily contact in service interactions. The dynamics of extended physical contact between women of different racial and class positions complicate and intensify the gendered performance of emotional labor. Body labor not only demands that the service worker present and comport her body in an appropriate fashion but also that she induces customers' positive feelings about their own bodies. This is a highly complicated enterprise in a culture that sets unattainable standards for female beauty and pathologizes intimate, nurturing physical contact between women, while it normalizes unequal relations in the exchange of body services.

By investigating the understudied area of body-related service occupations through an intersectional race, gender, and class analysis, this study of body labor reformulates the concept of emotional labor to dramatize howthe feeling rules governing its exchange are shaped by interlocking oppressions that operate at the macro level (Hill Collins 1991) and then emerge as different styles of emotional service at the micro level.

Background for the Study

In this section, I provide context for my study by describing nail salons as a niche for Korean immigrant women's work and discussing the dynamics of race and ethnicity in its development. As one of the few arenas in which immigrant and nativeborn women encounter each other in regular, sustained, physical contact, Korean immigrant women–owned nail salons in New York City illuminate the complex performance and production of race, gender, and class as they are constructed in feminized work sites in the global service economy. Since the early 1980s, Korean women in New York City have pioneered this new ethnic niche with more than 2,000 Korean-owned nail salons throughout the metropolitan area, or approximately 70 percent of the total, as estimated by the Korean American Nail Association of New York. Each salon employs an average of five workers, suggesting an occupational niche of roughly 10,000 women. While the New York State licensing bureau does not keep track of nail salon licenses by ethnic group, their figures reveal an overall 41-percent growth in the nail industry (from 7,562 licensed nail technicians in 1996 to 10,684 in 2000) in New York City, Westchester County, and Nassau County. These numbers undercount a sizable number of women who do not possess licenses or legal working status.

While concentrating on Korean immigrant women, this study examines both race and ethnicity as salient categories of analysis. I designate the salon owners and workers according to ethnicity, but I recognize shared racial positions that push not only Korean but also other Asian immigrant women into this niche. For example, in New York, there is a significant presence of Chinese- and Vietnamese- as well as Korean-owned nail salons, and on the West Coast, the niche is almost solely dominated by Vietnamese women (*www.nailsmag.com*). Common factors such as limited English-language ability, unrecognized professional credentials from their countries of origin, undocumented immigration status, and coethnic resources in the form of labor, start-up capital, and social networks explain why Asian immigrant women of various ethnic groups cluster in the nail salon industry. Similarities across Asian ethnic groups include not only the human capital of the women themselves but also the conditions of the labor market and the U.S. racial hierarchy that they encounter. Through their shared race, gender, and class locations, Asian women have been coveted as productive and docile workers, whose "nimble fingers" (Ong 1987) make them desirable and exploitable in an increasingly feminized, impoverished, and unprotected labor force (Cheng and Bonacich 1984; Hu-DeHart 1999). Racialized perceptions of Asian women as skilled in detailed handiwork and massage further contribute to customers' preference for their manicuring services, as evidenced by the fact that many customers racially identify the salons as owned by Asians or "Orientals," as opposed to by specific ethnic group.

In sum, because it would be methodologically unsound to generalize findings based on a limited sample of Korean women to include all Asian immigrant women in the nail industry, this study maintains ethnicity as the significant category for describing the workers and owners but frames differences between the customers and variation in service interactions according to race. Thus, I discuss the different dimensions of Korean-immigrant women's performance of body labor through the integrative lens of race, gender, and class rather than a more specific focus on Korean ethnicity.[1]

Research Design and Method

This study situates itself within feminist methodology and epistemology by beginning from the standpoint of women to investigate the "relations of ruling" in contemporary capitalist society (Smith 1987). At the same time, it does not privilege gender as the only or the most important framework for defining and investigating differences and aims instead for an understanding of race, gender, and class as crosscutting forces. By examining contrasting patterns of body labor between women of different racial and class backgrounds, this study reconstructs theories of emotional labor by addressing its embodied dimensions and the simultaneous influence of gender, race, and class on its performance. In doing so, it follows the extended case method of making critical interventions in existing theory by explaining anomalies between similar phenomena, rather than seeking generalizations toward the discovery of new theory, as in the contrasting approach of grounded theory. According to Burawoy (1991, 281), the primary architect of the extended case method, "The importance of the single case lies in what it tells us about society as a whole rather than about the population of similar cases." Thus, my study examines cases of specific nail salons, not to formulate generalizations about all similar nail salons but instead to explain how social forces influence variation in the service interactions at these sites.

The data collection for this project involved 14 months of fieldwork in New York City nail salons. The research design included in-depth interviews (N = 62) and participant observation at three sites: (1) "Uptown Nails," located in a predominantly white, middle- and upper-class commercial area; (2) "Downtown Nails," located in a predominantly Black (African American and Caribbean) working- and lower-middle-class commercial neighborhood; and (3) "Crosstown Nails," located in a racially mixed lower-middle and middle-class residential and commercial area. I spent at least 50 hours at each salon over the course of several months. In the case of Crosstown Nails, which was located near my home, visits were shorter (2 to 3 hours) and more frequent (several times a week). The other two salons required long commutes, so I usually visited once a week for 6 to 7 hours.

In addition to hundreds of unstructured conversational interviews conducted as a participant-observer, the research included in-depth structured interviews with 10 Korean nail salon owners, 10 Korean nail salon workers, 15 Black customers, and 15 white customers. The customers interviewed at each salon are as follows. Uptown Nails included a lawyer, professor, pharmacist, flight attendant, secretary, personal trainer, accessories importer, homemaker (formerly a computer programmer), fashion designer, and real estate broker. Customers interviewed at Downtown Nails included a package clerk, student/waitress, student/mother, grocery cashier, ambulatory service driver, county government administrative assistant, laboratory technician, nanny, therapist, and elementary school principal. At Crosstown Nails, I interviewed 10 customers (five white, five Black). The white customers included a bartender, high school teacher, hairdresser, homemaker, and retired insurance bookkeeper. The Black customers included a clinical researcher, theater technician/musician, management consultant, homemaker, and student.

In-depth interviews averaged 45 minutes for customers and two hours for owners and workers. Customers were interviewed in English at the salon while they were having their manicures, and when necessary, a follow-up meeting or telephone interview was arranged. Owners and workers were interviewed in both Korean and English, depending on their preference and level of fluency. Bilingual research assistants helped with translation, transcription, and follow-up interviews. I tape-recorded interviews in which consent was given, but in cases in which respondents refused, I took extensive handwritten notes that I typed immediately afterward. Both customers and service providers are referred to by pseudonyms that approximate the names they use in the salons. This convention captures the naturalistic setting where even coworkers commonly refer to each other by the "American name" that they employ at work. I have added a surname to citations and descriptions of owners and workers to differentiate customers from service providers. . . .

Findings

The Contours of Body Labor

Body labor involves the exchange of body-related services for a wage and the performance of physical and emotional labor in this exchange. My study's findings illustrate three dimensions of body labor: (1) the physical labor of attending to the bodily appearance and pleasure of customers, (2) the emotional labor of managing feelings to display certain feeling states and to create and respond to customers' feelings regarding the servicing of their bodies, and (3) variation in the performance of body labor as explained through the intersection of gender with race and class. These dimensions vary across the different research sites and emerge as three distinct patterns of body labor provision: (1) high-service body labor involving physical pampering and emotional attentiveness serving mostly middle- and upper-class white female customers, (2) expressive body labor involving artistry in technical skills and communication of respect and fairness when serving mostly working- and lower-middle-class African American and Caribbean female customers, and (3) routinized body labor involving efficient, competent physical labor and courteous but minimal emotional labor when serving mostly lower-middle and middle-class racially mixed female customers. The data presentation admittedly flattens some of the variation within each site to clarify distinctions between them, but this typology highlights the dominant physical and emotional style of service at each salon.

Uptown Nails: High-Service Body Labor

A seasoned Korean manicurist who has worked at Uptown Nails for nearly 10 years, Esther Lee is in high demand for her relaxing and invigorating hand massages. She energetically kneads, strokes, and pushes pressure points, finishing off the massage by holding each of the customer's hands between her own and alternately rubbing, slapping, and gently pounding them with the flare that has wooed many a customer into a regular nail

salon habit. Margie, a white single woman in her mid-30s who works for an accounting firm, smiles appreciatively and squeezes Esther's hand: "I swear, I couldn't stay in my job without this!" Esther reciprocates a warm, somewhat shy smile.

Uptown Nails boasts leafy green plants, glossy framed pictures of white fashion models showing off well-manicured hands, recent fashion magazine subscriptions stacked neatly on a coffee table, and classical CDs on the stereo system. The salon has been in operation for 13 years, and three of the six employees have worked there for more than 10 years. The customers sit quietly sipping their cappuccinos, updating their appointment books, or at times politely conversing with each other about the weather or the color of the nail polish they are wearing. Located in a prosperous business district of Manhattan, an Uptown Nails manicuring experience involves not only the filing and polishing of nails but attention to the customer's physical and emotional comfort. From the gentle removal of undernail dirt, to the careful trimming of cuticles and buffing of calluses, to the massaging of hands and feet, Korean manicurists literally rub up against their customers, who are mostly white middle- and upper-class women. The owner, one of the earliest pioneers in the nail salon industry, currently operates six very profitable salons in prime Manhattan locations and visits this salon only once a week to take care of paperwork. The owner, manager, and employees are all middle-aged Korean women with fluent English language ability, reflecting the greater expectations for communications with customers. The physical dimensions of body labor in Uptown Nails, including hot cotton towels, bowls of warm soaking solution, sanitized utensils, and calming background music, all indicate considerable attention to creating a pleasurable sensory experience for the customer. Particular attention is given to avoiding nicks and cuts and sterilizing and apologizing profusely when they occur.

In addition to this extensive physical pampering, Uptown Nails prioritizes the emotional needs of customers regarding the servicing of their bodies. The mostly white middle-class customers at this salon place great importance on emotional attentiveness as a crucial component of the service interaction. Kathy, a personal trainer, elaborated,

> Having them done is a pleasure, a luxury. Doing them myself is tedious, having them done is a treat. It's the whole idea of going and having something nice done for myself. If I do them myself, it's just routine upkeep of my body—like washing your hair or keeping your clothes clean. . . . Of course it makes it more enjoyable if they are friendly and can talk to you. If they can't remember my name that's okay, but I think they should recognize me.

The proper performance of body labor thus transforms a hygienic process, otherwise equated with washing hair or clothes, into a richly rewarding physical and emotional experience. The satisfaction Kathy experiences from the manicure derives not only from the appearance of the nails but the feeling of being special that accompanies attentive body servicing. To generate this feeling, customers expect the manicurist to display a caring demeanor and engage in pleasant one-on-one conversation with them.

Service providers recognize customers' high expectations with regard to both the physical and emotional dimensions of body labor, and they respond accordingly. Judy Cha, a 34-year-old who immigrated in 1993, describes the emotional and physical stressors that accompany high-service body labor, particularly giving massages to earn tips and engaging in conversation.

> Three years ago we didn't give a lot of massages but now customers ask more and more. It makes me weak and really tired. . . . I guess because I don't have the right training to do it in a way that doesn't tire my body. Some manicurists give massage all the time to get tips, but sometimes I don't even ask them if I'm tired. Owners keep asking you to ask them, but on days I'm not feeling well, I don't ask. . . . One of my biggest fears working in the salon is, what if I don't understand what the customer is saying? They don't really talk in detail, just say, "how is the weather." But in order to have a deeper relationship, I need to get past that and to improve my English. It makes it very stressful.

Thus, manicurists work hard to conform to the high service expectations of middle-class white women, but while the performance of caring, attentive emotional labor is noticeably higher than that afforded in the other research sites, it often does not meet customers' expectations. In particular, many Uptown Nails customers disapprove of the use of Korean language by the manicurists as a violation of proper attentiveness in beauty service transactions and suspect that they are being talked about (Kang 1997).

Cathy Hong, a 32-year-old manicurist who immigrated in 1999, sums up the assumptions many of the Uptown Nails customers have regarding access to a regular manicure delivered with high-service body labor: "These women get their nails done regularly because it has become a habit to them, they take if for granted. Just as we wash our face daily, American women get their nails done."

Downtown Nails: Expressive Body Labor

Entering another borough, the scene inside Downtown Nails differs as radically as the neighborhoods in which these two salons are located. Squeezed between a Caribbean bakery and a discount clothing store, a worn-out signboard displays the single word "NAILS" and a painting of a graceful, well-manicured hand holding a long-stemmed rose and pointing to a staircase leading to the second-story entrance. Upon being buzzed in through the locked door, the customer is greeted with a display of hundreds of brightly colored airbrushed nail tips lining an entire wall. The noise level in the salon is high, as various electronic nail-sculpting tools create a constant buzz to match the flow of the lively conversations among the mostly Black customers. On a weekend afternoon, Downtown Nails is filled to capacity, and the wait for a preferred "nail artist" can be more than an hour. Mostly Caribbean and African American women, the customers engage in animated conversations while sharing coco buns and currant rolls from the downstairs bakery. The banter ranges from vivid accounts of a recent mugging near the salon to news about the pay freeze in the nearby hospital where many of the women work as nurses or technicians.

A far cry from the spa-like pampering experience of Uptown Nails, a nail job at Downtown Nails is closer to a stint on a factory assembly line: highly mechanized and potentially toxic. Absent are the elaborate sanitizing machines and solutions, let alone the soft pampering touches. Despite these appearances, body labor at Downtown Nails involves a complex mix of physical and emotional labor that accommodates customers' desires to express a unique sense of self through their nail designs and their expectations that service providers demonstrate both individual respect and appreciation to the community.

The manicurists, or nail artists, provide less of the traditional, attentive style of emotional labor but focus their emotional management on communicating a sense of respect and fairness. These women tend to be more recent immigrants from more working-class backgrounds with less English-language fluency and are more likely to be working without legal immigration status or licenses. The owners, Mr. and Mrs. Lee, are a married couple, both formerly school teachers, who immigrated in 1981 to pursue better educational opportunities for their children. Two years after their arrival, they opened a salon in this location because the rent was affordable, the customer base was strong, and they reside in a nearby neighborhood. The customers at Downtown Nails span a broad range in socioeconomic status but most are working to lower-middle class.

The importance of the physical appearance of the nails themselves as opposed to the pampering experience of receiving these services is dramatized by customers' concern with the design of the nails versus the massage and other services that customers at Uptown Nails regard as integral and Downtown Nails customers view as extraneous. Jamilla, a 26-year-old African American part-time student and waitress, proudly displays her inch-and-a-half-long nails, each one adorned with the skyline of New York City in bold black, framed by an orange and yellow sunset. A regular patron of Downtown Nails for six years, she explains why she is willing to spend "$50–$60 every two weeks" for elaborate hand-painted designs:

> Because I don't like looking like anyone else. My nails say "me." They're the first thing people notice about me. I have big hands for a female. I never had those long, thin ladylike fingers. My father used to say my hands were bigger than his. I want long nails because they make my hands look more feminine.

Indicating a preference for nails that reflect very different norms of femininity than the demure, pastel tones prevalent at Uptown Nails, Jamilla elaborates further on her nail aesthetics. "It all depends on my mood. Like this design makes me feel like I'm on top of the city, like it can't bring me down [laughing]. . . . No one's gonna mess with you when you got nails like these." Jamilla's pride in having originally designed nails that no one else can reproduce suggests the importance of her nails as an expression of her individuality that also communicate a sense of self-efficacy and protection, as indicated in her comments that no one would "mess" with a woman with nails like hers. To meet the expectations of customers such as Jamilla, body labor at Downtown Nails calls for development of expertise in sculpting and painting original nail designs rather than in the soothing, pampering services offered at Uptown Nails. Thus, the physical demands of body labor are not less but simply of a different type.

Similarly, the emotional dimensions of body labor at Downtown Nails are not different in degree so much as kind. The customer's race and class location intersect to produce much lower expectations among working-class Black customers for emotional attentiveness than the white middle-class women at Uptown Nails. While it is clearly less attentive, Serena, an African American grocery store cashier, assesses the emotional labor at Downtown Nails positively.

> It's very good, I'm satisfied with it. They really just do the nails, no massages. That's fine with me. I just go in with my Walkman and listen to some good music and maybe just have a little basic conversation.

Customers at Downtown Nails rarely are on a first-name basis with the service providers, and their preference for a particular manicurist is based much more on her technical skills than her emotional attentiveness. Serena elaborated,

> There are a few people I like and I go to whoever's open, but I'll stay away from certain people. I know they're not good cause I hear other people complain—I see someone come back and say that their nail cracked the next day, or I see someone get nicked with a filer. . . . No, it's not because they're rude or anything, it's because I know they don't do a good job. . . . Just like some people just can't do hair, some people just can't do nails.

> [Regarding relations with her current manicurist] I feel comfortable with her, but it's more that she does an excellent job. If a wrap cracks or looks funny or I lose a nail, I'm not going back to her no matter how nice she is.

While many working-class Black customers like Serena give little importance to a caring, attentive emotional display, they demand another style of emotional labor.

Emotional labor at Downtown Nails calls less for sensitivity to pampering of individual customers and more for demonstration of values of respect and fairness that recognize the complex dynamics of Korean businesses operating in Black neighborhoods. This includes efforts such as sponsoring a Christmas party to thank customers for their patronage, participating in community events, displaying Afrocentric designs, and playing R&B and rap music. Mrs. Lee, the co-owner of the salon, allows regulars to run an informal tab when they are short of money and keeps a change jar that customers dip into for bus fare, telephone calls, or other incidentals. It is not uncommon for customers to drop by even when they are not getting their nails done to use the bathroom or leave shopping bags behind the front desk while they complete errands. These efforts at "giving back to the community" entail a distinct form of emotional labor that conforms not to white middle-class women's feeling rules of privilege and pampering but to Black working-class women's concerns about being treated with respect and fairness.

Jamilla described the importance of a sense of fairness and respect to Black customers and how this demands a particular form of emotional labor from Korean manicurists.

> It's kind of a Catch-22. Some customers feel like they're getting disrespected if you don't refer back to them or if you're having a side conversation. Then the Koreans get upset and think African Americans have an attitude, which then makes them talk more about us. You see, in the African American community, you can't outright say anything you want to say because we always have our guard up. We get it all the time, from the cops or whoever. I've seen it in the Hispanic community too—this thing about honor and respect. "Don't disrespect me just because I'm Black or Hispanic. What I say does count."

Thus, while the caring, pampering style of service is virtually absent at Downtown Nails, another form of emotional labor is necessary to negotiate and avoid conflicts with customers that can quickly become racialized into heated confrontations (Lee 2002). Serena described a scene at another salon that illustrates how the failure to perform appropriately respectful emotional labor can quickly erupt into shouting matches that take on racialized and anti-immigrant overtones: "I've seen some customers really go off on them, 'You're not in your country, speak English.'" Her comments underscore how the race and class of the neighborhood complicate the processes of emotional management inside the salons.

Although disagreements between Downtown Nails' customers and workers do arise, at times resulting in heated exchanges, the relations in the salon are congenial overall, as the expressive style of emotional labor enables customers and service providers to voice and, for the most part, "work out" their differences. Mrs. Lee explained that she prefers serving Black customers for this reason and actually moved back to working in a low-income Black neighborhood after working for a period in Long Island.

> Working in the white neighborhood didn't match my personality. I don't deal well with picky customers. . . . In the Black neighborhood, it's more relaxed. They don't leave tips but they don't expect so much service either. . . . [In Long Island] they want you to go slow and spend time

with them. Here I just concentrate on doing a good job and working quickly.

Service providers invest less energy in displaying and creating convivial feeling states, which in some cases allows for a genuine affinity with Black customers and less of a sense of burnout from the effort involved in the manufacture of falsely convivial feelings.

Expressive body labor thus prioritizes both the meanings of the nails as a form of self-expression to working-class Black customers and the expression of symbolic but tangible efforts to respond to the feeling rules of respect and fairness governing Korean immigrant service providers in predominantly Black working-class neighborhoods.

Crosstown Nails: Routinized Body Labor

Located on the second floor above a fashionable boutique, Crosstown Nails is clean but sparse and utilitarian. In many ways, this salon is representative of the most prevalent style of service offered in Korean-owned nail salons: fast, cheap, basic manicures and pedicures with no frills. The McDonald's of the nail salon industry, Crosstown Nails offers a manicure that is standardized and predictable in both its physical and emotional aspects.

This salon often has customers waiting, but even when it is busy, the line moves quickly as each customer is whisked in and out of the manicuring seat with crisp efficiency. The customer chooses her nail color, presents it to the manicurist who asks her to specify the desired shape of the nail, and then soaks her nails briefly in a softening solution. Depending on her preference, her nails are either trimmed or pushed back. The manicurist offers to give a massage, but it is perfunctory and lasts usually not more than a minute. After carefully layering on two coats of polish and a quick-drying topcoat, the customer moves to a heated hand dryer where she converses with other customers or more often "zones out."

Many customers come from the neighboring hospital during lunch hour or after work. Situated on the edge of a fashionable, high-rent, racially diverse residential district and a lower-income but also racially mixed neighborhood, Crosstown Nails captures the broad range of customer interactions that many Korean service providers negotiate in a given day. In large, high-immigrant-receiving cities such as New York, service interactions often involve multiracial rather than binary interactions between Korean and Blacks or Koreans and whites.

Susan Lee, age 39, founded Crosstown Nails in 1989 and is the sole owner. Divorced with one son, age 10, she emigrated in 1982 from Seoul with her husband, a graduate student. She graduated college with a degree in tourism and worked as a travel agent in Korea. In New York City, she first worked in a retail store in Manhattan, then began to work in a nail salon in Brooklyn to support her husband while he studied. After their marriage ended, she brought her mother from Korea in 1988 and with her help opened a convenience store, which failed shortly thereafter. She then opened Crosstown Nails a year later, and the business has thrived.

The secret of Crosstown Nail's success is its ability to appeal to customers who lack excess disposable income and normally would not indulge in a professional manicure but are attracted by the convenience and price. Julia, a white bartender, commented,

> I'm kind of a ragamuffin, so it kind of surprises me that I get them done as often as I do, which is still much less than most people in the city. It's just so easy to do here, and cheap.

Julia's description of herself as a "ragamuffin" suggests that she does not adhere to strict codes of femininity in her dress or other beauty routines, as indicated by her casual peasant skirt and no makeup. Nonetheless, easy and cheap access draws her into purchasing regular manicures.

Many customers at Crosstown Nails seek manicures not as a pampering experience or as creative expression but as a utilitarian measure to enhance their self presentation at work. Merna, an Afro-Caribbean clinical researcher, explained,

> I only get them done about every two months. I don't want to get attached to it. For some women it's such a ritual, it becomes a job—maintaining the tips and stuff. I'm presenting my hands all day long

so it's worth it to me to spend some time and money to make sure they look good.

Merna regards manicured nails as a professional asset more than a core aspect of a gendered self. Thus, the style of her nails and the meaning she gives to them is more similar to the white middle-class customers at Crosstown Nails than to the Black working-class customers at Downtown Nails.

In general, middle-class Black customers like Merna mostly exhibited similar nail aesthetics to those of middle-class white women, suggesting the greater importance of class over race in influencing nail styles and expectations of body labor, particularly in routinized settings such as Crosstown Nails.

Discussion

The concept of emotional labor addresses how service providers present and manipulate their feelings to communicate a sense of caring and attentiveness to customers, or in Hochschild's (1983, 6) words, where "the emotional style of offering service is part of the service itself." This study of interactions in Korean-owned nail salons enriches the literature on emotional labor by expanding it to include embodied dimensions, or body labor. The embodied aspects of emotional labor not only heighten the intensity of commercialized feeling exchanges but they also point out variation in these exchanges beyond the white middle-class settings explored by most researchers. Nail salon services, and body labor more generally, are gendered work processes, but they are enacted in different forms according to the influences of race and class.

In what ways is nail salon work gendered? In what ways are these gendered work processes remolded by race and class? Understanding the influence of race and class on the gendered performance of body labor in Korean-owned nail salons illuminates how gendered work processes reflect and reproduce racial and class inequalities at the level of social structures. Nail salon work is gendered in four major dimensions: (1) It involves mostly female actors, as both service providers and customers; (2) it focuses on the construction of beauty according to feminine norms; (3) it is situated in feminized,

semiprivate spaces; and (4) it involves the gendered performance of emotional labor.

In describing each of these dimensions, I do not emphasize how socialized gender roles are acted out in these establishments, but rather how gender operates as a social institution that lays the groundwork for the very existence of these businesses and frames the interactions that occur within them. Thus, I conceptualize these small businesses according to the model of gendered institutions (Marx Ferree and Hall 1996) and examine how they are constructed from the ground up through gendered ideologies, relations, and practices that sustain systematic gender inequality at the micro level of sex differences, at the meso level of group conflict, and the macro levels of power, social control, and the division of labor. At the same time, I argue that as gendered institutions, they cannot be separated from forces of racial and class inequality.

If, as Paul Gilroy (1993, 85) asserted, "gender is the modality in which race is lived," then race, and I argue class as well, are lived in these nail salons and other body-service sites as differences in gendered styles of body labor. Interactions in Korean female immigrant-owned nail salons illustrate how the gendered practices of body labor become the locus of expressing and negotiating race and class hierarchies between white, Black, and Asian women. High-service body labor, as performed at Uptown Nails, is similar to the style of caring, attentive emotional labor practiced by Hochschild's flight attendants and conforms to the feeling rules of white middle-class women. Expressive body labor focuses on the physical appearance and artistry of the nails and the communication of respect and fairness in serving mostly working- and lower-middle-class African American and Caribbean women customers at Downtown Nails. Routinized body labor stresses efficiency, predictability, affordability, and competency in physical labor and a courteous but no-frills style of emotional labor geared toward mostly lower-middle- and middle-class racially mixed female customers at Crosstown Nails.

These patterns of body labor conform to the racial and class positions of the customers and the associated feeling rules that define their service expectations. At Uptown Nails, race, gender, and class intersect to produce an emotionally and physically pampering form of body labor that conforms to the expectations of white, professional women for caring and attentive service. These women have high expectations regarding massages, cleanliness, sensitive touch, and friendly conversation while Black, working-class women at Downtown Nails expect minimal pampering and focus on the appearance, originality, and durability of the nails themselves. At Crosstown Nails, class prevails over race as both Black and white women of middling socioeconomic status view the nails instrumentally as a no-nonsense professional asset rather than conforming to traditional notions of pampered femininity. Thus, they trade off the physical pleasure and emotional attentiveness of high-service treatment for the convenience and price of routinized body labor.

Black middle-class women at Crosstown Nails share this instrumental view of nails and a preference for a routinized, hassle-free manicure. The style of nails and the meaning given to them by Black middle-class women radically differ from the working-class Black women at Downtown Nails, who value nail art as a form of self-expression and demand emotional labor that communicates respect and fairness. This contrast between the Black middle-class and working-class women customers at Crosstown and Downtown Nails again suggests the greater salience of class over race in determining the type of body labor.

What structural factors explain the differences in the provision of body labor in these three sites? These body labor types, while enacted at the micro level, reflect the social conditions of the neighborhoods in which the salons are located and the clientele they serve. Because of the reliance on tips in white middle-class neighborhoods, service providers have greater incentive to cater to the emotional needs of customers such as those at Uptown Nails to increase their earnings. In the Black working-class neighborhoods where tipping is not a widespread practice, nail salon workers guarantee their economic livelihood by establishing a base of regular customers who seek them out for their technical and artistic abilities more than their emo-

tional or physical attentiveness. In routinized body labor settings serving lower-middle-class women of mixed races, service providers maximize their earnings by generating a high turnover of customers who receive satisfactory but not special emotional and physical treatment.

These patterns of body labor service reflect and reproduce racial and class inequalities between women. Korean service providers learn to respond to white middle- and upper-class customers' emotional pampering and physical pleasure, thereby reinforcing the invisible sense of privilege claimed by these customers. The expressive practices of creating artful nails and troubleshooting potential problems with Black working-class customers, while helping to smooth relations, can also serve to emphasize racial meanings in these interactions and enforce a sense of difference. The routinized style of body labor reflects the generic social position of women whose bodies are neither privileged nor pathologized but simply treated with routine efficiency.

Conclusions

Exchanges of manicuring services set up complex emotional and embodied interactions between diverse women. In introducing and exploring the dimensions of body labor, this article challenges the scholarship on emotional labor to take more seriously the growth in body-related service jobs and to address the differences in these service interactions not simply in terms of gendered processes but through the lens of race, gender, and class intersections. Thus, not only does the concept of body labor add embodied dimensions to emotional labor, but it also makes it more applicable to low-wage service work performed by immigrant women of color.

This study situates the practice of body labor in Korean-owned nail salons within the restructuring of the global economy and the transplantation of the practices of enhancing bodily appearance from private households into new forms of public urban space. A manicure is no longer something a woman gives herself, her daughter, or a girlfriend in the quiet of her own bathroom, but it is something that she increasingly purchases in a nail salon.

In purchasing these services, she not only expands the boundaries of the service economy to include formerly private regimens of personal hygiene, but she also encounters the "other," often an immigrant woman of different racial and class background through physical contact that can generate highly charged feelings on both sides. These feelings manifest and are worked out differently in distinct styles of body labor that emerge through the intersection of gendered work processes with customers' racial and class positions and their associated service expectations.

Although so far I have drawn parallels between this process of exchanging body services for a wage with the commercialization of feelings in emotional labor, another parallel can be drawn to the encroachment of the capitalist system into the area of social reproduction. Nakano Glenn (1992) and others have illuminated how the performance of household work such as cleaning, cooking, and caring for children and the elderly has become increasingly part of the capitalist market, and these low-paying, unprotected jobs (nanny, elderly caregiver, nurses, aide) are most often filled by immigrant women of color. This study has illustrated how similar to these dynamics of commodifying reproductive labor and farming it out at low wages to less privileged women, body services and the emotional labor accompanying it (what I have conceptualized as body labor) have become increasingly commercialized and designated as racialized immigrant women's work.

Additional dimensions of body labor that I will explore in further studies include (1) the impact of this work on the women who perform it and the ways they conform to or resist its pressures, (2) the role of managers in supervising body labor, (3) the variation between body labor in nonessential beauty services such as nail salon work versus the work of social reproduction, and, as previously mentioned, (4) the ethnic-specific dimensions of Korean-Black and Korean-white relations. While this article has concentrated on my case study of nail salons, the concept of body labor can be applied to many other occupations, especially female-dominated service professions in which service providers and customers are of different race and class origins, including hairdressers, masseuses, nannies, nurses, doctors, personal trainers, and prostitutes.

Finally, in mapping out the racial, gendered, and classed complexity of body labor, this article highlights a kernel of social change that lies in negotiating service interactions between women of different classes, racial and ethnic backgrounds, and immigrant statuses. While these interactions often mimic structures of power and privilege, they also create opportunities to contest these structures. The Korean salon owner of Downtown Nails learns to respect and show appreciation for Black working-class patrons. Korean manicurists at Uptown Nails assert their knowledge and expertise over their white middle-class customers. Routinized service at Crosstown Nails equalizes treatment of women across race and class.

From the customer's side, a weekly trip to the local nail salon can become a lesson in relating to a woman of a radically different social position, whom she would rarely encounter in her own milieu. As these emotional and embodied interactions reflect larger systems of status and power, by rewriting the unspoken feeling rules of these interactions, women can take small but important steps in the creation of more equal relations with other women. Nakano Glenn (2002, 16–17) wrote that "contesting race and gender hierarchies may involve challenging everyday assumptions and practices, take forms that do not involve direct confrontation, and occur in locations not considered political." Exchanges involving body labor in Korean-owned nail salons are one such location where these everyday assumptions and practices can be recognized and possibly renegotiated.

Note

1. I will examine the ethnic-specific dimensions of customer interactions in the historical context of Korean-Black relations more fully in a separate article.

References

Anderson, Margaret, and Patricia Hill Collins. 2001. *Race, class, and gender: An anthology.* Belmont, CA: Wadsworth.

Baca Zinn, Maxine. 1989. Family, race, and poverty in the eighties. *Signs: Journal of Women in Culture and Society* 14: 856–74.

Burawoy, Michael. 1991. *Ethnography unbound.* Berkeley: University of California Press.

Chapkis, Wendy. 1986. *Beauty secrets.* Boston: South End.

Cheng, Lucie, and Edna Bonacich. 1984. *Labor immigration under capitalism: Asian workers in the United States before World War 2.* Berkeley: University of California Press.

Frank, Arthur W. 1990. Bringing bodies back in: A decade review. *Theory, Culture, and Society* 7: 131–62.

Gilroy, Paul. 1993. *The Black Atlantic: Modernity and double consciousness.* Cambridge, MA: Harvard University Press.

Hall, Elaine J. 1993. Waitering/waitressing: Engendering the work of table servers. *Gender & Society* 7: 329–46.

Hill Collins, Patricia. 1991. *Black feminist thought: Knowledge, consciousness, and the politics of empowerment.* New York: Routledge.

Hochschild, Arlie. 1983. *The managed heart: The commercialization of human feeling.* Berkeley: University of California Press.

hooks, bell. 1981. *Ain't I a woman: Black women and feminism.* Boston: South End.

———. 1990. *Black looks: Race and representation.* Boston: South End.

Hu-DeHart, Evelyn. 1999. *Across the Pacific: Asian Americans and globalization.* Philadelphia: Temple University Press.

Hurtado, Aida. 1989. Relating to privilege: Seduction and rejection in the subordination of white women and women of color. *Signs: Journal of Women in Culture and Society* 14: 833–55.

Kand, Miliann. 1997. Manicuring race, gender, and class: Service interactions in New York City Korean nail salons. *Race, Gender, and Class,* 4: 143–64.

Lee, Jee-Young Jennifer. 2002. *Civility in the city: Blacks, Jews, and Koreans in urban America.* Cambridge, MA: Harvard University Press.

Leidner, Robin. 1993. *Fast food, fast talk: Service work and the routinization of everyday life.* Berkeley: University of California Press.

———. 1999. Emotional labor in servicework. *Annals of the American Academy of Political and Social Science* 561: 81–95.

Lively, Kathryn. 2000. Reciprocal emotion management:Working together to maintain stratification in private law firms. *Work and Occupations* 27: 32–63.

Macdonald, Cameron. 1996. Shadow mothers: Nannies, au pairs, and invisible work. In *Working*

in the service society, edited by Cameron Lynne Macdonald and Carmen Sirianni. Philadelphia: Temple University Press.

Marx Ferree, Myra, and Elaine J. Hall. 1996. Rethinking stratification from a feminist perspective: Gender, race, and class in mainstream textbooks. *American Sociological Review* 61: 929–50.

Nakano Glenn, Evelyn. 1992. From servitude to service work: Historical continuities in the racial division of paid reproductive labor. *Signs: Journal of Women in Culture and Society* 18: 1–43.

———. 2002. *Unequal freedom: How race and gender shaped American citizenship and labor.* Cambridge, MA: Harvard University Press.

Ngan-Ling Chow, Esther. 1994. Asian American women at work. In *Women of color in U.S. society,* edited by Maxine Baca Zinn and Bonnie Dill Thornton. Philadelphia: Temple University Press.

Ong, Aihwa. 1987. *Spirits of resistance and capitalist discipline: Factory women in Malaysia.* Albany: State University of New York Press.

Pierce, Jennifer L. 1995. *Gender trials: Emotional lives in contemporary law firms.* Berkeley: University of California Press.

Schmitt, Frederika E., and Patricia Yancey Martin. 1999. Unobtrusive mobilization by an institutionalized rape crisis center: "All we do comes from victims." *Gender & Society* 13: 364–84.

Smith, Dorothy. 1987. *The everyday world as problematic: A feminist sociology.* Boston: Northeastern University Press.

Steinberg, Ronnie, and Deborah Figart. 1999. Emotional labor since The Managed Heart. *Annals of the American Academy of Political and Social Science* 561: 8–26.

Wharton, Amy. 1999. The psychological consequences of emotional labor. *Annals of the American Academy of Political and Social Science* 561: 158–77.

Food for Thought and Application Questions

1. Clarify the ways in which work in the nail salons is *gendered.*

2. Describe how differences in clientele influence the way that Korean immigrant women manage their service-providing behavior. Discuss both the physical and emotional aspects of body labor in this regard.

3. Brainstorm about what other kinds of body labor or service activities might result in similar variations in physical and emotional labor due to the intersection of gender, race, and class (that is, the context which is defined by clientele). ✦

26
Chicanas Modernize Domestic Service

Mary Romero

Introduction

Domestic service may once have carried "the shreds of genteel respectability," but as Lewis Coser pointed out, in 20th century America it has been an occupation "so stigmatized that it can hardly attract potential recruits among ordinary citizens and must increasingly turn to a pool of otherwise 'undesirable' foreigners" (Coser 1974, p. 39). Along with the stigma of servitude and lowstatus, David Katzman noted two other characteristics that make the occupation unattractive to workers: it "offers no opportunities for mobility and it is highly personalized in both tasks and employer-employee relationships" (Katzman 1978, p. 378). Both the shortage of domestic workers and the declining need for servants caused by labor-saving devices in the home are factors that, Coser argued (1974, p. 39), make the servant role obsolete. Future household workers, he predicted, will become a new profession in which "families will no longer be able greedily to devour the personality of their servants." "Servants" may indeed be obsolete. But the need for household workers is expanding to keep pace with increasing numbers of women in the labor force.

Several researchers have identified one structural change that has modernized the occupation of domestic service. Historical studies by Katzman (1978) and Clark-Lewis (1983) identified the shift from live-in to live-out as contributing to major changes in working conditions. Glenn ([1985], p. 143), in her study of Japanese-American women in the Bay Area, attributed non-residential jobs to the modernization of domestic work by bringing it closer to industrialized wage work: "Work and non-work life are clearly separated, and the basis for employment is more clearly contractual—that is, the worker sells a given amount of labor time for an agreed-upon wage." Katzman (1978, p. 378) characterized the "hourly 'cleaning lady,'" as replacing "the uniformed maid who was part of the household." Even with the change to hourly work, though, the relationship between domestics and mistresses have retained characteristics of the master-servant relationship. Recent studies on the experiences of minority women employed as domestics indicate that the extraction of emotional labor, described by Coser as obsolete, still persists.[1] My own work on Chicana domestics supports these findings by showing that the occupation still has traits of servanthood. The mistress maintains a benevolent attitude towards "her" domestic, demanding loyalty and deference. She will treat the employee with the type of kindness reserved for domestic animals or pets and children, or at times even as a "non-person." Interpersonal relationships continue to be the major factor in job satisfaction and job tenure. However, my findings also suggest a broader range of relationships co-existing in the occupation.

The focus of this paper is to identify modernizing trends in domestic service and to explore how domestics can create a meaningful work environment. Chicanas engaged in domestic service find that the occupation poses a paradox: on one hand, cleaning houses is degrading and embarrassing; on the other, domestic service can be higher paying, more autonomous, and less dehumanizing than other low-status, low-skilled occupations available to them. The challenge is to manage this paradox in everyday life and to modernize the working conditions. Analysis of 25 Chicanas' work histories show how each weighed her options and made choices based on the work situation that provided the most advantages.

The data were derived from participant observation, in-depth interviews, and collecting life histories of current and former domestic workers. I analyzed the experiences of Chicanas employed as private household workers in a major western urban area. Two current and one former domestic worker known to the researcher provided entry into an informal network. Each interview subject was asked to recommend other potential interviewees. Churches and social service agencies were also used to identify domestics. Interviewees ranged in age from 29 to sixty-eight. All but one of the women had been married. Four of the women were single heads-of-household. The other women were currently living with husbands employed in blue collar jobs, such as construction and factory work. All of the women had children. The smallest family consisted of one child and the largest family had seven children. At the time of the interview, the women who were single heads-of-household were financially supporting no more than two children. Nine women had completed high school, but seven had no high school experience. One interviewee had never attended school at all. The remaining eight had at least a sixth grade education. All of the women were U.S. citizens. None of the women in this study belonged to a union.

In analyzing their work histories, in particular the reasons given for leaving or returning to domestic service, I was struck by the way Chicanas make the most of their options. Domestic service is only one of several low-paying, low-status jobs the women held during their lives. They had been hired as waitresses, laundresses, janitors, farmworkers, nurse aides, fast food servers and various types of line workers in poultry farms and car washes. In general, these were jobs with no benefits or where workers are subject to frequent layoffs and little chance for promotion. In comparing domestic service to other available work options all of the women identified certain advantages. Mrs. Rojas, for example, concluded that domestic service offered independence:

> When you work like in a hospital or something, you're under somebody. They're telling you what to do or this is not right. But housecleaning is different. You're free. You're not under no pressure, especially if you find a person who really trusts you all the way. You have no problems.

Unable to find employment offering job security, advancement, or benefits, these Chicanas made a calculated attempt to modernize the one occupation offering some advantages by minimizing control and personalism. Domestics use several strategies in their struggle for control: (1) increasing opportunities for job flexibility; (2) increasing pay and benefits; (3) establishing and maintaining an informal labor arrangement specifying tasks; (4) minimizing contact with employers; (5) defining themselves as expert housekeepers; and (6) creating a business-like environment. The critical locus of their struggle is to define the work on the basis of a contract—by the house or apartment—not as hourly work. Examination of the strategies used by the Chicanas reveal differences from the experience of other contemporary women of color employed as domestics. Unlike many of the black domestics studied in the East, these Chicanas were not sole supporters of the family, nor union members. Unlike the Japanese-American women in Glenn's study, most of the Chicanas were second or third generation and were much younger. The Chicanas that I interviewed had more formal education, and for the most part were not being replaced by newly arrived immigrants.[2] The most important difference is that the Chicana domestics have restructured the work by transforming it from wage labor to labor services.

The Restructuring of Domestic Service

Job Flexibility

Chicanas, like other women employed in domestic service (Glenn 1981, 1985), work for several employers. Having a different employer every day allows domestics more independence than having only one employer.[3] This alternative provides domestics with the leeway to quit, replacing employers without affecting the rest of the work week.

The women experience great latitude in negotiating both a flexible schedule and the length of the working day. Personal arrangements and verbal contracts between employer and employee make it easy to negotiate a half day's work or to skip a day. As Mrs. Garcia, a 54-year-old domestic, explained:

> You can change the dates if you can't go a certain day and if you have an appointment, you can go later, and work later, just as long as you get the work done.... I try to be there at the same time, but if I don't get there for some reason or another, I don't have to think I'm going to lose my job or something.

The flexibility of day work is important to women with small children who need to attend to illnesses and school schedules. The cost of day care can be a burden for middle class women; it is especially onerous for low-paid workers. In many cases, the issue of child care for preschool children can be resolved by taking them to work, as in the case of Mrs. Rivera, a 33-year-old mother of two:

> I could take my kids with me. There were never any restrictions to the children. Most of the people I've worked for like kids, so I just take the kids with me. It's silly to have to work and pay a sitter. It won't work.

Flexibility was not limited to rearranging a particular day or week; domestic workers could easily rearrange the work week to fit their needs during a particular period in their life. For instance, many of the older women had reduced their work week to three or four days a week, whereas the younger women who needed more income were more likely to be cleaning two apartments a day and working six days a week. A few women, like Mrs. Lovato, used the flexibility to work as a domestic part-time during times of economic crisis:

> I worked for Coors (brewery) for about three years and I would still do housecleaning, sort of part-time in the morning.

Payment and Benefits

Older women recalled earning $1.25 an hour in the early '60s and $3.25 in the '70s, but most of the women are now averaging between seven and eight dollars an hour—a lot more than other jobs they have had. For many women, the higher pay earned in domestic service reduced the financial need to work six days a week.

Payment in cash was frequently cited as an important aspect of domestic work. As with so many working-class families, even when there is a working husband, many live from pay check to pay check, with little if any money left over for unplanned or extra expenses. Extra cash is particularly important to families with school-age children who need lunch money or cash for class trips, gym clothes, or school supplies. Also, extra cash is important in supplementing the families' meals, especially towards the end of the week. Without the ready cash, end-of-the-week cooking ingredients are frequently limited to flour and beans.

In all but two cases, employment in domestic service was not reported to the IRS and these women expressed relief that income tax was not filed. Underreporting income to the IRS appeared to be partially the result of their husbands' fear of raising the family into a higher tax bracket. But it is also the case that the women did not know how to file income tax and felt uncomfortable about requesting employers to do so. However, three women expressed concern about social security and urged their employers to submit the required paper work. Two of the oldest women were receiving social security benefits as a result of their long-term employers' concern over their welfare.

One third of the women received benefits unknown to other domestics or other holders of low-status jobs. Nine Chicanas who had worked for years for particular employers reported paid vacations. This benefit usually involved no more than one or two paid days per employer. Christmas bonuses were more common than annual raises. However, nine reported annual raises and three of the women increased their wages annually by requesting raises or quitting one employer and raising the cost for new employers.

Negotiating Specific Tasks

Chicanas established verbal contracts with employers. When starting a new employer, the domestic would work one day, and if the employer was satisfied with the work, the two would agree upon a work schedule and the specific tasks to be accomplished. Mrs. Rodriquez describes the ideal situation:

> Once the person learns that you're going to do the job they just totally leave you to your own. It's like it's your own home.

The ideal is similar to informal arrangements reported by Glenn. However, half of the women explained the ideal situation was achieved after some supervision and negotiation. Such an experience is alluded to in Mrs. Portillo's explanation of why she left an employer:

> I don't want somebody right behind me telling me what to do. I will not work like that and that's why I didn't stay any longer with this lady.

Fifteen of the Chicanas interviewed made a practice of carefully distinguishing specific tasks considered part of the agreement from other tasks which would only be undertaken for additional pay. While informal work arrangements frequently implied a set number of hours the typical arrangement was referred to as "charging by the house" or a "flat rate." Mrs. Salazar explained the verbal contract as follows:

> When you say you're going to clean a house, after you find out how big it is, you tell them (the employer) "I'll clean it for say 60 dollars." You're not saying how long you're going to be there. To me, that was just a contract between you and the customer and after awhile when you've been there awhile you know how fast you can work and I was doing it in less than eight hours.

Mrs. Lopez expressed her preference for "charging by the house":

> I never liked to work by the hour because if I would work by the hour the lady would just go crazy loading me up with work, with more work and more work to do.

Similar to the dialectic between employer and employee described by Glenn, there was an ongoing negotiation as the domestic attempted to maintain the agreement while the employer attempted to lengthen the working day or add more tasks. Unlike the report on Japanese-American domestics,

however, Chicana domestics developed procedures for handling "extras." One way to avoid extra tasks was to prepare a monthly or bimonthly schedule for rotating particular tasks, such as cleaning the stove or refrigerator. Another practice was to establish an understanding with the employer that if one task was added, one would be eliminated. If the employer did not identify the tasks to be eliminated, the employee simply selected one and explained that there was not enough time for both.

> My cousin said, "do the same thing every time you come in, as far as changing the sheets, vacuum and dust, and window sills, pictures on the walls, and stuff like that unless they ask you to do something extra. Then, maybe don't clean the tile in the bathroom, or just do the windows that really need it, so you can have some time to do this other stuff that they wanted you to do extra." And she said, "never do more than what they ask you to do, because if you do then you're not really getting paid for it."

Employers feared that domestics were cheating on their time. Three women reported that past employers insisted they work until the very last second, leaving little if any paid time for putting away appliances or cleaning materials and ignoring the additional time required to complete a task. One domestic recalled employers bringing her lunch to her on the stairs or elsewhere in the house so that she would not take a lunch break. However, domestics, like Mrs. Sanchez, viewed the work as "averaging out":

> Suppose one day they (employers) may be out of town and that day you go to work. You won't have much work to do, but you'll get paid the same. And then maybe some other time they're going to have company and you end up working a little more and you still get paid the same. So it averages about the same, you know, throughout the month.

Chicana domestics, not unlike black and Japanese-American domestics (Rollins 1985; Coley 1981; Dill 1979; Katzman 1981; Glenn [1985]), did not necessarily find an affective relationship the ingredient for a satisfying working relationship. In fact, the opposite was the case, because affective relationships provided more opportunities for exploitation. Frequently, close friendships resulted in fictitious kinship references, such as a young employer adopting the domestic as a surrogate mother. Redefining the work obligation as a "family" obligation placed the domestic in a difficult position. One older domestic explained how the personal nature of the relationship created an atmosphere conducive to manipulation: "Some people use their generosity to pressure you." Maintaining the conditions of the verbal contract became difficult because requests for extra work were made as requests from a friend rather than an employer.

Minimizing Contact With Employers

In order to create meaningful work, domestics needed to remove employers from controlling decisions that structure the work and reduce the domestic to unskilled labor and housecleaning to mindless hourly work. Furthermore, the domestics wanted to eliminate the stigma of servitude, or being "hired help," which implies unskilled labor. The Chicanas defined their work as being different from maid's work. Mrs. Fernandez, a 35-year-old domestic, pointed to the distinction in the following account:

> They (the employer's children) started to introduce me to their friends as their maid. "This is our maid Angela." I would say "I'm not your maid. I've come to clean your house and a maid is someone who takes care of you and lives here or comes in everyday and I come once a week and it is to take care of what you've messed up. I'm not your maid. I'm your housekeeper."

Domestics commonly reported conflict over the work process. Some employers gave detailed instructions on how to clean their home: washing the floor on hands and knees, using newspaper instead of paper towels on the windows, or even which direction to scrub the wall. Mrs. Portillo, a retired domestic with 30 years experience, expressed the frustration of such a situation:

> I used to have one lady that used to work right along with me. I worked with her three years. I found it hard. I was taking orders. I'm not the type to want to take or-

ders. I know what I'm going to do. I know what general house cleaning is.

Mrs. Sanchez voiced the general consensus that the less interaction with employers the better the working conditions: "The conflicts have been mostly with people who stay at home and really just demand the impossible." Five domestics even commented that they select employers on the basis of whether the employer worked outside the home.

Chicanas argued that working women are more appreciative of having the housework done, and are relieved to turn over the planning and execution of cleaning to the domestic. Unemployed women were perceived as "picky" and not willing to relinquish control. Three domestics made the analysis that unemployed women feel guilty because they are not doing the work themselves and, thus, have to retain control and responsibility for the housework.

> I think women that weren't working were the ones that always had something to complain about. The ones that did work were always satisfied. I've never come across a lady that works that has not been satisfied. Those that are home and have the time to do it themselves, and don't want to do it, they are the ones that are always complaining, you know, not satisfied, they always want more and more. You can't really satisfy them.

Mrs. Lopez classified the type of employer she was working with by their attitude in the first few minutes of their first encounter:

> I have had ladies that have said "I know you know what to do so I'll leave it to you" or they pull out their cleaning stuff and tell you "this is for this and this is for that" and I say "I know I've done this before. Oh, ok, I'll let you do it."

Supervision and the monitoring of workers not only control the work process but reminds the worker of her subordinate position in society. Offering unsolicited advice about cleaning techniques, such as scrubbing floors on hands and knees rather than with a mop, or the safest way to bend while picking up the vacuum cleaner and moving heavy furniture, symbolizes a level of servitude. Asking a domestic to scrub floors on hands and knees, not a common practice of housewives today, is experienced as demeaning. The inferior status of the domestic is also evident in the employer's instructions on how to bend instead of offering assistance.

Becoming an Expert

The Chicana domestics' strategy of defining themselves as expert cleaners or housekeepers was one more step forward in modernizing domestic service. It is a unique strategy not found among the blacks studied by Rollins or the Japanese-Americans in Glenn's study. This strategy served to modernize the employee/employer relationship, creating an ideal situation in which employers turned over responsibility for the housework to the domestic. Establishing themselves as expert house-cleaners involved defining a routine set of tasks that did not include personal services such as babysitting, laundry, or ironing.[4] Mrs. Montoya's statement illustrates the equation of personal services with maid's work:

> I figure I'm not there to be their personal maid. I'm there to do their housecleaning—their upkeep of the house. Most of the women I work for are professionals and so they feel it's not my job to run around behind them. Just to keep their house maintenance clean and that's all they ask.

The women interviewed considered themselves experts. They were aware of the broad range of knowledge they had acquired from cleaning a variety of homes. This knowledge included the removal of stains on various surfaces, tips for reorganizing the home, and the pros and cons of certain brands of appliances. A source of pride among the women was the fact that they had introduced a labor-saving device or tactic into the employer's home. Mrs. Garcia's experience in removing stains illustrates the assistance that domestics give employers:

> They (employers) just wipe their stoves and then complain "this doesn't come off anymore." They never took a SOS pad or a scrub brush to scrub it off. They expect it just to come off because they wiped. . . . Their kitchen floors would have kool-aid stains or they would have it on the counters, so I would just pour Chlorox on it

and the Chlorox would just bring it right up and they would say "but you'll ruin it!" "No it will be alright." "Are you sure?" I never ruined anything from helping them out.

Mrs. Cortez's habit of providing cleaning hints illustrates how many employers willingly accept the expertise of the domestic.

> I cut out pieces of cleaning (information) that tell you how to do this an easy way . . . I'll take them and paste them on like their pantry door and I'll put them there and then when they go to open (the pantry door) they say "Oh, that's a good idea." So then they start doing it that way.

As expert cleaners, the women take responsibility for all decisions regarding the structure of the work process, the pace of the housework, and the selection of work materials. Ideally the domestic would enter the employer's home, decide where to begin, and arrange the appliances and cleaning products accordingly. She would pace herself to finish in a certain number of hours. If she needs to leave early she can speed up and not take a break; in other cases, a more leisurely pace would be indicated.

Half of the women recalled offering employers advice on the care of appliances and the best detergent or cleaning utensil for a particular surface. The Chicanas also attempt to routinize and rationalize the housework by reorganizing family practices and introducing new methods, perhaps cleaning neglected areas of the house to create additional space or rearranging the furniture. Mrs. Rodriquez described her approach as follows:

> I take one room and give it a full general cleaning which was walls, windows, everything, and from there I would do the rest light housework. Then the next week, I would take another room and give that a general cleaning and go to the rest lightly until I had all the house done real good and after that it was just a matter of keeping it up.

Taking responsibility frequently included finding replacements during their absence.

> I worked for my mother-in-law sometimes and if she was sick or if she was go-

ing out of town, I'd do some of the houses that she does every week and she really couldn't leave without somebody going to do something because it would be really a mess when she came back and it would be more work on her. So I would go and fill in for her.

The domestics did not view themselves as "one of the family." They also retained a separation between tasks completed for their employers and the "work of love" given to their families. The Chicanas attempted to enforce a new set of norms modernizing the domestic-mistress relationship into a customer-vendor relationship. In their struggle to transform the occupation, the Chicanas altered the employer's role from mistress to client or customer. This new definition of the relationship lessened the opportunity for psychological exploitation and the extraction of emotional labor. Chicanas identified particular tasks that would add to the problem of psychological exploitation. For instance, cooking Mexican food for employers was a request refused by all but two of the women. Their reasons for refusing the request suggest that they made a division between paid tasks and "work of love" and took precautions against selling their personhood.

> I only cook for my family, I didn't want to share my culture with them (employers).

In order to convince employers to accept the new working relationship, private household workers had to present the advantages. One strategy used to convince the employer that she did not want to be a supervisor was to create a situation on the part of the employer that demanded more detailed supervision. This included such tactics as doing only the tasks requested and nothing else, not bothering to inform the employer that the worker had used the last vacuum bag or had used up cleaning materials, and refusing to offer the employer assistance in fixing a simple mechanical problem in an appliance. Consequently, employers who refused to shift control and responsibility were confronted with domestics who took no interest in or responsibility for completing the housework.

To redefine their work as skilled labor, Chicanas capitalized on the fact that work-

ing women are no longer interested in supervising the work of private household workers. Women hiring domestics to escape the double day syndrome cannot reap the benefits of the work if they supervise the activities of a "menial laborer." Acknowledging housework as skilled labor affirms the worth of the housewives' housework. In shifting housecleaning to "expert housekeepers," the housewife fulfills her responsibility to the family by obtaining skilled services; and, in doing so, she defines the work as difficult and time consuming, requiring skilled labor.

Creating a Business-Like Environment

Just as in other female-dominated occupations, such as nursing and teaching, private household workers lack authority (Spencer 1987; Ritzer 1977; Corley & Mauksch 1987) and must therefore rely on the employers' cooperation in accepting them as expert housekeepers. Rios' account of an employer's daughter expecting her to subordinate illustrates the role some employers play in eliminating any aspects of servitude in the occupation.

> I told a young lady something about leaving her underclothes thrown around, and she asked me what was I there for? I went straight in, called her mother and told her the situation. Her mother came home from work and let the young lady have it. She (the mother) was thoroughly upset. I was not there to be her (the daughter's) personal maid and she was told that in no uncertain terms.

Analysis of the informal networks used by both [employers and] employees points to a key role in establishing a business-like environment. The informal network between employers and employees serves to socialize employers and employees to the value of modernizing trends in the occupation. Chicana work histories revealed that, particularly for younger workers, the introduction to domestic service involved an informal apprenticeship. The new recruit accompanied a relative to work for several days or weeks until deciding she was ready to work alone. Domestics identified these training sessions as providing experience in cleaning, learning about new products or appliances, and discovering the pros and cons of structuring the work in particular ways.

> She would go look it over and see if I missed anything or like in the bathroom you have to polish all the chrome and I didn't know that so I cleaned it and it was clean but she's the one that gave me all these tips on polishing up the chrome and stuff.

Most important, new workers were socialized to expect certain working conditions, and wages, and they learned ways to negotiate with employers.

Employers were similarly tied to the network. Employers asked domestics for the names of interested persons to work for neighbors, while domestics asked employers for the names of their friends interested in hiring housekeepers. Domestics were often very careful in their recommendations:

> They'll (friends) call and see if I know anybody that needs help but I have to know the person, and if I don't think the person is going to do the job, I will not send them . . . I'm very careful who I send—who I recommend.

In assisting friends and neighbors in finding workers, employers informed potential employers of existing conditions and thereby helped to create certain expectations. In using the network, Chicanas could be reasonably assured that new employers were socialized to appropriate expectations.

> I right away tell them what I do and what I expect to get paid and they already know because of their friends because they have already discussed my work.

Employers' involvement in modernizing the occupation may not be limited to exposing new employers to contemporary expectations. Two domestics reported that employers actually applied pressure on other employers to upgrade working conditions. Both domestics worked for employers who set standards of fairness and urged their friends and neighbors to conform—for instance, by complying with federal regulations by filing income tax and social security forms. Mrs. Salazar had such an employer:

> I don't ask for raises anymore. I have one woman who kind of sets the pace and

she's given me a raise almost every year and then she hints around to some of the other ones that she knows what I work for and then they all bring it up to her standards.

The controlled environment created by the use of the informal network provides the avenue for Chicanas to establish their self-defintion as experts and their informal work arrangement as a business-like relationship.

Conclusion

Faced with limited job opportunities, Chicanas turned to domestic service and restructured the occupation to resemble a business-like arrangement. The Chicana domestics defined themselves as expert cleaners hired to do general housework. They urged their employers to turn over the planning along with the execution of the work. They considered themselves skilled laborers who were well-able to schedule tasks, determine cleaning techniques, select appropriate work materials, and set the work pace. Verbal agreements specifying tasks served to minimize supervision and increase the degree of autonomy. Eliminating the employer from a supervisory role removed the worker from a subordinate position. Domestics' ability to select and change employers became a critical source of autonomy and control in what would otherwise be a powerless, subservient position.

Chicanas employed as day workers in private households are moving away from "wage work" and selling their "labor time," toward a "flat rate" in which a "job" is exchanged for a specific amount of money. In this situation, any efficiency realized by the worker saves her time and can sometimes be converted to profit that will accrue to her. The Chicanas are modernizing domestic work in the direction of a petty bourgeois relation of customer-vendor rather than the preindustrial relation of mistress-servant or even the capitalistic relation of wage worker-employer. This arrangement is most successful with employed housewives who readily accept the skills of domestics. The strategy to modernize domestic service by selling labor services rather than labor power is also useful in eliminating potentially exploitative aspects of the domestic-mistress relationship.

Notes

1. Recurring themes in the mistress/maid relationship that appear in recent studies are: the extraction of emotional labor, maintenance of status and control with an informal and companionable relationship, and the struggle for control as a crucial source of conflict. Cock (1980) and Rollins (1985) identified the personal nature of the relationship between domestics and their employers as primarily one of psychological exploitation. Exploitation is most visible in the expectation of emotional cheap manual labor, and is a common experience among black women in the East (Rollins 1985; Coley 1981; Dill 1979), Japanese-American domestics in the Bay area (Glenn 1985), West Indians in New York (Colen 1986), and Chicanas in the Southwest (Romero 1986; 1987).

2. Presently Mexican immigrants do not represent competition, but the Chicanas indicate they are incorporating Mexican women into their networks and urge them not to lower standards. Several women expressed concern over the willingness of Vietnamese immigrants to work for less pay, and do gardening along with household chores. For the most part, Chicanas experience a domestic's market and, therefore, have the latitude to select employers that show respect and professional behavior.

3. In recent years some of the women were working for two employers in one day, cleaning two houses. This pattern was particularly common when employers lived in condominiums or apartments.

4. Older Chicanas recalled babysitting, ironing, cooking and doing laundry, but in recent years they rarely did such tasks. Even younger Chicanas in their thirties, some with 12 years experience, only did ironing or laundry for employers they started with 10 years ago.

References

Clark-Lewis, E. 1983. "From 'servant' to 'dayworker': A study of selected household service workers in Washington, D.C., 1900–1926." Ph.D. Dissertation, University of Maryland.

Cock, J. 1980. "Maids and madams: A study in the politics of exploitation." Johannesburg: Raven Press.

Colen, S. 1986. " 'With respect and feelings': Voices of West Indian child care and domestic workers in New York City." In J. B. Cole (Ed.), *All American Women: Lines That Divide, Ties That Bind.* New York: Free Press:46–70.

Coley, S. M. 1981. "And still I rise: An exploratory study of contemporary black private household workers." Unpublished Ph.D. Dissertation, Bryn Mawr College.

Corley, M. C. & H. O. Mauksch. 1987. "Registered nurses, gender, and commitment." In A. Statham, E. M. Miller and H. 0. Mauksch (Eds.), *The Worth of Women's Work: A Qualitative Synthesis.* Albany: State University of New York Press:135–149.

Coser, L. 1974. "Servants: The obsolescence of an occupational role." *Social Forces,* 52:31–40.

Davidoff, L. 1976. "The rationalization of housework." In D. L. Baker and S. Allen (Eds.), *Dependence and Exploitation in Work and Marriage.* New York: Longman:121–151.

Dill, B. T. 1979. "Across the boundaries of race and class: An exploration of the relationship between work and family among black female domestic servants." Ph.D. Dissertation, New York University.

Glenn, E. N. 1985. *Issei, Nisei, War Bride: Three Generations of Japanese American Women in Domestic Service.* Philadelphia: Temple University Press.

——. 1981. "Occupational ghettoization: Japanese-American women and domestic service, 1905–1970." *Ethnicity,* 8(4):352–386.

Grossman, A. S. 1980. "Women in domestic work: Yesterday and today." *Monthly Labor Review,* (Aug.):17–21.

Katzman, D. M. 1981. *Seven Days a Week: Women and Domestic Service in Industrializing America.* Chicago: University of Illinois Press.

——. 1978. "Domestic service women's work." In A. H. Stromberg and S. Harkess (Eds.), *Women Working: Theories and Facts in Perspective.* Palo Alto: Mayfield Publishing Company:377–391.

Ritzer, G. 1977. *Working: Conflict and Change.* Englewood Cliffs, New Jersey: Prentice-Hall, Inc.

Rollins, J. 1985. *Between Women: Domestics and Their Employers.* Philadelphia: Temple University Press.

Romero, M. 1987. "Day work in suburbs: The work experience of Chicana private housekeepers." In A. Statham, E. M. Miller, and H. O. Mauksch

(Eds.), *The Worth of Women's Work: A Qualitative Synthesis*. Albany: State University of New York Press:77–91.

———. 1986. "Domestic service in the transition from rural to urban life: The case of la Chicana." *Women's Studies*, 13(4):199–222.

Spencer, D. A. 1987. "Public schoolteaching: A suitable job for a woman?" In A. Statham, E. M. Miller, and H. O. Mauksch (Eds.), *The Worth of Women's Work: A Qualitative Synthesis*. Albany: State University of New York Press:167–186.

Food for Thought and Application Questions

1. In Chapter 17, Amott and Matthaei argue that in order to understand women's disparate work experiences it is necessary to examine the interaction of gender, race, and class in the context of both history and place. Identify the particular combination of statuses and circumstances that enabled the Chicana domestics studied by Romero to successfully modernize their work while many other workers in low level occupations were unable to do so. What aspects of Chicana domestics' *work situation* were associated with successful attempts at modernization? What *personal characteristics* affected their success?

2. Compare the strategies used to improve work conditions, job security, and pay described in this chapter to those used by teachers (Chapter 21). How do gender, race, and class appear to affect the "activist" strategies employed? ✦

Unit Five

Policy and Assessment

Social policy develops as a response to emergent social concerns, deriving from legislation as well as changing social norms and practices. Over a four decade period that spanned the last part of the twentieth century, workplace activity by women created pressures for change in at least two major institutional arenas: work and family. In many ways, policies to address these changes lagged behind the observable evolution in women's participation in the work force and the issues that emerged from this. By the mid- to late-1980s, however, there was increasing pressure at the federal level of government and in corporations to address issues that came with the dramatic increase in women's labor force participation.

Policies responding to women's employment existed throughout the twentieth century. Many of the policies followed laws that were intended to protect women from particular burdens or hardships in employment, hence the term *protective legislation*. Sterling (1996) summarized protective legislation of the early 1900s as being of two types. One type was intended to safeguard women's health and improve working conditions. Women were working in sweatshops and factories that were poorly lighted, poorly ventilated, and often unsanitary. These laws sought minimum wages, mandatory rest periods, improved working conditions, and a maximum number of hours that a woman could work per week. The second type of protective legislation was discriminatory in nature, barring women from certain types of jobs, including mining, bar tending, and late night work. There was also controversy surrounding the passage of such laws. Some women would benefit because their work conditions would improve as would their pay. Indeed, when the National Women's Party submitted a proposed Equal Rights Amendment to the U.S. House of Representatives in 1923, it was felt that such an amendment would jeopardize legislation that protected women workers. Others felt that such legislation would have employers replace women and hire men because there would be no economic advantage to hiring women (Sterling 1996).

Minimum wage laws that were proposed intended to improve the situation of working women. These laws were not supported early in the twentieth century, and it took until 1938, with the passage of the Fair Labor Standard Act, for a minimum wage. This act also defined the maximum number of hours one could work for an employer (44 hours). The Act applied equally to male and female workers (Sterling 1996). The Equal Pay act of 1963 and Title VII of the 1964 Civil Rights act, which prohibited sex discrimination in employment, provided the legal impetus for employers to establish policies of non-discrimination. The Equal Employment Opportunity Commission (EEOC) was established to enforce Title VII and assure non-discrimination (Rossi 1996), and monitored the practices of employers. Also within this legal framework, Affirmative Action programs were established to remedy inequalities (Summers 1996), and sexual harassment was defined as sex discrimination in employment (Rossi 1996). With regard to sexual harassment, employers were held responsible for providing a work environment that was free of sexual harassment and a means by which complaints about harassing behavior could be addressed and remedied (Bowes-Sperry and Tata 1999).

The legal changes that were intended to remove overt forms of employment discrimination against women spawned the identification of related but often less obvious practices that created barriers to women's access, mobility, and success in positions of authority. What was less clearly identified until the 1980s was how women's employment was forcing a redefinition of the boundaries between work and the family. While women added new economic responsibilities, there was often little adjustment with regard to family and home life responsibilities. Indeed, the term *second shift*, popularized by Hochschild's research, resonated with many employed women. Yet the management of a work-family balance was largely left to the individual (or individual family unit), and women were left with the responsibility to negotiate time off from employment for family matters. As might be expected, some women were more successful than others in doing so.

In the late 1980s, during the (first) Bush presidency and the 99th Congress, pressure from the changing demographics of the work force—and particularly the employment of mothers of very young children—spurred the introduction of federal legislation to provide for job-protected leave for family and medical reasons (Brannen 1996). While not passed during the (first) Bush presidency, the issues that prompted the introduction of the legislation remained viable. In fact, a number of states passed family-medical leave legislation despite its being stalled at the federal level. In 1993, during the Clinton administration, the Family and Medical Leave Act (FMLA) was passed. It incorporated "parental leave"—a broadly based concept that included either parent or both parents—and protected the parent's job for up to twelve weeks (Brannen 1996). Importantly, by the time the legislation had passed at the federal level, a number of the country's largest corporations had already incorporated the base-line requirements of the 1993 Act into corporate policy.

The articles in the present section address issues of policy and assessment, asking not only what policies are in place with regard to women's employment, but also how these policies work and whether reconceptualization is needed. The first article in this section provides an overview of the emergence of the work/family intersection as a social issue. In the selection, Dubeck examines the steps corporations have taken to address issues associated with women's employment. Drawing on *Working Mother* magazine's 100 Best Companies for working women, Dubeck highlights the changing nature of criteria for the "best" given the accumulation of research addressing the issues associated with women and work.

In the second selection, Mainiero and Sullivan challenge traditional models (generally male-defined models) of career, arguing that existing models are inadequate for today's work force (the GenXers), particularly with regard to women. Noting that many highly talented and highly trained women value authenticity, balance, and challenge in their careers, Mainiero and Sullivan propose an alternative career model, the "kaleidoscope career model." Their model emphasizes different patterns among priorities at different times in one's career, departing significantly from the traditional model where steady upward movement defines careers. They argue that corporations will need to change their practices in order to attract and retain talented women, and the authors provide guidelines that corporations could incorporate in order to secure the commitment of such women. One of the strengths of this article is that Mainiero and Sullivan provide a framework for "seeing things differently," and then suggest ways in which new practices can be incorporated into organizations.

The third selection in this unit, Gerstel and McGonagle explore the early impact of the Family and Medical Leave Act of 1993 (FMLA) as a major step toward providing institutional support networks for working family members. By examining both the "need" for leave and the "taking" of leave, they identify the benefits and constraints provided by the legislation. In addition, they discuss limitations of the FMLA, including the issues of *unpaid* family leave, the narrow definition of family, and problems with workplace responsiveness. Their article suggests the FMLA is only a first step toward solving issues associated with balancing work and family.

In the final selection in this unit, Glass examines the impact of employer-sponsored work-family policies on women's wages. Policies such as flexible scheduling, reduced hours of work, telecommuting, and childcare assistance are the focus of her interest. She notes that women are concerned that the use of such benefits come with a penalty of blocked career opportunities or lower wages. Glass examines the extent to which the use of these work innovations affect women's wage growth, and in particular, whether they act to depress earnings. In as-

sessing the impact of policy use, Glass pays attention to the employee's status, whether they changed employers, and whether the use of specific benefits (versus the availability of a broad set of benefits) influence wage growth. Glass research is important in that it is a systematic assessment of work-family benefits, and it allows us to gain an understanding of the "costs" that are embedded in the use of such benefits.

References

Bowes-Sperry, Lynne and Jasmine Tata. (1999). "A Multiperspective framework on sexual harassment: Reviewing two decades of research." In Gary N. Powell, Ed., *Handbook of Gender and Work*, Thousand Oaks, CA: Sage. 263–280.

Brannen, Kathleen C. 1996. "Job-protected leave for family and medical reasons." In P. Dubeck and K. Borman, eds. *Women and Work: A Handbook*. New York: Garland, 274–277.

Rossi, Mary Ann. 1996. "Women's rights in the labor market." In P. Dubeck and K. Borman, eds. *Women and Work: A Handbook*. New York: Garland: 255–257.

Sterling, David L. 1996. "Women's work and protective legislation." In P. Dubeck and K. Borman, eds. *Women and Work: A Handbook*. New York: Garland. 251–254.

Summers, Russel J. 1996. "Affirmative action." In P. Dubeck and K. Borman, eds. *Women and Work: A Handbook*. New York: Garland: 257–259. ✦

27

Are We There Yet?

Reflections on Work and Family as an Emergent Social Issue

Paula J. Dubeck

I want to begin with two brief stories of my past. The first came during my first year as a faculty member at the University of Cincinnati. It was 1974 and my second academic job. The department had ordered a nameplate for my door and, finally, it had arrived and was being installed. I was in a meeting in my office at the time, so the door was closed. When I opened it, I looked at the nameplate, and saw: *Paul A. Dubeck*. Seeing that nameplate reminded me that not everyone associated with a university envisioned that a female could also be a faculty member.

The second incident occurred 15 years later, when I spoke at a luncheon of an organization of women in communication. At that time, I was director of the department's Center for the Study of Work and Family (the Kunz Center), and I chose to speak about the changing composition of the work force, the competing demands of work and family, and the need for employers to respond to a variety of work/family issues, particularly with regard to mothers with children. My presentation was followed by a talk by a representative of a major consumer products corporation in Cincinnati. She stated clearly and concisely that her company viewed work and family as *separate* spheres and that the company did not focus on issues relating to family. In that moment, the work/family issues I had discussed (and supported with data) were brushed aside as unimportant for working women.

I use these two examples because of what they represent with regard to the study of work and family. In the first case, women in my cohort were truly "new" to most of academe; except for colleges of nursing and education, female faculty members were few and far between. Academe was not an isolated case, however. Examining the numbers, or even more tellingly the percentages, other high-status, male-dominated professions showed women were rare. In the 1970s, however, the number of women entering many of the traditionally male-dominated professions and occupations increased rapidly, and by the end of the 1990s, women represented a significant proportion of new entrants to professions such as law, medicine, and academe (U.S. Census 2001). Similarly, for women in college, this period showed a major shift in the majors selected by women. For example, in the early 1970s, education was the most frequent major of female college graduates (approximately 1 of every 4 women); by contrast, only 1 of 20 earned a degree in business. By approximately 1985, more than 1 out of 5 females earning bachelor degrees did so in business (U.S. Department of Education 1981, 1987). My second example illustrates that such changes had not become widely apparent in the 1980s.

Factors Bringing Work and Family Into Focus

Despite the position of some corporations that work and family were separate spheres, by 1989, mounting evidence suggested that this was not a tenable position for the future. A number of factors had converged in a way that made an emphasis on work and family an issue to be dealt with on a number of fronts. For example, data from the U.S. census shows that among married women with husbands present, 50 percent were in the labor force in 1980 (Figure 27.1); more than 60 percent of those with children from age 6–17 were in the labor force. By 1985, over half of the married women with children under the age of 6 were in the labor force (U.S. Bureau of Census 2001).

This demographic change also brought attention to a number of problems that previously were "below the surface" of social awareness. For example, people began to

Figure 27.1

Women's Labor Force Participation Rate By Marital Status and Presence of Children,
1960-2000

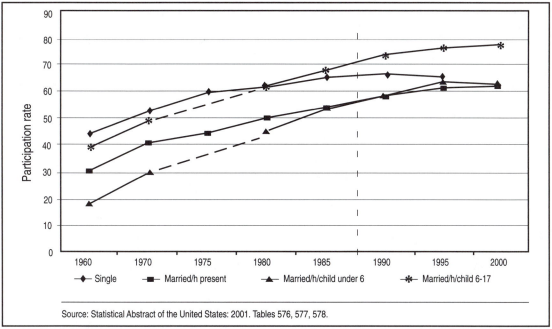

Source: Statistical Abstract of the United States: 2001. Tables 576, 577, 578.

voice concern about childcare and the problem of latchkey kids (Menaghan 1991;
Menaghan and Parcel 1991). In addition, the
profile of women's employment was beginning to change. Younger women had work
histories that looked increasingly like those
of men. Specifically, more women had a pattern of continuous labor force participation,
rather than interrupted participation, even
with children present (Reskin and Padavic
1994).

It was not only the rising employment of
women that brought the issue of work and
family into social awareness. It also had to do
with the positions women were hired into.
That is, women moved into positions of leadership and influence. Essentially, they moved
into traditionally male-dominated positions
of status, such as management, law, and medicine. These were positions in which skills
were valuable and an employer's investment
in training was high; further, it was costly to
replace a person who left (Schwartz 1992).

To be sure, the willingness of corporations
to embrace this "new" source of skilled labor

was slow, and women were often steered to positions that were less central to an
organization's mission. When women entered
the ranks of management they were often directed to human resource positions (Powell
1999; Reskin and Padavic 1994; Stroh and
Reilly 1999); in law firms, they were directed
to family law, estates, and wills (Epstein 1993).
But over time two things occurred. First,
women challenged practices that placed them
in peripheral positions. As a result, positions
that were more central to the primary work of
the organization became accessible (see, for
example Blair-Loy 1999; Davies-Netzley 1998;
Epstein 1993). Second, employers began to
take notice of *turnover* among management
women. They were leaving management positions at a rate higher than that of men, and this
turnover was viewed as costly to companies
(Schwartz 1989, 1992).

Academic/Print Media

The changes in women's employment,
their employment opportunities and issues
surrounding careers were well monitored in
sociological research. Increasingly research

began to address issues of work and family. Figure 27.2 presents data on sociology journal articles that have "work and family" referenced in their text from 1980 to 2000.

These data from JSTOR, a computerbased search, show that a consideration of work and family issues had been present throughout the 1980s, peaked in the early 1990s, and then decreased. Early studies included such topics as the effects of mother's work on children (Menaghan 1991) and marital quality of dual earner couples (see Vannoy and Philliber 1992).

These data contrast with findings from the same time period on work and family "books in print;" books on work and family were relatively absent until 1989 (Figure 27.3). Such publications have continued since then at high rates. One could argue that the research in the decade of the 1980s was a necessary precursor to books being published; it provided the knowledge base upon which they could be written. And there is merit to that argument.

However, timeliness is also one of the criteria that can justify the publication of a book. As such, the number of books published on work and family can be viewed as an indicator of the salience of an issue—and its rising salience over time.

Importantly, it was not until the mid- to late-1980s that the popular press—news magazines and newspapers—began to focus on working mothers. This is shown in Figure 27.4. The data here, from an *Infotrac* search, present the number of articles (including academic articles) that have "working mother" in their title, abstract, or citation. The dramatic increase comes in 1987, continues in 1988, and then is sustained throughout the 1990s.

The significance of this attention is found not only in the numbers. Particular early publications also helped to frame the discussion of issues in the work/family debate: Two of these were Arlie Hochschild's 1987 book, *The Second Shift,* and a 1989 article by Felice Schwartz.

Hochschild presented and analyzed scenarios about the situation of married women who worked full-time. In particular, she explored how the traditional gen-

Figure 27.2
Journal Articles With "Work And Family" Referenced in Text, 1980-2000

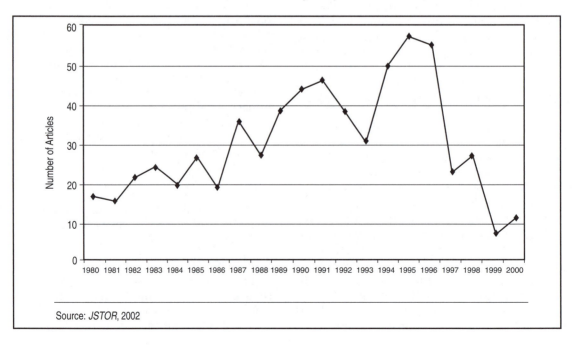

Source: *JSTOR,* 2002

Figure 27.3
"Work and Family" Books in Print, 1980-2000

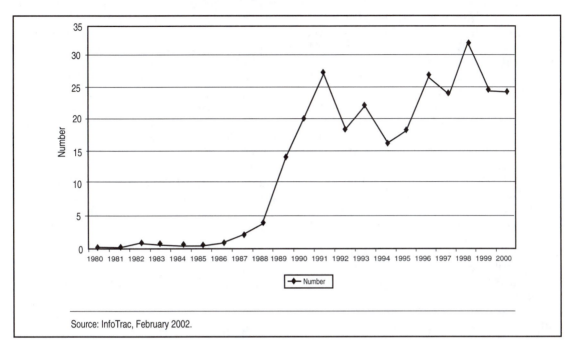

Source: InfoTrac, February 2002.

Figure 27.4
Articles With "Working Mother" in Their Title, Abstract, or Citation, 1980-2001

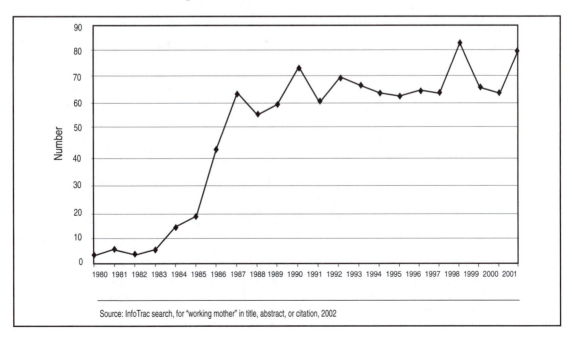

Source: InfoTrac search, for "working mother" in title, abstract, or citation, 2002

der-based division of labor in the household—men responsible for economic well-being and women responsible for the home—had not changed, despite wives' full-time participation in the labor force. Hochschild (1987) argued that after working all day on their paying job, wives come home to a second job, the traditional tasks of household care/responsibility. This she labeled the *second shift*. Hochschild's analysis of that cultural lag and its consequences—for marriages, husbands, children, and employment—has stimulated a considerable amount of research on the distribution of household tasks (Bianchi et al. 2000; Blair 1996; Orbuch and Eyster 1997), family relations and stress (Glass and Camarigg 1992; Menaghan 1991; Moen and Yu 2000), flex time opportunities, and family friendly corporate policies (Blair-Loy and Wharton 2002; Glass and Estes 1997; Wharton 1994).

The second publication, Felice Schwartz's controversial article, "Management Women and the New Facts of Life," was published in the *Harvard Business Review* in 1989. Schwartz began her article with the following statement:

> The cost of employing women in management is greater than the cost of employing men. This is a jarring statement, partly because it is true, but mostly because it is something people are reluctant to talk about. A new study by one multinational corporation shows that the rate of turnover in management positions is 2-1/2 times higher among top-performing women than it is among men . . .

> Career interruptions, plateauing, and turnover are expensive. The money corporations invest in recruitment training, and development is less likely to produce top executives among women than among men, and the invaluable company experience that developing executives acquire at every level as they move up through management ranks is more often lost. (p. 65)

Schwartz argued that corporations should be ready to pay that extra price in order to keep talented women on board. She also proposed that corporations develop two tracks for female managers: (1) the career-primary track and (2) the career and family track (subsequently labeled the "mommy track"). For "career-primary" women, Schwartz proposed that corporations develop practices that support the movement of high aspiring and achieving women into the upper ranks of the corporation. These would include early identification, providing the same opportunities and responsibility as early-identified male stars, mentoring, support groups, and special training. For career-and-family (or "mommy track") women, Schwartz proposed that corporations accommodate pregnancy and motherhood with a variety of supportive measures. Flexible work schedules, paid parental leave for the birth of a child, phased-in time back at work after the birth of a child, and support for childcare options were just some of these (Schwartz 1989). She argued that support early in the career of a career-and-family woman would pay benefits to the firm later (after the major child rearing years were over) with committed, high achieving middle managers (see also Schwartz 1992).

While the immediate discussions of Schwartz's article centered on the controversial "two track" system, particularly the "mommy track," a number of the changes proposed by Schwartz are what we define today as "family-friendly" corporate policies (Glass and Estes 1997). Also, her proposals to support "career primary" women highlighted areas where high achieving women lacked support and signaled the need for corporations to address the factors that resulted in a high level of turnover among female managers.

Why is this important? The previous diagrams (Figures 27.1–4) show the demographic change of women's labor force participation and the increasing public attention through the media. Thus, as participation increased, the ramifications of that participation spread in a way that no longer justified treating "work" and "family" as separate spheres in everyday work life. Furthermore, research on work/family issues began to link questions about women's opportunities in the work force with those of work/family conflict.

Corporate Responsiveness

The increasing attention given to work and family in the media and in academic publications directed one focus of inquiry to the work setting and employer responsiveness to the needs of employees. How *did* employers respond to the rapid influx of women, particularly to the managerial and professional ranks of the organization?

One way to investigate this has been to examine corporate policies. Various surveys by consulting firms suggest that by the early 1990s, most major corporations had policies or programs to help relieve work/family pressures. A Family and Work Institute report issued in 1991 indicated that nearly two-thirds of the *Fortune* 500 companies had instituted some type of family-responsive program (Glass and Estes 1997). Family-responsive programs, however, can and do vary widely. For example, some corporations might develop a childcare referral service or establish a policy on flex-time; others might develop on-site childcare or pay some of the cost of childcare for employees. As such, global percentages referring to "some type of" childcare program may be misleading with regard to the nature of work/family support provided.

Also, Glass and Estes (1997) noted that institute and consulting firm studies about family-responsive programs generally have higher estimates of such programs in corporations compared to those found by the U.S. Bureau of Labor Statistics. For example, Glass and Estes noted that a 1991 Survey by Hewitt, a consulting organization, found that 53 percent of the employers surveyed made flexible scheduling available to employees, while the BLS found 11 percent of workers had it available. One of the factors that accounts for the difference in estimate, according to Glass and Estes (1997), was the size of firm; larger firms generally have more benefits (p. 297). Another is the extent to which something like flexible scheduling reached from the top to the bottom levels of the organization (Finnigan 2001).

Examination of the 100 Best

To examine whether the accumulating information on work/family issues has had an impact on work environments, I reviewed 12 years of rankings of the "best companies" for working mothers. These rankings, done by *Working Mother* magazine, were begun in 1986. My comments focus on the years 1990 to 2001, because I was only able to secure detailed reports from 1990 on.

The *Working Mother's* annual "best" list begins with companies nominating themselves for being considered as "one of the best." The nomination process requires that companies complete an extensive (100-page) questionnaire about their practices. In 2001, the magazine's published (although brief) overview of the evaluation strategy included the following:

> First eligible companies . . . completed the comprehensive application which included questions about a company's culture, employee population, and policies on work/life and women's advancement. We designed the application to focus on the availability and tracking of programs, plus the accountibility of managers overseeing them. We also required applying companies to send supporting documents such as benefits handbooks and the results of employee surveys.
>
> With the help of . . . a nationally respected industrial research firm . . . we validated the applications carefully for completeness and accuracy, then awarded scores. Companies accumulated points based on the types of benefits offered, how widely available they are, and usage rates. We weighted the scoring system so that smaller companies could compete. After compiling a preliminary list, we [fine-tuned it]. This year, we focused on three issues, *flex* because it's essential for working moms; *advancement* because that's critical to the work side of work/life balance in companies; and *equitable distribution* of benefits.
>
> After we finalized the list of 100 winning companies, our writers and in-house researchers verified the information yet again. . . . Companies that applied but didn't make the grade got feedback showing which areas need improvement. (p. 94)

To be sure, the self-nominating procedure does not assure a representative or random sample of firms. At the same time, the depth of examination implied in the evaluation process suggests that being in the "Top 100" is a desirable designation for employers. Notably, when this survey began, only 30 companies were listed as the "best" places for mothers to work. In 1990, the number had climbed to 75, and in 1991, to 85; only in 1992 was there a list of the "Top 100." Finally, editors from the magazine note that when they initiated the survey, they virtually had to beg for submissions. In 2001, *Working Mother* would not divulge the number of applications they reviewed, but they referred to it as "more than a thousand" (personal communication).

My interest in the *Working Mother* survey centered on two things: (1) the criteria used for their assessment and how these changed over the decade and (2) the industries represented by the top companies. I expected that the criteria for evaluation had changed over the 12 years to reflect our increasing understanding about work/family issues in an organizational context. Less was anticipated with regard to industries represented. I only expected that those with very high percentages of female employees would be regularly found among the "best."

Criteria for Evaluation

Working Mother organized the criteria for evaluating companies in two ways, by general categories and by specific measures within categories. In 1986, three general categories were used: (1) pay (compared with competition); (2) opportunities for women to advance; and (3) family-friendly benefits. In 1988 a fourth category, support for childcare, was added.

In 1996 two additional categories were added: flexibility, alternative schedules, and leave for new parents. In 1998, a category labeled support for work/life balance was added. These categories "accumulated" with the only reduction in categories coming in 2001, when the first category (pay compared to the competition) was dropped.

Specific Criteria and Expansion of Criteria

Table 27.1 details the specific measures within categories that have been used, by their year of use. An examination of these measures shows the increasing number of measures from 1990 through 2001 (consistent with the added categories of assessment). Each year after 1990, at least one new measure was added. Also, some measures were dropped, and some were redefined. The measure of family sick days in 1990 was redefined as child sick days in 1991. The work/life measure of 1998 is a more general measure that becomes refined in 1999 to include managerial pay tied to employee satisfaction, training supervisors on helping employees with work/life conflicts, and an active task force on work/life issues.

Some changes also came about because of legal changes. For example, pregnancy leave changed from being equated with disability leave to a leave covered by the Family and Medical Leave Act (FMLA) of 1993. Beginning in 1995, corporations were asked to indicate the number of weeks that the employee is given leave at full pay (see Note 12 [of Table 27.1]).

Other interesting criteria were used to assess the "working mother friendliness" of employers. For example, three categories (ABC Member, ABC Champion, and ABC Participant; the last replaces the first after 1996) refer to participation in the American Business Collaboration. ABC is a group of corporate employers who responded to the increasing number of women and dual income families in the labor force by investing in improved childcare in the communities in which they operated. Twenty-one corporations pledged $100 million to improve childcare and were defined as the "champions." The "participant" group members are corporations who invest in their communities although they may not be part of the initial 21 corporations.

A second set of criteria I want to highlight has to do with *linking managerial pay to the advancement of women and to employee satisfaction.* By 1999, these measures had been incorporated into the evaluation process, reflecting an understanding that gender researchers have been "championing" with regard to the advancement of women and changing organizational practices: *You must make it count for your managers. They are the*

Table 27.1
Criteria for Evaluating Company Programs, Working Mother *Magazine, 1999–2001*

Year	1990	91	92	93	94	95	96	97	98	99	00	01
No. of female mgrs/ professionals/VPs	•	•	•	•	•	•	•	•	•	•	•	•
Childcare centers	•	•	•	•	•	•	•	•	•	•	•	•
Standard maternity leave	•											
Pre-tax set asides	•	•	•	•	•	•	•	•	•	•		•
R & R (1)	•	•	•	•		•	•	•	•	•		•
Family sick days	•											
Sick child days			•	•	•	•	•	•	•	•	•	•
Stock ownership	•	•							•			
Leave for childbirth	•	•	•	•	•	•	•	•	•	•	•	•
Leave (11)						•(12)	•	•	•	•	•	•
Disability (partial pay after childbirth)		•	•	•					•	•	•	•
Disability plus (full salary for at least some of the time after childbirth)		•	•	•					•	•	•	•
No disability: must use accrued sick and vacation days		•	•	•								
Part time (no. of employees)		•	•(3)	•	•	•	•	•	•	•	•	•
Flextime	•	•	•	•	•	•	•	•	•	•	•	•
Job sharing	•	•	•	•	•	•	•	•	•	•	•	•
Work at home	•	•	•	•	•	•	•	•	•	•	•	•
Highest paid (2)			•	•	•	•	•	•	•	•	•	•
Compressed workweeks			•	•	•	•	•	•	•	•	•	•
Phase back for new mother's (part-time or work at home)				•	•	•	•	•	•	•	•	•
Dependent care find (4)					•	•	•	•	•	•	•	•
ABC member (5)					•	•						
ABC champion (9)					•	•	•	•	•	•	•	
ABC participant (10)							•	•	•	•	•	•
Health insurance (6)					•	•	•	•	•			
Mgrs advancement (7)						•	•	•				•
Mgr training (8)						•	•	•				•
Adoption aid (13)	•	•	•	•	•	•	•	•	•	•	•	•
NAEYC accreditation (14)								•	•	•	•	
Paid time off (15)								•	•			
Reduced work option (16)								•				
Lactation program (17)									•	•		
Work/Life (18)									•			•
Paternity leave (19)										•	•	•
Mgr pay tied to flex use (20)										•	•	
Mgr pay tied to advancement of women										•	•	•
Mgr pay tied to employee satisfaction										•	•	•
Work life (21)										•	•	•
Network of family childcare homes (22)										•	•	•
Childcare backup (23)											•	•
Women's support group (24)						•						

Notes:

(1) Resource and referral service to help parents find childcare or elder care.

(2) Percentage of females among the highest paid top 20% of all workers at the company.

(3) If part-timers are eligible for benefits, such as health insurance, the minimum number of hours they must work is in parentheses (change in definition).

(4) Money that's been earmarked by the company to pay for child and elder care services.

> **Table 27.1 (Cont)**
> *Criteria for Evaluating Company Programs,* Working Mother *Magazine, 1999–2001*
>
> (5) Company participates in the American Business Collaboration for Quality Dependent Care, a coalition of businesses that has put out more than $26 million to expand and improve child and elder care around the country. An ABC Champion is one of the 11 corporations that helped found and fund the American Business Collaboration.
> (6) Percentage of health insurance paid for by employer.
> (7) Measures managers on women's advancement.
> (8) Training for manager on alternative schedules—how to manage flexible work arrangements.
> (9) One of 21 leadership companies in the American Business Collaboration. The 21 have collectively pledged $100 million over six years to expand and improve child and elder care services across the country.
> (10) One of over 100 companies that help fund local projects of the Collaboration.
> (11) Leave: Number of women/men who took leave after birth of child.
> (12) Family and Medical Leave Act plus number of weeks employee given full pay given.
> (13) Maximum reimbursement employees can receive to pay for cost of adopting a child.
> (14) Childcare center meets standard for health, safety, and education established by the National Association for the Education of Young Children.
> (15) Number (usually based on service) of vacation, sick, and personal days allowed per year.
> (16) Ability of full-time employees to cut back hours for specified period of time; benefits are retained and job is guaranteed.
> (17) Company provides a private space and other aids to nursing mothers such as breast pumps or access to lactation consultant.
> (18) Work/life: Ways in which company promotes work/life balance; for example, by providing counseling, support groups, training of managers, and executives making public statements in support of this issue.
> (19) Paternity leave with job guarantee.
> (20) Manager pay tied to flex use by employees.
> (21) Work/Life
> • Manager's pay tied to employee satisfaction.
> • Supervisors get instructions on helping employee with work/life conflicts.
> • Company has active task force to work on work/life issues.
> (22) Number of homes financially supported by the company.
> (23) Before- and after-school care; sliding scale fees or direct subsidies; summer programs; backup care; sick-child care.
> (24) Women's support group—a company backed group dedicated to the advancement of women.

critical initial support system for employees. Tying practices to managerial pay is one way of doing this.

Overall, the criteria used to evaluate employers changed in ways that reflected our changing knowledge base. What I found interesting, as well, was the extent to which a number of organizations rated reasonably well on the more stringent of these criteria. For example, in 2001, 48 of the companies had managerial pay tied to employee satisfaction and 45 had it tied to the advancement of women. Similarly, the job-guaranteed time off for childbirth was measured in terms of *paid leave beyond the FMLA requirement.* Across the "100 Best" in 2001, the number of weeks of leave ranged widely,

from the minimum legal guarantee of 12 weeks to 56 weeks. Yet over one third ($n = 37$) of the firms provided full pay during "new mom" leave. Only three firms had no policy with regard to pay after childbirth. The remainder provided partial pay. These firms, as such, went beyond the minimum requirements of the FMLA of 1993.

The Employers

These observations bring me to my second area of interest with the *Working Mother* survey: employers. As one might expect, the Top 100 employers covered the range of business sectors. I focused on the business sectors for the "Top 10" employers for the years from 1990 to 2001. During this period, manufacturing dropped out of the Top 10, and financial services increased. Technology and information services and pharmaceuticais did not change in their representation over this period. In 2001, consumer products regained a position in the Top 10, after dropping out for the prior two years.

The pattern illustrated by the companies over the 12 years reflects the growth of service sector employment, although the infrequent representation of health services goes against that trend. Corporations in the areas of financial services and technology and information services represent the growth sectors of the 1980s and 1990s. These employers also are likely to be structured differently—more flexibly—from traditional manufacturing concerns. As such, they are likely to respond to employment issues in a more flexible fashion than are older organizatonal forms.

These are also sectors that employ a high percentage of women. Among the Top 10 companies in 2001, for example, nearly half (47 percent) of their employees were female. Also, on average, women comprised 36 percent of employees in the top 20 percent of the pay scale; they were 35 percent of the middle managers and 23 percent of executives. What these numbers imply is that these are companies that have been aggressive in hiring and promoting women. In doing so, they have instituted a number of practices that actively support their employment, including those that respond to work and family issues. They are also large companies, a fact that is consistent with previous research on the provision of work/family benefits (Glass and Estes 1997).

Ideally, these companies were also viewed as leaders in responding to work/family concerns. In relation to this, if the application numbers referred to by *Working Mother* magazine are true, then it signifies that the importance now given to the magazine's ranking and the practices of these orgarnzations may, indeed, set the standard for others, including smaller organizations.

Implications

What, then, have we gained from the information explosion that helped define work and family as a salient social issue? And what are the areas that now warrant attention?

Consequences of Media Visibility

One important consequence of this dramatic rise in research and writing on work and family is that it has fundamentally transformed the way we think about the spheres of work and of family. No longer do we frame discussions in terms of separate entities; rather, the joined terms "work and family" convey an *image of overlapping institutions*. A second and related consequence is that some concepts that developed from the study of work and family have become a regular part of our language. Two come to mind: One is "the second shift;" another is "family-friendly."

Third, the advancement of women in organizations is *not* viewed as a separate issue from work/family concerns. Work and family has *not* replaced the concern for assuring opportunity and support for women's mobility up the corporate ladder. Rather, good places for women and mothers to work are those that deal aggressively with both issues.

A fourth consequence is the continuing evidence that shows that instituting family-friendly policies is a financial advantage to the employer. Schwartz's assertion about the cost of managerial women is not necessarily true. Women managers do not necessarily cost more than men—if the organization develops effective programs that address both the career-primary and career-and-family woman. Family-friendly programs are one step toward such a realization. In 1999, for example, Prudential reported that its "comprehensive resource and referral service costs the company $1.4 million annually. But . . . it saved more than $7 million, from fewer absences and lower turnover, as a result of program use by over 3,000 employees. . . . [It] saved another $227,000 by opening up a backup childcare center in Newark, NJ . . . which reduced attrition and absenteeism significantly" (*Working Mother*, p. 98).

Other research has confirmed the financial advantage associated with family-friendly programs (Hammonds 1996; Schwartz 1992). Thus, family-friendly programs can be defined as a good business practice that makes sense.

Issues That Remain

Four issues, however, remain on the landscape. The first of these is the extent to which work/family support programs are available from the top to the bottom of the organizational hierarchy. In many organizations—even among the Top 10 of the 2001 list—work/family benefits provided to managers do not automatically apply to those in rank and file positions (Finnigan 2001). As such, the challenge of responding to work/family *at all levels* remains.

The second emerging issue concerns the careers of middle-age women whose children are in their teens or older. These would be similar to the career-and-family women who, Schwartz (1989) argued, would exhibit a high level of commitment to the organization. Research by Gordan and Whelan (1998) began looking at career interests of women in such positions. They suggested that middle-aged women in middle management have different needs and interests than men in the same position and age group. If that is the case, corporations will need to address the differences in order to capitalize on the talents of middle-age women.

The third issue is the notion of "face time," or on-site hours. It has emerged as a concern of employees, *because* of the practice of using on-site hours as a measure of employee performance (WFD Consulting 2001). Because flexible work practices include working at remote sites (including home), there is the potential for penalizing those who have taken advantage of this opportunity. A better understanding of "face time" and its effects will be required in order to assess the extent to which it will diminish the advantages of flexible work practices.

Finally, there is some research suggesting a work and family backlash. Arguably, an increasing proportion of workers do not believe that they benefit from work/family support policies, and that they bear additional burdens when co-workers take advantage of such policies (Young 1999). This can become a countervailing pressure that diminishes the value of flexibility options for employees. Such sentiments also play into the issue of "face time" and its use as a measure of employee performance. Again, an understanding of these dynamics is an important aspect of developing effective programs that are beneficial to the broadest group of employees.

References

Bianchi, Suzanne M., Melissa A. Milkie, Liana C. Sayer, and John P. Robinson. 2000. "Is Anyone Doing the Housework? Trends in the Gender Division of Household Labor." *Social Forces* 79: 191–228.

Blair, Sampson Lee. 1996. "Gender Segregation of Housework." Pp. 391–395 in *Women and Work: A Handbook*, edited by Paula J. Dubeck and Kathryn Borman. New York: Garland Publishing.

Blair-Loy, Mary. 1999. "Career Patterns of Executive Women in Finance: An Optimal Matching Analysis." *American Journal of Sociology* 104: 1346–1397.

Blair-Loy, Mary and Amy S. Wharton. 2002. "Employees' Use of Work Family Policies and the Workplace Social Context." *Social Forces* 80: 813–845.

Davies-Netzley, Sally Ann. 1998. "Women above the Glass Ceiling: Perceptions on Corporate Mobility and Strategies for Success." *Gender and Society* 12: 339–355.

Epstein, Cynthia Fuchs. 1993. *Women in Law*. Urbana: University of Illinois Press.

Finnigan, Annie. 2001. "The Inside Story." *Working Mother*, October, pp. 65–72.

Glass, Jennifer and Valerie Camarigg. 1992. "Gender, Parenthood, and Job-Family Compatibility." *American Journal of Sociology* 98: 131–151.

Glass, Jennifer, L. and Sarah Beth Estes. 1997. "The Family Responsive Workplace." *Annual Review of Sociology* 23: 289–314.

Gordon, Judith R., and Karen S. Whelan. 1998. "Sucessful Professional Women in Midlife: How Organizations Can More Effectively Understand and Respond to the Challenges." *Academy of Management Executive* 12: 8–23.

Hammonds, Keith H. 1996. "Balancing Work and Family: Big Returns for Companies Willing to Give Family Strategies a Chance." *Business Week*, September 16. (*http://www.businessweek.com/1996/38/960916.htm*).

Hochschild, Arlie Russell. 1987. *The Second Shift*. New York: Viking Penguin.

Menaghan, Elizabeth G. 1991. "Work Experiences and Family Interaction Processes: The Long Reach of the Job?" *Annual Review of Sociology* 17: 419–444.

Menaghan, Elizabeth and Toby L. Parcel. 1991. "Determining Children's Home Environments: The Impact of Maternal Characteristics and

Current Occupational and Family Conditions." *Journal of Marriage and the Family* 53: 417–431.

Moen, Phyllis and Yan Yu. 2000. "Effective Work/Life Strategies: Working Couples, Work Conditions, Gender and Life Quality." *Social Problems* 47: 291–326.

Orbuch, Terri L. and Sandra L. Eyster. 1997. "Division of Household Labor among Black Couples and White Couples." *Social Forces* 76: 301–322.

Powell, Gary N. 1999. "Reflections on the Glass Ceiling: Recent Trends and Future Prospects." Pp. 325–345 in *Handbook of Gender and Work*, edited by Gary N. Powell. Thousand Oaks, CA: Sage Publication.

Reskin, Barbara and Irene Padavic. 1994. *Women and Men at Work*. Thousand Oaks, CA: Pine Forge Press.

Schwartz, Felice N. 1989. "Management Women and the New Facts of Life." *Harvard Business Review* (January–February): 65–76.

———. 1992. *Breaking with Tradition*. New York: Warner Books.

Stroh, Linda K. and Anne H. Reilly. 1999. "Gender and Careers: Present Experiences and Emerging Trends." Pp. 307–324 in *Handbook of Gender and Work*, edited by Gary N. Powell. Thousand Oaks, CA: Sage.

U.S. Bureau of the Census. 2001. *Statistical Abstract of the United States: 2001* (121st ed.) Washington, DC: U.S. Government Printing Office.

U.S. Department of Education. 1981. *Degrees Awarded to Women*. Washington, DC: U.S. Government Printing Office.

U.S. Department of Education. Center for Education Statistics. 1987. "Bachelor's and Higher Degrees Conferred in 1985–86." Bulletin. Washington, DC: Office of Education Research and Improvement.

Vannoy, Dana and William W. Philliber. 1992. "Wife's Employment and Quality of Marriage." *Journal of Marriage and the Family* 54: 387–398.

WFD Consulting. 2001. "Corporate America's Move to Remote Work May Be Limited by Heavy Workloads and Face Time Cultures." (*www.wfd.com/new_site/news/face_t.html*).

Wharton, Carol S. 1994. "Finding Time for the Second Shift: The Impact of Flexible Work Schedules on Women's Double Days." *Gender and Society* 8: 189–205.

Working Mother Magazine. 1999. "The 100 Best Companies for Women: Prudential." October, p. 98.

Young, Mary B. 1999. "Work-Family Backlash: Begging the Question, What's Fair?" *Annals*, AAPSS 562: 32–46.

Food for Thought and Application Questions

1. Evaluate the extent to which work-family issues remain central to today's public by monitoring publication information. Using computer-based services (such as InfoTrac), monitor articles in the public media and in academic research concerning work-family issues, working mothers, and family-friendly policies. How do these more recent patterns compare with those identified by the author? Based on the information you gathered, how would you assess the salience of work-family issues today?

2. Find issues of *Working Mother* magazine published since 2001. What types of firms or industries are represented by the "top ten firms to work for"; by the "top 100"? Is there variation across the years? If so, how would you explain the variation?

3. Take one of the issues that remain to be addressed (as defined by the author)—an example would be "face time"—and research the extent to which it is important today. Based on what you find, decide whether you would or would not include this as an important work-family issue today. Justify your decision. ✦

28
Kaleidoscope Careers

An Alternate Explanation for the 'Opt-Out' Revolution

Lisa A. Mainiero
Sherry E. Sullivan

The media coverage on "the opt-out revolution," a term coined to describe the alarming talent drain of highly trained women who choose not to aspire to the corporate executive suite, has been explosive and controversial. Twenty years ago, working women imagined they would pursue their careers, bring home the bacon, fry it up in a pan, split child care with their sensitive, understanding, feminist husbands, and have a relaxing glass of wine at the end of the day. But the complications of balancing work with non-work demands have led some women to voluntarily exit the corporate rat race. Are women leaving corporations in droves because they find the balance between their work and non-work lives far too skewed? Or has the "opt-out revolution," a term suggested by the *New York Times Magazine*, been overblown and exaggerated?

Executives who have read headlines profiling women such as Karen Hughes (White House Chief Strategist for President George W. Bush), Brenda Barnes (President and CEO of PepsiCo's North America division), and Maureen Smith (President of the Fox Family Channel and the Fox Kids Network) who left their jobs to spend time with family, would believe that indeed this is the case. While analyzing last year's media coverage, a reader would assume that women are failing to achieve the top posts in their Fortune 500 firms because: (1) highly educated women are leaving the workforce, thus reducing the number of female contenders for top positions; (2) women aren't willing to work as hard as men for the top spots; (3) women are too timid or too passive to claim their reward; (4) women don't want power; or (5) women find there are more psychological and social rewards for staying home. The thesis of the popular press is that work demands are incompatible with family needs; therefore, women leave the work force to concentrate on family.

But do these popular press accounts of women leaving the workforce tell the full story? We think not. The answer lies in more complex issues and trends resulting from a major paradigm shift in how careers are developed, created, and utilized—by women and by men—that is the real story magazine writers and news reporters have missed.

It Makes Great Copy, But What's Really Going On?

To support the claim that women are not interested in the executive suite, the *New York Times Magazine* article focused on a small, elite sample of Princeton graduates who represented a socio-economic stratum that allowed them the privilege to leave their careers behind. The article reported that more than a third of women with MBAs are not working full time; merely 16 percent of women have made it to partner in the law field; only 16 percent of corporate officers in *Fortune* 500 companies are women; and only 38 percent of Harvard MBA women from the classes of 1981, 1985, and 1991 work full time. Census data also reveal an increase in stay-at-home moms who hold graduate degrees, as 22 percent of mothers with graduate degrees are home full-time with their children. In addition, the article noted that fewer women with MBAs than men remained in the full-time work force through mid-career. Citing a Catalyst survey that suggested that 26 percent of the women within three levels of the upper echelon aren't interested in the CEO position, it was conveniently omitted that 55 percent of those surveyed do want the top job, and an additional 19 percent are undecided.

While there is a trend indicating a drop off in workplace participation among working mothers, and statistics show some married mothers work only part of the year, part time, or stay home while their children are young, women are nonetheless making inroads into the executive suite. *Fortune* magazine, in addition to its 2003 article titled, "Power: Do Women Really Want It?" dutifully lists its yearly *"Power 50 Women"* of American and global businesses, highlighting women who have achieved executive positions in Fortune 500 firms. From these statistics, it is clear that women are making slow but sure inroads in various industries, even those characterized as "old-boys clubs." For example, women in the entertainment industry now occupy almost 30 percent of all executive and production slots at senior vice president or higher at the major film studios, and the number of women in traditionally male-dominated fields of financial services, law, and insurance are increasing. There are more women in the pipeline for executive slots, but progress is slow.

Nonetheless, data from the Current Population Survey indicate that although working mothers are more likely to work full-time than 20 years ago, only 37 percent of them worked full-time year round compared to 54 percent of women without children and 66 percent of men. The percentage of women entrepreneurs and small business owners also is growing directly in proportion to the loss of qualified talent from major corporations. A recent Fortune-Yankelovich survey discovered an astonishing number of women were considering other career and personal options at mid-life, such as starting their own businesses, changing jobs, returning to school, taking time off, making major personal changes, or simply leaving their jobs.

This exodus of women from corporations demands answers—and solutions. The answer to the question: "Are women leaving organizations for non work or advancement reasons?" isn't a simple "yes" or "no" but requires an examination of the complex interplay between non-work demands and lack of advancement opportunities for women. Three reasons have been suggested as underpinnings for this phenomenon: (1) generational differences and shifts in work values; (2)

work-family balance issues; and (3) discrimination against women in the workforce.

Turnover Rates: Family Reasons, Lack of Advancement, or Changing Values?

The most frequent assumption by members of the popular press is that women are leaving corporations because they need to resign for family reasons. Although it may be true that many women leave work to care for family, not all women are leaving corporations for that reason alone. Research has indicated that women's turnover intentions were not predicted by family structure (e.g., dual earner status or number of children). Instead, women reported they were leaving for the same reasons as male managers: lack of career opportunities in their current company and other work-related predictors of turnover, such as job dissatisfaction and low organizational commitment. A comprehensive review on turnover found the turnover rate for women is actually similar to that of men, with women being more likely than men to remain in the work force as they age. Moreover, researchers have found that managers who had been promoted were less likely to resign than nonpromoted managers, and promoted women were less likely to resign than promoted men. In general, when opportunities for career advancement are poor, managers—regardless of gender—leave, but when opportunities for career advancement exist, women remain loyal.

Lack of advancement opportunities may be the foremost reason why women leave corporations. According to Catalyst, women hold only 15.7 percent of the Fortune 500 corporate officer positions, and despite progress, men still dominate the executive suite in many industries, including higher education. Only 47 percent of women faculty have tenure compared to 65 percent for men and only 18 percent of full professors at doctoral universities are women. Karen Lyness and Donna Thompson, in a comparative study of 69 men and women executives, found women reported greater barriers to career advancement, citing roadblocks including: lack of general management or line experience (79 percent agreement), exclusion from informal networks (77 percent agreement), stereotypes about women's roles and abilities (72 percent agreement), and failure of top leaders to assume accountability for women's advancement (68 percent agreement). Sixty-seven percent agreed "commitment to personal/family responsibilities" was the most important challenge for women.

Finally, generational differences in values between GenXers and Baby Boomers may serve as one explanation for the "opt-out" phenomenon. Baby Boomers, typically defined as the generation born between 1946 and 1960, witnessed great political, religious, and social upheavals as they watched the Vietnam War, Watergate, and the advancement of feminism shape their generation. GenXers, born between 1961–1982, grew up with financial, family and social insecurity, rapid technological change, and increased diversity. Today's GenX workers are the former latch-key kids who watched their Baby Boomer parents work long hours only to be downsized out of their jobs. Researchers posit such generational differences may have affected GenXers' work ethic and their willingness to work long hours as the price for material success. Catalyst tested the assumption that GenXers bring different expectations to the workplace, finding that 76 percent want a compressed work week and 59 percent want to telecommute or have flexible working arrangements. GenXers also rated personal/family goals higher than career goals.

The Research: Time for a New Model of Careers

New trends in career research have articulated the concept of boundaryless careers, in which workers are no longer bound to the idea of traditional career with steady upward movement within one firm, and are motivated more by self-fulfillment and balancing work/nonwork than the stability and security of the past. Although the concept of the boundaryless career became a hallmark of research about careers only in the last decade, this model has been used by women for decades out of necessity. The needs of caring

for children, coping with aging parents or ailing spouses, personal demands, trailing spouse issues, and outright discrimination in the workplace have led women to pursue discontinuous, interrupted, and even "sideways" careers.

While trends such as the generational differences between GenXers and Baby Boomers, issues of balance and work/nonwork conflict, and discrimination against women may have contributed to the drop off in workplace participation among women, we think the issues run much deeper and suggest a new career model for workers in the 21st century. The career shifts, changes, transitions, and compromises employees are making in their careers provide interesting material for study. As researchers, we felt it was time to articulate a new model for careers in a way that deconstructs what employees are doing today: How do women's careers unfold? What meaning does "career" have? And which factors are salient in the transitions they make in their careers?

For our research, we took a complex, multiple-pronged, three-study approach. First, we conducted an online survey of over 100 high achieving women, primarily professionals, managers, and business entrepreneurs. Participants were asked to explicate transitions they made in their careers and the reasons why. Second, we conducted a larger, more detailed online survey of professionals (837 men and 810 women) to compare differences in career motivations and transitions between men and women. This survey was quite large and offered us the opportunity to compare men and women at different points in their life span. In addition to the results of these two surveys, we wanted to gain insights into some of the transitions and setbacks associated with women's and men's careers. Therefore, we orchestrated a series of lengthy online "conversations" with 22 men and 5 women about their careers. Because we examined only women in the first study, we intentionally oversampled men for Study 2. In contrast to the high-profile, senior-level women executives often featured in the popular press, our sample included women (and men) from different levels and backgrounds to more realistically capture the careers of most working professionals.

Voices of Women: Defining Careers Differently

In defining a new model of careers that includes career interruptions, employment gaps, top-outs, opt-outs, as well as the new values of the current generation, we were intrigued to find that women and men described their careers quite differently. Many women examined the opportunities, roadblocks, and possibilities, then forged their own approach to a career without regard for traditional career models and standard measures of achievement. They rejected the concept of linear career progression, preferring instead to create non-traditional, self-crafted careers that suited their objectives, needs, and life criteria.

Consider Lynn's career description. Lynn is a 43-year-old mother of three who has an MBA. She describes the reasons she "opted out":

> I left college for a great career opportunity at a local phone company. I worked as a marketing manager for awhile, starting off as a staff assistant and moving up to the manager's spot. I loved my work and did it well. But over time I realized there was no way I was going to be president of that company and started to think about other options. My husband had taken a job up in Hartford, CT, and I was pregnant—finally. I struggled getting pregnant and did not want to take any chances with this baby. So I left the dream job and stayed home while raising my three children, at least while they were young. I figured I would go back to work after the first one, and I did, part-time for awhile, but that didn't work out. Then I returned to work, helping my husband in his consulting practice for awhile. I even took client assignments. But we got on each other's nerves and the work wasn't fulfilling enough. I needed a job where I could be home for the bus in the afternoon and still have a challenge. I found employment in my town as a Museum Curator—who would have thought. The job is not challenging but I can be close to home and available to my chil-

dren. I am thinking of starting my own antique shop in town, because I love antiques, and that would be more fulfilling for me.

Lynn temporarily opted out for a combination of reasons, including the lack of advancement opportunities and the birth of a child. Contrast her description to that of Lori, a single professional with no children, who changed her career course because of a failed relationship. She forged a path in a male-dominated field by developing a childhood passion into a job that offered both challenge and the chance to fulfill a cherished dream:

> First I was a photographer . . . then a concert promoter . . . but like many women I know, the most transforming career decision was motivated by the need to make a leap into the void at the ruination of a cherished love relationship. I was devastated when the man I lived with and was crazy about dumped me for four or five other (and rather unremarkable) women, and I needed a life raft—something new and challenging to throw my energies into. . . . Since high school I had been fascinated by shipwrecks and sunken treasure. One day during the long post-love crisis period, I learned of a marine archaeological field school to be taught in the Netherlands Antilles by some of Mel Fisher's crew, so I [went] and fell in love with historic shipwreck archaeological search and recovery and all of the research and learning that goes along with it. . . . Now more than a decade later I live in Key West, Florida, having created my own business as a professional in the field of historic shipwrecks. Though it is not a picnic carving a niche in a profession almost exclusively dominated by men, I am happy I made the leap because the work is fascinating beyond my imaginings!

Both Lynn's and Lori's career descriptions illustrate the interplay of work and nonwork factors on women's career development. Lynn's and Lori's career descriptions are interesting because instead of emphasizing the negative outcomes of trying to balance work and nonwork that we often read about in the popular press, these women chose to blend their work and nonwork lives. Their career decisions were a natural outgrowth of the opportunities that were presented to them and the choices they made to fulfill their dreams within the context of the relationships around them. . . .

Contrast Lynn's and Lori's careers with this career history from a male respondent, John, recounting his extraordinarily accomplished but quite linear career in banking:

> I started with [my bank] over 25 years ago as a part-time teller. I have had the opportunity, over the course of my career with the bank, to be involved in various areas of the organization. These areas include Branch Management, Management of the Accounting and Proof areas, Director of Deposit Operations, Management of Consumer Loans, Management of the Mortgage Field Rep teams [names other areas, etc.]. I currently serve as First Vice President and I am now responsible for the Bank's 50-branch network and growth of our deposit portfolio, the Alternative Financial Services Area, the Trust Department, as well as departments that support branch operations and sales management. I have had the pleasure of having a one bank career. I grew up in the organization. Having been given the opportunity to work in various areas of the organization, I feel that I have a broad view of the bank and have interacted with a vast majority of the people in the organization. I now serve as a member of the Executive Management Team of the bank with responsibilities for the development and implementation of the organization's strategic and business plans.

Not all men in our research demonstrated such extremely linear career paths, but men as a group were more likely to follow traditional career paths associated with one industry (though not necessarily one firm) than women. Our research asks: Is Lynn's career any less valid because she took time off to be with her children? Is Lori's career not a "career" because it is variable and disjointed? We think not. The fact that Lynn and Lori crafted together a series of job opportunities, some part-time, some full-time, constitutes a career as much as the linear career in a single institution as described by John. The difference is that these women created a career on their own terms, blending and in-

tegrating rather than segregating the work and non-work facets of their lives, while striving to obtain greater job challenge and personal fulfillment.

Our analysis of the women's responses to the first survey, from which Lynn's and Lori's career descriptions are taken, helped us to understand the nature and character of women's careers. The women surveyed indicated that they were more likely to have non-traditional careers, characterized by various career interruptions that required attention to non-work needs, than traditional linear careers as described by the men. These nonwork needs went beyond childcare concerns and encompassed many needs including the quest for spiritual fulfillment and the need to be true to oneself, as illustrated by this comment from Ruth:

> I left the corporate world at age 48 to start my own business fulfilling a long desire to be my own boss and be aligned with my spiritual belief and need to help others reach their full potential.

Similarly, other women discussed their career transitions being triggered by the need to care for themselves, especially after experiencing a serious illness. Consider the comments of Robin, a 53-year-old attorney:

> When I changed careers 4 years ago, I did so not only because I wanted to accept the challenge of a new career but also because I wanted to put more of a balance in my life, with adding more time for family and friends. In 1990, I collapsed during a trial and learned it was chronic fatigue syndrome. I was out of work for 18 months. I [was] determined to get back and [be] healthy and add more relaxation time into my life.

Others faced direct and indirect discrimination, as illustrated by the following comments:

> . . . that as a woman I needed to be more credentialed than my male counterparts in order to be treated half as well. Always heard the excuse that men in my field were paid more because they were heads of households.

> Most of the changes I have made were because of feelings of being underappreciated, undervalued, or underpaid.

I have experienced sexism, harassment, and outright hostility.

When some of the women in our study found internal advancement opportunities blocked, like a growing number of women, they opted out and started their own businesses. Between 1997 and 2002, the Center for Women's Business Research reported that the number of women-owned firms increased by 14 percent, for an estimated 6.2 million U.S. firms owned by women.[32] Twenty-nine-year-old Laura is one of the growing number of women making the transition out of the corporate world:

> I now manage my own career—I am in control of how much money I am able to make, rather than relying on a male dominated corporate world dictating when I will get promoted and how much I will get paid. I have flexible hours so can find the time to work out, travel, and spend time with family and friends. I am so much happier as a person.

In sharp contrast to the traditional model as illustrated by John, the careers of the women in our study were characterized by the need to seek challenges and learning opportunities but were curtailed by the lack of advancement opportunities, and outright discrimination. Their career interruptions were shaped by non-work issues—including the need for personal fulfillment, balance, and to nurture oneself. The women in our studies didn't ask for or want special treatment. They worked long hours and held themselves to high performance standards. They emphasized the intrinsic rewards of quality performance. But they were immensely frustrated by the lack of job challenge, discrimination, and the exhaustion that comes from trying to do it all.

Kaleidoscope Careers: A New Model for a New Generation

Despite great changes in social and workplace norms as well as advances in gender equality, we were surprised to find such dramatic differences between the careers of men and women throughout the research. In sharp contrast to men, the career histories of women are relational. Their career decisions were normally part of a larger and intricate web of interconnected issues, people, and aspects that had to come together in a delicately balanced package. In our research, we saw women making decisions about their career options after considering the impact their decisions will have on others. Listen to the explanations of these two (typical) women:

> Most of my career changes have been influenced by family reasons. When I had my first child, the company for which I worked did not have options like flex-time or the ability to accept the fact that you can work from home. In my current position and company, I have a lot more say over my schedule and am able to delegate to several people in order to keep my work load reasonable. These benefits are keeping me in this position, although I have felt that it is time for me to move on career-wise. My family would be very disrupted by a position that required me to put in extensive overtime which any new job that paid my current salary would demand.

> After I had put a number of years into the job, I looked at my husband—worn down from travel, working hard on weekends—and I said, "Something's gotta give." So it was me. How long were we going to go on like that? My husband had needs, my children were saying they needed me more, my parents needed someone to take them to the doctor's appointments they made, my brother's marriage ended in divorce . . . there was so much going on that I could not do the 9 to 5 anymore. So I gave up the big job where I wasn't going anywhere fast anyway and became a copy editor and now work from home, make my own hours, and work when I can.

As a means of understanding the "opt-out" or career interruption phenomenon, we developed the kaleidoscope model. Like a kaleidoscope that produces changing patterns when the tube is rotated and its glass chips fall into new arrangements, women shift the pattern of their careers by rotating different aspects of their lives to arrange their roles and relationships in new ways. Women's careers, like kaleidoscopes, are relational.

Each action taken by a woman in her career is viewed as having profound and long lasting effects on others around her. Each career action, therefore, is evaluated in light of the impact such decisions may have on her relationships with others, rather than based upon insulated actions as an independent actor on her own.

Although research has focused on "work/family conflict"—with family often narrowly defined as a husband and children—non-work issues (e.g., a woman's own physical and psychological well-being, family issues, elder care, volunteerism) must be viewed as much more than a career constraint. For women, making career decisions while considering their impact on others may be inherent. Researcher Shelley Taylor and associates discovered a biobehavioral stress response in females that describes a "tend and befriend" response, rather than a "fight or flight" response, demonstrating how ingrained attachments and caregiving may be in women. For women, we do not believe the concept of "career" can be summarily divorced from a larger understanding of "context." In our kaleidoscope model, "family" and "context" are more broadly defined as the set of connections representing individuals who deserve consideration as a weight in the decision, each with their own needs, wants, and desires that must be evaluated as parts of the whole.

The women in our research made career decisions from a lens of ***relationalism***—they factored in the needs of their children, spouses, aging parents, friends, and even co-workers and clients—as part of the total gestalt of their careers. Men, on the other hand, tended to examine career decisions from the perspective of goal orientation and independent action—acting first for the benefit of career. Men tended to keep their work and non-work lives separate—and often could do this because the women in their lives managed the delicate interplay between work and non-work issues. For example, significantly more women than men (41.1 percent women, 24.4 percent men) stated, "I made changes in my career due to family demands," while more men than women reported family demands were "not a factor" (40.2 percent

men, 30.1 percent women). More women than men (42.7 percent women, 15.0 percent men) reported "My spouse moved to another geographical location and I followed." In addition to family issues, women were more likely to make career transitions because of a yearning for self-improvement (30.1 percent women and 19.3 percent men) "I wanted to simplify and reduce stress.") and greater challenge (23.5 percent women, 17.3 percent men) "I was bored and wanted greater challenge." On the other hand, significantly more men than women reported reasons associated with career achievements or goal-orientation: "An opportunity presented itself for more money, greater security" (30.7 percent men, 24.4 percent women), or "A risky opportunity presented greater long term payoff" (18.1 percent men, 11.8 percent women). Surprisingly, corporate politics was an equal opportunity player for both men and women; there was no difference by gender when corporate politics was nominated as the reason for career transitions. The reasons why men and women made career transitions are summarized in Figure 28.1 and Table 28.1.

Consider again the working of a kaleidoscope: as one part moves, the other parts change. Women, who utilize a relational model in attending to their worlds, understand that any decision they make for themselves creates changes in others' lives. Women evaluate the choices and options available through the lens of the kaleidoscope to determine the best fit among their relationships, work constraints, and opportunities. As one decision is made, it affects the outcome of the kaleidoscope pattern. Rather than singularly striving for career goals, the women in our research determined the set of options in that kaleidoscope that mark the best fit at the time, always considering the impact of their decisions on others in their lives.

Why is the kaleidoscope model a revolutionary new approach to the study of careers? The contribution of the kaleidoscope model is that it provides context to the study of careers and puts *gender* in the foreground. Researchers in the area of work-family-nonwork domains have long noted the bifurcation of "work" versus "family." Yet the

Figure 28.1
Career Transition Percentages for Men and Women (n=837 Men, 810 Women)

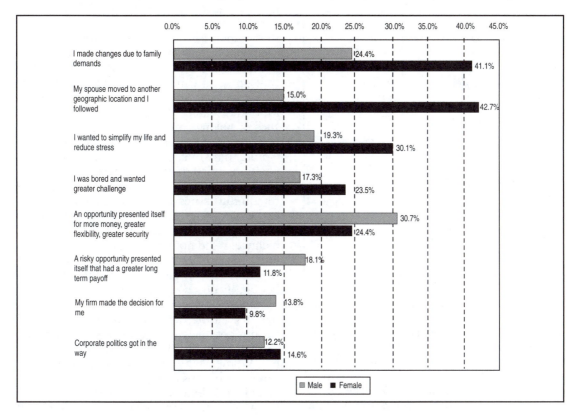

women in our studies saw work/family concerns as more of a gestalt in their lives—"I must find the fit that is right for me given my circumstances and context—rather than a division of "work" versus "family" with both concepts treated in isolation. A woman's context—her family, relationships, caregiving needs—offers decision-making parameters for her in any decision about her career. She is relational. Her context does not exist in isolation; rather it is the difference between *figure* and *ground* in the complex decision-making interplay that is associated with careers.

We offer the kaleidoscope metaphor as a new way of thinking about careers emanating from gender issues, valuing gender and context rather than making it "invisible" in the study of careers. . . . The voices of the women in our research tell us that women are more interested in creating a career *their*

way, through lateral but challenging assignments, opportunities that fit their lives, entrepreneurial activities, or flexible scheduling, rather than focusing on advancement for the sake of advancement. This is not to say that women are not interested in advancement; they are. Lots of women are. But the women in our research were more interested in making the career *suit* their lives, rather than allowing the career to *overtake* their lives.

Parameters of the Kaleidoscope: The ABC Model

The relational model is not new. When the ethic of care, connection, and relationalism concept was first introduced by Carol Gilligan, she wrote about the impact of relationships on moral development, not careers. Joan Gallos introduced relationalism as a concept for

Table 28.1
Sample Percentages for Men and Women
Regarding Career Items (Study 2)
(N = 837 men, 810 women)

Linear Career Items:	Men	Women
I have pursued my career goals at several different firms all within the same industry	25.5*	17.6
I was promoted several times after working hard to achieve my goals	31.8*	25.1
I have developed a certain level of expertise in my field	42.9*	28.6
I enjoy using my skills and talents in a variety of different ways	17.9*	11.7
Nonwork/Family Related Items:		
Nothing is more important to me than my family	4.7	18.8*
Family needs necessitated that I change jobs or careers so that I could achieve a better balance for my work and family	14.2	29.4*
I took a break from work/career to care for family, children, or elders	5.6	27.7*

Note: (*) denotes significance levels at the p < .05 level or higher.[36]

studying women's careers, and researchers Gary Powell and Lisa Mainiero allowed an interpretation of relationalism in discussing the complexities of women's careers as part of their "river of time" metaphor. Other researchers have discussed the need for a "dual agenda" that allows for an integration of work and family in the workplace. Our model goes beyond these original precepts, however, to examine the importance of three key career issues women must face: authenticity, balance, and challenge. . . .

Figure 28.2 illustrates how three key parameters shift over a typical woman professional's life span. The three parameters that predominated choices about the "fit" of their lives and careers include questions about:

Authenticity: *Can I be myself in the midst of all of this and still be authentic?*

Balance: *If I make this career decision, can I balance the parts of my life well so that there can be a coherent whole?*

Challenge: *Will I be sufficiently challenged if I accept this career option?*

Each of these parameters, or decision-making questions, were active as significant posts throughout a woman's career. We found, however, that certain issues predominated at different points in the life span, becoming the parameter that caused a pivot in the woman's decision making about her career. The remaining aspects, still active, are not irrelevant but take on a secondary role at that point in time. For example, most of the women in our samples discussed their needs for finding career challenges in early career. Issues of balance and authenticity were of secondary concern, but nonetheless important. A woman may make a career decision to take a position offering more responsibility, because challenge is the key pivot at that time, but the remaining issues (balance, authenticity) become secondary. In mid-career, women were predominately concerned about the issue of balance. It did not matter whether the woman had a husband or children or whether she was single. She was concerned about balancing her family needs as a priority, or, as in the case of single women, soliciting eldercare for aging parents, aiding the concerns and interests of various nephews and nieces, or searching for a companion with whom she could balance her life. Women may make adjustments to their career ambitions at that point to take on more flexible schedules. In late career, women in our research were asking the question, "Is that all there is?" Desire for authenticity, being true to herself, and making decisions that suited her above others predominated her career and life decisions. At this point, we found most women were interested in challenges, but on their own terms, making decisions in an authentic, meaningful way, and the issue of balance, while still active, had receded to the background.

We call this the "ABC Model of Kaleidoscope Careers." Just as a kaleidoscope uses three mirrors to create infinite patterns, our kaleidoscope career model has three "mirrors" or parameters (authenticity, balance, and challenge) that combine in different ways throughout a woman's life, reflecting the unique patterns of her career. . . . For example, at one point, she may delay having children in order to devote more energy to her career. At another point, she may subjugate career ambitions for the sake of her family needs. Later in life, she may forge ahead, searching for meaning and spirituality in her life. Somewhere in

Figure 28.2
The ABC Model of Kaleidoscope Careers for Women

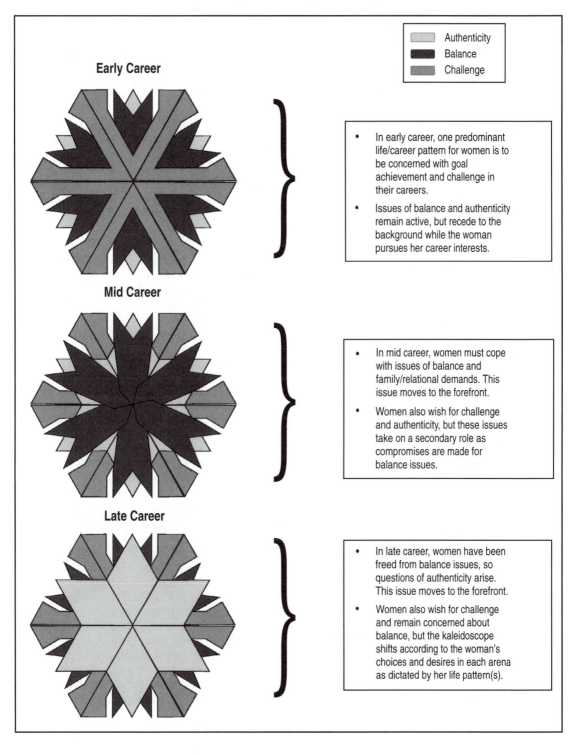

the middle she may be most concerned about balance and relationships in her life. Her context shapes her choices. Therefore, "opting-out" becomes a natural decision based on the fit of the colors of her kaleidoscope at that point in time. Her career does not dictate her life. Instead, she shapes her career to fit her life as marked by her distinct and changing personal kaleidoscope patterns over her life span.

Do Men Value Family and Flexibility? Yes, But Their Timing Is Different

Our research also allowed for an opportunity to examine men's careers as a counterpoint to women's careers. Men's careers had a linear, or sequential aspect—challenges first, concerns about the self, then a later focus on balance and others—that was far more straightforward than the complex kaleidoscope patterns and multiplicity of career/family decision making of women. Although previous research based on gender archetypes has focused on the influence of relationships on women and achievement for men, we do not believe such distinctions are quite that clear cut. Our research showed that men came to value relationships more once they had made progress in their careers. In the words of two men in the online sample (Study 3):

I have made many personal sacrifices for success. While I was a good provider, the time and dedication to my job left little time and energy to enjoy my family. This really hit home seven years ago when my mother passed away and I realized that certain things, like one's success and accomplishments, are not as important as one's family. [Since then] I have made conscious efforts to form relationships with my own family. (62-year-old male executive)

My wife chose the harder career and stayed home with our three sons while I went to work. Having worked for one firm my entire career, I grew up with the company and found the company has been very supportive when I needed time. The real issue was me. I did not ask for much time. We needed the money and I

worked a lot of overtime in the early years. As time passed, the balancing issue became more of an issue. I knew there had to be tradeoffs. Supporting my family meant working hard, getting the promotions and increasing my pay. I found . . . balance means making choices. [So] I picked a few things I would participate with (soccer, scouts, vacation). (50-year-old male vice president)

The men in our sample focused on realizing career ambitions, challenge, and developing their skills first, but came to value personal relationships more over time. This difference in perspective, and of timing of the pivotal values of family relationships vis-à-vis career, marks a profound contrast between women and men and explains why women's careers do not fit neatly into the traditional career stage models (developed with men's careers in mind). It also explains why women's career decisions may mystify corporate decision-makers and male executives, who are confounded by successful women jumping off the career ladder just as they were about to achieve a position of prominence in their careers. While men tend to follow a sequential pattern, focusing first on their careers and then on their families later in life, we found women tend to simultaneously focus on the context of relationships throughout their lives, considering all three parameters—authenticity, balance, and challenge—of the kaleidoscope model at each personal decision point before making any life-changing decisions.

Looking at the life span, we find that women and men are negotiating different time constraints associated with their career decisions, and these timing and life span issues impact turnover. Firms that fail to understand these differences, and try to force women into the cookie-cutter traditional corporate linear model of long hours, face-time, and extensive travel don't realize that inflexible corporate polices contribute to women's turnover and result in an immeasurable loss of human capital for the firm. Criteria based on the traditional linear career model work against women who are immersed in their relational context and may be saddled with more non-work responsibilities than men.

The Upcoming Labor Shortage: What Should Organizations Do?

The U.S. Bureau of Labor Statistics forecasts an upcoming labor shortage in the year 2012 unless organizations effectively retain and utilize human capital. To answer the question about the talent drain that prefaced this article, executives must realize that a complex set of factors—lack of advancement options due to discrimination, blending work and relationships, and the need for authenticity, balance, and challenge—have a great influence on women's career decisions. To create workplaces that do not suffer from a talent drain of women—and GenX men, for that matter—it is imperative that firms urgently begin the process of initiating policies that improve retention *now*.

Many firms expect that providing "family-friendly" policies, such as allowing parental leave, subsidizing day care, and orthodontics coverage in benefits policies is sufficient to make their firms attractive to potential recruits. But what firms traditionally think is "family-friendly" simply isn't. With the new GenX mentality, firms will need to do more than simply offer cosmetic benefits. Firms will need to undergo normative change, restructure their policies concerning careers, benefits, and pay, and re-examine central assumptions about how work gets done in a way that embraces kaleidoscope thinking.

There are two important caveats to implementing successful work/life programs. First, organizations must be truly committed to work/life programs and not use them solely for the purpose of publicity. If organizations have work/life policies but foster a hostile culture that makes use of these programs unacceptable, the policies become worthless and will fail to produce the positive intended.

Second, establishing work/life programs is not enough. Our research shows that women make career decisions based on a complex and interrelated set of factors, including job challenge and opportunities for advancement. While work/life programs are a beginning, they must be coupled with challenging jobs and advancement opportunities for women. Gender-based inequities in wages, job placements, and training opportunities must be eliminated. We offer recommendations, summarized in Table 28.2, that address what firms should do to re-structure the fabric, policies, and norms of organizations to provide true "kaleidoscope" environments.

Assumption #1: What firms *think* is sufficient: "We offer flexible schedules for those jobs that are appropriate."

What firms *should* do: Completely redesign the way work is done in a way that supports work/life integration.

Many firms, especially those commonly noted in publications such as *Working Mother* magazine, *Fortune* magazine, NAFE (the National Association of Female Executives) as well as those profiled in Catalyst publications, offer flexible schedules. However, flexible scheduling often is offered with caveats that include special circumstances or for certain types of work. A norm of flexible work, with rewards for those who effectively perform on such schedules, must be created throughout the workforce for firms to be truly family-friendly. For example, at Sun Microsystems, an overwhelming 95 percent of its workforce uses flexible schedules. But flexibility, on its own, is not enough.

Researchers from MIT's Workplace Center, a think tank that examines work-life issues, suggest that basic assumptions about how work is designed must be challenged. Instead of assuming that employees should demonstrate their commitment and ambition through long hours, face-time and travel, firms need to recognize their employees have both work and personal obligations. Work should be redesigned around this "dual agenda". . . .

With the new technologies that are available, work can be redesigned around the concept of performance outcomes rather than hours logged sitting in an office—with rewards based on outcomes not hours worked. When employees can make recommendations for improved work schedules and see their valid suggestions implemented and rewarded, then work will be re-designed so that it is truly family-friendly.

Assumption #2: What firms *think* is sufficient: "Linear career paths are the status quo."

Table 28.2

*Recommended Changes for Organizations Committed to the Retention and
Advancement of Women*

What Corporations Think is Sufficient To Be "Family-Friendly"	New Approaches for Firms Committed to the Advancement and Retention of Women
Offer flexible schedules where appropriate.	Redesign work so it can be made flexible. Provide "tech for flex" (technology for flexibility) so that workers can work remotely from their offices at all hours of the day. Allow videoconferencing to eliminate unnecessary travel. Reward and promote individuals who effectively use flexible schedules and are role models for others.
Linear career paths.	Real acceptance of kaleidoscope thinking and alternative career paths, including meaningful opportunities to "opt-back-in." Build on-ramps as well as off-ramps so that professionals and workers of all types can take a career interruption and return at a later point. Reward women who return with advancement possibilities. Maintain employee alumni networks for communication purposes.
State support for the advancement of women.	Make top level managers accountable for turnover and advancement rates of women. Provide career succession plans that include time off for career interruptions, with rewards attached for re-entry. Monitor the number of men and women in the "pipeline" for general and upper management positions. Consider early field experiences for women who have not yet taken a career interruption, and profit and loss experience to women who return once they have re-acclimated.
Traditional reward system based on face time, long hours, and travel commitments.	Create reward systems based on outcomes and actual performance, not face time. Eliminate gender discrimination in wages and benefits, and gender inequities in training and promotion systems. Include feedback from family and friends as part of evaluation process. Reward managers for developing unique compensation packages.
Provide family-friendly programs.	In addition to programs, create an organizational culture that encourages and rewards the use of such programs. Redefine "family" beyond children and provide programs that support caregiving. Consider radical new benefits, such as tuition reimbursement programs for employee children offered based on length of service, or on-site summer camp programs for employee children on site. Allow for corporate sabbaticals to encourage fresh new thinking for long-term employees.
Tacit lip-service to government and community efforts to create programs that value families.	Provide lobbying efforts for governmental initiatives to support working parents, such as paid day care, increased paid options for staying home, and the rights of parents and caregivers to a shorter work week without fear of penalty.

What firms *should* do: Adopt kaleidoscope thinking and create new, open-ended career paths for women and men.

Realizing that the kaleidoscope model suggests that women may need to take time off to handle various aspects of their lives, career pathways can be created so that women may do so without penalty of losing their jobs entirely. Corporations need to create better "on ramps" as well as "off ramps"—positions that allow for career interruptions or part-time downscaling of the work at hand. For example, Deloitte, Touche Tomatsu has created a five-year unpaid leave policy as a means of facilitating career interruptions for employees who wish to take time off to settle family or personal concerns. IBM has long been a leader in developing "alumni relations" networks, allowing for policies that re-admit employees in good standing to the firm. These so-called "boomerangs" may not return to jobs equivalent to their previous level, but they usually are placed within the former area of responsibility. Paid and unpaid corporate sabbaticals are slowly catching on, with some firms like General Mills offering one-year leaves to women on global assignments so that they can obtain international experience needed for corporate advancement. . . .

Firms wishing to retain talented women need to examine the level of challenge and support they are providing, and ensure that professional women gain critical field experience early in their careers—ahead of their child rearing years—and that training continues throughout their careers. Some activities that might support kaleidoscope thinking include: long-term succession planning that allows for career interruptions; training programs that allow for re-acclimation to the workforce; alumni networks that keep former employees "in the know"; . . . and above all, the corporate expectation that employees will be welcomed back with open arms. . . . By creating a corporate culture that allows for and respects all pathways—staying in, opting-out, stop-out, interrupted, boomerangs, returnees, alumni, laid-offs, part-timers—the kaleidoscope model will be realized not as a barrier, but as a natural process of career management.

Assumption #3: What firms *think* is sufficient: "But we say we support the advancement of women."

What firms *should* do: Make managers accountable for advancement goals.

Women have made great strides in gaining entrance to firms and cracking the glass ceiling. Despite these advances, women still largely remain stuck in middle management. Researchers have found there were significant differences in the criticality, visibility, and breadth of responsibility in management positions held by men and women. Women were more likely to be placed in positions where they lacked authority to influence others, lacked network support, and experienced greater stress.

Although some corporations are now making a concerted effort to improve the pipeline of women to executive positions in their firms, women in the largest U.S. firms still hold less than 10 percent of the profit-and-loss line jobs that eventually lead to the top organizational positions. In an effort to promote and retain women, firms must provide real advancement opportunities that allow for executive development. Companies can benchmark the practices of other firms to improve their own poli-

cies. For example, NAFE's Top 30 companies focus on not only how many women hold senior profit and loss positions, but also how many women in middle management have experience to be viable pipeline candidates. Some activities that can help support the advancement of women include: monitoring the number of women and men rotating into operating roles; formal job rotation policies that identify and train high potential women; developing women's networks; . . . and offering women leadership forums, conferences, and training programs that sharpen the type of bottom line skills that lead to career advancement.

Further, managers must be held accountable for the promotion and advancement of women, and rewarded for doing so. Research has found that structured hiring and promotion procedures that hold managers accountable reduce decision-making biases. . . . Rewards should be based on the attainment of these goals and managers must be held accountable if these goals are not met.

Assumption #4: What firms *think* is sufficient: "We have a traditional reward system, based on seniority, performance, and bonuses."

What firms *should* do: Alter performance evaluation and reward systems to pay and promote employees fairly based on project work, the outcomes of their performance, and how they balance work/nonwork demands.

Evaluation and pay for performance systems have not kept pace with the changing workplace. Women who take advantage of flexibility discover their pay is disadvantaged, making it less attractive to remain employed. For example, 90 percent of U.S. legal firms offer part-time career options to employees but only about 4 percent choose this option because 33 percent of legal professionals believe it will hurt their careers and their pay. . . . Nonetheless, the economic costs of leaving a firm are often overlooked. Ann Crittenden, in her book *The Price of Motherhood* detailed the large, and often hidden costs, to women who take time off to rear children. The "mommy tax" or the forgone income of a college-educated woman is usually greater than one million dollars, producing a bigger wage gap between mothers and women without children than the wage gap between young men and women. . . .

One method of rewarding employees for balancing their work and non-work demands is to expand 360 feedback evaluation systems to include family and friends. For example, Ford Motor Company's total leadership program includes using evaluations of managers' roles as parents, spouses, and community members as part of their overall evaluations as leaders. Including non-work aspects into evaluation methods and revamping pay systems so that workers are paid based on their project outcomes rather than the number of hours they work fits the kaleidoscope model. Additionally . . . firms should extend family benefits to give employees an allowance to be spent on benefits of their choice rather than imposing "one size-fits all" programs that may be of little use to some workers (e.g., value of childcare programs to single employees without children).

Assumption #5: What firms *think* is sufficient: "We don't need to offer any additional benefits beyond what other firms are offering to be considered family-friendly."

What firms *should* do: Recognize flexible schedules and other work/life programs are not perks but necessities.

Many of the women we studied talked about forgoing career opportunities in order to care for ailing family members, to be near aging parents, and to care for small children. Likewise, many of the men regretted not spending more time with family. But while the list of corporations that offer favorable parental leave or work-life programs is increasing, stellar examples are still rare.

Corporations must adopt kaleidoscope-oriented job policies, such as time banks of paid parental leave, reduced-hour careers, job-sharing opportunities, and options for career interruptions to retain workers caught in a parental work bind. We further suggest that similar programs be developed to help working women manage eldercare issues (e.g., paid leave, subsidized daycare for the elderly).

Other possible initiatives to validate work outside the office, eliminate stress, and develop a more holistic approach to work include: reducing the length of the paid work-week; increasing paid vacation time; . . . creating more quality part-time jobs, with pro-rated benefits and pension plans; . . . and providing paid tuition reimbursement programs for loyal employees. . . . Some countries have initiated policies that provide considerable support for working parents. The international examples of note include:

- In the Netherlands, maternity benefits include four to six weeks of pre-birth leave and 16 weeks of after-birth leave with 100 percent salary. Parental leave laws allow parents, after twelve months on the job, to take up to thirteen weeks full-time or six months part-time unpaid leave to care for children up to four years old. Surprisingly, these laws even cover those working less than 20 hours per week.

- In Sweden, new mothers receive a year's paid leave, the right to work a six-hour day with full benefits until their child enters primary school, and a government stipend to help pay childcare expenses. Married couples are taxed independently; women earning less than their husbands are taxed at a lower rate, making it economically worthwhile for her to work.

Until recently, programs to encourage work/life balance have been treated with a passing nod and little real change. With the advantages of technology, firms can help reshape career paths to recognize the increasing complexities of kaleidoscope careers. By creating more acceptable nontraditional careers paths within the firm; by broadening compensation policies to encompass alternative forms of work; by abolishing obsolete norms such as face time, long hours, or travel as a surrogate measure for commitment and promotability; by rewarding managers who provide support to the development of women; and by creating cultures that truly support work/life balance, corporations will have an easier time recruiting, retaining, and shaping talent.

Editor's note: For information on studies, please see original article.

Selected References

Babcock, L. and Laschever, S. 2003. *Women don't ask: Negotiation and the gender divide.* Princeton University Press.

Belkin, L. 2003. "Q: Why don't more women choose to get to the top? A: They choose not to." *New York Times Magazine,* 26 October, 42–47, 58, 85.

Brett, J. M., and L. K. Stroh. 2003. "Working 61 hours plus a week: Why do managers do it?" *Journal of Applied Psychology,* 88 (1): 67–78.

Catalyst, 2003. "Women in corporate leadership."

Griffeth, R. W., P. W. Horn, and S. Gaertner. 2000. "A meta-analysis of antecedents and correlates of employee turnover: Update, moderator tests, and research implications for the next millennium." *Journal of Management,* 26 (3): 563–588.

Lyness, K. S. and D. E. Thompson. 2000. Climbing the corporate ladder: Do female and male executives follow the same route? *Journal of Applied Psychology,* 85 (1), 86–101.

Mero, J. & Sellers, P. 2003. "Power: Do women really want it?" *Fortune,* October 148 (8): 80–88.

Powell, G. 1999. "Reflections on the glass ceiling." *Handbook of Gender and Work,* Thousand Oaks, CA: Sage. 325–370

Ragins, B. R., B. Townsend, and M. Mattis. 1998. "Gender gap in the executive suite: CEOs and female executives report on breaking the glass ceiling." *Academy of Management Executive,* 12 (1): 28–42.

Rapoport, R., L. Bailyn, J. K. Fletcher, and B. Pruitt. 2002. *Beyond work-family balance: Advancing gender equity and workplace performance.* San Francisco, CA: Jossey-Bass.

Reprinted from: Lisa A. Mainiero and Sherry E. Sullivan, "Kaleidoscope Careers: An Alternate Explanation for the 'Opt-Out' Revolution." In *Academy of Management Executive,* Vol. 19, No. 1, pp. 106–123. Copyright © 2005 by the Academy of Management.

Food for Thought and Application Questions

1. Someone could argue that a kaleidoscope career model is biased in favor of women, so that they could "reap corporate benefits" when they haven't "given their all" continuously to the corporation over the years. How would you address this argument? Is this a model biased in favor of women or is it gender neutral?

2. Interview a woman who has had a long career history (20 or more years) and a man with approximately the same length of career. Gather information on the jobs they have had—any promotions, work interruptions—and find out how they would divine their career paths. Include information on family formation and how they viewed their work life once married with children. Evaluate how each one's career path meshes with the kaleidoscope career model.

3. The authors suggest that firms redesign the way work is done in order to realize the "dual agenda" of career and family. Brainstorm about ways this *could* be done and how firms might evaluate work performance with these new ways of doing things. ✦

29

Job Leaves and the Limits of the Family and Medical Leave Act

The Effects of Gender, Race, and Family

Naomi Gerstel
Katherine McGonagle

Magazine articles, op-ed pieces, and popular books now regularly address how job obligations impinge on family ties and how family obligations interfere with job responsibilities. . . . Notably, it took White middle-class mothers' entrance into the labor market to force revision of mainstream media images and political policies concerning the families of employees. With the entrance of such White women, especially mothers, into the paid labor force, family caregiving became simultaneously more visible and more threatened. Concomitantly, pressure on politicians and organizations to attend to the family needs of employees intensified (Families and Work Institute 1991).

Some scholars believe that the tide is now turning in favor of government intervention, pointing to the proliferation in recent years of bills in the U.S. Congress addressing the "accommodation" of employers to family needs (Burstein, Bricher, & Einwohner 1995). In their recent review of family responsive workplaces, Glass and Estes (1997) write that "one of the major family needs addressed through workplace initiatives are those policies that reduce work to provide time for family caregiving" (p. 294). The

Family and Medical Leave Act (FMLA, 1993) is the major federal initiative to respond to this set of needs. In this article, we analyze the need for and use of those job leaves designated by the FMLA.

The FMLA was signed into law by President Clinton in 1993 after protracted debate and at least a decade of delay.[1] Its central provisions include a guarantee that people employed for more than 12 months (or 1,250 hours) in companies with at least 50 employees within 75 miles of their work site can take up to 12 weeks unpaid leave per year. Without losing their jobs, these workers can take that leave to care for newborn or newly adopted children, for seriously ill spouses, children, or parents, or to recover from their own serious health conditions, including pregnancy. Serious illnesses and health conditions are defined as those requiring at least one night in the hospital or continuing treatment by a health care provider.

Each of these provisions was the result of protracted political debates with an extensive coalition joining together to negotiate each part and each compromise. In his 1998 state of the union address, Clinton proudly claimed the FMLA as the first bill he signed into law and suggested that 15 million citizens had taken such a family leave since its inception. It was touted as a "gender neutral" [FMLA, 1993, Section 2 (b) 4] bill that extended its rights and protections to men as well as women.

Although its passage was clearly a major political victory, its limitations—especially lack of provision for remuneration, allowable leave length (12 weeks), and scope (including only a limited proportion of employees as well as a narrow definition of the family)—were also clearly the results of coalition politics. As Elison (1997) writes, "The FMLA is targeted to cover those within the primary sector of the labor market who are more likely to have access to financial and familial resources. Families with these characteristics would tend to be White, middle class, and married" (p. 312). . . . Very little research has examined empirically the extent to which the need for job leaves and their use are tied to these differences in social characteristics. This article begins to do so.

This article focuses on three issues. First, we analyze the extent to which Americans say they need to take the kind of job leaves designated by the FMLA. Second . . . we analyze who actually takes such leaves. Third, we focus on three limits on leave use: pay, scope, and workplace responsiveness. We argue that whereas the act may have been passed as an attempt at gender-neutral policy, the opportunities it ensures are not only highly gendered but also restricted by race and family characteristics.

Literature Review

We will briefly review two sets of literature: (a) caregiving to families and (b) job leaves to do that caregiving.

Literature on Caregiving

The FMLA (1993) provides for leaves when an individual is sick, gives birth, or needs to provide for a sick child, spouse, or parent. Even prior to the passage of the act, both men and women not surprisingly took time off for their own sickness—African American men most often, White women least often, with only women generally taking time off for childbirth (Spalter-Roth & Hartmann, 1990). Much literature shows that Americans also spend a great deal of time caring not only for spouses and young children but for adult children and elderly parents. Such kin work—like domestic work more generally—is unevenly distributed within and across families.

Within families, gender matters. Both husbands and wives believe that it is women who should keep in touch with and care for kin (Brody 1990; Gatz, Bengston, & Blum 1990; Mancini & Blieszner 1989). There is much evidence to suggest that women do, in fact, provide more care than do men to a range of kin—including those covered by the act, such as elderly parents and adult children, as well as those not covered, such as siblings and more distant kin (Abel 1991; Di Leonardo 1987; Eriksen 1998). . . . Gerstel and Gallagher (1996) find that this labor adds about an extra work week to women's monthly load.

Although the evidence is far more debated and limited here, some studies also suggest that race shapes caregiving. In particular, African Americans seem more likely than Whites to value intensive kin ties and have expectations for care from them. Some studies suggest that African Americans are also more likely to provide care to a range of family members. However, here the evidence is more mixed. . . . (Collins 1994; Jarrett 1997; Lee, Peek, & Coward 1998; Roschelle 1997). . . . Although there is even less evidence on Latinos, Hogan et al. (1993) suggest that Mexican Americans resemble African Americans more than Whites in their patterns of caregiving.

A number of authors have documented the ways this often demanding but taken-for-granted caregiving produces heightened levels of psychological distress (Gallagher, Wrabetz, Lovett, DelMaestro, & Rose 1989; Gerstel & Gallagher 1993). When combined with employment, caregiving is particularly likely to be stressful. . . . Schor (1992) suggests recent surveys show parents increasingly want to limit their time on the job so they can give care to family members. These findings suggest a clear, although variegated, need for job leaves.

Literature on Job Leaves

Turning to the literature on job leaves, we find little discussion of employees' perceived need for job leaves to provide for family members; there is somewhat more research on the use of such leaves, especially maternity leaves.

Klerman (1993) estimated that about one third of all new mothers took maternity leave before the passage of the act. . . . Comparing national (Current Population Survey) data from the pre-FMLA (1992–1993) with the post-FMLA (1994–1995) period, Waldfogel (in press) suggests that whereas changes in the continuity of employment were negligible, there was an increase in leave taking among mothers. These effects, however, were primarily among those mothers with children younger than 1 year who worked in medium-size (100 to 499 employees) firms. . . .

Although these researchers have begun to examine the effects of leave legislation on the actual use of leaves, there are limits on their ability to specify such effects. . . . Moreover, all these studies of change are limited to maternity leave; although there are clearly benefits to looking at such specific types of leave, none assesses the overall need for or use of job leaves to provide care for the range of family members who are covered by the FMLA. As Ross (1998) notes, "Perhaps the most substantial effects of the FMLA on labor market behaviors will be among the population of employed caregivers as a whole, not just recent mothers" (p. 21). . . .

. . . Hyde et al. (1996) found that prior to the passage of the FMLA, women took an average of 9 weeks (3 weeks less than that provided by the act) of maternity leave. Importantly, they found most women returned to work earlier than they might otherwise have for two reasons: They needed the money, and the leaves allowed were too short.

Research shows that shorter maternity leaves are associated with job attrition (Glass & Riley 1998) and, especially when combined with other risk factors such as a troubled marriage, increased symptoms of depression (Hyde et al. 1996). Such symptoms, in turn, may produce lowered job productivity (Hyde 1995).

Research Questions

In this article, we examine both the need for and use of job leaves after the passage of the FMLA. Although we do not have data before and after the passage of the FMLA that might allow us to assess the act's effects, we do have national data that allow us to analyze the need for and use of a range of job leaves since it was passed. Our data, unlike that used in most other studies, asked respondents directly about needing and taking job leaves to provide care for the range of family members covered by the act.

In this article, we analyze the following three questions:

1. Who needs job leaves to care for family members, or how does such perceived need vary by gender, family characteristics (including marital and parental status), race, or class position?

2. Who actually takes a leave, and what are the characteristics of (including reasons for and length of) their leaves?

3. What explains the difference between those who need leaves and those who take them?

Data and Method Sample

This article uses data from a national survey conducted under the auspices of the Congressional Commission on the Family and Medical Leave Act. As the first national survey of leave needing and taking, this employee survey randomly sampled the telephone household population of the conterminous United States, age 18 years and older who had been employed for pay any time between January 1, 1994, and the time of the interview (a time span of approximately 18 months). The field period was from June to August 1995.

The population was divided into three sample subtypes based on responses to the following questions: "Since January 1, 1994, have you [or another family member] taken time off from work to care for a newborn, newly adopted, or new foster child or for your [or their] own serious health condition, the serious health condition of your [or their] child, spouse, or parent that lasted more than 3 days or required an overnight hospital stay?" If the informant answered no, he or she was asked the following: "Since January 1, 1994, did you [or another family member] need but not take time off from work?" Informants were told to include vacation and sick time when thinking about leave.[2] These questions were used to form the following three sample subtypes: (a) leave takers, consisting of persons who did take a leave in the required time period for the reasons described; (b) leave needers, consisting of persons who did not take a leave but needed to take one in the required time period for the reasons described; (c) employed—only persons who did not take or need to take a leave in the defined time period but who met the age and employment criteria for eligibility. . . .

. . . Data on leaves taken, leaves needed, the length and reason for leave, and various social and demographic characteristics of the respondent were obtained during the telephone interview with a total of 2,253 respondents. Weighted response rates were 73 percent for leave takers, 76 percent for leave needers, and 71 percent for employed-only persons. . . .

Findings

Needing Leaves

A fifth of employees said they needed a leave from jobs for reasons covered by the act. Who are they? Table 29.1 presents the proportion of persons needing to take a leave regardless of whether they actually did so. These results show that certain demographic groups are significantly more likely to perceive a need for a leave. Specifically, women are

more likely than are men, and those with children in the household younger than 18 are significantly more likely than those without such children to perceive a need for a leave. In addition, race and income matter: Those with less money and non-Whites, particularly African Americans, are significantly more likely to report needing a leave.

[T]he results from the logistic regression models . . . show, even after controls this same set of social characteristics exert independent and significant effects: women, African Americans, those with low income, and those with dependent children are still significantly more likely to perceive pressure to take time off from their work than are men, Whites, or Latinos, those with more income, and those with no children at home.[3]

Table 29.1
t-Tests for Leave Needers: Demographic Characteristics

Characteristics	Percentage Needing Leave	SE	t
Gender			
Male	16.3	1.00	−4.39**
Female	24.6	1.60	
Income			
Less than $30,000	23.9	1.50	2.33**
Greater than $30,000	19.7	1.00	
Race			
White	18.7	.80	−3.07**
Not White	25.6	2.10	
Black	26.9	3.20	2.27**
Not Black	19.4	.80	
Latino	25.9	3.60	1.71*
Not Latino	19.6	.80	
Other race	22.1	4.00	.51
Not other race	20.0	.80	
Married/partner			
Yes	20.4	.90	.50
No	19.6	1.40	
Union			
Yes	21.9	2.00	.96
No	19.8	.90	
Children (younger than 18 in household)			
Yes	24.9	1.30	5.12**
No	16.5	1.00	

Source: Adapted from SUDAAN (1992) to generate standard error.
NOTE: Those who perceived a need to take a leave regardless of whether they actually took a leave. Unweighted total $N = 2,253$; $n = 1,218$ takers (54.1 percent), $n = 206$ needers (9.1 percent) and $n = 829$ employed only (36.8 percent). Weighted total $N = 11,916$; $n = 1,997.44$ takers (16.8 percent), $n = 403.52$ needers (3.4 percent), and $n = 9,515.1$ employed only (79.9 percent).
*.05<p<.10; ** p= .05.

In concert, these findings suggest that it is not simply family and work characteristics typically associated with gender and race that explain their effects: net of other familial factors (such as marriage, parenthood, or household income) or job characteristics (such as union membership), women and African Americans are still significantly more likely to perceive a need to take a leave from their jobs.

Taking Leaves

When we turn to leave taking, we find quite a different picture. A majority (83 percent) of those who need leaves actually take them. . . . [Yet], a great deal of inequality remains between those who do and do not take leaves.

The analysis presented in Table 29.2 . . . [is] based on the subset of individuals who reported that they needed to take a leave. We find that just as women are more likely to report needing a leave (see Table 29.1), they are significantly more likely than men to take a leave. Other factors that shaped need—both low income and the presence of children in the household—do not affect leave taking. In fact, those with more income are actually more likely to take a leave, although not significantly so. (Note, however, that most of those with or without children and most of those with high as well as low income in fact take the leaves they report they need.) When we turn to race, we see a very different pattern. At the bivariate level, there is an important reversal: whereas we showed earlier that African Americans are more likely to report needing leaves, they are significantly less likely to take them than any other racial group, including not only Whites but also Latinos and others.

Table 29.2
t-Tests for Leave Takers: Demographic Characteristics

Characteristics	Percentage Needing Leave	SE	t
Gender			
Male	80.0	2.00	-2.34**
Female	85.7	1.40	
Income			
Less than $30,000	81.4	1.80	-1.08
Greater than $30,000	84.0	1.60	
Race			
White	84.2	1.30	1.53
Not White	80.0	2.40	
Black	76.0	3.80	-2.04**
Not Black	84.0	1.20	
Latino	84.1	3.70	.26
Not Latino	83.1	1.20	
Other race	82.5	5.30	-.13
Not other race	83.2	1.20	
Married/partner			
Yes	84.2	1.40	1.30
No	80.8	2.20	
Union			
Yes	84.0	2.50	.32
No	83.1	1.30	
Children			
Yes	82.8	1.70	-.34
No	83.6	1.60	

NOTE: Those who actually took leave (among those who perceived a need to take a leave): Unweighted total N = 1,424; n = 1,218 takers (85.5 percent); n =206 needers (15.5 percent). Weighted total N = 2,400.96; n = 1,997.44 takers (82.2 percent), n = 403.5 needers (16.8 percent). See Table 29.1 for description of variables and standard error. ** p<(.05).

. . . [Ex]amin[ing] predictors of leave taking in the subgroup of respondents who needed to take a leave, results show that gender remains significant when other factors are controlled: women are significantly more likely to take a leave than are men. Importantly . . . [i]t is married women (or those with partners) who are significantly more likely to take a leave than are married men; single women who perceive a need for a leave are not more likely to take those leaves than are single men. This finding underlines the remaining power of husband's breadwinning to keep them always on the job (see Bianchi 1996) and suggests marriage (rather than simply gender) still promotes the feminization of caregiving. . . .

Beyond gender differences . . . neither income nor the presence of children has a significant effect on leave taking. Recall that we found that those with less income, similar to those with more children, were significantly more likely to need a leave.

Moreover . . . African Americans (men and women alike) are significantly less likely than their White counterparts to take a leave, even though . . . they are significantly more likely to perceive a need for such a leave. That is, this racial difference is significant even with controls for the important resource of household income.

We also found that, net of other factors . . . the chances that African American women will take a leave is only about half that of White women . . . and African American men are only about three quarters as likely as White men to take a leave . . . ; in contrast, Latina women are approximately equal to White women, and Latino men are approximately equal to White men. (Note that White women are about 1.7 times more likely than are White men to take a leave. . .)

Reasons for Taking Leaves

People take leaves for numerous reasons. Whereas the majority of leaves are to care for oneself (64 percent), slightly more than one third (36 percent) are taken to care for other people—most often children (22 percent, including 14 percent for births and adoptions and 8 percent for a child's illness) but also parents (7 percent), spouses (3 percent), or some other relative (4 percent). Analyzing reasons for taking leaves, we again find a significant gender effect. Of those who do take a leave, men are significantly more likely to do so for themselves than are women, even if we count taking maternity disability as taking leave for oneself. In contrast, women are much more likely than men to take leaves for other people. They were about twice as likely to take a leave for their child's health condition, about twice as likely to take a leave for their parents' health, and four times as likely to take a leave for other relatives' health.

Examining the reasons for taking leave, the differences by race are no longer significant, and the differences by income reverse themselves. Those with more income are significantly less likely to take leaves for themselves and more likely to take leaves for others. That may well be a result of the fact that the less affluent can only afford to take leaves when they are too sick themselves to go to work, whereas the more affluent have the luxury of altruism for others as well as better health themselves.

The Limits of the Act

The passage of the FMLA was, in many ways, a major step forward. It allows leave from a job with a legal guarantee that the job will be there on the leave taker's return. Nonetheless, numerous critics of the FMLA point to many limitations. Here we will focus on three of these: that the leaves (a) are unpaid, (b) are narrow in scope, and (c) do not ensure workplace responsiveness. These three limitations help explain the uneven use of leaves by those who need it.

Unpaid Leaves

Because the FMLA provides only unpaid leaves to covered employees, it encourages families to provide care but does so without ensuring the income caregivers often need and want to support their families. Among those who took a leave, 47 percent took a paid leave, and 33 percent took a partially paid leave. The fact that leaves are unpaid is the most common reason for not being able to take a leave: of those who needed leaves but did not take them, the majority (64 percent) said they did not take a leave because they could not afford one; about half of those who did take leaves said they returned to work because they could not afford the extra needed time off. Moreover, of those whose leaves were unpaid or only partially paid, about one quarter had to borrow money during their leaves, and 11 percent received public assistance while on leave.[4] This helps explain why on one hand, it is married women—who have husbands to support them—who are more likely to take a leave and why, on the other hand, those with more obligations (such as dependent children to support) cannot easily avail themselves of the leaves they say they need.

Overall, then, one of the criticisms of the act made by proponents of leaves was that low-paid workers would not be able to afford to use it. We find that it is more difficult for precisely these workers to take a leave, even though our analysis also suggests they are more likely to need a leave.

The Act's Scope: Employee Coverage and Definition of the Family

The FMLA is of limited scope in two ways. First, it covers only a narrow band of employees; second, it contains a narrow conception of the family. These help explain some of the inequalities in leave taking.

Coverage of Employees

One of the major limitations of the act is those employees that it covers: it excludes seasonal and temporary workers as well as those who work in firms with fewer than 50 employees. Our analysis shows that those who reported themselves to be working in organizations that fit FMLA criteria for coverage are more likely to include the relatively affluent. Slightly more than a third (39 percent) of those who make $20,000 or less worked for such firms in contrast to two thirds of those who make $50,000 or more. African Americans (74 percent) are significantly more likely than non-Latino Whites (54 percent) or Latinos (48 percent) to work for such firms (although there is little difference between women and men).

Importantly, however, whether an individual reported he or she worked for a firm that fit the criteria set out by the FMLA is not associated with leave taking. . . . [We found] that those in such firms who perceive a need for a leave are no more likely to take that leave than those in firms that do not fit these criteria. Although we do not have longitudinal data that would allow us to ascertain its precise effects, these findings do begin to suggest that the act has limited impact.

Narrow Definition of the Family

A second way the scope of the act is limited lies in its definition of the family. Its proponents made much of its broad coverage: it not only covers leaves for mothers and fathers to care for birth and adopted children but also leaves to care for spouses and elderly parents. This broad, "gender-neutral" coverage allowed a large coalition to form in the support of the act's passage. However, it does not cover that wide range of kin (such as siblings, grandparents, aunts, or uncles), in-laws, and "fictive" kin (nonblood ties) who routinely need and receive care from those close to them. It does not cover those who are not legally married, including gays and lesbians who cannot legally marry.[5]

Our analysis suggests that numerous respondents need to (and some do) take leaves from work to care for relatives and nonrelatives not covered by the act. . . . [A]bout 4 percent spontaneously mentioned they took leave for those (kin and nonkin) not covered by the definition of the family used by the act. . . . There is good reason to think that this is a conservative estimate. The only reason we have these limited data is that the initial screening question was misunderstood by some respondents. . . . Nonetheless, these individuals said they took leave for nonspecified kin or nonkin. It is likely, then, that if we had a specific question on other kin and nonkin for whom individuals needed and took a leave, we would find the numbers to be considerably higher.

. . . The act thus prioritizes a very narrow definition of the family and, in doing so, legitimates and supports a narrow range of caregiving.

Workplace Responsiveness

A third limit on the use of leaves emerges from inadequate workplace responsiveness.

State-mandated family policies may clash with organizational cultures and norms; these often require the demonstration of loyalty by workplace attendance visible to bosses, colleagues, subordinates, and clients. Even when the organizational culture seems responsive to family concerns, researchers suggest that managers may not be committed to or may even discourage family-friendly policy such as family leaves, especially for lower level employees (Fried 1998; Glass 1998; Hochschild 1997). Consequently, workplace responses to official policy may increase inequalities in leave taking.

We found differences, especially by gender and income, in the responsiveness of workplaces to the need for leave. Women were significantly more likely than men to say that when they took a leave, they "felt pressure to return to work by bosses and co-workers" (26 percent vs. 19 percent). Especially if they were not married, economic pressures forced them to return. Whereas the differences by race were not significant, class differences were. Compared to those with more income, those with less income were significantly more likely to feel such pressure to return to work (28 percent vs. 21 percent), and they were also significantly more likely to report they had been denied time off to attend to family medical concerns (4 percent vs. 10 percent). Such analyses suggest that some groups already disadvantaged are less likely to take leaves because their workplaces and bosses are less friendly to their families. As Galinksy et al. (1997) argue, the implementation of policies by managers and their legitimization by organizational ethos may be even more important than official policy in determining whether employees take leave or experience conflict when trying to do so.

Summary and Conclusion

The FMLA is a de jure recognition that work and family are profoundly entwined. Even if our nation's family leave policy still lags far behind that of most other industrialized nations (Kammerman & Kahn 1995), it at least provides some recognition that families do not simply persist. Americans have to

expend a great deal of time and effort to maintain them and the health of their members. Through the FMLA, the state has begun to support those efforts.

We found considerable demand for job leave over the 18-month period after the passage of the FMLA. . . . Unfortunately, the data we used produce a snapshot or cross-sectional view of family leaves; as such, we cannot examine the extent to which the FMLA caused changes in these leaves. Although confined to the period following its passage, our analysis at least suggests that the act may exacerbate the inequalities it could diminish.

Although we found that relatively advantaged workers were more likely to report they were covered by the act than were those less advantaged, our analyses also suggested that such coverage—controlling for other factors—was not itself associated with an increased likelihood of taking a leave. . . .

Our analysis does suggest rather large effects of social characteristics on leave taking. Most obviously, gender continues to matter. A large number of men took leaves; however, their leaves were typically taken when they themselves got sick as well as occasionally to care for some other family members (especially a sick wife). Women were more likely than men to say they needed leaves, to take leaves, and to take longer leaves. Moreover, the leaves they did take were more likely than men's to be for other people. A particular group likely to take the leaves needed is women who have spouses or partners to support them. To some extent, these figures are likely the outcome of norms that emphasize women as caregivers. We also still suspect the influence of economic factors associated with gender. Future research should examine the effect of personal income rather than just the household income reported with these data. We hypothesize that such analysis will show that it is wives whose husbands earn a higher proportion of the family income who are particularly likely to take such leaves.

Other family characteristics also shape leave taking, and these too are highly gendered. In some ways, having children at home hurts: Although women with children are more likely to say they need leaves, they are not more likely to be able to take them than are women who are not mothers. Although motherhood increases the length of leaves for wives, fatherhood reduces the amount of time husbands take leave. Hyde et al.'s (1996) remarks on the shorter leaves fathers took before the passage of the act still ring true:

> In the twentieth century, the good provider role has been an important component of male identity. . . . For men, then, a high degree of family commitment might not manifest itself in taking a long leave, but rather in taking a short leave so as to get back to work quickly, do well on the job, and earn money to support his wife and new child, at least under conditions of unpaid leaves. (p. 102)

At the same time, Hochschild (1997) reminds us that jobs can be more comforting than the demanding and sometimes stressful caregiving of family members. More generally, gender-neutral state policy can reinforce gender inequality if the wider social context, consisting of gender inequality in family caregiving as well as in material opportunities and rewards, remains in force (see Fraser 1994; Orloff 1996).

A related argument applies to race. African Americans need leaves more than do Whites, but they are unable to take them as often as Whites. At least to some extent, this racial difference is likely a result of the higher rates of morbidity and various health problems among African Americans (Cockerham 1995) as well as an outcome of the act's narrow definition of the family. Some research also would seem to suggest that this racial difference in leave taking is rooted in differential economic resources (e.g., Lee et al. 1998). However, racial differences were maintained even when household income was controlled. To explore these racial differences further, additional measures of per capita economic resources and the people to whom those resources are distributed should be included in future research.

Current inequalities may be further reinforced by the medical definition of *need* embodied in the FMLA. The act requires the provision of unpaid leave only when an employee cares for a relative with a sickness or injury requiring at least one overnight stay in a hospital or continuing treatment by a health care worker. On one hand, this may reduce health care costs by substituting the unpaid leave of family members for costly medical professionals. On the other hand, it omits common health problems and may produce a greater reliance on health care providers to show need. Those with less money have less access to health care providers or the legal services needed to validate the seriousness of their illnesses. In an analysis of court cases concerning the FMLA, Wisensale (1998) found that one of the most common areas of litigation concerns employee-employer disputes over the seriousness of illness. Bills promoted by employers are now winding their way through Congress to narrow still further the health conditions that may be considered in granting job leaves.

. . . Additional changes are beginning to address other inequities built into the act. The 1997 extended family leave policy allows employees to use family leave to accompany elderly relatives to professional appointments or participate in school activities related to their child's educational attainment. This, however, only adds 24 hours during a 12-month period and remains unpaid. In 1998, the National Partnership for Women and Families issued a call for an expanded leave policy—one not only providing wage replacement but also extending to smaller companies. In his 1999 state of the union address, Clinton endorsed one of these, saying that the FMLA needs to be expanded to cover workers in firms with 25 employees. In concert with a broadened definition of family and enforcement at the workplace, such extensions will begin to address the inequities in leave taking analyzed here.

Notes

1. We write "at least a decade" because many versions of some part or another of the Family and Medical Leave Act (FMLA) have appeared since World War II when the Women's Bureau of the Department of Labor recommended a 6-week prenatal period and 2-month postbirth leave for women.

2. If workers have any available paid leave (e.g., vacation time), employers may require they use it up as part of FMLA leave (unless the un-

ion contract specifies otherwise) (Schwartz 1996).

3. We also found a significant gender/age interaction. Young men are less likely than are older men to report needing a leave, whereas young women are more likely than are older women to report needing a leave (data not shown). This may mean that young males are especially likely to feel they should give priority to building careers, whereas young women are especially prone not only to give birth but take care of family members (including but not limited to children because the effects of gender are net of children), which of course may have negative implications for their careers.

4. This is prior to the implementation of the current welfare laws, which may reduce the number able and willing to obtain public assistance payments while on leave.

5. It does cover lesbians and gays as parents but not as partners (Lenhoff 1998).

References

Abel, E. K. (1991). *Who Cares for the Elderly? Public Policy and the Experiences of Adult Daughters*. Philadelphia: Temple University Press.

Bianchi, S. (1996). Changing economic roles of women and men. In R. Farley (Ed.), *State of the Union: America in the 1990s: Economic Trends*. Vol. 1. New York: Russell Sage.

Brody, E. M. (1990). *Women in the Middle: Their Parent Care Years*. New York: Springer.

Burstein, P., Bricher, M. P., & Einwohner, R. (1995). Policy alternatives and political change: Work, family and gender on the congressional agenda. *American Sociological Review*, 60, 67–83.

Cockerham, W. (1995). *Medical sociology*. Englewood Cliffs, NJ: Prentice Hall.

Collins, P. H. (1994). Shifting the center: Race, class, and feminist theorizing about motherhood. In E. N. Glenn, G. Chang, & L. R. Forcey (Eds.), *Mothering: Ideology, Experience, and Agency*. New York: Routledge.

Di Leonardo, M. (1987). The female world of cards and holidays: Women, families and the work of kinship. *Signs*, 12, 441–453.

Elison, S. K. (1997). The Family and Medical Leave Act of 1993. *Journal of Family Issues*, 18(1), 30–54.

Eriksen, S. (1998). Sisterhood and brotherhood: An exploration of sibling ties in adult life. Unpublished Ph.D. dissertation, University of Massachusetts, Amherst.

Family and Medical Leave Act, Pub. L. No.103–3, 139 Cong. Rec. (1993).

Families and Work Institute. (1991). *Corporate Reference Guide to Work Family Program*. New York: Author.

Fraser, N. (1994). After the family wage: Gender equity and the welfare state. *Political Theory*, 22, 609–630.

Fried, M. (1998). *Taking Time*. Philadelphia: Temple University Press.

Gallagher, D., Wrabetz, A., Lovett, S., DelMaestro, S., & Rose, J. (1989). Depression and other negative effects in family caregivers. In E. Light & B. D. Lebowitz (Eds.), *Alzheimer's Disease Treatment and Family Stress* (pp. 218–244). Rockville, MD: Department of Health and Human Services.

Gatz, M. Bengston, V. L., & Blum, M. J. (1990). Caregiving families. In J. E. Birren & K. W. Schaie (Eds.), *Handbook of the Psychology of Aging*, 3rd ed. (pp. 404–426). New York: Academic Press.

Gerstel, N., & Gallagher, S. (1993). Kinkeeping and distress: Gender, recipients of care and work-family conflict. *Journal of Marriage and the Family*, 55, 598–608.

——. (1996). Caring for kith and kin: Gender, employment, and the privatization of care. *Social Problems*, 41(4), 519–539.

Glass, J. (1998, November). How responsive is the family responsive workplace—and to whom? Paper presented at Conference on Work and Family: Today's Realities, Tomorrow's Visions, Boston.

Glass, J., & Estes, S. B. (1997). The family responsive workplace. *Annual Review of Sociology*, 23, 289–313.

Glass, J., & Riley, L. (1998). Family responsive policies and employee retention following childbirth. *Social Forces*, 76, 1401–1435.

Hochschild, A. (1997). *The Time Bind*. New York: Metropolitan.

Hogan, D., Eggebeen, D., & Clogg, C. C. (1993). The structure of intergenerational exchanges in American families. *American Journal of Sociology*, 98, 1428–1458.

Hyde, J. (1995). Women and maternity leave: Empirical data and public policy. *Psychology of Women Quarterly*, 19, 299–313.

Hyde, J. S., Essex, M. J., Clark, R., Klein, M. H., & Byrd, J. (1996). Parental leave: Policy and research. *Journal of Social Issue*, 52, 91–109.

Jarrett, R. L. (1997). African American family and parenting strategies in impoverished neighborhoods. *Qualitative Sociology*, 20, 275–288.

Kammerman, S., & Kahn, A. J. (1995). *Starting Right*. New York: Oxford University Press.

Klerman, J. (1993). Characterizing leave for maternity. RAND Labor and Population Program.

Working Paper 93–94. Santa Monica, CA: RAND.

Klerman, J., & Leibowitz, A. (1997). Labor supply effects of state maternity leave legislation. In F. Blau and R. Ehrenberg (Eds.), *Gender and Family Issues in the Workplace*. New York: Russell Sage.

Lee, G. R., Peek, C. C., & Coward, R. T. (1998). Race differences in filial responsibility expectations among older parents. *Journal of Marriage and the Family, 60,* 404–412.

Lenhoff, D. (1998, June). Discussion. Presented at Fifth Women's Policy Research Conference on Women's Progress: Perspectives on the Past, Blueprint for the Future, Washington, D.C.

Mancini, J. A., & Blieszner, R. (1989). Aging parents and adult children. *Journal of Marriage and the Family, 51,* 275–290.

Orloff, A. (1996). Gender in the welfare state. *Annual Review of Sociology, 22,* 51–78.

Roschelle, A. (1997). *No More Kin: Exploring Race, Gender and Class in Social Networks*. Thousand Oaks, CA: Sage.

Ross, K. E. (1998). Labor pains: The effects of the Family and Medical Leave Act on recent mothers' returns to paid work after childbirth. Unpublished paper, Syracuse University, Center for Policy Research.

Schor, J. (1992). *The Overworked American*. New York: Basic Books.

Spalter-Roth, R., & Hartmann, H. (1990). *Unnecessary Losses: Costs to Americans of the Lack of Family and Medical Leave*. Washington, D.C.: Institute for Women's Policy Research.

Waldfogel, J. (in press). The impact of the Family and Medical Leave Act. *Journal of Policy Analysis and Management,* 18(2).

Wisensale, S. (1998, June). The Family and Medical Leave Act in court: An analysis of important legal decisions five years after implementation. Presented at IWPR Conference on Women's Progress: Perspectives on the Past, Blueprint for the Future, Washington, D.C.

Food for Thought and Application Questions

1. According to the findings of this research, who—males vs. females or single vs. married—are more likely to report the need of taking a leave and who are in fact more likely to take a leave? How do gender, class, and race shape the discrepancy between the need and reality of taking leave?

2. The authors argue that the FMLA is narrow in its application. Discuss the ways in which the law "narrows" its application and how this differentially affects groups—again, thinking in terms of how groups defined by gender, race, and class and their intersection are affected. Discuss two ways to change the law so that the application is more broadly based. What are the implications of these changes for employers and employees? Is there any downside to such changes? What are they? How would you respond to these issues? ✦

30

Blessing or Curse?

Work-Family Policies and Mothers' Wage Growth Over Time

Jennifer Glass

Much research in the past has focused on the benefits of work-family policies for business in the form of increased productivity and decreased turnover (e.g., see Baltes, Briggs, Huff, Wright, & Neuman, 1999). Less attention has focused on the benefits to workers and their families, despite the widespread belief that such policies are valued and sought after by workers, especially mothers of young children. These policies include flexible scheduling, telecommuting, reduced or part-time hours of work, and child care assistance. Although these work innovations may make caregiving of family members easier, a substantial literature documents the dearth of employees who actually use these policies when offered because of the fear they will be punished with lower raises or blocked mobility (Fried, 1998; Golden, 2001; Hochschild, 1997; Perlow, 1998; Thompson, Beauvais, & Lyness, 1999). Mothers frequently report that they or their colleagues who have taken advantage of such policies have suffered as a result or that supervisors have made it clear such policies are only for employees who are not serious about career advancement (Crittenden, 2001; Williams, 2001).

However, this literature has its limitations. First, the qualitative accounts of large corporations studied by Fried (1998) and Hochschild (1997) may not apply to the majority of workers who work for small firms. These workers may feel freer to negotiate nontraditional work arrangements or use them without penalty. Second, many of these accounts

(Perlow, 1998; Thompson et al., 1999) feature the experiences of white-collar professional and managerial workers, for whom long hours and continuous availability are increasingly a normative expectation of employment and a precondition for upward mobility (Jacobs & Gerson, 2001). Yet only about 40% of all women workers are managers and professionals who can reasonably expect significant career mobility with their current employer (Bureau of Labor Statistics [BLS], 2001c). Although workers in clerical, service, and blue-collar jobs could theoretically suffer wage penalties or deterioration in the conditions of work if they use work-family policies, the threat of blocked mobility as the source of subsequently stagnating earnings is likely to be less salient.

Perhaps most important, the predictions that lower wage growth and blocked mobility will result from the use of work-family policies have yet to be empirically tested with a representative sample of workers followed across time. In fact, very few studies have looked at the impact of family-responsive policies on wages at all. Gariety and Shaffer (2001) and Johnson and Provan (1995) looked at the impact of work-family policies on wages in cross-section and generally concluded that policies either had no effect or a small positive net effect on wages for men and women. However, Johnson and Provan asked only about the availability of policies, not the actual use of such policies, and neither study was able to track the impact of policies on wage growth over time. Given the empirical tendency for work-family benefits to be more available in larger and more profitable firms, and then primarily to their most valued professional and managerial workers (Golden, 2001), this net positive association in cross-section is not surprising. In sum, the question of whether work-family policies actually hurt or help the earnings of workers who use them is still open, in large part, because the detailed longitudinal work history data necessary to answer the question have been unavailable.

The analysis here follows a unique and innovative sample of employed mothers for whom detailed information on policy availability and use have been collected over a number of years and over multiple job changes to determine the impact of work-family policies on their wage growth over time. Mothers of young children were targeted for several reasons—first and foremost, they are the group most likely to value and take advantage of policy innovations to accommodate family caregiving (Blair-Loy & Wharton, 2002; Galinsky, Bond, & Swanberg, 1998; Kiser, 1998; Thompson et al., 1999); second, they are the group whose policy use is likely to be interpreted by employers or supervisors as indicators of lower commitment or performance (Weeden, 2001); and third, they are the group who already empirically display blocked mobility and a wage penalty for having children (Budig & England, 2001; Waldfogel, 1997a), although the explanation of these effects is still hotly disputed.

Background

Ascertaining the impact of employer policies on mothers' wages is particularly important because mothers' earnings constitute an ever-increasing proportion of household income among U.S. families with dependent children. In dual-earner families with children (the most prevalent family form) wives' earnings now account for 40% of the family's income (BLS, 2001c). Among single mothers, 79% of whom are employed, mother's earnings are even more crucial given the typically small amounts of child support received from absent fathers and the trend toward reductions in state support for mother-only families (BLS, 2001b). These two family types represent more than three-fourths of all households with dependent children in the United States (U.S. Census Bureau, 1999). Children's economic welfare increasingly depends on the ability of their mothers to garner sufficient income from their labor force activity.

However, trends in women's earnings over the past 20 years reveal that mothers are the group of women who have shown the slowest wage growth over time, now accounting for most of the so-called gender gap in the average wages of employed women and men (Budig & England, 2001; Waldfogel, 1997b). Although single women and married women without children now earn almost as much as similarly situated men, women with children earn roughly one half as much as men with equivalent qualifications. Quite commonly, this gap has been explained as the result of mothers' decisions to work fewer hours, change jobs more frequently, or experience multiple spells out of the labor force to accommodate childbearing. However, recent cohorts of young women have increasingly worked full-time and continuously throughout their childbearing years (Rexroat, 1992; Spain & Bianchi, 1996) yet show the same pattern of wage stagnation following motherhood as earlier cohorts of women.[1]

Paradoxically, work-family policies have been seen as the cause of this wage stagnation and its solution. Causally, if employed mothers seek out jobs with features that accommodate their caregiving responsibilities but such jobs generally offer lower wages to workers, then mother's wages will fall behind other groups of workers. Some analysts believe that the labor market is so inflexibly structured that only peripheral, low-paying jobs offer the short work hours and greater schedule flexibility that mothers need to continue labor force participation. Others believe that mothers' wage stagnation is caused precisely by the failure of the market to provide work-family policies such as schedule flexibility and reduced work hours. The consequences among mothers who remain in these inflexible jobs are stress, fatigue, frequent absenteeism, and career interruptions that impair wage growth. Mothers are either condemned to the labor market purgatory of low wage part-time jobs to accommodate family care or are the fatigued victims of inflexible full-time jobs that lower their productivity. If work-family policies became commonplace across a broad range of jobs, however, such unpalatable choices (and the motherhood wage gap they create) would disappear.

This optimistic scenario cannot yet be tested—work-family policies are not yet ubiquitous, though they are more common in recent years. Empirical data *can* address two central questions: (a) whether, ceteris paribus, mothers who use work-family policies show weaker wage growth than their counterparts who do not and (b) if so, whether this occurs because jobs offering work-family policies are lower paying than other similar jobs or whether mothers who use policies pay an individual wage penalty. Although it is logical to believe that mothers who use work-family policies are more productive workers, employers may nevertheless penalize workers who use their policies in comparison to workers who do not require any special managerial accommodations. The size of this penalty determines whether the diffusion of work-family policies across a wide range of occupations and industries would have any effect on the motherhood wage gap.

Should Mothers Using Work-Family Policies Experience Weaker Wage Growth?

One version of the empirical research on work-family policies suggests not. Research has documented support for the notions that the lack of work-family policies hampers mothers' productivity and that the presence of family accommodations improves it. Rodgers (1992) reported that a much higher proportion of women than men in Fortune 500 companies said that work-family problems affected their ability to concentrate at work. Among a sample of mothers, work-family incompatibility decreased concentration and alertness in an experimental task (Barling & MacEwen, 1991). Googins (1991) noted that lack of workplace flexibility was associated with depression among women, whereas difficulties with child care reduced psychological well-being in studies by Ross and Mirowsky (1988) and Galinsky (1994). The empirical evidence also suggests that using work-family policies reduces the job stress and fatigue, turnover, and labor force interruptions that reduce productivity per hour among mothers (see, e.g., Baltes et al., 1999; Glass & Estes, 1997). Friedman and Greenhaus (2000) looked at wages in a cross-sectional sample of business school graduates and found that the earnings gap between women with and without children was smaller in family-responsive firms.

However, this optimistic read of the evidence is counterbalanced by a more pessimistic possibility. It may also be the case that employers who offer child care assistance, flexible schedules, or other family benefits to employees do so to recruit workers willing to accept lower wages to their firms. Firms paying higher wages may have no need to offer such accommodations to attract or keep workers. In general, research has failed to support the notion that women's lower wages are created by compensating differentials in women-dominated jobs, which are most heavily populated by mothers (Budig & England, 2001; Estes & Glass, 1996). However, anecdotal evidence of this exists—fast food and other service franchises have experimented with child care subsidies as a low-cost way to increase the supply of workers without raising the wages of all workers. If work-family amenities disproportionately characterize the lowest wage firms, workers who do not use policies should suffer the same wage penalties over time as workers who do, thus providing a crucial test of this hypothesis.

Whether or not mostly lower wage employers offer work-family policies, work-family policy use could still reduce wage growth. Available evidence suggests that all kinds of employers increasingly offer work-family accommodations (Beers, 2000), but they may only penalize those workers who use them (Fried, 1998; Perlow, 1998). If employers prefer workers who display continuous availability and unfettered work commitment by not using any work-family accommodations, mothers are uniquely handicapped. Mothers often cannot, and do not want to, put in the long overtime hours mandated in the structure of many managerial and professional jobs (Epstein, 1999). Mothers on flexible schedules or who work from home may not be instantly available in crisis situations for employers. Furthermore, employers may overgeneralize from negative experiences with some work-family policy users to all those using policies, a process commonly referred to as statistical discrimination. Employers might then prefer to train and promote those who do not take advantage of flexible employment practices or reduced work hours irrespective of current productivity (Fried, 1998; Hochschild, 1997). Under these conditions, work-family policy use might be of no benefit or actually lower mothers' wage growth over time.

Are All Jobs the Same?
Are All Work-Family Policies the Same?

Which jobs best fit the circumstances conducive to employer discrimination against workers using work-family policies? The answer would seem to be managerial and professional jobs, because they typically require longer work hours and higher levels of work commitment than production, clerical, or service jobs (Epstein, 1999; Jacobs & Gerson, 2004). These jobs are also characterized by possibilities for on-the-job training and promotion that are more often denied workers in other job categories (Blair-Loy, 2003). Pressures to conform to workplace norms of continuous availability are therefore stronger in the high-stakes competition for upward mobility. Thus, employer penalties for the use of work-family policies among mothers should be concentrated among the managerial and professional ranks.

Diversity among the types of work-family polices offered by employers complicates across-the-board predictions about their effects on mothers' wage growth. Some policies are more intrusive in the workplace than others and hamper managerial control more than others. I rely here on the typology of work-family practices developed in earlier work (Glass & Riley, 1998): (a) those that promote reductions in work hours, (b) those that promote schedule flexibility in the time and place of hours worked, and (c) those that provide concrete assistance with child care, family emergencies or illnesses, and other family responsibilities, either through formal policies or informal social support from supervisors and coworkers. Work reduction policies enable mothers to meet their caregiving responsibilities by performing care themselves. Direct assistance policies enable women to substitute others' caregiving labor for their own, thus freeing workers' time for their employers' needs. Schedule flexibility policies fall somewhere in the middle—they allow women to schedule some time to perform their own caregiving, but in addition to the time normally spent on paid work tasks.

Given employer preferences for long work hours and continuous availability (Schor, 1991), I expect work reduction policies to show the least positive impacts on wage growth, followed by flexibility and direct assistance policies. Reduced work opportunities, especially part-time work (as opposed to job sharing) are quite common. Although some research has shown part-time work experience to be almost as valuable as full-time work experience in enhancing women's wage growth (Ferber & Waldfogel, 1998; Waldfogel, 1997a), the more typical view is that such work retards wage growth (Rosenfeld, 1996). The issue is still unsettled, in large part, because of the tremendous diversity in the quality and mobility opportunities of part-time jobs (Tilly, 1996). Flextime and telecommuting arrangements are almost as common, especially in clerical and professional jobs, though limited among service and retail workers who must be available for clients or customers (Beers, 2000; Golden, 2001). Yet little research has looked at the impact of flexible scheduling on subsequent wage growth (for a notable exception, see Weeden, 2001). Direct assistance policies are the rarest forms of employer assistance, generally restricted to large firms in protected, high-profit sectors of the economy. For example, virtually no small firms provide on-site child care or monetary subsidies for child care, and less than 5% of employers overall do (BLS, 2001a). However, where available, child care assistance would seem to have the greatest impact on mother's work availability and thus show the smallest wage penalty.

Methodological Issues

A number of methodological issues have prevented empirical analysis of the impact of work-family policies on wages in the past. Unmeasured heterogeneity among employed mothers that could affect their distribution across firms that do and do not offer work-family policies, organizational differences among jobs and firms that determine whether policies get offered, and instability in the work careers of employed mothers all make isolation of the effects of policy use on wage growth quite difficult.

Unmeasured heterogeneity among employed mothers complicates any attempt to adequately measure the impact of work-family policy use on wage growth. If mothers with strong family identities and weak career commitment are disproportionately likely to take jobs with extensive family accommodations, their subsequent wage growth may reflect not their use of family policies but their underlying weak work involvement. Those mothers with strong work identities may disproportionately fill jobs without family accommodations or choose not to use work-family policies when offered, instead relying on supportive partners or paid helpers to care for their families. The data used here are unique in that questions concerning work commitment are available for all mothers as well as direct measures of the importance of work-family accommodations in their decision to take their current job. These measures can control for sources of selectivity bias among the mothers who have and use family responsive policies at work.

There are also close associations between the type of family responsive policies offered by employers and the sectoral location of jobs in the economy (industry, occupation, firm size, etc.). Analyses must therefore carefully control for the impact of organizational and occupational characteristics on wage growth (see Dietch & Huffman, 2003, for a more lengthy discussion of this issue). This avoids confusion over the true causes of wage growth—prosperity in the employing firm, manifesting itself in generous employer policies and high wages, or the usage of employer policies that allow the mother to be a more productive worker. The fact that workers in prosperous firms show larger wage growth over time may be because of their generally favorable market position, not the use of work-family policies offered by the firm.

The same causal problem occurs for occupational categories within firms. Managerial and professional workers more often have access to work-family accommodations than production or service workers, while typically experiencing more rapid wage growth as well. This association could produce a positive bias in the effects of policy use on subsequent wage growth if not adequately controlled. Because this sample exhibits great diversity in firm size and occupational distribution, these sectoral differences in employment characteristics can be controlled to isolate the impact of family responsive policy on wages.

Finally, instability in mothers' employment complicates the interpretation of work-family policy use. Past policy use may have a smaller impact on current wages if there has been an employer change, especially if the current employer has no information about past behavior. In this way, mothers may be able to "mask" nonconforming behavior when their children are very young by changing employers. The potential benefits of job changing, however, must be counterbalanced against the negative wage effects of employer changes because job tenure and seniority tend to increase wages. The mothers in this sample were followed over a 7-year period, including all employer changes. The effects of job changes on wage growth and the mitigating effects of job changes on past policy use can therefore be observed.

Analysis Plan

The analyses reported here were guided by the two empirical questions posed earlier:

1. Controlling for unobserved heterogeneity among mothers and observable job and organizational characteristics, does work-family policy use advance or retard mothers' wage growth over time? Under Question 1, I further explore

   - whether all types of work-family accommodations are equally helpful or harmful in advancing mothers' wages;

   - whether the effects of work-family policy use on wage growth are stronger for managers and professionals than other workers;

   - whether effects of policy use are employer specific or follow workers as they change employers.

2. Is there evidence that employers who offer work-family policies systematically pay their workers less than employers who do not, as a way of enticing workers to a lower wage firm?

Method

Data

The data to be used come from four waves of longitudinal data on 195 mothers first interviewed when employed and pregnant in 1991 to 1992. The initial random sample of pregnant employees came from five midwestern counties (served by four regional hospitals) who were employed at least 20 hours per week at the time they became pregnant and subsequently gave birth between December 1991 and September 1992. All women using the hospitals for maternity care were eligible to participate. The effective response rate for the original survey was 83% ($N = 321$). Demographic comparisons with national data showed this sample was representative of U.S. mothers in age, education, occupational distribution, family size, and marital status, but not race (Whites were overrepresented). Two more waves of data collection followed at 6-month intervals until the infants were 1 year old. After another 6 years, the respondents from the original panel were recontacted. The respondents at this last wave of data collection had children approximately 7 years old. Attrition over time reduced the sample to 61% of the original respondents ($N = 196$). . . . The first three waves of data ending in 1993 investigated which workplace policies reduced employer turnover among childbearing women in the 1st year postpartum and what motivated employers to institute (or fail to institute) those policies. The fourth wave of data collection in 1999 focused on the impact of employer policies on these mothers' job mobility and wage growth over time.

This is the first data set to obtain detailed information on the availability and use of a diverse set of family responsive policies over a substantial period of time and across possible employer changes and spells out of the labor force. It represents mothers in large and small firms and across a diverse set of occupations and industries. It contains baseline information on women's work commitment and work preferences to control for unmeasured heterogeneity in career orientation that might affect productivity and hence wage growth over time. No existing panel surveys contain the richness and variety of measures on mothers' employment.

Retrospective employment histories were obtained from these mothers in 1999 and combined with the prospective information on their wages and working conditions from childbirth to 1 year postpartum to trace the impact of family responsive policies on wage growth over time. Data collection efforts focused on the availability of work-family policies and respondents' use of those policies during the 7-year period, to make sure policy effects stem from respondents' actual use rather than the typical association between high wages and generous fringe benefits.

For each work-family policy (including flexible work scheduling, ability to work at home, ability to reduce work hours, and child care assistance) in each job held, respondents were asked whether they have any such arrangement available to them and whether they used the policy if available. If so, respondents were asked to describe the arrangement, indicate when it began, and whether they felt that arrangement helped them meet their work responsibilities. The data make no distinction between formal and informal work-family accommodations; that is, respondents were instructed to report any accommodation they had available to them, whether official policy or an informal arrangement with supervisors or coworkers. . . . Because the 1990s were a period of relative prosperity and wage growth even for workers near the bottom of the income distribution, most women experienced wage growth over time (BLS, 2001c).

Results

Table 30.1 displays means and standard deviations for all variables in the analysis. The average wage gain from 1992 to 1999 was U.S. $6.07 per hour across all workers still employed in 1999 (note that this figure does not control for inflation). Managers and professional workers averaged an $8.66 gain, while workers in all other occupations averaged a $5.08 wage gain. Overall, the mothers in this sample exhibited a high degree of labor force attachment, not atypical of women in recent cohorts who were employed prior to childbirth. Although 59% of the sample had an additional child by 1999 (not surprising because most of the original sample was experiencing a first birth), few of the respondents had experienced a labor force withdrawal lasting 6 months or more, and average months in the labor force across the 7-year period were 60 out of 84 possible months. More than 70 of the 162 respondents remained with the same employer across the entire time series. However, job changing was not uncommon, with the average number of employer changes at a little more than one. About one third of the sample consistently worked in a managerial or professional job across this time period, while about 40% reported holding managerial or professional occupation in 1999, the last year surveyed. The majority (56.2%) worked for firms with fewer than 50 employees; however, the mean number of employees was 388 because of the significant presence of very large employers in the sample. Only five respondents were self-employed in 1999 (not in table).

Turning to the policy variables, Table 30.1 shows that only 29% of the sample reported that employer family policies were important considerations when they took their current job, with that number divided roughly equally between those who reported looking for schedule flexibility and those who looked for reduced work hours. In contrast, larger numbers reported having such policies available to them on their current job. Although 26% reported being able to work from home and 37% reported some form of child care assistance, a whopping 52% reported either working a reduced-hour schedule or being able to do so, while 82% reported having some flexibility available to them. These policy availability estimates are considerably higher than those found in BLS surveys. The difference is probably due to two significant factors: (a) This sample is limited to mothers of young children, a group that many scholars believe are most likely to adapt their work lives around their domestic responsibilities and (b) the survey instrument used here explicitly asked respondents whether they had access to accommodations regardless of whether these were officially sanctioned by their employers or were

informal arrangements made with supervisors or coworkers. For example, many more respondents said they could informally rearrange schedules when needed (55%) than said they had access to a formal flextime policy (27%). Looking at policy use "among those mothers who report policies available to them," this survey yielded relatively high utilization rates. In 1999, 60% of those who could work from home did so, while 55% of those with schedule flexibility were taking advantage of that on a regular basis. However, only about 40% were taking advantage of employer-sponsored child care assistance, and a mere 23% of those who said they could work reduced hours were actually doing so in 1999. Looking at past use across the entire sample from 1992 to 1999, mean number of months on a flexible schedule was about 26 but only 6 for working at home and 13 for working reduced hours. Months using child care assistance averaged 28.

[In the first analysis of] wage change from 1992 to 1999 with all the different work-family policies included . . . [it was found that] months of reduced work hours showed significant and negative effects on wage growth over time, as expected, whereas months of schedule flexibility showed no significant effect. Unexpectedly, months of child care assistance also showed a significant and negative effect on wage growth, despite its assumed link to stronger work availability.

[In the second analysis] several additional findings emerge. First, the impacts of working at home and working reduced hours seem confined to mothers employed continuously in professional or managerial jobs, as expected. When the interactions with managerial and professional status were entered into the model, the negative main effects for reduced work hours and work at home became nonsignificant. Months of flexibility in work location and reduced work hours showed no significant impact for those ever employed in clerical, service, or blue-collar jobs over the time series. Second, mothers who changed jobs at least once during this interval experienced smaller penalties for policy use. . . . The interaction of job changes and flexibility in work location was so large that it completely canceled the penalty for

Table 30.1
Descriptive Statistics and Variable Descriptions, Employed Mothers,
N = 159

Variable	M	SD
Wage gain (Time 2 hourly wage minus Time 1 hourly wage)	6.36	11.92
Months in the labor force (Number of months in the labor force from Time 1 to Time 2[a])	59.69	32.25
Number of job changes (Must involve a change from one employer to another)	1.13	1.14
Work commitment (If you were to get enough money to live as comfortably as you'd like, would you continue to work for pay? 1 = yes, 0 = no)	.64	.48
Manager/professional (Coded "1" if Time 1 occupation and Time 2 occupation were managerial or professional. All else coded "0")	.36	.48
Firm size (Firm size at Time 2)	393.05	676.67
Employer tenure (Number of months respondent has worked for Time 2 employer)	86.83	67.74
New child (Coded "1" if respondent had additional children between Time 1 and Time 2)	.59	.62
Specific policy mattered (Coded "1" if respondent reported that a particular family-friendly policy mattered in the decision to take her Time 2 job):		
Flexibility in work schedule	.14	.35
Flexibility in work location	.02	.14
Reduced work hours	.13	.34
Available policy (Coded "1" if respondent had a particular family policy available to her):		
Flexibility in work schedule	.89	.67
Flexibility in work location	.26	.44
Reduced work hours	.56	.50
Employer assistance with child care	.39	.49
Months of flexibility in work schedule (Aggregated job tenure [in months] for all jobs in which [a] respondent reported working a flexible schedule on a routine basis, [b] respondent *agreed* or *strongly agreed* with the statement "It would not be hard for me to take time off during my work day to take care of personal or family matters.")	26.48	31.88
Months of flexibility in work location (Aggregated job tenure [in months] for all jobs in which respondent worked 5 or more hours at home per week)	6.25	17.99
Months of reduced work hours (Aggregated job tenure [in months] for all jobs in which respondent worked fewer than 30 hours per week)	13.13	27.20
Months of child care assistance (Aggregated job tenure [in months] for all jobs in which respondent had any employer assistance with child care, including flexible spending account, money/vouchers, information/referral, on-site child care)	28.03	34.13

a. Time 1 = 1992, Time 2 = 1999.

policy use among managerial and professional mothers. This consistent pattern of effects for mothers who changed jobs is intriguing. It suggests either that women who use work-family policies can negate the signaling function of policy use from future earnings by changing to employers who are ignorant of their past policy use or that these women are strategically moving to employers who offer policies they can use without a wage penalty.

To investigate this issue, I calculated the percentages of women who had changed employers and were still using any of the family-responsive policies in their current job. The figures indicate that most women who changed employers and had used policies in the past were not continuing policy use at their present job. Among those who had ever changed employers, 69% had used flexible scheduling at some point in time; however, only 20% used a flexible schedule at their current job. A smaller number, 21%, had ever worked from home, but only 10% were currently working from home.

Although 61% of the employer changers has used some form of child care assistance in the past, only 10% were currently using some form of child care assistance. Finally, only 26% of the employer changers had ever worked fewer than 30 hours per week, and an even smaller 9% were currently working reduced hours in their new job. Although not definitive, these figures suggest that the ameliorative effects of job changing primarily occur because new employers are unaware or unaffected by mothers' past policy use. Note that job changing itself carried a hefty wage penalty, however . . . leaving mothers with the unpleasant choice of continuing with an employer and being penalized for policy use or losing the accrued advantages of firm seniority and experience to move to a different employer.

I hypothesized that the effects of direct assistance policies, such as child care, would be least detrimental to mother's wages, whereas flexibility policies would fall somewhere in the middle, and work reduction policies would be most detrimental. The [data analysis] support a modified ordering of these effects. Child care assistance did show only a small negative im-

pact, and only among those who remained continuously with the same employer, whereas reduced work hours showed a large and consistent negative effect on wages for professional and managerial workers, moderated only partially for those who changed jobs over time. However, using a flexible work schedule showed no significant impact on wage growth among any group of workers, while working from home had large negative effects only for managers and professionals who never changed jobs.

[T]he results for models of schedule flexibility and work at home [showed that] months of schedule flexibility had no significant effect on wage growth when averaged across all workers; . . . [yet] schedule flexibility more strongly impaired the wage growth of women in high-status and high-paying jobs relative to other jobs. . . .

Moving to flexibility in work location, [the analysis showed] a significant negative effect of working from home on wage growth among all mothers. . . . [T]he effect of working at home was concentrated among managers and professionals, while those women who changed employers at least once showed much smaller net effects of telecommuting on their wage growth. This group would include those who contract for short periods of time for skilled work, including accounting and computer processing.

For work at home, similar to schedule flexibility, sheer policy "availability" had no impact on wage growth. Evidence that employers who offered these policies paid less than other employers could not be detected here. Nor was there evidence that self-selection into jobs with these flexibility policies affects wage growth. . . .

[F]inally . . . [the results of analysis seem] to indicate that part-time workers searched for the best wages by changing employers rather than staying with one employer and hoping for wage increases over time. Employers may not reward work experience among part-time workers as they do full-time workers.

The availability of reduced work from one's employer was the only policy that by its sheer availability showed a consistently significant negative effect on mothers' wage growth. This means that the group of employers who offered part-time work also slowed wage increases over time for all their workers. However, this did not account for the slower wage growth of mothers who actually worked reduced hours.

There was no indication that employers offering child care assistance slowed wage growth in return for all their workers. If anything, the evidence suggests that employers offering child care assistance might have offered higher wages than others.

Discussion

Do Mothers Using Work-Family Policies Experience Weaker Wage Growth?

The results from this longitudinal analysis show that the use of work-family policies did not appear to benefit mothers' wages across the 1990s and sometimes hindered their wage growth. The negative wage impacts depended heavily on the type of accommodation used, the primary occupation of the respondent, and the respondent's continuity with a single employer. Although all four policies studied (schedule flexibility, telecommuting, reduced work hours, and child care assistance) showed some negative impact on wage growth for at least some workers, schedule flexibility and child care assistance showed mostly nonsignificant or mild impacts overall. By contrast, months spent working from home or working fewer than 30 hours per week (accommodations that reduce the physical time employees spend at their workplace) were heavily penalized, though only for managerial and professional workers. Wherever significant negative effects existed, they were almost always more intense for managerial and professional workers. The analysis revealed that the wage effects of months worked at home, worked at reduced hours, and worked with flexible scheduling were significantly more negative for mothers employed as managers or professionals than for mothers employed in other occupations. Mothers in lower status occupations, though less likely to have work-family policies at their place of employment, were better able to use those poli-

cies without penalty. This pattern fits the description of rigid workplace norms for long hours and continuous availability in professional occupations noted by Epstein (1999), Fried (1998), and Blair-Loy (2003).

Finally, the analysis showed that changing employers could often ameliorate the negative effects of using work-family policies, although this entailed losing any benefits of firm-specific human capital. For example, working a significant number of hours at home negatively affected the wages of those managerial/professional mothers who stayed with one employer but only marginally reduced the wage growth of those who changed jobs, suggesting that job changing can ameliorate past wage depression from telecommuting. Among those managerial or professional mothers who ever worked fewer than 30 hours a week, changing employers at least once reduced the cumulative negative effect by one third. Among all workers, the cumulative negative impact of receiving child care assistance was offset by a single employer change.

Simulating the wage losses experienced for each work-family policy showed that mothers who ever worked at home at least 5 hours per week in a managerial or professional job with a single employer faced an average 27% lower wage gain than mothers avoiding work at home, making $2.36 less per hour. Mothers employed fewer than 30 hours a week showed sharply lower wage gains over time as well. Mothers ever employed fewer than 30 hours a week with a single employer over time lost an average 22% of their expected wage gain, earning $1.90 less per hour. Comparable losses for using child care assistance were 10% on average ($.86 per hour), with a scant 9% for flexible scheduling 9% ($.78 per hour).

Simulating continuous use of each policy over the entire 7-year period produces more drastic estimates of effects, particularly for work at home and reduced hours of work. Again using managerial and professional women who do not change employers as the reference group and holding all other variables at their means, continuously working from home 5 or more hours per week would result in an estimated 58% lower wage gain over time, or a loss of $5.03 per hour. Continuously reduced hours of work over this period results in a 49.6% loss, or $4.30 per hour. These simulated losses are not trivial and, if confirmed by future studies, may go a long way toward explaining the stagnation of many mothers' wages despite their increases in labor force attachment.

Do Employees Who Offer Work-Family Policies Systematically Pay Their Workers Less Than Employers Who Do Not?

These models also tested for the presence of compensating differentials and unmeasured heterogeneity among mothers using family responsive policies, which might account for any effects of policy use on wage growth. I turn first to the question of whether policy availability depressed wage growth as employers offered policies in lieu of wages to attract greater labor supply among mothers. Scant evidence supported the idea that compensating differentials depress wages when employers offer work-family policies. I found that policy use indicators were often significant and negative but availability indicators were not, with the sole exception of the availability of part-time work that depressed wage growth among all workers in the sample. Nor did availability indicators ever lower the effect size of policy use variables. Thus, it was an individual mother's use of family responsive policy that depressed wage growth, not the availability of policies in her workplace. As has been shown elsewhere, the results here suggest that employers who offer family accommodations often offer higher-than-average wages because wages and benefits require significant employer profits and employee productivity (note the positive association between child care benefits and wage growth, for example).

The models also do not generally support the view that mothers who self-select into family-accommodating jobs seek to maximize utilities other than wages and might be less productive workers than other mothers as a result. Net of their occupation, experience, and use of family policies, mothers who reported that they actively accepted jobs because of the availability of flexible scheduling or telecommuting showed no lower wage gains over time. Specifically choosing an employer because of the availability of part-time work did show a weak and inconsistent association with lowered wage growth over time. This suggests that some mothers may be selecting part-time jobs because they are less ambitious or productive workers. In no specification, however, did this self-selection lower or alter the impact of policy use on wage growth. Rather, self-selection had its own independent effect on wage growth over time.

Conclusions

The results here suggest that work-family policies do not increase mothers' success in the labor market or ameliorate the wage retardation evidenced by mothers in large longitudinal studies of the labor force. At best, policy use was benign or neutral in effect for most of those studied (workers in clerical, service, or blue-collar jobs) and for two of the policies studied (employer child care assistance and schedule flexibility). The schedule flexibility findings may be particularly important because this was the accommodation most frequently offered to employed mothers. Rearranging work times and days to better mesh with family responsibilities did not seem to increase or seriously hamper wage growth.

However, use of accommodations that diminished employee "face time" in the workplace and most directly freed employee time to perform caregiving tasks led to potentially serious wage penalties for those in more lucrative managerial and professional careers. Whatever productivity gains are produced by these policies are more than offset by the negative reaction of employers to those who are not continuously available for work. These work-family policies may be reinforcing traditionally female responsibilities for caregiving that signal weaker commitment and dedication to employers. Similar to the experiences of workers in more progressive European social welfare states, reduced hour and homework policies may cement the subordinate position of women in the private sector labor force, while still permitting women to maintain employment throughout their childbearing years (Silver & Goldscheider, 1994).

These results need further extension and replication before such a scenario is accepted. The sample here consists only of mothers. It is impossible even with longitudinal data to ascertain the wage growth of these individual mothers had they not used work-family policies but had instead withdrawn from the labor force or changed jobs more frequently. Only a quasi-experimental design could accomplish that. As well, the results here cannot show whether the widespread adoption of family responsive policies might not increase mothers' wages overall relative to other groups of workers through their indirect effects on labor force continuity and employer tenure. This possibility could coexist with the finding that policy use still disadvantages mothers relative to those mothers who do not use any forms of employer assistance. Furthermore, the negative effects on wage growth found here for a sample of employed mothers may not exist for men or women without children who use flexible employment practices. Weeden (2001) found positive short-term effects of schedule flexibility on men's wages. Although some scholars have hypothesized that the use of family responsive policies might be more negative for men than for women because that violates gender expectations regarding work and family priorities (Allen & Russell, 1999; Ferber & Waldfogel, 1998), the limited empirical evidence available at present indicates that men may perhaps fare better than women who use family policies (Gariety & Shaffer, 2001; Weeden, 2001).

Finally, the results here consider the effects of using only one policy at a time. Although the intercorrelations among the policy use variables in this sample hover near zero (the only significant correlation was .22 between months of flexible hours and months working at home), some mothers did use multiple policies during their work careers either simultaneously or sequentially. Whether the disadvantages of policy use are additive or exponential in their effects on wage growth remains a topic for a larger sample. All these limitations point to the need for more systematic exploration of the impact of work innovations on a broad sample of workers followed over time.

Notes

1. This is troubling, in that work-family policies have been touted as one way to decrease the job-churning and labor force interruptions characteristic of mothers' employment patterns and have been shown empirically to do just that (Glass & Riley, 1998).

References

Allen, T. D., & Russell, J. E. A. (1999). Parental leave of absence: Some not so family-friendly implications. *Journal of Applied Social Psychology, 29,* 166–191.

Baltes, B., Briggs, T. E., Huff, J. W., Wright, J. A., & Neuman, G. A. (1999). Flexible and compressed workweek schedules: A meta-analysis of their effects on work-related criteria. *Journal of Applied Psychology, 84,* 496–513.

Barling, J., & MacEwen, K. E. (1991). Maternal employment experiences, attention problems and behavioral performance: A mediational model. *Journal of Organizational Behavior, 12,* 495–505.

Beers, T. (2000, June). Flexible schedules and shift work: Replacing the "9 to 5" workday? *Monthly Labor Review,* pp. 33–40.

Blair-Loy, M. (2003). *Competing devotions: Career and family among women executives.* Cambridge, MA: Harvard University Press.

Blair-Loy, M., & Wharton, A. (2002). Employees' use of work-family policies and the workplace social context. *Social Forces, 80,* 813–845.

Budig, M., & England, P. (2001). The wage penalty for motherhood. *American Sociological Review, 66,* 204–225.

Bureau of Labor Statistics, U.S. Department of Labor. (2001a). *Employee benefits in private industry 1999.* Available at *www.bls.gov/ncs/ebs/sp/ebnr0006.pdf.*

———. (2001b). *Employment characteristics of families in 2000.* Available at *www.bls.gov/news.release/famee.nr0.htm.*

———. (2001c). *Highlights of women's earnings in 2000.* Available at *www.bls.gov/cps/cpswom2000.pdf.*

Crittenden, A. (2001). *The Price of Motherhood.* New York: Metropolitan Books.

Dietch, C., & Huffman, M. (2003). Family responsive benefits and the two-tiered labor market. In R. Hertz & N. Marshall (Eds.), *Work and family* (n.p.). Berkeley: University of California Press.

Epstein, C. F. (1999). *The part-time paradox: Time norms, professional lives, family, and gender.* New York: Routledge.

Estes, S. B., & Glass, J. (1996). Job changes following childbirth. *Work and Occupations, 23,* 405-436.

Ferber, M., & Waldfogel, J. (1998, May). The long-term consequences of nontraditional employment. *Monthly Labor Review,* pp. 3–12.

Fried, M. (1998). *Taking time: Parental leave policy and corporate culture.* Philadelphia: Temple University Press.

Friedman, S., & Greenhaus, J. (2000). *Work and family—Allies or enemies?* New York: Oxford University Press.

Galinsky, E. (1994). Families and work: The importance of the quality of the work environment. In S. L. Kagan & B. Weissbound (Eds.), *Putting families first* (pp. 112–136). San Francisco: Jossey-Bass.

Galinsky, E., Bond, J. T., & Swanberg, J. (1998). *The 1997 Study of the Changing Work Force.* New York: Families and Work Institute.

Gariety, B. S., & Shaffer, S. (2001, March). Wage differentials associated with flextime. *Monthly Labor Review,* pp. 68–75.

Glass, J., & Estes, S. B. (1997). The family responsive workplace. *Annual Review of Sociology, 23,* 289–313.

Glass, J., & Riley, L. (1998). Family responsive policies and employee retention following childbirth. *Social Forces, 76,* 1401–1435.

Golden, L. (2001). Flexible work schedules: Which workers get them? *American Behavioral Scientist, 44,* 1157–1178.

Googins, B. K. (1991). *Work/family conflicts: Private lives–public responses.* New York: Auburn House.

Hochschild, A. (1997). *The time bind: When work becomes home and home becomes work.* New York: Metropolitan Books.

Jacobs, J., & Gerson, K. (2001). Overworked individuals or overworked families: Explaining trends in work, leisure and family time. *Work and Occupations, 28,* 40–63.

——. (2004). *The time divide: Balancing work and family in contemporary society.* Cambridge, MA: Harvard University Press.

Johnson, N., & Provan, K. (1995). The relationship between work/family benefits and wages: A test of competing predictions. *Journal of Socio-Economics, 24,* 571–584.

Kiser, J. (1998, January/February). Behind the scenes at a "family friendly" workplace. *Dollars and Sense,* pp. 19–21.

Perlow, L. (1998). Boundary control: The social ordering of work and family time in a high-tech corporation. *Administrative Science Quarterly, 43,* 328–357.

Pleck, J. (1993). Are "family supportive" employer policies relevant to men? In J. Hood (Ed.), *Men, work, and family* (pp. 217–237). Newbury Park, CA: Sage.

Rexroat, C. (1992). Changes in the employment continuity of succeeding cohorts of young women. *Work and Occupations, 19,* 18–34.

Rodgers, C. (1992). The flexible workplace: What have we learned? *Human Resource Management, 31* (3), 183–199.

Rosenfeld, R. (1996). Women's work histories. *Population and Development Review, 22,* S199–S222.

Ross, C., & Mirowsky, J. (1988). Child care and emotional adjustment to wives' employment. *Journal of Health and Social Behavior, 29,* 127–138.

Schor, J. (1991). *The Overworked American.* New York: Basic Books.

Silver, H., & Goldscheider, F. (1994). Flexible work and housework: Work and family constraints on women's domestic labor. *Social Forces, 72,* 1103–1119.

Spain, D., & Bianchi, S. (1996). *Balancing act: Motherhood, marriage, and employment among American women.* New York: Russell Sage.

Thompson, C., Beauvais, L., & Lyness, K. (1999). When work-family benefits are not enough: The influence of work-family culture on benefit utilization, organizational attachment and work-family conflict. *Journal of Vocational Behavior, 54,* 392–415.

Tilly, C. (1996). *Half a job: Bad and good part-time jobs in a changing economy.* Philadelphia: Temple University Press.

U.S. Census Bureau. (1999). America's families and living arrangements (Table FG2, CPS, March, 1999). Available at http://www.census.gov/population/socdemo/hh-fam/p20-537/1999/tabFG2.pdf.

Waldfogel, J. (1997a). The effect of children on women's wages. *American Sociological Review, 62,* 209–217.

——. (1997b). Working mothers then and now: A cross-cohort analysis of the effects of maternity leave on women's pay. In F. Blau & R. Ehrenberg (Eds.), *Gender and family issues in the workplace* (pp. 92–126). New York: Russell Sage.

Weeden, K. (2001). *Is there a flexiglass ceiling? The impact of flexible work arrangements on wages and wage growth.* Unpublished manuscript, Cornell University.

Williams, J. (2001). *Unbending gender: Why work and family conflict and what we can do about it.* New York: Oxford University Press.

Reprinted from: Jennifer Glass, "Blessing or Curse? Work-Family Policies and Mothers' Wage Growth Over Time." In *Work and Occupations*, Vol. 31, No. 3: 367–394. Copyright © 2004 by Sage Publications.

Food for Thought and Application Questions

1. Among the variety of work-family accommodations that employers make available, which (if any) of those have no apparent affect on mothers' wages? Which ones (if any) retard mothers' wages? Do these effects apply to all categories of employed mothers?

2. Assume you were asked to advise the CEO and Human Resource Director of an organization that employs mainly professional workers. Their concern is to assure fairness in the wages of their professional employees. They have also told you that many of their professionals are young with young children. What could you tell them about family-friendly practices that appear to influence the wages of mothers? Brainstorm about steps that could be taken to prevent a wage penalty for mothers. ✦

Appendix I: 2004 Salary Survey

A Long Way to Go. . .

Equal pay for equal work? In this year's annual NAFE salary survey, we see that pay parity is still far from reality for women. For the following chart—which looks at selected positions in 20 different industries—NAFE has once again collected data from federal agencies and private trade and consulting firms to pull together an overall picture of what men and women are making across the country.

The numbers speak for themselves: whether we're talking about high-tech, health care, finance, social work, or education, men are consistently compensated at a higher rate than their female co-workers. And women who have attained the top positions in their fields fare no better. CEOs, directors, and managers in fields ranging from advertising to health care management consistently make less than their male counterparts for doing the same work.

Yes, we can take our daughters to work, and yes, things are better than they were 50 years ago, when women earned only about 60 percent of what men earned. But judging by the numbers in the following salary survey, we still have a long road ahead of us.

Note: All salaries are median unless otherwise noted.

—Compiled by Christine Larson with Jennifer Osborn and Katherine Lee

Accounting*

All IMA Members*

(accountants, managers, certified management accountants, certified financial accountants)

	Women	Men
For all IMA Members	$72,773	$94,314
With 1–5 years experience	$72,534	$85,019
6–10 years experience	$72,823	$90,451
11–15 years experience	$77,051	$94,062
16–20 years experience	$87,131	$112,336
20+ years of experience	$85,375	$119,628

Source: Institute of Management Accountants, 2004
*Average total compensation, including salary and bonus
**Bureau of Labor Statistics (BLS)-based Estimate

	Women	Men
Accountants and auditors**	$39,312	$54,132
Bookkeepers, accountants, and auditing clerks	$26,624	$30,940

Source: The Bureau of Labor Statistics (BLS), 2003
**Based on weekly median income, which is multiplied by 52 to yield yearly salaries

Advertising*

	Women	Men
CEO	$155,000	$163,000
Creative Director	$113,000	$115,000
Media Director	$76,000	$84,000
Copywriter	$55,000	$60,000
Art Director	$54,000	$55,000
Account Executive	$49,000	$56,000

Source: Advertising Age, 2003
*Average base salary

	Women	Men
Marketing and sales managers	$47,008	$66,092

	Women	Men
Advertising sales agents	$30,888	$45,760

Source: BLS-based estimates, 2003

Banking/Financial Services

Accounting, Finance, and Banking*

	Women	Men
Financial analyst	$58,989	$59,846
Internal audit	$43,353	$56,372
Cost accounting	$50,056	$48,460
Cash management	$39,003	$67,053
Credit analyst	$56,631	$55,780
Management consultant	$57,570	$83,356
Payroll	$41,597	$41,831

Source: CareerBank.com Salary Survey Report, 2003
*Total cash compensation

	Women	Men
Bank tellers	$20,436	N/A**

Source: BLS-based estimate, 2003
**BLS data not available when fewer than 50,000 people work in that category

Insurance

	Women	Men
Claims adjusters, appraisers, examiners, investigators	$33,696	$45,136
Insurance sales agents	$31,668	$51,012

Source: BLS-based estimate

	Women	Men
Securities, commodities, financial services sales agents	$36,348	$65,260

Source: BLS-based estimate

Book Publishing

	Women	Men
Exec/Senior VP	$176,000	$208,000
Editorial Director/Editor in Chief	$79,000	$88,000
Editor	$45,000	$44,000
Sales Director/Manager	$81,000	$89,000
Marketing Director/Manager	$54,000	$64,200
Promotion Director/Manager	$44,250	$50,080

Source: Publishers Weekly, 2004

Education

College and University Professors*

	Women	Men
Professor	$92,937	$102,408
Associate Professor	$65,495	$70,332
Assistant	$55,284	$61,011
Instructor	$38,571	$40,740
Lecturer	$42,999	$48,946

Source: American Association of University Professors, March–April, 2004
*Salaries for professors with doctorates teaching in private and public universities

Pre-K-12 Education

	Women	Men
Teachers, pre-K/K	$25,636	N/A**
Teachers, elementary/middle	$39,364	$43,836
Teachers, secondary school	$42,848	$46,956
Teachers, special education	$40,820	$45,240
Teachers' aides	$17,888	$21,944

Source: BLS-based estimates
**BLS data not available when fewer than 50,000 people work in that category

Engineering

	Women	Men
Civil Engineer	$61,000	$78,000

Source: American Society of Civil Engineers, the Institute of Industrial Engineers, and the National Society of Professional Engineers, The Engineering Income and Salary Survey, 2004

	Women	Men
Senior Mechanical Engineer	$72,000	$76,360
Project Mechanical Engineer	$58,000	$59,134
Staff Mechanical Engineer	$54,000	$52,000
Junior Mechanical Engineer	$50,000	$47,500

Source: Comission on Professionals in Science and Technology Salaries of Scientists, Engineers, and Technicians: A Summary of Salary Surveys, 2003

Health Care

Health Care Management (Non-Hospital)*

	Women	Men
CEO	$152,673	$195,783
Practice Administrator	$111,854	$129,151
COO	$84,034	$123,655
Ambulatory/ Clinical Services Director	$68,698	$77,187

Source: Medical Group Management Association, Management Compensation Survey 2003
*Total compensation

Physicians*

	Women	Men
Allergy/Immunology	$190,983	$254,289
Anesthesiology	$258,253	$322,543
Dermatology	$223,874	$277,757
Emergency medicine	$191,883	$213,793
Family practice (w/o OB)	$131,016	$156,998
Internal medicine: general	$135,960	$161,696
OB/GYN	$216,012	$247,601
Ophthalmology	$224,570	$276,614
Pediatrics	$136,642	$167,242
Psychiatry	$149,218	$162,527
Radiation oncology	$339,544	$389,925
Surgery: general	$212,030	$257,249
Surgery: neurological	$337,031	$487,000

Source: Medical Group Management Association, Physician Compensation and Production Survey, 2003
*Total compensation

Nursing and Health-Related Fields

	Women	Men
Dental assistants	$25,480	N/A**
Registered nurses	$46,124	$52,312
Physical therapists	$43,524	N/A**
Psychologists	$48,776	N/A**
Pharmacists	$70,928	$79,716
Physicians and surgeons	$51,428	$87,204

Source: BLS-based estimates
**BLS data not available when fewer than 50,000 people work in that category

Human Resources

	Women	Men
Human resources, training, labor relations specialists	$40,248	$49,972
Management analyst	$50,804	$65,884

Source: BLS-based estimates

Law

	Women	Men
Lawyers	$73,476	$84,188
Paralegal/Legal assistant	$35,620	N/A

Source: BLS-based data

Library Science

University, College, and Research Libraries*

	Women	Men
Director	$151,081	$155,172
Associate director	$96,899	$98,732
Department head, reference	$65,685	$65,008

	Women	Men
Head librarian, branch	$63,117	$69,160
Reference librarian, 10–14 years experience	$46,937	$46,837
Reference librarian 0–5 years experience	$38,399	$39,958

Source: Association of Research Libraries, ARL Annual Salary Survey, 2003–04
*Average salary

	Women	Men
Librarians	$41,028	Not available

Source: BLS-based estimates

Media

Magazine Publishing*

	Women	Men
Editor in chief/editorial director	$79,130	$104,132
Executive editor	$75,508	$85,588
Managing editor	$55,983	$62,574
Senior editor	$57,385	$65,377

Source: Folio, National Magazine Salary Survey, 2004
*Salaries are mean

Newspaper Publishing

	Women	Men
Journalists	$37,731	$46,758

Source: Indiana University, "The American Journalist in the 21st Century," 2003

	Women	Men
TV/Radio news		
News director/TV	$68,000	$67,800
News director/radio	$40,000	$32,000

Source: Radio Television News Directors Association/Ball State University annual survey, 2004

Nonprofits*

CEOs

	Women	Men
CEO/Executive director	$84,070	$84,825

Source: The NonProfit Times 2004
*Average salaries

Association Executives

	Women	Men
Administration	$55,000	$88,400
Fundraising/Development	$70,000	$70,297
Government/Lobbying	$73,907	$96,655
Membership development	$61,273	$75,000

Source: American Society of Association Executives, Association Executive Compensation and Benefits Study, 2003

Office Administration/Clerical

	Women	Men
Secretaries and administrative assistants	$27,612	$29,796
Receptionists and information clerks	$23,192	$26,000
General office clerks	$26,104	$26,104
Administrative support supervisors	$26,676	$30,368
Data-entry keyers	$25,376	$27,508

Source: BLS-based estimates

Public Relations

	Women	Men
All PR professionals	$56,820	$79,307
Ages 26–30	$53,202	$59,146
Ages 31–35	$67,558	$75,550
Ages 36–40	$80,481	$99,572
Ages 41–50	$80,926	$103,600
Age 51+	$81,815	$99,614

Source: PR Wee Salary Survey 2004

	Women	Men
Public relations specialists	$41,860	N/A**

Source: BLS-based estimate, 2003
**BLS data not available when fewer than 50,000 people work in that category

Retail

	Women	Men
First-line supervisors/ managers of retail workers	$25,792	$36,660
Buyers, wholesale and retail	$34,840	$42,224
Retail salespersons	$19,864	$31,148

Source: BLS-based estimates

Real Estate

	Women	Men
Property, real estate, community association managers	$33,176	$44,148
Real estate brokers, sales agents	$31,616	$49,556

Source: BLS-based estimates

Sales and Marketing*

	Women	Men
Director or manager, sales	$91,238	$126,159
Director or manager, marketing	$84,008	$111,348

Source: Sales & Marketing Management, 2003
*Average salary

Science

Chemists, Physicists, Social Scientists

	Women	Men
Chemists, except biochemistry	$74,000	$85,000
Physical and related scientists	$62,000	$80,000
Social scientists	$56,000	$68,000

Source: Commission on Professionals in Science and Technology, data derived from National Science Foundation, 2001 Survey of Doctorate Recipients

Geoscience

	Women	Men
Geoscientists	$55,000	$71,083

Source: Commission on Professionals in Science and Technology, data derived from American Geogical Institute, Compensation of Geoscientists, 2001

Life Scientists

	Women	Men
Life and related scientists	$58,000	$70,000
Medical scientists	$57,000	$80,000
Biological scientists	$58,000	$68,000

Source: Commission on Professionals in Science and Technology, data derived from National Science Foundation, 2001 Survey of Doctorate Recipients

Technology*

Management Compensation

	Women	Men
Vice president	$127,833	$131,625
CIO	$129,000	$135,750
Senior manager	$109,950	$109,759
Project manager	$84,500	$93,800

Staff Compensation

	Women	Men
Web infrastructure	$69,850	$87,750
Database analysis and devt.	$68,002	$78,088
Application development	$71,500	$77,480
Web design, development	$66,500	$62,250

Source: Information Week, 2004
*Median cash compensation (including salary and cash bonus)

Travel*

	Women	Men
Owner/executive	$32,797	$48,519
Manager	$40,730	$55,465
Frontline travel agent	$27,077	$30,769

Source: The Travel Institute, 2003
*Annual compensation

Appendix II: Data and Information on Women's Labor Force Participation

Basic Facts about Women in the Labor Force, 2004[1]

- Of the 116 million women age 16 years and over in the United States, 68 million were labor force participants—working or looking for work.

- With a labor force participation rate of 59.2 percent, women represented 46 percent of the total United States labor force.

- Women of color made up 13.4 percent of the labor force in 2002.

- Labor force participation rates for women, by race, were: black, 61.5 percent; white, 58.9 percent; Asian, 57.6 percent; and Hispanic, 56.1 percent.

- The higher a person's educational attainment, the more likely she will be in the labor force. The labor force participation rates for women age 25 years and over by educational attainment:
  - with less than a high school diploma—32.5 percent;
  - with a high school diploma—54.1 percent;
  - some college, no degree—64.3 percent;
  - associate degree—71.5;
  - and bachelor's degree and higher—72.8 percent.

- Greater educational attainment usually results in lower unemployment rates: women with less than a high school diploma—10.0 percent; with a high school diploma—4.9 percent; some college, no degree—4.7 percent; and bachelor's degree and higher—2.7 percent.

- Of working women, seventy-four percent (74 percent) worked full time and 26 percent worked part time.

- Approximately 4 million women were self-employed in nonagricultural industries. These self-employed women represented nearly 6 percent of all employed women.

- Women between the ages of 55 and 64 have steadily increased their labor force participation rates from 42.0 percent in 1985 to 49.2 percent in 1995 and to 56.6 percent in 2003.

- In 2000, the average retirement age for women in 2000 was just under 63 compared to 65 in 1965.

- In 2004, 70.7 of mothers with children under 18 were in the labor force; 77.5 percent of mothers with children age 6 to 17 were in the labor force, and 62.2 percent of mothers with children under the age of 6 were in the labor force. By contrast, in 1980, these percentages were 56.6 percent, 64.3 percent, and 46.8 percent respectively. In 1955, these percentages were 27 percent, 38.4 percent, and 18.2 percent respectively.[2]

- The median income for married couple families in 2001 was $60,335; for female-headed families (with no husband present), the median income was $25,745.[2]

- In 2003, single mothers had a labor force participation rate of 78.1 percent.[5]

- Median annual earnings for African-American women working full-time, year round, in 2004, was $26,992; for comparable white women, median annual earnings was $32,036; for comparable Hispanic women in 2003, median annual earnings was $22,369. Asian-American women had the highest annual earnings for full-time workers in 2003 at $32,774.[4]

- Census Data from 2003 show that 26.5 percent of African-American women lived in poverty. That contrasts sharply with 9.2 percent of white women living in poverty and 12 percent of Asian-American women living in poverty. The rate, however, was similar to that of Hispanic women, of which 24.4 percent lived in poverty.[4]

Women and Education[2]

- In 2003, with regard to education for women age 25 and over: 85.7 percent of white women, 80.3 percent of black women, 86 percent of Asian women, and 57.8 percent of Hispanic women had completed high school.

- In 2003, with regard to educational attainment for women age 25 and over: 25.9 percent of white women had earned at least a Bachelor's degree; 17.8 percent of African-American women had done so; 46.1 percent of Asian-American women had done so; and 11.6 percent of Hispanic women had done so.

- In 2002, women earned 57.4 percent of all Bachelor's degrees in the United States, 58.7 percent of all Master's degrees, and 46.3 percent of all doctorates.

- In 2001, women earned 43.3 percent of medical degrees (M.D.), 38.6 percent of dentistry degrees (D.D.S. or D.M.D.), 47.3 percent of law degrees (LL.B. or J.D.), and 32 percent of theological degrees (B.D., M.Div., M.H.L.).

Women in Various Occupations

- The seven occupations with the *highest median weekly earnings among women* who worked full-time in 2004 were:
  - pharmacists, $1,432;
  - chief executives, $1,310;
  - lawyers, $1,255;
  - computer and information systems managers, $1,288;
  - computer software engineers, $1,149;
  - computer programmers, $1,006;
  - physicians and surgeons, $978; and
  - human resource managers, $958

- Women comprised 50.5 percent of managerial and professional specialty positions in the United States in 2003.

- In 2002, African American women comprised 5.1 percent of management, professional, and related occupations; Asian women made up 2.4 percent and Latinas made up 3.1 percent.[3]

- In the *Fortune* 500 Companies, women comprise 15.7 percent of corporate officers, are 13.6 percent of the members of Boards of Directors, are 7.9 percent of those with the highest titles (e.g., CEO, Senior VP), and represent 5.2 percent of top earners in their companies. Eight women are CEOs of *Fortune* 500 companies.[3]

- Women of color held only 1.6 percent of corporate officer positions in 2002 and held 2 percent of the Board of Directors seats in the *Fortune* 1000 companies; nearly two-thirds of women of color who are corporate officers are African-American women.[3]

- Among professional occupations, women are *least* represented in architecture and engineering occupations; women are 22 percent of architects, 14.9 percent of chemical engineers, 8.7 percent of civil engineers, 7.1 percent of electrical engineers, and 5.5 percent of mechanical engineers.

- Among education professionals, women are 97.8 percent of preschool and kindergarten teachers, 81.7 percent of elementary and middle school teachers, 55 percent of secondary school teachers, and 44.9 percent of post-secondary (college level) teachers.[2]

- Across all occupations, women are least represented in natural resource, construction, and maintenance occupations. They are 2.5 percent of brick masons, 1.6 percent of carpenters, 2.6 percent of cement masons, 2.1 percent of electricians, 1.0 percent of plumbers, and 6.7 percent of painters.[2]

- In 2003, women made up 29.1 percent of all lawyers; women were 16.8 percent of partners in law firms and comprised 14.9 percent of the General Counsels of Fortune 500 companies.[6]

Notes

1. Source: U.S. Department of Labor, Bureau of Labor Statistics. 2005. *Women in the Labor Force, 2004* and *Quick Facts on Older Workers. www.dol.gov/bls/wb/factsheets*.

2. Source: U.S. Census Bureau, Statistical Abstract of the United States. 2004–2005. Tables 212, 213, 284, 286, and/or 287.

3. Source: Catalyst. 2004. Facts about Working Women. *www.catalystwomen.org*.

4. Source: Institute for Women's Policy Research. "African-American Women Work More, Earn Less." News release March 29, 2005.

5. Source: Catalyst. "Quick Takes: Working and Stay-at-home Mothers" 2005.

6. Source: Catalyst. "Quick Takes: Women in Law" 2004. ✦

Figure II.1 and II.2
Charts on Earnings for Full-Time Wage and Salary Workers

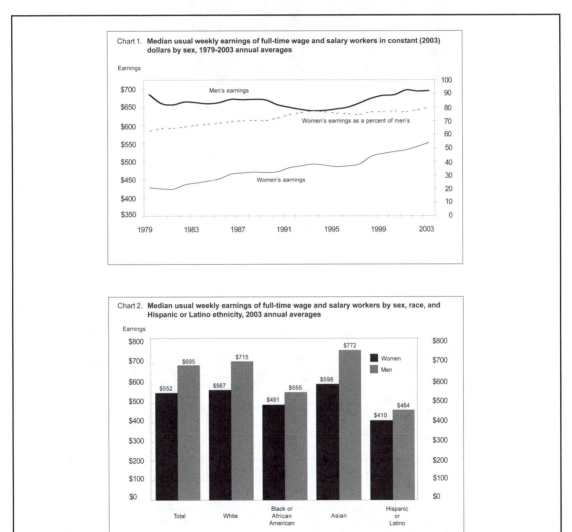

Source: U.S. Census Bureau, Current Population Survey, 2004 Annual Social and Economic Supplement

Source: Highlights of Women's Earnings, 2003. Bureau of Labor Statistics, Women's Bureau. *http://www.dol.gov/wb/media/reports/main.htm*

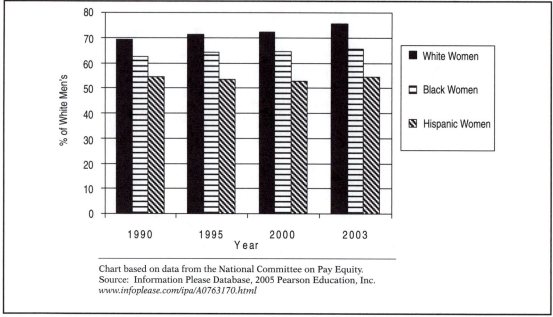

Figure II.3
The Wage Gap: Median Annual Earnings as Percentage of White Men's Median Annual Earnings, 1990-2003

Chart based on data from the National Committee on Pay Equity.
Source: Information Please Database, 2005 Pearson Education, Inc.
www.infoplease.com/ipa/A0763170.html

Figure II.4
Mothers in the Labor Force, 1955-2004, by Age of Children

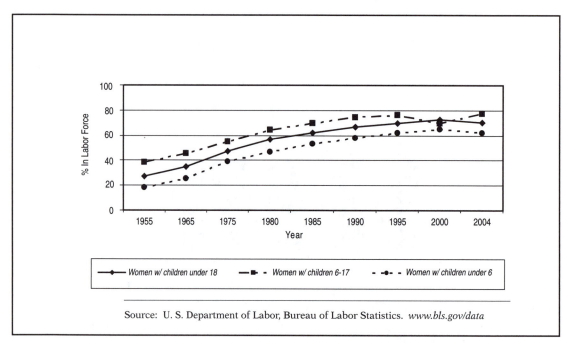

Source: U. S. Department of Labor, Bureau of Labor Statistics. *www.bls.gov/data*